Hungary

Steve Fallon

Hungary

2nd edition

Published by
Lonely Planet Publications
Head Office: PO Box 617, Hawthorn, Vic 3122, Australia
Branches: 155 Filbert St, Suite 251, Oakland, CA 94607, USA
               10 Barley Mow Passage, Chiswick, London W4 4PH, UK
               71 bis rue du Cardinal Lemoine, 75005 Paris, France

Printed by
Colorcraft Ltd, Hong Kong

Photographs by
Bertold Daum
Steve Fallon
Peter Gyulavary
Mark Honan
Hungarian Tourist Board

Front cover: Thermal bath at Gellert Hotel, Budapest (The Image Bank, Michael Pasdzior)

First Published
February 1994

This Edition
July 1997

Although the authors and publisher have tried to make the information as accurate as possible, they accept no responsibility for any loss, injury or inconvenience sustained by any person using this book.

National Library of Australia Cataloguing in Publication Data

Fallon, Steve.
    Hungary.

    Includes index.
    ISBN 0 86442 452 3.

    1. Hungary – Guidebooks. I. Title. (Series: Lonely Planet travel survival kit).

914.390454

Steve Fallon

Born in Boston, Massachusetts, Steve Fallon can't remember a time when he was not obsessed with travel, other cultures and languages. As a teenager he worked at an assortment of jobs to finance trips to Europe and South America, and he graduated from Georgetown University in 1975 with a Bachelor of Science in modern languages. The following year he taught English at the University of Silesia near Katowice, Poland. After he had worked for several years for a Gannett newspaper and obtained a master's degree in journalism, his fascination with the 'new' Asia took him to Hong Kong, where he lived and worked for 13 years for a variety of publications and was editor of *Business Traveller* magazine. In 1987, he put journalism on hold and opened Wanderlust Books, Asia's only travel bookshop. Steve lived in Budapest for 2½ years from where he wrote *Hungary* and *Slovenia* before moving to London in 1994. He has written or contributed to a number of other Lonely Planet titles, including *France* and the *Europe on a shoestring* series.

From the Author

This one too (two-oh!) is for Michael Rothschild, the point on the map, and for Anny – long may she wave. Friends in Budapest who were helpful and hospitable, as always, included Ildikó Nagy Moran and the Szirti family – Zsóka, István (Steve) and Bea. Tourinform remains the most authoritative and knowledgeable source of information on Hungary and things Hungarian; *köszönöm szépen* to staff throughout Magyarország, but especially to Ágnes Padányi and Katalin Koronczi in the capital. Cate Tower and Judy Finn showed me where Budapest plays after dark, and I am grateful. Dr Zsuzsa Medgyes of M&G Marketing's *Idegenforgalmi Kézikönyv* showed me the way, again and again.

From the Publisher

This book was edited at Lonely Planet in Melbourne by Bethune Carmichael with assistance from Darren Elder, Anne Mulvaney, Lynn McGaurr, Chris Wyness, Suzi Petkovski, Peter D'Onghia and Mary Neighbour. Tony Fankhauser drew the maps, designed and laid out the book with assistance from Mark Griffiths, Tamsin Wilson, Jenny Jones, Jacqui Saunders, Trudi Canavan and Michelle Lewis. Tony and Rachel Black drew the illustrations, and Simon Bracken designed the cover. Thanks to Brigitte Barta and Mary Neighbour for proofing. Thanks also to Dan Levin and Al Sharifian for their computer wizardry.

Warning & Request

Things change – prices go up, schedules change, good places go bad and bad places go bankrupt – nothing stays the same. So, if you find things better or worse, recently opened or long since closed, please tell us and help make the next edition even more accurate and useful.

We value all of the feedback we receive from travellers. Julie Young coordinates a small team who read and acknowledge every letter, postcard and e-mail, and ensure that every morsel of information finds its way to the appropriate authors, editors and publishers.

Everyone who writes to us will find their name in the next edition of the appropriate guide and will also receive a free subscription to our quarterly newsletter, *Planet Talk*. The very best contributions will be rewarded with a free Lonely Planet guide.

Excerpts from your correspondence may appear in updates (which we add to the end pages of reprints); new editions of this guide; in our newsletter, *Planet Talk*; or in the Postcards section of our Web site – so please let us know if you don't want your letter published or your name acknowledged.

Thanks

Many thanks to the travellers who used the last edition and wrote to us with helpful hints, useful advice and interesting anecdotes:

G Ambrus, J Bailey, Graham Balfry, R Beauchamp, Ingrid Bey, Elizabeth & Helen Bostock, Robert & Razan Brooker, Livia Cattaneo, Lucy Church, Alessandro Colizzi, Sophy D'Angelo, L Davis-Miller, Susan L Duhl, R Ercolanoni, Paul Falvo, Hugh Finsten, Leslie Fuzess, Hank Guzik, Karen, Helene Haurehed, Brent Holt, Jacqueline Jago, Donna Jones, Katie Jones, Donna Kernohan, Dawn Kovacs, Rob Lober, Gabor Lovei, Timothy Mason, Noelle Murphy, Don Newton, HT Oosterheerd, Susan Pasley, Lies Peeters, Stephanie J Petschat, DJ Priestley, Sally Quinn, Peter Ramsden, E Relizeller, Grant Roberts, JE Saville, Margaret Sheriff, Clare Springell, Janey Stone, N Stubbs, Andras Toth, Andrew Ungar, Dot Vali, John Waddington-Feather, Johnathon Wilde, John Williams, Pieter Wolters, Enrique Yarza, Kispal Zsolt.

Contents

Map Legend

BOUNDARIES

............International Boundary
............Regional Boundary

ROUTES

............Freeway
............Highway
............Major Road
............Unsealed Road or Track
............Minor Road
............City Road
............City Street
............Railway
............Underground Railway
............Tram
............Walking Track
............Walking Tour
............Cable Car or Chairlift

AREA FEATURES

............Parks
............Built-Up Area
............Pedestrian Mall
............Market
............Cemetery
............Forest
............Beach or Desert
............Rocks

HYDROGRAPHIC FEATURES

............Coastline
............River, Creek
............Intermittent River or Creek
............Rapids, Waterfalls
............Lake, Intermittent Lake
............Canal
............Swamp

SYMBOLS

CAPITAL		National Capital
Capital		Regional Capital
CITY		Major City
City		City
Town		Town
Village		Village
		Place to Stay, Place to Eat
		Cafe, Pub or Bar
		Post Office, Telephone
		Tourist Information, Bank
		Transport, Parking
		Museum, Youth Hostel
		Caravan Park, Camping Ground
		Church, Cathedral
		Mosque, Synagogue
		Buddhist Temple, Hindu Temple
		Hospital, Police Station

............Embassy, Petrol Station
............Airport, Airfield
............Swimming Pool, Gardens
............Shopping Centre, Zoo
............Winery or Vineyard, Picnic Site
A25 ....One Way Street, Route Number
............Stately Home, Monument
............Castle, Tomb
............Cave, Hut or Chalet
............Mountain or Hill, Lookout
............Pass, Spring
............Metro Station
............River Flow
............Archaeological Site or Ruins
............Ancient or City Wall
............Cliff or Escarpment, Tunnel
............Railway Station

Note: not all symbols displayed above appear in this book

Map Index

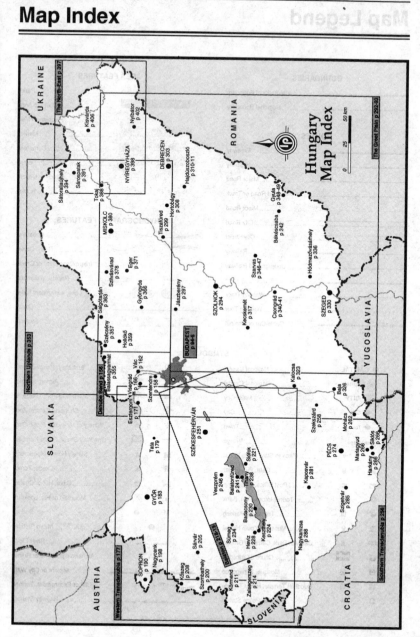

Hungary
Map Index

0 25 50 km

The North-East p 397

UKRAINE

ROMANIA

Kisvárda p 406

Nyírbátor p 402

Sárospatak p 391

Sátoraljaújhely p 394

NYÍREGYHÁZA p 398

DEBRECEN p 303

Hajdúszoboszló p 310–11

Tokaj p 388

MISKOLC p 380

Tiszafüred p 299

Hortobágy p 308

Szilvásvárad p 378

Eger p 371

Salgótarján p 363

Gyöngyös p 366

Jászberény p 297

SZOLNOK p 294

Kecskemét p 317

Szarvas p 346–47

Békéscsaba p 342

Gyula p 348–49

Hódmezővásárhely p 336

Csongrád p 340–41

SZEGED p 330

The Great Plain p 292–93

Northern Uplands p 353

Szécsény p 357

Hollókő p 359

Vác p 162

BUDAPEST p 94–5

Danube Bend p 156

Balassagyarmat p 355

Esztergom p 171 Visegrád p 166

Szentendre p 158

Kalocsa p 323

Baja p 326

YUGOSLAVIA

SLOVAKIA

Tata p 179

GYŐR p 183

SZÉKESFEHÉRVÁR p 251

Szekszárd p 258

Mohács p 262

PÉCS p 274

Mágócs p 266 Siklós p 266 Harkány p 266

Veszprém p 246

Balatonfüred p 241

Siófok p 221

Tihany p 238

Badacsony p 230

Kaposvár p 281

Szigetvár p 285

Western Transdanubia p 177

SOPRON p 190

Nagycenk p 198

Sárvár p 205

Sümeg p 234

Hévíz p 228

Keszthely p 224

Nagykanizsa p 288

Balaton p 216–19

Kőszeg p 206

Szombathely p 200

Körmend p 211

Zalaegerszeg p 214

Southern Transdanubia p 256

AUSTRIA

SLOVENIA

CROATIA

Introduction

Hungary (Magyarország) is a kidney-shaped country in the heart of Europe whose impact on the continent's history has been far greater than its present size and population would suggest. Hungarians – who call themselves the Magyar – speak a language and form a culture unlike any other in the region; this distinctiveness has been both a source of pride and an obstacle for more than 1100 years. Firmly entrenched in the Communist Soviet bloc until the late 1980s, Hungary is now an independent republic making its own decisions and policies.

Hungarian nationalism has been the cause and the result of an often paranoiac fear of being gobbled up by neighbouring countries – particularly the 'sea of Slavs' that surrounds much of the country. Yet, despite endless occupations and wars, the Hung-arians have been able to retain their own identity without shutting themselves off from the world. Now more than ever Hungary looks to Europe for its future.

Given its geographic situation and its experience in welcoming travellers, Hungary is the best place to enter Eastern Europe. While some of its neighbours may have more dramatic scenery or older and more important monuments, Hungary is the country most geared and stable for tourists, and travel here is essentially hassle-free. Visitors with special interests – fishing, horse riding, botany, bird-watching, cycling, thermal spas, Jewish culture – will find Hungary a treasure trove. And, by Western standards, it is still a bargain destination, with very affordable food, lodging and transport.

Under the Communist regime most of the

government's attention and money went to the capital, Budapest. As a result, foreign visitors rarely ventured beyond this splendid city on the Danube, except on a day trip to the Danube Bend or to Lake Balaton. These places should be visited, but don't ignore other towns and regions off the beaten track including: *a tanya világ* ('the farm world') of the southern Plain, the ethnically rich North-East, the Villány Hills in Southern Transdanubia, covered in vineyards; and the traditional Őrség region of the far west. This is not a case of 'authentic' versus 'touristy'; a supermarket check-out counter in Budapest is as much a part of the real Hungary today as a village greengrocer's in the Zemplén Hills. But life in the provinces is more redolent of times past – simpler, slower, often more friendly.

The first half of this decade were not glory days for Hungary. Serious economic problems affected all aspects of daily life, and the majority of Hungarians were very disappointed with what the change to a capitalist economy had brought them. A joke making the rounds at the time illustrates the prevailing sentiment: 'What's worse than Communism?' went the question. Answer: 'Apparently what comes after it.'

Thankfully, those days (and feelings) appear to be on their way out. Foreign investment is up, living standards are rising, many people have that little bit of extra cash for a new freezer or a winter holiday in the Canary Islands, many war-ravaged buildings are getting much needed face-lifts, and membership of the European Union – an 'acceptance' that Hungary has craved for a long, long time – appears to be within reach. The present may not be stellar, but the future for Hungary and its people is certainly looking rosier.

Of course, we would have known all that had we listened carefully to the words of a man they call 'the greatest Hungarian' – a 19th-century reformer and patriot who did more for his nation than any other:

Many people think that Hungary was;
I like to believe that she will be!
Count István Széchenyi, (1830)

Facts about the Country

HISTORY

Early Inhabitants

The Carpathian Basin, in which Hungary lies, has been populated for hundreds of thousands of years. Human bone fragments found at Vértesszőlős near Tata in Transdanubia in the 1960s, and believed to be half a million years old, suggest that Palaeolithic and later Neanderthal humans were attracted to the area by warm-water springs, hunting reindeer, bear and mammoth. Stone Age pottery shards have also been found at Istállóskő Cave near Szilvásvárad in northern Hungary.

Around 5000 BC, during the Neolithic period, changes in the climate forced much of this wildlife to migrate northward. The domestication of animals and the first forms of agriculture appeared, as indeed they did in much of Europe. Remnants of the Körös culture suggest that these goddess-worshipping people lived in the Szeged area at this time.

Indo-European tribes from the Balkans stormed the Carpathian Basin from the south in horse-drawn wheeled carts in about 2000 BC, bringing with them copper tools and weapons. After the introduction of more durable bronze, forts were built and a military elite developed.

Over the next millennium, invaders from the west (Illyrians, Thracians) and east (Scythians) brought iron, but the metal was not in common use until the Celts arrived in about the 3rd century BC. They introduced glass and crafted some of the fine gold jewellery that can still be seen in museums throughout Hungary.

Around the beginning of the Christian era, the Romans conquered the area west of the Danube River and established the province of Pannonia. Later victories over the Celts extended their domination across the Tisza River as far as Dacia (now Transylvania in Romania). The Romans brought writing, viticulture and stone architecture, and established garrison towns, the remains of which can still be seen in Óbuda (Aquincum), Szombathely (Savaria), Pécs (Sophianae) and Sopron (Scarabantia). They also built baths near the region's thermal waters and introduced the new religion of Christianity.

The Great Migrations

The first of the so-called Great Migrations of nomadic peoples from Asia reached the eastern outposts of the Roman Empire late in the 2nd century AD, and in 270 the Romans abandoned Dacia. Within two centuries, they were also forced to flee Pannonia by the Huns, whose short-lived empire was established by Attila. He had earlier conquered the Magyars near the lower Volga River, and for centuries the two groups were erroneously thought to have common ancestry. Attila remains a very common given name in Hungary, however.

Germanic tribes such as the Goths, Longobards and Gepids occupied the region for the next century and a half until the Avars, a powerful Turkic people, gained control of the Carpathian Basin in the 6th century. They in turn were subdued by Charlemagne in 796 and converted to Christianity. By that time, the Carpathian Basin was virtually unpopulated except for scattered groups of Turkic and Germanic tribes on the plains and Slavs in the northern hills.

The Magyars & the Conquest

The origin of the Magyars is a complicated issue, not in the least helped by the similarity in English of the words 'Hun' and 'Hungary', which are not related. One thing is certain: Magyars are part of the Finno-Ugric group of peoples, who inhabited the forests somewhere between the middle Volga River and the Ural Mountains in western Siberia as early as 4000 BC.

In about 2000 BC population growth forced the Finnish-Estonian branch to move westward, ultimately reaching the Baltic

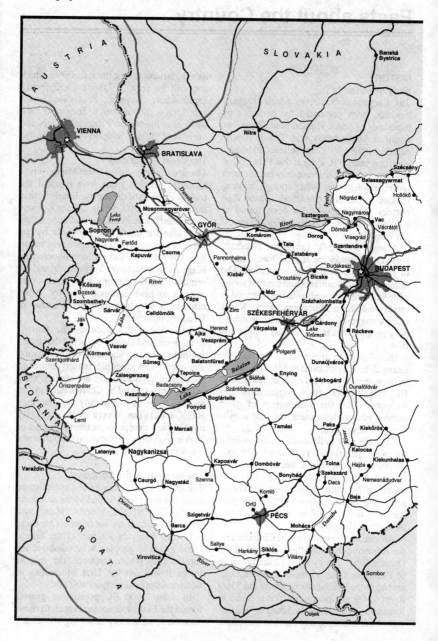

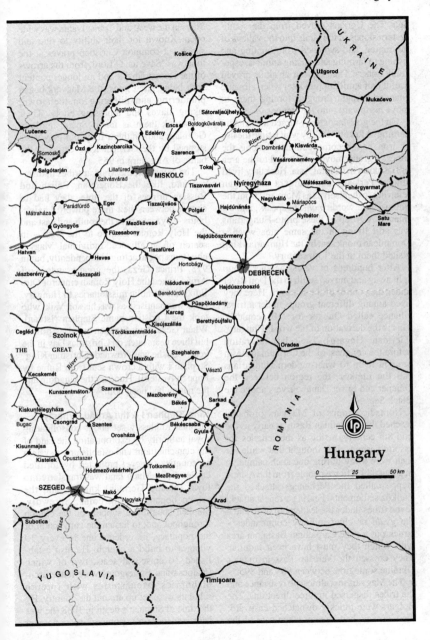

Hungary

0   25   50 km

Sea. The Ugrians moved from the south-eastern slopes of the Urals into the valleys of the region, and switched from hunting and fishing to farming and raising animals, especially horses. Their equestrian skills proved useful half a millennium later when climatic changes brought drought, forcing them to move northward onto the steppes.

On the grasslands, they turned to nomadic herding. After 500 BC, by which time the use of iron had become common among the tribes, a group moved westward to the area of Bashkiria in Central Asia. Here they lived among Persians and Bulgars and began referring to themselves as Magyars (from the Finno-Ugric words *mon*, 'to speak', and *er*, 'man'). A group of these proto-Hungarians was still living in the same area when a Dominican monk sent by the Hungarian king visited them in the 13th century.

After hundreds of years, another group split away and moved south to the Don River under the control of the Khazars. Here they lived among different groups under a tribal alliance called Onogur (or '10 peoples'). This is the derivation of the word 'Hungary' (German: Ungarn). Their last migration before the conquest of the Carpathian Basin brought them to what modern Hungarians call the Etelköz, the region between the Dnieper and lower Danube rivers above the Black Sea.

Nomadic groups of Magyars probably reached the Carpathian Basin as early as the mid-8th century, acting as mercenaries for assorted armies. It is thought that while the men were away during one such campaign in about 889, a fierce people from the Asiatic steppe called the Pechenegs attacked the Etelköz settlements. Fearing a repeat attack, seven tribes under the leadership of Árpád – the *gyula* or chief military commander – struck out for the Carpathian Basin, an area with which they must have been familiar. They crossed the Verecke Pass in today's Ukraine some time between 893 and 895.

The Magyars met almost no resistance and the tribes dispersed in three directions. The Bulgars were quickly dispatched eastward; the Germans had already taken care of the Slavs in the west; and Transylvania was wide open. Known for their ability to ride and shoot – a common Christian prayer at the time was 'Save us, O Lord, from the arrows of the Hungarians' – and no longer content with being hired guns, the Magyars began plundering and pillaging on their own, taking slaves and amassing booty. Their raids took them as far as Spain, northern Germany and southern Italy, but they were stopped by the German King Otto I at the battle of Augsburg in 955.

The defeat left the Magyar tribes in disarray and, like the Bohemian, Polish and Russian princes of the time, they had to choose between their more powerful neighbours – Byzantium to the south and east and the Holy Roman Empire to the west – in search of an alliance. Individual Magyar chieftains began acting independently, but in 973, Prince Géza, the great-grandson of Árpád, asked the Holy Roman emperor Otto II to send Catholic missionaries to Hungary. Géza was baptised, as was his son Vajk, who took the Christian name Stephen (István). When Géza died, Stephen ruled as prince, but three years later, on Christmas Day in the year 1000, he was crowned 'Christian King' Stephen I with a crown sent from Rome by Pope Sylvester II. Hungary the kingdom and the nation had been born.

King Stephen I & the Árpád Dynasty

Stephen ruthlessly set about consolidating royal authority by expropriating the land of the clan chieftains and establishing a system of counties *(megye)* protected by fortified castles *(vár)*. Much land was transferred to loyal (mostly German) knights, and the crown began minting coins. Shrewdly, Stephen sought the support of the church throughout and, to hasten the conversion of the populace, he ordered one in every 10 villages to build a church. He also established 10 episcopal seats, two of which (Kalocsa and Esztergom) were made archbishoprics. Monasteries with foreign scholars were set up around the country. By the time of Stephen's death in 1038 (he was later made a saint), Hungary was a nascent

Christian country, increasingly westward-looking and multi-ethnic.

But the next two and a half centuries – the reign of the House of Árpád – would test the new kingdom to the limit. The period was one of relentless struggles between rival claimants to the throne, which weakened the young nation's defences against its powerful neighbours. There was a brief hiatus under King Ladislas I (László; ruled 1077-95), who fended off attacks from Byzantium, and under his successor Koloman the Bookish (Könyves Kálmán), who encouraged literature, art and the writing of chronicles until his death in 1116.

Tension flared again when the Byzantine emperor made a grab for Hungary's provinces in Dalmatia and Croatia, which it had attached by the turn of the 12th century. Béla III, a powerful ruler from 1172 to 1196 who had a permanent residence built at Esztergom (then an alternative royal seat to Székesfehérvár), stopped him. Béla's son, Andrew II (András; ruled 1205-35), however, weakened the crown when he gave in to the barons' demands for more land, for the most part in order to fund his crusades. This led to the Golden Bull, a kind of Magna Carta signed at Székesfehérvár in 1222, which limited some of the king's powers in favour of the nobility.

When Béla IV (ruled 1235-70) tried to regain the estates, the barons were able to oppose him on equal terms. Fearing Mongol expansion and realising he could not count on local help, Béla looked to the West and brought in German and Slovak settlers. His efforts were in vain. In 1241 the Mongol hordes raced through the country, virtually burning Hungary to the ground and killing an estimated one-third of its two million people.

To rebuild the country as fast as possible, Béla invited Germans and Saxons to settle in Transdanubia, Transylvania and the Great Plain. He also built a string of defensive hilltop castles (including the ones at Buda and Visegrád). But in a bid to appease the nobility, he handed over large tracts of land to the barons. This enhanced their position

and quest for independence still further. At the time of Béla's death, anarchy reigned in Hungary. The Árpád line died out with the death of the heirless Andrew III in 1301.

Medieval Hungary

The struggle for the Hungarian throne after the death of Andrew III involved several European dynasties, but it was Charles Robert (Károly Róbert) of the French House of Anjou who finally won out (with the pope's blessing) and ruled until 1342. Charles Robert was an able administrator who managed to break the power of the provincial barons (though much of the land remained in private hands) and sought links with his neighbours. In 1335, he met the Polish and Czech kings at the new royal palace in Visegrád to discuss territorial disputes and to forge an alliance that would smash Vienna's control of trade.

Under his son and successor, Louis the Great (Nagy Lajos), Hungary returned to a policy of conquest. A brilliant military strategist, Louis (ruled 1342-82) acquired southern territory in the Balkans as far as Dalmatia and as far north as Poland. But his successes were short-lived and the menace of the Ottoman Turks had begun.

As Louis had borne no sons, one of his daughters, Mary, succeeded him. Predictably, this was deemed unacceptable by the barons, who rose up against the 'petticoat throne'. Within a short time, Mary's husband, Sigismund (Zsigmond) of Luxembourg, was crowned king. Sigismund's long reign (1387-1437) brought peace at home, and there was a great flowering of Gothic art and architecture in Hungary. But while he was able to procure the coveted crown of Bohemia and was made Holy Roman emperor during his rule, he was unable to stop the march of the Turks up through the Balkans.

A Transylvanian general of Romanian origin called János Hunyadi began his career at the court of Sigismund and, after the king's death, acted as regent. His victory over the Turks at Belgrade (Hungarian: Nándorfehérvár) in 1456 checked the Ottoman advance into Hungary for 70 years and assured the coronation of his son Matthias (Mátyás) Corvinus, the greatest ruler of medieval Hungary.

Wisely, Matthias (ruled 1458-90) maintained a mercenary force through taxation of the nobility, and this 'Black Army' conquered Moravia, Bohemia and even parts of Austria. Not only did Matthias make Hungary one of Central Europe's leading powers, but under his rule the nation enjoyed something of a golden age. His second wife, the Neapolitan Queen Beatrice, brought artisans from Italy who completely rebuilt and extended the Gothic palace at Visegrád; the beauty and sheer size of the Renaissance residence they built was beyond comparison in Europe at the time. Matthias was celebrated for his fairness and justice, and Hungarian mythology is full of stories illustrating 'Good King' Matthias' love of his subjects.

But while Matthias busied himself with centralising power for the crown, he ignored the growing Turkish threat. His successor Vladislav II (Úlászló) of the Bohemian Jagiellonian dynasty was unable to maintain even royal authority as members of the diet (assembly) met to approve royal decrees, squandered royal funds and expropriated land. In 1514, what had begun as a crusade organised by the power-hungry archbishop of Esztergom, Tamás Bakócz, turned into a peasant uprising against the landlords under the leadership of György Dózsa. The revolt was brutally repressed, some 70,000 peasants were tortured and executed, and Dózsa was burned alive on a red-hot iron throne. The retrograde Tripartitum Law that followed codified the rights and privileges of the barons and nobles and reduced the peasantry to perpetual serfdom. By the time Louis II (Lajos) took the throne in 1516 at the tender age of nine, he couldn't rely on either side.

The Battle of Mohács & Turkish Occupation

The defeat of the ragtag Hungarian army by the Ottoman Turks at Mohács in 1526 is a watershed in Hungarian history. On the battlefield near this small Southern Transdanubian town, a relatively prosperous and independent medieval Hungary died, sending the nation into a tailspin of partition, foreign domination and despair that can still be felt today.

It would be foolish to put all the blame on the weak and indecisive boy-king Louis or on his commander-in-chief Pál Tomori, the archbishop of Kalocsa. Bickering among the nobility and the brutal crackdown of the Dózsa uprising a dozen years earlier had severely weakened Hungary's military power, and there was virtually nothing left in the royal coffers. By 1526, the Ottoman sultan Süleyman the Magnificent had taken much of the Balkans, including Belgrade, and was poised to march on Buda and then Vienna with a force of 100,000 men.

Unable – or unwilling – to wait for reinforcements from Transylvania under the command of his rival John Szapolyai (Zápolyai János), Louis rushed south with a motley army of 25,000 to battle the Turks and was soundly thrashed in less than two hours. Along with bishops, nobles and an estimated 20,000 soldiers, the king himself was killed – an ignoble death by drowning in a stream as he retreated. John Szapolyai, who had sat out the events in the castle at Tokaj, was crowned king three months later but, despite grovelling before the Turks, was never able to exploit the power he had sought so madly. Greed, self-interest and ambition had led Hungary to defeat itself.

After Buda Castle fell to the Turks in 1541, Hungary was divided into three parts. Though heroic resistance continued against the Turks, most notably at Kőszeg (1532), Eger (1552) and Szigetvár (1566), the division would remain intact for more than a century and a half. The central part, including Buda, went to the Turks while parts of Transdanubia and what is now Slovakia were governed by the Austrian House of Habsburg assisted by the Hungarian nobility based at Bratislava (Hungarian: Pozsony). The principality of Transylvania east of the Tisza River prospered as a vassal state of the

Ottoman Empire, initially under Szapolyai's son John Sigismund (Zsigmond János).

The Turkish occupation was marked by constant fighting among these three parties; Catholic 'Royal Hungary' was pitted against not only the Turks but the Protestant Transylvanian princes. Gábor Bethlen, who ruled Transylvania from 1613 to 1629, tried to end the incessant warfare by conquering Royal Hungary with a mercenary army of Heyduck peasants and some Turkish assistance. But the Habsburgs and the Hungarians themselves viewed the Ottomans as the greatest threat to Europe since the Mongols and blocked the advance.

Although Transylvania enjoyed something of a cultural renaissance during this period, the Turkish-occupied central part of Hungary suffered greatly, with most people fleeing from the devastated Great Plain to the northern hills or to the *khas* towns, which were under the protection of the sultans. For rump Hungary, the occupation was known as the 'century of decline'. The Turks did little building apart from a few bath houses and some civic structures in Pécs and Szigetvár; for the most part, they converted churches into mosques and used existing public buildings for administration.

As Turkish power began to wane in the 17th century, Hungarian resistance to the Habsburgs, who had used Royal Hungary as a buffer zone between Vienna and the Turks, increased. A plot inspired by the palatine Ferenc Wesselényi was foiled in 1670 and a revolt by Imre Thököly (1682) and his army of *kuruc* (anti-Habsburg mercenaries) put down. But with the help of the Polish army, Austrian and Hungarian forces liberated Buda in 1686. An imperial army under Eugene of Savoy wiped out the last Turkish army in Hungary at the Battle of Zenta (now Senta in Yugoslavia) 13 years later.

Habsburg Rule

The expulsion of the Turks did not result in a free and independent Hungary, and the policies of the Catholic Habsburgs' Counter-Reformation and heavy taxation further alienated the nobility. In 1703, the Transyl-

vanian prince Ferenc Rákóczi II assembled an army of kuruc forces against the Austrians. The war dragged on for eight years, during which time the Habsburgs were 'deposed' as the rulers of Hungary by the rebels, but superior imperial forces and lack of funds forced the kuruc to negotiate a separate peace with Vienna behind Rákóczı's back. The 1703-11 War of Independence had failed, but Rákóczi was the first leader to unite Hungarians against the Habsburgs.

Though the compromise had brought the fighting to an end, Hungary was now a mere province of the Habsburg Empire. With the ascension of Maria Theresa to the throne in 1740, the Hungarian nobility pledged their 'lives and blood' to her at the diet in Bratislava in exchange for concessions. Thus began the period of enlightened absolutism that would continue under the rule of her son, the 'hatted king' (so-called as he was never crowned in Hungary) Joseph II, who ruled for a decade from 1780.

Under the reigns of Maria Theresa and Joseph, Hungary made great steps forward economically and culturally. The depopulated areas in the east and south were settled by Romanians and Serbs while German Swabians went to Transdanubia. Attempts to modernise society by dissolving the all-powerful (and corrupt) religious orders, abolishing serfdom and replacing 'neutral' Latin with German as the official language of state administration were opposed by the Hungarian nobility, and Joseph rescinded most on his death bed.

Dissenting voices could still be heard, and the ideals of the French Revolution began to take root in certain intellectual circles in Hungary. In 1795 Ignác Martonovics, a former Franciscan priest, and six other prorepublican Jacobins were beheaded at Vérmező (Blood Meadow) in Buda for plotting against the Crown.

At this time almost 90% of the population worked the land, and it was primarily through agriculture that modernisation came to Hungary. Liberalism and social reform found their greatest supporters among certain members of the aristocracy. Count György Festetics (1755-1819), for example, founded Europe's first agricultural college at Keszthely. Count István Széchenyi (1791-1860), a true Renaissance man and called 'the greatest Hungarian' by his contemporaries, advocated the abolition of serfdom and returned much of his own land to the peasants, regulated the Tisza and Danube rivers for commerce and irrigation, and promoted horse racing among the upper classes to improve breeding stock for use in agriculture.

But the proponents of gradual reform were quickly superseded by a more radical faction demanding more immediate action. The group included such men as Miklós Wesselényi, Ferenc Deák and the poet Ferenc Kölcsey, but the dominant figure was Lajos Kossuth (1802-94). It was this dynamic lawyer and journalist who would lead Hungary to its greatest confrontation ever with the Habsburgs.

The 1848-49 War of Independence & the Dual Monarchy

The Habsburg Empire began to weaken as Hungarian nationalism increased early in the 19th century. The Hungarians, suspicious of Napoleon's policies, ignored French appeals to revolt against Vienna, and certain reforms were introduced: the replacement of Latin, the official language of administration, with Magyar; a law allowing serfs alternative means of discharging their feudal obligations of service; and increased Hungarian representation in the Council of State.

But the reforms were too limited and too late, and the diet became more defiant in its dealings with the crown. At the same time, the wave of revolution sweeping Europe spurred the more radical faction on. In 1848, liberal Count Lajos Batthyány was made prime minister of the new Hungarian ministry, which counted Deák, Kossuth and Széchenyi as members. The Habsburgs also reluctantly agreed to abolish serfdom and proclaim equality under the law. On 15 March, a group calling itself the Youth of March led by the poet Sándor Petőfi took to the streets to press for even more radical reforms and revolution. Habsburg patience was wearing thin.

In September, Habsburg forces under the governor of Croatia, Josip Jelačić, launched an attack on Hungary and Batthyány's government was dissolved. A national defence commission was hastily formed and the government moved to Debrecen, where Kossuth was elected leader. In April 1849, the parliament declared Hungary's full independence and the dethronement of the Habsburgs.

The new Habsburg emperor, Franz Joseph (1848-1916), was nothing like his feeble-minded predecessor Ferdinand V and quickly took action. He sought the assistance of Tsar Nicholas I, who obliged him with 200,000 troops. Already support for the revolution was crumbling, particularly in areas of mixed population where the Magyars were seen as oppressors. Weak and vastly outnumbered, the rebel troops were defeated by the summer of 1849.

A series of brutal reprisals ensued in the aftermath of the revolution. Batthyány and 13 generals (the so-called Martyrs of Arad) were executed and Kossuth went into exile in Turkey, (Petőfi had been killed in battle). Habsburg troops then went around the country systematically blowing up castles and fortifications lest they be used by resurgent rebels. What little of medieval Hungary that was left after the Turks and the 1703-11 War of Independence was now reduced to rubble.

Hungary was again merged into the empire as a conquered province and 'neo-absolutism' was the order of the day. Passive resistance among Hungarians and disastrous military defeats for the Habsburgs in 1859 and 1865, however, pushed Franz Joseph to the negotiating table with liberal Hungarians under Deák's leadership.

The result was the Compromise of 1867 (*Ausgleich* in German, which actually means 'reconciliation'), creating the Dual Monarchy of Austria the empire and Hungary the kingdom. It was a federated state of two parliaments and two capitals – Vienna and Budapest (the city that would be incorporated six years later when Buda, Pest and Óbuda united). Only defence, foreign relations and customs were shared. Hungary was even allowed a small army.

This so-called Age of Dualism would carry on until 1918 and spark an economic, cultural and intellectual rebirth in Hungary. Agriculture developed, factories were founded and the composers Franz (Ferenc) Liszt and Ferenc Erkel were making beautiful music. The middle class, dominated by Germans and Jews in Pest, burgeoned and the capital entered into a frenzy of building. Much of what you see in Budapest today – from the grand boulevards and their Eclectic-style apartment blocks to the Parliament building and Matthias Church in the Castle District – was built at this time. The apex of this golden age was the six-month exhibition in 1896 celebrating the millennium of the Magyar conquest (*honfoglalás*).

But all was not well in the kingdom. The city-based working class had almost no rights, and the situation in the countryside has remained almost unchanged since the Middle Ages. Minorities under Hungarian control, such as Czechs, Slovaks, Croatians and Romanians, were under increased pressure to 'Magyarise' and saw their new rulers as oppressors. Increasingly they worked to dismember the empire.

WWI, the Republic of Councils & Trianon

In July 1914, a month to the day after the assassination of the heir to the Habsburg throne, Archduke Franz Ferdinand, by Bosnian Serbs in Sarajevo, the Dual Monarchy entered WWI as an ally of the German Empire. The result was disastrous with heavy destruction and hundreds of thousands killed on the Russian and Italian fronts. At the armistice in 1918 the fate of the Dual Monarchy (and Hungary as a multinational kingdom) was sealed.

A republic under the leadership of Count

Hungary before the 1920 Trianon Treaty

Mihály Károlyi was set up immediately after the war, and the Habsburg monarchy was dethroned for the third and final time. But the fledgling republic would not last long. Widespread destitution, the occupation of Hungary by the Allies and the success of the Bolshevik revolution in Russia had radicalised much of the Budapest working class. In March 1919 a group of Hungarian Communists under Béla Kun seized power. The so-called Republic of Councils (*Tanácsköztársaság*) set out to nationalise industry and private property and build a fairer society, but opposition to the regime unleashed a reign of 'red terror'. Kun and his comrades were overthrown in just five months by troops from Romania, which occupied the capital.

In 1920, the Allies drew up a postwar settlement under the Treaty of Trianon that enlarged some countries, truncated others and created several 'successor states'. As one of the defeated countries and with large numbers of minorities clamouring for independence within its borders, Hungary stood to lose more than most. Hungary was reduced to one-third its historical size and, while it was now largely a uniform nation-state, for millions of ethnic Hungarians in Romania, Yugoslavia and Czechoslovakia, the tables had turned: they were now the minorities.

'Trianon' became the singularly most hated word in Hungary, and the *diktátum* is often reviled today as if it were imposed on the nation just yesterday. Many of the problems it created remain to this day, and it has coloured Hungary's relations with its neighbours for more than three-quarters of a century.

The Horthy Years & WWII

In 1920, in Hungary's first secret-ballot election, parliament chose a kingdom as the form of state and elected Admiral Miklós Horthy as its regent, who would remain so until the latter days of WWII. The arrangement confused even US President Franklin D Roosevelt in the early days of the war. After being briefed by an aide on the government

and leadership of Hungary, he reportedly said: 'Let me see if I understand you right. Hungary is a kingdom without a king run by a regent who's an admiral without a navy?'

Horthy launched a 'white terror' – every bit as brutal as the 'red' one of Béla Kun – that attacked Communists and Jews for their role in the Republic of Councils. As the regime was consolidated, it showed itself to be extremely rightist and conservative, advocating 'traditional values' and the status quo. Though the country had the basics of a parliamentary system, Horthy was all-powerful – what is now referred to as a 'strong man' – and very few reforms were enacted. Indeed, the lot of the working class and the peasantry worsened.

One thing everyone agreed on was that the return of lost territories was essential for Hungary's development. Early on, Prime Minister István Bethlen was able to secure the return of Pécs, illegally occupied by Yugoslavia, and the citizens of Sopron voted in a plebiscite to return to Hungary from Austria, but it was not enough. Hungary could not count on France, Britain or the USA to help recoup its land and sought help from the fascist governments of Germany and Italy. Hungary's move to the right intensified throughout the 1930s, though it remained silent when WWII broke out in September 1939.

Horthy hoped an alliance would not mean actually having to enter the war, but after recovering northern Transylvania and part of Croatia through German efforts, he was forced to join the Axis in June 1941. The war was as disastrous for Hungary as the 1914-18 one had been, and hundreds of thousands of Hungarian troops died while retreating from Stalingrad, where they'd been used as cannon fodder. Realising too late that his country was again on the losing side, Horthy began negotiating a separate peace with the Allies.

The result was the total occupation of Hungary by the German army in March 1944. Under pressure, Horthy installed Ferenc Szálasi, the deranged leader of the Nazi Arrow Cross Party, and was deported to

Germany. (Horthy later moved to Portugal, where he died in 1957. Despite some public outcry, Horthy's body was returned to Hungary in September 1993 and reburied in the family plot at Kenderes, east of Szolnok. His role in history is now being re-examined by revisionist historians.)

The Arrow Cross moved quickly to quash any opposition, and thousands of liberal politicians and labour leaders were arrested. At the same time, the puppet government introduced anti-Jewish legislation similar to that in Germany, and Jews, relatively safe under Horthy, were rounded up by Hungarian Nazis into ghettos. In the summer of 1944, less than a year before the war's end, some 400,000 Jewish men, women and children were deported to Auschwitz and other labour camps, where they were savagely murdered, starved or succumbed to disease.

Hungary now became an international battleground for the first time since the Turkish occupation, and bombs began falling on Budapest. The resistance movement drew support from many sides, including the Communists. Fierce fighting continued in the countryside, especially near Debrecen and Székesfehérvár, and by Christmas the Soviet army had surrounded Budapest. When the Germans and Hungarian Nazis rejected a settlement, the siege of the capital began. By the time the German war machine surrendered in April 1945, many of Budapest's homes, historical buildings, churches and all the Danube bridges had been destroyed.

The People's Republic

When free elections were held in November 1945, the Independent Smallholders Party took 57% of the vote. But Soviet political officers, backed by the occupation forces, insisted that three other parties – including the Social Democrats and Communists – form a coalition. Limited democracy prevailed, and land-reform laws, sponsored by the Communist minister of agriculture, Imre Nagy, were enacted, wiping away the prewar feudal structure. Hungary also experienced the worst hyperinflation the world has ever

known, with notes worth up to 10,000 trillion pengő issued before the new forint was introduced.

Within a couple of years, the Communists were ready to grab total power. After a rigged election held under a complicated new electoral law in 1947, they declared their candidate Mátyás Rákosi victorious. The Social Democrats were forced to merge with the Communists into the Hungarian Socialist Workers Party.

Rákosi, a big fan of Stalin, began a process of nationalisation and unfeasibly fast industrialisation at the expense of agriculture. Peasants were forced into collective farms, and all produce had to be delivered to the state. A network of spies and informers exposed 'class enemies' to the secret police (ÁVO), who had them jailed for spying (such as Cardinal József Mindszenty), sent into internal exile or condemned to labour camps like the notorious one at Recsk in the Mátra Hills. It is estimated that during this period a quarter of the adult population faced police or judicial proceedings.

Bitter feuding within the party began, and purges and Stalinesque show trials became the norm. László Rajk, the Communist minister of the interior (which also controlled the ÁVO) was executed for 'Titoism'; his successor János Kádár was tortured and jailed. In August 1949, Hungary was proclaimed a 'people's republic'.

After the death of Stalin in March 1953 and Krushchev's denunciation of him three years later, Rákosi's tenure was up and the terror began to abate. Under pressure from within the party, Rákosi's successor, Ernő Gerő, rehabilitated Rajk posthumously and readmitted Nagy, who had been expelled from the party a year earlier for suggesting reforms. But Gerő was as much a hardliner as Rákosi had been, and in October 1956 during Rajk's reburial, murmured calls for a real reform of the system – 'Communism with a human face' – were made.

The 1956 Uprising

The nation's greatest tragedy – an event that for a while shook the world and Communism and pitted Hungarian against Hungarian – began on 23 October when some 50,000 university students assembled at Bem tér in Buda, shouting anti-Soviet slogans and demanding that Nagy be named prime minister. That night a crowd pulled down the colossal statue of Stalin near Heroes' Square and shots were fired by ÁVH (the renamed ÁVO) agents on another group gathering outside Hungarian Radio headquarters in Pest. Hungary was in revolution.

Two days later Nagy formed a government (which included János Kádár), and for a short time it appeared that he might be successful in transforming Hungary into a neutral, multiparty state. But on 1 November Soviet tanks and troops crossed into Hungary and within 72 hours began attacking Budapest and other centres. Kádár, who had slipped away from Budapest to join the Russian invaders, was installed as leader.

Fierce street fighting continued for several days – encouraged by Radio Free Europe broadcasts and promises of support from the West, embroiled at the time in the Suez crisis. When it was over, 25,000 people were dead. Then the reprisals – the worst in Hungarian history – began. An estimated 20,000 people were arrested and 2000 – including Nagy and his associates – were executed. Another 250,000 refugees fled Hungary through Austria. The government lost what little credibility it had had and the nation some of its most competent and talented citizens. As for the physical scars, look at almost any building in Pest: the bullet holes and shrapnel on the exterior walls still cry out in silent fury.

Hungary under Kádár

The transformation of János Kádár from traitor and most hated man in the land to respected reformer is one of the most astonishing *tours de force* of the 20th century. No doubt it will keep historians busy well into the next.

After the reprisals and the consolidation of his regime, Kádár began a programme to liberalise the social and economic structure based on compromise. (His most quoted line

is 'Whoever is not against us is with us' – a reversal of the Stalinist adage.) In 1968, he and the economist Rezső Nyers unveiled the New Economic Mechanism (NEM) to introduce elements of a market to the planned economy. But even this proved too daring for many party conservatives. Nyers was ousted and the NEM chipped away.

Kádár survived that power struggle and went on to introduce greater consumerism and market socialism. By the mid-1970s Hungary was light years ahead of any other Soviet bloc country in its standard of living, freedom of movement and opportunities to criticise the government. People may have had to wait seven years for a Lada car or 12 for a telephone, but most Hungarians could enjoy at least access to a second house in the countryside and a decent material life. The 'Hungarian model' attracted much Western attention – and investment.

But things began to sour in the 1980s. The Kádár system of 'goulash socialism', which had seemed 'timeless and everlasting' as one Hungarian writer put it, was incapable of dealing with such 'un-socialist' problems as unemployment, soaring inflation and the largest per-capita foreign debt in the region. Kádár and the 'old guard' refused to hear talk about party reforms and were dismissed in May 1988.

János Kádár in 1963

Renewal & Change

Three reformers – Nyers, Károly Grósz and Imre Pozsgay – took power. Party conservatives at first put a lid on real change by demanding a retreat from political liberalisation in exchange for their support of the new regime's economic policies. But the tide had already turned. Throughout the summer and autumn of 1988, new political parties were formed and old ones revived. In February 1989 Pozsgay, seeing the handwriting on the wall as Mikhail Gorbachev kissed babies and launched his reforms in the Soviet Union, announced that the events of 1956 had been a 'popular uprising', not the 'counter-revolution' the regime had always said it was. Four months later hundreds of thousands of people attended the reburial of Imre Nagy and other victims of 1956.

In September 1989, again at Pozsgay's instigation, Hungary cut away the electrified wire fence separating it from Austria. The move released a wave of East Germans holidaying in Hungary into the West and the gap attracted thousands more. The collapse of the Communist regimes around the region was now unstoppable. What Hungarians now call *az átkos 40 év* ('the accursed 40 years') had come to an end.

The Republic of Hungary Again

In October 1989, on the 33rd anniversary of the 1956 Uprising, the nation once again became the Republic of Hungary. At their party congress the Communists surrendered their monopoly on power, paving the way for free elections in March 1990. The party's name was changed from the Hungarian Socialist Workers' Party to simply the Hungarian Socialist Party (MSZP).

The MSZP's new programme advocated social democracy and a free-market economy, but this was not enough to shake off the stigma of four decades of autocratic rule. The 1990 vote was won by the centrist Hungarian Democratic Forum (MDF), which advocated a gradual transition to capitalism. The social-democratic Alliance of Free Democrats (SZDSZ), which had called for much faster change, came second and the

Socialists trailed far behind. As Gorbachev looked on, Hungary changed political systems with scarcely a murmur and the last Soviet troops left Hungary in June 1991.

In coalition with two smaller parties – the Independent Smallholders (FKgP) and the Christian Democrats (KDNP) – the MDF provided Hungary with sound government during its painful transition to a full market economy. Those years saw Hungary's northern (Czechoslovakia) and southern neighbours (Yugoslavia) split apart along ethnic lines. Prime Minister József Antall did little to improve relations with Slovakia, Romania and Yugoslavia by claiming to be the 'emotional and spiritual' prime minister of the large Hungarian minorities in those countries. In mid-1993 the MDF was forced to expel István Csurka, a party vice president, after he made ultranationalistic and anti-Semitic statements that tarnished Hungary's image as a bastion of moderation and stability in a volatile region. Antall died after a long fight with cancer in December 1993 and was replaced by Interior Minister Péter Boross.

Despite initial successes in curbing inflation and lowering interest rates, a host of economic problems slowed the pace of development, and the government's laissez-faire policies did not help. But like most people in the region, Hungarians had unrealistically expected a much faster improvement in their living standards. Most of them – 76% according to a poll in mid-1993 – were 'very disappointed'.

In the elections of May 1994 the Socialist Party, led by Gyula Horn, won an absolute majority in parliament. This in no way implied a return to the past, and Horn was quick to point out that it was in fact his party that had initiated the whole reform process in the first place. (As foreign minister in 1989 Horn had played a key role in opening the border with Austria.) Árpád Göncz of the SZDSZ was elected for a second five-year term as president of the republic in 1995. In March 1996, Horn was re-elected Socialist Party leader and confirmed that he would push ahead with the party's economic stabilisation programme and seek closer political and military ties with the West.

Kings, Saints, Strong Men & Premiers

The following is a list of the most important monarchs, rulers, dictators and leaders in Hungarian history. Names are given in English, with the Magyar equivalents in brackets. The dates refer to their reign or term of office.

Árpád Dynasty
Árpád 886-907
Géza 972-997
Stephen I (István) 1000-38
Ladislas I (László) 1077-95
Coloman the Bookish (Könyves Kálmán) 1095-1116
Béla III 1173-96
Andrew II (András or Endre) 1205-35
Béla IV 1235-70
Andrew III 1290-1301

Mixed Dynasties
Charles Robert (Károly Róbert) 1307-42
Louis the Great (Nagy Lajos) 1342-82
Mary (Mária) 1383-87
Sigismund (Zsigmond) 1387-1437
János Hunyadi (regent) 1445-56
Matthias (Mátyás) Corvinus 1458-90
Vladislav II (Ulászló) 1490-1516
Louis II (Lajos) 1516-26
John Szapolyai (Zápolyai János) 1526-40

Habsburg Dynasty
Ferdinand I (Ferdinánd) 1526-64
Maximilian II (Miksa) 1564-76
Leopold I (Lipót) 1655-1705
Maria Theresa (Mária Terézia) 1740-80
Joseph II (József) 1780-90
Ferdinand V 1835-48
Franz Joseph (Ferenc József) 1848-1916
Charles IV (Károly) 1916-18

Political Leaders
Mihály Károlyi 1919
Béla Kun 1919
Miklós Horthy (regent) 1920-44
Ferenc Szálasi 1944-45
Mátyás Rákosi 1947-56
János Kádár 1956-88
Károly Grósz 1988-90
József Antall 1990-93
Péter Baross 1993-94
Gyula Horn 1994-

GEOGRAPHY

Hungary lies in the Carpathian Basin and almost in the centre of Europe. It shares borders with seven countries: Austria, Slovakia, Ukraine, Romania, Yugoslavia, Croatia and Slovenia. The country covers just over 93,000 sq km – roughly 1% of Europe's total land mass.

There are three basic topographies: the low-lying regions of the Great Plain (Nagyalföld) in the east, centre and south-east, and of the Little Plain (Kisalföld) in the north-west, which together account for two-thirds of Hungary's territory; the northern mountain ranges; and the hilly regions of Transdanubia in the west and south-west. The biggest rivers are the Danube (417 km in Hungary) and the Tisza (598 km), which divide the country into thirds, and the Dráva, forming the south-western border with Croatia. The country has well over 1000 lakes (of which the largest is Balaton), and is strewn with thermal springs.

Main Regions

Hungary's topographical divisions do not accurately reflect the country's cultural and subtler geographical differences, nor do the 19 administrative counties *(megye)* help travellers much. Instead, Hungary can be divided into eight main regions: Budapest and its environs; the Danube Bend; Western Transdanubia; the Balaton region of central Transdanubia; Southern Transdanubia; the Great Plain; the Northern Uplands; and the North-East.

Greater Budapest, by far Hungary's largest city, with about two million people, has for its borders Csepel Island in the Danube River to the south, the start of the Great Plain in the east, the Buda Hills to the west and the Danube Bend in the north. The Danube bisects the city, with flat Pest on the east side (or the left bank as you follow the flow of the river) and hilly Buda to the west. A dozen thermal or therapeutic baths make use of the city's hot springs.

The Danube Bend is the point at which the river, flowing east across Europe, is forced southward by two small ranges. It is a hilly

Hungary's
Regions

area of great beauty and historical significance and an easy day trip from the capital. The Bend's main city is Esztergom.

Transdanubia – the area 'across the Danube' (or west of it) – has great variety. Western Transdanubia is both hilly and flat (the Little Plain is to the north), and its chief centres are Győr, Sopron and Szombathely. The centre of Transdanubia is dominated by Balaton, the largest lake in Europe outside Scandinavia. Székesfehérvár is the largest city here. Southern Transdanubia, with Pécs as its 'capital', is less hilly but richer in minerals. Wine is produced in all three parts of Transdanubia.

The Great Plain, often referred to as the *puszta*, is a prairie scarcely 200m above sea level that stretches for hundreds of km east of the Danube. The central part, the most industrialised area of the Plain, has Szolnok as its major town. The Eastern Plain is largely saline grassland and given over to stock-breeding; Debrecen is the main seat.

The Southern Plain is agriculturally rich, with cereal crops and fruit in abundance and the occasional farmstead breaking the monotony. Market towns that have grown into cities here are Kecskemét and Szeged.

The so-called Northern Uplands is Hungary's 'mountainous' region and has peaks averaging between 400 and 800m; the highest is Kékes in the Mátra Hills, which reaches just over 1000m. Abutting the forested hills and valleys are lush vineyards and industry (though much of that is now in decline). Miskolc and Eger are the Northern Uplands' main cities.

North-East Hungary is much lower than the Northern Uplands but not quite as flat as the Great Plain. It is a fruit-growing region and ethnically quite heterogeneous with the bulk of the nation's Gypsy population. Nyíregyháza is the main centre.

Habitation

About 70% of Hungary is under cultivation

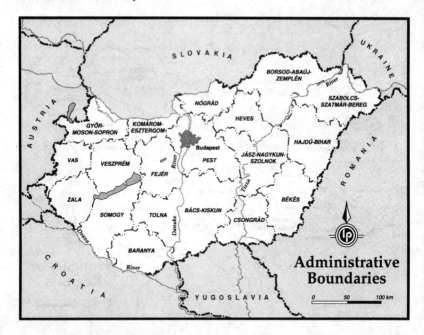

Administrative
Boundaries

0   50   100 km

in some form or another; 14% of it is forested. The population density is 110 people per sq km, and about 61% of the total live in towns or cities. More than half of Hungary's 3500 communities lie in Transdanubia.

Towns – and even some cities – are of three basic types depending on the region. The radial system, with roads leading to the open fields, is common on the Eastern Plain. The single street with houses clustered on and off it is the usual pattern in the Northern Uplands and much of Transdanubia, while some towns on the Southern Plain take the form of a chessboard. Houses in some Hungarian communities are spaced far apart, especially in parts of Southern Transdanubia and the Southern Plain.

CLIMATE
Hungary has a temperate climate – variable but generally very pleasant. If you think of the Carpathian Basin as a saucer, you'll get an idea of how it all works. The Dinaric

Mountains lie to the south-west, the Alps to the west, and the Carpathians to the north, east and south-east. These ranges determine Hungary's three climatic zones: Mediterranean in the south, Continental in the east and Atlantic in the west.

In Southern Transdanubia, spring arrives early and its famous Indian summers can stretch into early November. Winters are mild and wet. The Great Plain has the most extreme seasonal differences, with very cold, windy winters and hot, usually dry summers (though sudden storms are a common occurrence on the Plain in summer). The climate of the Northern Uplands is also Continental, but it gets more sun in autumn and winter than any other part of Hungary.

Spring arrives early in April in Budapest and Western Transdanubia and usually ends in showers. Summers can be very hot and humid (especially in the capital). It rains most of November and doesn't usually get

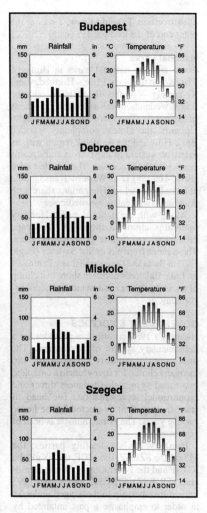

number of hours of sunshine a year stands at about 2000 – among the highest in Europe. From April to the end of September, you can expect the sun to shine for about 10 hours a day. Precipitation varies according to the region. The climate charts on these pages show you what to expect and when to expect it.

ECOLOGY & ENVIRONMENT

Pollution – a legacy of the former Communist regime – is a large and costly problem in Hungary. The Soviet-designed nuclear power generator at Paks in Southern Transdanubia produces about one-third of the nation's electricity. Low-grade coal that continues to fuel some industry and heat homes creates sulphur dioxide and acid rain that threatens the forests of the Northern Uplands. Automobiles manufactured in the former Soviet bloc, especially the two-stroke East German Trabants, have raised nitrogen oxide levels in some Hungarian cities to among the highest in Europe. Waste created by the Soviet military, particularly buried toxic chemicals and routinely dumped jet fuel, threatens the soil, the ground-water supply, rivers and lakes. The over-use of nitrate fertilisers in agriculture has caused the ground water beneath the Plain and Lake Balaton to become contaminated with phosphates.

Government funding for the environment is minimal, though some work has been carried on in the cities worst hit, including Esztergom, Veszprém and Debrecen. Yet even at an accelerated rate the total cleanup and rebuilding of Hungary, including some areas flattened by Soviet bombing drills, is expected to take at least another decade.

FLORA & FAUNA
Flora

Hungary is home to more than two thousand flowering plant species, many of which are not normally found at this latitude. A lot of the flora in the Villány Hills of Southern Transdanubia, for example, is usually seen only around the Mediterranean, and the salty Hortobágy region on the Eastern Plain hosts

cold until mid-December. Winters are relatively short, often cloudy and damp but sometimes brilliantly sunny. What little snow this area gets tends to disappear after a few days.

The mean average temperature in Hungary is 11°C. January is the coldest month (4°C) and July the hottest (28°C). The many plants normally found by the seashore. The Gemenc Forest on the Danube near Szekszárd, the Little Balaton in the centre of Transdanubia and the Tisza River backwater east of Kecskemét are all important wetlands. Most of the trees in the nation's forests are beech, oak and birch, with only a small percentage being fir.

Fauna

There are a lot of common European animals here (deer, wild hare, boar, otter) as well as some rare species (wild cat, lake bat, Pannonian lizard). But three-quarters of the country's 450 vertebrates are birds, especially waterfowl attracted by the rivers, lakes and wetlands. Parts of the Great Plain and the Northern Uplands are important nesting or migratory areas for hundreds of bird species.

The majestic stork

Cruelty to Animals

Hungarians as a whole are extremely fond of animals and every self-respecting small town has at least one *állat-díszhal bolt*, a pet shop selling everything from puppies and hamsters to tropical fish. They are especially fond of dogs (you can't miss the mop-like *puli* or the giant white *komondor* breeds indigenous to Hungary), and people of all ages go gaga over a particularly friendly or

attractive one. I should know; I was at the other end of the lead for 2½ years.

National Parks

There are five national parks in Hungary. The two on the Great Plain – Hortobágy and Kiskunság – protect the wildlife and the fragile wetlands, marsh and saline grasslands of the puszta. Two more are in the Northern Uplands: the almost completely wooded Bükk Hills and the Aggtelek region with its extensive system of karst caves and streams hewn into the limestone. The smallest park (Fertő-Hanság) is in Western Transdanubia at Lake Fertő, which Hungarians share with Austrians (who call it Neusiedlersee).

Along with the national parks, Hungary maintains almost a thousand 'landscape protection' and 'nature preservation' areas. These range from places like Sashegy (Eagle Hill) in Buda and the entire Tihany Peninsula on Lake Balaton's northern shore to a clump of ancient oak trees in downtown Hajdúböszörmény.

GOVERNMENT & POLITICS

Hungary's 1989 constitution provides for a parliamentary system of government. The unicameral assembly consists of 386 members chosen for four years in a complex, two-round system that balances direct and proportional representation. The head of state, the president, is elected by the house for five years. The prime minister is head of government.

Hungary has six leading parties: the MSZP, the SZDSZ, the MDF, the FKgP, the KDNP and the Federation of Young Democrats (FIDESZ). FIDESZ, which until 1993 limited membership to those aged under 35 in order to emphasise a past untainted by Communism, privilege and corruption, looked set for a significant role in government in the early 1990s. But its controversial leader Viktor Orbán moved the party to the centre-right and they did poorly in the 1994 elections.

The party in charge of the ruling coalition at present is the MSZP with 278 seats; the SZDSZ hold 69. The next elections will be in 1998. None of the parties represent the far right or the far left, which is not surprising in a nation that saw both fascism and Stalinist Communism in power within five years of each other.

In foreign policy, Hungary has taken a more assertive role in recent years as it looks to full integration into Western Europe, including membership of the EU and NATO. While Hungary refused to get involved in the civil war in what was then Yugoslavia – despite some extremist calls to 'protect' the large Hungarian minority in Vojvodina – it has since allowed NATO to open a military base at Taszár in Southern Transdanubia for troops and supplies funnelling into the US-run northern zone of the peacekeeping operation in Bosnia.

In Romania, the landslide re-election of the former Communist regime in 1991 (replaced by a centre-right government five years later) and resurgent nationalism in some cities with large Hungarian populations like Cluj-Napoca (Hungarian: Kolozsvár) raised tensions, but Hungary dealt with the problem on the international stage. In October 1996 the two countries signed a wide-ranging treaty in which Romania pledged to respect the individual rights of its two million ethnic Hungarians, while Hungary renounced forever any claim on Romanian territory.

One of the biggest thorns in Hungary's side in the 1990s has been Slovakia's work on the Danube dam at Gabčikovo (see aside in the Danube Bend chapter). Though Hungary signed a basic agreement with Slovakia – home to some 600,000 ethnic Hungarians – in March 1995, it took the Slovakian government a full year to ratify it. Relations between the two countries remain very strained.

ECONOMY

Hungary's painful economic restructuring since 1989 finally appears to be paying off. After seeing their living standards decline through the first half of this decade, Hungarians can at last be optimistic that they will be able to approach the economic level of their Western neighbours in the coming years.

Because Hungary started to liberalise its economy under socialism long before the other countries of Eastern Europe did, both Hungarians and foreigners had high hopes for a rapid rise in the standard of living when Communist structures were dismantled. But, instead of producing a solid market economy leading to greater growth, unemployment soared from virtually nil to as high as 14% in the spring of 1994, inflation topped 35% and the forint lost half its value from 1992 to 1996.

Unemployment and inflation might be ugly economic realities in some Western countries, but for a population shielded for more than 40 years by Communist, the damage came as a shock. Hungarians, for example, never had to pay tax. Suddenly employees were not only confronted with a maximum rate of 40% tax on their incomes but had to shell out hard-earned forint for ÁFA, a value-added tax covering the purchase of all goods, including some food and books. A bankruptcy law helped to dispose of many very sick companies, but it also brought job insecurity and job losses.

Hungary's economic titans recognised early on that they could not rely on the local population to restructure antiquated companies and infrastructure; funds and modern management techniques had to come from outside the country. After a slow start, Hungary's approach to privatisation, which relies heavily on foreign investment, has been a driving force behind the turnaround. The government's plans were for more than 80% of the economy to be privatised before the end of 1997.

Hungary has received more than 40% of all capital invested by foreign companies in Eastern Europe. Taking advantage of the country's low wages and skilled-labour base, European, Asian and North American companies have established automobile assembly plants, high-tech electronics factories and light manufacturing works in the country. As a result, unemployment has dropped to just over 10%, though most of the jobs are in relatively prosperous Budapest and Transdanubia. North-eastern Hungary, traditionally an economic 'black hole', has largely been passed over, and unemployment still reaches double digits in many towns and villages there.

The sale of utilities and state enterprises, in large part to Western investors, is beginning to show tangible benefits. For instance, Hungary leads Eastern Europe in the modernisation of its antiquated telephone system. It carved up the country into regions with private telephone companies and sold off a large chunk of Matáv, the national phone company. As a result, getting a line in or out of Budapest is not always the frustrating and time-consuming experience it used to be, and even dialling to and from small villages is not like trying to connect with Mars.

Another example of economic progress is the modern motorway linking Budapest with Vienna. Hungary pioneered the use of a private company to build and operate the toll road. Some critics might argue that it is an unfair burden to pay for use of the road, but anyone who travelled on its perilous predecessor welcomes the change.

To a large extent Hungary had no option but to rely on foreign investors to pay for the country's modernisation. There simply wasn't any money left in the government's coffers. During the spend-thrift days of the former regime, little heed was paid to the consequences of the cost of Hungary's relatively generous social services and leisure facilities.

Over-borrowing – and the over-spending of hard currency – resulted in Hungary's foreign debt rising to a dangerously high level. Foreign debt climbed throughout the 1990s from around US$20 billion to over US$30 billion but is now falling thanks to decent exports and the continued inflow of foreign capital. Some critics charge that money that should be going to cushion Hungarians against hard-hitting economic reforms has instead been redirected to pay off the country's interest payments.

Reducing the national social-security bill,

a big drain on the country as the birth-rate remains static and the population gets older, has been one of the toughest challenges facing the government. Because of the large role the so-called shadow (or black market) economy plays, Hungary simply cannot raise enough funds through taxes to meet its budget commitments. Domestic interest rates have been forced up as the government has lured savings away from citizens into bonds and bills.

Despite the political risk in chopping back on social-security benefits, government officials in Hungary remain committed to tough budgetary measures. In March 1995 austerity measures were introduced in a bid to cut public spending. Domestic borrowing has declined, allowing interest rates to drop to 24% – well below their 1995 high of 34%. Inflation, which stood at about 32% in 1995, has been brought down to a still unacceptable 20%.

There have, of course, been ulterior motives for Hungary's new-found economic discipline: the country is determined to become a member of the European Union. Nearly two-thirds of all exports go to EU countries, and most Hungarians believe that the country will be able to join the EU by the year 2000. In order to qualify, however, Hungary must get its economic house in order. This explains why politicians in Hungary, whatever their party persuasion, are united in continuing the country's tough economic reforms.

POPULATION & PEOPLE
When the Italian-American Nobel Prize-winning physicist Enrico Fermi (1901-54) was asked whether he believed extraterrestrials existed, he replied: 'Of course they do... they are already here among us. They are called Hungarians'. Dr Fermi was, of course, referring to the Magyars, an Asiatic people of obscure origins who do not speak an Indo-European language and make up the vast majority of Hungary's 10.4 million people. Almost five million Magyars live outside the national borders, mostly as a result of the Trianon Treaty, WWII and the

1956 Uprising. The estimated two million Hungarians in Romanian Transylvania constitute the largest ethnic minority in Europe, and there are another 600,000 in Slovakia, 650,000 in Yugoslavia and Croatia, 200,000 in Ukraine and 70,000 in Austria. Immigrants to the USA, Canada, Australia and Israel add up to over one million.

Though Hungary is a very homogeneous country, several non-Magyar minorities make their home here. The largest group is the Gypsies, who number around a quarter of a million. Other minorities include Germans (1.6%), Slovaks (1.1%) and Croatians or other South Slavs (0.9%). The number of Romanians in Hungary is officially put at about 25,000, but the real total is almost certainly higher.

Most of these minorities can be found in the border areas and are engaged in agriculture, though there was a large movement to the cities in the 1940s and 1950s. Germans are centred in Western Transdanubia and Pécs; South Slavs in Southern Transdanubia; Slovaks in Transdanubia and the Great Plain; and Gypsies in the Northern Uplands and North-East. Hungarians may not all be Magyars, but they are united by the Hungarian language.

Hungary's relative affluence, stability and relaxed border surveillance after 1989 made it a magnet for illegal immigrants and refugees escaping economic hardship and war from as close as Bosnia and as far away as China. Romanians, Ukrainians, Transylvanian Hungarians and mainland Chinese could be seen hawking their wares on city streets and in flea markets throughout the country in the early 1990s. But there was a severe crackdown in 1994 and many of the more 'visible' illegals were placed in detention camps – including a controversial one at Kerepestarcsa outside Budapest.

For the most part, ethnic minorities in Hungary suffer no outright discrimination and their rights are inscribed in the constitution: 'The national and ethnic minorities living in the Republic of Hungary are participants in the power of the people and constituent components of the State'. By law they are guaranteed participation in public life, the promotion of their cultures and the use of their languages – in schools, too. Discrimination against national, ethnic, racial or religious groups is punishable by law. Yet this has not stopped occasional attacks on non-white foreigners, a rise in anti-Semitism and the widespread hatred of and discrimination against Gypsies.

Life expectancy in Hungary is very low by European standards: 67 years for men, 74 for women. The nation also has one of Europe's lowest birth rates (-0.1%). Sadly, it also claims the dubious distinction of having the highest suicide rate in the world (see the aside in the Great Plain chapter).

EDUCATION

Hungary is a well-educated society with a literacy rate of about 98%. School is compulsory for children until the age of 16, and the more than three-quarters who leave have completed the eight primary grades.

The education system generally follows the German model. The primary or elementary school (*általános iskola*) is followed by four years of secondary education, which can either be in grammar (*gimnázium*) or vocational (*szakiskola*) schools. About 30% of those aged over 18 have secondary-school certificates. College and university matriculation is very competitive – places are few and entrance requirements pretty stiff. Still, about 10% of the population have university degrees, a quarter of them in engineering and economics.

Hungary has an international reputation in certain areas of specialised education. A unique method of music education devised by the composer Zoltán Kodály (1882-1967) is widespread. The Pető Institute in Budapest has a very high success rate in teaching children with cerebral palsy to walk. Sadly, many people who are experts in fields like science (in which Hungarians excel and have the Nobel Prizes to prove it) are being lured to Western Europe and the USA by higher wages and better living and working conditions.

ARTS

Hungarian art has been both stunted and spurred on by the monumental events in the nation's history. King Stephen's conversion to Catholicism brought Romanesque and Gothic art and architecture, while the Turkish occupation nipped most of Hungary's Renaissance in the bud. The Habsburgs opened the doors to baroque influences. The arts thrived under the Dual Monarchy, then through truncation and even under fascism. The early days of Communism brought the art celebrating wheat sheaves and muscle-bound steelworkers to a less-than-impressed populace, but much money was spent on music and 'correct art' like classical theatre.

It would be foolish – if not impossible – to ignore folk art when discussing fine art in Hungary. The two have been inextricably linked for several centuries and have greatly influenced one another. The music of Béla Bartók and the ceramic sculptures of Margit Kovács are deeply rooted in traditional culture. You'll see many fine examples of folk baroque and neoclassical peasant houses throughout Hungary, especially in Southern Transdanubia and around Lake Balaton.

Music & Dance

Hungary has made many contributions to the music world, but one person stands above all others: Franz Liszt. Liszt (1811-86), who established the Academy of Music in Budapest, liked to describe himself as part Gypsy, and some of his works, notably *Hungarian Rhapsodies*, echo Gypsy music.

Ferenc Erkel (1810-93) is the father of Hungarian opera and two of his works – the stirringly nationalist *Bánk Bán*, based on József Katona's play, and *László Hunyadi* – are standards at the State Opera House in Budapest. Erkel also composed the music for the Hungarian national anthem. Imre Kálmán (1882-1953) was Hungary's most celebrated composer of operettas. *The Queen of the Csárdás* is his most popular – and extravagant – work.

Béla Bartók (1881-1945) and Zoltán Ko-

Composer Franz Liszt (1811-86)

dály (1882-1967) made the first systematic study of Hungarian folk music together, travelling and recording throughout the linguistic region in 1906. Both integrated some of their findings into their own compositions – Bartók in *Bluebeard's Castle*, for example, and Kodály in his *Peacock Variations*. Bartók made a further study of Balkan folk music and continued to compose; Kodály went on to establish his own method of musical education with preliminary emphasis on voice instruction. The system is in widespread use in Hungary and the Kodály Institute in Kecskemét attracts students from all over the world.

It's important to distinguish between Gypsy music and real Hungarian folk music. Gypsy music as it is known and played in Hungarian restaurants from Budapest to Boston is urban schmaltz and based on recruiting tunes *(verbunkos)* played during the Rákóczi independence war. At least two fiddles, a bass and a cymbalom (a curious stringed instrument played with sticks) are *de rigueur*; if you want to hear this saccharine czardas music, almost any hotel restaurant in the land can oblige, or you can buy a tape or CD by Sándor Lakatos or his son Déki.

To confuse matters even further, real Gypsy music does not use instruments but is sung as a cappella (though sometimes it is backed with guitar and percussion); a very good tape of Hungarian Gypsy folk songs is *Magyarországi Cigány Népdalok*, produced by Hungaroton. The best modern Gypsy group is Kalyi Jag (Black Fire), led by Gusztav Várga, which comes from the North-East. The group plays all sorts of unconventional instruments and gives performances from time to time at Budapest *táncházak* (dance houses).

The táncház is an excellent place to hear Hungarian folk music and learn to dance. It's all good fun and they're easy to find in Budapest, where the dance-house revival began, although it hasn't really spread from there (villagers now prefer videos, game shows and weekend discos).

Hungarian folk musicians play violins, zithers, hurdy-gurdies, bagpipes and lutes on a five-note scale. There are lots of different groups but ones to watch out for are Méta and Muzsikás (especially when Marta Sebestyén sings). Anyone playing the haunting music of the Csángó region in eastern Transylvania is also a good bet.

Traditional Yiddish music is less known than Gypsy music but is of similar origin, having once been closely associated with Central European folk music. Until WWI so-called *klezmer* dance bands were led by the violin and cymbalom, but the influence of Yiddish theatre and the first wax recordings inspired a switch to the clarinet, which is the predominant instrument today. In 1990 the Budapest Klezmer Band was formed to revive this happy mix of jazz and big-band sound.

Hungary has ballet companies based in Budapest, Győr, Pécs and Szeged. Groups like the State Folk Ensemble perform dances essentially for tourists throughout the year; visit a táncház instead.

There are many symphony orchestras both in the capital and provincial cities. Among the best are the Budapest Festival Orchestra and the Hungarian Radio & Television Orchestra.

Literature

No one could have put it better than the poet Gyula Illyés (1902-83): 'The Hungarian language,' he wrote, 'is at one and the same time our softest cradle and our most solid coffin'. The difficulty and subtlety of the Magyar tongue has excluded most outsiders from Hungarian literature and, though it would be wonderful to be able to read the swashbuckling odes and love poems of Bálint Balassi (1554-94) or Miklós Zrínyi's *Peril of Sziget* (1651) in the original, most people will have to make do with what they can find in English translation.

Sándor Petőfi (1823-49) is Hungary's most celebrated and accessible poet, and a line from his work *National Song* became the rallying cry for the 1848-49 War of Independence, in which Petőfi fought and died. A deeply philosophical play called *The Tragedy of Man* by Imre Madách (1823-64), published a decade after Hungary's defeat in the War of Independence, is still considered to be the country's greatest classical drama.

The defeat in 1849 led many writers to look to Romanticism for inspiration and solace: heroes, winners, knights in shining armour. Petőfi's comrade-in-arms, János

Composer Béla Bartók (1881-1945)

Arany (1817-82), whose name is synonymous with impeccable Hungarian, wrote epic poetry *(Toldi Trilogy)* and ballads.

Another friend of Petőfi, the prolific novelist Mór Jókai (1825-1904), wrote of heroism and honesty in such wonderful works as *The Man with the Golden Touch* and *Black Diamonds*. This 'Hungarian Dickens' still enjoys widespread popularity. Another perennial favourite, Kálmán Mikszáth (1847-1910), wrote satirical tales like *The Good Palóc People* and *St Peter's Umbrella* in which he poked fun at the declining gentry. Apparently the former US president Theodore Roosevelt enjoyed the latter work so much that he insisted on visiting the ageing novelist during a European tour in 1910.

Zsigmond Móricz (1879-1942) was a very different type of writer. His works, very much in the tradition of the French naturalist Émile Zola (1840-1902), examined the harsh reality of peasant life in turn-of-the-century Hungary. His contemporary, Mihály Babits (1883-1941), poet and the editor of the influential literary magazine *Nyugat* (West), made the rejuvenation of Hungarian literature his lifelong work.

Two 20th-century poets are unsurpassed in Hungarian letters. Endre Ady (1877-1919), who is sometimes described as a successor to Petőfi, was a reformer who ruthlessly attacked the complacency and materialism of early 20th-century Hungary. The socialist Attila József (1905-1937) wrote of alienation and turmoil in a technological age; *By the Danube* is brilliant even in English translation. József fell afoul of both the underground Communist movement and the Horthy regime. Tragically, he threw himself under a train near Lake Balaton at the age of 32.

György Konrád (1933-), Péter Nádas (1942-) and Péter Esterházy (1950-) are three of Hungary's most important contemporary writers. Konrád's *A Feast in the Garden* (1985) is an almost autobiographical account of the fate of the Jewish community in a small eastern Hungarian town. *A Book of Memoirs* by Nádas concerns the decline of Communism in the style of Thomas Mann. Eszterházy's *A Little Hungarian Pornography* is a difficult but enjoyable read.

Film

The scarcity of government grants has severely limited the production of quality Hungarian films recently, but a handful are still produced every year. For classics, look out for anything by Oscar-winning István Szabó *(Sweet Emma, Dear Böbe)*, Miklós Jancsó *(The Red and the White)* and Péter Bacsó *(The Witness, Live Show)*. György Szomjas' *Junk Film*, Lívia Gyarmathy's *The Joy of Cheating*, Gábor Dettre's *Diary of the Hurdy-Gurdy Man*, György Molnár's *Anna's Film* and Marcell Iványi's award-winning *Wind* are more recent films showing the great talent of their directors.

Painting & Architecture

You won't find as much Romanesque and Gothic art and architecture in Hungary as you would in Slovakia or the Czech Republic – the Mongols, Turks and Habsburgs destroyed most of it – but the abbey churches at Ják and Lébény are fine examples of Romanesque architecture, and there are important Gothic churches in Nyírbátor and Sopron. For Gothic paintings, have a look at the 15th-century altarpieces done by various masters at the Christian Museum in Esztergom. The Corpus Christi Chapel in the cathedral in Pécs and the Royal Palace at Visegrád contain valuable Renaissance works of art.

Baroque abounds in Hungary; you'll see architectural examples in virtually every town in the land. For something on a grand scale, visit the Esterházy Palace at Fertőd or the Minorite church in Eger. The ornately carved altars in the Minorite church at Nyírbátor and the Abbey Church in Tihany are baroque masterpieces. The greatest painters of this style were the 18th-century fresco artists Anton Maulbertsch (Ascension Church frescos at Sümeg) and István Dorffmeister (Bishop's Palace, Szombathely).

Distinctly Hungarian art and architecture didn't come into their own until the mid-19th century when Mihály Pollack, József Hild and Miklós Ybl were changing the face of Budapest or running around the country building mansions and cathedrals. The romantic nationalist school of heroic paintings, best exemplified by Bertalan Székely (1835-1910) and Gyula Benczúr (1844-1920), gratefully gave way to the realism of Mihály Munkácsy (1844-1900), the painter of the puszta. But the greatest painters from this period were Tivadar Csontváry (1853-1919) and József Rippl-Rónai (1861-1927), whose best works are on exhibit at their own museums in Pécs and Kaposvár. Favourite artists of the 20th century include Victor Vasarely (1908-), the so-called father of op art, and the sculptor Amerigo Tot (1909-84).

The Romantic Eclectic style of Ödön Lechner (Budapest Museum of Applied Art) and Hungarian Art Nouveau (Reök Palace in Szeged) brought unique architecture to Hungary at the end of the 19th century and the start of the 20th. Fans of Art Nouveau will find in Hungary some of the best examples of that style outside Brussels and Vienna.

Postwar architecture in Hungary is almost completely forgettable. One exception is the work of Imre Makovecz, who has developed his own 'organic' style (not always popular locally) using unusual materials like tree trunks and turf. His work is everywhere, but among the best (or strangest) examples are the cultural centres at Sárospatak and Szigetvár, the Lutheran church in Siófok and the award-winning Hungarian Pavilion at the 1992 Expo in Seville.

Folk Art

Hungary has one of the richest folk traditions in Europe and, quite apart from its music, this is where the country comes to the fore in art. Many urban Hungarians probably wouldn't want to hear that, considering folk art a bit *déclassé* and its elevation the work of the Communist regime, but it's true.

From the beginning of the 18th century, as segments of the Hungarian peasantry became more prosperous, ordinary people tried to make their world more beautiful by painting and decorating objects and clothing. It's important to remember two things when looking at folk art. First, with very few exceptions (eg the 'primitive' paintings in Kecskemét's Museum of Naive Artists), only practical objects used daily were decorated. Second, this is not 'court art' or the work of artisans making Chinese cloisonné or Russian Fabergé eggs. It is the work of ordinary people trying to express the simple world around them in a new and different way. Some of it is excellent and occasionally you will spot the work of a true genius who probably never ventured beyond his or her village or farm.

Sadly, outside museums most folk art in Hungary is dead (though the ethnic Hungarian regions of Transylvanian in Romania are a different story). But through isolation or a refusal to let go for economic or aesthetic reasons, pockets remain throughout the country. Ignore the central *népművészeti bolt* (folk-art shop) you'll find in most towns: they're mostly full of mass-produced kitsch.

The main centre of cottage weaving has always been the Sárköz region in Southern Transdanubia – its distinctive black and red fabric is copied everywhere. Simpler homespun material can be found in the North-East, especially around the Tiszahát. Because of the abundance of reeds in these once marshy areas, the people here became skilled at cane weaving as well.

Decorative canteens made using horse hair

Three groups stand out for their embroidery, the apogee of Hungarian folk art: the Palóc people of the Northern Uplands, especially around the village of Hollókő; the Mátyó from Mezőkövesd; and the women of Kalocsa. The various differences and distinctions are discussed in the appropriate chapters, but to my mind no one works a needle like a Mátyó seamstress. The heavy woollen waterproof coats called *szűr*, once worn by herders on the Great Plain, were masterfully embroidered by men using thick, 'furry' yarn.

Folk pottery is world-class, and no Hungarian kitchen is complete without a couple of pairs of matched plates or shallow bowls hanging on the walls. The centre of this industry is the Great Plain – Hódmezővásárhely, Karcag and Tiszafüred, in particular – though fine examples also come from Transdanubia, especially from the Őrség region. There are jugs, pitchers, plates, bowls and cups, but the rarest and most attractive are the inscribed pots *(írókázás fazékok)* usually celebrating a wedding day or in the form of people or animals like the Miska jugs from the Tisza River region.

Folk woodcarving

Nádudvar near Hajdúszoboszló specialises in striking black pottery – far superior to the greyish stuff produced in Mohács in Southern Transdanubia.

Objects carved from wood or bone – mangling boards, honey-cake moulds, mirror cases, tobacco holders, saltcellars – were usually the work of idle herders or farmers in winter. The shepherds and swineherds of Somogy County south of Lake Balaton and the cowherds of the Hortobágy excelled at this work, and their illustrations of celebrations and the local 'Robin Hood' outlaws are always fun to look at.

Everyone made and decorated their own furniture in the old days, especially cupboards for the *tiszta szoba* (parlour) and trousseau chests with tulips painted on them, the *tulipán láda*. But for my money the best furniture in Hungary are the tables and chairs made of golden spotted poplar from the Gemenc Forest near Tolna. The oaken chests decorated with geometrical shapes from the Ormánság region of Southern Transdanubia are superior to the run-of-the-mill tulip chests.

One art form that ventures into the realm of fine art is ceiling and wall folk painting. Among the best examples of the former can

Water jug from the Great Plain

be found in churches, especially in the North-East (Tákos), the Northern Uplands (Füzér) and the Ormánság. The women of Kalocsa also specialise in wall painting, some of them so colourfully over-wrought as to be garish.

SOCIETY & CONDUCT
Traditional Culture
Traditional ceremonies and practices are dying, if not completely dead, in Hungary – even in the villages. Weddings, births and deaths are marked in modern European ways, though occasional differences crop up, particularly among certain minority groups like the Germans and Slovaks.

Apart from the Busójárás festival in Mohács, Farsang and other pre-Lenten carnivals are now celebrated at balls and private parties and some people go in costume. The sprinkling of water or perfume on young girls on Easter Monday is now rare (except in Hollókő), though the Christmas tradition of Betlehemzés, where young men and boys carry model churches containing a manger from door to door, can still be seen in some parts of the countryside. A popular event for city folk with tenuous ties to the countryside is the *disnótor*, the slaughtering of a pig followed by an orgy of feasting and drinking. (The butchering is done somewhere out the back by an able-bodied peasant.) Wine-harvest festivals, now commercial events with rock bands and a late-night outdoor disco, occur throughout the wine-growing regions in September and October.

Sport & Leisure
While economic difficulties have forced many Hungarians to take on a second job, this supplementary income is often used to take a holiday or buy goods like deep-freezers, VCRs or CD players, which are standard features in urban Hungarian homes nowadays. Most people put in a relatively short working day at their primary job (from about 8.30 am to 4 pm, finishing even earlier on Fridays), and everyone has weekends off to pursue other jobs or personal interests. In their spare time, Hungarians read a lot, listen to music, watch a lot of TV and videos and play sport.

Swimming is extremely popular – even small towns usually have both indoor and outdoor pools open to the public – as is water polo. For its size, Hungary has done extremely well in the Olympics. At the 1996 Olympic Games in Atlanta, for example, they finished 12th overall out of 197 countries, with 21 medals, including seven gold. (They ranked eighth in 1992 at Barcelona with 30 medals, 11 of them gold.) Chess is also hugely popular.

Football (soccer) is by far and away the favourite spectator sport, and people still talk about the 'match of the century' at Wembley in 1953 when Hungary beat England 6-3 – the first time England lost a match at home.

In August, most people head for the hills, Lake Balaton or, nowadays, abroad and they usually have some time off at other times of the year, too. Many urban dwellers own or have access to a small country cottage, or at least a plot of land, where they can play at being vintners at weekends or perhaps distil a little of their own fruit *pálinka* (brandy).

Social Life
In general Hungarians are not uninhibited like the Romanians or sentimental Slavs who will laugh or cry at the drop of a hat (or a drink). They are reserved, very formal people. Forget the impassioned, devil-may-care Gypsy stereotype – it doesn't exist. The national anthem calls Hungarians 'a people torn by fate' and the overall mood is one of *honfibú* (literally 'patriotic sorrow', but really a penchant for the blues) with a sufficient amount of hope to keep most people going.

This mood certainly predates Communism. To illustrate what she calls the 'dark streak in the Hungarian temperament', the veteran US foreign correspondent Flora Lewis recounts a story in *Europe: A Tapestry of Nations* that was the talk of Europe in the early 1930s. 'It was said,' she writes, 'that a song called *Gloomy Sunday* so deeply moved otherwise normal people (in Budapest) that whenever it was played, they

Last Name First

Unusual outside Asia, Hungarians reverse their names in all usages, and their 'last' name (or surname) *always* comes first. For example, 'John Smith' is not 'János Kovács' to Hungarians but 'Kovács János', while 'Elizabeth Taylor' is 'Szabó Erzsébet' and 'Francis Flour' 'is Liszt Ferenc' for example.

Most titles also follow: 'Mr John Smith' is 'Kovács János úr'. Many women follow the practice of taking their husband's full name. If Elizabeth were married to John, she might be 'Kovács Jánosné' or (increasingly popular among professional women) 'Kovácsné Szabó Erzsébet'.

To avoid confusion, all Hungarian names in this guide are written in the usual Western manner – including the names of museums, theatres etc – if they are translated into English. Thus the 'Arany János színház' in Budapest is the 'János Arany Theatre' in English. Addresses are always written in Hungarian as they appear on street signs: 'Kossuth Lajos utca', 'Arany János tér' etc. ∎

would rush to commit suicide by jumping off a Danube bridge.' The song has been covered in English by several artists, including Billie Holiday and Sinéad O'Connor.

Hungarians are almost always extremely polite in social interaction, and the language can be very courtly – even when doing business with the butcher or having your hair cut. An older man will often kiss a woman's hand, and the standard greeting for youngsters to their elders is *Csókolom* ('I kiss it' – 'it' being the hand, of course). People of all ages – even close friends – shake hands profusely when meeting up. But while all this gentility certainly oils the wheels that turn a sometimes difficult society, it can be used to keep 'outsiders' (foreigners and other Hungarians) at a distance. Perhaps as an extension of this desire to keep everything running as smoothly as possible, Hungarians are always extremely helpful and on the ball in an emergency – be it an accident, a robbery or simply helping someone who's lost their way.

Like Spaniards, Poles and others with a Catholic background, Hungarians celebrate name days more than birthdays. Name days are usually the Catholic feast day of their patron saint, but less holy names have a date too. All Hungarian calendars list them and you can also find them in the English-language weeklies in Budapest; there's even a telephone number to call that tells Hungarians which name is being remembered that day. Flowers, cakes or a bottle of wine are the usual gifts, and tradition dictates that you can present them up to eight days after the event.

Drinking is an important part of social life in a country that has produced wine and fruit brandies for thousands of years. Consumption is high; only France and Germany drink more alcohol per capita. Alcoholism in Hungary is not as visible to the outsider as it is, say, in Poland, but it's there nonetheless: in the smoky *borozó* (wine bar) that opens at dawn and does a brisk business all day, or in the kitchen as the working mother downs another half-litre of vodka while trying to cope with her job, household chores and family. Official figures suggest that as many as 6% of the population are fully fledged alcoholics, but some experts say that 40% to 50% of all males drink 'problematically'. There is little pressure for others (particularly women) to drink, and if you really don't want that glass of apricot brandy your host hands you, refuse politely.

Hungarians let their hair – and most of their clothes – down in summer at lake and riverside resorts; going topless is almost the norm for women. In warm weather everywhere you'll see more public displays of affection on the streets than perhaps any place else in the world. It's all very romantic, but beware: in the remoter corners of city parks you may even stumble upon more passionate displays (which always seems to embarrass the stumbler more than the active participants).

Dos & Don'ts

For outsiders, there are no special rules governing interpersonal relationships or conduct, though Hungarians themselves are very sensitive to things like *viszonzás*, the back-scratching system of returned favours that was especially used (and abused) during the Communist regime. That won't affect you, though.

If you're invited to someone's home, bring a bunch of flowers (available in profusion all year) or a bottle of good local wine. You can talk about anything, but money is a touchy subject. Traditionally, the discussion or manifestation of wealth – wearing flashy jewellery, for example – was considered gauche here as it was throughout Eastern Europe. Nowadays no one thinks they have enough money, and those still in the low-paying public sector are often jealous of people who have made the leap to better jobs in the private sector. Your salary – piddling as you may think it is back home – will astonish most Hungarians. Though it's almost impossible to calculate (the 'black economy' being so widespread and important), a decent salary for a worker or university graduate starting out in Hungary at present is about 25,000 Ft a month.

RELIGION

Throughout history, religion in Hungary has often been a question of expediency. Under King Stephen, Catholicism won the battle for dominance over Orthodoxy and, while the majority of Hungarians were quite happily Protestants by the end of the 16th century, many donned a new mantle during the Counter-Reformation under the Habsburgs. During the Turkish occupation thousands of Hungarians converted to Islam – though not always willingly.

As a result, Hungarians tend to have a more pragmatic approach to religion than most of their neighbours, and almost none of the bigotry. It has even been suggested that this generally sceptical view of matters of faith has led to Hungarians' high rate of success in science and mathematics. Except in villages and on the most important holy days (Easter, the Assumption of Mary, Christmas), churches are never full. The Jewish community in Budapest, though, has seen a great revitalisation in recent years.

Of those Hungarians declaring religious affiliation, about 68% say they are Roman Catholic, 21% Reformed (Calvinist) Protestant and 6% Evangelical (Lutheran) Protestant. There are also small Greek Catholic and Orthodox congregations. Hungary's Jews number about 80,000, down from a prewar population of almost 10 times that size. Some 400,000 died during deportation under the fascist Arrow Cross in 1944 or were murdered in Nazi concentration camps. Many others emigrated after 1956.

LANGUAGE

Hungarians like to boast that their language ranks with Japanese and Arabic as among the world's most difficult. All languages are hard for non-native speakers to master, but it is true, Hungarian is very difficult to learn. This should not put you off attempting a few words and phrases, however. Without some German, that's the only way you'll make yourself understood in the more remote parts of Hungary.

Hungarian (which is also known as Magyar) belongs to the Finno-Ugric language group and is distantly related only to Finnish (with five million speakers), Estonian (one million) and about a dozen other languages with far fewer speakers in Russia and western Siberia. It is not an Indo-European language, meaning that English is closer to French, Russian and Hindi in vocabulary and structure than it is to Hungarian. As a result you'll spot few words that you are likely to recognise – with the exception of things like *disco* or *hello*, the slangy way young Hungarians say 'goodbye'. Attempting to order a beer or a glass of wine in pseudo-Spanish or French, for example, will get you nowhere; the words for these are *sör* and *bor*.

For assorted reasons (as a reaction against the compulsory study of Russian in all schools until the late 1980s being one of them), Hungarians tend to speak only Hungarian. Even when they do have a smattering of a foreign language, they lack experience or are hesitant to speak it. Attempt a few words in Hungarian (*Magyar*) and they will be impressed, take it as a compliment and be extremely encouraging.

The next-best language for getting around in Hungary is German. Historical ties, geographical proximity and the fact that it was the preferred language of the literati up to this century have given it almost semi-official status. Still, apart from in Budapest and Transdanubia, the frequency and quality of spoken German is low. Though this is changing slowly, English is rarely heard outside the capital; if you're desperate, look for someone young, preferably under the age of 25. For obvious reasons, Russian is best avoided; there seems to be almost a national paranoia about speaking it, and many people revel in how little they know 'despite all those years in class'. Italian is understood more and more in Hungary because of tourism. French and Spanish are almost useless.

Pronunciation

Hungarian is not difficult to pronounce – though it may look strange with all those accents. Unlike English, Hungarian is a 'one-for-one' language: the pronunciation of each vowel and consonant is always the same. Stress falls on the first syllable (no exceptions), making the language sound a bit staccato at times.

Consonants in Hungarian are pronounced more or less as in English with about a dozen exceptions (listed below). Double consonants (**ll**, **tt**, **dd**) are not pronounced as one letter as in English but lengthened so you can almost hear them as separate letters. Also, what we would call consonant clusters (**cs**, **zs**, **gy**, **sz**) are separate letters in Hungarian and appear that way in the telephone directory and listings. For example, the word *cukor* ('sugar') appears in the dictionary before *csak* ('only').

c	'ts' as in 'hats'
cs	'ch' as in 'church'
gy	'dj' like the 'j' in 'jury' with your tongue pressed against the roof of your mouth
j	'y' as in 'yes'

ly	also like the 'y' in 'yes'
ny	like the 'ni' in 'onion'
r	pronounced with the tip of your tongue; a slightly trilled Spanish or Scottish 'r'
s	'sh' as in 'shop'
sz	's' as in 'salt'; an easy way to remember it is the important Magyar word *szex*
ty	like 'tube' in British English (rare)
w	'v' as in 'vat' (appears in foreign words only)
zs	's' as in 'pleasure'

Vowels are going to give you a lot more trouble, and the difference between an **a**, **e** or **o** with and without an accent mark is great. *Hát* means 'back' while *hat* means 'six'; *kérek* means 'I want' while *kerek* means 'round'.

The pronunciation of vowels is more difficult to describe than consonants. Try to imagine a Briton with a standard 'TV' accent or an American from Boston pronouncing the following sounds:

a	'o' as in hot
á	'a' as in 'father' or 'Shah'
e	'e' as in 'set'
é	'a' as in 'say' but without that 'y' sound
i	almost like 'i' in 'hit'
í	'ee' as in 'feet'
o	'o' as in 'open'
ó	a longer version of the above
ö	like the 'o' in 'worse' but without any 'r' sound
ő	a longer version of **ö**
u	'u' as in 'pull'
ú	'oo' as in 'food'
ü	a tough one ... 'ü' as in German *fünf*
ű	even tougher ... a longer, breathier version of the above

As in many other languages, verbs in Hungarian have a formal and familiar form in the singular and plural. Formal (form) is used with strangers, older people, your 'superiors', officials and service people. The familiar form (fam) is reserved for friends, pets, children and sometimes foreigners but is used much more frequently and sooner than it is in, say, French. Almost all young people use it among themselves – even when they're strangers. In the following phrases, the formal 'you' *(Ön* and *Önök)* is given except in situations where you'd obviously be trying to establish a more personal relationship.

If you want more Hungarian words and phrases than there is space here, you should consult Lonely Planet's *Eastern* or *Central Europe phrasebooks.*

Greetings & Civilities
Hello.
   Jó napot kívánok. (form)
   Szia or szervusz. (fam)
Goodbye.
   Viszontlátásra. (form)
   Szia or szervusz. (fam)
Good day.
   Jó napot. (most common greeting)
Good morning.
   Jó reggelt.
Good evening.
   Jó estét.
Please.
   Kérem. (asking for something)
   Tessék. (handing something/inviting)
Thank you. (very much)
   Köszönöm (szépen).
   Köszi. (fam)
You're welcome.
   Szívesen.
Yes.
   Igen.
No.
   Nem.
Maybe.
   Talán.
Excuse me.
   Legyen szíves. (for attention)
   Bocsánat. (stepping on someone's toe)
I'm sorry.
   Sajnálom or Elnézést.
How are you?
   Hogy van? (form)
   Hogy vagy? (fam)

I'm fine, thanks.
   Köszönöm, jól.

Language Difficulties
Please write it down.
   Kérem, írja le.
Would you please show me (on the map)?
   Meg tudná nekem mutatni (a térképen)?
I understand.
   Értem.
I don't understand.
   Nem értem.
I don't speak Hungarian.
   Nem beszélek magyarul.
Do you speak English (French/German/Italian)?
   Beszél angolul (franciául/németül/olaszul)?
Does anyone here speak English?
   Van itt valaki, aki angolul beszél?
How do you say ... in Hungarian?
   Hogy mondják magyarul ...?

Paperwork
surname	*családnév*
given name	*utónév*
date of birth	*születési dátum*
place of birth	*születési hely*
nationality/ citizenship	*nemzetiség/ állampolgárság*
sex (male/female)	*nem (férfi/nő)*
passport	*útlevél*
identification card (ID)	*személyi igazolvány*

Small Talk
What is your name?
   Hogy hívják? (form)
   Mi a neved? (fam)
My name is ...
   A nevem ...
I'm a ... tourist/student.
   Turista/diák.
Are you married?
   Ön férjezett? (to a woman)
   Ön nős? (to a man)
Do you like Hungary?
   Tetszik neki Magyarország?
I like it very much.
   Nagyon tetszik.

Where are you from?
Honnan jön?
I am American (British/Australian/
Canadian/a New Zealander).
*Amerikai (brit/ausztrál/kanadai/
új-zélandi) vagyok.*
I have a visa/permit.
Nekem van vízum/engedély.
How old are you?
Hány éves vagy? (fam)
Hány éves? (form)
I am 25 years old.
Húszonöt éves vagyok.
Just a minute.
Egy pillanat.
May I?
Lehet? (general permission)
Szabad? (eg for a chair)
It's all right.
Rendben van.
No problem.
Nem baj.

Getting Around

I want to go to (Esztergom/Debrecen/Pécs).
*(Esztergomba/Debrecenbe/Pécsre)
akarok menni.*
I want to book a seat to (Prague/Paris/
Moscow).
*Szeretnék heljet foglalni (Prágába/
Párizsba/Moszkvába).*

What time does ...	Mikor
leave/arrive?	indul/érkezik ...?
the bus/tram	az autóbusz/a villamos
the train	a vonat
the boat/ferry	a hajó/komp.
the airplane	a repülőgép

How long does the trip take?
Mennyi ideig tart az út?
The train is delayed/on time/early
*A vonat késik/pontosan/korábban
érkezik.*
The train is cancelled.
A vonat nem jár.
Do I need to change?
Át kell szállnom?

You must change trains.
Át kell szállni.
You must change platforms.
Másik vágányhoz kell menni.

left-luggage	csomagmegőrző
ticket	jegy
one-way ticket	egy útra/csak oda
return (round-trip) ticket	oda-vissza/ retúrjegy
train station	vasútállomás/ pályaudvar
bus station	autóbuszállomás
platform	vágány
ticket office	jegyiroda/pénztár
timetable	menetrend

I'd like to hire a car.
Autót szeretnék bérelni.

I'd like to hire a ...	... szeretnék kölcsönözni
bicycle	kerékpárt/
motorcycle	motorkerékpárt
horse	lovat

I'd like to hire a guide.
Szeretnék kérni egy idegenvezetőt.

Directions

How do I get to ...?
Hogy jutok ...?
Where is ...?
Hol van ...?
Is it near/far?
Közel/messze van?

What ... is this?	Ez melyik ...?
street/road	utca/út
street number	házszám
city district	kerület
town	város
village	falu/község

(Go) straight ahead.
(Menyen) egyenesen előre.
(Turn) left.
(Forduljon) balra.
(Turn) right.
(Forduljon) jobbra.

at the traffic lights	a közlekedési
next/second/third	lámpánál
corner	kevetkező/második/h
up/down	armadik saroknál
behind/in front	fent/lent
opposite	mögött/előtt
here/there/	szemben
everywhere	itt/ott/
north	mindenhol
south	észak
east	dél
west	kelet
	nyugat

I want to call this number.
Szeretném felhívni ezt a számot.
I'd like to change some money/
travellers' cheques.
Szeretnék pénzt/utazási csekket váltani.

beach	strand
bridge	híd
castle	vár
cathedral	székesegyház
church	templom
synagogue	zsinagóga
island	sziget
lake	tó
square/main square	tér/fő tér
market	piac
mosque	mecset
palace	palota
mansion	kastély
ruins	romok
tower	torony

Useful Signs

ENTRANCE	BEJÁRAT
EXIT	KIJÁRAT
OCCUPIED (RESERVED)	FOGLALT
TOILET	TOALETT or WC
MEN'S ROOM	FÉRFIAK or URAK
LADIES' ROOM	NŐK OR HÖLGYEK
INFORMATION	INFORMÁCIÓ or FELVILÁGOSÍTÁS
OPEN/CLOSED	NYITVA/ZÁRVA
PROHIBITED	TILOS
TRAIN STATION	VASÚTÁLLOMÁS or PÁLYAUDVAR ■

Accommodation

I'm looking for a/ the ...	... keresem.
guesthouse	a fogadót
camping ground	camping or kemping
youth hostel	ifjúsági szálló
hotel	szállodát
manager/owner	a főnököt/a tulajdonosot
rooms available	szoba kiadó (German: Zimmer frei)

Around Town

Where is ...?	Hol van ...?
a bank/exchange office	bank/pénzváltó
the city centre	a város központ a centrum
the ... embassy	a ... nagykövetség
the hospital	a kórház
the market	a piac
the police station	rendőrkapitányság
the post office	a posta
a public toilet	nyilvános WC
a restaurant	étterem
the telephone centre	telefonközpont
tourist information office	idegenforgalmi iroda

Do you have a ... available?	Van szabad ...?
bed	ágyuk
cheap room	olcsó szobájuk
single/double room	egyágyas szobájuk/ kétágyas szobájuk
for one/two nights	egy/kettő éjszakára

What is the address?
Mi a cím?

How much is it per night/per person?
Mennyibe kerül
éjszakánként/személyenként?
Is service included?
A kiszolgálás benne van?
Can I see the room?
Megnézhetem a szobát?
Where is the toilet/bathroom?
Hol van a WC/fürdőszoba?
It is very dirty/noisy/expensive.
Ez nagyon piskos/zajos/drága.
I am/We are leaving.
El megyek/El megyünk.

Do you have ...?	*Van ...?*
a clean sheet	*tiszta lepedő*
hot water	*meleg víz*
a key	*kulcs*
a shower	*zuhany*

Food

(See also the Menu Reader under Food and the Drinks section in the Facts for the Visitor chapter.)

breakfast	*reggeli*
lunch	*ebéd*
dinner (supper)	*vacsora*
the menu	*az étlap*
set (daily) menu	*napi menü*
food stall	*laci konyha/ pecsenyesütő*
grocery store	*élelmiszer*
delicatessen	*csemege*
market	*piac*
restaurant	*étterem* or *vendéglő*

I am hungry/thirsty.
Éhes/szomjas vagyok.
The menu, please.
Az étlapot, kérem.
The bill, please.
A számlát, kérem or *Fizetek.*
I would like the set lunch, please.
Mai menüt kérnék.
Is service included in the bill?
Az ár tartalmazza a kiszolgálást?
I am a vegetarian.
Vegetáriánus vagyok.

I would like some ...
Kérnék ...
Another ... please.
Még egy ... kérek szépen.

I don't eat ...	*Nem eszem ...*
pork	*disznóhúst*
fish	*halat*
beer	*sör*
bread	*kenyér*
chicken	*csirke*
coffee	*kávé*
eggs	*tojás*
fish	*hal*
food	*étel*
fruit	*gyümölcs*
fruit juice	*gyümölcslé*
meat	*hús*
milk	*tej*
mineral water	*ásvány víz*
pepper	*bors*
pork	*disznóhús*
salt	*só*
soup	*leves*
sugar	*cukor*
tea	*tea*
vegetables	*zöldség*
water	*víz*
wine	*bor*
hot/cold	*meleg/hideg*
with/without sugar	*cukorral/cukor nélkül*
with/without ice	*jéggel/jég nélkül*

Shopping

How much does it cost?
Mennyibe kerül?
I would like to buy this.
Szeretném megvenni ezt.
It's too expensive for me.
Ez túl drága nekem.
Can I look at it?
Megnézhetem?
I'm just looking.
Csak nézegetek.

I'm looking for ...	*Keresem ...*
the chemist (pharmacy)	*a patikát*

clothing	*ruhát*
souvenirs	*emléktárgyat*

Time & Dates

When/At what time?
Mikor/Hány órakor?

today	*ma*
tonight	*ma este*
tomorrow	*holnap*
the day after tomorrow	*holnapután*
yesterday	*tegnap*
all day/every day	*egész nap/minden nap*
Monday	*hétfő*
Tuesday	*kedd*
Wednesday	*szerda*
Thursday	*csütörtök*
Friday	*péntek*
Saturday	*szombat*
Sunday	*vasárnap*
January	*január*
February	*február*
March	*március*
April	*április*
May	*május*
June	*június*
July	*július*
August	*augusztus*
September	*szeptember*
October	*október*
November	*november*
December	*december*

What time is it?
Hány óra?
It's ... o'clock.
... óra van.

in the morning	*reggel*
in the evening	*este*
Noon.	*Dél.*
Midnight.	*Éjfél.*
1.15	*negyed kettő* ('one-quarter of two')
1.30	*fél kettő* ('half of two')
1.45	*háromnegyed kettő* ('three-quarters of two')

Numbers

0	*nulla*
1	*egy*
2	*kettő*
3	*három*
4	*négy*
5	*öt*
6	*hat*
7	*hét*
8	*nyolc*
9	*kilenc*
10	*tíz*
11	*tizenegy*
12	*tizenkettő*
13	*tizenhárom*
14	*tizennégy*
15	*tizenöt*
16	*tizenhat*
17	*tizenhét*
18	*tizennyolc*
19	*tizenkilenc*
20	*húsz*
21	*huszonegy*
22	*huszonkettő*
30	*harmincs*
40	*negyven*
50	*ötven*
60	*hatvan*
70	*hetven*
80	*nyolcvan*
90	*kilencven*
100	*száz*
101	*százegy*
110	*száztíz.*
1000	*ezer*
1 million	*egymillió*

Health

I'm diabetic/epileptic/asthmatic.
Cukorbeteg/epilepsziás/asztmás vagyok.
I'm allergic to penicillin/antibiotics.
Penicillinre/antibiotikumra allergiás vagyok.

I've got diarrhoea.
Hasmenésem van.
I feel nauseous.
Hányingerem van.

antiseptic	*fertőzésgátló*
aspirin	*aszpirin*
condoms	*óvszer/gumi*
contraceptive	*fogamzásgátló*
medicine	*orvosság*
suntan lotion/	*napozókrém/*
sunblock cream	*fényvédőkrém*

tampons   *tampon*

Emergencies

Help!	*Segítség!*
Go away!	*Menjen el!*
Leave me alone!	*Hagyjon békén!*
Keep your hands to yourself!	*Ne fogdosson!*

Call a doctor/the police.
Hívjon orvost/rendőrt.

Facts for the Visitor

PLANNING
When to Go
Every season has its attractions in Hungary, but do yourself a favour and drop the romantic notion of a winter on the *puszta*. Aside from being cold and often bleak, winter sees museums and other tourist sights closed or their hours sharply curtailed (see the Business Hours section). Animal-rights activists will also want to skip this season: half the women are draped in furry dead things throughout much of the winter.

Though it can be pretty wet in May and early June, spring is just glorious in Hungary. The Hungarian summer is warm, sunny and unusually long, but the resorts are very crowded in late July and August. If you avoid Lake Balaton and perhaps the Mátra Hills, you'll be OK. The summer fashions and beach wear are daringly brief, even by Western standards. Like Paris and Rome, Budapest comes to a grinding halt in August (called 'the cucumber-growing season' here because that's about the only thing happening), which is the most uncomfortable month to be in cities and towns. Remember that only a few offices, large hotels and shops have air conditioning.

Autumn is beautiful, particularly in the hills around Budapest and in the Northern Uplands. In Transdanubia and on the Great Plain it's harvest and vintage time. November is one of the rainiest months of the year, however.

For more information, see the Climate section in the Facts about the Country chapter.

Maps
Cartographia, Hungary's largest map-making company, produces national, regional and hiking maps (scales 1:10,000 to 1:40,000) as well as city plans, though newcomers like Zentai & Zentai, Sollun, Dimap are now also publishing city and town maps.

Cartographia's *Magyarország Autóatlasza*
(Road Atlas of Hungary, 990 Ft), with 23 road maps on a scale of 1:360,000 and thumbnail plans of virtually every community in the land, is indispensable if you plan to do a lot of travelling, especially by car. They also publish a folding 1:500,000 scale *Hungary* map (300 Ft).

The *Budapest Atlas* (650 Ft), also from Cartographia, has 40 detailed maps of the city, an index with all the new street names and some descriptive information in English.

What to Bring
There are no particular items of clothing to remember – an umbrella in late spring and autumn, a warm hat (everyone wears them) in winter – unless you plan to do some serious hiking or other sport. A swimsuit for use in the mixed-sex thermal spas and pools is a good idea as are plastic sandals or thongs (flip-flops).

In general, Hungarian dress is very casual; many people attend even the opera in denim. Men needn't bother bringing a tie; it will be seldom – if ever – used.

If you plan to stay at hostels and college dormitories, pack or buy a towel and a plastic soap container when you arrive. Bedclothes are almost always provided, though you might want to take along your own sheet bag. You'll sleep easier with a padlock on one of the storage lockers provided at hostels.

Other items you might need include a torch (flashlight), an adapter plug for electrical appliances (such as a cup or coil immersion heater to make your own tea or instant coffee), a universal bath/sink plug (a plastic film canister sometimes works), sunglasses, a few clothes pegs and premoistened towelettes or a large cotton handkerchief that you can soak in fountains and use to cool off while touring cities and towns in the warmer months.

SUGGESTED ITINERARIES
Depending on the length of your stay, you

finds); the Imre Patkó Collection (Asian and African art) in Győr; the Applied Arts Museum (furniture) and the Hungarian Commerce & Catering Museum (antique cookware) in Budapest.

two days
    Budapest
one week
    Budapest, the Danube Bend and one or two of the following: Eger, Sopron, Pécs, Kecskemét
two weeks
    Budapest, the Danube Bend, the north shore of Lake Balaton, Kőszeg, and two or three of the following: Eger, Sopron, Pécs, Kecskemét, Szeged, Eger

HIGHLIGHTS
Historic Towns

Many of Hungary's historic towns, including Eger, Győr, Székesfehérvár and Veszprém, were rebuilt in the baroque style during the 18th century. Sopron and Kőszeg are among the few Hungarian towns with a strong medieval flavour. The greatest monuments of the Turkish period are in Pécs. Kecskemét has wonderful examples of Art Nouveau architecture.

Castles & Palaces

Hungary's most famous castles are those that resisted the Turkish onslaught in Eger, Kőszeg and Szigetvár. Though in ruins, the citadel at Visegrád evokes the power of medieval Hungary. Those at Siklós, Sümeg, Hollókő and Boldogkőváralja have dramatic locations. Among Hungary's finest palaces are the Esterházy Palace at Fertőd, the Festetics Palace at Keszthely, the Széchenyi Mansion at Nagycenk and the Bishop's Palace at Veszprém.

Museums & Galleries

The following museums stand out not just for what they contain but for how they display it: the Christian Museum in Esztergom (Gothic paintings); the Storno Collection in Sopron (Romanesque and Gothic furnishings); the Zsolnay Museum (Art Nouveau porcelain) and the Csontváry Museum in Pécs; the Palóc Museum in Balassagyarmat (folklore collection); the Ferenc Móra Museum in Szeged (Avar

Churches & Synagogues

The following is just a sampling of Hungary's most beautiful houses of worship. They represent no particular architectural preference, though many are outstanding examples of their type: the baroque Minorite church in Eger; the Gothic Calvinist church in Nyírbátor; the Art Nouveau synagogue in Szeged; the baroque cathedral at Kalocsa; Sümeg's Church of the Ascension (for its frescos); the Gothic Old Synagogue in Sopron; the Abbey Church in Tihany and the Minorite church in Nyírbátor for their carved wooden altars; the Romantic Nationalist Szolnok Synagogue (now the Szolnok Gallery); the Romanesque church at Őriszentpéter; and Pécs Synagogue.

Outdoor Activities

Among the top outdoor activities in Hungary are bird-watching in the Hortobágy region, hiking in the Zemplén, riding the narrow-gauge railway from Miskolc into the Bükk Hills, canoeing on the Tisza River, caving in Aggtelek and cycling in the Danube Bend area.

Hotels

For lots of atmosphere, the following budget hotels can't be beaten: the Lujza Blaha in Balatonfüred; the Duna in Baja; the Csokonai in Kaposvár; the Aranystrucc in Kőszeg; the Kastély at the Esterházy Palace in Fertőd; the Tisza in Szeged; and the Szilvás in Szilvásvárad.

These are my favourites of the more expensive (though not prohibitively so) hotels in Hungary: Senator House in Eger; the Fiume in Békéscsaba; the Aranykereszt in Gyula; the Klastrom in Győr; the Kalocsa in Kalocsa; the Savaria in Szombathely; and the Tisza in Szolnok.

TOURIST OFFICES
Local Tourist Offices

The Hungarian Tourist Board (HTB), a branch of the Ministry of Industry & Trade, has established a chain of some 30 tourist information offices called Tourinform in many parts of Hungary, and these are the best places to ask general questions and pick up brochures. The main Tourinform office (☎ 1-117 9800; fax 1-117 9578; e-mail tourinform@hungary.com) is in Budapest at V Sütő utca 2.

If your query is about private accommodation, international train transportation or changing money, you should turn to a commercial travel agency; every Hungarian town has at least one (and usually several) of them. Ibusz remains visible (though it is scaling back considerably in favour of its banking interests) and has representative offices abroad (see the following list). Another national travel agency with offices around the country is Cooptourist. Regional travel agencies in provincial centres (Dunatours, Balatontourist, Mecsek Tourist etc) are often more familiar with their own local area.

The travel agency Express used to serve the youth and student market exclusively, but it now also sells outbound package tours to local people. It issues ISIC (student), FIYTO (youth) and Hostelling International (HI) cards. It can also issue discounted BIJ train tickets to anyone under the age of 26. Some Express offices also know about accommodation in student dormitories in July and the first three weeks of August.

Tourist Offices Abroad

The HTB has offices in seven countries, including:

Austria
Parkring 12, III/6, 1010 Vienna (☎ 0222-513 9122; fax 0222-513 1201)

Germany
Berliner Strasse 72, 60311 Frankfurt-am-Main (☎ 069-929 1190; fax 069-929 11918)

Italy
Via dei Monti Parioli 38, 00197 Rome (☎ 06-321 24 09; fax 06-321 13 73)

Netherlands
PO Box 91644, 2509 EE The Hague (☎ 070-320 9092; fax 070-327 2833)

Russia
Ulica Krasnaya Presnya 1-7, 123242 Moscow (☎ /fax 095-255 5231)

UK
PO Box 4336, London SW18 4XE (☎ /fax 0171-871 4009)

USA
150 East 58th St, 33/F, New York, NY 10155 (☎ 212-355 0240; fax 212-207 4103)

Ibusz has representative offices in eight countries:

Austria
Krugerstrasse 4, 1010 Vienna (☎ 0222-515 550; fax 0222-515 5535)

France
27 Rue du 4 Septembre, 75002 Paris (☎ 0147 42 50 25; fax 0147 42 58 56)

Germany
Mauritiussteinweg 114-116, 50676 Cologne (☎ 0221-206 450; fax 0221-206 4520)

Poland
Ulica Marszalkowska 80, 00517 Warsaw (☎ 022-259 915; fax 022-256 859)

Russia
Krasnopresenskaya naberezhnaja 12, Suite 921, Moscow 123610 (☎ 095-253 2921; fax 095-253 0084)

Sweden
Beridarebanan 1, Stockholm 10326 (☎ 08-232 030; fax 08-243 741)

Switzerland
Bederstrasse 97, Zürich 8002 (☎ 01-201 1760; fax 01-202 6538)

UK
Danube Travel, 6 Conduit St, London W1R 9TG (☎ 0171-491 3588; fax 0171-493 6963)

In countries without an HTB or Ibusz office, contact Malév Hungarian Airlines, which has offices in some three dozen countries worldwide, including the following:

Belgium
Cantersteen 49, Brussels 1000 (☎ 02-511 1878; fax 02-514 5844)

Canada
175 Bloor St East, Suite 712, Toronto, Ont M4W 3R8 (☎ 416-944 0093; fax 416-944 0095)

Japan
Sun Travel Service, Sumito Building, 5/F, 5-12-2 Minami-Aoyama, Minato-ku, Tokyo (☎ 03-3406 8870; fax 03-3406 8364)

Netherlands
  Noortse Bosch, Vijzelgracht 52, 1017 HS Amsterdam (☎ 020-623 4336; fax 020-638 1206)
Spain
  Calle Princessa 10, Madrid 28008 (☎ 1-548 2289; fax 1-548 2329)

Tourist Publications

The HTB produces many free brochures and pamphlets in English. Some of them are just colourful pap while others are extremely useful and written with style and humour. They are often available at HTB, Ibusz and Malév Hungarian Airlines offices abroad; in Hungary you'll find them at Tourinform offices, independent travel bureaus and agencies, Malév offices and expensive hotels.

The titles listed below are general ones; more specialised publications appear under other headings in this chapter.

Programme in Ungarn/in Hungary
  a monthly national listing of events, from ballet and puppet shows to sport and conferences, in German and English
Calendar of Events
  annual listing of festivals and other events around the country
Budapest Panorama
  a scaled-down version of *Programme* for the capital
Southern Transdanubia: Viva Pannonia and *On the Trails of Tradition: Northern Hungary*
  two of a half-dozen colourful and useful brochures that focus on Hungary's main regions
Camping and *Accommodation*
  complete listings of camping grounds and accommodation around the country, with telephone numbers and a star-rating system so you have an idea of how much each charges
Folk Art in Hungary
  a well-written and sensible 'idiot's guide' to traditional art and culture
The Flavours of Hungary
  an introduction to Hungarian food with recipes and recommended accompanying wines
Get Fit in Hungary
  a brief but useful guide to Hungary's 'active' offerings
Land of Spas
  some two dozen of the more than 100 thermal baths in a nutshell

Jewish Relics in Hungary
  Jewish museums, sights and traditions in contemporary Hungary

The HTB also has a number of videos for sale on the country's various regions as well as on subjects ranging from history *(King Matthias and the Hungarian Renaissance, Turkish Monuments in Hungary)* and tradition *(Folk Art, Shalom)* to sport *(Hungary by Bicycle, Angling in Hungary)*. They cost US$8/$10 per 30-minute PAL/NTSC video, plus US$6 postage for up to six cassettes.

VISAS & DOCUMENTS
Passport

Almost everyone entering Hungary must have a valid passport, though citizens of Germany and France need only produce their national identity card on arrival. Because of the large number of illegal immigrants in Hungary, identification checks are not uncommon, especially in Budapest. It's a good idea to carry your passport or other identification at all times.

Visas

Citizens of the USA, Canada, most European countries and South Africa do not require visas to visit Hungary for stays of up to 90 days. Nationals of Australia, Hong Kong, Japan and New Zealand (among others) still need them. If you hold a passport from one of these countries, check current visa requirements at an embassy or consulate or any HTB or Malév office.

Single-entry visas valid for between 30 and 90 days (the length of stay depends on your passport) are issued at Hungarian consulates upon receipt of US$32/£26 and three photos. A double-entry tourist visa costs US$60/£48, and you must have five photos. If you know you'll be visiting Hungary twice, get a double-entry visa to avoid having to apply again somewhere else. A multiple-entry visa is US$100/£86. Some consulates charge US$15/£10 extra for express service (10 minutes as opposed to overnight). Single and double-entry visas are valid for six months prior to use. Multiple entries are good for a year.

Be sure to get a tourist rather than a transit visa; the latter – available for single (US$30/£26), double (US$50/£42) and multiple entries (US$60/£48) – is only good for a stay of 48 hours and cannot be extended. On a transit visa you must enter and leave through different border crossings and have a visa (if required) for the next country you visit. A tourist visa can be extended at the central police station (rendőrkapitányság) of any city or town, provided you do so 48 hours before it expires.

Visas are issued at most international highway border crossings and the airport, but this usually involves a wait and there are not always photo booths nearby if you've forgotten mug shots. Visas are never issued on trains and seldom to passengers on international buses.

Your hotel, hostel, camping ground or private room booked through an agency anywhere in the country will register your address with the police as required. In other situations (eg if you're staying with friends or relatives), you have to take care of this yourself within 72 hours. Don't worry if you haven't got round to it; it's a hangover from the old regime, and enforcement has been fairly lax. Address registration forms for foreigners (lakcímbejelentő lap külföldiek részére) are available at main post offices.

Photocopies

The hassles brought on by losing your passport can be considerably reduced if you have a record of its number and issue date, or even better, photocopies of the relevant data pages. A photocopy of your birth certificate can also be useful.

Also add the serial numbers of your travellers' cheques (cross them off as you cash them) and photocopies of your credit cards, airline ticket and other travel documents. Keep all this emergency material separate from your passport, cheques and cash, and leave extra copies with someone you can rely on back home. Add some emergency money, say US$50 in cash, to this

separate stash as well. If you do lose your passport, notify the police immediately to get a statement, and contact your nearest consulate.

Travel Insurance

You should seriously consider taking out travel insurance. This not only covers you for medical expenses and luggage theft or loss but also for cancellation or delays in your travel arrangements. (You could fall seriously ill two days before departure, for example.) Cover depends on your insurance and type of airline ticket, so ask both your insurer and your ticket-issuing agency to explain where you stand. Ticket loss is also covered by travel insurance.

Paying for your airline ticket with a credit card often provides limited travel accident insurance, and you may be able to reclaim the payment if the operator doesn't deliver. In the UK, for instance, institutions issuing credit cards are required by law to reimburse consumers if a company goes into liquidation and the amount in contention is more than UK£100. Ask your credit card company what it's prepared to cover.

Driving Licence & Permits

If you don't hold a European driving licence and plan to drive in Hungary, obtain an International Driving Permit from your local automobile association before you leave – you'll need a passport photo and a valid local licence. They are usually inexpensive and valid for one year only.

Camping Card International

Your local automobile association also issues the Camping Card International, which is basically a camping ground ID. These cards are also available from your local camping federation, and sometimes on the spot at camping grounds. They incorporate third-party insurance for damage you may cause, and some camping grounds in Hungary offer a small discount if you sign in with one.

Hostel Card

A hostel card is sometimes useful in Hungary. No hostels require that you be a hostelling association member, but they sometimes charge less if you have a card. Some hostels will issue one on the spot or after a few stays; Express, with offices around Hungary, will issue you an HI card for 1200 Ft.

Student & Youth Cards

The most useful of these is the International Student Identity Card (ISIC), a plastic ID-style card with your photograph, which provides discounts on some forms of transport and cheap or free admission to museums, sights and even films. If you're aged under 26, but not a student, you can apply for a GO25 card issued by the Federation of International Youth Travel Organisations (FIYTO), which gives much the same discounts and benefits as an ISIC. Express sells both ISIC and FIYTO cards for 500 Ft each.

EMBASSIES

Hungarian Embassies Abroad

Hungarian embassies around the world include the following:

Albania
    Rruga Skanderbeg 16, Tirana (☎ 42-322 38)
Australia
    17 Beale Crescent, Deakin, ACT 2600 (☎ 02-6282 3226)
    Edgecliff Centre, Suite 405, 203-233 New South Head Road, Edgecliff, NSW 2027 (☎ 02-9328 7859)
Austria
    1 Bankgasse 4-6, 1010 Vienna (☎ 0222-535 3389)
Bulgaria
    Ul 6 Septemvri 57, Sofia 1000 (☎ 02-662 021)
Canada
    299 Waverley St, Ottawa, Ont K2P 0V9 (☎ 613-230 2717)
    102 Bloor St West, Suite 1005, Toronto, Ont M5S 1M8 (☎ 416-923 3596)
Croatia
    Ul Cvietno Naselje 17/b, 41000 Zagreb (☎ 041-610 430)

Czech Republic
    Ul Badeniho 1, 12537 Prague 6 (☎ 02-365 041)
Denmark
    Stranvejen 170, Charlottenlund, 2920 Copenhagen (☎ 31 63 16 88)
France
    92 Rue Bonaparte, 75006 Paris (☎ 01 43 54 66 96)
Germany
    Unter den Linden 76, 10177 Berlin (☎ 030-220 2561)
    Turmstrasse 30, 53175 Bonn-Plittersdorf (☎ 0228-371 112)
    Vollmannstrasse 2, 81927 Munich (☎ 089-911 032)
Greece
    Kalvou 16, Paleo Psyhiko, 15452 Athens (☎ 01-671 4889)
Ireland
    2 Fitzwilliam Place, Dublin 2 (☎ 01-661 2902)
Italy
    Via dei Villini 12-16, 0161 Rome (☎ 06-4423 0598)
Japan
    14-17 Mita 2-chome, Minato-ku, Tokyo 108 (☎ 03-798 8801)
Netherlands
    Hogeweg 14, 2585 JD, The Hague (☎ 070-350 0404)
Norway
    Sophus Lies gt 3, Oslo 0264 (☎ 22 55 24 18)
Poland
    Ul Chopina 2, 00559 Warsaw (☎ 02-628 4451)
Romania
    Strada Calderon 63-65, Bucharest (☎ 090-614 6621)
Russia
    Ul Mosfilmovskaya 62, Moscow (☎ 095-143 8611)
    Ul Marata 15, St Petersburg (☎ 812-312 64 58)
Slovakia
    Sedlárska ul 3, 81425 Bratislava (☎ 07-330 541)
Slovenia
    Ul Konrada Babnika 5, Ljubljana 1000 (☎ 061-152 1882)
South Africa
    959 Arcadia St, 0132 Pretoria (☎ 012-433 030)
    14 Fernwood Ave, Newlands, 7700 Cape Town (☎ 021-641 547)
Sweden
    Strandvägen 74, Stockholm 11527 (☎ 08-661 67 62)
UK
    35/b Eaton Place, London SW1X 8BY (☎ 0171-235 2664)
Ukraine
    Ul Rejterskaya 33, 252901 Kiev (☎ 044-212 4134)

USA
3910 Shoemaker St NW, Washington, DC 20008 (☎ 202-362 6730)
223 East 52nd St, New York, NY 10022 (☎ 212-752 0661)
Yugoslavia
Ul Ivana Milutinovica 74, Belgrade 11000 (☎ 011-444 0472)

Foreign Embassies in Hungary

Selected countries with representation in Budapest (where the telephone code is 1) follow. The Roman numerals preceding the street name indicates the *kerület*, or district, in the capital.

Albania
VI Bajza utca 26 (☎ 322 7251)
Australia
XII Királyhágó tér 8-9 (☎ 201 8899)
Austria
VI Benczúr utca 16 (☎ 269 6700)
Bulgaria
VI Andrássy út 115 (☎ 322 0836)
Canada
XII Budakeszi út 32 (☎ 275 1200)
China
VI Benczúr utca 17 (☎ 322 4872)
Croatia
XII Nógrádi utca 28/b (☎ 155 1522)
Czech Republic
VI Délibáb utca 30 (☎ 351 0065)
Denmark
XII Határőr út 37 (☎ 155 7320)
France
VI Lendvay utca 27 (☎ 132 4980)
Germany
XIV Stefánia út 101-103 (☎ 251 8999)
Ireland
V Szabadság tér 7 (☎ 302 9600)
Israel
II Fullánk utca 8 (☎ 200 0781)
Italy
XIV Stefánia út 95 (☎ 343 6065)
Japan
XII Zalai út 7 (☎ 275 1275)
Netherlands
II Füge utca 5-7 (☎ 326 5301)
Norway
XII Határőr út 35 (☎ 155 1729)
Poland
VI Városligeti fasor 16 (☎ 351 1300)
Romania
XIV Thököly út 72 (☎ 268 0271)
Russia
VI Bajza utca 35 (☎ 302 5230)

Slovakia
XIV Stefánia út 22-24 (☎ 251 1700)
Slovenia
II Cseppkő utca 68 (☎ 250 8180)
South Africa
VIII Rákóczi út 1-3 (☎ 267 4566)
Sweden
XIV Ajtósi Dürer sor 27/a (☎ 268 0804)
UK
V Harmincad utca 6 (☎ 266 2888)
Ukraine
XII Nógrádi utca 8 (☎ 155 2443)
USA
V Szabadság tér 12 (☎ 267 4400)
Yugoslavia
VI Dózsa György út 92/b (☎ 342 0566)

CUSTOMS

You can bring into Hungary the usual personal effects, 500 cigarettes, three bottles of wine and a litre of spirits. Importing illegal drugs, pirated CDs and cassettes, offensive weapons and paprika(!) is taboo. When leaving the country, you are not supposed to take out valuable antiques without a 'museum certificate' (available from the place of purchase). Restrictions on the import/export of forint won't affect most travellers; the limit now is 200,000 Ft (but make sure you double-check the figure if you do plan to carry out that much money).

Customs inspections at most border crossings and the airport are pretty cursory. The one exception is Romania. Hungarian police believe this country has become a conduit for drug traffickers from Asia into Western Europe since the collapse of Yugoslavia. In summer there may be very long delays for motorists.

MONEY
Costs

The high rate of inflation (over 20%) and the systematic devaluation of the forint has made life very difficult for Hungarians earning local salaries, but for foreign travellers the country remains a bargain destination for food, lodging and transport. If you stay in private rooms, eat at medium-priced restaurants and travel 2nd-class on trains, you should get by on around US$25 a day without scrimping. Those putting up in hostels, dormitories or camping grounds and eating at self-service restaurants or food stalls will cut costs substantially.

Because of the rapidly changing value of the forint, many hotels now quote their rates in Deutschmarks. In such cases, we have done the same. For restaurants, transport, articles in shops etc we always quote prices in forint.

Currency

The Hungarian forint (Ft) is divided into 100 fillér, worthless little aluminium coins that are no longer minted and will soon be withdrawn from circulation. There are coins of 10, 20 and 50 fillér and one, two, five, 10, 20, 50, 100 and 200 Ft.

Notes come in five denominations: 50, 100, 500, 1000 and 5000 Ft. The brown 50 Ft note, which may have been withdrawn from circulation by the time you read this, bears the likeness of the 18th-century independence leader Ferenc Rákóczi II on the front and our hero mounted on horseback fighting the Habsburgs on the back.

The 100 Ft note is burgundy and features the national hero Lajos Kossuth on one side and a peasant couple in a horse-drawn cart escaping a puszta storm on the other.

The early 20th-century poet Endre Ady and Elizabeth Bridge in Budapest are on the blue 500 Ft note, while the 1000 Ft, coloured green, has the composer Béla Bartók and Ferenc Medgyessy's sculpture *Nursing Mother*.

The ugly orange-brown 5000 Ft note bears a portrait of the 19th-century reformer and statesman Count István Széchenyi. On the reverse side there's a marking in Braille, and an etching of the Academy of Science that was done not from a picture contemporary with the great count (who founded it) but from a modern photo – look closely and you'll see four Eastern European cars, including a Trabant.

A new 10,000 Ft note will soon be introduced.

Currency Exchange

Australia	A$1	=	130 Ft/DM1.26
Canada	C$1	=	126 Ft/DM1.22
France	1FF	=	31 Ft/DM.29
Germany	DM1	=	104 Ft
Japan	¥100	=	139 Ft/DM1.35
UK	UK£1	=	276 Ft/DM2.66
US	US$1	=	170 Ft/DM1.64

Changing Money

The hassle of trying to change travellers' cheques at the weekend, rip-off bureaux de change and the allure of the black market have all gone the way of the dodo in Hungary; automatic teller machines (ATMs) accepting any number of credit and cash cards are here and here to stay throughout the country.

It's always useful to carry a little foreign cash, preferably US dollars or Deutschmarks, and travellers' cheques in case your cash card doesn't work or you go over your limit on your credit card. American Express, Visa and Thomas Cook are the most recognisable brands of travellers' cheques in Hungary.

You can exchange cash, travellers' cheques and Eurocheques up to 30,000 Ft per transaction at banks (the National Savings Bank – Országos Takarékpénztár or OTP – has branches almost everywhere and charges no commission on travellers' cheques) and travel agents, which will usually take a commission of 1% to 2%. Post offices almost always change cash, but rarely cheques. Using private money-change bureaus can be convenient but expensive.

Ibusz and K&H banks everywhere will give you a cash advance on your Visa card; in Budapest, Ibusz Bank maintains a 24-hour exchange office at V Apáczai Csere János utca 1, near the Duna Marriott hotel. American Express is at V Deák Ferenc utca 10 in the capital, and there's an ATM there dispensing cash forint and travellers' cheques in US dollars. But be warned that this service costs 3% and Amex offers a poor exchange rate.

Though the forint became more or less convertible at the start of 1996, you should exchange only what you think you'll need over the next couple of days or to see you through the weekend. You are allowed to change leftover forint back into hard currency, but the procedure is still complicated, restrictive and somewhat expensive. You must have the official exchange receipts with the date and your passport number clearly legible, the limit is half the total on each of your transactions up to US$300, and you'll be charged a 7% commission. Getting US dollars for your dollar travellers' cheques is expensive, too. Amex, for example, first changes your dollars into forint at a low buying rate and then changes the forint into dollars at a high selling rate.

It's senseless to make use of the black market to change money. The advantage is virtually nil, it's illegal and you are almost sure to be ripped off anyway.

Credit cards are becoming more accepted in Hungary, especially American Express, Visa and MasterCard. You'll be able to use them at up-market restaurants, shops, hotels, car-rental firms, travel agencies and – something new – petrol stations.

Having money wired to Hungary through Thomas Cook or American Express is fairly straightforward; for the latter you don't need to be a card holder and it takes less than a day. You should know the sender's full name, the exact amount and the reference number when you're picking up the cash. With a passport or other ID you'll be given the amount in US dollars or forint. The sender pays the service fee (eg US$28 for $100, US$73 for $500, US$124 for $1000). Western Union's money transfer system (☎ 1-267 4282) is also popular.

Tipping & Bargaining

Hungary is a very tip-conscious society and virtually everyone routinely tips waiters, hairdressers, taxi drivers and even doctors, dentists and some petrol-station attendants about 10% (or even a generous 15%). If you were less than impressed with the service at the restaurant, the joyride in the taxi or the way someone cut your hair, leave next to

nothing or nothing at all. He or she will get the message.

The way you tip in restaurants is unusual. You never leave the money on the table – this is considered both rude and stupid in Hungary – but tell the waiter how much you're paying in total. If the bill is 630 Ft, you're paying with a 1000 Ft note and you think the waiter deserves the extra 10%, first ask if service is included (some restaurants in Budapest and other big cities add it to the bill automatically). If it isn't, say you're paying 700 Ft or that you want 300 Ft back. Don't worry if the 'bill waiter' is not the same one who served and impressed you: tips are always shared.

Bargaining was never the done thing under Communism. Except for the privileged class, everyone paid the same amount by weight and volume for items freely available, including a scoop of ice cream. You'll never be able to do it in shops (though a more advanced young capitalist may knock off 10% for a display model or something shop-soiled). You may haggle in flea markets or with individuals selling folk crafts, but even this is not as commonplace as it is in other parts of Eastern Europe.

Taxes & Refunds

ÁFA, a value-added tax (VAT) of between 12% and 25%, covers the purchase of all new goods in Hungary. It is almost always included in the quoted price but sometimes it is on top, so be wary. Visitors are not exempt, but they can claim refunds for total purchases of more than 25,000 Ft. However, claiming your money is a bit complicated. You must take the goods out of the country within 90 days, the ÁFA receipts (available from the shops where you made the purchases) should be stamped by customs at the border and the claim has to be made within six months of the purchase. Two outfits in Budapest that can help with refunds are Europe Tax Free Shopping Hungary (☎ 1-212 4734) at II Bég utca 3-5 and Interimport (☎ 1-206 6702) at XI Budafoki út 111. They charge a service fee of about 10%.

Some car-rental firms nowadays will

exempt you from paying the ÁFA in advance by having you sign a statement saying you do not intend on staying in Hungary more than 180 days.

POST & COMMUNICATIONS

The Hungarian Postal Service (Magyar Posta) has improved somewhat in recent years; its trendy British-designed logo of a stylised St Stephen's crown and the introduction of new uniforms have helped it limp into the 20th century. But post offices are usually still crowded, and the staff have not improved their foreign-language skills much.

Postal Rates

Letters sent within Budapest cost 16 Ft; for the rest of Hungary it's 24 Ft. Foreign air mail is 75 to 80 Ft for up to 20g and 150 to 160 Ft for 20 to 100g base rate plus 10 Ft per 10g air-mail charge. Postcards are 50 to 70 Ft.

Sending & Receiving Mail

To beat the crowds at the post office, ask at kiosks or stationery shops if they sell stamps, and drop your letters and postcards into letterboxes on the street.

If you must deal with the post office, you'll be relieved to learn that most people are there to pay electric, gas and telephone bills. To get in and out with a minimum of fuss, look for the window marked with the symbol of an envelope. Make sure the destination of your letter is written clearly, and simply hand it over to the clerk. He or she will apply the stamps for you, postmark it and send it on its way.

If you are trying to send a parcel, look for the sign 'Csomagfeladás' or 'Csomagfelvétel'. Packages must not weigh more than two kg or the contents be worth more than 10,000 Ft, or else you'll face a Kafkaesque nightmare of permits and more queues; try to send small packages. Books and printed matter are exceptions. You can send up to two kg in one box for between 900 and 936 Ft and up to five kg for 2250 to 2340 Ft.

Hungarian addresses start with the name of the recipient, followed by the postal code

and city or town and then the street name and number. The postal code consists of four digits. The first indicates the city/town, the second and third the district and the last the neighbourhood.

Mail addressed to poste restante in any town or city will go to the main post office (*főposta*). All post marked 'Poste Restante, Budapest' goes to the post office at V Petőfi Sándor utca 13-15. When picking up mail, look for the sign 'Postán maradó küldemények'. Don't forget identification. Since the family name always comes first in Hungarian usage, have the sender underline your last name, as letters are often misfiled under foreigners' first names.

You can have your mail delivered to American Express (1052 Budapest, Deák Ferenc utca) if you have an Amex credit card or travellers' cheques.

Telephone

Hungary's telephone system has gone from being one of the most antiquated in the region to one of the most modern in a few short years. You can make domestic and international calls from most public telephones, which are usually in good working order. To avoid having to carry a purse or pocket full of change, buy a telephone card from any post office. These come in message units of 50 (500 Ft), 100 (750 Ft) and 120 (100 Ft). Telephone boxes with a black and white arrow and red target on the door and the word 'Visszahívható' display a telephone number, which can be phoned back.

All localities in Hungary have a two-digit telephone area code, except for Budapest, which simply has a '1'. Local codes appear in the Information headings in this book.

To make a local call, pick up the receiver and listen for the neutral and continuous dial tone. Then dial the local number (seven digits in Budapest, six elsewhere). For a trunk call in Hungary, dial ☎ 06 and wait for the second, more musical, tone. Then dial – and don't forget the two-digit area code. You must also dial ☎ 06 if ringing a mobile telephone, whose area codes are usually ☎ 60.

The procedure for making an international

call is the same except that you dial ☎ 00, followed by the country and area codes and then the number. International phone charges are: 60 Ft per minute to neighbouring countries; 80 Ft for most of Western Europe; 160 Ft to North America, Australia and New Zealand; 180 to 220 Ft to East Asia and the Pacific; 220 Ft to the Middle East; and 250 Ft to south Asia. The country code for Hungary is ☎ 36.

You can also get straight through to an operator based in your home country by dialling the 'country direct' number from a public phone (charges are reversed), but you need a coin or phone card for the initial connection. Beware that some of the services listed below are very expensive.

Australia Direct ☎ 00-800 06111
Britain Direct (BT) ☎ 00-800 04411
Britain (Mercury) ☎ 00-800 04412
Canada Direct ☎ 00-800 01211
New Zealand Direct ☎ 00-800 06411
USA Direct (AT&T) ☎ 00-800 01111
USA MCI ☎ 00-800 01411
USA Sprint Express ☎ 00-800 01877

Other numbers you may find useful include:

international directory assistance in English
   ☎ 267 5555
domestic operator ☎ 01
international operator ☎ 09
time in Hungarian ☎ 08

Fax, Telegraph & E-mail
You can send telexes and faxes from most main post offices around Hungary; for information on how to get on to the Internet, see the list of cybercafés and public-access Internet servers under Information in the Budapest section.

BOOKS
There's no shortage of books on Hungary and things Hungarian – from travel guides and histories to travelogues. Once the biggest bargain in Hungary, books are becoming more expensive, though they haven't reached Western prices yet. Quality has also improved: the colour reproduction in some of the pictorials and coffee-table books on sale is first rate. For tourist publications, see the earlier Tourist Offices section.

Lonely Planet
Both Lonely Planet's *Eastern Europe on a shoestring* and *Central Europe on a shoestring* contain Hungary chapters. The Lonely Planet *Eastern Europe phrasebook* contains lengthy sections of useful words and expressions in Hungarian.

Travel
Travellers writing 'diary' accounts usually treat Hungary rather cursorily as they make tracks for 'more exotic' Romania or points beyond. But Patrick Leigh Fermor, in describing his 1933 walk through Hungary en route to Constantinople in *Between the Woods and the Water* (Penguin), wrote the classic account of the country. Brian Hall's tempered love affair with the still Communist Budapest of the 1980s, described in *Stealing from a Deep Place* (Minerva), is sensitive but never cloying. *The Double Eagle: Vienna, Budapest and Prague* by Stephen Brook (Picador) is a cultural and political commentary on the three major Habsburg cities through the eyes of a modern traveller.

History & Politics
The Corvina History of Hungary (Corvina), written by seven leading historians and edited by Péter Hanák, is fairly comprehensive but rather dull. *Hungary: A Brief History* (also from Corvina) is a light, almost silly history by geologist-cum-journalist István Lázár. *A History of Modern Hungary* (Longman) by Jörg K Hoensch covers the period from 1867 to 1994 in a balanced, though somewhat dry, way. Another serious work from Longman is *The Hungarian Revolution of 1956*, edited by György Litván. *Budapest 1900* (Weidenfeld) by John Lukacs is an illustrated social history of the capital at the height of its glory.

More in the spirit of *Boy's Own* is Géza Gárdonyi's swashbuckling *Eclipse of the Crescent Moon* (Corvina), written in 1901;

it's an excellent fictionalised account of the 1552 siege of Eger Castle. *In the Name of the Working Class* (Fontana) is a very readable account of the events leading to the 1956 revolution by Budapest's then chief of police, Sándor Kopácsi.

For clear, insightful interpretations of what led to the collapse of Communism in 1989, read *We the People* (Granta) by Timothy Garton Ash or Misha Glenny's updated *The Rebirth of History* (Penguin).

If you've ever wondered how censorship actually worked under Communism and how writers dealt with it, pick up a copy of *The Velvet Prison* by Miklós Haraszti (IB Tauris).

General

The City of Budapest publishes a number of small topical guidebooks in its Our Budapest series, including *Budapest for Children, Nightlights: A Tour of Our Locals, Budapest Courtyards Parks & Forests* etc. Those intent on seeing Budapest's main museums in depth might be interested in *The Museums of Budapest* (Corvina), a colourful souvenir album with useful text.

A Guide to Hungarian Wine by József Katona is a brief but useful introduction to what's on offer. Ornithologists will want to pick up a copy of *The Birds of Hungary* (Helm) or *Where to Watch Birds in Eastern Europe* (Hamlyn), both by Gerard Gorman. The latter contains a 40-page chapter on Hungary.

For travel agents and those requiring lots of detail, nothing beats *Hungary Handbook (Idegenforgalmi Kézikönyv* in Hungarian), which contains tourist data from hundreds of sources in one volume and is updated every other year (even Tourinform relies on it!). You can order it through M & G Marketing (Üllői út 71, 1091 Budapest; ☎ /fax 1-216 5239). It may soon be available on CD rom.

Homage to the Eighth District by Giorgio & Nicola Pressburger (Readers International) is the poignant account of life in what was a Jewish working-class section of Budapest during and after WWII. The twin brothers emigrated to Italy in 1956. Tibor

Fischer's *Under the Frog* (Penguin) is an amusing account of a basketball team's antics in the Hungary of the early 1950s.

Corvina publishes a number of small albums on subjects ranging from traditional dress to Hungarian cuisine, but the real gem is *Hungarian Ethnography and Folklore* by Iván Balassa & Gyula Ortutay, an 800-page opus that weighs in at three kg and leaves no question on traditional culture unanswered. It's out of print but can still be found in Budapest and some provincial bookshops. Highly recommended.

Hungarian Folk Art (Corvina) by Tamás Hofer and Edit Fél is an over-sized picture book that offers a good introduction to the subject.

ONLINE SERVICES

Tourinform has a homepage with tourist information on the Internet at http:// www .hungary.com/tourinform.

NEWSPAPERS & MAGAZINES

Hungary has seen a frenzy of new specialised publications appear and disappear in recent years. As in many European countries, printed news has strong political affiliations. The two main exceptions are the highly respected news magazine *Heti Világgazdaság* (World Economy Weekly), better known as *HVG*, and the former Communist Party mouthpiece *Népszabadság* (People's Freedom), which is now completely independent and, curiously, has the highest circulation of any newspaper.

Hungary counts three weekly English-language newspapers: the *Budapest Week* tabloid, which has ample coverage of news and cultural events but sometimes reads like a college newspaper; the more serious *Budapest Sun* broadsheet, with a particularly useful Style supplement with entertainment listings; and the *Budapest Business Journal*, an almost archival publication of financial news and business features.

Western newspapers in English available on the day of publication at many large kiosks and expensive hotels in Budapest include the *International Herald Tribune*, the European edition of the *Wall Street Journal*, the *Guardian International* and the *Financial Times*.

Other English-language periodicals include the *Hungarian Observer*, published sporadically by the government throughout the year, and the erudite *Hungarian Quarterly*, which examines a wide variety of issues in great depth and is a valuable source of current Hungarian thinking in translation.

RADIO & TV

State-owned Magyar Televízió (MTV) has two stations (TV 1 and TV 2), and there are four local cable stations including Top TV, the Hungarian response to MTV (the music – not the Magyar – one). TVs equipped with satellite dishes and the necessary decoders can receive Sky TV and CNN among other channels.

Hungarian Radio has three stations named after Lajos Kossuth, Sándor Petőfi and Béla Bartók. Radio Bridge (102.1 Mhz on the FM band) has hourly news broadcasts in English, news features at 8 am on weekdays and a good late-night jazz show.

VIDEO SYSTEMS

If you want to record or buy video tapes to play back home, you won't get the picture if the image registration systems are different. Like most of Australia and Europe, Hungary uses PAL, which is incompatible with the North American and Japanese NTSC system or the SECAM system used in France.

PHOTOGRAPHY & VIDEO

All the major brands of film are readily available and you can have your film developed in one hour at many locations in Budapest, including any of the 18 Fotex outlets (VII Rákóczi út 2, V Váci utca 9 etc).

Film prices vary, but basically 24 exposures of 100 ASA Kodacolor II, Agfa or Fujifilm will cost from 550 to 650 Ft and 36 exposures between 790 and 930 Ft. Ektachrome 100 is 1240 Ft. Developing print film costs about 420 Ft a roll; for the prints themselves, you choose the size and pay accordingly (10x13 cm prints cost 52 Ft

each). Slide film costs 520 Ft to process. Video film like TDK EHG 30/45 minutes costs 990/1310 Ft.

TIME

Hungary lies in one time zone. Winter time is GMT plus one hour and in summer it's GMT plus two hours. Clocks are advanced at 2 am on the last Sunday in March and set back at 3 am on the last Sunday in October. Without taking daylight-saving times into account, when it's noon in Budapest, it's:

11 pm in Auckland
1 pm in Athens
noon in Belgrade
noon in Berlin
noon in Bratislava
1 pm in Bucharest
7 pm in Hong Kong
11 am in London
2 pm in Moscow
6 am in New York
noon in Prague
3 am in San Francisco
9 pm in Sydney
8 pm in Tokyo
6 am in Toronto
noon in Vienna
noon in Warsaw
noon in Zagreb

An important note on the way Hungarians tell time: 7.30 (am or pm in conversation) is 'half eight' *(fél nyolc óra)*. So a film at 7.30 pm could appear on the schedule as 'f8', 'f20', '½ 8' or '½ 20'. A quarter to the hour has ¾ in front ('¾ 8' means 7.45) while quarter past is ¼ of the next hour ('¼ 9' means 8.15).

ELECTRICITY

The electric current in Hungary is 220V, 50 Hz AC. Plugs are the European type with two round pins. Do not attempt to plug an American appliance into a Hungarian outlet without a transformer.

WEIGHTS & MEASURES

Hungary uses the metric system – there's a conversion table at the back of this book. In supermarkets and outdoor markets, fresh food is sold by weight or by piece *(darab)*. When ordering by weight, you specify kg or *deka* (decagrams – 50 dg is equal to half a kg or a little more than one pound).

Beer at a *söröző* (pub) is served as a *pohár* (one-third of a litre) or a *korsó* (half a litre). Wine in old-fashioned *borozó* (wine bars) is served by the *deci* (decilitre, 0.1 litre), but in more modern places it comes by the ill-defined 'glass'.

LAUNDRY

Laundries *(patyolat)* are fairly common in Hungary, especially in Budapest, though they're never self-service. You can elect to have your laundry done in six hours or one, two or three days (and pay accordingly).

Dry-cleaning is appalling except at big international hotels: suits and dresses are often ruined and buttons go missing. There is never any packaging and don't expect hangers.

TOILETS

Public toilets in Hungary are invariably staffed by an old *néné* (auntie), who mops the floor continuously, hands out sheets of grade AAA sandpaper and has seen it all. The usual charge is 20 to 50 Ft a go.

HEALTH

No special inoculations are needed before visiting Hungary, and there are no trouble-some snakes or creepy-crawlies to worry about. Mosquitoes are a real scourge around lakes and rivers, so be armed with insect repellent *(rovarírtó)*. One insect that can bring on more than just an itch is the forest tick *(kullancs)*, which burrows under the skin causing inflammation and even enceph-alitis. You might consider getting the vaccination against tick encephalitis if you plan to do a lot of hiking and camping in Transdanubia or the Northern Uplands between May and September.

The number of AIDS cases is relatively low in Hungary, but remember that the border has only really been open for less than a decade, and those could multiply in a very short time, particularly as Budapest becomes more and more the sex capital of Eastern Europe. Two AIDS hot lines operate in Budapest: ☎ 1-138 2419 between 6 am and 4 pm, and ☎ 1-138 4555 between 4 pm and 6 am.

First-aid and ambulance services are free for citizens of the UK, Scandinavian and most Eastern European countries, though follow-up treatment must be paid for. Treatment at a public outpatient clinic *(rendelő intézet)* costs little, but doctors working pri-vately sometimes charge much more. Very roughly, a consultation in a doctor's surgery *(orvosi rendelő)* starts at 2000 Ft, while a home visit costs from 4500 Ft.

Dental work is usually of a high standard and cheap by Western standards (at least the Austrians seem to think so, judging from the numbers who regularly cross the border to have their teeth fixed). Some dentists adver-tise in the English-language press in Budapest.

Most large towns and Budapest's 23 dis-tricts have an all-night pharmacy open every day; a sign on the door of any pharmacy will help you locate the closest 24-hour one.

WOMEN TRAVELLERS

Hungarian men can be very sexist in their thinking, but women do not suffer any par-ticular form of harassment (though rape and domestic violence get little media coverage here). Most men – even drunks – are effu-sively polite with women. Women may not be made to feel especially welcome when eating or drinking alone, but it's really no different here than in many other countries in Europe. If you can handle yourself in a less than comfortable situation, you'll be fine.

Two organisations dealing with women's issues are:

Women United Against Violence
    PO Box 660, Budapest 1462 (☎ 1-216 5900, help
    line ☎ 1-216 1670)
Feminist Network
    PO Box 701, Budapest 1399

GAY & LESBIAN TRAVELLERS

There's not much gay life beyond Budapest

unless you take it with you, but a couple of national organisations might be able to help with information. (See the Budapest section for listings in the capital). Contact the following for more information:

Rainbow Association for Homosexual Rights
PO Box 690, Budapest 1293
Mások
PO Box 388, Budapest 1461 (☎ 1-137 0327)

DISABLED TRAVELLERS

Hungary has a very long way to go before it becomes user-friendly for the physically challenged (one positive step: the 5000 Ft note has markings in Braille). Wheelchair ramps, toilets fitted for the disabled and so on are virtually nonexistent. Contact the following for more information:

Hungarian Disabled Association (MEOSZ)
San Marco utca 76, Budapest 1035 (☎ 1-188 2388)

SENIOR TRAVELLERS

Senior citizens are sometimes entitled to discounts in Hungary on things like public transport, museum admission fees etc, provided they show proof of their age. In some cases you might need a special pass. The minimum qualifying age is generally 60 or 65 for men and slightly younger for women.

TRAVEL WITH CHILDREN

Successful travel with young children requires planning and effort. Don't try to overdo things; even for adults, packing too much into the time available can cause problems. Make sure the activities include the kids as well – balance that morning at Budapest's Museum of Fine Arts with an afternoon at the nearby Grand Circus or a performance at the puppet theatre. Include children in the trip planning; if they've helped to work out where you will be going, they will be much more interested when they get there. Lonely Planet's *Travel with Children* by Maureen Wheeler is a good resource. Most car-rental firms in Hungary have children's safety seats for hire at a nominal cost, but it is essential that you book them in advance. The same goes for highchairs and cots (cribs); they're standard in many restaurants and hotels but numbers are limited. The choice of baby food, infant formulas, soy and cow's milk, disposable nappies (diapers) and the like can be as great in Hungarian supermarkets these days as it is back home, but the opening hours may be quite different. Don't get caught out at the weekend.

DANGERS & ANNOYANCES

Hungary is hardly a violent or dangerous society, but crime has increased dramatically in the 1990s (or has at least been reported in the media more consistently). In fact, the number of murders in the country dropped to 241 in 1995 from 310 the year before – a decrease of 22%.

Violence is seldom directed against travellers, though racially motivated attacks by skinheads against Gypsies, Africans and Arabs are not unknown, and the murder of a British tourist on Margaret Island in Budapest in the summer of 1995 has turned that idyllic spot into a ghost town after dark.

As a traveller you are most vulnerable to car thieves, pickpockets and taxi louts. To avoid having your car ripped off, take the usual precautions. Most Hungarian car thieves are not after fancy Western models as they're too difficult to get rid of. But Volkswagens, Audis and the like are very popular, and they're easy to dismantle and ship abroad. Don't leave anything of value inside the car, even if it is hidden.

Pickpocketing is most common in flea markets and on certain forms of transport in Budapest (see Dangers & Annoyances in that chapter for details). Always put your wallet in your front pocket, hold your purse close to your body and keep your backpack or baggage in sight. And watch out for tricks. The usual method on the street is for someone to distract you by running into you and then apologising profusely – as an accomplice takes off with the goods.

Taking a taxi in the provinces is seldom a problem. For information about arriving at your destination in a Budapest taxi without tears (or bruises), see Getting Around in that chapter.

In the event of an emergency anywhere in Hungary, the following are the most important national numbers:

Police ☎ 107
Fire ☎ 105
Ambulance ☎ 104 (☎ 1-111 1666 in English)
Car assistance ☎ 1-155 0379 (nationwide) or 1-252 8000 (Hungarian Automobile Club) in Budapest

BUSINESS HOURS

With rare exceptions, the opening hours *(nyitvatartás)* of a business, museum or government office are posted on the front door. Grocery stores and supermarkets are usually open on weekdays from 7 am to 7 pm, but there's always at least one 'nonstop' around – convenience stores open round the clock and selling basic food items, bottled drinks and cigarettes, have sprung up all over the country. Always look for one by the train station first.

Department stores, clothiers and bookshops keep shorter hours: roughly from 10 am to 6 pm on weekdays (though some stay open until 7 or 8 pm on Thursday) and 9 am to 1 pm on Saturday. And it's hell trying to remember the opening hours of certain businesses – such as laundries. Many private shops close early each Friday and during most of August. Restaurants in Budapest can stay open till midnight or even later, but don't arrive at one in the provinces after 9 pm and expect to get much to eat.

Bank hours vary but generally they're open from 8 am to 3 or 4 pm and to 1 pm on Friday. The main post office in any town, city or Budapest district (usually the ones listed in the Information sections of this book) is open from 8 am to 6 or 7 pm on weekdays and to 1 pm on Saturday. Branch offices close much earlier – usually at 3.30 pm – and are not open on weekends.

With few exceptions, museums in Hungary are open from 10 am to 6 pm Tuesday to Sunday from April to October and to 4 pm the rest of the year.

PUBLIC HOLIDAYS & SPECIAL EVENTS

Hungary has nine public holidays: New Year's Day, 1848 Revolution Day (15 March), Easter Monday, International Labour Day (1 May), Whit Monday (May/June), St Stephen's Day (20 August), 1956 Remembrance Day (23 October), Christmas Day and Boxing Day.

Hungary's most outstanding annual events are the Budapest Spring Festival (mid-March to mid-April), Hortobágy Equestrian Days (late June), Sopron Early Music Days (late June), Búcsú (Farewell) Festival in Budapest (late June), Győr Summer Cultural Festival (late June to late July), Pannon Festival in Pécs (July and August), Szentendre Summer Festival (July), Kőszeg Street Theatre Festival (late July), Savaria International Dance Competition in Szombathely (July), Debrecen Jazz Days (July), Szeged Open-Air Festival (mid-July to August), Eurowoodstock on Diáksziget (Student Island) north of Budapest (August), Eger Wine Harvest Festival

Busó carnival mask from Mohács

(September), Budapest Autumn Arts Festival (mid-September to mid-October), and the Budapest Marathon (early October).

St Stephen's Day (20 August) is celebrated with sporting events, parades and fireworks nationwide. On the same day there's a Floral Festival in Debrecen and a bridge fair in nearby Hortobágy. Formula 1 car races are held in early August at the Hungaroring near Mogyoród, 24 km northeast of Budapest.

ACTIVITIES

While Hungary is more of an 'educational' experience than an 'active' one, when compared with, say, Australia or Canada, there's still plenty to do here. You could forsake many of the country's sights and spend the entire time here boating, bird-watching or folk-dancing. In fact, the government is stressing what it calls 'exclusive' tourism to expand its base of visitors, particularly repeat ones.

Hungarians love a day out in the country to escape their relatively cramped quarters and the pollution of the towns and cities, and nothing is more sacred than the kirándulás (outing), which can be a day of horse riding or just a picnic of gulyás cooked in a bogrács (kettle) in the open air by a river or lake.

Cycling

The possibilities for cyclists are many in Hungary. The slopes of northern Hungary can be challenging, while Transdanubia is much gentler; the Great Plain is flat though windy (and in summer, hot). The problem is bicycle rentals: they're hard to come by in Hungary. Your best bets are camping grounds, resort hotels or Budapest's Margaret Island in season. Bicycles can be taken on trains but not on buses or trams.

Remember when planning your itinerary that bicycles are banned from the motorways (and national motorways Nos 0 to 9), and they must be equipped with lights and reflectors. Riding mountain bikes is becoming increasingly popular, especially in the Buda Hills and in the Börzsöny range north of the Danube Bend.

The HTB publishes useful pamphlets called *Hungary by Bike* and *Bicycle Tours in Eastern Hungary* with recommended routes and basic sketch maps. *Hungary by Bicycle*, in Hungarian, German and English, can be found in some Budapest bookshops.

In Budapest, the Hungarian Bicycle Touring Association (MKTSZ; ☎ 1-217 7208) at VIII Kalvin tér 9 can supply more information. For bike tours around Hungary lasting eight to 12 days, contact Velo-Touring (☎ 1-302 1648) at VI Vörösmarty utca 61. All-inclusive prices range from DM1190 to DM1380.

Hiking & Trekking

Though Hungary does not have high mountains, you can enjoy good hiking in the forests around Visegrád, Esztergom, Badacsony, Kőszeg and Budapest. North of Eger are the Bükk Hills and, south of Kecskemét, the Bugac Puszta, both national parks with marked hiking trails.

Cartographia's greatest contribution to humanity is its three dozen hiking maps (1:20,000 to 1:60,000) to the hills, forests, rivers and lakes of Hungary. Most are available from its outlet in Budapest (see Maps in the Orientation section of that chapter). On hiking maps, paths appear as a red line and usually with a letter, an abbreviation in Hungarian, indicating the colour-coding of the trail. Colours are painted on trees and markers and are 'K' for blue, 'P' for red, 'S' for yellow and 'Z' for green.

The Hungarian Friends of Nature Federation (MTSZ; ☎ 1-111 2467) in Budapest at VI Bajcsy-Zsilinszky út 31 organises hiking competitions around the country.

Swimming

Swimming is extremely popular in Hungary, and most towns have both a covered and outdoor pool, allowing enthusiasts to get into the water all year. The entry fee is low (usually between 100 and 200 Ft), and you can often rent swimming costumes and bathing caps (the latter are mandatory in some indoor pools for both sexes). All pools have a locker system. Find one, get changed in it or beside it and call over the attendant. He or she will lock the door with your clothes inside and hand you a numbered tag to tie on your costume. Lakes and rivers of any size have a grassy *strand* (beach) with showers and changing facilities.

Thermal Baths

Since Roman times settlers have been enjoying Hungary's ample thermal waters, and today there are no fewer than 100 open to the public throughout the country. Many spas, such as those at Hajdúszoboszló, Sárvár, Gyula and on Margaret Island in Budapest, are very serious affairs indeed, and people come to 'take the waters' for specific complaints, be they respiratory, muscular or gynaecological. Many spa hotels at such places offer cure packages (including accommodation, board, use of the spa and other facilities, medical examination, etc) that last a week or longer. Danubius Travel (☎ 1-117 3115) at V Szervita tér 8 in Budapest can book the best packages.

But most people use the spas just to relax (they're also an excellent cure for a hangover). The most unusual in the country is the thermal lake in Hévíz (see the Hévíz section of the Lake Balaton chapter), but the Cave Baths in Miskolc-tapolca, the outdoor thermal pools at Harkány, the Castle Baths at Gyula and Budapest's Turkish-style baths like the Rác, the Király and the Rudas also have their own following. Some good spas are recommended in the relevant sections of this book.

The procedure for getting into the warm water is similar to the one for swimming pools, though in Budapest's baths you will sometimes be given a number and will have to wait until it's called (if you can't get help, you can learn how to say your number in Hungarian while you wait – see the Language section) or until it appears on the electronic board. Though some of the local spas and baths look a little rough around the edges, they are clean and the water is changed daily. You might consider taking along a pair of plastic sandals or flip-flops, however; athlete's foot is not unknown in these places. You should tip the attendant 30 to 40 Ft.

Windsurfing

Wherever there's water, a bit of wind and a camp site, you'll find sailboards for rent (on Lake Tisza at Tokaj, on Lake Pécs or on Lake Velence, for example), but the main place for the sport is Lake Balaton, especially at Kiliántelep and Balatonszemes. The best time for the sport is early and late summer, as the wind tends to die down in July and August.

Boating & Kayaking

Qualified sailors can rent boats at locations around the lake, including Balatonfüred, Tihany, Siófok, Fonyód and Balatonboglár. Motorboats are banned on Lake Balaton, so the only place you'll get to do any waterskiing is at Füred Camping in Balatonfüred, where a cable tow does the job.

There are many canoe and kayak trips available. Following the Danube from Rajka to Mohács (386 km) or the Tisza River from Tiszabecs to Szeged (570 km) are popular runs, but there are less congested waterways and shorter trips like the 210-km stretch of the Körös and Tisza rivers from Békés to Szeged or the Rába River from Szentgotthárd to Győr (205 km).

The HTB publishes a brochure titled *Water Tours in Hungary*, which is a gold mine of information for planning itineraries and rentals and learning the rules and regulations. Many travel agencies organise kayak and canoe tours lasting from seven days to two weeks, but the best is Jezer Sport which has offices in Budapest (☎ 1-165 3879; XI Kende utca 19) and in Cegléd (☎ 53-312 575; Köztársaság utca 16), 23 km west of the Tisza River on the Central Plain. Prices start at 2450 Ft for a two-day tour with accommodation.

The Hungarian Friends of Nature Federation (see the previous Hiking & Trekking section) publishes an excellent series of water-tour maps (*vízitúrázók térképei*).

Fishing

You'll see people fishing in waterways everywhere, but Lake Balaton and the Tisza River – especially at the Kisköre Reservoir south-west of Tiszafüred, which is said to be the second-best spot for fresh-water angling in Europe after the Danube Delta in Romania – are the most popular. The best source for information and permits is the Hungarian National Angling Association (Mohosz; ☎ 1-131 3199) in Budapest at VI Ó utca 3.

Hunting

Whether you like it or not, hunting is big business in Hungary. Roe and red deer, mouflon, wild pigs, hare, pheasant and duck abound, and other game exists in smaller numbers. Strict rules apply, and you must do your hunting through the main hunting organisations. The gory details are provided by Mavad (☎ 1-201 6445) at I Úri utca 39, and Pannonvad (☎ 1-175 4089) at I Várfok utca 15/b, both in Budapest.

Horse Riding

There's a saying in Hungarian that the Magyars were 'created by God to sit on horseback'. Judging from the number of stables, riding schools and courses around the country, that is still true today.

A lot of the riding in Hungary is the follow-the-leader variety up to a castle or through open fields, but larger schools have horses for more advanced equestrians that can be taken into the hills or across the puszta. These schools also offer lessons. Not surprisingly, the best centres are on the Great Plain – at Máta near Hortobágy, Lajosmizse and Bugacspuszta near Kecskemét and Solt, north of Kalocsa. But you don't have to travel that far to get into the saddle. In Transdanubia you'll find good schools at Nagycenk and Tamási (north-west of Szekszárd). Around Lake Balaton they're at Szántódpuszta and Keszthely, and Gizellatelep near Visegrád has some of the best horse flesh in the country. But nothing beats mounting a Lippizaner at the stud farm in Szilvásvárad.

It's risky – particularly in the high season – to show up at a riding centre without a booking. Do this through the local tourist office, or in Budapest you can contact Ibusz (Leisure Department; ☎ 1-118 2967) at V Ferenciek tere 10, which organises 10-day riding tours in Transdanubia, the Danube Bend and the Great Plain. Prices range from DM1500 to DM2000. Two other Budapest-based agencies specialising in horse riding and excursions are Pegazus (☎ 1-117 1552), V Ferenciek tere 5, and Top Sí (☎ 1-266 7444), V Királyi Pál utca 8.

Bird-Watching

It may come as something of a surprise, but Hungary has some of the best bird-watching areas in Europe. Indeed, some 310 of the continent's 400-odd species have been sighted in the Hortobágy region alone. The arrival of the storks in the Northern Uplands and the North-East in spring is a wonderful sight.

First of all you should get a copy of Gerard Gorman's *The Birds of Hungary* (Helm) or at least his *Where to Watch Birds in Eastern Europe* (Hamlyn). The best areas overall are the Hortobágy region, the Mátra Hills, Aggtelek and Little Balaton, but the Buda Hills and even places like Tata attract a wide range of birds. Spring and autumn are good for sightings, but the best month is May. A Debrecen-based company called Aquila and the Hungarian Ornithological and Nature Conservation Society (MME) offer guided bird-watching tours of the Hortobágy (see that section in the Great Plain chapter).

LANGUAGE COURSES

Schools teaching Hungarian to foreigners have proliferated – at least in Budapest – over the past five years, but they vary tremendously in quality, approach and success rates. Unfortunately many believe the (very wrong) adage: 'If you can speak a language, you can teach it'. Establish whether your teacher has a degree in the Hungarian language and whether he or she has ever taught foreigners. You should be following a text or at least a comprehensive series of photocopies produced by your teacher. Remember also that you'll never get anywhere by simply sitting in class and not studying at home or practising with native speakers.

Reliable schools in the capital include:

Hungarian Language School
  VI Eötvös utca 25/a (☎ 1-112 5899)
Arany János Language School
  VI Csengery utca 68 (☎ 1-111 8870)

The granddaddy of all Hungarian language schools is the Debrecen Summer University in Debrecen, which organises intensive two and four-week courses in July and August and 80-hour advanced courses in winter. The emphasis is not just on language but the whole Magyar picture: history, culture, literature and art. The four-week (120-hour) course costs US$840, including board and lodging in a triple room (singles and doubles are available at extra cost). For more information, contact the Debreceni Nyári Egyetem (☎ /fax 52-329 117), PO Box 35, Debrecen 4010.

WORK

Travellers on tourist visas in Hungary are not supposed to accept employment, but many end up teaching, doing a little writing for the English-language press or even working for foreign firms without permits. Check the telephone book or advertisements for English-language schools in the *Budapest Week* or *Budapest Sun*; there are also job listings, but pay is generally pretty low. You can do much better teaching privately (800 to 1200 Ft per 45-minute 'hour') once you've built up the contacts. Babysitting for expatriates pays about 1000 ft an hour.

Obtaining an official work permit involves a Byzantine paper chase with Hungarian bureaucracy and, at the end of it all, you'll have to pay Hungarian income tax. First you'll need a letter of support from your prospective employer to get a one-year renewable residency. You'll need copies of your birth certificate and school transcript or academic record officially translated into Hungarian (1000 Ft). A medical exam and AIDS test (3200 Ft) is also mandatory. The

office in Budapest dealing with foreigners' registrations is Keokh (☎ 1-118 0800) at VI Városligeti fasor 46-48.

ACCOMMODATION

Except during the peak summer season – July and August – in places like Budapest, parts of Lake Balaton, the Danube Bend and the Mátra Hills, you should have no problem finding accommodation to fit your budget in Hungary. Camp sites are plentiful, college dormitories open their doors to guests during summer and other holiday periods, large trade-union holiday homes have been converted into hostels and hotels, and family-run pensions are popping up everywhere. It's unusual even for a small town not to have a hotel, and the paying-guest service is as common as B&Bs are in Britain and Ireland.

The price quoted should be the price you pay, but it is not as cut-and-dried as that. There's a 10% turnover tax on all hotels, though this should be included in the price you are quoted. In the past, all hotels and pensions included breakfast in their rates, but this is changing and now some don't. Certain places insist on a 'mandatory breakfast' and charge you from 300 Ft even if you don't want it (and it's never the huge buffet served in other Eastern European countries). If that's their policy, they're probably not going to change it for you.

Tourist offices and bureaus charge you a small fee for booking a private room or other accommodation, and there's usually a surcharge if you stay less than four nights. Many cities and towns levy a local tourist tax of about 100 Ft per person per night – sometimes only after the first 48 hours though. Those under 18 years of age or staying at camping grounds may be exempt.

On the whole, Hungarians do not travel alone and they assume other people don't either. As a result it is often difficult to get single rooms. Outside expensive hotels, a room is designated a single, double or triple according to how many beds it has and not by the number of occupants. If they try to charge just you for a double, insist – pleasantly – that you are alone. You should be able to negotiate the price down depending on the location, season and staff.

Inflation is running above 20% at present, so prices will almost certainly be higher than those quoted in this book, although they shouldn't change much when quoted in Deutschmarks, and the relative differences between various establishments in forint should stay the same. The rate usually increases in April for the summer season – often by as much as 30%. Where possible, we've indicated seasonal price differences in this book (eg 'doubles are 1800 to 3200 Ft').

Camping

Hungary has more than 200 camping grounds, and these are the cheapest places to stay. Small, private camping grounds accommodating as few as six tents are usually preferable to the large, noisy, 'official' camping grounds. Prices vary from about 400 to 1880 Ft for two adults plus tent at one, two and three-star sites. The sites around Lake Balaton are more expensive and an additional tourist tax of 60 to 150 Ft is levied in some areas, usually after the first night. Some sites on the Great Plain have poor drainage.

Most camping grounds are open from May to September (though some open in April and close in October) and rent small bungalows (üdölőház or faház) for around 1200 Ft to those without tents. In midsummer the bungalows may all be booked, so it pays to check with the local tourist office before making the trip. Holders of the Camping Card International (see the previous Visas & Documents section) sometimes get a 10% discount. Camping 'wild' is prohibited in Hungary.

For more information, contact the Hungarian Camping and Caravanning Club (MCCC; ☎ 1-133 6536) in Budapest at VIII Üllői út 6.

Hostels & Student Dormitories

Despite all the 'hostels' listed in the HI/Hungarian Youth Hostel Federation handbook, an HI card doesn't get you very far in Hungary. With the exception of those

in Budapest, most of the youth hostels (ifjúsági szálló) are in places well off the beaten track. Generally, the only year-round hostels are in Budapest.

Hostel beds cost 700 to 1900 Ft, depending on room size, in Budapest and considerably less elsewhere. An HI card is not required, although you occasionally get 10% off with one. There's no age limit at the hostels, they remain open all day and are often good places to meet other travellers.

From 1 July to 20 August only, Hungary's cheapest rooms are available in vacant student dormitories, known as kollégium or diákszálló, where beds in double, triple and quadruple rooms begin around 400 Ft per person. There's no need to show a student or hostel card, and it usually won't get you any discount. Express offices can generally tell you which dormitories to try, and they'll sometimes call ahead to reserve your bed.

The Hungarian Youth Hostel Federation (MISZSZ; ☎ 1-131 9705) is based in Budapest at VI Bajcsy-Zsilinszky út 31 II/3.

Tourist Hostels

There's another class of accommodation that is similar to Western youth hostels but not included in hostel handbooks. A tourist hostel (turistaszálló) offers beds in separate dormitories for men and women. There are no rules (for example, there are no curfews, smoking and drinking are allowed in the rooms, etc). Tourist hostels are found in many cities and most stay open all year. The overnight fee will be around 600 Ft and in winter you might have a whole room to yourself. Though often run-down, tourist hotels in the countryside are good, cheap places to stay and can be found near castles or on mountain peaks. In cities, however, they're often full of down-and-outers who drink, smoke and snore a lot.

Private Rooms & Farmhouses

Hungary's 'paying-guest service' (fizető-vendég szolgálat) is a great deal and still relatively cheap. Expect to pay from 1200 to 2500 Ft for a single, or 1500 to 4000 Ft for a double, depending on whether the room is

1st, 2nd or 3rd class. Private rooms at Lake Balaton are slightly more expensive. Single rooms are often hard to come by, and you'll usually have to pay a 20% or 30% supplement if you stay less than four nights. Some agencies also have entire flats for rent without the owner in residence. These can be a good deal if there are four or more of you travelling together and you want to stay put for a while.

Private rooms are assigned by travel agencies, which take your money and give you a voucher bearing the address or sometimes even the key to the flat. If the first room you're offered seems too expensive, ask if they have something cheaper. There are usually several agencies offering private rooms, so ask around if the price seems higher than usual or the location inconvenient.

If you decide to take a private room, you'll share a house or flat with a Hungarian family. The toilet facilities are usually communal, but otherwise you can close your door and enjoy as much privacy as you please. All 1st and some 2nd and 3rd-class rooms have shared kitchen facilities. In Budapest you may have to take a room far from the centre of town, but public transport is good and cheap.

Individuals at train stations in Budapest may offer you an unofficial private room. The prices these people ask are often higher than those at the agencies, and you will have nowhere to complain in case of problems. Sometimes these people misrepresent the location or quality of their rooms to convince you to go with them. In resort areas look for houses with signs reading 'szoba kiadó' or 'Zimmer frei', advertising private rooms in Hungarian or German.

'Village tourism' *(falusi turizmus)*, which means staying at a farmhouse, is in no way as developed as it is in, say, Slovenia, and most of the places are truly remote, but the price is right: from as low as 350 Ft per person per night. The HTB publishes a catalogue called *Village Tourism*, available at most Tourinform offices, which lists farmhouses accepting paying guests. By their very nature, these places are well off the beaten track and you'll have to have your own transport.

Pensions

Privately run pensions *(panzió)*, which form the biggest growth area in the Hungarian hospitality industry, are really just little hotels of four to six rooms charging from 2000 Ft in the provinces and 4500 Ft in Budapest for a double with shower. They are usually new, very clean and have an attached restaurant, bar or coffee shop.

Most pensions in Budapest (where their number equals the number of hotel rooms) are up in the Buda Hills, while in the provinces they're often two or three km out of town. Thus they're best for people travelling under their own steam, and visiting Austrians and Germans seem to favour them. But that's changing too, and you'll sometimes find them downtown in cities like Győr, Sopron and Pécs, along the Danube Bend and on Lake Balaton. Always ask to see a room first as they can be quite different. Those under the roof – so-called 'mansard rooms' – are cramped but cheaper. You are sometimes allowed to use the kitchen at a pension.

Hotels

Hotels, called *szálló* or *szálloda*, can run the gamut from luxurious five-star palaces like the Kempinski Corvinus in Budapest to the derelict Béke (Peace) hotel you can still find in a few Hungarian towns and small cities. The cheapest hotel rooms are more expensive than private rooms, but they are a real bargain by international standards (from 1500 Ft single, 2500 Ft double). A hotel may be the answer if you're only staying one night or if you arrive too late to get a private room through an agency.

Two-star hotels usually have rooms with private bathroom, whereas at one-star hotels the bathroom is usually down the hall. Breakfast – a meal at which the Hungarians decidedly do not excel – is usually (but not always) included in the room price. Expect ersatz coffee, weak tea, unsweetened lemon 'juice', tiny triangles of processed 'cheese' and stale bread.

For the big splurge, if you're romantically inclined, or if you're travelling with a rich uncle or aunt, check Hungary's network of castle and mansion hotels, *kastély szálló* or *kúria szálló*. These need not break the bank: the ones at Egervár or Fertőd in Western Transdanubia, for example, charge only about 1000 Ft. But most of the fancy castle hotels have three stars and cost 4500 Ft and upward for a double.

Other Accommodation

Accommodation choices don't stop there. Farmhouses can be rented on the Southern Plain, cottages for hire dot the hills on the northern side of Lake Balaton, and some people travel to Csongrád just to stay in the 200-year-old fishing cottages there. Peasant houses done up in traditional style are popular in Transdanubia and the Northern Uplands – the Palóc ones in Hollókő are nice. Budapest and Tiszafüred have boat hotels.

FOOD

Much has been written about Hungarian food – some of it silly, much of it downright false. It's true that Hungarian cuisine has had many outside influences and that it makes great use of paprika. But it's pretty mild stuff; a taco with salsa or balti chicken will taste a lot more 'fiery' to you. Paprika in its many varieties is used predominantly with sour cream or in *rántás*, a heavy roux of pork lard and flour added to vegetables. Most meat dishes – and Hungarians eat an astonishing amount of flesh – are breaded and fried or baked.

Hungary's reputation as a food centre dates partly from the last century and partly from the chilly days of Communism. In the heady days following the advent of the Dual Monarchy and right up to WWII, food became a passion among well-to-do city folk, and writers and poets sang its praises. This was the 'gilded age' of the famous chefs Károly Gundel and József Dobos and of Gypsy fiddlers like Jancsi Rigo and Gyula Benczi, an age when nothing was too extrav-

agant. The world took note and Hungarian restaurants sprouted in cities around the world – including a 'Café Budapest' in Boston, Massachusetts – complete with imported Gypsy bands and waiters who sounded like Bela Lugosi and Zsa Zsa Gabor.

After the war, Hungary's gastronomic reputation lived on – most notably because everything else in the region was so bad. Hungarian food was, as one observer noted, 'a bright spot in a culinary black hole'. But most of the best chefs, including Gundel himself, had voted with their feet and left the country in the 1950s, and restaurants were put under state control. The reality and the reputation of Hungarian food had diverged.

Although inexpensive by Western standards and served in huge portions, Hungarian food today remains heavy and, frankly, can be unhealthy. Meat, sour cream and fat abound and, except in season, *saláta* means a plate of pickled beets, cabbage and peppers. There are a few bright spots – though they seldom have much to do with Hungarian cuisine as such. Vegetarian restaurants and particularly salad bars are opening up, and ethnic food – from Chinese and Middle-Eastern to Italian – is all the rage. If Hungarian food can't (or won't) lighten up, foreign imports are going to have to do the job.

Basics

On the whole, Hungarians are not big breakfast eaters, preferring a cup of tea or coffee with an unadorned bread roll at home or on the way to work. (It is said that Hungarians will 'eat bread with bread'.) Lunch, eaten at 1 pm, is often the main meal and can consist of two or three courses, though this is changing in the cities. Dinner is less substantial when eaten at home.

It is important to note various sauces and cooking methods unique to Hungarian food. *Pörkölt* (stew) is what almost everyone calls 'goulash' abroad; the addition of sour cream makes the dish, whatever it may be, *paprikás*. *Gulyás* or *gulyásleves* is a thickish soup of beef, usually eaten as a main course. *Halászlé*, fish soup with paprika and one of the spicier dishes around, is also a main dish. Things stuffed *(töltött)* with meat and rice, such as cabbage or peppers, are cooked in *rántás*, tomato sauce or sour cream. As a savoury, *palacsinta* (pancakes) can be prepared in a similar way, but they also appear as a dessert with chocolate and nuts. *Lecsó* is a tasty stewed sauce of peppers, tomatoes and onions served with meat.

Pork is the preferred meat, followed by beef. Chicken and goose legs and turkey breasts – though not much else of the birds – make it to most menus. Freshwater fish from Lake Balaton (such as *fogas*, or pike-perch) or the Tisza River is plentiful, but quite expensive and often overcooked. Lamb and mutton are rarely eaten.

A main course usually comes with some sort of starch and a little garnish of pickles. Vegetables and salads must be ordered separately. A typical menu will have up to 10 pork and beef dishes, a couple of fish ones and only one poultry dish.

Vegetarian Food Such a carnivorous country is suspicious of non-meat eaters. 'You don't want meat? Then go to Romania!' I once heard a waiter snarl at an optimistic vegetarian. Outside the country's few vegetarian (or partly vegetarian) restaurants, you'll have to make do with what's on the regular menu or shop for yourself in the markets. The selection of fresh vegetables and fruit is not great in the dead of winter, but come spring a cycle of bounty begins: from strawberries and raspberries and cherries through all the stone fruits to apples and pears and nuts.

In restaurants, vegetarians can usually order fried mushroom caps *(gombafejek rántva)*, pasta dishes with cheese like *túrós csusza* and *sztrapacska*, or plain little dumplings *(galuszka)*. Salad as it's usually known around the world is called *vitamin saláta* here and only available at expensive restaurants when in season; everything else is *savanyúság*, or pickled things. When they're boiled, vegetables *(zöldség)* are 'English-style' or *angolos*. The traditional way of preparing vegetables is in *főzelék*, where they're fried or boiled and then mixed into a roux with sour cream.

Lángos, a deep-fried dough with various toppings, is sold on streets throughout the country.

Restaurants

Eateries in Hungary are rated according to class *(osztály)*, which is usually abbreviated 'I. O', 'II. O' etc on a sign somewhere inside. But these categories speak of price more than quality and the dishes served. In general, it's more useful to know the names of the types of Hungarian restaurants – though distinctions can sometimes be a bit blurred.

An *étterem* is a restaurant with a large selection, including international dishes, and is usually more expensive. A *vendéglő* or *kisvendéglő* is smaller and is supposed to serve regional dishes or 'home cooking', but the name is now 'cute' enough for a lot of large places to use it. An *étkezde* is something like a vendéglő but cheaper, smaller and often with counter seating. The overused term *csárda* originally signified a country inn with a rustic atmosphere, Gypsy music and hearty local dishes. Now any place that strings dry paprikas on the wall is a csárda. Most restaurants offer a good-value set menu *(menü)* of two or three courses at lunch.

A *bisztró* is a much less expensive sit-down place that is usually *önkiszolgáló* (self-service). A *büfé* is cheaper still with a very limited menu. Here you eat while standing at counters.

Most butcher shops *(hentesáru bolt)* have a büfé inside selling boiled or fried *kolbász* (sausage), *wirsli* (frankfurts), roast chicken, bread and pickles. Point to what you want; the staff will weigh it all and hand you a slip of paper with the price. You pay at the *pénztar* (cashier) and hand the stamped receipt back to the staff for your food. Food stalls, known as *Laci konyha* ('Larry's kitchen') or *pecsenyesütő*, sell the same sorts of things, as well as fish when they're by lakes or rivers. At these last few places you pay for everything, including a dollop of mustard for your kolbász, and eat with your hands.

An *eszpresszó* is essentially a coffee house, but they usually sell alcoholic drinks and light snacks. A *cukrászda* serves cakes, pastries and ice cream.

It is not unknown for waiters to try to rip you off once they see you are a foreigner. They may try to bring you an unordered dish; simply say *azt nem rendeltem, köszönöm* ('I didn't order that, thank you') and don't touch it. Bills are not normally padded, but 'mistakes' are sometimes made. If you think there's a discrepancy, ask for the menu and check the bill carefully. The most common ruse is to bring you the most expensive beer or wine when you order a draught or a glass. Ask the price. If you've been taken for more than 15% or 20% of the bill, call for the manager. Otherwise just don't leave a tip (see the section on Tipping & Bargaining earlier in this chapter).

Not everyone likes the Gypsy bands that go from table to table playing in some touristy restaurants and csárdas. If you're not interested in making a request (and paying roughly 500 to 1000 Ft per song), ignore them. This is perfectly acceptable, and they will get the message.

Menu Reader

Most sit-down restaurants in Budapest will be able to dig up a menu in English or at least one in German for you, but this is not always the case in the provinces. Many English menus have not been updated in years, and the language is sometimes so bad as to be indecipherable. The following is a sample menu as it would appear in many restaurants in Hungary. It's far from complete but it gives a good idea of what to expect. For more food, see the Language section in the Facts about the Country chapter.

Előételek – Appetisers
   rántott gombafejek – breaded, fried mushrooms
   hortobágyi palacsinta – meat pancakes with paprika sauce
   libamáj pástétom – goose-liver paté

Levesek – Soups
   gombaleves – mushroom soup
   bableves – bean soup
   jókai bableves – bean soup with meat
   csontleves – consommé
   újházi tyúkhúsleves – chicken broth with noodles
   meggyleves – cold sour-cherry soup (summer)

Saláták – Salads
   vitamin saláta – seasonal mixed salad
   vegyes saláta – mixed salad of pickles
   cékla saláta – pickled beetroot
   ecetes almapaprika – pickled peppers
   paradicsom saláta – tomato salad
   uborka saláta – sliced pickled-cucumber salad

Zöldség – Vegetables
   gomba – mushrooms
   káposzta – cabbage
   karfiol – cauliflower
   sárgarépa – carrots
   spárga – asparagus
   spenót – spinach
   zöldbab – string (French) beans
   zöldborsó – peas

Köretek – Side Dishes
   galuska – dumplings
   sült hasábburgonya – chips (French fries)
   főzelék – hungarian-style vegetables
   rizi-bizi – rice with peas

Készételek – Ready-Made Dishes
   gulyás – beef goulash soup
   halászlé – spicy fish soup
   pörkölt – stew (many types)
   csirkepaprikás – chicken paprika
   töltött paprika/káposzta – stuffed peppers/cabbage

Frissensültek – Dishes Made to Order
   hagymás rostélyos – beef sirloin with fried onions
   rántott hátszínszelet – breaded, fried rump steak
   borjú bécsiszelet – Wiener schnitzel
   sült csirkecomb – roast chicken thigh
   sült libacomb – roast goose leg
   rántott pulykamell – breaded turkey breast
   sült libamáj – roast goose liver
   sertésborda – pork chop
   brassói aprópecsenye – braised pork brassó-style
   cigánypecsenye – roast pork Gypsy-style
   csülök – smoked pork knuckle
   rántott ponty – fried carp
   fogas – Balaton pike perch

Cooking Methods
  sült or *sütve* – fried
  rántva or *rántott* – breaded and fried
  párolt – steamed
  roston – grilled
  főtt or *főve* – boiled
  füstölt – smoked
  pirított – braised

Édességek or *Tészták* – Desserts
  rétes – strudel
  somlói galuska – sponge cake with chocolate and
    whipped cream
  gundel palacsinta – flambéed pancake with
    chocolate and nuts
  dobos torta – multilayered chocolate and cream
    cake with caramelised brown sugar top

Gyümölcs – Fruit
  alma – apple
  banán – banana
  cseresznye – cherries
  eper – strawberries
  körte – pear
  málna – raspberries
  meggy – sour cherries
  narancs – orange
  őszibarack – peach
  sárgabarack – apricot
  szilva – plum
  szőlő – grapes

DRINKS
Wine

Wine has been produced in Hungary for thousands of years, and it remains important economically and socially. You'll find it available by the glass or bottle everywhere – at wine bars (very basic affairs by Western standards), food stalls, restaurants, supermarkets and 'nonstops' (buinesses providing 24-hour service). It is always very cheap.

Foreigners used to drinking wine are generally disappointed by the Hungarian variety. Under Communism, most of what wasn't consumed at home went to the Soviet Union where, frankly, they were happy to drink anything. This and state control offered little incentive to upgrade antiquated standards of wine-making and to apply modern methods to traditional grape varieties.

All of that is changing – and fast. 'Boutique' Hungarian chateaux like Gere, GIA and Thummerer have begun producing very good wines, and joint ventures with Austrian and Italian vintners are changing the face of the industry.

There are some 20 wine-growing areas in Hungary – in Transdanubia, the Northern Uplands and the Great Plain, but more than one-third of the vines grow in the sandy soil of the Great Plain. Of course it's all a matter of taste, but the most distinctive reds come from Villány and Szekszárd in Southern Transdanubia and the best whites come from around Lake Balaton and the Mátra Hills. The reds and whites from Eger and Tokaj are much better known abroad, however.

When choosing wine, look for the words *minőség bor* (quality wine), the closest thing Hungary has to *appellation controlée*. Vintage is not as important here as it is in France or Germany, and the quality of a label can vary widely from bottle to bottle. On a Hungarian wine label, the first word indicates where the wine comes from. The second word is the grape varietal.

For dry whites, look for Badacsonyi Kéknyelű or Szürkebarát, Mőcsényi or Boglári Chardonnay or Debrői Hárslevelű. Olasz Rizling and Egri Leányka tend to be on the sweet side, though nowhere near the Tokaji Aszú dessert wines, which are rated according to the number of *puttony* (butts) of sweet essence added to other base wines.

Dependable reds are Villányi Merlot, Pinot Noir and Cabernet Sauvignon, Szekszárdi Kékfrankos and Nagyrédei Cabernet Franc. The celebrated Egri Bikavér (Eger Bull's Blood) is a full-bodied red high in acid and tannin. As in Germany and Austria, people usually order a bottle or glass of mineral water along with their wine.

In summer, spritzers (wine coolers) of red or white wine and mineral water are consumed in large quantities.

Important wine words include:

bor – wine
borozó – wine bar
borpince – wine cellar
édes – sweet
fehér bor – white wine
féledes – semisweet
félszáraz – semidry/medium

fröccs – spritzer/wine cooler
itallap – drinks/wine list
vörös bor – red wine
pezsgő – champagne/sparkling wine
pohár – glass (size varies)
rozé – rosé
száraz – dry
üveg – bottle

Beer

Hungary produces a number of its own beers for national distribution (Dreher, Kőbanyai), though some are usually found only near where they are brewed (eg Kanizsai in Nagykanizsa and Szalon in Pécs). Bottled Austrian and German beer like Gösser, Holstein and Zipfer – either imported or brewed here under licence – are readily available as are Czech imports like Pilsner Urquell and Staropramen.

Beer is available in pubs and shops in half-litre bottles and imported cans, and many licensed pubs and bars now sell their own draught beers in one-half or one-third litre glasses. Locally brewed and imported beer in Hungary is almost always lager, though occasionally you'll find Dreher stout.

Important beer words include:

barna sör – dark beer/stout
csapolt sör – draught beer
egészségére! – cheers!
korsó – mug (half litre)
pohár – glass (one-third litre)
sör – beer
söröző – pub/beer hall
sörpince – beer cellar
világos sör – lager

Other Drinks

An alcoholic drink that is as Hungarian as wine is *pálinka*, a strong brandy distilled from a variety of fruits but most commonly from plums or apricots. There are many different types and qualities but the best is Óbarack, the double-distilled 'Old Apricot', and anything with *kóser* (kosher) on the label.

Hungarian liqueurs are usually unbearably sweet and taste artificial, though the Zwack brand is reliable. Zwack also produces Unicum, a bitter apéritif that has been around since 1790.

The Austrian emperor Joseph II christened the liqueur when he tasted it and supposedly exclaimed *'Das ist ein Unikum!'* ('This is a unique drink!'). It's an acquired taste.

Most international soft drink brands are available in Hungary, but mineral water seems to be the most popular libation for teetotallers in pubs and bars. Fruit juice is usually canned or boxed fruit 'drink' with lots of sugar added.

Useful words include:

almalé – apple juice
ásvány víz – mineral water
barackpálinka – apricot brandy
cappuccino – coffee with whipped cream
    (see *tejes kávé*)
körtepálinka – pear brandy
limonádé – lemonade
narancslé – orange juice
őszibarack pálinka – peach brandy
szilvapálinka – plum brandy
tejes kávé – cappuccino (milky coffee with froth)
üdítő ital – soft drink

ENTERTAINMENT

Hungary is a very culture-oriented society, and the arts – especially music – are dear to the hearts of most people. Many cities and even some large towns have a symphony or chamber orchestra, an ornate theatre where plays and musicals are staged, and a cultural centre where other events take place. Outside Budapest, cultural life is especially active in Győr, Sopron, Szombathely, Pécs, Kecskemét, Szeged, Debrecen and Eger. Festivals in spring, summer and autumn are scheduled in cities throughout Hungary (see the Public Holidays & Special Events section earlier in this chapter), and some of them, like Budapest Spring, attract many visitors from abroad. Some useful words to remember are *színház* (theatre), *pénztár* (box office), *jegy* (ticket) and *elkelt* (sold out).

Unfortunately, the loss of state subsidies in recent years has forced many smaller festivals and groups to cut back their events and performances. And theatre troupes, which must now rely on box-office receipts, are abandoning classical and avant-garde drama in favour of imported musical productions like *Macskák (Cats)* or *Sakk (Chess)*. Still, there's always something going on to suit every taste, and usually you'll be spoiled for choice, especially in Budapest.

Your best source of information for performances nationwide is *Programme in Hungary*; *Budapest Week* and *Budapest Sun* are good for the capital. The most complete listing of plays, concerts, exhibitions and films can be found in the weekly *Pesti Műsor* and the freebie *Pesti Esti*. Unfortunately, they're only in Hungarian.

Tickets, which seldom cost more than 1000 Ft (except during special festivals), can be purchased at the venue, but it's always safer to get them in advance, particularly in smaller towns where the production may be the big event of the month and the place to be seen. You'll find the addresses of ticket offices and information sources under individual cities and towns.

Of course, it's not all Mozart and Brecht. Hungary is now on the circuit for many pop and rock bands – hey, the Stones, Michael Jackson and Tina Turner were all there within a year of each other in the mid-1990s – and concerts of an international standing are frequent in Budapest. Táncház, an evening of Hungarian folk music and some traditional dance, is great entertainment and a great way to meet Hungarians. You'll seldom find táncház outside the capital though.

Be aware that many foreign films are dubbed into Hungarian, so try asking the ticket seller if the film is dubbed (*szinkronizált* or *magyarul beszélő*), or only has Hungarian subtitles (*feliratos*) and retains the original

soundtrack. All the films listed in the English-language weeklies are in the latter category. Seats are assigned in most cinemas, and admission is usually less than 200 Ft. In theatres, there are *bal* (left) and *jobb* (right) seats with the same numbers so make sure you know which one you are. To make sure you arrive at the correct time, see the Time section earlier in this chapter.

Discos – which range from those in Budapest's rollicking palaces to unpretentious get-togethers in provincial sport halls – are the most popular form of entertainment for young people and are always good fun. Striptease and sex shows attract foreigners and the well-heeled Hungarian *új gazdag* (nouveau riche).

THINGS TO BUY

Hungarian shops are well stocked and the quality of the products is generally high. Food, alcohol, books and folk-music recordings are affordable and there is an excellent selection. Traditional products include folk-art embroidery and ceramics, wall hangings, painted wooden toys and boxes, dolls, all forms of basketry and porcelain (especially Herend, Zsolnay or the cheaper Kalocsa). Feather or goose-down goods like pillows and duvets (comforters) are of excellent quality. Foodstuffs that are expensive or difficult to buy elsewhere – goose liver (both fresh and potted), caviar and some prepared meats like Pick salami – make nice gifts as do the many varieties of paprika. Some of Hungary's new 'boutique' wines – especially the ones with imaginative labels – make good, inexpensive gifts. A bottle of five or six-puttonyos dessert Tokaj always goes down well.

Getting There & Away

AIR

Airports & Airlines

Malév Hungarian Airlines, the national carrier, flies direct to Budapest Ferihegy airport to/from the USA and more than 30 European cities. Other destinations include Bangkok, Cairo, Damascus and Tel Aviv.

Malév, Delta, Lufthansa, Alitalia and Air France flights arrive and depart from Ferihegy Terminal 2, about five km east of Terminal 1, which all other international airlines use. The general information number at Ferihegy is ☎ 1-296 9696. Otherwise, call ☎ 1-296 7373/7155 for departures/arrivals at Ferihegy Terminal 1, or ☎ 1-296 7831/8977 for departures/arrivals at Ferihegy Terminal 2.

Buying Tickets

At present basic return excursion tickets (with fixed dates and heavy penalties if you change them) are about UK£220 (£170 in the low season) from London on British Airways and US$500 from New York on Malév. A return excursion ticket valid for three months on Lauda Air from Hong Kong or Bangkok to Vienna is US$1400 to US$1600. From Budapest you should be able to fly return to New York/London/Bangkok on Malév for 60,000/29,000/90,000 Ft. Most destinations in Continental Europe are around 35,000 to 40,000 Ft return.

Return flights from Budapest to other cities in the former Soviet bloc are relatively inexpensive but still much dearer than travel by train or bus: to fly to Moscow costs 58,210 Ft return, to Warsaw 29,350 Ft, to Prague 26,300 Ft.

Malév has no student discounts on flights originating in Hungary, but there is a youth fare available to persons aged 25 years or younger, which is usually about 30% cheaper than the normal fare. London, for example, is just under 20,000 Ft. Youth fares to Moscow/ Warsaw/Prague, which can only

be bought a week in advance, are 18,000/13,350/12,250 Ft.

One of the cheapest and most reliable agencies for tickets in Budapest is Tradesco Tours (☎ 1-268 0038) at VII Rákóczi út 4. Its office in Los Angeles (☎ 310-649 5808) also offers excellent discount packages. You can reach them on the Internet at http://www.geninc.com/tradescotours or write to 6033 West Century Blvd, Suite 670, Los Angeles, CA 90045. Another reliable agency in Budapest is Vista Travel (☎ 1-269 6032) at VII Károly körút 21.

For information on air taxis to provincial cities in Hungary, see the Getting Around chapter.

The USA

Malév and Delta both have services to/from New York (JFK airport) and Atlanta.

Europe

Malév flies to Budapest from Amsterdam, Athens, Barcelona, Belgrade, Berlin, Brussels, Bucharest, Cologne, Copenhagen, Düsseldorf, Frankfurt, Hamburg, Helsinki, Istanbul, Kiev, Larnaca, London, Madrid, Milan, Moscow, Munich, Paris, Prague, Rome, Sofia, St Petersburg, Stuttgart, Stockholm, Thessaloniki, Tirana, Vienna, Warsaw and Zürich.

Other airlines serving Budapest include: Aeroflot (Moscow), Air France (Paris), Air Lithuania (Vilnus), Air Malta (Malta), Air Ukraine (Kiev), Alitalia (Rome and Milan), Austrian Airlines (Vienna), Balkan (Sofia), British Airways (London), Czech Airlines (Prague), Finnair (Helsinki), Iberia (Madrid, Barcelona), KLM (Amsterdam), LOT (Warsaw), Lufthansa/United (Düsseldorf, Frankfurt, Hamburg, Munich, Stuttgart), Sabena (Brussels), Swissair (Geneva, Zürich), Tarom Romanian (Bucharest) and Tunisair (Tunis).

Middle East

Malév and El Al have a daily flight to/from Tel Aviv; Malév and Egyptair serve Cairo between two and four times a week. Malév also flies nonstop twice a week to Beirut. There are three flights a week to Damascus on Malév and Syrian Arab and one nonstop a week with Tunis on Tunisair.

Asia

Malév now flies nonstop to/from Bangkok twice a week. From Hong Kong there are two weekly flights on Lauda Air to Vienna and four a week from Bangkok. Lufthansa (via Frankfurt) and British Airways (via London) also offer good deals from Asia.

LAND

Budapest is well connected to all surrounding countries by road, rail and even river. Trains arrive in Budapest from every neighbouring capital, and in summer there's a hydrofoil service between Vienna and Budapest. The main entry points for international trains to Hungary include: Sopron and Hegyeshalom (from Vienna and most of Western Europe); Szombathely (from Graz); Komárom and Szob (from Prague and Berlin); Miskolc (from Košice, Kraków and Warsaw); Nyíregyháza (from Lvov, Moscow and St Petersburg); Békéscsaba (from Bucharest via Arad and Timişoara); Szeged (from Subotica); Pécs (from Osijek); and Nagykanizsa (from Zagreb and Ljubljana).

By road there's a bus service to/from all neighbouring countries and this is often the cheapest way to go. In Budapest, buses to/from Western Europe and several neighbouring countries use the bus station at V Erzsébet tér (☎ 1-117 2562) near Deák tér, while those serving most – but not all – Eastern European countries as well as Turkey and Sweden go from the one at Népstadion (☎ 1-252 1896) at XIV Hungária körút 48-52 (metro: Népstadion).

Timetables for both domestic and international trains and buses use the 24-hour system. Remember that 0.05 means five minutes past midnight (12.05 am).

On many (though not all) bus and train timetables, Hungarians tend to use the Hungarian name for cities and towns in neighbouring countries. Many of these are in what once was Hungarian territory and the names are used by the Hungarian-speaking minorities who live there. You should at least be familiar with the more important ones to help decipher bus and (less so) train timetables. (See the Alternative Place Names appendix in the back of this book).

Bus

Volánbusz (literally 'steering wheel bus'), in conjunction with Eurolines, sells 30 and 60-day passes allowing unlimited travel in some 18 European countries, including Hungary. One caveat: you are not allowed to travel on the same line more than twice. Adults pay US$359/49,200 Ft or US$434/59,400 Ft; the youth/senior passes for the same periods cost US$309/42,300 Ft and US$389/53,500 Ft.

Erzsébet tér Bus Station The Volánbusz international bus office (☎ 1-117 2562) upstairs at the Erzsébet tér bus station is open weekdays from 6 am to 7 pm (6 pm in winter) and 6.30 am to 4 pm on weekends. There's a Eurolines/Volánbusz bus service three times a week (Monday, Friday, Saturday) throughout the year from Rotterdam to Budapest via Amsterdam, Düsseldorf and Frankfurt (1615 km, 21 hours, US$115/15,900 Ft one way, US$187/25,900 Ft return, with a 10% discount for those under 26 or over 60 years of age). From early June to late September the Amsterdam bus runs four times a week and in July and early August it runs daily. The run from Amsterdam to Budapest is through Austria, precluding the need for a Czech or Slovak visa. In Amsterdam tickets are sold by Eurolines Nederland (☎ 020-627 5151), Rokin 10. In Budapest you can buy them upstairs at the Erzsébet tér bus station. In summer this bus is often full, so try to book ahead.

A similar service from Brussels to Budapest (1395 km, 19 hours, US$107/14,700 Ft one way, US$179/24,700 Ft return) also operates three times a week (Wednesday, Thursday, Sunday) with an additional trip on

Monday from July to mid-September. In Brussels, seek information from Eurolines' Belgian office (☎ 02-217 0025) at 50 Place de Brouckère.

Other international buses departing from Budapest's Erzsébet tér station and their one-way fares include those to: Bratislava (daily, 200 km, US$10/1370 Ft); Florence (one or two weekly, 1025 km, 16½ hours, US$74/10,200 Ft); Hamburg (once a week, 1215 km, 18½ hours, US$101/14,000 Ft); Milan (one or two a week, 1080 km, 17 hours); Munich (three to six a week, 701 km, 10 hours, US$77/10,600 Ft); Paris (two to three times weekly, 1525 km, 22½ hours, US$101/13,900 Ft); Prague (two to four times weekly, US$26/3530 Ft); and Rome (one to three times weekly, 1310 km, 21½ hours, US$89/11,900 Ft). From June to mid-September a bus on Friday heads for Poreč (US$40/5600 Ft) and Rovinj (US$43/5900 Ft) on the Istrian Peninsula in Croatia, stopping at Ljubljana, Koper and Piran (19 hours, US$38/5200 Ft) in Slovenia along the way. It's best to reserve seats on these long-distance buses a few days in advance, especially in summer.

From July to early September, buses run between Budapest and London via Vienna and Brussels on Monday, Wednesday, Thursday and Sunday (1770 km, 26 hours, US$125/17,300 Ft one way, US$193/26,700 Ft return). In London check with Eurolines (☎ 0171-730 8235) at the Victoria coach station or ring ☎ 01582-404511 for reservations. In Paris enquire about Hungary-bound buses at the Gare Routière Internationale (☎ 1-49 72 51 51), 28 Avenue du Général de Gaulle (metro: Galliéni).

Three buses daily make the run between Vienna's Autobusbahnhof Wien-Mitte and Erzsébet tér, departing from Vienna at 7 am and 5 and 7 pm and from Budapest at 7 am, noon and 5 pm daily (254 km, US$28/2990 Ft one way, US$40/4490 Ft return). From mid-May to September additional buses depart Vienna daily at 11 am and 3 pm and Budapest at 9 am and 7 pm. In Budapest you can make enquiries at the Erzsébet tér station and in Vienna at Autobusbahnhof Wien-

Mitte (☎ 0222-712 0453), Landstrasser Hauptstrasse 1/b.

Népstadion Bus Station By far the cheapest and easiest way by far to go from Hungary to Romania is by bus from the Népstadion station (☎ 1-252 1896). There are buses to Oradea (daily, 260 km, six hours), Arad (six a week, 276 km, seven hours), Timişoara (weekly, 327 km, eight hours), Cluj-Napoca (daily, 413 km, 9½ hours) and Brasov (six a week, 790 km, 17½ hours, US$36/5020 Ft). A return ticket is about 50% more than a one-way ticket.

The international ticket window at Népstadion bus station is open weekdays from 5.30 am to 6 pm and Saturday from 5.30 am to 4 pm. On Sunday try paying the driver. The clerks at Népstadion speak no English, so study the posted timetables and then write down what you want. The names of the Romanian cities in question are in Hungarian; see the Alternative Place Names appendix. Remember that there can be long delays at highway border crossings into Romania (especially in summer), though it's worse westbound than eastbound.

Other useful international buses from Népstadion include those to Subotica in Yugoslavia (daily, 216 km), Istanbul (five a week, 1375 km, 25 hours), Tatranská Lomnica in Slovakia (twice a week, 311 km, seven hours) and Zakopane in Poland (twice a week, US$15).

Budapest is not the only Hungarian city with buses serving neighbouring countries. For example, from Harkány, 22 km south of Pécs, you can catch a bus to several towns in Croatia, and there are buses from Pécs to Osijek (Croatia), from Barcs and Nagykanizsa to Zagreb (Croatia), from Lenti to Ljubljana (Slovenia) and from Szeged to Arad and Timişoara (both in Romania). See Getting There & Away in the individual town and city entries for more specific information.

Train

Magyar Államvasutak, which translates as Hungarian State Railways and is universally known as MÁV, links up with the European rail network in all directions, running trains as far as London (via Paris or Brussels), Stockholm (via Malmö), St Petersburg, Istanbul and Rome. The international trains listed below are expresses, and quite a few require seat reservations. On long hauls, sleepers are almost always available in both 1st and 2nd class, and couchettes are available in 2nd class. Surprisingly, not all express trains have dining or even buffet cars. Make sure you bring along some snacks and drinks as vendors can be few and far between and quite pricey (eg 250 Ft for a thimble-sized cup of coffee). Hungarian trains are hardly luxurious, but generally they are clean and punctual.

Almost all international trains now arrive and depart from the Keleti (Eastern) train station (☎ 1-113 6835); trains to Oradea in Romania leave from Nyugati (Western) station (☎ 1-149 0115), while Déli (Southern) station (☎ 1-175 6293) handles trains to/from Zagreb and Rijeka. But these are not hard-and-fast rules, so always make sure you check which station the train leaves from when you buy a ticket.

To reduce confusion, specify your train by its name (these are listed in the sections following and on the posted schedule) when requesting information or buying a ticket. You can get information and buy tickets at the three train stations, but it's easier to communicate with the information staff at MÁV's central ticket office (☎ 1-322 9035/8275) at VI Andrássy út 35 in Budapest. It is open weekdays from 9 am to 5 or 6 pm.

If you just want to get across the border, local trains are cheaper than international expresses, especially if you're on a one-way trip. Concession fares between cities of the former socialist countries are only available on return tickets.

Tickets & Discounts Everyone gets a 30% to 50% discount on return fares to the Czech Republic, Croatia, Poland, Romania, Russia, Ukraine, Belarus, Lithuania and Latvia; it's a generous 70% to Slovakia. Also, there's a 40% concession on return fares to six

selected cities: Prague and Brno in the Czech Republic, and Warsaw, Kraków, Katowice and Gdynia in Poland. Thus, the 2nd-class one-way fare to Prague is 7500 Ft but only 9200 Ft return. The comparable fares to Warsaw are 7913 Ft and 9495 Ft and to Moscow 18,600 Ft and 22,300 Ft.

For tickets to destinations in Western Europe you'll pay the same as everywhere else unless you're aged under 26 and qualify for a BIJ (Billet International de Jeunesse) ticket, which cuts international fares by up to about 30% (ask at MÁV or Express). The following are sample one-way fares from Budapest (the return trip is double): Amsterdam 31,000 Ft; Berlin 14,800 Ft; London 41,472 Ft; Munich 13,851 Ft; Rome 15,200 Ft. There's a discounted return fare (about 30% off) to Vienna of 8000 Ft if you come back to Budapest within four days. Three daily EuroCity (EC) trains to Vienna and points beyond charge a supplement of 1000 to 1500 Ft. The 1st-class seats are always 50% more expensive than 2nd class.

An international seat reservation costs 500 Ft. Fines of 100 Ft are levied on passengers without tickets or seat reservations where they are mandatory. Costs for sleepers depend on the destination, but a two-berth sleeper in a 1st-class cabin is 6600 Ft per person to Munich (4400 Ft in 2nd class). A couchette in a compartment for six people is 3000 Ft. Tickets are valid for 60 days from purchase and stopovers are permitted.

Budapest is no longer the bargain basement that it once was for tickets on the Trans-Siberian or the Trans-Mongolian railways. In fact, MÁV will only write you a ticket to Moscow; you have to buy the onward ticket from there (from about US$250, depending on the routing). Of course, if you are coming back to Budapest from Moscow you get the 40% discount, making the return ticket to the Russian capital only 22,300 Ft.

MÁV sells Inter-Rail passes in one to seven zones to those under 26 years of age. The price for any one zone is US$265 and passes are valid for 15 days; Hungary is in Zone D along with the Czech Republic,

Slovakia, Poland, Croatia, Bulgaria and Romania. Multizone passes are better value and are valid for one month: two zones is US$315, three zones US$255, and all zones – a 'Global' pass – is US$400. Several types of Eurail pass are available, but the cheapest – good for 15 days – is $630. It's almost impossible for a Eurail pass to pay for itself in Hungary, so plan your Eurail travel days carefully.

As with the buses and planes, international train tickets can now be purchased with forint, and there is no requirement to produce official exchange receipts. Travellers' cheques and credit cards are not accepted, however.

When pricing train tickets from Western Europe remember that airfares (especially those out of London) often match or beat surface alternatives in terms of cost. For example a return airfare from London to Budapest is available through discount travel agents off season for around UK£170. By comparison, a two-month return ticket by rail to Budapest costs UK£368/£301 for adults/youths. The BIJ return ticket from London to Budapest is UK£269. In London, the entertainment listings magazine *Time Out*, the Sunday papers, the *Evening Standard* and *Exchange & Mart* carry ads for cheap airfares. Also look out for the free magazine *TNT*. You can often pick it up outside the main train and tube stations and at discount travel agencies.

A special Eastbound Explorer ticket from London to Prague, Budapest and Kraków and back (and valid for two months) is available for UK£286 to people aged under 26 from Campus Travel (☎ 0171-730 3402), 52 Grosvenor Gardens, London SW1W OAG.

Western & Central Europe Some eight trains a day link Vienna with Budapest (3¼ hours) via Hegyeshalom. Most of them leave from Vienna's Westbahnhof, including the *Orient Express* arriving from Paris (18 hours) via Munich, the *Arrabona*, the EC *Bartók Béla* from Frankfurt (12 hours) via Salzburg, the EC *Liszt Ferenc* from Dortmund (15 hours) via Frankfurt, the *Dacia Express* and the

Avala bound for Belgrade (11 hours). The early-morning EC *Lehár*, however, departs from Vienna's Südbahnhof and the *Beograd Express* arrives and departs from Budapest's 'fourth' station – Kelenföld in Buda. None requires a seat reservation, though they're highly recommended in summer.

In addition, up to 10 trains leave Vienna's Südbahnhof every day for Sopron (75 minutes) via Ebenfurth; as many as a dozen a day also serve Sopron from Wiener Neustadt (easily accessible from Vienna). Some seven trains daily make the three-hour trip from Graz to Szombathely.

There are four trains a day from Berlin's Lichtenberg station to Budapest (about 14 hours) via Prague, Bratislava and Štúrovo: the *Metropol*, the EC *Commenius*, the *Hungária* and the *Csárdás* (from Malmö; 22 hours). Two additional trains, the *Amicus* and *Pannónia*, run from Prague to Budapest (nine hours).

Slovakia & Poland Every day two trains, the *Polonia* and the *Báthory*, leave Warsaw for Budapest (12 hours) via Katowice, Bratislava and Štúrovo. The *Karpaty* from Warsaw passes through Kraków and Košice before reaching Miskolc, where you can change for Budapest. The *Cracovia* runs from Kraków to Budapest (12 hours) and Pécs via Košice. Another train, the *Rákóczi*, links Košice with Budapest (four hours), and in summer there's an extension to Poprad Tatry, 100 km north-west of Košice. The *Bem* connects Szczecin in north-western Poland with Budapest (18 hours) via Poznan Wrocław and Lučenec.

Five local trains a day cover the 90 km from Miskolc and Košice (two hours). The two-km hop from Sátoraljaújhely to Slovenské Nové Mesto is only a four-minute ride by train.

Romania From Bucharest to Budapest (14 hours) you can choose among four trains: the *Alutus*, the *Dacia Express*, the *Ister* and the *Pannónia*, all via Arad. Three of these require seat reservations. The *Karpaty* goes to Bucharest from Miskolc.

There are two connections daily from

Cluj-Napoca to Budapest (seven hours, via Oradea): the *Corona* (from Braşov) and the *Claudiopolis*. These trains require a seat reservation. Two other trains, the *Partium* and *Varadinum*, link Budapest and Oradea only.

There's only one local train a day linking Baia Mare in northern Romania with Budapest (eight hours) via Satu Mare and Debrecen. Otherwise you'll have to take one of two local trains from Debrecen across the border to Valea lui Mihai and catch a Romanian train.

Bulgaria & Yugoslavia The *Balkán*, departing from Istanbul (28 hours), links Budapest with Sofia (15 hours) via Belgrade. Other trains between Budapest and Belgrade via Subotica (six hours) include the *Beograd Express*, the *Hunyadi*, the *Avala* and the *Hellas* (which runs from Thessaloniki in Greece, via Skopje, and takes 23 hours). Be warned that the *Beograd Express* arrives and departs from Kelenföld station in Buda. You must reserve your seats on some of these trains.

The *Pushkin Express* from Belgrade and Subotica to Moscow goes through Szeged, Kecskemét, Szolnok and Debrecen. Otherwise there are five local trains (no reservations needed) making the 1¾-hour journey between Subotica and Szeged every day.

Croatia & Slovenia You can get to Budapest from Zagreb (six hours) on four trains, all of them via Siófok on Lake Balaton: the *Adriatica* from Rijeka (11 hours); *Maestral* from Split (16 hours), the *Avas*, and the *Venezia Express* via Ljubljana (eight hours). The *Dráva*, which originates in Venice, also travels via Ljubljana.

Ukraine & Russia From Moscow to Budapest (28 hours) there's only the *Tisza Express*, which travels via Kiev and Lvov in Ukraine. The *Pushkin Express* between Belgrade and Moscow can be caught in Szeged, Kecskemét, Szolnok or Debrecen. The *Tisza Express* has an extension to/from St Peters-burg, which joins the line at Lvov. Most nationalities require a transit visa to travel through Ukraine.

Car & Motorcycle

Of the 70 border crossings Hungary maintains with its seven neighbours, 15 (mostly in the north and north-east) are restricted to local citizens from both sides of the border. Fortunately, that no longer includes the Esztergom-Štúrovo ferry crossing, which is now one of the easiest and most central ways to enter Hungary from Slovakia.

The following is a list of border crossings that are open to all motorists (clockwise from Austria). The Hungarian checkpoint appears first, the foreign checkpoint (or nearby town) follows, and references to cities or big towns are inserted in brackets after each.

Austria
 Szentgotthárd (27 km south-west of Körmend)/Jennersdorf
 Rábafüzes (five km north of Szentgotthárd)/Heiligenkreuz
 Bucsu (13 km west of Szombathely)/Schachendorf
 Kőszeg/Rattersdorf
 Kópháza (11 km north of Sopron)/Deutschkreutz
 Sopron (seven km north-west of the city)/Klingenbach
 Fertőd/Pamhagen
 Hegyeshalom (51 km north-west of Győr)/Nickelsdorf

Croatia
 Udvar (12 km south of Mohács/Knezevo
 Drávaszabolcs (nine km south of Harkány)/Donji Miholjac (49 km north-west of Osijek)
 Barcs (32 km south-west of Szigetvár)/Terezino Polje
 Berzence (24 km west of Nagyatád)/Gola
 Letenye (26 km west of Nagykanizsa)/Gorican

Romania
 Csengersima (40 km south-east of Mátészalka)/Petea (11 km north-west of Satu Mare)
 Ártánd (25 km south-east of Berettyóújfalu)/Borş (14 km north-west of Oradea)
 Kötegyán (20 km north-east of Gyula)/Salonta
 Gyula/Varşand (66 km north of Arad)
 Lökösháza (26 km south of Gyula)/Curtici
 Nagylak (52 km west of Szeged)/Nădlac (54 km west of Arad)

Slovakia
    Rajka (18 km north-west of Moson-
       magyaróvár)/Rusovce
    Vámosszabadi (13 km north of Győr)/Medvedov
    Komárom/Komárno
    Parassapuszta (40 km north of Vác)/Šahy
    Balassagyarmat/Slovenské Darmoty
    Somoskőújfalu (eight km north of Salgótarján)/
       Filakovo
    Bánréve (43 km north-west of Miskolc)/Král
    Tornyosnémeti (60 km north-east of Miskolc)/
       Milhost
    Sátoraljaújhely/Slovenské Nové Mesto

Slovenia
    Rédics (nine km south-west of Lenti)/Dolga Vas
    Bajánsenye (60 km west of Zalaegerszeg)/Hodoš

Ukraine
    Záhony (23 km north of Kisvárda)/Chop (23 km
      south of Užvgorod)

Yugoslavia
    Rözske (16 km south-west of Szeged)/Horgošv
      (30 km north-east of Subotica)
    Tompa (30 km south of Kiskunhalas)/Kelebija
      (11 km north-west of Subotica)
    Hercegszántó (32 km south of Baja)/Bački Breg
      (28 km north-west of Sombor)
    Kelebia (31 km south of Kiskunhalas)/Subotica

On Foot & Bicycle

To save the cost of an international ticket or
just for fun, you may consider walking
across the frontier into or out of Hungary.
But many border guards frown on this practice, particularly in Romania, Yugoslavia
and Croatia; try hitching a ride instead.
Cyclists may have a problem crossing
Hungarian stations connected to main roads
since bicycles are banned on motorways and
national highways with single-digit route
numbers.

There are three crossings to/from Slovakia
where you won't have any problems. The
Esztergom-Štúrovo ferry is now open to
international traffic and bicycles are allowed
on board. At Komárom, 88 km north-west of
Budapest, a bridge over the Danube connects
the city with Komárno. At Sátoraljaújhely,
north-east of Miskolc, another highway
border crossing over the Ronyva River links
the centre of town with Slovenské Nové
Mesto.

To/from Romania, the easiest place to
cross on foot is Nagylak/Nădlac between
Szeged and Arad. There are eight unreserved
local trains a day from Szeged to Nagylak
(47 km, 1¼ hours) near the border. After
crossing into Romania you must walk or take
a taxi six km to Nădlac, where you'll find
four local trains a day to Arad (52 km, 1½
hours).

Slovenia-bound, take a train from Budapest to Zalaegerszeg (252 km via Tapolca,
four hours by express train), then one of 10
trains daily from there to Rédics (49 km,
1½ hours), which is only a couple of km
from the main highway border crossing into
Slovenia. From the border it's an interesting
five-km downhill walk through Lendava to
the bus station, where you'll have a choice
of six buses daily to Ljubljana (212 km, four
hours) and many more to Maribor (92 km).

RIVER

A hydrofoil service on the Danube from
Budapest to Vienna (282 km, 5½ hours)
operates daily from April to early November
and twice daily from mid-July to early September. Fares are high: US$70/$102 one
way/return, but ISIC student-card holders
get a 20% discount. Taking along a bicycle
costs just under US$10 each way.

Ferries arrive and depart from the International Landing Stage (*Nemzetközi hajóállomás*) on Belgrád rakpart in Pest, just north
of Szabadság Bridge. In April and from early
September to early November there's a
sailing at 9 am; from May to early September, the boat leaves at 8 am. There's a second
sailing at 1.30 pm from mid-July to early
September. The boat docks at the Reichs-
brücke pier near Mexikoplatz in Vienna. The
departure times from Vienna are the same as
those from Budapest except that the extra
boat from mid-July to early September
leaves at 1.10 pm.

Tickets are available in Budapest from
Mahart Tours (☎ 1-118 1704) at the pier. The
small office there is open from 8 am to 4 pm
on weekdays. At weekends the ticket

window is open from 8 am to noon. In Vienna, get them from Mahart Tours (☎ 0222-729 2161) at Karlsplatz 2-8.

DEPARTURE TAXES
An air passenger duty *(illeték)* of between 3000 and 4000 Ft is levied on all air tickets written in Hungary. There are no other departure or port taxes.

WARNING
This chapter is particularly vulnerable to change – prices for international travel are volatile, routes are introduced and cancelled, schedules change, special deals come and go, and rules and visa requirements are amended. Airlines seem to take a perverse pleasure in making price structures and regulations as complicated as possible; you should check directly with the airline or travel agent to make sure you understand how a fare (and ticket you may buy) works. In addition, the travel industry is highly competitive and there are many schemes and bonuses. The upshot of this is that you should get opinions, quotes and advice from as many airlines and travel agents as possible before you part with your hard-earned cash. The details given in this chapter should be regarded as pointers and are not a substitute for careful, up-to-date research.

Getting Around

Local people complain about it, but Hungary's domestic transport system is efficient, comprehensive and inexpensive – they should only come to Britain! The average Hungarian train may look like it's been through a couple of wars, and you'll wait a month of Sundays for a bus in most cities, but almost everything runs to schedule, and most towns and cities are easily negotiated on foot.

AIR

There are no scheduled flights within Hungary. The cost of domestic air taxis is prohibitive – eg 35,000 Ft to Szeged and back (you must pay for a return flight whether or not you return) – and the trips can take almost as long as the train when you add the time required to get to/from the airports. Several better-known firms with offices in Budapest are Indicator (☎ 1-201 5962), I Lovas utca 19; Air Service Hungary (☎ 1-185 1344), XII Kőérberki út 36; and Aviaexpress (☎ 1-157 7791) at Ferihegy Terminal 1.

BUS

Hungary's Volán buses are a good alternative to the trains, and bus fares are only slightly more expensive than comparable 2nd-class train fares. In Southern Transdanubia and parts of the Great Plain, buses are essential unless you are prepared to make several time-consuming changes on the train. For short trips around the Danube Bend or Lake Balaton areas, buses are highly recommended.

In cities and large towns it is usually possible to catch at least one direct bus a day to fairly far-flung areas of the country (Pécs to Sopron, for example, or Debrecen to Szeged).

Of course, not everyone likes bus travel, but in Hungary it's a better way to see the deep countryside than train – the parts 'somewhere behind the back of God', as people say here. Seats on Volán buses are spaced far enough apart for you to be able to fit your pack between your knees. A few large bus stations have luggage rooms, but they generally close by 6 pm. Check your bag in at the train station, which is almost always next door anyway.

National buses arrive and depart from long-distance bus stations (*távolsági-autóbusz pályaudvar*), not the local stations, which are called *helyi* or *városiautóbusz pályaudvar*. Often, though, these are found side-by-side or share the same space. Arrive early to confirm the correct departure bay (*kocsiállás*), and be sure to check the individual schedule posted at the stop itself; the times shown can be different, and recent additions are not always on the main boards.

Tickets are usually purchased directly from the driver, who provides change and a receipt. There are sometimes queues for intercity buses (especially on Friday afternoon) so it's wise to arrive at the bus stop early. Smoking is not allowed on buses in Hungary. A 10-minute rest stop is made about every 1½ hours.

People in the countryside use intercity buses for short stages, and there are always many stops (which drivers do not usually announce). If you plan to do a lot of travelling by bus, buy a copy of the national road atlas (see Maps in the Facts for the Visitor chapter), and watch for signs when entering or leaving a settlement. Otherwise just point to your destination on the map and ask your neighbour: *Szóljon kérem, mikor kell leszállnom?* ('Could you tell me when to get off?').

Posted bus schedules and timetables can be horribly confusing if you don't speak Hungarian. The basics to remember when reading a timetable are that *indulás* means 'departures' and *érkezés* means 'arrivals'. Timetable symbols include the following:

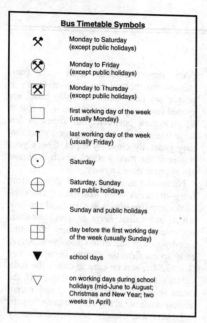

Bus Timetable Symbols

☓ Monday to Saturday (except public holidays)

⊗ Monday to Friday (except public holidays)

⊠ Monday to Thursday (except public holidays)

☐ first working day of the week (usually Monday)

↑ last working day of the week (usually Friday)

⊙ Saturday

⊕ Saturday, Sunday and public holidays

+ Sunday and public holidays

⊞ day before the first working day of the week (usually Sunday)

▼ school days

▽ on working days during school holidays (mid-June to August; Christmas and New Year; two weeks in April)

Numbers one to seven in a circle refer to the days of the week, beginning with Monday. Written footnotes you could see include *naponta* (daily), *hétköznap* (weekdays), *munkanapokon* (on workdays), *munkaszüneti napok kivételével naponta* (daily except holidays), *szabadnap kivételével naponta* (daily except Saturday), *szabad és munkaszüneti napokon* (on Saturday and holidays), *munkaszuneti napokon* (on holidays), *iskolai napokon* (on school days) and *szabadnap* (on Saturday).

For bus services to destinations south and west of Budapest, go to the bus station on V Erzsébet tér (☎1-117 2966/1-118 2122). The Népstadion bus station (☎1-252 4496/1-252 1896) serves cities and towns to the north and the east. The bus station on the Pest side of Árpád Bridge (☎1-129 1450) is the place to catch buses for the Danube Bend.

TRAIN

MÁV operates comfortable, reliable and uncrowded train services on some 8000 km of track. Second-class train fares in Hungary are 176 Ft for 50 km, 424 Ft for 100 km, 848 Ft for 200 km or 1548 Ft for 500 km. First class is 50% more (264/636/1272/2322 Ft respectively).

All main railway lines converge on Budapest, though many secondary lines link provincial cities and towns. There are three main train stations in Budapest: Keleti station (to the Northern Uplands and the North-East), Nyugati (Great Plain and the Danube Bend) and Déli (Transdanubia and Lake Balaton).

There are several types of train. Express ('Ex' on the timetable) trains, of which there are only a handful, usually require a seat reservation costing 55 Ft. The two dozen or so InterCity (IC) trains levy a 200 Ft supplement. These stop at main centres only. Seat reservations may be compulsory (indicated on the timetable by an 'R' in a box), mandatory on trains departing from Budapest (an 'R' in a circle) or simply available (just plain 'R'). The other types of train are *gyorsvonat* (fast trains) and *személyvonat* (passenger trains). The latter are the real milk runs and stop at every hamlet. If you buy your ticket on the train rather than in the station, there's a 200 Ft surcharge.

One-way *(egy útra)* and return *(retúrjegy)* tickets are available at stations, MÁV's main ticket office (☎ 1-322 9035) at VI Andrássy út 35 and at certain travel agencies. An unlimited travel pass for all trains in Hungary is available for 5800/8700 Ft in 2nd/1st class for seven days and 8340/12,510 Ft for 10 days, but you'd have to travel like the wind to make it pay for itself. Reservation charges are additional. Passes sold by agencies abroad allow five days of train travel in 15 days for US$55 and 10 days in a month for US$69.

Depending on the station, departures and arrivals are announced by loudspeaker or on an electronic board and are always on a printed timetable – yellow for departures *(indul)* and white for arrivals *(érkezik)*. On these, fast trains are marked in red, local trains in black. *Vágány* indicates the platform from which the train departs or arrives; for the other symbols and abbreviations used, see the Bus section. The huge paper rolls in glass cases that you'll see in some stations show the schedules for every train in the country. Look for the route number on the map posted nearby. If you plan to do a lot of travelling by train, get yourself a copy of MÁV's official timetable *(Menetrend;* 400 Ft), which is available at most large stations and at the MÁV office on Andrássy út. It has explanatory notes in English.

All railway stations have left-luggage offices, many of which stay open 24 hours a day. You often have to pay the fee (about 70 Ft) at another office (usually marked *pénztár).* You can freight a bicycle for 106 Ft per 100 km.

The following are distances and approximate times to provincial cities from Budapest, usually via express trains (on which you might expect to cover from 65 to 70 km/h):

Danube Bend
Esztergom – 53 km (1½ hours, slow trains only)
Szentendre – 20 km (40 minutes on the HÉV commuter railway)

Transdanubia
Győr – 131 km (two hours)
Sopron – 216 km (three hours)
Szombathely – 236 km (3½ hours)
Pécs – 228 km (three hours)

Balaton
Siófok – 115 km (1½ hours)
Balatonfüred – 132 km (two hours)
Veszprém – 112 km (1¾ hours)
Székesfehérvár – 67 km (50 minutes)

Great Plain
Szolnok – 100 km (1¼ hours)
Kecskemét – 106 km (1½ hours)
Debrecen – 221 km (three hours)
Békéscsaba – 196 km (2½ hours)
Szeged – 191 km (2½ hours)

The North
Nyíregyháza – 270 km (four hours)
Eger – 143 km (two hours)
Miskolc – 183 km (2¼ hours)
Sátoraljaújhely – 267 km (3½ hours)

MÁV runs some vintage steam-train *(nosztalgiavonat)* trips around Lake Balaton and along the Danube Bend in summer, and narrow-gauge trains *(keskeny nyomközű vonat)* can be found in many wooded and hilly areas of the country. The latter are usually taken as a round trip by holiday-makers, but in some cases they can be useful for getting from A to B (Miskolc to Lillafüred and the Bükk, for example, or from Baja to Szekszárd via the Gemenc Forest). Narrow-gauge trains are run by United Forest Railways (ÁEV); MÁV passes are not valid on them. The only other private line in Hungary (called GySEV) links Győr and Sopron with Ebenfurth in Austria. MÁV pass-holders have to pay an extra 100 Ft when riding between these cities.

CAR & MOTORCYCLE

Roads in Hungary are generally good and there are three basic types. Motorways, preceded by an 'M', link Budapest with Lake Balaton and with Vienna and run part of the way to Miskolc and Kecskemét. National highways are numbered by a single digit and fan out mostly from Budapest. Secondary and tertiary roads have two or three digits.

Fuels of 91, 92, 95 (unleaded) and 98 octane, as well as diesel, are widely available; prices range from 120 to 130 Ft a litre (104 Ft for diesel). Payment with a credit card is now possible at many stations, including the branches of the national chain MOL. Third-party insurance is compulsory. If your car is registered in the EU, it is assumed you have insurance, but other motorists must be able to show a Green Card or will have to buy insurance at the border.

The Yellow Angels of the Hungarian Automobile Club do basic repairs free of charge in the event of a breakdown if you belong to an affiliated organisation such as AAA in the USA or AA in the UK. They can be reached 24 hours a day at ☎ 06-1-155 0379 (nationwide) or ☎ 1-252 8000 in Budapest.

Road Rules

You must drive on the right. Speed limits for

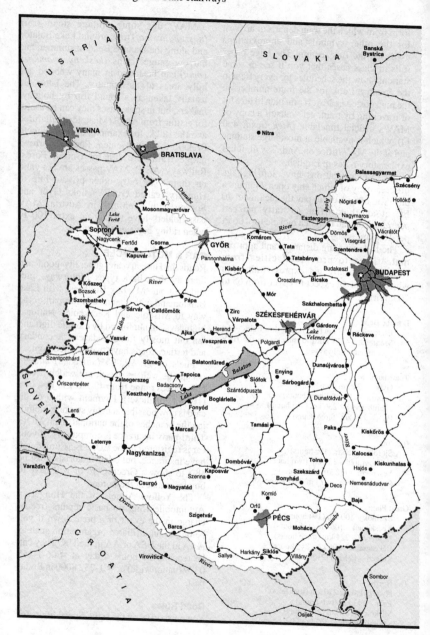

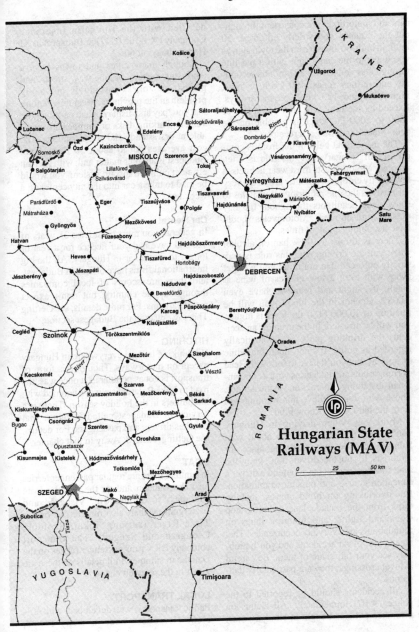

Hungarian State
Railways (MÁV)

cars and motorbikes are consistent throughout the country and strictly enforced: 50 km/h in built-up areas (from the town sign as you enter to the same sign with a red line through it as you leave); 80 km/h on secondary and tertiary roads; 100 km/h on most highways; and 120 km/h on motorways. Exceeding the limit will earn you a fine of 1000 to 2000 Ft, which is payable on the spot. Make sure you get a receipt.

The use of seat belts in the front is compulsory in Hungary, but this rule is often ignored. Motorcyclists must wear helmets, a law strictly enforced. Another law taken very seriously is the one requiring all vehicles to show their headlights throughout the day outside built-up areas. Motorcycles should have headlights on at all times.

There is almost a 100% ban on alcohol when you are driving, and this rule is *very* strictly enforced. Do not think you will get away with even a few glasses of wine at lunch; if caught and found to have even 0.008% alcohol in the blood, you will be fined up to 30,000 Ft. If the level is higher, you will be arrested. In the event of an accident, the drinking party is automatically regarded as guilty. It's not much fun while on holiday, but you'll have to follow the lead of Hungarians and take turns with a companion in abstaining at parties and at meal times. Those who don't believe this warning will learn the hard way; I know I did.

Mind you, when driving in Hungary you'll want to keep your wits about you; Hungary can be quite a trying place for motorists. It's not that drivers don't know the road rules; everyone has to attend a driver's education course and pass an examination. But overtaking on blind curves, making turns from the outside lane, running stop signs and lights, and jumping lanes on roundabouts are everyday occurrences. That means a lot of car accidents and you'll probably see your fair share of them. Be careful at level crossings; they are particularly dangerous.

All accidents should be reported to the police (☎ 07) immediately. All claims on insurance policies bought in Hungary must be filed with the Hungária Insurance Company (☎ 1-166 0247) in Budapest at XI Hamszabégyi út 60.

Though many cities and towns have a confusing system of one-way streets and pedestrian zones, parking is not a big problem in the provinces. Most now require that you 'pay and display' when parking your vehicle. Parking disks or coupons are available at newsstands and petrol stations. The cost averages out to about 30 Ft an hour. Budapest is another matter and, with such an efficient public-transport system, you would be mad to take a car into the city centre on a weekday.

Car Rental

In general, you must be at least 21 years of age and have had your licence for a year or longer to rent a car in Hungary. All the big international firms have offices in Budapest, and there are scores of local companies throughout the country, but don't expect many bargains. For more details, see Getting There & Away in the Budapest section.

HITCHING

Hitchhiking is legal everywhere in Hungary except on motorways. Though this form of transport is not as popular as it once was, the road to Lake Balaton is always jammed with hitchhikers in the holiday season. There is a service in Budapest called Kenguru that matches drivers and passengers. For details, see Getting There & Away in that chapter.

BOAT

In summer there are regular passenger ferries on Lake Balaton and on the Danube from Budapest to Szentendre, Visegrád and Esztergom. Mahart also runs ferries on the Tisza River (serving Tokaj, Szolnok, Csongrád and Szeged). The transport company BKV runs passenger ferries on the Danube in summer. Full details on these are given in the relevant chapters.

LOCAL TRANSPORT

Public transport is well developed, with efficient city buses and, in many towns, trolleybuses. Four cities – Budapest, Szeged, Miskolc and Debrecen – also have trams and there's an extensive metro (underground or subway) system and a suburban railway known as the HÉV in the capital.

You'll probably make extensive use of public transport in Budapest but little (if any) in provincial towns and cities: with very few exceptions, most places are quite manageable on foot, and bus services are not all that frequent. Generally, city buses meet incoming long-distance trains; hop onto anything standing outside and you'll get close to the centre of town.

You must purchase your ticket (generally about 50 Ft) at newsstands or ticket windows beforehand and cancel it once aboard. Passes valid for a day to a month are available in the capital; these are very convenient (single-journey tickets are not always easy to buy) and good value if you're moving around a lot. In the provinces, such passes (if available) are only useful if you're staying a long time.

Boarding without a ticket ('riding black', as the Hungarians say) is an offence and you'll be put off and fined about 600 Ft on the spot. Time was when a foreigner could claim not to understand the system and perhaps be let off with a warning. But those were the days when a ride cost a couple of forints and no one really cared. Now that the bus and tram companies are trying to turn a profit, public transport is considered expensive by local people and you'll have to pay like everyone else. Don't try to argue; the inspector has heard it all before.

Taxi

Taxis are plentiful and, if you are charged the correct fare, very reasonably priced. Flag fall varies, but a fair price is anything between 50 and 100 Ft, with the charge per km between 90 and 150 Ft, depending on whether you booked it by telephone or hailed it on the street. The best places to find taxis are in ranks at bus and railway stations, big hotels, near markets and on the main square. But you can flag down cruising taxis anywhere at any time. At night, taxis illuminate

A Street by Any Other Name

After WWII, most streets, squares and parks in Hungary were renamed after people, dates or political groups that have since become anathema to the independent, non-communist Hungary of today. Since April 1989, names have been changed yet again at a frantic pace and with a determination that some people feel borders on the psychotic; Cartographia's *Budapest Atlas* lists upwards of 400 new street names in the capital alone. Sometimes it's just been a case of returning a street or square to its original (perhaps medieval) name – from Lenin útja, say, to Szent korona útja (Street of the Holy Crown). Other times the name is new.

The result has been confusion, with the very old, the very young and tourists using the new (or original) names and almost everyone else still calling them what they were before 1989. Ferenciek tere (Square of the Franciscans) in Budapest is a good example: many people between the ages of 30 and 65 still call it Felszabadulás tér (Liberation Square), which honours the Soviet army's role in liberating Budapest.

The following list includes the most common place names to be disposed of in Hungary. It's not necessary to know who the people were or what the dates signify; the average Hungarian doesn't have a clue. Just remember that if you see any one of these names on an old map, it's very likely to have been changed:

Április 4
Bacsó Béla
Béke (Peace)
Beloiannisz
Dimitrov
Engels Frigyes
Felszabadulás (Liberation)
Fürst Sándor
Hamburger Jenő
Kun Béla
Lenin
Magyar-Szovjet barátság (Hungarian-Soviet Friendship)
Marx Károly
Néphadsereg (People's Army)
November 7
Rózsa Ferenc
Ságvári Endre
Sallai Imre
Somogyi Béla
Tanácsköztársaság (Council of the Republics)
Tolbuhin
Úttörő (Young Pioneer)
Vörös Hadsereg (Red Army)
Vörös október (Red October)

their sign on the roof when vacant. If an independent taxi (see the Getting Around section of the Budapest chapter) stops on the street, wave it on and wait for one with the logo of a reputable firm printed on its door.

Taking a taxi in the provinces is almost always without incident, and because fewer people take them than in Budapest the driver will usually be courteous and helpful. It's a different case altogether in Budapest, and you should be on your guard at all times when taking a taxi in the capital. If all goes well, passengers usually tip drivers about 10% (or round up to the nearest 100 Ft, even if it means tipping a little less or a little more).

Budapest

There's no other city in Hungary like Budapest. With a population of around two million people, the metropolis is home to almost 20% of the total population. As Hungary's capital, it is the administrative, business and cultural centre; virtually everything starts, finishes or is taking place in Budapest. There is more to see and do here for visitors than anywhere else in the country.

But the beauty of Budapest is what really makes it stand apart. Straddling a gentle curve in the Danube, it is flanked by the Buda Hills on the west bank and what is really the start of the Great Plain to the east. Architecturally, it is a gem. Though it may lack the medieval buildings so ubiquitous in Prague, there is enough baroque, neoclassical, Eclectic and Art Nouveau architecture here to satisfy anyone. Overall, however, Budapest has a turn-of-the-century feel to it, for it was then – during the industrial boom and the capital's 'golden age' – that most of today's city was built. In some places, particularly

HIGHLIGHTS

Top Twelve

Though it's all a matter of taste and interest, the following could be considered the top sights and activities in Budapest; at least a few of them should be included on every traveller's itinerary. For those with more time or an interest in seeing the city in greater depth, there are a dozen walking tours to follow later on. The 'top 12' listed below (in no particular order) can also be found on the walking tours.

Unless specified otherwise, all museums in Budapest are open Tuesday to Sunday from 10 am to 6 pm between April and October and from 10 am to 4 pm on the same days during the rest of the year. The entrance fee is anything between 60 and 200 Ft, though a few museums have free days.

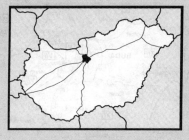

- the view of Pest from Fishermen's Bastion on Castle Hill in district I (Walking Tour 1)
- the view of Buda from the waterfront tram No 2 on the Pest side (Walking Tour 6)
- a night at the State Opera House, VI Andrássy út 22 (Walking Tour 9)
- the period furniture and bric-a-brac at the Applied Arts Museum, IX Üllői út 33-37 (Walking Tour 11)
- a soak at any of the following thermal baths: Gellért, XI Kelenhegyi út 4, and Rudas, I Döbrentei tér 9 (Walking Tour 2); Király, II Fő utca 84 (Walking Tour 3); Széchenyi, XIV Állatkerti út 11, City Park (Walking Tour 9)
- the two icons of Hungarian nationhood: the Crown of St Stephen at the National Museum, VIII Múzeum körút 14-16 (Walking Tour 11), and the saint-king's mortal remains in the Basilica of St Stephen, Bajcsy-Zsilinszky út (Walking Tour 6)
- the wonderfully renovated Central Market Hall (Nagycsarnok) on IX Fővám tér (Walking Tour 11), or the more traditional outdoor market at XIII Lehel tér (Walking Tour 6)
- the Old Masters and symbolist collections at the Museum of Fine Arts, XIV Hősök tere (Walking Tour 9)
- the descent (for better views) on the Libegő (chair lift) from János-hegy in the Buda Hills to Zugligeti út (Walking Tour 12)
- the Judaica collection at the Jewish Museum, VII Dohány utca 2 (Walking Tour 10)
- a slice of anything in the Művész café, VI Andrássy út 29 (Walking Tour 9)
- a browse and a purchase at the Ecseri flea market, XIX Nagykőrösi út (see Markets)

along the two ring roads and up Andrássy út to the City Park, Budapest's nickname – 'the Paris of Eastern Europe' – is well deserved. Nearly every building has some interesting or unusual detail – from Art Nouveau tiles and neoclassical reliefs to bullet holes left over from WWII or the 1956 Uprising.

In fact, Budapest's scars are not well hidden. Industrial and automobile pollution have exacerbated the decay, but in recent years the rebuilding and renovations have been nothing short of astonishing.

Budapest is at its best in the spring and summer or just after dark when Castle Hill is bathed in a warm yellow light. Stroll along the river front (Duna korzó) on the Pest side or across any of the bridges past young couples embracing passionately. It's then that you'll feel the romance of a city that, despite all attempts both from within and outside to destroy it, has never died.

HISTORY

Strictly speaking, the story of Budapest begins as recently as 1873 when hilly, residential Buda merged with flat, industrial Pest and historic Óbuda to the north to form what

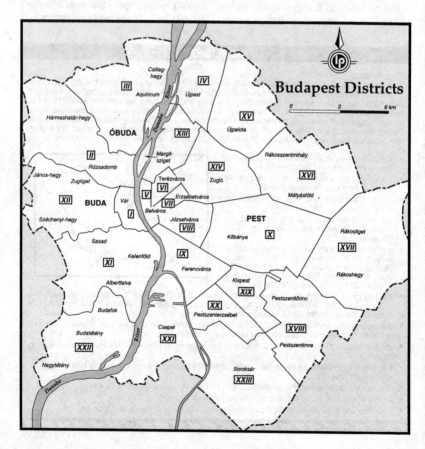

Budapest Districts

was first called Pest-Buda. But like everything here, it's not that simple.

The Romans had an important settlement here called Aquincum until the 5th century, when the Great Migrations began. The Magyars settled nearby half a millennium later, but Buda and Pest were no more than villages until the 12th century, when foreign merchants and tradespeople settled. In the 13th century, King Béla IV built a fortress here, but it was King Charles Robert who moved the court from Visegrád to Buda 50 years later. His son Louis the Great (Nagy Lajos) began the construction of a royal palace.

The Mongols burned Buda and Pest to the ground in 1241, and thus began a pattern of destruction and rebuilding that would last until this century. Under the Turks, the two towns lost most of their populations, and when the Turks were defeated by the Habsburgs in the late 17th century, Buda Castle was in ruins. The 1848 Revolution, WWII and the 1956 Uprising all took their toll. In the final days of WWII, for example, all seven bridges linking the two sides of the river were blown up by the retreating Germans and a large part of the city was in ruins.

ORIENTATION

Budapest is in the north-central part of Hungary, some 250 km south-east of Vienna. It is a large, sprawling city and, with few exceptions (eg Buda Hills, City Park, some excursions), the areas beyond the Nagykörút (literally the 'big ring road') in Pest and west of Moszkva tér in Buda are residential or industrial and of little interest to visitors. It is a well laid-out city and almost never confusing.

If you look at a full-size map of Budapest you'll see that two ring roads – the big one and the semicircular Kiskörút (the 'little ring road') – link some of the bridges across the Danube and essentially define downtown Pest. The Nagykörút consists of Szent István körút, Teréz körút, Erzsébet körút, József körút and Ferenc körút. The Kiskörút comprises Károly körút, Múzeum körút and Vámház körút. Important boulevards like Bajcsy-Zsilinszky út, leafy Andrássy út, Rákóczi út and Üllői út fan out from the ring roads, creating large squares and circles.

Buda is dominated by Castle and Gellért hills. The main roads here are Margit körút (the only part of either ring road that crosses the river), Fő utca and Attila út on either side of Castle Hill, and Hegyalja út and Bartók Béla út running west and south-west.

Many visitors will arrive at one of the three train stations: Keleti (Eastern), Nyugati (Western) and Déli (Southern). See the Getting There & Away section later in this chapter for details. All of them are on one of the three metro lines, which converge at Deák tér, a busy square a few minutes walk north-east of the inner town.

Budapest is divided into 23 kerület, or districts, which usually also have traditional names like Lipótváros (Leopold Town) or Víziváros (Watertown). While these can sometimes help visitors negotiate their way around (all of Castle Hill is in district I, for example, and the inner town is district V), I've divided the city into a dozen walks for easy touring. The Roman numeral appearing before each street address signifies the district.

Maps

The best folding map to the city is Cartographia's *Budapest City Map* available everywhere for about 250 Ft. If you plan to see the city thoroughly or stay beyond just a few days, the *Budapest Atlas* (650 Ft), also from Cartographia, is indispensable. It has 40 detailed maps (1:30,000) of the city, an index with all the new street names and some descriptive information in English. The 1:20,000 format (1200 Ft) with 28 maps is larger but easier to read.

Cartographia has its own outlet at VI Bajcsy-Zsilinszky út 37 (metro: Arany János utca), but it's not self-service. A better bet would be the small shop in the Párizsi Udvar at V Ferenciek tere 11 (metro: Ferenciek tere) or the larger Libri map shop at VII Nyár utca 1 (metro: Blaha Lujza tér) open weekdays from 9 am to 5 pm.

BUDAPEST

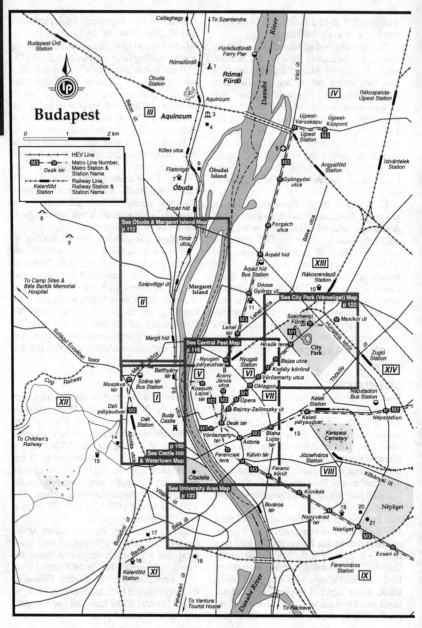

Budapest

0   1   2 km

HÉV Line

M3—Ⓜ — Metro Line Number, Metro Station & Station Name
Deák tér

— Railway Line, Railway Station & Station Name
Kelenföld Station

To Szentendre

Csillaghegy

Budapest-Ürő Station

Punkósdfürdő Ferry Pier

Rómaifürdő

Rómaifürdő

Óbuda Station

Vácí út

Rákospalota-Újpest Station

IV

Aquincum

III Aquincum

Kőles utca

Óbudai Island

Újpest-Városkapu

Újpest-Központ Ⓜ M3

Újpest Station

Angyalföld Station

Istvántelek Station

Filatorigát

Óbuda

Gyöngyösi utca

Óbudai Island

Forgách utca

Béke utca

Árpád híd

Árpád híd

Árpád híd Bus Station

Dózsa György út

Rákosrendező Station

XIII

See Óbuda & Margaret Island Map p 112

Timár utca

Margaret Island

Szépvölgyi út

II

To Camp Sites & Béla Bartók Memorial Hospital

See City Park (Városliget) Map p 122

Lehel tér

Lehel utca

Széchenyi Fürdő

Mexikói út

City Park

Zugló Station

XIV

Margit híd

Hősök tere

Bajza utca

Kodály körönd

Vörösmarty utca

Hungária körút

Thököly

Margit körút

See Central Pest Map p 116

Nyugati pályaudvar

Nyugati Station

VI

Batthyány tér

Arany János utca

Oktogon

VII

Népstadion Bus Station

Szilágyi Erzsébet fasor

Moszkva tér

Szena tér Bus Station

V

Kossuth Lajos tér

Opera

Bajcsy-Zsilinszky út

Keleti Station

Népstadion Ⓜ M2

Fő utca

I

Déli pályaudvar

Ⓜ M2

Buda Castle

Déli Station

Deák tér

Keleti pályaudvar

XII

Cog Railway

To Children's Railway

Alkotás utca

Vörösmarty tér

Astoria

Blaha Lujza tér

Kerepesi Cemetery

13

Ferenciek tere

Kálvin tér

p 100

See Castle Hill & Watertown Map

Citadella

Ferenc körút

M3

Józsefváros Station

VIII

Kőbányai út

See University Area Map p 133

Villányi út

Boráros tér

Klinikák

IX

Ferencváros Station

Budaörsi út

Béla út

Nagyvárad tér

19   20

Népliget

21

Népliget M3

XI

Kelenföld Station

Bartók

18

Fehérvári út

To Ventura Tourist Hostel

Danube River

To Ráckeve

Ecseri út

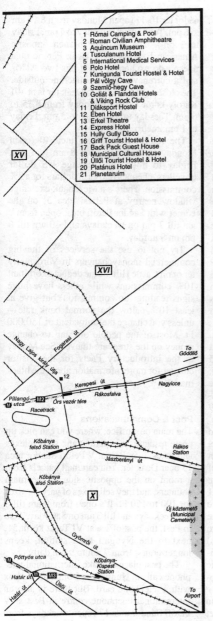

1 Római Camping & Pool
2 Roman Civilian Amphitheatre
3 Aquincum Museum
4 Tusculanum Hotel
5 International Medical Services
6 Polo Hotel
7 Kunigunda Tourist Hostel & Hotel
8 Pál völgy Cave
9 Szemlő-hegy Cave
10 Goliát & Flandria Hotels
   & Viking Rock Club
11 Diáksport Hostel
12 Ében Hotel
13 Erkel Theatre
14 Express Hotel
15 Hully Gully Disco
16 Griff Tourist Hostel & Hotel
17 Back Pack Guest House
18 Municipal Cultural House
19 Üllői Tourist Hostel & Hotel
20 Platánus Hotel
21 Planetaruim

XV

XVI

Nagy Lajos király útja

Fogarasi út

To Gödöllő

■ 12

Kerepesi út

Rákosfalva

Nagyicce

Pillangó utca   M2

Örs vezér tére

Racetrack

Köbánya felső Station

Rákos Station

Jászberényi út

Köbánya alsó Station

X

Új köztemető (Municipal Cemetery)

Gyömrői út

Pöttyös utca

Köbánya-Kispest Station

Határ út   M3

Határ út   Üllői út

To Airport

INFORMATION
Tourist Offices

Most of the agencies listed under Travel Agencies, below, and the ones listed under Private Rooms in the Places to Stay section later in this chapter, provide information and often brochures and maps. But the best single source of information – bar none – is Tourinform (☎ 1-117 9800; fax 1-117 9578; e-mail tourinform@hungary.com) in Pest at V Sütő utca 2, just off Deák tér. It's open every day from 8 am to 8 pm. They have a second office (☎ 1-132 0597) at the Nyugati train station, next to platform No 10, which is open daily from 7 am to 8 pm. Though the staff can't book you accommodation, they'll send you somewhere that does and will help with anything else – from maps and ferry schedules to where to find vegetarian food.

The MÁV ticket office (☎ 1-322 9035 or ☎ 1-322 8275) in Pest at VI Andrássy út 35 (metro: Opera) sells international train tickets and can make advance seat reservations for domestic express trains at the same price you'd pay at the station. They accept cash only and are open weekdays from 9 am to 5 pm (6 pm in summer).

Assistance and/or advice for motorists is available at the Magyar Autóklub (☎ 1-212 2821), II Rómer Flóris utca 4/a off Margit körút near Margaret Bridge. There's another Magyar Autóklub office opposite the Budapest Operetta Theatre at VI Nagymező utca 20.

Money

Most agencies will exchange foreign currency, but the rate is seldom in your favour. Automatic teller machines (ATMs) can be found outside banks everywhere in the capital these days. Ibusz and any K&H bank branch will give you a cash advance on your Visa card, Eurocard or MasterCard; Ibusz Bank maintains a 24-hour exchange office at V Apáczai Csere János utca 1, near the Duna Marriott hotel. The American Express office (☎ 1-267 2020) at V Deák Ferenc utca 10, a block up from Vörösmarty tér towards Deák tér, has an ATM dispensing cash forint and travellers' cheques in US dollars. It changes its own travellers' cheques at a rate about 3% lower than the banks. To convert US dollar travellers' cheques into dollars cash here incurs about a 6% to 7% commission. Amex is open from 9 am to 5.30 (or 6.30 pm) seven days a week. Citibank card holders should go to Citibank (☎ 268 8888) at V Vörösmarty tér 4.

As elsewhere in Hungary, the OTP (National Savings Bank) changes travellers' cheques without commission, but get there at least an hour before closing to be sure the foreign-exchange counter is still open.

The OTP branch closest to Keleti train station is at VIII Rákóczi út 84 (open Monday from 8.15 am to 6 pm, Tuesday to Thursday to 3 pm, Friday to 1 pm). The small private exchange office just inside the Europa Cinema on the right at VIII Rákóczi út 82 often gives a slightly better rate than the bank for cash (open on weekdays from 9 am to 6 pm, weekends to 1 pm). The K&H bank at the Ibusz office inside Keleti train station itself also changes travellers' cheques at a good rate. It's open weekdays from 8 am to 6.30 pm and Saturday to 1 pm.

The OTP branch with foreign exchange facilities closest to Nyugati train station is at XIII Tátra utca 10 (open Monday from 8.15 am to 6 pm, Tuesday to Thursday to 3 pm, Friday to 1 pm). The K&H bank beside platform No 10 inside Nyugati (open weekdays from 8.15 am to 6 pm, Saturday from 9 am to 3 pm) gives a good rate for travellers' cheques. The GWK exchange bureau next to Tourinform in the station is also reasonable.

The OTP branch closest to Déli train station is at I Alagút utca 3, on the corner of Attila út (open Monday from 8.15 to 6 pm, Tuesday to Thursday to 4 pm, Friday to 1 pm). The K&H bank in the Ibusz office downstairs at the entrance to the metro in the same station (open weekdays from 8 am to noon and 12.45 to 6 pm, Saturday to 1 pm) changes travellers' cheques without commission. The Máv Tours office in the same concourse will change certain Eastern European currencies into forint.

Not far from the international bus station on Erzsébet tér is the OTP bank at V József nádor tér 10-11 (open Monday from 8.15 am to 6 pm, Tuesday to Thursday to 4 pm, Friday to 1 pm). The big OTP branch opposite American Express on V Deák Ferenc utca doesn't do exchange, but it has two ATMs and a currency-exchange machine outside. The closest OTP branch to Deák tér is at VII Károly körút 1 (open Monday from 8.15 to 6 pm, Tuesday to Thursday to 3 pm, Friday to 1 pm; metro: Astoria).

The K&H bank at Váci utca 40 (open Monday to Thursday from 8 am to 1 pm, Friday to noon) will change US dollar travellers' cheques into cash dollars for a 3% commission. There's a Mezőbank exchange window nearby at Párizsi utca 3, on the corner with Sándor Petőfi utca, open from 9 am till 7 pm on weekdays and 10 am till 6 pm on Saturday.

Try not to use the services of the big commercial moneychangers in Vörösmarty tér or on Castle Hill. Some deduct exorbitant 10% commissions while others have huge signs reading 'no commission' but give at least 10% below the normal bank rate – unless you change the equivalent of 150,000 Ft. Most of the people offering to change money on the street are thieves. See Money in the introductory Facts for the Visitor chapter for more information about the black market.

Post & Communications

The main post office, where you can pick up poste restante, mail letters and send telexes and faxes, is in Pest at V Petőfi Sándor utca 13 near Deák tér. You can mail parcels from a room on the opposite side of the main counters, and they sell boxes of varying sizes for 100 to 150 Ft. It's open from 8 am till 8 pm weekdays and till 3 pm on Saturday. Also in Pest, the post office at VI Teréz körút 51, next to the Nyugati train station, keeps longer hours: from 7 am to 9 pm daily.

The best place to make international telephone calls in Hungary is from a phone box with a telephone card. But there is also an international telephone centre in Pest at V Petőfi Sándor utca 17 (open weekdays from

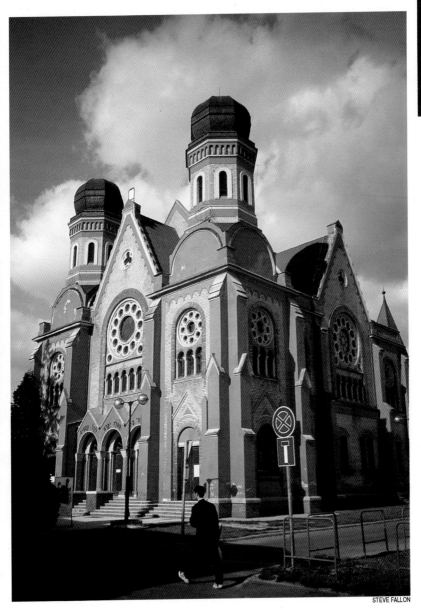

STEVE FALLON

Synagogue, Zalaegerszeg, Western Transdanubia

Top: Chain Bridge, Budapest
Left: Serbian Orthodox Church, Ráckeve, Around Budapest
Right: Turkish-era pool at the Rudás Baths in Buda

8 am to 8 pm, Saturday from 9 am to 3 pm). Budapest's telephone code is ☎ 1.

Internet Budapest now has a half-dozen cybercafés and public-access Internet servers, and that number is certain to grow. Among the biggest (and by all accounts best) are:

Internext Studio
   VIII József körút 40
   e-mail: reg@mail.inext.hu
Info Shop
   V Múzeum körút 17
   e-mail: geoseva@omk.omikk.hu

Travel Agencies

In Pest, the main Ibusz office (☎ 118 1120), V Ferenciek tere 10, supplies free travel brochures, and the staff are usually very good about answering general questions. They also change money and rent private rooms.

Express (☎ 111 9898), V Zoltán utca 10 (metro: Kossuth Lajos tér), open Monday to Thursday from 8 am to 4 pm, Friday to 3 pm, sells BIJ train tickets with a 30% discount on fares to Western Europe to those under the age of 26. The main Express office (☎ 117 8600) at V Semmelweis utca 4 (metro: Astoria) and Wasteels (☎ 210 2802) on platform No 9 at Keleti train station also sell these tickets. You must have an ISIC card (available from Express for 500 Ft) to get the student fare.

Other helpful agencies in Pest are Budapest Tourist (☎ 117 3555) at V Roosevelt tér 5 and Cooptourist (☎ 112 1017) nearby at Kossuth Lajos tér 13-15. In Buda, aside from the agencies at Déli train station mentioned in Places to Stay, there's an Express office (☎ 185 3173) at XI Bartók Béla út 34 (see the University Area map), and a Cooptourist (☎ 166 5349) at No 4 of the same street. These agencies are usually open on weekdays from 8 am till 5 pm and on Saturday in summer till noon or 1 pm.

If the queues are very long at the MÁV ticket office, head for Ibusz (☎ 322 1656) at VII Dob utca 1 (metro: Astoria or Deák tér),

which sells the same tickets and can also make seat reservations. It's open weekdays from 9 am to 5 pm.

Bookshops

One of the best English-language bookshop in Budapest is Bestsellers, V Október 6 utca 11 (metro: Arany János), which has novels, travel guides, magazines and newspapers. It's open weekdays from 9 am till 6.30 pm and on Saturday from 10 am to 6 pm. There's another branch close by at the Central European University, Nádor utca 9.

The Libri-Studium Academia Bookshop at Vaci utca 22 has a good selection of English books (including guides), as has the Kodex Bookshop at Honved utca 5, where you will find Hungarian books on the ground floor and foreign books on the 1st floor. The Párisi Konyvesbolt at Petofi Sandor utca 2 specialises in maps and travel guides. There is also a small foreign-language bookshop at Gerloczy utca 7. A bit further away, Pendragon Trading Kft at Raoul Wallenberg utca 9-11 has a good stock of foreign-language books, which includes guides and fiction.

For antique and second-hand books (mostly Hungarian and German) try Antikvárium, V Ferenciek tere 3 (metro: Ferenciek tere). Other good used bookshops are at VIII Múzeum körút 15 (metro: Kálvin tér), V Szent István körút 1-3 (metro: Nyugati pályaudvar) and VI Bajcsy-Zsilinszky út 34 (metro: Arany János utca).

For Hungarian authors in translation, try the Writers' Bookshop (Írók boltja) at VI Andrássy út 45. With coffee and tables for use while browsing, it is one of the most comfortable bookshops in the city and was a popular literary café for most of the first half of this century.

The best place for foreign newspapers and magazines is the small bookshop in the Corvinus Kempinski hotel at V Erzsébet tér 7-8; the outdoor kiosk on V Deák Ferenc utca as you enter Vörösmarty tér; the Hírker newsstand in the subway below Nyugati tér; and the shop on the ground floor of the telephone centre at Petőfi Sándor utca 17.

Cultural Centres

The Institut Français (☎ 202 1133) at Fő utca 17 is open Tuesday to Friday from 1 to 7 pm and Saturday from 10 am to 1 pm.

The Italian Institute of Culture (☎ 118 8144) is at VIII Bródy Sándor utca 8. The America House Library on XIV Zichy Géza utca is open Tuesday to Friday from 11 am to 4 pm.

Laundry

Two central laundries are at V József nádor tér 9 (metro: Vörösmarty tér) and VII Rákóczi út 8/b (metro: Astoria). The latter has better hours and is open on Saturday morning. They're not self-service (they never are in Hungary); you elect to have your laundry done in six or 24 hours and pay accordingly (from about 600 Ft). The best – and most expensive – dry-cleaning service is available at the Corvinus Kempinski hotel.

Medical Services

International Medical Services (☎ 129 8423 or 250 3829 after hours), XIII Váci út 202 (metro: Újpest-Városkapu) is a private medical clinic open 24 hours a day. Consultations usually cost from 2300 to 4000 Ft. Home visits cost around 4500 Ft.

A dental clinic specialising in treating foreigners is Dental Co-op (☎ 176 3600), XII Zugligeti út 60 (bus No 158), open weekdays from 9 am to 6 pm (from 1 pm on Thursday).

Emergency

If you need to report a lost or stolen passport or credit card or a crime, go to the central police station (☎ 112 3456) at V Deák Ferenc utca 16-18. If possible, bring along a Hungarian-speaker or dredge up what little German you have. The office in Budapest dealing with foreigners' registrations is Keokh (☎ 118 0800) at VI Városligeti fasor 46-48 (metro: Hősök tere).

In the event of an emergency, the following are the most important telephone numbers:

Police ☎ 107
Fire ☎ 105
Ambulance ☎ 104 or ☎ 111 1666

Dangers & Annoyances

No parts of Budapest are 'off-limits' to visitors, although some locals now avoid Margaret Island after dark, following the murder of a British tourist there in the summer of 1995.

As in the rest of Hungary, you are most vulnerable in the capital to car thieves, pickpockets and taxi louts. To avoid having your car ripped off (some 50 are stolen every day in Budapest), follow the usual security procedures. Don't park it in a dark street, and make sure the burglar alarm is armed (though these often go off for no reason and are usually ignored) or at least have a steering-wheel lock in place.

Pickpocketing is most common in markets, the castle area and Váci utca, and on certain buses (No 7) and trams (Nos 2, 4 and 6); in the past, metro No 1 (the yellow line) has been plagued by thieves who work in gangs.

Taking a taxi in Budapest can be an expensive – even violent – experience. For more information, see Taxi in the Getting Around section later in this chapter.

WALKING TOURS

Budapest is an excellent city for walking, and there are sights around every corner – from a brightly tiled gem of an Art Nouveau building to peasant women fresh in from the countryside or Transylvania hawking their colourful wares.

The following 12 tours can easily be done on foot individually or in tandem with the preceding or following ones; the highlights listed in the aside can be found along the way. Don't worry about doing every tour or even finishing one; linger as long as you like in a museum or market that takes your fancy, do a little shopping or even visit one of the city's fine thermal spas along the way.

Walking Tour 1: Castle Hill

Castle Hill, a one-km-long limestone plateau in Buda 170m above the Danube, contains Budapest's most important medieval monuments and some of its best museums. It is the premier sight for visitors to the city and, with its grand views and so many things to see, you should start your touring here. Castle Hill sits on a 28-km network of caves formed by thermal springs. The caves were supposedly used by the Turks for military purposes and then as air-raid shelters during WWII. Castle Hill lies entirely in district I.

All the sights listed here can be found on the Castle Hill & Watertown map (see p 100).

The walled Castle area consists of two distinct parts: the Old Town (Vár), where commoners lived in the Middle Ages (the current owners of the coveted burgher houses here are no longer so common) and the Royal Palace (Budavári Palota), the original site of the castle built by Béla IV in the 13th century. To get to the former (where we'll start), take the red metro line to Moszkva tér and walk up Várfok utca (southeast above the square) to Vienna Gate, the northern entrance to the Old Town. A small bus labelled 'Várbusz' or sometimes 'Dísz tér' follows the same route from the start of Várfok utca.

If you want to begin with all the museums in the Royal Palace, there are a number of options. The easiest is the Sikló, a funicular that takes passengers up in two minutes from Clark Ádám tér to Szent György tér between 7.30 am and 10 pm (150/80 Ft for adults/children). Alternatively, you can walk up the Király lépcső, steps that lead from Hunyadi János út north of Clark Ádám tér, or the ones that go to the southern end of the Royal Palace from Szarvas tér. Bus No 16 from Erzsébet tér (almost opposite the Corvinus Kempinski hotel) in Pest terminates at Dísz tér.

The best way to see the **Old Town** is to stroll along the four medieval streets that more or less converge on Szentháromság tér, poking your head into the attractive little courtyards (an acceptable activity) and visiting the odd museum. But be selective: it would take you at least two full days to see everything on Castle Hill. A brief tour of the Old Town in one of the horse-drawn *fiacres* standing in Szentháromság tér will cost about 400 to 500 Ft.

You can start your tour by climbing to the top of **Vienna Gate** (Bécsi kapu), rebuilt in 1936 to mark the 250th anniversary of the retaking of the castle from the Turks. It's not all that huge, but when loquacious Hungarian children natter on, their parents tell them: 'Be quiet, your mouth is as big as the Vienna Gate!' The large building to the west with the superb tiled roof is the **National Archives** (1920). Across the square, a weekend market in the Middle Ages, a **Lutheran church** with the words 'A Mighty Fortress is Our God' written in Hungarian marks the start of Táncsics Mihály utca. On the west side of Bécsi kapu tér there's an attractive group of houses, especially No 7 with its medallions of classical poets and philosophers and the one with a round corner window at No 8.

Táncsics Mihály utca is a narrow street of little houses painted in pastel colours and adorned with frescos and statues. Most have plaques with the word *műemlék* ('memorial') attesting to their historical importance. The one at Táncsics Mihály utca 9, for example, cites that Lajos Kossuth was imprisoned there from 1837 to 1840 'for his homeland'. In the entrances to many of the courtyards, you'll notice lots of **sedilia** (sedile in the singular) – stone niches dating as far back as the 13th century. Historians are still debating their function. Some say they were merchant stalls, while others think servants cooled their heels here while their masters (or mistresses) paid a visit to the occupant.

Parts of the **medieval synagogue** at Táncsics Mihály utca 26 date from the 14th century, and a small museum contains religious objects and writings. It's open from May to October only, from 10 am till 5 pm Tuesday to Sunday. Across the road to the south-east at No 7 is the **Music History Museum** in an 18th-century palace with a lovely courtyard. As the name suggests, it traces the development of music and musical instruments in Hungary; the violin maker's workbench and the unusual 18th-century sextet table are particularly interesting. The paintings on loan from the Museum of Fine Arts all have musical themes. A special room upstairs is devoted to the work of Béla

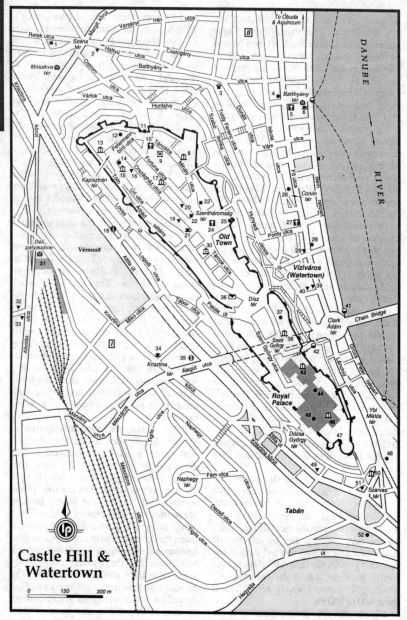

Castle Hill & Watertown

0   150   300 m

PLACES TO STAY		40	Taverna Ressaikos	27	Capuchin Church
1	Büro Pension &		Restaurant	28	Institut Français
	Söröző a Szent	49	Tabáni Kakas	30	Golden Eagle
	Jupáthoz		Restaurant		Pharmacy
	Restaurant	51	Aranyszarvas	31	Déli Railway Station
3	Donáti Hostel		Restaurant	35	OTP Bank
	(Summer Only)			36	Post Office
7	Dunapart Boat Hotel	**OTHER**		37	Castle Theatre
22	Kulturinnov Hotel	4	Market		(Várszínház)
23	Budapest Hilton Hotel	5	St Anne's Church	38	Sándor Palace &
		8	Music History		Historical
PLACES TO EAT			Museum		Waxworks Museum
2	Nagyi Palacsintázúya	9	Medieval Synagogue	41	Tram Stop No 19
6	Angelika	10	Lutheran Church	42	Funicular (Lower
16	Akadémia Self-	11	Vienna Gate		Station)
	Service Restaurant	12	National Archives	43	Ludwig Museum
19	Fekete Holló	13	Military History	44	National Gallery
	Restaurant		Museum	45	Széchenyi National
20	Fortuna Späten	14	Magdalene Tower		Library
	Restaurant	15	Telephone Museum	46	Budapest History
21	Ruszwurm Café	17	Museum of Catering		Museum
29	Jardin de Paris		& Commerce	47	Ferdinand Gate
32	Gerber Banya-Tanya	18	Cooptourist	48	Castle Garden Kiosk
	Restaurant	24	Matthias Church	50	Medical History
33	Il Treno Pizzeria	25	Fishermen's Bastion		Museum
34	Caffè Déryné	26	Budai Vigadó	52	Rác Baths
39	Seoul House		(Concert Hall)		

Bartók (lots of scores), and concerts are sometimes held in Kodály Hall.

The controversial **Budapest Hilton** hotel, which incorporates parts of a 14th-century Dominican church and a baroque Jesuit college, is at Hess András tér 1. Have a look at the little red hedgehog above the doorway at house No 3, which was an inn in the 14th century.

If you walk north along Fortuna utca, another street of decorated houses, you'll soon reach one of Budapest's most interesting small museums: the **Museum of Catering & Commerce** at I Fortuna utca 4. An entire 19th-century cake shop has been relocated to the three rooms of the catering (left-hand) section of the museum, complete with a pastry kitchen. There are moulds for every occasion, a marble-lined icebox and an antique ice-cream maker. Much is made of those great confectioners Emil Gerbeaud and József Dobos of *Dobos torta* (a kind of cake) fame.

Across the entrance way, the commerce collection traces retail trade in the capital. Along with electric toys and advertisements

that still work, there's an exhibit on the hyperinflation that Hungary suffered after WWII when a basket of money would buy no more than four eggs. Among the many posters, my favourite is that of WWI Allied troops surrendering to Austro-Hungarian soldiers who are lustily drinking beer from the first Hungarian brewery. Before you leave, check the great old pub sign, depicting a satyr and foaming mug, in the courtyard out the back.

Fortuna utca leads back into Bécsi kapu tér, but if you continue west along Petermann bíró utca you'll reach Kapisztrán tér. The large white building to the north houses the **Military History Museum** (the entrance is to the west side on Tóth Árpád sétány). The museum has more weapons inside than a Los Angeles crack house, but if you look to either side of the museum gate you'll see cannonballs fired in 1848 at what was then a military barracks. Around the corner, along the so-called **Anjou Bastion** (Anjou bástya) with all the cannons, lies the grave of Abdurrahman, the last Turkish governor of Budapest, who was killed here in 1686. 'He was a heroic foe,' reads the tablet. 'May he rest in peace.'

The large steeple in Kapisztrán tér, visible for km to the west of Castle Hill, is the **Mary Magdalene Tower**, with a reconstructed window and a bit of foundation being all that is left of the church once reserved for Hungarian-speakers in this district. It was used as a mosque during the Turkish occupation and was hit in an air raid in WWII.

From Kapisztrán tér, walk south on Országház utca, being careful not to miss the sedile in the entrance to No 9 and the medieval houses painted white, lime and tangerine at Nos 18, 20 and 22. György Seregi, a blacksmith at No 16, does unusual stuff with wrought iron.

The next street to the west running parallel, Úri utca, has some interesting courtyards, especially No 19 with a sundial and what looks like a tomb. There are more Gothic sedilia at Nos 32 and 36. The **Telephone Museum** at Úri utca 49 is housed in an old Clarist monastery. Tree-lined Tóth Árpád sétány, the next 'street' over, follows the west wall from the Anjou Bastion to Dísz tér and has some great views of the Buda Hills.

On the corner of Úri utca and Szentháromság utca is a mounted **statue of András Hadik**, a field marshal in the wars against the Turks. If you were wondering (and we knew you were) why the steed's brass testicles are so shiny, well, it's a student tradition to give them a stroke before taking an exam. Szentháromság utca leads east into the square of that name.

In the centre of the square there's a **Holy Trinity statue**, another one of the 'plague pillars' put up by grateful, healthy citizens in the 18th century. Szentháromság tér is dominated by the Old Town's two most famous sights: Matthias Church, originally reserved for German-speakers, and beyond it the Fishermen's Bastion.

Bits of **Matthias Church** – so named because the 15th-century Renaissance king Matthias Corvinus was married here – date back some 500 years, notably the carvings above the southern entrance. But basically the church is a neo-Gothic creation designed by the architect Frigyes Schulek in the late 19th century. The church has a colourful tile roof and a lovely tower; the interior is remarkable for its stained-glass windows and frescos by the Romantic painters Károly Lotz and Bertalan Székely. They also did the wall decorations, an unusual mixture of folk, Art Nouveau and Turkish designs.

Escape the crowds by walking down the steps to the right of the main altar to the crypt, which leads to the **Museum of Ecclesiastical Art**. It has monstrances, reliquaries, chalices – that sort of thing – but you'll get some interesting views of the chancel from high up in the Royal Oratory. There are usually organ concerts in the church on weekend evenings, continuing a tradition that began in 1867 when Franz Liszt's *Hungarian Coronation Mass* was first played here for the coronation of Franz Joseph and Elizabeth as king and queen of Hungary.

The **Fishermen's Bastion** is another neo-Gothic masquerade that most visitors (and Hungarians) believe is much older. But who cares? It looks medieval and still offers among the best views in Budapest. Built as a viewing platform in 1905 by Schulek, the name was taken from the guild of fishermen responsible for defending this stretch of the wall in the Middle Ages. The seven gleaming white turrets represent the Magyar tribes who entered the Carpathian Basin in the late 9th century. Nearby is an equestrian statue of St Stephen (977-1038), Hungary's first king.

The **Golden Eagle Pharmacy** (Aranysas patikaház), just north of Dísz tér at Tárnok utca 18, probably looks exactly the way it did in Buda Castle in the 17th century, though it was moved to its present site 100 years later. The miniature of Christ as a pharmacist is unusual: the mock-up of an alchemist's lab with dried bats, tiny crocodiles and eye of newt in jars is straight out of the Addams Family.

From Dísz tér, walk south along Színház utca to Szent György tér. Along the way you'll pass the **Castle Theatre** on the left, built in 1736 as a Carmelite church and monastery, and across from it the bombed-out **Ministry of Defence**, another wartime casualty. The restored **Sándor Palace** opposite, which is to be turned into the prime minister's office, now contains the tacky **Historical Waxworks Museum**. It is open from mid-March to October daily except Tuesday and costs an outrageous 350 Ft for a guided tour.

On the south-east side of Szent György tér is an enormous statue of the *turul*, an eagle-like totem of the ancient Magyars (see aside in the Western Transdanubia chapter). The steps nearby lead to the Royal Palace.

The **Royal Palace** has been burned, bombed, razed, rebuilt and redesigned at least half a dozen times over the past seven centuries. What you see today clinging to the southern end of Castle Hill is an 18th and early 20th-century amalgam reconstructed after the last war, during which it was bombed to bits. Ironically, the palace was never used by the Habsburgs.

The first part of the palace (Wing A), which can be entered from the courtyard facing west, houses the **Ludwig Museum** of modern Hungarian and foreign art (Andy Warhol, Roy Lichtenstein, Keith Haring etc). It's free on Tuesday.

Return to the square facing the Danube to get to Wing C or walk under the massive archway protected by snarling lions to Wing D to enter the National Gallery. If you take the second route, you'll pass a Romantic-style fountain called **Matthias Well** which tells the story of Szép Ilonka (Beautiful Helen), a poor girl who fell in love with the young King Matthias. Upon learning his identity and feeling unworthy, she died of a broken heart. (If you want to bail out of the tour now, there's a lift to the right of the archway that will take you down to Dózsa György tér and the bus stop for Pest.)

The **National Gallery** (free entry on Saturday) is devoted exclusively to Hungarian art from the Middle Ages. It is an over-whelmingly large collection, and you won't recognise many names among the 19th and 20th-century artists on the 1st, 2nd and 3rd floors. But keep an eye open for works by the Romantic painters József Borsos, Gyula

Benczúr and Mihály Munkácsy and the impressionists Jenő Gyárfás and Pál Merse Szinyei.

Personal favourites include the harrowing depictions of war and the dispossessed by László Mednyánszky, the unique portraits by József Rippl-Rónai, the mammoth canvases by Tivadar Csontváry and the paintings of carnivals by the modern artist Vilmos Aba-Novák. On no account should you miss the Gothic and Renaissance altars, panel paintings and sculptures on the 1st floor, especially the recently restored Altar of St John the Baptist from Kisszebes (a town now in Romania) and the 16th-century painted wooden ceiling in the next room.

Wing F of the palace on the west side of Lion Court contains the **Széchenyi National Library**, which has occasional exhibits. You can peruse the stacks by paying a small daily user's fee.

The **Budapest History Museum** in Wing E to the south (open daily except Tuesday, free entry on Wednesday) traces the 2000 years of the city on three floors of jumbled (but improving) exhibits. A cassette player with a 30-minute tour in English is available for 250 Ft. About the only things really worth seeing here are the Gothic statues of courtiers, squires and saints discovered by chance in 1974 during excavations. They're in a climate-controlled room on the ground floor.

Restored palace rooms dating from the 15th century can be entered from the basement. Three vaulted halls, one with a magnificent door frame in red marble bearing the seal of Queen Beatrice and tiles with a raven and a ring (the seal of her husband King Matthias Corvinus), lead to the **Gothic Hall**, the **Royal Cellar** and the 14th-century **Tower Chapel**.

From the museum, exit through the rear doors into the palace gardens. **Ferdinand Gate** under the conical **Mace Tower** will bring you to a set of steps. These descend to Szarvas tér in the Tabán district.

Walking Tour 2: Gellért Hill & the Tabán
Gellért-hegy, a 235m rocky hill south-east of

Raoul Wallenberg

Of all the 'righteous gentiles' honoured by Jews around the world, none is as well known as Raoul Wallenberg, the Swedish diplomat and business-man who rescued as many as 35,000 Hungarian Jews during WWII.

Wallenberg, who came from a long line of bankers and diplomats, began working in 1936 for a trading firm whose president was a Hungar-ian Jew. In July 1944 the Swedish Foreign Ministry, at the request of Jewish and refugee organisations in the USA, sent the 32-year-old Wallenberg on a rescue mission to Budapest as an attaché to the embassy there. By that time, almost half a million Jews in Hungary had been to Nazi death camps.

Wallenberg immediately began issuing Swedish safe-conduct passes (called 'Wal-lenberg passports') and set up a series of 'safe houses' flying the flag of neutral countries where they could seek asylum. He even followed German deportation trains and 'death marches', distributing food and clothing and freeing some 500 people along the way.

When the Soviet army entered Budapest in January 1945, Wallenberg reported to the authorities, but in the wartime confusion was arrested for espionage and sent to Moscow. In the early 1950s, responding to reports that Wallenberg had been seen alive in a labour camp, the Soviet Union announced that he had in fact died of a heart attack in 1947. Several reports over the next two decades suggested Wallenberg was still alive, but none was ever confirmed. ■

the Castle, is crowned with a fortress of sorts and the Independence Monument, Buda-pest's unofficial symbol. From Gellért Hill, you can't beat the views of the Royal Palace or the Danube and its fine bridges, and the Jubilee Park on the south side is an ideal spot for a picnic. The Tabán, the area between the two hills and stretching north-west as far as Déli train station, is associated with the Serbs, who settled here after fleeing from the Turks in the early 18th century. Later it became known for its restaurants and wine gardens – a kind of Montmartre for Budapest – but was levelled in the 1930s after being condemned as a health hazard. Today the two areas are given over to private homes, parks and three Turkish-style public baths that make good use of the springs gushing from deep below Gellért Hill.

Unless indicated otherwise, the items listed in the following tour can be found on *the south-west corner of the Central Pest map (see p 116).*

If you're starting the tour from Castle Hill, exit via Ferdinand Gate and walk south from Szarvas tér to **Elizabeth Bridge**, the big white span rebuilt after the war and opened to great fanfare in 1964. To the west is a large gushing fountain and a statue of St Gellért, an Italian missionary invited to Hungary by King Stephen. The stairs lead to the top of the hill. Though bus No 27 runs from Móricz Zsigmond körtér to the top of the hill, I'll begin at Szent Gellért tér, which is accessible from Pest on bus No 7 or tram Nos 47 and 49 and from the Buda side on bus No 86 and tram Nos 18 and 19.

Bartók Béla út runs south-west from the square and leads to Móricz Zsigmond körtér, a busy 'circular square' or circus. Nearby, on Műegyetem rakpart along the river before Petőfi Bridge, stands the **Technical Univer-**

sity (see the University Areas map), whose students were the first to march on 23 October 1956. There are no real sights in this area, but the street is full of students, hostels, bars, restaurants and all-night grocery stores.

Szent Gellért tér faces Szabadság Bridge, which opened for the millenary exhibition in 1896, was destroyed by German bombs during WWII and was then rebuilt in 1946. The square is dominated by the Gellért hotel, an Art Nouveau pile (1918) and the city's favourite old-world hotel. If you don't want to fork out the US$100 minimum to stay here (as every celebrity in the world seems to have done, judging from the guest book), you can take the waters in the cathedral-like baths or use the indoor and outdoor swimming pools (see the Activities section in this chapter). The entrance is around the corner on Kelenhegyi út.

Directly north on the small hill above the hotel is the Cliff Chapel built into a cave in 1926. It was the seat of the Paulite order until the late 1940s when the priests were arrested and the cave sealed off. It was reopened earlier in the decade and reconsecrated; the main altar with a symbolic fish is made partly of Zsolnay ceramic. The monastery behind the church with its neo-Gothic turrets is visible from Szabadság Bridge.

From the church, a small path – Verejték utca (literally 'Perspiration Street') – leads to Jubilee Park and a walkway named after Dezső Szabó, a controversial writer killed in the last days of WWII. You'll pass a funny bust of this rather angry-looking and large man along the way as you ascend through what were once vineyards. Another route to follow is along Kelenhegyi út. At No 12-14 is the interesting Art Nouveau Studio Building (1903), which has enormous rooms once used to construct huge socialist realist monuments. Continue up Kelenhegyi út and turn north on Minerva utca. No 1, the Swedish Embassy during the war, is where the diplomat Raoul Wallenberg helped save the lives of thousands of Hungarian Jews (see aside). The short flight of steps rejoins Verejték utca.

Towering above you is the Citadella, a fortress that never saw warfare. Built by the Habsburgs after the 1848-49 War of Independence to 'defend' the city from further insurrection, by the time it was ready the political climate had changed and the Citadella had become obsolete. It was given to the city in the 1890s and parts of it were symbolically blown to pieces. Between June and mid-September, an unbelievably expensive (3700 Ft) sound-and-light show is staged here most nights at 10.30 pm and midnight. Ring ☎ 112 4037 for information.

There's not much inside the Citadella today except for a hotel/hostel, a casino and restaurant, a pleasant outdoor café and about a dozen display cases reviewing the history of the city. To the east along Citadella sétány stands the Independence Monument, the lovely lady with the palm proclaiming freedom throughout the city and the land. It was erected in 1947 in tribute to the Soviet soldiers who died liberating Hungary in 1945. But many Hungarians choose not to remember that fact any more and both the victims names in Cyrillic letters on the plinth and the statues of the Soviet soldiers have been removed. In actual fact, the Independence Monument had been designed by the politically 'flexible' sculptor Zsigmond Kisfaludi Strobl for the ultra-right government of Admiral Miklós Horthy. After the war, when pro-Communist monuments were in short supply, Kisfaludi Strobl passed it off as a memorial to the Soviets.

If you walk west a few minutes, you'll come to what is the best vantage point in Budapest. The trail below leads to the St Gellért Monument, marking the spot where the bishop was hurled to his death in a spiked barrel in 1046 by pagan Hungarians resisting conversion. Across busy Hegyalja út at Döbrentei tér 9 is the second of the area's thermal baths, the Rudas, and the most Turkish of all with its octagonal pool, domed cupola with coloured glass and massive columns. If you're not male or don't have the inclination to visit, you can have a 'drinking cure' by visiting the ivócsarnok (pump room), which is below the bridge and within sight of the bath. A half-litre of the smelly hot water – meant to cure whatever ails you – is just a few forint. To the north through the underpass is a statue of the much revered Habsburg empress and Hungarian queen, Elizabeth (1837-98).

As you walk north along Döbrentei utca, have a look at the plaques at No 15. These mark the water level on the Danube during two devastating floods in 1775 and 1838. What's interesting about them is that they are in German, Serbian and Hungarian, attesting to the mixed population that used to live here. The **Tabán Parish Church** on the east side of Szarvas tér dates from the early 18th century. Across from it, at I Apród utca 1-3, is the **Medical History Museum** (see Castle Hill & Watertown map) named in honour of Ignác Semmelweis, the 19th-century physician known as 'the saviour of mothers'. He discovered the cause of life-threatening childbirth fever. The exhibits trace the history of medicine from Greco-Roman times, and yet another antique pharmacy makes its appearance.

To the east of the museum on Ybl Miklós tér is a lovely renovated building with a fountain known as the **Castle Garden Kiosk**. Once a pump house for Castle Hill, it was designed by Ybl in 1879 and is now a casino. The dilapidated steps and archways across the road, the **Castle Bazaar**, functioned as a pleasure park with shops until about 20 years ago.

Return to Szarvas tér and turn right on Attila út. In the park across the road you'll see a yellow block with a domed roof: this is the **Rác Bath**. It's Ybl on the outside and pure Turkish within.

There's not a heck of a lot to see along Attila út (though the neighbourhood seems to figure in Hungarian literature pretty often). The lift at the bottom of the Széchenyi Library on Dózsa György tér can whisk you back up to Castle Hill, but if you carry on you'll see the entrance to the **Alagút**, the tunnel under Castle Hill that leads to Chain Bridge. Have a look at the old clock maker's at I Krisztina körút 34, the street running parallel to the west.

The large park just ahead of you to the

north is the **Vérmező**, the 'Blood Field' where Ignác Martonovics and six other pro-republican intellectuals were beheaded in 1795 for plotting against the Habsburgs (see the Castle Hill & Watertown map). Déli station, an eyesore completed in 1977, is across the Vérmező to the west.

Walking Tour 3: Watertown

Víziváros is the narrow area between the Danube and Castle Hill that widens as it approaches Rózsadomb (Rose Hill) and Óbuda to the north-west and north, spreading as far west as Moszkva tér, one of the main transport hubs in Buda. In the Middle Ages, those involved in trades, crafts and fishing – the commoners who couldn't make the socio-economic ascent to the Old Town on Castle Hill – lived here. Under the Turks many of churches here were used as mosques, and baths were built, one of which is still functioning. Today Watertown is an area of apartment blocks, shops and small businesses. It is the heart of urban Buda.

Unless otherwise indicated, sights in this section can be found initially on the Castle Hill & Watertown map (see p 100) and later on the Óbuda & Margaret Island map (see p 112). Notice will be given when to make the switch.

Watertown actually begins at Ybl Miklós tér, but the best place to begin a stroll is at **Clark Ádám tér**. You can reach it on foot from Batthyány tér by walking south along the river or via tram No 19 from Szent Gellért tér. Bus No 16 from Deák tér stops here on its way to/from Castle Hill.

The square is named after the Scottish engineer who supervised the building of **Chain Bridge**, leading from the square, and who designed the tunnel, which took eight months to carve out of the limestone. (The bridge was actually the idea of Count István Széchenyi and is officially named after him.) When the bridge opened in 1849, it was unique for two reasons: it was the first link between Buda and Pest, and the nobility – previously exempted from all taxation – had to pay up like everybody else. The curious sculpture hidden in the bushes to the south that looks like a stretched doughnut is the **0-km stone**; all roads to and from the capital are measured from this point. The dilapidated, weed-covered building with the arcade on the north-west corner was a café before the war.

Fő utca is the main street running through Watertown and dates from Roman times. A French restaurant, popular with staff at the post-modern Institut Français across the road, is in the medieval house below street level at No 20 and has interesting Chinese reliefs above and below the windows. At the former **Capuchin church** at No 30, turned into a mosque by the Turks, you can see the remains of Islamic-style ogee-arch doors and windows on the south side. Around the corner there's the seal of King Matthias Corvinus – a raven and a ring – and the little square is called Corvin tér. The Eclectic building on the north side at No 8 is the **Budai Vigadó**, much less grand than its Pest counterpart and home to the State Folk Ensemble.

Lots of churches can be found along this route, but only one or two are worth a look inside. The neo-Gothic one on Szílagyi Dezső tér is the **Calvinist church** built at the end of the last century. The boat moored along the Danube is a hotel operated by North Koreans. The open deck is a pleasant place for an afternoon drink in the warmer months.

The next square is **Batthyány tér**, the centre of Watertown and the best place to snap a picture of the Parliament building across the Danube. In the centre of the square is the entrance both to the red metro and the HÉV suburban line to Szentendre.

On the south of Batthyány tér is **St Anne's Church**, whose completion in 1805 was the culmination of more than six decades' work because of the interruption caused by floods and an earthquake. It has one of the loveliest baroque interiors of any church in Budapest. The attached building at No 7 was an inn until 1724, then the church presbytery and now a fine café. Batthyány tér was called Upper Market Square in the Middle Ages, but the **market hall** (1902) to the west now

contains just a supermarket and department store. Have a look at the double courtyard at No 4, which housed an elegant inn in the 18th century.

From here on, most sights can be found on the Óbuda & Margaret Island map (see p 112).

A couple of streets north is Nagy Imre tér, with the enormous **Military Court of Justice** on the northern side. Here Imre Nagy and others were tried and sentenced to death in 1958. It was also the site of the notorious **Fő utca prison** where many lesser mortals (but heroes nonetheless) were incarcerated and tortured. It is not pleasant place to linger.

Király Bath, parts of which date from 1580, is one block up at II Fő utca 84. Next to it across Ganz utca is the Greek Catholic **St Florian Chapel**, built in 1760 and dedicated to the patron saint of firefighters. The whole chapel was raised more than a metre in the 1930s after earlier flooding had washed up dirt and silt.

The next square up is **Bem tér**, named after the Pole József Bem who fought on the Hungarian side in the 1848-49 Independence War. In 1956 students from the Technical University rallied in front of the statue here at the start of the uprising.

At the western end of Bem utca at No 20 is the **Foundry Museum**. It may not be to everyone's taste, but it is a lot more interesting than it sounds. The exhibits (cast-iron stoves, bells, furniture) are housed in a foundry that was in use until the 1960s, and the massive ladles and cranes still stand, anxiously awaiting use.

Bem utca joins Margit körút, Buda's share of the 'big ring road', a few streets to the west. If you were to follow it south-west for 10 minutes or so, you'd reach **Széna tér** (see the Castle Hill & Watertown map). This square saw some of the heaviest fighting in Buda during the 1956 Uprising. Moszkva tér, the large square to the south-west, is an important centre for transport connections.

At Bem tér, Fő utca turns into Frankel Leó út, a tree-lined street of expensive antique shops. If you cross Margit körút and continue north, you'll reach Gül Baba utca on the left.

Aristocratic family arms in stone relief

This steep, narrow lane leads to the Tomb of Gül Baba, named after a 16th-century Muslim holy man. Gül Baba was a Dervish who took part in the capture of Buda in 1541 and is known in Hungary as the 'Father of Roses'. Halfway up, just past No 14, there is a set of steps that will take you to the tiny octagonal building and a lookout tower. The tomb is still a pilgrimage place for Muslims, and you must remove your shoes. It contains Islamic furnishings and is open from May to October from 10 am till 6 pm.

Walking north along Frankel Leó út, you'll pass the **Lukács Bath**, one of the city's dirtier spas, at No 25-29. At No 49 and tucked away in an apartment block is the **Újlak Synagogue** built in 1888 on the site of an older prayer house. It is the only functioning synagogue left on the Buda side. To the right of the entrance is an old umbrella maker – a dying breed in this era of cheap Asian imports.

Walking Tour 4: Óbuda & Aquincum

Ó means ancient in Hungarian and, as its name suggests, Óbuda is the oldest part of Budapest. The Romans established Aquin-

cum, the key military garrison of the Roman province of Pannonia and a civilian settlement, near here at the end of the 1st century. When the Magyars came, they named it Buda, which became Óbuda when the Royal Palace was built on Castle Hill and turned into the real centre. Like the Tabán area to the south, Óbuda today is only a shadow of its former self.

Most visitors on their way to Szentendre are put off by what they see of Óbuda from the highway or HÉV commuter train. Prefabricated housing blocks seem to go on forever and the Árpád Bridge flyover splits the heart of the district (Flórián tér) in two. But behind all that are some of the most important Roman ruins in Hungary, noteworthy museums and small, quiet neighbourhoods that still recall the Óbuda of the turn of the century.

Most of the listed items can be found on the Óbuda & Margaret Island map (see p 112). However, some of the later, more northerly, items will be found on the Budapest map (see p 94-95). Notice will be given when to consult the latter.

Flórián tér is the historic centre of Óbuda. You can reach it on the HÉV train from Batthyány tér (Árpád híd stop) or bus No 86 from many points along the Danube on the Buda side. Most people coming from Pest will catch the red metro line to Batthyány tér and board the HÉV. But if you're up near the City Park (Városliget), walk south-east to the intersection of Hungária körút and Thököly út and catch the No 1 tram, which avoids Buda and crosses Árpád Bridge into Óbuda.

Archaeology buffs taking the No 86 bus should descend at Nagyszombat utca (for HÉV passengers, it's the Tímár utca stop), about 800m south of Flórián tér on Pacsirtamező utca, to explore the **Roman Military Amphitheatre** built in the 2nd century for the garrisons. It could accommodate up to 15,000 spectators and was larger than the Colosseum in Rome. The rest of the military camp extended from here north to Flórián tér. The broken-down **Roman Camp Museum** at Pacsirtamező utca 63 has bits and bobs – mostly tools – on display in a dusty room.

If you walk north-west along Bécsi út (the old road to Vienna) from here, you'll reach the **Kiscelli Museum** which towers above Kiscelli utca on the left at No 106. Housed in an 18th-century monastery, later a barracks that was badly damaged in WWII and again in 1956, the exhibits painlessly tell the story of Budapest since liberation from the Turks. The museum has an impressive art collection (Rippl-Rónai, Lajos Tihanyi, István Csók) and a complete 19th-century apothecary moved here from Kálvin tér, but the best are the rooms furnished in Empire, Biedermeier and Art Nouveau furniture that give you a good idea how the affluent merchant class lived in Budapest in the last century.

The yellow baroque **Óbuda Parish Church** dominates the east side of Flórián tér. There's a massive rococo pulpit inside. The large neoclassical building beside the Aquincum hotel at III Lajos utca 163 is the former **Óbuda Synagogue** and now houses sound studios of Hungarian Television (MTV).

A branch of the **Budapest Gallery** directly opposite at Lajos utca 158 has some of the more interesting avant-garde exhibitions in Budapest and has a standing exhibit of works by Pál Pátzay, whose sculptures can be seen throughout the city (for example, the fountain on Tárnok utca on Castle Hill).

In the subway below Flórián tér are Roman objects found in the area; sadly, many of them have been vandalised and covered in graffiti. Still more Roman ruins can be found in the middle of a vast housing estate north-west of Flórián tér at Meggyfa utca 19-21. This is the so-called **Hercules Villa**, whose name derives from the astonishing 3rd-century floor mosaics found in what was a Roman villa.

Two squares north-east of Flórián tér and through the subway contain Óbuda's most important museums. In the former Zichy Mansion at III Szentlélek tér 6-7 is the **Vasarely Museum** devoted to the works of the

'Father of op art', Victor Varsarely (or Vásárhelyi Győző before he emigrated to Paris in 1930). The works, especially ones like *Dirac* and *Tlinko-F*, are excellent and fun to watch as they swell and move around the canvas. On the 1st floor are some of the unusual advertisements Vasarely did for French firms before the war. In the courtyard of the same building (enter at Fő 1) is the unique **Kassák Museum**, a three-room art gallery with some real gems of early 20th-century avant-garde art.

Fő tér is a restored square of baroque houses, public buildings and restaurants. At No 4, the **Zsigmond Kun Collection** displays folk art amassed by a wealthy ethnographer in his 18th-century townhouse. Most of the pottery and ceramics are from Mezőtúr near the Tisza River, but there are some rare Moravian and Swabian pieces and Transylvanian furniture and textiles. The attendants are very proud of the collection, so be prepared for some lengthy explanations. And don't ask about the priceless tile stove that a workman knocked over a few years ago unless you want to see a grown woman cry.

Walking east from Fő tér, in the middle of the street you'll see a group of odd metal sculptures of rather worried-looking women with umbrellas. It is the work of the prolific Imre Varga, who seems to have sat on both sides of the fence politically for decades – sculpting Béla Kun and Lenin as easily as he did St Stephen and Queen St Elizabeth. The **Imre Varga Collection** is housed in a charming townhouse nearby at III Laktanya utca 7.

The HÉV or bus Nos 34 and 43 from Szentlélek tér head north for a few stops to the Roman civilian town of **Aquincum**, the most complete in Hungary. A **Roman aqueduct** used to pass this way from a spring in the nearby park, and remains have been preserved in the median strip of the highway alongside the HÉV railway line. The prosperous town's heyday was in the 2nd and 3rd centuries, lasting until the Huns and assorted other hordes came and ruined everything. Who knows? Had the Romans stayed on,

Hungarian might now be spoken with a lilting Italian accent.

From here on, consult the Budapest map for the location of sights (see p 94-95).

Aquincum had paved streets and fairly sumptuous single-storey houses with courtyards, fountains and mosaic floors as well as sophisticated drainage and heating systems. Not all that is easily apparent today as you walk among the ruins, but you can see their outlines as well as those of the big public baths, market, an early Christian church and a temple dedicated to Mithra, the chief deity of a religion that once rivalled Christianity in its number of believers (see aside).

Mithra & the Great Sacrifice

Mithraism, the worship of the god Mithra, originated in Persia. As Roman rule extended into Asia, the religion became extremely popular with traders, imperial slaves and mercenaries of the Roman army and spread rapidly throughout the empire in the 1st and 2nd centuries AD. The Roman emperors eventually accepted the new faith, and Mithraism was the principle rival of Christianity until Constantine came to the throne in the 4th century.

Mithraism was a mysterious religion with devotees sworn to secrecy. What little is known of Mithra (or Mithras), the god of justice and social contract, has been deduced from reliefs and icons found in sanctuaries and temples like the one at Aquincum. Most of these portray Mithra clad in a Persian-style cap and tunic and sacrificing a white bull in front of Sol, the sun god. From the bull's blood and semen, sprout grain, grapes and living creatures. Sol's wife Soma, the moon, begins her cycle and time is born.

Mithraism and Christianity competed so strongly because of the striking similarity in many of their rituals. Both involve the birth of a deity on 25 December, shepherds, death and resurrection and baptism. Devotees knelt when they worshipped and a common meal – a 'communion' of bread and water – was a regular feature of the liturgy. ∎

The **Aquincum Museum**, Szentendrei út 139, tries to put it all in perspective – unfortunately only in Hungarian. Keep an eye open for the unique 3rd-century water organ (and the mosaic illustrating how it was played), pottery moulds, and floor mosaics from the governor's palace across the river on Óbuda Island. Most of the big sculptures and stone sarcophagi are outside to the left of the museum or behind it along a covered walkway. The complex is open from 9 am till 5 or 6 pm (Monday excluded) from mid-April to October.

Across Szentendrei út is the **Civilian Amphitheatre**, about half the size of the one reserved for the garrisons. Much is left to the imagination, but you can still see the small cubicles where lions were kept and the 'Gate of Death' to the west through which slain gladiators were carried.

North of Aquincum are the outer suburbs of **Rómaifürdő** and **Csillaghegy**, both of them on the HÉV line. The holiday area of Rómaifürdő (Roman Bath) has an open-air thermal pool in a big park and Budapest's largest camping ground. The swimming pool and 'beach' in Csillaghegy is one of the most popular in the city. From the HÉV stop, walk west along Ürömi út for a few minutes to Pusztakúti út.

Walking Tour 5: Margaret Island

Neither Buda nor Pest, 2.5-km-long Margaret Island (Margit-sziget) in the middle of the Danube was always the domain of one religious order or another until the Turks came and turned what was then called the Island of Rabbits into – appropriately enough – a harem, from which all infidels were barred. It's been a public park open to everyone since the mid-19th century, though you may encounter some harem-like activity if you stray too far off the path in the twilight. Unfortunately the island is no longer considered safe at night, and you should probably not walk there alone after dark.

With its large swimming complex, thermal spa, gardens and shaded walkways, the island is a lovely place to spend an afternoon away from the city. You can walk anywhere – on the paths, the shoreline, the grass – but don't try to camp: that's strictly *tilos* (forbidden).

Cross over to Margaret Island from Pest or Buda via tram No 4 or 6. Bus No 26 covers the length of the island as it makes the run between Nyugati station and Árpád Bridge. Cars are allowed on Margaret Island from Árpád Bridge only as far as the two big hotels at the north-eastern end. The rest is reserved for pedestrians and bicyclists. If you follow the shoreline in winter, you'll see thermal water gushing from beneath the island into the river.

You can walk the length of Margaret Island in one direction and return on bus No 26. Or you can rent a bicycle from one of two stands. The first, open between March and October, is on the west side just past the stadium as you walk from Margaret Bridge. It charges 220/800 Ft per hour/day for a basic three-speed, 390 Ft an hour for a tandem bike, and a pedal coach is 740 Ft. The other is at the Bringóvár refreshment stand, near the Japanese Garden in the north of the island and open all year. A bike costs 380 Ft per hour and a pedal coach from 880 to 1400 Ft, depending on how many adults and kids it seats. A twirl around the island in one of the horse-drawn coaches near the hotels costs from 700 Ft per person.

In the roundabout at the end of the access road, the **Centennial Monument** marks the union of Buda, Pest and Óbuda in 1873. A quarter of a century ago was an entirely different era, and the sculptor filled the strange cone with all sorts of socialist symbols. They remain – as if contained in a partially open time capsule.

Margaret Island boasts two popular swimming pools on its west side. The first is the indoor/outdoor **National**, officially named after the Olympic swimming champion Alfréd Hajós, who won the 100m and 1200m races at the first modern Olympiad in 1896 and actually built the place. The **Palatinus**, a large complex of outdoor pools, huge water slides and strands to the north, is a madhouse on a hot summer afternoon, but a good place to watch Hungarians at play. If you want to take all your clothes off, there are single-sex sunbathing decks on the roof of the main building.

Just before you reach the Palatinus, you'll pass the ruins of the 13th-century **Franciscan church and monastery** of which only the tower and a wall still stand. The Habsburg archduke Joseph built a summer residence here when he inherited the island in 1867. It was later converted into a hotel that ran until after WWII.

The octagonal **water tower** (1911) to the north-east rises above the **open-air theatre**, used for opera and plays in summer. Beyond the roundabout is the **Japanese Garden** with lily pads, carp and a small wooden bridge. The raised gazebo in front of you neither plays music nor gushes water, but it's called the **Musical Fountain**, a replica of one in Transylvania.

The Romans used the thermal springs in the north-eastern part of the island and today these sit atop the Margit-sziget Thermal hotel (entrance on the south side). The **thermal bath** is the cleanest, most modern in Budapest, but lacks atmosphere because of that. It's also by far the most expensive at 1200 Ft a go, but you also get to use the swimming pool.

South of the posh Ramada Grand hotel is the reconstructed Romanesque **Church of St Michael**. Its 15th-century bell is real enough; it mysteriously appeared one night in 1914 under the roots of a tree that had been knocked over in a storm. It was probably buried there by monks at the time of the Turkish invasion.

More ruins – but more important ones – lie a few steps south. These are the former **Dominican church and convent** built by Béla IV whose scribes played an important role in the continuation of Hungarian scholarship. Its most famous resident was Béla's daughter, St Margaret (1242-71). As the story goes, the king promised to commit his daughter to a life of devotion in a nunnery if the Mongols were driven from the land. They were and she was – at nine years of age. Still, she seemed to enjoy it – if we're to believe the *Lives of the Saints* – especially the mortification-of-the-flesh parts. St Margaret, only canonised in 1943, commands something of a cult following in Hungary. A red

BUDAPEST

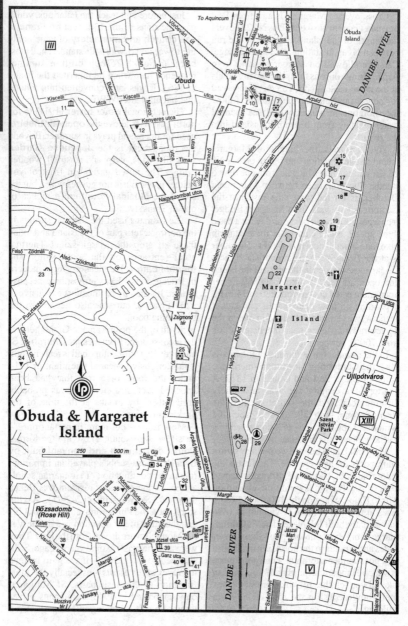

To Aquincum

III

Óbuda

Kiscelli

11

12

13

14

Nagyszombat utca

23

24

Óbuda & Margaret Island

0   250   500 m

Rózsadomb
(Rose Hill)

36

37

38

35

33

34

32

31

39

40

41

42

DANUBE RIVER

Óbuda
Island

Árpád híd

15

16

17

18

19

20

21

Margaret

22

Island

26

27

28

29

Margit híd

Margit

DANUBE RIVER

Újlipótváros

XIII

Szent
István
Park

30

See Central Pest Map

Jászai
Mari
tér

V

PLACES TO STAY
13 San Marco Pension
17 Thermal Hotel & Bath
18 Ramada Grand Hotel
37 Papillon Pension

PLACES TO EAT
1   Don Stefano Pizzeria
5   Sípos Halászkert Restaurant
10 Kéhli Restaurant
12 Kisbuda Gyöngye Restaurant
24 Vadrózsa Restaurant
30 Móri Restaurant
31 Hong Kong Pearl Garden Restaurant
    & Gasztró Butcher Shop
32 La Prima Pizzeria
36 Les Amis Restaurant
38 Marxim Pizzeria
41 Kacsa Restaurant

OTHER
2   Town Hall
3   Imre Varga Sculptures
4   Zsigmond Kun Collection
6   Vasarely Museum
7   Former Óbuda Synagogue
8   Óbuda Parish Church
9   Budapest Gallery
11 Kiscelli Museum
14 Roman Military Amphitheatre
15 Japanese Garden
16 Bringóvár Bike Rentals
19 Church of St Michael
20 Water Tower & Open-Air Theatre
21 Dominican Church & Convent
22 Palatinus Pools
23 Szemlő-hegy Cave
25 Újlak Synagogue
26 Franciscan Church & Monastery Ruins
27 National Pool
28 Bike Rentals & Stadium
29 Centennial Monument
33 Lukács Bath
34 Gül Baba's Tomb
35 Magyar Autóklub
39 Foundry Museum
40 Király Bath
42 Military Court of Justice

marble sepulchre cover marks her original resting place, and there's a much visited shrine with votives nearby.

Walking Tour 6: István körút & Bajcsy-Zsilinszky út

This relatively brief walk crosses over into Pest and follows Szent István körút, the northernmost stretch of the Big Ring Road, to Nyugati tér and then south to Deák tér. You can reach Jászai Mari tér, the start of the walk, via tram Nos 4 and 6 from either side of the river or simply by walking over the bridge from Margaret Island. If you're coming from the inner town in Pest, hop on the waterfront tram No 2 to the terminus.

The following items can be found initially on the Óbuda & Margaret Island map (see p 112). Later on, look for them on the Central Pest map (see p 116).

Two buildings of very different styles and functions face Jászai Mari tér, which is split in two by the foot of the bridge. To the north is an elegant 19th-century block of flats called **Palatinus House**. The modern building south of the square (V Széchenyi rakpart 19) is the **White House**, the former headquarters of the Central Committee of the Hungarian Socialist Workers' Party. It now contains offices of many members of Parliament. If you walk a bit farther north to Szent István Park in the direction of the Calvinist church, with its tall, ugly belfry, you'll see a rarity in Budapest: a row of Bauhaus-style apartments. They may not look like much today after decades of bad copies, but they were the bee's knees when they were built in the late 1920s.

The area north of Szent István körút is called **Újlipótváros** (New Leopold Town) to distinguish it from Lipótváros around Parliament. (Archduke Leopold was the grandson of Habsburg Empress Maria Theresa.) It is a wonderful neighbourhood of tree-lined streets, cafés and boutiques and vaguely reminiscent of uptown Manhattan. The area was upper middle class and Jewish before the war, and many of the 'safe houses' organised by the Swedish diplomat Raoul Wallenberg during WWII were here. A street named after this great man two blocks to the north bears a commemorative plaque.

If you've got the munchies this early on, stop into the Mézes Kuckó (literally 'Honey Nook'), a tiny bakery at Jászai Mari tér 4/a. Their nut and honey cookies are to die for. It is open weekdays from 9 am to 6 pm and to 1 pm on Saturday.

Szent István körút is an interesting street to traipse along; as elsewhere on the Big

Ring Road, most of the Eclectic-style buildings, decorated with Atlases, reliefs and other details, were erected in the last part of the 19th century. Don't hesitate to explore the inner courtyards here and farther on – if Dublin is celebrated for its doors and London for its squares, Budapest should be celebrated for its courtyards.

This stretch of the boulevard is also good for shopping. The **Antikvarium** at No 3, a second-hand bookshop, has excellent old prints and maps for browsing in the chest of drawers at the back. Falk Miksa utca, the next street on the right, and running south, is loaded with pricey antique shops (especially Nos 19 and 32). You can get an idea of what Hungarians are off-loading these days from the second-hand Báv shop on the corner.

The attractive theatre on your left as you continue along Szent István körút is the **Vígszínház** (Gaiety Theatre), a popular venue for comedies and musicals that has recently been renovated. When it was built in 1896, the theatre was criticised for being too far out of the city.

Henceforth, you can find sights on the Central Pest map (see p 116).

You might recognise the large iron and glass structure on Nyugati tér (once known as Marx tér) if you arrived by train from points east or Romania. It's the **Western train station** (Nyugati pályaudvar) built in 1877 by the Paris-based Eiffel company. In the early 1970s a train actually crashed through the enormous glass screen on the main façade when its brakes failed, coming to rest at the tram line. The old restaurant room to the right now houses one of the world's most elegant McDonald's. British travellers will be amused to learn that a 'cheeseburger' in Hungarian is *sajtburger*, roughly pronounced 'SHITE-burger'.

If you look north up Váci út from Nyugati tér, you can see the twin spires of the **Lehel tér church**, a 60-year-old copy of the 13th-century Romanesque church (now in ruins) at Zsámbék, 33 km west of Budapest. The open-air **Lehel tér market** is one of the most colourful in the city.

From Nyugati tér, walk south on Bajcsy-Zsilinszky út for about a km to the **Basilica of St Stephen**, the main sight on this street. This neoclassical structure was built over the course of half a century and not completed until 1906. Much of the interruption had to do with the fiasco in 1868 when the dome collapsed. No one was killed but it certainly must have frightened the horses. The basilica is rather dark and gloomy inside; disappointing for the city's largest and most important Catholic church.

To the right as you enter is a small **treasury** of ecclesiastical objects. Behind the main altar in a small chapel rests the basilica's major draw card: the **Holy Right** (also known as the Holy Dexter). It is the mummified right hand of St Stephen (King Stephen I) and an object of great devotion. Like the Crown of St Stephen in the National Museum, it too was snatched by the bad guys after WWII but was soon, er, handed back.

To view it, follow the signs for 'Szent Jobb' (yes, it's to the right). You have to put a 50 Ft coin into a little machine in front of it to light up the glass casket containing the Right. At almost 1000 years of age, it is – unsurprisingly – not a pretty sight. The treasury and chapel are open from 10 am to 5 pm (4 pm in winter). Concerts are held here on Monday at 7 pm from July to September.

Bajcsy-Zsilinszky út ends at Deák tér, a busy square and the only place where the three metro lines converge. In the subway below near the entrance to the metro is the **Underground Museum**, which gives the history of the three lines and plans for the future. Much emphasis is put on the little yellow metro – Continental Europe's first underground railway – which opened for the millenary celebrations in 1896 and was completely renovated for the millecentenary celebrations in 1996. The best thing in the tiny museum, which costs a metro ticket to get in, are the two old coaches with curved wooden benches. The track they're sitting on and the platform were actually part of the system until some diversions were made in 1973.

In the early part of the century, big foreign insurance companies built their offices at

Deák tér, with huge ones still standing at No 2 and across at No 6. Madách Imre út, running east from the Little Ring Road, was originally designed to be as big and grand a boulevard as nearby Andrássy út. But WWII nipped the plan in the bud and it now ends abruptly after just two blocks.

Walking Tour 7: Northern Inner Town
This district, also called Lipótváros, is full of offices, ministries and 19th-century apartment blocks.

The sights listed here can be found on the Central Pest map (see p 116).

From Deák tér, walk north through Erzsébet tér and west on József Attila utca toward the Danube. **Roosevelt tér**, named after the long-serving (1933-45) American president in 1947, is at the foot of Chain Bridge and offers the best view of Castle Hill.

The statue in the middle of the square is of Ferenc Deák, the Hungarian minister largely responsible for the Compromise in 1867, which brought about the Dual Monarchy of Austria and Hungary. The statues on the west side are of an Austrian and a Hungarian child holding hands in peaceful bliss. The Magyar kid's hair is tussled and he is naked; the Osztrák is demurely covered in a robe, his hair coiffed.

The Art Nouveau building with the gold tiles to the east (Nos 5-6) is the **Gresham Palace**, built by an English insurance company in 1907. There were plans to turn it into a hotel a few years ago, but first they had to dislodge the elderly tenants who refused to budge and then it was found to be structurally unsound. Walk through the passageway below to see the enormous glass dome and intricate wrought-iron gates with peacocks. The **Academy of Sciences**, founded by the late great Count István Széchenyi, is at the northern end of the square. You may recognise it from the verso of the 5000 Ft note.

Szabadság tér (Independence Square), one of the largest squares in the city but ruined by all the parked cars, is a few minutes to the north-east. It has one of Budapest's few remaining monuments to the Soviet army. On the east side at No 12 is the US Embassy, where Cardinal József Mindszenty took refuge for 15 years until leaving for Vienna in 1971 (see aside in the Danube Bend chapter).

South of the embassy is the former **Post Office Savings Bank**, now part of the **Hungarian National Bank** (MNB) next door. The former, an Art Nouveau extravaganza of colourful tiles and folk motifs built by Ödön Lechner in 1900, is completely restored; go around the corner for a better view from Hold utca. (Until recently this street was called Rosenberg házáspár utca in honour of the married couple executed for espionage in the USA in 1953.) Have a look, too, at the reliefs on the MNB building that illustrate trade and commerce through history: Arab camel traders, African rug merchants, Chinese tea salesmen – and the inevitable attorney witnessing contracts.

The large white and yellow building on the west side of the square housed the Budapest Stock Exchange when it was built in 1906. It is now the **headquarters of MTV** – Magyar Televízió (Hungarian Television).

North-west of Szabadság tér is Kossuth Lajos tér, the site of Budapest's most photographed building: the **Parliament** (Országház). This is where the national government sits. Built in 1902, this colossal structure (it has almost 700 rooms and 18 courtyards) is a blend of many architectural styles and in sum works very well. Sadly – though the stonemasons are surely laughing all the way to the bank – the Parliament was surfaced with a porous form of limestone that does not resist pollution very well. Renovations began almost 70 years ago and will continue until the building crumbles.

The Parliament's rooms and halls – all neo-Gothic and baroque murals, gold tracery and marble – are dazzling. You can join a tour (500/200 Ft for adults/students), when Parliament is not in session, daily except Monday and Tuesday. Tours in English leave from Gate XII at 10 am Wednesday to Friday and from Gate VI on weekends (tours in German leave from the same gates on the

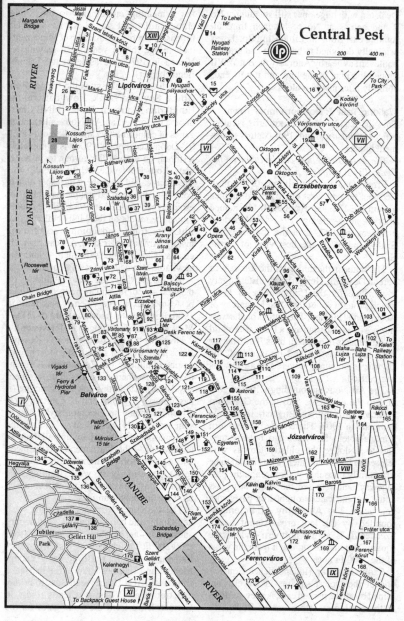

Central Pest

0   200   400 m

To Lehel

Margaret
Bridge

Jászai
Mari tér

Szent István körút

Váci út

To Lehel

Nyugati
Railway
Station

XIII

Vígszínház utca

Balaton utca

Lipótváros

Nyugati
tér

Nyugati
pályaudvar

Falk Miksa utca

Markó

Szondi utca

Izabella utca

Kodály
körönd

Podmaniczky utca

Vörösmarty utca

VII

Honvéd utca

Alkotmány utca

Hold

VI

Vörösmarty utca

Andrássy út

Erzsébetváros

Kossuth
Lajos
tér

Báthory utca

Oktogon

Oktogon

Liszt
Ferenc
tér

Dob utca

Dózsa György út

Bajcsy-Zsilinszky út

Nagymező utca

Teréz körút

Szabadság
tér

Dessewffy utca

Király utca

Wesselényi utca

DANUBE

Akadémia utca

Nádor utca

Hajós utca

Opera

Paulay Ede utca

Király utca

Klauzál
tér

Dob utca

Erzsébet körút

Roosevelt
tér

Arany János utca

Arany
János
utca

V

Szent
István
tér

Bajcsy-
Zsilinszky
út

Nyár utca

Akácfa utca

Wesselényi utca

Chain Bridge

Zrínyi utca

Kazinczy utca

Nagy Diófa utca

Dob utca

József
Attila
utca

Erzsébet
tér

Deák
tér

Deák Ferenc tér

Dohány utca

Blaha
Lujza
tér

Blaha
Lujza
tér

To
Keleti
Railway
Station

Vigadó
tér

Ferry &
Hydrofoil
Pier

Belváros

Vörösmarty
tér

Deák Ferenc utca

Károly körút

Rákóczi út

Rákóczi tér

Petőfi
tér

Kossuth Lajos utca

Ferenciek
tere

Astoria

Kálvin
tér

Múzeum körút

Bródy Sándor utca

Gutenberg
tér

Józsefváros

VIII

Március
15 tér

Egyetem
tér

Krúdy utca

Döbrentei
tér

 Elizabeth
Bridge

Belgrád rakpart

Szerb utca

Üllői út

Baross

Kálvin
tér

József körút

Hegyalja

Döbrentei
tér

Szent Gellért rakpart

DANUBE

Fővám
tér

Vámház körút

Práter utca

Citadella
sétány

Jubilee
Park

Gellért Hill

Szabadság
Bridge

Csarnok
tér

Markusovszky
tér

Ferencváros

Ferenc körút

IX

Tűzoltó utca

Kelenhegyi
út

Szent
Gellért
tér

Bartók Béla út

XI

To Backpack Guest House

Műegyetem rakpart

RIVER

Kinizsi utca

Ferenc körút

PLACES TO STAY
10 City Ring Pension
21 Lotus Hostel
49 Medosz Hotel
79 Forum Hotel
80 Atrium Hyatt Hotel
91 Corvinus Kempinski
    Hotel
101 Metropol Hotel
102 Nemzeti Hotel
133 Duna Marriott Hotel
137 Citadella Hostel/Hotel
152 Ottó & Viktor's Hostel
    (Summer Only)
155 Astoria Hotel
171 Strawberry I Hostel
    (Summer Only)
173 Strawberry II Hostel
    (Summer Only)
176 Gellért Hotel & Baths

PLACES TO EAT
4 Mézes Kucko Bakery
6 123 Restaurant
9 Okay Italia
11 Miyako Ramen
    House
12 Don Pepe Pizzeria
13 Okay Italia
16 Chez Daniel Restau-
    rant
24 Semiramis Middle
    Eastern
    Restaurant
26 Szalai Café
29 Pick Ház Restaurant
32 Tiki/Luak Restaurant
38 Market & Tüköry
    Restaurant
42 Bel Canto Restaurant
46 Művész Café
51 Bombay Palace
    Restaurant
53 Falafel Faloda
57 Jorgosz Restaurant
61 Acapulco Restaurant
67 Café Kör
69 Durcin Sandwich Bar
70 Kisharang Étkezde
72 Xi Hu Restaurant
76 Lou Lou Restaurant
77 Self-Service
    Restaurant
81 Amadeus Restaurant
85 Gerbeaud Café
87 Golden Gastronomia
89 Sushi Restaurant
94 Hannah Kosher
    Restaurant
97 Kádár Étkezde
98 Lammu Takeaway
    Restaurant
99 Grill 99

100 New York Café
104 Chicago Restaurant
108 Orchidea Restaurant
112 Scampi Restaurant
114 Fausto's Restaurant
129 Bölcs Bagoly Self-
    Service Restaurant
131 Cyrano Restaurant
139 Capella Café
141 Govinda Indian
    Vegetarian Restaurant
142 Pertu Station Pub-
    Restaurant
143 Taverna Dionysos
146 Fatál & Chan-Chan
    Restaurants
148 Cabar Restaurant
149 Vegetárium
    Restaurant
153 Stop Restaurant
158 Múzeum Restaurant
160 Kalocsa Pince
    Restaurant
164 Görög Csemege
166 Il Treno Pizzeria

BARS & CLUBS
2 Jazz Café
8 Franklin Trocadero
    Club
14 Bahnhof Disco
18 Hades Jazztaurant
23 Becketts Pub
39 Mystery Bar
41 Picasso Point (Club)
43 Morrison's Music Pub
48 Rocktogon Club
54 Café Incognito
105 Black Horse Club
110 Portside Pub
119 No Limit Club
122 Merlin Jazz Club
140 Kalamajka Táncház
    (Club)
147 Fat Mo's Speakeasy
154 Janis Pub
156 Talk Talk Café
157 Action Bar
162 Nothing But the Blues
    Club
168 Guillotine Live Music
    Club
170 Fél Tíz Jazz Club
172 Paris Texas (Club)

**TOURIST OFFICES
& BOOKING AGENCIES**
20 Volántourist
27 Cooptourist
30 Express (Train
    Tickets)
33 Express (Hostel
    Bookings)

44 Színházak Központi
    Jegyiroda
    (Ticket Office)
50 MÁV Ticket Office
64 Dunatours
75 Budapest Tourist
83 Malév Office
84 Nemzeti Filharmónia
    Jegyiroda
    (Ticket Office)
117 Ibusz (Train Tickets)
118 Express (Main Office)
123 Ibusz Main Office
    (Private Rooms)
125 Tourinform

MUSEUMS
19 Ferenc Liszt Museum
25 Ethnography Museum
59 Stamp Museum
63 Post Office Museum
95 Electrotechnology
    Museum
113 Jewish Museum
159 National Museum
169 Museum of Applied
    Arts

OTHER
1 White House
3 Antikvárium
    Bookshop & Báv
    Shop
5 OTP Bank
7 Vígszínház (Gaiety
    Theatre)
15 Post Office
17 Budapest Puppet
    Theatre
22 Kaiser's Supermarket
28 Parliament
31 Imre Nagy Monument
34 MTV Building
35 Soviet Army Memorial
36 US Embassy
37 Hungarian National
    Bank Building
40 Cartographia Map
    Store
45 State Opera House
47 City Operetta Theatre
52 Ferenc Liszt Music
    Shop
55 Café Mediterán
56 Liszt Academy of
    Music
58 National Theatre
60 Madách Theatre
62 János Arany Theatre
65 Inka Car Rental
66 Basilica of St Stephen
68 Bestsellers Bookshop
(continued next page)

BUDAPEST

OTHER (cont.)	107	Rothschild Kosher	134	Rác Baths
71 Boutique des Vins		Supermarket	135	Ivócsarnok
(Wine Shop)	109	Uránia Cinema	136	Rudas Baths
73 Central European	111	Laundrette	138	Independence
University	113	Great Synagogue		Monument
74 Duna Palota	115	OTP Bank	144	International Ferry
75 Gresham Palace	116	K&H Bank		Pier
78 Academy of Science	120	Holló Atelier (Folk	145	K&H Bank
82 Pesti Vigadó (Concert		Craft)	150	Serbian Orthodox
Hall)	121	City Hall		Church
86 OTP Bank	123	Parizsi Udvar	151	Demi John Wine Shop
88 American Express	124	Main Post Office	161	Ervin Szabó Library
90 UK Embassy	126	International	163	Kenguru Ride Service
92 Erzsébet tér Bus		Telephone Centre	165	Joseph Town Market
Station	127	International	167	Corvin Cinema
93 Central Police Station		Bookstore	174	Central Market Hall
96 Ghetto Market	128	Folkart Centrum		(Nagycsarnok)
103 Julius Meinl	130	Inner Town Parish	175	Cliff Chapel
Supermarket		Church		
106 Map Store	132	Ibusz 24-Hour Office		

same days at 11 am). For information, go to Gate X.

Opposite Parliament at V Kossuth Lajos tér 12 is the **Ethnography Museum**. As Hungary's largest indoor folk collection, it is a big disappointment. The building itself, designed in 1893 to house the Supreme Court, is worth a look – especially the massive central hall with its marble columns and ceiling fresco of *Justice* by Károly Lotz. But the 13 rooms on the 1st floor devoted to folk art and culture from the 18th century on contain worn-out exhibits that look like they haven't been changed or dusted in decades. Still, it's an easy introduction to traditional Hungarian life, the labels are also in English and the mock-ups of peasant houses from the Őrség and Sárköz regions of Transdanubia are pretty well done.

South of the museum and past the Ministry of Agriculture in Vértanúk tere is a **statue of Imre Nagy**, the reformist Communist prime minister executed in 1958 for his role in the uprising two years before. It was unveiled to great ceremony in the summer of 1996.

Walking Tour 8: Inner Town

The Belváros is the heart of Budapest and contains the most expensive real estate in the city. But this inner town has something of a split personality. North of Ferenciek tere is the 'have' side with the flashiest boutiques, the biggest hotels, some expensive restaurants and the most tourists. You'll often hear more German, Italian and English spoken here than Hungarian. Until recently the south was the 'have not' section – studenty, quieter and more Hungarian. Now it too has become pedestrian and is filling up with trendy clubs, cafés and restaurants. It is the beginning of what is now called the SoKo district – short for 'south of Kossuth' utca.

The sights listed here can be found on the Central Pest map (see p 116).

You can decide which part of the inner town you want to explore first; we'll start with the latter. Busy Ferenciek tere, which divides the inner town at Szabad sajtó út, is on the blue metro line and can be reached by bus No 7 from Buda or points east in Pest. To get here from the end of the last tour, take bus No 15 or tram No 2 along the Danube.

The centre of this part of the inner town is Egyetem tér (University Square), a five-minute walk south along Károly Mihály utca from Ferenciek tere. The square's name refers to the branch of the prestigious **Loránd Eötvös Science University** (ELTE) at No 1-3. Next to the university building is the

University Church, a lovely baroque structure built in 1748. Inside are a carved pulpit and pews and over the altar a copy of the Black Madonna of Częstochowa so revered in Poland. The church is often full of young people – presumably those who haven't paid a visit to András Hadik's horse on Castle Hill (see Walking Tour 1).

Kecskeméti utca runs south-east from the square to Kálvin tér. It is a leafy street with a number of cafés, clubs and restaurants. At the end, near the Korona hotel on Kálvin tér, there's a plaque marking the location of the **Kecskemét Gate**, part of the medieval city wall that was pulled down in the 1700s. If you want to see a largish section still standing, turn north on Magyar utca to No 28 and go through the passageway to the courtyard that leads to Múzeum körút. You can't miss the walls.

Just north of Egyetem tér at V Károlyi Mihály utca 16, the **Literature Museum** has rooms devoted to Sándor Petőfi, Endre Ady, Mór Jókai and Attila József. But even these great authors' works are not easy to obtain (or translate) in English and probably won't mean much to most travellers. The building with the multicoloured dome nearby at V Ferenciek tere 10 is the **University Library**.

South-west of the square, at Szerb utca and Veres Pálne utca, stands the **Serbian Orthodox church** built by Serbs fleeing the Turks in the 17th century. The iconostasis is worth a look, but entry to the church is sometimes difficult.

There are a couple of interesting sights along **Veres Pálné utca**. The building at No 19 has bronze reliefs above the 2nd floor illustrating various stages of building in the capital. At the corner of the next street, Papnövelde utca, the large university library building at No 4-10 is topped with little Greek temples on either side of the block. A few steps north, Szivárvány köz – Rainbow Alley – is one of the narrowest streets in the city.

The best way to see the posher side of the inner town is to walk up pedestrian Váci utca, the capital's premier – and most expensive – shopping street. This was the total length of Pest in the Middle Ages. At V Ferenciek tere 5, walk through the **Párizsi Udvar** (Parisian Court), a decorated arcade with a domed ceiling, out onto tiny Kigyó utca. Váci utca is immediately to the west.

Váci utca has boutiques with designer clothes, antique jewellery shops, pubs and some bookshops for browsing. Until recently it was Budapest's answer to Regent St and the only place where luxury goods were easily obtainable. Now that sort of thing is available everywhere.

Make a little detour by turning right (east) on Haris köz – once a privately owned street – and continue across Petőfi Sándor utca to Kamermayer Károly tér, a lovely little square with antique shops and boutiques, an old umbrella maker's, an artsy café and, in the centre, a statue of Mr Kamermayer, united Budapest's first mayor. On the south-east corner of the square at V Városház utca 7 is the green **Pest county hall** (the city of Budapest is in the county of Pest), a large neoclassical building with three courtyards that you can walk through during office hours. North of the square at V Városház utca 9-11 is the 18th-century **city hall**, a rambling red and yellow structure that is the largest baroque building in the city.

Szervita tér is at the northern end of Városház utca. Naturally there's a **baroque church** (1732), but much more interesting are the buildings to the west. You'd probably never guess, but the modern one at No 5 was built in 1912. Look up to the gable at No 3; the Art Nouveau mosaic of *Hungaria* dates from the turn of the century. You can return to Váci utca via Régiposta utca.

Many of the buildings on Váci utca are worth a closer look, but as it's a narrow street you'll have to crane your neck or walk into one of the side lanes for a better view. **Thonet House** at 11/a is another masterpiece built by Ödön Lechner (1890), and the **Philanthia** flower shop at No 9 has an original Art Nouveau interior. To the west, at Régiposta utca 13, there's a relief of an old postal coach by the ceramist Margit Kovács of Szentendre. The souvenir shop here always displays items of the same colour in its front window.

At the top of Váci utca, across from Kristóf tér with the little **fishergirl well**, is a brick outline of the foundations of the **Vác Gate**, part of the old city wall. The street leads into **Vörösmarty tér**, an enormous square of smart shops, galleries, airline offices and, in the warmer months, an outdoor market of stalls selling tourist schlock and artists who will draw your portrait or caricature. Suitable for framing – maybe...

In the centre is a statue of the 19th-century poet after whom Vörösmarty tér was named. It is made of Italian marble and is protected in winter with a straw and burlap covering. The first stop of the little yellow metro line is also in the square, and at the northern end is **Gerbeaud**, Budapest's fanciest and most famous café and cake shop. Stop here for at least a cup of coffee and a dobos torta. The Kisgerbeaud cake shop on the east side of the building does takeaway.

The despised modern building on the west side of Vörösmarty tér (No 1) contains a large music shop and the main ticket office for concerts in the city. South of it at Deák utca 5 is the sumptuous **Bank Palace**, built in 1915 and completely renovated. It now houses the Budapest Stock Exchange.

The **Pesti Vigadó**, the Romantic-style concert hall built in 1865 but badly damaged during the war, faces the river on Vigadó tér to the west. But before proceeding, have a look in the foyer at Vigadó utca 6. It has one of the strange lifts nicknamed 'Pater Noster' (supposedly their resemblance to a large rosary) that can still be found in some public buildings here. It's a rotating series of individual cubicles that run continuously; you hop on just as one reaches the floor level. If you were wondering what happens at the top, stay on and find out (don't worry; you'll live).

A pleasant way to return to Ferenciek tere is along the **Duna korzó**, the riverside walkway between Chain and Elizabeth bridges and above Belgrád rakpart that is full of cafés, musicians and handicraft stalls by day and hookers and hustlers by night. The Duna korzó leads into Petőfi tér, named after the poet of the 1848-49 Independence War and the scene of political rallies (both legal and illegal) over subsequent years. Március 15 tér, which marks the date of the outbreak of the revolution, abuts it to the south.

On the east side of Március 15 tér, sitting uncomfortably close to the Elizabeth Bridge flyover, is the **Inner Town parish church** where a Romanesque church was first built in the 12th century within a Roman fortress. You can see a few bits of the fort, **Contra Aquincum**, outside in the centre of the square. The church was rebuilt in the 14th and 18th centuries, and you can easily spot Gothic and baroque elements both inside and out. Two of the side chapels have 16th-century Renaissance tabernacles and the fifth one on the right is pure Gothic. There's a mihrab (Muslim prayer nook) in the chancel from the time when the Turks used the church as a mosque.

Behind the church is the arts faculty of ELTE. The two grand buildings flanking the western end of Ferenciek tere on Szabad sajtó út are the so-called **Klotild Palaces** built in 1902.

Walking Tour 9: Andrássy út & the City Park

This is a rather long tour starting at Deák tér and following the most attractive boulevard in Budapest. The yellow metro runs just below Andrássy út from Deák tér to the City Park, so if you begin to lose your stamina, just go down and jump on.

The listed sights can first be found on the Central Pest map (see p 116). Later, where indicated, you should turn to the City Park map (see p 122).

Join Andrássy út a short way north of Deák tér as it splits away from Bajcsy-Zsilinszky út. This section of Andrássy is lined with plane trees – cool and pleasant on a warm day. The **Post Office Museum** is at No 3. While the exhibits won't do much for you, the museum is housed in the seven-room apartment of a wealthy turn-of-the-century businessman and is among the best preserved in the city. Even the communal staircase and hallway are richly decorated with fantastic murals. In the museum itself, much is made of Tivadár Puskás, a Hungarian associate of Thomas Edison, and of the latter's very brief visit to Budapest in 1891.

The neo-Renaissance **State Opera House** on the left at No 22 was designed by Miklós Ybl in 1884, and for many it is the city's most beautiful building. The interior is especially lovely and once again sparkles after a total overhaul in the 1980s. If you cannot attend a concert or an opera, join one of the tours every day at 3 and 4 pm. Tickets (500/250 Ft for adults/students) are available from the office on the east side of the building (Hajós utca), and the tour includes a brief musical performance. When buying tickets to a performance, avoid the cheapest ones as you'll have to enter by a side entrance for the top floor and miss all the grand *salles*.

The building across from the Opera House, the so-called **Drechsler House**, was designed by the Art Nouveau master builder Ödön Lechner in 1882 and now houses the **State Ballet Institute**. You can explore the interior courtyard from the west side (Dalszínház utca), but go around the corner for something even more magical: an Art Deco gem embellished with monkey faces, globes and geometric designs that is now the **János Arany Theatre** (also called the New Theatre) at VI Paulay Ede utca 35.

The old-world **Művész** (Artist) café at Andrássy út 29 serves some of the best pastries in the city 24 hours a day. Across the street is the theatre avenue of Nagymező utca, hardly 'the Broadway of Budapest' but counting a number of theatres. The main MÁV ticket and information centre is nearby at Andrássy út 35.

The **Divatcsarnok** at No 39, the fanciest emporium in town when it opened as the Grand Parisian in 1911, is now just another Hungarian department store (Centrum) except for the so-called **Lotz Hall** on the mezzanine floor. The room is positively dripping with gilt, frescos and marquetry.

The Big Ring Road meets Andrássy út at **Oktogon**, a busy intersection full of fast-food places, shops and people selling junk on the street. Teréz körút runs to the northwest (where we'll make a quick detour) and for a block to the south-east where it

becomes Erzsébet körút. Until 1989 both were named Lenin körút.

This stretch of Teréz körút looks much like the rest of the boulevard, with grand apartment blocks and lovely courtyards (check the superb one at No 33). The little Butterfly shop at Teréz körút 20 *(not* the one next door called Vajassütemények) has the best ice cream in the city.

Beyond Oktogon, Andrássy út is lined with very grand buildings, housing such institutions as the **Budapest Puppet Theatre** (No 69), the **Academy of Fine Arts** at No 71 and **MÁV** headquarters at No 73-75. The former **secret police building** at No 60 has a ghastly history, for it was here that many activists of whatever political side that was out of fashion before and after WWII were taken for interrogation and torture. The plaque outside reads in part: 'We cannot forget the horror of terror, and the victims will always be remembered'.

The **Ferenc Liszt Memorial Museum** is across the street (entrance at VI Vörösmarty utca 35). The composer lived in the apartment on the 1st floor from 1881 until his death in 1886, and the four rooms are filled with his pianos (including a tiny glass one), composer's table, portraits and personal effects. It's open weekdays till 6 pm and on Saturday till 5 pm.

From here on, listed items can be found on the City Park map (see p 122).

The next square (more accurately a circus) is Kodály körönd, one of the most beautiful in the city, though the four neo-Renaissance townhouses are in bad shape, especially the former residence of the composer Zoltán Kodály at No 1. Just beyond the circus at VI Andrássy út 98 is the neo-Renaissance **Palavicini Palace**, the seat of a profascist family who once owned most of the town of Szilvásvárad in the Bükk Hills.

The last stretch of Andrássy út and the surrounding neighbourhoods are packed with stunning old mansions that are among the most desirable addresses in the city. It won't come as a surprise to see that embassies, ministries, political parties and multinationals have moved in.

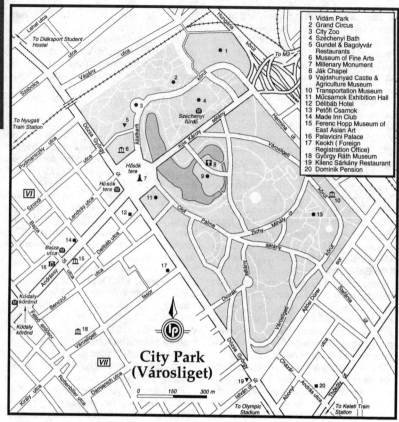

1 Vidám Park
2 Grand Circus
3 City Zoo
4 Széchenyi Bath
5 Gundel & Bagolyvár
   Restaurants
6 Museum of Fine Arts
7 Millenary Monument
8 Ják Chapel
9 Vajdahunyad Castle &
   Agriculture Museum
10 Transportation Museum
11 Műcsarnok Exhibition Hall
12 Délibáb Hotel
13 Petőfi Csarnok
14 Made Inn Club
15 Ferenc Hopp Museum of
   East Asian Art
16 Palavicini Palace
17 Keokh (Foreign
   Registration Office)
18 György Ráth Museum
19 Kilenc Sárkány Restaurant
20 Dominik Pension

City Park
(Városliget)

The **Ferenc Hopp Museum of East Asian Art** is at VI Andrássy út 103 in the former villa of its collector and benefactor. Founded in 1919, the museum has a fairly good collection of Indonesian *wayang* puppets, Indian statuary and lamaist sculpture and scroll paintings from Tibet. There's an 18th-century Chinese moon gate in the back garden, but most of the Chinese and Japanese collection of ceramics and porcelain, textiles and sculpture is housed in the **György Ráth Museum** at VI Városligeti fasor 12, a few minutes walk south on Bajza utca and then

west. It's an incredibly beautiful Art Nouveau residence.

Andrássy út ends at **Hősök tere** (Heroes Square), which has the nation's most solemn monument – with an empty coffin representing one of the unknown insurgents from the 1956 Uprising below it – and guard of honour. This is where visiting dignitaries are taken to lay wreaths and pay their respects.

The square is essentially the **Millenary Monument**, a 36m pillar backed by colonnades to the right and left. About to take off from the top of the pillar is the Angel Gabriel, who is offering Vajk – the future King

Stephen – the Hungarian crown. At the base are Árpád and the six other Magyar chieftains who occupied the Carpathian Basin in the late 9th century. The statues and reliefs in and on the colonnades are of rulers and statesmen. The four allegorical figures atop are (from left to right): Work & Welfare, War, Peace, Knowledge & Glory.

South of the square is the **Műcsarnok**, an exhibition hall built around the time of the millenary exhibition in 1896 and renovated a century later. It is used for temporary art exhibits. South of the hall, along the parade grounds of Dózsa György út, stood the 25m statue of Joseph Stalin pulled down by demonstrators on the first night of the 1956 Uprising.

Across Heroes' Square to the north is the **Museum of Fine Arts** (1906), housing the city's outstanding collection of foreign works. The Old Masters collection is the most complete, with thousands of works from the Flemish, Spanish, Italian, German, French and British schools between the 13th and 18th centuries. Other sections include 19th and 20th-century paintings, watercolours and graphics, sculpture and Egyptian and Greco-Roman artefacts. One particularly fine exhibit displays *fin-de-siècle* symbolist works.

Heroes' Square sits at the entrance to the **Városliget** (City Park), which hosted most of the events during Hungary's 1000th anniversary celebrations in 1896. Almost a square km in area, it is the largest park in Budapest and still has plenty to entertain visitors. This is not Margaret Island though; don't count on a quiet stroll under the trees. Instead, expect to have fun at a ramshackle amusement park, a large thermal bath, a couple of museums or a large concert hall.

The **City Zoo** (Állatkert) is a five-minute walk to the west along Állatkerti út, past **Gundel**, Budapest's – and Hungary's – most famous restaurant. The zoo has a good collection of animals (big cats, rhinos, hippopotamuses), but unfortunately most are in cramped, dirty quarters which are, however, being renovated. Some visitors come here just to look at the Art Nouveau animal houses

built in the early part of this century, such as the **Elephant House** with pachyderm heads in beetle-green Zsolnay ceramic and the **Palm House** built by the Eiffel company of Paris. The zoo is open every day from 9 am till 7 pm in summer and to 4 pm in winter. Nearby is the permanent **Grand Circus,** which has performances weekdays (except Monday and Tuesday) at 3 pm and 7 pm and on weekends at 10 am.

The large castle on the little island in the lake, which is transformed into a skating rink in winter, is **Vajdahunyad Castle**, partly modelled after a fortress in Transylvania, but with Gothic, Romanesque and baroque wings and additions to reflect architectural styles from all over Hungary. The castle was erected as a temporary canvas structure for the millenary exhibition in 1896 but proved so popular that the same architect was commissioned to build it in stone.

The stunning baroque wing, incorporating designs from castles and mansions around the country, now houses the **Agricultural Museum**. After a visit here there's not much you won't know about Hungarian fruit production, cereals, wool, poultry and pig slaughtering – if that's what you want. The little church opposite is called **Ják Chapel**, but only its portal is copied from the 13th-century Abbey Church in Ják in Western Transdanubia.

The statue of the **hooded scribe** south of the chapel is that of Anonymous, the unknown chronicler at the court of King Béla III who wrote a history of the early Magyars. Writers (real and aspirant) touch his pen for inspiration. In the park south of the Agricultural Museum, Americans – or anyone who's ever looked at a greenback – will spot a familiar face. The **statue of George Washington** was erected by Hungarian Americans in 1906.

The gigantic 'wedding cake' building north-east of the lake just off XIV Kós Károly sétány is the **Széchenyi Bath**, which has indoor and outdoor thermal pools open year-round. It's an unusual bath for Budapest for three reasons: its immense size; its bright, clean look; and its water temperatures, which really are what the wall plaques say they are. East of the bath is **Vidám Park**, a rumble-tumble little amusement ground with a rickety wooden roller coaster, Ferris wheel and fun house that would be the perfect setting for one of those luna park murder mysteries or films. Most of the amusements are open only between April and September.

OK, it doesn't sound like a crowd-pleaser, but the **Transportation Museum**, in the City Park at XIV Városligeti körút 11, is one of the most enjoyable in Budapest and great for children. In an old and a new wing there are scale models of ancient trains (some of which run), classic turn-of-the-century automobiles and lots of those old wooden bicycles they called 'bone-shakers'. There are a few hands-on exhibits and lots of show-and-tell from the attendants. Outside are pieces from the original Danube bridges that were retrieved after the bombings of WWII. The museum's **air and space-travel exhibit** is housed in the Petőfi Csarnok, a large hall nearby at XIV Zichy Mihály utca 14, better known for its rock and pop concerts (see the Entertainment section).

The surrounding streets on the south-east corner of the City Park are loaded with gorgeous buildings, residences and embassies. Some of my favourites are on **Stefánia út** (for example, the Geological Institute at No 14), but for something close by, just walk across Hermina utca to the Art Nouveau masterpiece at No 49, which now houses the Institute for the Blind.

Walking Tour 10: Oktogon to Blaha Lujza tér

The Big Ring Road slices district VII (also called Erzsébetváros or Elizabeth Town) in two between these busy squares. The eastern side is a rather poor area with little of interest to visitors except the Keleti train station on Baross tér. The western side, bounded by the Little Ring Road, has always been predominantly Jewish, and this was the ghetto where Jews were forced to live behind wooden fences when the Nazis occupied Hungary in 1944. From an estimated 800,000 people nationwide before the war, the Jewish population has dwindled to about 80,000 through wartime executions, deportations and emigration.

The sights listed below can be found on the Central Pest map (see p 116) unless otherwise indicated.

Your starting point, Oktogon, is on the yellow metro line. It can also be reached via tram Nos 4 and 6 from both Buda and Pest.

The **Liszt Academy of Music** is one block east of Oktogon at Liszt tér 8; and the small **Stamp Museum** is at VII Hársfa utca 47 to the south-east. The academy, built in 1907, attracts students from all over the world and is one of the top venues in Budapest for concerts. The interior, richly embellished with Zsolnay porcelain and frescos, is worth a look even if you're not attending a performance. But there are always cheap tickets available to something – perhaps a recital. The box office is at the end of the main hall from the entrance at Király utca 64.

If you walk west on Király utca you'll pass a lovely neo-Gothic house (No 47) built in 1847, and, almost opposite, the **Church of St Teresa** (1811) with a massive neoclassical altar and chandelier. **Klauzál tér**, the heart of the old Jewish quarter, is a couple of streets south down Csányi utca.

The square and surrounding streets still give you a feeling of prewar Budapest. Signs of a continued Jewish presence are still evident – in a kosher bakery at Kazinczy utca 28, a delicatessen at Kazinczy utca 41, a butcher's at Dob utca 35 and the tumble-down Frölich cake shop and café at No 22, which has old Jewish favourites.

There are about half a dozen synagogues and prayer houses in the district once reserved for conservatives, the orthodox, Poles, Sephardics, etc. The **Orthodox Synagogue**, at VII Kazinczy utca 29-31 (or enter from Dob utca 35), has been given a face-lift as has the Moorish **Conservative Synagogue** (1872) at VII Rumbach Sebestyén utca 11.

But none compares with the **Great Synagogue** at VII Dohány utca 2-8, the largest anywhere in the world outside New York. Built in 1859 with romantic and Moorish elements, the copper-domed synagogue has been under renovation since 1988 with funds raised by the Hungarian government and a New York-based charity headed by the actor Tony Curtis, whose parents emigrated from Hungary in the 1920s. The organ, dating back to 1859, has been completely rebuilt and concerts are held here in summer.

The **Jewish Museum** is in the annexe to the left, next to the plaque noting that Theodore Herzl, the father of modern Zionism, was born at this site in 1860. The museum's four rooms contain objects related to religious and everyday life, and an interesting hand written book of the local Burial Society from the 18th century. The last room – dark and sombre – relates the events of 1944-45, including the infamous mass murder of doctors and patients at a hospital on Maros utca. The museum is open from April to October on weekdays from 10 am to 3 pm and on Sunday to 1 pm.

The **Holocaust Memorial** (Imre Varga, 1989) on the Wesselényi utca side of the synagogue stands over the mass graves of those murdered by the Nazis in 1944-45. On the leaves of the metal 'tree' are the family names of some of the 400,000 victims. Nearby, in front of Dob utca 12, there's an unusual antifascist **monument to Carl Lutz**, a Swiss consul who, like Raoul Wallenberg, provided Jews with false papers during the war. It portrays an angel on high sending down a golden bolt of cloth to a victim.

The **Electrotechnology Museum** at VII Kazinczy utca 21 doesn't sound like everyone's cup of tea, but the staff are very enthusiastic and some of the exhibits are unusual enough to warrant a visit. Its collection of electricity-consumption meters, one of the largest in the world, is not very inspiring though they have one that was installed in the apartment of 'Rákosi Mátyás elvtárs' (Comrade Mátyás Rákosi), the Communist Party secretary on his 60th birthday in 1952.

The staff will also show you how the alarm system of the barbed-wire fence between Hungary and Austria worked. Apparently high winds triggered alarms through the entire system and it was often switched off –

allowing those in the know to make a dash for it. There's also an exhibit on the nesting platforms that the electric company kindly builds for storks throughout the country so they won't interfere with the wires and electrocute themselves. The museum is open Tuesday to Saturday from 11 am till 5 pm.

Rákóczi út, a busy shopping street, leads to **Blaha Lujza tér**, named after a leading turn-of-the-century actor. The subway under the square is one of the most lively in the city, with hustlers, beggars, peasants selling their wares, Peruvian musicians and, of course, pickpockets. The 18th-century **St Rókus Chapel**, at Rákóczi út 27/a, is a cool oasis away from all the chaos.

North of Blaha Lujza tér at Erzsébet körút 9-11 is the Art Nouveau New York Palace and the famous **New York Café**, scene of many a literary gathering over the years. Find your way through the scaffolding – it's been here since the 1956 Uprising – have a cup of coffee and enjoy the splendour.

The city's 'other' opera house, the **Erkel Theatre**, is at VIII Köztársaság tér 30, southeast of this stretch of Rákóczi út (see the Budapest map). From the outside, you'd never guess it was built in 1911. The building at No 26-27 is the former **Communist Party headquarters** from which members of the secret police were dragged and shot by demonstrators on 30 October 1956.

Rákóczi út ends at Baross tér and **Keleti train station**. It was built in 1884 and renovated a century later. About half-a-km south on Fiumei út (tram No 23 or 24) is the entrance to **Kerepesi Cemetery** (see the Budapest map), Budapest's Highgate or Père Lachaise and deathly quiet during the week. The flower shop at the entrance sometimes has maps for sale, but you can strike out on your own, looking at the graves of creative and courageous men and women whose names have now been given to streets, squares and bridges.

Some of the mausoleums are worthy of a Pharaoh, especially those of statesmen and national heroes like Lajos Kossuth, Ferenc Deák and Lajos Batthyány; others are quite moving (Lujza Blaha, Endre Ady). Plot 21 contains the graves of many who died in the 1956 Uprising. Near the huge mausoleum for party honchos, which is topped with the words 'I lived for Communism, for the people', is the simple grave of János Kádár, who died in 1989, and his wife Mária Tamáska. The grave of József Antall, 'new' Hungary's first prime minister, who died in 1993, is marked by a simple cross.

If you're into necropolises, you can reach the **Új köztemető**, Budapest's huge 'new municipal cemetery' on the far eastern side of town in district X, on bus No 95 from Baross tér or tram No 28 from Blaha Lujza tér. It would be just another huge city cemetery if Imre Nagy, prime minister during the 1956 Uprising, and 2000 others hadn't been buried here in unmarked graves (plot Nos 300-301) after executions in the late 1940s and 1950s.

Today, the area has been turned into a moving **National Pantheon**, which stipulates that 'Only with a Hungarian soul can you pass through the gate'. The Transylvanian-style notched posts mark the graves of some of the victims. The area is about a 30-minute walk from the entrance; walk eastward on the main road till you reach the end (and a yellow building), then head north. There are some signs pointing the way to '300, 301 parcela' but not enough, so be alert. At peak periods you can take a microbus marked *'temető jarat'* around the cemetery or hire a taxi at the gate.

Walking Tour 11: Blaha Lujza tér to Petőfi Bridge

From Blaha Lujza tér, the Big Ring Road runs through district VIII, also called Józsefváros or Joseph Town. The west side transforms itself from a neighbourhood of lovely 19th-century townhouses and villas around the Little Ring Road to a large student quarter. East of the boulevard is the rough-and-tumble district so poignantly described in the Pressburger brothers' *Homage to the Eighth District*. Dilapidated entrances give way to dark and foreboding courtyards with few traces left of the dignified comfort

enjoyed by the bourgeois residents in the early part of the century. It is also the area where much of the fighting in October 1956 took place.

The sights listed below can be found on the Central Pest map unless otherwise indicated (see p 116).

Rákóczi tér, the only real square on the Big Ring Road, is as good a place as any to get a feel for this area. It is the site of the busy **Joseph Town Market**, erected in 1897 and renovated in the early 1990s after a bad fire. The square is also the unofficial headquarters of Budapest's low-rent prostitutes who you'll see calling out to anyone who'll listen in Hungarian or German as early as 8 am. Sex-show and topless nightclubs line both József körút and Ferenc körút to the south.

Across the boulevard, Bródy Sándor utca runs west from Gutenberg tér (with a lovely Art Nouveau building at No 4) to the old **Hungarian Radio Building** at No 5-7, where shots were first fired on 23 October 1956. Beyond it, at VIII Múzeum körút 14-16, is the **National Museum**, the largest in the country.

The museum, designed by Mihály Pollack, opened in 1847 and a year later was the scene of a momentous event (though, as always, not recognised as such at the time). On 15 March a crowd gathered to hear the poet Sándor Petőfi recite *Nemzeti Dal* (National Song), a prelude to the 1848-49 Revolution.

The National Museum contains the most cherished object in Hungary: the **Crown of St Stephen** (see aside).

It is on display, together with the ceremonial sword, orb, and the oldest object among the coronation regalia, the 10th-century sceptre with a crystal head, in a darkened room to the left as you enter the museum. In another glass case is the crimson silk coronation robe stitched by nuns at Veszprém in 1031. The silver chests in the room were used to carry the regalia during the coronations of Franz Joseph in 1867 and of the last Habsburg king of Hungary, Charles IV, in 1916.

At the time of writing the museum was

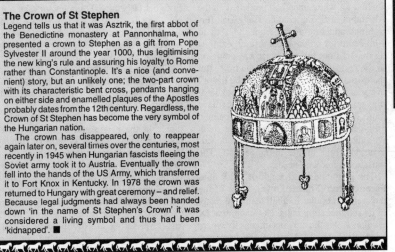

The Crown of St Stephen
Legend tells us that it was Asztrik, the first abbot of the Benedictine monastery at Pannonhalma, who presented a crown to Stephen as a gift from Pope Sylvester II around the year 1000, thus legitimising the new king's rule and assuring his loyalty to Rome rather than Constantinople. It's a nice (and convenient) story, but an unlikely one; the two-part crown with its characteristic bent cross, pendants hanging on either side and enamelled plaques of the Apostles probably dates from the 12th century. Regardless, the Crown of St Stephen has become the very symbol of the Hungarian nation.

The crown has disappeared, only to reappear again later on, several times over the centuries, most recently in 1945 when Hungarian fascists fleeing the Soviet army took it to Austria. Eventually the crown fell into the hands of the US Army, which transferred it to Fort Knox in Kentucky. In 1978 the crown was returned to Hungary with great ceremony – and relief. Because legal judgments had always been handed down 'in the name of St Stephen's Crown' it was considered a living symbol and thus had been 'kidnapped'. ■

undergoing a massive reorganisation, but exhibits in the past have traced the history of the Carpathian Basin from earliest times, of the Magyar people to 1849 and of Hungary in the 19th and 20th centuries in 16 comprehensive rooms. Watch out for the reconstructed 3rd-century Roman villa from Pannonia, the treasury room with pre-Conquest gold jewellery, a second treasury room with later gold objects (including the 11th-century Monomachus crown), the Turkish tent, the stunning baroque library and Beethoven's Broadwood piano that toured world capitals in 1992. The Decorative Hall (Dísz Terem) on the 2nd floor has been reserved for temporary exhibitions in the past. There's an enormous 3rd-century Roman mosaic from Balácapuszta, near Veszprém, at the foot of the steps on the ground floor.

You may enjoy walking around the **Museum Gardens**, laid out in 1856. The column to the left of the museum entrance once stood at the Forum in Rome. Have a look at some of the villas and public buildings on Pollack Mihály tér behind the museum and the white wrought-iron gate in the centre.

You can wander back to the Big Ring Road through any of the small streets. If you follow Baross utca eastward from Kálvin tér, drop into the **Ervin Szabó Library**, built in 1887. With its gypsum ornaments, faded gold tracery and enormous chandeliers, you'll never see a another public reading room like it.

Farther east, across the boulevard, the old **Telephone Exchange Building** (1910) on Horváthy Mihály tér has reliefs of classical figures using the then newfangled invention. The Art Deco **Corvin Cinema** at the southern end of Kisfaludy utca in the middle of a square flanked by Regency-like houses has been restored to its former glory.

Directly to the west at IX Üllői út 33-37 is Hungary's Victoria & Albert: the **Applied Arts Museum**. In fact, the London museum was the inspiration when this museum was founded in 1864. The building, designed by Ödön Lechner and decorated with Zsolnay ceramic tiles, was completed for the millenary exhibition but was badly damaged during WWII and again in 1956.

The museum's galleries, which surround a white-on-white main hall modelled on the Alhambra in Spain, contain Hungarian furnishings and bric-a-brac from the 18th to 19th centuries on the ground floor; exhibits on the 1st floor tell you what was going on in the rest of Europe at the same time. But the displays on the 2nd floor on the history of trades and crafts (glass making, bookbinding, gold smithing, leatherwork etc) have more life to them. Don't miss the painted 18th-century coffered ceiling in the room with the old printing presses, or the stained-glass skylight in the entrance hall. The museum is free on Tuesday.

The neighbourhood south of Üllői út is **Ferencváros** (Francis Town), home of the city's most popular football team and many of its rougher supporters. (Its stadium at IX Üllői út 129 is the only one in the city where booze is banned.) Most of the area was washed away in the Great Flood of 1838. The area to the west toward the Little Ring Road is dominated by the **Economics University** on Fővám tér and is full of hostels, little clubs and inexpensive places to eat. Pop into the university (entrance on the west side facing the river) for a look at its beautiful central courtyard and glass atrium. The imposing **Central Market Hall**, built for the millenary exhibition, reopened in 1996 after a major face-lift. It is now the nicest covered market in the city.

Walking Tour 12: Buda Hills

With 'peaks' reaching over 500m, a comprehensive system of trails and no lack of unusual transport, the Buda Hills are the city's true playground and a welcome respite from hot, dusty Pest in summer. This is not an area of sights – though there are one or two. Come here just to relax and enjoy yourself. If you're walking, take along a copy of Cartographia's 1:30,000 *A Budai hegység* map (No 6) to complement the trail markers. See Hiking & Trekking in the Facts for the Visitor chapter for the colour-code system used in Hungary.

Heading for the hills is more than half the fun. From the Moszkva tér metro station in Buda, walk westward along Szilágyi Erzsébet fasor for 10 minutes (or take tram No 18 or bus No 56 for two stops) to the circular high-rise Budapest hotel. Opposite is the terminus of the **cog railway** (Fogaskerekű). Built in 1874, the cog climbs for 3.5 km to **Széchenyi-hegy**, one of the prettiest residential areas in the city. The railway runs all year till midnight and costs the same as a tram or bus.

At Széchenyi-hegy, you can stop for a picnic in the park south of the station or board the narrow-gauge **children's railway** (Gyermekvasút), two minutes to the south on Rege utca. The railway was built in 1951 by Pioneers (socialist Scouts) and is staffed entirely by children – the engineer excepted – who will sell you tickets and tell you where to get off. The little train chugs along for 12 km, terminating at **Hűvös-völgy** (Chilly Valley). There are walks fanning out from any of the stops along the way, or you can return to Moszkva tér on tram No 56 from Hűvös-völgy. The train operates hourly, year-round, every day except Monday.

A more interesting way down, though, is to get off at **János-hegy**, the fourth stop and the highest point (527m) in the hills. There's an old lookout tower (1910) here, with excellent views of the city, and some good walks. About 700m west of the station is the **chair lift** (libegő), which will take you down to Zugligeti út. From here bus No 158 returns to Moszkva tér. The chair lift runs from 9 am till 5 pm between mid-May and mid-September and an hour earlier the rest of the year. The one-way fare is 100/60 Ft for adults/children.

Hármashatár-hegy (Three Border Hill) is less crowded even in the peak season and is a great spot for a picnic, hiking or watching the gliders push off from the hillside. The view is 360° and worth the trip alone. There's also a lovely restaurant here with a large open terrace. You can reach this hill by taking bus No 86 in Buda to III Kolosy tér from where bus Nos 65 and 65/a depart. The No 65 will take you to the top; No 65/a stops at the Fenyőgyöngy restaurant on Szépvölgyi út at the base.

Top: Millenary Monument at Heroes' Square, Budapest
Bottom: Windows & statue reliefs, Budapest

STEVE FALLON

STEVE FALLON

HUNGARIAN TOURIST BOARD

Top: Hollókő village, Hollókő, Northern Uplands
Left: Abbey Church, Ják, Western Transdanubia
Right: Market in Jurisics tér, Kőszeg, Western Transdanubia

Museums

The names and addresses of the museums mentioned in the Highlights aside and Walking Tours sections are listed here for easy reference.

Agriculture
  Vajdahunyad Castle, XIV City Park
Air & Space Travel
  Petőfi Csarnok, XIV Zichy Mihály utca 14, City Park
Applied Arts
  IX Üllői út 33-37
Aquincum
  III Szentendrei út 139
Béla Bartók Memorial House
  II Csalán út 29
Budapest Gallery
  III Lajos utca 158
Budapest History
  Royal Palace (Wing E), I Szent György tér, Castle Hill
Catering & Commerce
  I Fortuna utca 4
Ecclesiastical Art
  Matthias Church, I Szentháromság tér, Castle Hill
Electrotechnology
  VII Kazinczy utca 21
Ethnography
  V Kossuth tér 12
Fine Arts
  XIV Hősök tere
Foundry
  II Bem József utca 20
Golden Eagle Pharmacy
  I Tárnok utca 18
Gül Baba's Tomb
  II Gül Baba utca
Hercules Villa
  III Meggyfa utca 19-21
Historical Waxworks
  I Színház utca, Castle Hill
Ferenc Hopp East Asian Art
  VI Andrássy út 103
Jewish
  VII Dohány utca 2
Kassák
  III Fő tér 1

Kiscelli
  III Kiscelli utca 106
Zsigmond Kun Collection
  III Fő tér 4
Ferenc Liszt Memorial
  VI Vörösmarty utca 35
Literature
  V Károlyi Mihály utca 16
Ludwig
  Royal Place (Wing A), I Szent György tér, Castle Hill
Medical History
  I Apród utca 1-3
Medieval Synagogue
  I Táncsics Mihály utca 26
Military History
  I Tóth Árpád sétány 40
Music History
  I Táncsics Mihály utca 7
National
  VIII Múzeum körút 14-16
National Gallery
  Royal Palace (Wings B-D), I Szent György tér, Castle Hill
Post Office
  VI Andrássy út 3
György Ráth Collection
  VI Városligeti fasor 12
Roman Camp
  III Pacsirtamező utca 63
Stamp
  VII Hársfa utca 47
Telephone
  I Úri utca 49
Transportation
  XIV Városligeti körút 11, City Park
Underground
  V Deák tér metro
Imre Varga Collection
  III Laktanya utca 7
Victor Vasarely
  III Szentlélek tér 6-7

Returning from Hármashatár on bus No 65 or 65/a, you might want to stop at **Pál-völgy Cave** at II Szépvölgyi út 162 (get off at Szikla utca). The cave, noted for its stalactites and bats, is the third largest in Hungary. Unfortunately, visitors only get to see about 500m of it on half-hour guided tours (120 Ft), which run every hour. It's open every day except Monday from 9 am till 4 pm.

A more beautiful cave, with stalactites, stalagmites and weird grape-like formations, is the one at **Szemlő-hegy**, about a km south-east of Pálvölgyi at II Pusztaszeri út 35 (there's a map at the ticket office showing you the way). If you're heading for Szemlő-hegy Cave from Kolosy tér, take bus No 29. It keeps the same hours as the Pál-völgy Cave, but is closed Tuesday instead of Monday.

The only other sight in the vicinity is the **Béla Bartók Memorial House** at II Csalán út 29, which is also on the No 29 bus route. The house was the composer's residence from 1932-40 before he emigrated to the USA, and contains artefacts related to his life and work. The old Edison recorder (complete with wax cylinders) he used to record Hungarian folk music in Transylvania is on display, as well as furniture and other objects he collected. Concerts are held in the music hall most Friday evenings, and outside in the garden in summer.

ACTIVITIES
Cycling

Parts of Budapest, including Margaret, Óbudai and Csepel islands and the Buda Hills, are excellent places for cycling. The only places to rent a bicycle are the two stalls on Margaret Island (see Walking Tour 5). The Friends of City Cycling Group (☎ 280 0888), V Curia utca 3, publishes a useful cycling map of Budapest. One called *Budapest on Bike* and published by Frigoria can be found in most bookshops.

Horse Riding

In a nation of equestrians, the chances for riding in the capital are surprisingly limited. Wait till you get to the *puszta* or Transdanubia if you're looking for a serious gallop.

Riding schools near Budapest include the Petneházy Country Club (☎ 176 5992) at II Feketefej utca 2 near Budakeszi and the National Riding School (☎ 113 5210) at VIII Kerepesi út 7.

Thermal Baths

'Taking the waters' at one of the city's many spas is a real Budapest experience, so try to go at least once. Some date from Turkish times, others are Art Nouveau wonders, while one or two are spic-and-span modern establishments.

Generally, entry to the baths is 220 Ft (indicated if otherwise), which allows you to stay for two hours on weekdays and an hour and a half at weekends. They offer a full range of serious medical treatments as well as services like massage (450/900 Ft for 15/30 minutes) and pedicure. Specify what you want when buying your ticket(s). For the procedure for getting out of your street clothes and into the water, see Thermal Baths in the Facts for the Visitor chapter. The baths may sometimes look a bit rough around the edges, but they are clean and the water is changed continuously. You may want to wear rubber sandals though.

Please note that some of the baths become gay venues on male-only days – especially the Király and Rác; to a degree, the Gellért always is. Not much actually goes on except for some intensive cruising, but those not into it may feel uncomfortable.

Gellért
XI Kelenhegyi út 4; men and women (separate sections): weekdays 6 am to 7 pm, weekends 6 am to 2 pm. 300 Ft. Soaking in this Art Nouveau palace has been likened to taking a bath in a cathedral.

Király
II Fő utca 84; men: Monday, Wednesday, Friday 6.30 am to 7 pm; women: Tuesday, Thursday 6.30 am to 7 pm and Saturday till noon. The pools date from 1570.

Lukács
II Frankel Leó út 25-29; men and women weekdays 6 am to 7 pm, weekends 6 am to 5 pm. This sprawling 19th-century establishment has everything from thermal and mud baths to a swimming pool.

Rác
I Hadnagy utca 8-10; women: Monday, Wednesday, Friday 6.30 am to 7 pm; men: Tuesday, Thursday, Saturday 6.30 am to 7 pm. The 19th-century exterior hides a Turkish core.

Rudas
I Döbrentei tér 9; men only: weekdays 6 am to 7 pm, weekends 6 am to 1 pm. This is the most Turkish of all the baths.

Széchenyi
XIV Állatkerti út 11; men and women (separate sections): weekdays 6 am to 7 pm, weekends 6 am to 4 pm. This enormous bath is very bright inside – something unusual in Budapest.

Thermal
Margit-sziget Thermal hotel, XIII Margaret Island; men and women: every day 7 am to 8 pm. This is the most up-market (and, at 1200 Ft, most expensive) bath in the city.

Swimming

Every town of any size in Hungary has at least one indoor and outdoor pool (*úszoda*), and Budapest boasts dozens. They're always excellent places to get in a few laps (if indoor), cool off on a hot summer's day (if outdoor) or watch all the posers strut their stuff.

Indoor swimming pools usually require the use of a bathing cap, so bring your own or wear the plastic one provided, rented or sold for a nominal fee.

The system inside is similar to that at the baths except that rather than a cabin or cubicle, sometimes there are just lockers. Get changed and call the attendant, who will lock it, write the time on a chalkboard and hand you a key.

The following is a list of the best indoor and outdoor pools in the city. The latter are open from May to September unless specified. Addresses for the swimming pools attached to the thermal baths can be found in the previous Thermal Baths section.

Taking the waters at Széchenyi Baths

Csillághegyi
III Pusztakúti út 3. The indoor and outdoor pools are open weekdays 6 am to 7 pm, Saturday 6 am to 4 pm, Sunday 6 am to noon. Nudist section on southern slope. 150 Ft.

Gellért
XI Kelenhegyi út 4. The indoor and outdoor pools, with a wave machine and nicely landscaped gardens, are open every day from 6 am till 7 pm daily except Sunday, when they close at 4 pm. You can sunbathe nude on the rooftop. 800 Ft.

Alfréd Hajós (National)
XIII Margaret Island. The indoor (only) pool is open weekdays from 6 am to 5 pm and weekends from 6 am to 6 pm if no competitions are on. 150 Ft.

Palatinus
XIII Margaret Island. The greatest series of pools in the capital are open 8 am to 6 pm every day in season. There are separate-sex roof decks for nude sunbathing. 170 Ft.

Római
III Rozgonyi Piroska utca 2. The outdoor cold-water thermal pools are open every day from 8 am to 7 pm. 150 Ft.

Thermal
Margit-sziget Thermal hotel, XIII Margaret Island. The indoor pool is open every day 7 am to 7 pm. 1200 Ft.

ORGANISED TOURS
City Tours

Many travel agencies, including Ibusz and Cityrama Gray Line (☎ 131 0043), V Báthory utca 22 offer three-hour city tours from 2900/1500 Ft per adult/child and excursions farther afield to the Danube Bend (8900/4500 Ft) and Lake Balaton (9900/5000 Ft) lasting between nine and 10 hours. Budatours (☎ 153 0558) charges adults 2400 Ft for a two-hour tour in one of a dozen languages. Buses depart from the Gresham Palace at V Roosevelt tér 5. Citrobuses (☎ 185 3388) make a continuous loop from Gellért tér over to Pest and back to Castle and Gellért hills with 10 stops along the way daily in season between 9.30 am and 6 pm. You can get on and off as you like, the tickets cost 2800/1600 Ft for adults/children and they are valid for four days.

Hungaria Koncert (☎ 117 2754) has a number of specialist tours including one that focuses on Budapest's Jewish heritage most Tuesdays and Thursdays in season at 1.30 pm. The four to five-hour programme (4000/3500 Ft adults/students) includes a visit to the Great Synagogue, a walking tour of the ghetto, cantor music and a concert by the Budapest Klezmer Band. The concert alone costs 2900/2400 Ft. Tickets are available from locations throughout the city, including the Duna Palota at V Zrínyi utca and at the entrance to the synagogue.

River Tours

From May to September there are two-hour Mahart cruises (500/250 Ft adults/children) on the Danube daily at noon and 7 pm. In April the cruise at noon operates on Sunday and holidays only. You can buy your ticket and board the boat at a small ticket office by the river at Vigadó tér (metro: Vörösmarty tér). Other more expensive cruises such as the ones on the Legenda are heavily promoted around town ('selection of 14 languages!'), but try to find the much cheaper Mahart boat. The night lights of the city rising to Buda Castle, Parliament, Gellért Hill and the Citadella make the evening trip far more attractive than the afternoon one, and the timing doesn't conflict with the rest of your sightseeing.

PLACES TO STAY
Camping

The largest camping ground in Budapest is *Római Camping* (☎ 168 6260), III Szentendrei út 189, with space for more than 2500 happy campers in a shady park north of the city. To get there take the HÉV suburban railway from the Batthyány tér metro station to the Rómaifürdő station, which is within sight of the camping ground. Though the facility is open all year, cabins are available only from mid-April to mid-October at 2000 Ft double in 3rd category and 3000 Ft per double in 2nd category. They have about 45 cabins in total, but they're often full. Use of the adjacent swimming pool, with lots of green grass on which to stretch out, is included.

Up in the Buda Hills, *Hárshegyi Camping* (☎ 200 8803), II Hárshegyi út 7, is open from Easter to mid-October. Take bus No 22 from Moszkva tér and watch for the signs on the right. Camping here costs 500 Ft per person and per tent. The seventy 3rd-category

duplex cabins without bath are 1600 Ft for a single/double, or 2400 Ft for a triple. There are also six 2nd-category rooms with bath at 4500 Ft single/double and ten 1st-category bungalows with bath at 5000 Ft for a single/double.

A somewhat more convenient camping ground for those without their own transport is *Zugligeti Niche Camping* (☎ 200 8346), XII Zugligeti út 101, at the bottom station of the Buda Hills chair lift (take bus No 158 from Moszkva tér to the terminus). It's about 1500 Ft for two people to camp on one of the small hillside terraces. In addition, there's one on-site caravan at 2250 Ft for a double, one bungalow at 2550 Ft for two people and two rooms at 3300 Ft for a double or 4950 Ft for four people. Their reception area and snack bar are in a couple of old Budapest trams parked at the entrance. Zugligeti Niche is open from March to mid-November and the friendly staff speak English.

Tündérhegyi Camping, farther up the hill at II Szilassy út 8 (mobile ☎ 60-336 256), is even smaller, accommodating a total of 150 people. But it has a couple of trailers for rent and bungalows with kitchen and bathroom starting at about 4000 Ft for two. It's open all year. A büfé and two small swimming pools are open in summer. Take bus No 28 from Moszkva tér (Várfok utca side).

Hostels & Student Dormitories

Hostelling International (HI) has an office at Keleti train station open daily from 7 am to 11 pm (to 10 pm in winter) and will make bookings. The Express office (☎ 131 7777) for booking hostel beds is at V Szabadság tér 16, a block from the Kossuth Lajos tér (open Monday to Thursday from 8 am to 4.30 pm, Friday until 2.30 pm). The main Express office at V Semmelweis utca 4 (metro: Astoria) also has information during business hours, though they don't make bookings. You can also go directly to the hostels. Hostel or student cards are not required at any of the hostels, although they'll sometimes get you a 10% discount. The two Express offices are open all year, but only a few of the hostels are.

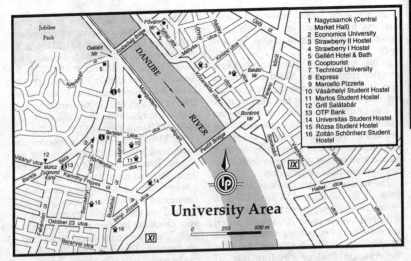

Map legend:
1 Nagycsarnok (Central Market Hall)
2 Economics University
3 Strawberry II Hostel
4 Strawberry I Hostel
5 Gellért Hotel & Bath
6 Cooptourist
7 Technical University
8 Express
9 Marcello Pizzeria
10 Vásárhelyi Student Hostel
11 Martos Student Hostel
12 Grill Salátabár
13 OTP Bank
14 Universitas Student Hostel
15 Rózsa Student Hostel
16 Zoltán Schönherz Student Hostel

University Area

If you've always dreamed of staying in a castle on the Danube you'll like the *Citadella* (☎ 166 5794) in the fortress above the Gellért hotel. In addition to hotel rooms (see the following section), they have five dormitories with 58 beds at 950 Ft per person. The dorms are usually booked by groups a week ahead, so call well in advance for a reservation.

Another popular hostel in Buda but quite a way out is *Back Pack Guest House* (☎ 185 5089), XI Takács Menyhért utca 33. A place in a seven-bed dorm is 700 Ft, in a five-bed dorm 800 Ft. Double rooms are available in winter only. There's a kitchen, laundry, lockers, TV lounge and no curfew, but it's cramped (and very sociable). Access is relatively easy on bus No 7 or 7/a (black number) from Keleti train station or Ferenciek tere.

One of Budapest's nicest yet least known places to stay is the *Csillebérc Youth Centre* (☎ 156 5772) at XII Konkoly Thege utca 21 in the Buda Hills. This huge complex was once a Pioneer camp, and it's in a quiet, wooded location. Csillebérc offers a 73-room hostel at DM18 to DM22 for doubles and DM23 to DM28 for triples, depending on the season (20% discount with an HI card, but not on singles). Two and four-bed bun-

galows with private bath are DM45 to DM60, and camping is DM4 per person plus DM5 per tent (or DM7 per person if you sleep in one of their fixed dormitory tents). All of the above and the many sporting facilities are available year-round and are easily accessible on bus No 21 (red number) from Moszkva tér to the end of the line, then bus No 90 to the first stop after the railway tracks (or a 10-minute downhill walk). Reception is open 24 hours a day.

In summer, private entrepreneurs rent vacant student dormitories from the universities and turn them into hostels, which they do their best to fill in order to make a profit. Competition is fierce and there are several rival hostel operators, so you can afford to shop around a bit. Prices average 700 to 1000 Ft for dormitory beds, and 1400 to 2400 Ft for singles and doubles.

Most of these hostels are open during the school summer holidays (July to 20 August), so at other times make sure a place is actually open before going far out of your way. Ask at Ibusz, Express or Tourinform, or call the hostel the night before. Functioning hostels usually have receptionists who speak English. The More Than Ways group (see the following) is the largest year-round operation, but their hostels are also the most crowded – great places to meet people and party.

In July and most of August, backpackers are often approached at Keleti and Nyugati train stations by representatives from the different hostels offering free minibus rides to their hostels. This is fine but if you want a double room, get a firm commitment that one will be available that night. Otherwise you could be stuck in a dormitory for days on end waiting for someone to leave. The hostels rarely have single rooms.

The most central hostel in Pest is the *Lotus* hostel on the 3rd floor of VI Teréz körút 56 (metro: Nyugati pályaudvar). A place in a 10 or 12-bed room is about 1000 Ft per person and 1650 Ft in a two-bed one. *Ottó & Viktor's* (☎ 267 0311), V Papnövelde utca 4-6, is in the Apáczai College building just off Egyetem tér, a few minutes walk from Ferenciek tere. Ottó & Viktor's offers 35 two, four and six-bed rooms from late June to late August only.

From late June to early September, the István Széchenyi College at IX Ráday utca 43-45, becomes *Strawberry I* (☎ 218 4190), a hostel with 54 double, triple and quad rooms and a popular student club. Nearby at IX Kinizsi utca 2-6, *Strawberry II* (☎ 217 3033) is another modern six-storey student residence, which functions in exactly the same way. These places are within walking distance from the Ferenc körút metro station and are a good bet in summer.

Most of the hostels belonging to the Technical University are west of the Ferenc körút metro station and in July and August it should be easy to find a bed there (though most function as regular student dormitories the rest of the year and are closed to travellers). One of the largest, and now run by More Than Ways, is the *Zoltán Schönherz College* (☎ 166 5021), XI Irinyi József utca 42 (tram No 4 from Ferenc körút metro station to the second stop west of the Danube). In July and August this 22-storey skyscraper offers four-bed rooms with shower at 1750 Ft per person.

Other summertime hostels in the large student residential area near the Schönherz College are *Universitas* (☎ 181 2313), at XI Irinyi József utca 9-11, with doubles from 1300 Ft per person; *Martos* (☎ 181 2171), XI Sztoczek József utca 7; *Vásárhelyi* (☎ 185 2216), XI Kruspér utca 2-4; *Ferenc Rózsa College* (☎ 166 6677), XI Bercsényi utca 28-30; and *Gábor Baross College* (☎ 185 1444), XI Bartók Béla út 17.

The More Than Ways chain operates nine youth hostels around Budapest in July and August. Towards the end of August, eight of them close and revert to being student dormitories; only one stays open year-round. In summer all the hostels are open 24 hours a day, and you can check in any time, but you must check out by 9 am or pay for another night. There's no curfew and an HI card is not required. The More Than Ways hostels can be noisy and a little chaotic at times, but they're fine if you only want a cheap place to crash and meet other travellers.

More Than Ways has its headquarters at the *Diáksport Hostel* (☎ 140 8585), XIII Dózsa György út 152, a two-minute walk from Dózsa György út metro station and open all year. Although this 122-bed hostel is usually the most crowded (hordes of backpackers), they offer a free minibus transfer in summer from there to any of their other hostels that still have beds available, so this is probably the best place to go first. The Diáksport charges 1850 Ft per person in singles or doubles, or 1300 Ft per person in dormitories with six beds. The singles and doubles are almost always full in summer (but often available in winter). There's a raucous 24-hour bar here called the Nonstop Party Pub.

Another More Than Ways place, the central but dumpy *Donáti Hostel* (☎ 201 1971), II Donáti utca 46, a five-minute walk from Batthyány tér in Buda, has only 44 dormitory beds (1200 Ft) and is open only in summer.

The *Express* (☎ 175 2528), more of a hotel than a hostel at XII Beethoven utca 7-9, several blocks south-west of Déli train station (take tram No 59 for two stops), charges 3150/5100/6750 Ft for singles/doubles/triples. The toilet and shower are down the hall and breakfast costs extra. There's a 10% discount for HI card holders.

Tourist Hostels

The Eravis hotel chain (☎ 204 0069) at Bartók Béla út 152 runs a dozen 'workers hostels', often next door or attached to one of its six moderately priced hotels. Generally, these hostels are contracted out to groups like the police, who billet bachelors and couples without proper housing here, but at least one floor is reserved for tourists. Accommodation is priced by the room (roughly 2500 to 3000 Ft for three or four beds), but you can usually talk your way into a single or share. The deal is the same as at the colleges – a sink in the room and showers and toilets in the corridor – and some have kitchens and refrigerators you can use.

In Pest, the most convenient of the tourist hostels is the *Üllői* (☎ 210 4445) at VIII Üllői út 94-98, within walking distance of the Népliget stop on the blue metro line. The dingy *Góliát* (☎ 270 1456) at XIII Kerekes utca 12-20 is in Angyalföld, north-east of the inner town and the Lehel market. Take bus No 4 from Deák tér or the blue metro to the Lehel stop and change to tram No 12 or 14.

In Buda, the *Ventura* (☎ 208 1232) at XI Fehérvári út 179 can be reached by tram No 47 from Pest, tram No 18 from Déli station or bus No 3 from Móricz Zsigmond tér. The *Griff* (☎ 204 2666) is at XI Bartók Béla út 152. Take bus No 7 or tram No 49 from Pest or tram No 19 from Batthyány tér.

Two other Eravis hostels – the *Touring* (☎ 250 3184) at III Pünkösdfürdő utca 38, about 10 minutes from the Békásmegyer HÉV station in Csillaghegy, and the *Kunigunda* (☎ 188 9328) at III Kunigunda utca 25-27, north of Óbuda at the terminus of bus No 6 from Nyugati station – are in quiet areas of district III, but are very far out. Consider them only as a last resort.

Private Rooms

The private rooms assigned by local travel agencies are reasonable value for money in Budapest. They generally cost from 1500 Ft per person or more, with a 20% supplement if you stay less than four nights. To get a single or a room in the centre of town, you may have to try several offices. There are lots of rooms available, and even in July and August you'll be able to find something. You'll probably need to buy an indexed city map to find your room though.

The following is a list of various agencies, beginning with those closest to the transportation terminals. Most are open only during normal business hours, so if you arrive late or on a weekend, try the Ibusz accommodation office (☎ 118 3925), at V Apáczai Csere János utca 1 near the Duna Marriott hotel (metro: Ferenciek tere), which never closes. If you arrive at Keleti train station between 11.10 pm and 4.30 am when the metro isn't running, catch night bus No 78 from outside the nearby Grand Hungária hotel at VII Rákóczi út 90 to Erzsébet Bridge. The centre's prices are higher than those of the following agencies, however, so only go there when the others are closed.

Tourinform does not arrange private accommodation but will send you to To-Ma Tour (☎ 153 0819) at V Október 6 utca 22.

Individuals on the street outside the train stations and the 24-hour Ibusz office may offer you an unofficial private room, but their prices are usually higher than those asked by the agencies and there is no quality control. They vary considerably and cases of travellers being promised an idyllic room in the centre of town, only to be taken to a dreary, cramped flat in some distant suburb are not unknown. You really have to use your own judgment here.

Near Keleti Train Station The Ibusz office in Keleti train station (open weekdays to 6 pm and Saturday to 4 pm) has private rooms from 1650 Ft, but there are few singles. Express opposite Ibusz also has private rooms.

Budapest Tourist at VII Baross tér 3, south-west of Keleti train station at the start of Rákóczi út, also arranges private rooms and changes money.

Near Nyugati Train Station Ibusz at Nyugati train station arranges private rooms. Also try Budapest Tourist (weekdays 9 am to 4.30 pm) in the underground concourse at the entrance to the metro below Nyugati train station. More rooms are for rent at Volántourist, VI Teréz körút 38, also near Nyugati. Another Cooptourist office is in the opposite direction at V Kossuth Lajos tér 13 across from Parliament (metro: Kossuth Lajos tér).

Near Erzsébet tér Bus Station Dunatours at VI Bajcsy-Zsilinszky út 17 behind St Stephen's Basilica has reasonable rooms. Also nearby is Ibusz at V Október 6 utca 8. One of the largest offices in the city offering private rooms is Budapest Tourist at the Gresham Palace at V Roosevelt tér 5 (open 8 am to 5.30 pm weekdays). Singles/doubles here are a costly 3000/4000 Ft.

Near the Hydrofoil Terminal Some of Budapest's least expensive private rooms – from 1000/2000 Ft for singles/doubles and flats from 2500 Ft – are available from Ibusz at V Ferenciek tere 5 (metro: Ferenciek tere). They're open weekdays to 7 pm and Saturday to 2 pm. The Ibusz 24-hour accommodation office at V Apáczai Csere János utca 1 is also within walking distance from both the pier and the Erzsébet tér bus station.

Near Déli Train Station At Déli train station private rooms are arranged by Ibusz at the entrance to the metro and open weekdays to 6 pm and Saturday to 1 pm, and by Budapest Tourist in the mall in front of the station. Also try Cooptourist, I Attila út 107, directly across the park in front of Déli train station.

Pensions

Budapest now has dozens of *panziók*, but most of them are in the outskirts of Pest or in the Buda Hills and not very convenient unless you have your own transport (preferably motorised). As in the rest of Hungary, pensions are popular with Germans and Austrians who like the homey atmosphere and the better breakfasts. Often pensions can cost as much as a moderate hotel, although there are some worthwhile exceptions.

In Pest the *Dominik* pension (☎ 343 7655), XIV Cházár András utca 3, beside a large church on Thököly út, is just two stops north-east of Keleti train station on bus No 7 (black number). The 33 rooms with shared bath are 3070/3880 for a single/double. This friendly pension is a convenient place to stay for a few nights.

A more expensive (but central) place in Pest is the *City Ring* pension (☎ 111 4450) at XIII Szent István körút 22. Singles range from DM67 to DM123, doubles from DM94 to DM156, depending on the season. Prices begin to descend if you stay more than five days.

In Buda, the *Büro* pension (☎ 212 2929) at II Dékán utca 3, just a block off the north side of Moszkva tér, looks basic from the outside but the rooms (which cost DM60/80/90 for a single/double/triple with bath) are comfortable and have TVs. The *Papillon* (☎ 212 4750) at II Rózsahegy utca 3/b has 20 rooms with bath costing 5000 to 6500 Ft for singles and 6500 to 8000 Ft for doubles, depending on the season. It has a decent restaurant attached.

A comfortable, very friendly place in Óbuda is the small, family-run *San Marco* pension (☎ 439 7525) at III San Marco utca 6. It has five spic-and-span rooms on the 2nd floor (three with private bath), a pleasant courtyard out the back and air conditioning. Doubles are 7000 Ft including breakfast.

In the Buda Hills, the 15-room *Beatrix* pension (☎ 176 3730) at II Széher út 3 charges DM50 to DM60 for singles with shared shower and DM60 to DM70 for doubles. Doubles with bath are DM70 to DM100, depending on the season. The Beatrix is an attractive, friendly place with a garden and can be reached on bus No 29, but it would be much more convenient to have your own transport for this one.

Hotels

Hotels in Budapest run the gamut from converted worker hostels at 2000 Ft per head to five-star properties charging over DM300 a night for a double. The low season for hotels in Budapest runs roughly from mid-October or November to March (not including the Christmas/New Year holidays). The high season is obviously summer, when prices can increase enormously. Almost without exception the price includes breakfast. If you're driving, parking at many of the central Pest hotels will be difficult.

Hotels – bottom end A one-star hotel room will cost more than a private room, though the management doesn't mind if you stay only one night. There are no cheap hotels right in the city centre, but the *Flandria* hotel (☎ 270 3181), XIII Szegedi út 27, is easily accessible on tram Nos 12 and 14 from the Lehel tér metro station. Rooms with shared bath in this 116-room tourist hotel cost DM26/37/50/63 for a single/double/triple/quad.

One of the best deals in town if there are a few of you is the *Góliát* hotel (☎ 270 1454), XIII Kerekes utca 12-20, two blocks away from the Flandria. This huge 11-storey block accommodates workers as well as tourists. A room with four beds will cost about 4000 Ft for the room whether you're alone or a group of four. The atmosphere in the Góliát can be a little rough at times.

The 15-room *Citadella* hotel/hostel (☎ 166 5794) on Gellért Hill charges 5000 Ft for a double with shared bath, 5500 Ft with a leaky shower, and 6000 Ft with bath.

Several inexpensive places are accessible on the HÉV line to Szentendre from Batthyány tér in Buda. The first is the one-star *Polo* hotel (☎ 250 0222) at III Mozaik utca 1-3 near the Filatorigat HÉV stop. You can't see the hotel from the station, but it's beside a service station, behind a long building that runs along the east side of the tracks. Doubles with shared bath are 3200 Ft, while the one double with private bath is 4200 Ft.

The 53-room *Touring* hotel (☎ 250 3184), III Pünkösdfürdő utca 38, in the north-west area of Budapest, has singles/doubles with shower for DM61/69 and triples/quads with shared bath for DM72/83 – good value for small groups. It's a 10-minute walk from Békásmegyer HÉV Station (ask directions from the station).

Hotels – middle In Pest, the old *Park* Hotel (☎ 313 1420), VIII Baross tér 10, directly across from Keleti train station, charges 4950/5950 Ft for a single/double without bath, or 6600/ 8900 Ft with shower, but it is often full. The *Metropol* hotel (☎ 342 1175), near Keleti at VII Rákóczi út 58 (metro: Blaha Lujza tér), has singles/doubles at DM40/70 without bath, or DM80/90 with bath.

A much better medium-priced hotel than these is the *Medosz* hotel (☎ 153 1700), VI Jókai tér 9 (metro: Oktogon). The 11 singles are DM44, the 53 doubles are DM68, and all have private bath. The *Délibáb* (☎ 342 9301) is at VI Délibáb utca 35 across from Heroes' Square and the City Park. Housed in an old Jewish orphanage, its 34 rooms (all with showers) are 5000 to 7000 Ft.

In Óbuda, the 82-room *Tusculanum* (☎ 188 7673) at III Záhony utca 10, just off Szentendrei út, is packed with groups, and is only a couple of hundred metres from the Aquincum HÉV stop. Singles/doubles are DM80/95.

The Eravis chain is a good bet for medium-priced hotels. Again, they're not always so ideally situated, but that's the price you (don't) have to pay for a hotel in the Hungarian capital. In Buda, the group's flagship property, the 108-room *Griff*, and the 148-room *Ventura* are both in the XIth district next to or attached to the tourist hostels of the same name (see the earlier Tourist Hotels section). The Griff is easier to get to, with singles/doubles with shower at DM57/ 75 in the low season and DM70/98 in summer. But the Ventura – all *faux* Art Deco in various shades of blue and purple – is a much more fun place to stay. Singles/doubles here are DM60/70 or DM90/100, depending on the season.

In Pest, the Eravis' *Ében* (☎ 252 3333) at XIV Nagy Lajos király útja 15-17 is an intimate 52-room hotel next to the Örs vezér tér stop on the red metro line. Attractively appointed with cable TVs and the odd bit of art on the walls, rooms with shower are DM45 to DM60 for singles, and DM60 to DM80 for doubles. The Ében's pub-restaurant is one of the better outlets in this category of hotel.

The 128-room *Platánus* hotel (☎ 210 2599) at VIII Könyves Kálmán körút 44, near the Népliget metro stop on the blue line, is moderately priced off-season (singles/doubles with shower are DM49/69), but rooms jump to DM99/119 in summer. The Platánus has a restaurant with Gypsy music nightly, a pub and a fitness centre with a well-equipped gym, sauna and aerobics room.

Hotels – top end In Pest, the *Nemzeti* (☎ 269 9310), with a beautifully renovated Art Nouveau exterior and inner courtyard, is centrally located at VIII József körút 4. Its 76 rooms (all with shower or bath) are relatively affordable in winter; singles/doubles are DM99/110 then but jump to DM150/190 in summer.

For location and atmosphere in Buda, you can't beat the *Kulturinnov* (☎ 155 0122), a 16-room hotel in the former Finance Ministry on Castle Hill at I Szentháromság tér 6. Chandeliers, artwork and a sprawling marble staircase greet you on entry, but the rooms, though clean and with private baths, are not half as grand. Singles/doubles are 8500/10,000 Ft.

The *Orion* (☎ 156 8583), tucked away in the Tabán district at I Döbrentei utca 13, is a cozy, 30-room hotel with a relaxed atmosphere and within walking distance of the castle. Most importantly, unlike most three-star hotels in Budapest, it has central air conditioning. Singles are DM95 to DM145 and doubles are DM130 to DM185.

If you want to be near the Danube, you can't get any closer than on the *Dunapart* (☎ 155 9001), a boat hotel moored along I Alsó rakpart at Szilágyi Dezső tér. Understandably, the 32 rooms are rather cramped, but the teak and brass fittings in the public areas and the pleasant restaurant and back deck make this former Black Sea cruiser

worth considering. Singles in high season are a pricey DM120 and doubles are DM150.

If you like the idea of staying in the Buda Hills, your first choice should be the *Panoráma* (☎ 395 5464) at XII Rege utca 21, next to the terminus of the Cog and Children's railways on Széchenyi-hegy. Built in the last century, this three-storey hotel with a strange tower still has an old-world feel to it despite renovations, and has all the mod cons. Singles are DM65 to DM115, and doubles are DM90 to DM150, all with bath. The 54 bungalows for four that ring the swimming pool out the back almost have a country feel to them.

The *Normafa* (☎ 156 3444), nearby at XII Eötvös út 52-54, is a newish place with 70 rooms. But for atmosphere, it should be a distant second choice to the Panoráma. Singles are DM60 to DM116 and doubles DM85 to DM158, depending on the season.

Hotels – luxury If price is really no object, choose any of the following four hotels for their unique location, special amenities or 'face-giving' qualities: the Gellért or Hilton in Buda, the Corvinus Kempinski in Pest or the Ramada Grand on Margaret Island. All are special for one reason or another and quite different.

Budapest's grande dame of hotels, the 233-room *Gellért* (☎ 185 2200) at XI Szent Gellért tér 1 is looking less tattered these days as renovations progress; some rooms are now very attractive. The thermal baths are free for guests, but with the exception of the terrace restaurant on the Kelenhegyi út side (which is open in summer) its other facilities are forgettable. Prices change depending on which way your room faces and what bathing facilities it has, but singles start at DM158, and doubles at DM326. Lower-level rooms facing the river can be noisy.

The 323-room *Budapest Hilton* (☎ 214 3000) at I Hess András tér 1 on Castle Hill was built carefully in and around a 14th-century church and baroque college (though it still has its detractors). It has great views of the city and the Danube and some good facilities, including a medieval wine cellar serving a good range of Hungarian vintages. Singles are from DM280 and doubles from DM365.

The *Ramada Grand* (☎ 311 1000) on Margaret Island has 164 rooms in what used to be the Grand hotel, built in 1873. Posh, quiet, with all the mod cons and connected to the Thermal spa via an underground corridor, it ain't cheap: singles are DM160 to DM280 and doubles DM210 to DM330. At these prices, you have your rights: demand a room with Biedermeier furniture, a balcony and a river view. Seniors get a 25% discount here.

The *Corvinus Kempinski* (☎ 266 1000) at V Erzsébet tér 7-8 is Budapest's (and Hungary's) most expensive hotel, with singles/doubles from DM350/430. Essentially for business travellers on hefty expense accounts, it has European service, American efficiency and Hungarian charm.

PLACES TO EAT
Food Markets & Self-Catering

The renovated Nagycsarnok (Central Market Hall) on IX Fővám tér is Budapest's finest market. There are some good food stalls on the upper level serving everything from Chinese spring rolls to German sausages. Among other colourful food markets in the city are the Joseph Town Market on VIII Rákóczi tér; the market on Hold utca near V Szabadság tér; the so-called Ghetto Market on VII Klauzál tér and the open-air market at Lehel tér in the XIIIth district. Markets are usually open weekdays to 6 pm and Saturday till 1 pm or 2 pm. Monday is always very quiet (if the markets aren't closed completely).

There are large supermarkets everywhere in Budapest these days, including the *Csemege Julius Meinl* on VIII Blaha Lujza tér and *Kaiser's* opposite Nyugati train station in Pest. *Rothschild* is another large chain with outlets throughout the city including one at the western end of Szent István körút.

The *Görög Csemege* is a Greek-style delicatessen at VIII József körút 31/b. The *cheese shop* at V Gerlóczy utca 3 sells a wide variety of Hungarian and imported cheeses. See Things to Buy for the best wine shops.

Fast Food & Cheap Eats

Fast-food places like McDonald's, Pizza Hut, Kentucky Fried Chicken, Dunkin' Donuts, Wendy's and Hungarian Paprika outlets abound in Budapest, but old-style self-service restaurants, the mainstay of both white and blue-collar workers in the old regime, where full meals cost under 300 Ft, are disappearing fast. One of just a few left in Pest is *Bölcs Bagoly*, centrally located at V Váci utca 33 and open weekdays from 11.30 am to 3 pm. There's a similar *self-service restaurant* at V Arany János utca 5 open weekdays from 11.30 am to 4 pm only. A bit more up-scale is the self-service upstairs at the *Pick Ház* beside the metro entrance on Kossuth Lajos tér. It's open weekdays from 9 am to 6 pm and on Saturday from 8 am to 1 pm.

Oddly enough, there are two self-service restaurants on Castle Hill: *Akadémia* above the police station at I Országház utca 30 (take the lift to the 3rd floor), open weekdays from 11.30 am to 2 pm, and another above the *Fortuna Späten* restaurant, across the street from the Hilton Hotel on I Fortuna utca. It is open weekdays from 11 am to 2.30 pm.

Bear in mind that, while cheap, self-service restaurants are the lowest common denominator in Hungarian food and usually serve very mediocre fare. Much better value at lunch are the butcher shops that serve cooked sausage and occasionally roast chicken such as the *Gasztró Hús-Hentesáru* at II Margít körút 2, opposite the first stop of tram Nos 4 and 6 on the west side of Margaret Bridge (open from Monday 7 am to 6 pm, Tuesday to Friday from 6 am to 7 pm and Saturday from 6 am to 1 pm). Also in Buda, the *Grill Salátabár* at XI Móricz Zsigmond körtér No 4 has excellent grilled chicken and even a salad bar.

Even better value are the wonderful little restaurants called étkezde – not unlike British 'cafs' – serving simple dishes that change every day. Two of the best are the *Kisharang* at V Október 6 utca 17 (open on

BUDAPEST

weekdays from 11 am to 8 pm, weekends to 3.30 pm) and *Kádár* in the former Jewish district at X Klauzál tér (open Tuesday to Saturday till 3.30 pm).

An excellent place for tasty takeaway open-face sandwiches is *Durcin* at V Október 6 utca 13. It is open weekdays from 8 am to 6 pm and Saturday from 9 am to 1 pm.

Pizza Pizza took Budapest by storm in the early 1990s, and pizzerias can be found everywhere now. Among the best places in Buda are *Il Treno* at XII Alkotás utca 15 (with a branch in Pest at VIII József körút 60) and *Marcello*, which is popular with students from the nearby university, at XI Bartók Béla út 40. It's open daily, except Sunday, from noon to 10 pm.

La Prima at II Margit körút 3 gets rave reviews for reasons I can't fathom; they serve 'ketchup pizza' as far as I can tell, but the salad bar is OK. *Marxim*, II Kisrókus utca 23, a five-minute walk from Moszkva tér (open Sunday to Thursday until 1 am, and till 2 am on Friday and Saturday), is popular among workers from the nearby city gas works and factories who appreciate the Gulag, Kulák, Lenin and Anarchismo pizzas and the campy Stalinist décor.

There are several pizza places on Nyugati tér, including *Okay Italia* (see Restaurants) at No 6 and *Don Pepe* at No 8, open till the very wee hours. *Don Stefano*, on III Harrer Pál utca behind the town hall on Fő tér in Óbuda, serves pizza till 9 pm.

Middle Eastern Middle Eastern fast food is now almost as popular as pizza. The *Semiramis* at V Alkotmány utca 20 is the old stand-by and still has the most authentic fare around. Seating is on two levels and it stays open till 9 pm every day but Sunday. Another excellent spot is *Cabar*, V Irányi utca 25, with Israeli-style turkey shwarma (260 Ft) and felafel (235 Ft). There's also a self-service salad bar – you'll be charged by the weight. It's open Monday to Saturday from 10 am to 11 pm. A very inexpensive place for

gyros is the *123* at XIII Szent István körút 13.

Golden Gastronomia, between Vörösmarty tér and Deák tér at V Bécsi utca 8, is a delicatessen with Middle Eastern pita sandwiches, lots of vegetarian dishes and decent salads. *Lammu*, east of the Klauzál tér market at VII Akácfa utca 40, is a tiny place with authentic gyros. About 10 minutes on foot east of Keleti station at VII Garay tér 13-14, the *Nilus* serves Egyptian dishes till 10 pm. *Aladdin* is another unpretentious place serving shwarma, gyros (190 Ft) and dips. It's north of Rákóczi tér at VIII Bérkocsis utca 23.

Restaurants
Very roughly, a two-course meal for one person with a glass of local wine or beer for around 500 Ft in Budapest is 'cheap', while a 'moderate' one hovers around 1000 Ft or slightly more. There's a pretty big jump to an 'expensive' meal (from 2000 Ft per head), and 'very expensive' is anything over that. Most restaurants are open till midnight, but it's best to arrive by 9 pm. It is advisable to book tables at those restaurants with telephone numbers provided.

Traditional Hungarian In Buda, the *Gerber Banya-Tanya*, near Déli station at XII Nagyenyed utca 3, serves better-than-average Hungarian dishes in a cellar restaurant. The *Fekete Holló* (Black Raven) at I Országház utca 10 is the most charming inexpensive eatery on Castle Hill – a district of mostly overpriced, touristy restaurants. If you really want to eat in one of these, go for the expensive *Alabárdos* (☎ 156 0851), I Országház utca 2. It's open for dinner till midnight every night but Sunday.

The *Aranyszarvas* (Golden Stag; ☎ 175 6451), set in an old 18th-century inn perched above Döbrentei tér at I Szarvas tér 1, serves – what else? – game dishes and has an outside terrace in summer. It's open till 2 am weekdays and till midnight on Sunday. If your cholesterol is down, the *Tabáni Kakas* (☎ 175 7165), not far away at I Attila út 27, will raise it for you – almost everything (mostly poultry dishes) is cooked in flavour-enhancing goose fat. It's open till midnight every day. Prices are moderate.

A more up-market place is *Kacsa* (☎ 201 9992) at II Fő utca 75. Kacsa is the place for duck, which is what its name means. It's a dressy, fairly elegant place with excellent service. That costs, so go only if someone's taking you.

Vadrózsa (☎ 326 5817 or ☎ 135 1118), in a beautiful neo-Renaissance villa at II Pentelei Molnár út 15 on Rózsadomb is the No 1 top-class restaurant in Buda, and one of your first choices if you've got the rich uncle or aunt in tow. It's filled with roses, antiques and soft piano music, and there's no menu – you choose off the cart of raw ingredients and specify the cooking style. Only dinner is served. Very, very expensive.

In Óbuda, try the fish soup at the *Sípos Halászkert* at III Szentlélek tér 8. In the evening there will probably be Gypsy music. Some people think *Kéhli* (☎ 250 4241) at III Mókus utca 22 in Óbuda has the best traditional Hungarian food (such as bone marrow on toast – better than it sounds) in town, but I prefer the *Kisbuda Gyöngye* (☎ 168 6402) at III Kenyeres utca 34. This is an attractive and cosy Hungarian restaurant (moderate to expensive) decorated with antiques, and manages to create the atmosphere of turn-of-the-century Óbuda. It's open for lunch and dinner till midnight Monday to Saturday and for lunch only on Sunday.

In Pest, try to have lunch at the little *Móri* restaurant at XIII Pozsonyi út 37, a short walk north of Szent István körút, which has excellent home-cooked Hungarian food. It's cheap and very popular with local customers, so be prepared to wait for a table. It's open weekdays from 10 am till 8 pm. The *Tüköry* at V Hold utca 15 is a Hungarian pub popular with workers from Magyar Televízió on Szabadság tér. The three-course daily menu – in Hungarian only – is an exceptionally good deal. *Fatál* (☎ 266 2607), V Váci utca 67, serves massive Hungarian meals on wooden platters in three rustic rooms daily from 11.30 am to 2 pm. Be sure to book.

The *Kalocsa Pince* at VIII Baross utca 10 is a reasonably priced Hungarian cellar restaurant with walls decorated by two 'painting women' from Kalocsa on the Southern Plain.

New Hungarian For lighter, more up-to-date Hungarian food it's hard to think of a better place than my favourite, the *Múzeum* restaurant (☎ 267 0375) at VIII Múzeum körút 12. Still going strong after more than a century, this restaurant near the National Museum is perfect if you want to dine in grand style without breaking the bank. It has very good fish and duck with fruit (specify this over the usual potatoes and cabbage) and is open every day, except Sunday, till 1 pm. Expensive.

If you're not discouraged by the prospect of spending something like 5000 Ft per person for dinner, *Gundel* (☎ 321 3550), next to the zoo directly behind the Museum of Fine Arts at XIV Állatkerti út 2, is the city's fanciest Hungarian restaurant, with a tradition dating back to 1894. Budapest cognoscenti, though, have now abandoned Gundel to the expense-account brigade and flock to *Bagolyvár* (☎ 321 3550), Gundel's little sister restaurant next door. It's open daily from noon to 10 pm.

Continental *Remíz* (☎ 275 1396), next to the tram depot (remíz) in Buda at II Budakeszi út 5, has gone from being a moderate 'find' to a relatively expensive up-market restaurant. It specialises in grilled dishes; the ribs are especially good. Open Tuesday through Sunday for lunch and dinner to 1 am.

Up in the Buda Hills, *Udvarház* (☎ 188 8780) at II Hármashatárhegyi út 2 has the most scenic location in Budapest, and the outside terrace is a delight in warmer months. The food can be very good. It's open in summer from 11 am till 11 pm every day but Monday, and only for dinner in winter till 11 pm. Expensive.

In Pest, *Café Kör* at V Sas utca 17 near the basilica is a great place for a light meal at any time between 9 am and 10 pm from Monday to Saturday. Salads and desserts are very good. One of the best new restaurants – some say *the* best around – is *Lou Lou* (☎ 112 4505) at V Vigyázó Ferenc utca 4. It's like a bistro with excellent daily specials; try the très garlicky lamb.

Amadeus (☎ 118 4677), V Apáczai Csere János utca 30, is a chichi Austrian-owned café-restaurant just north of Vigadó tér. It has excellent salads, steaks and – a rarity in Hungary – fresh prawns. Very expensive. If you really want to be in the thick of things, head for *Cyrano* (☎ 266 3096) at V Kristóf tér 7-8, the best restaurant in the immediate Váci utca area. Moderate to expensive.

French The *Jardin de Paris* (☎ 201 0047) at II Fő utca 20 is a regular haunt of the staff at the French Institute across the road – as good a recommendation as any. *Les Amis* (☎ 212 3173) at II Rómer Flóris utca 12 is a somewhat cramped little restaurant on the fringe of Rózsadomb that stays open late. The kitchen, too, is tiny, but the Franco-Hungarian dishes it produces are above average. Closed Sunday. Expensive.

Chez Daniel (☎ 302 4039) at VI Szív utca 32 serves as authentic cuisine Française as you'll find in Budapest. Excellent cheese board. It's open Tuesday to Saturday for lunch and dinner to 11 pm and on Sunday for lunch only to 3 pm. Expensive.

Italian The best budget Italian restaurant is the Italian-owned *Okay Italia* chain, with branches at XIII Szent István körút 20; V Nyugati tér 6 (the one favoured by 'those in the know'); and III Szentendrei út 36. Pizzas/pastas/Italian main courses start at 420/450/600 Ft. The very expensive *Scampi* (☎ 269 6026) at VII Dohány utca 10 specialises in Italian-ish seafood. It's open every day from noon till midnight. Its 780 Ft weekday lunch is good value.

Don't go to *Bel Canto* (☎ 269 2786), behind the Opera House at VI Dalszíház utca 8, for the food but for the song: opera-trained waiters burst into song at the drop of a plate. It's fun, but don't expect much conversation. Bel Canto is open till midnight. Expensive.

The most up-market Italian restaurant in town is *Fausto's* (☎ 322 7806) at VIII Dohány utca 5 with excellent pasta dishes, daily specials and desserts. Expensive.

Greek *Jorgosz* (☎ 141 0772), VII Csengery utca 24, has average food but the live bouzouki music livens up the surrounds. It's open every day from noon till midnight. Moderate. A better choice would be the more expensive *Taverna Ressaikos* (☎ 212 1612) on the Buda side at I Apor Péter utca 1. *Taverna Dionysos* (☎ 118 122) at V Belgrád rakpart 18 is always crowded.

Mexican *Acapulco* (☎ 322 6014), VII Erzsébet körút 39, is Budapest's most authentic Mexican/Mexican-American restaurant (not a difficult claim to make in these parts), but stick with the fajitas and margaritas. It's open for lunch and dinner every day. Moderate to expensive.

American No one goes to the *Chicago* (☎ 269 6753) at VII Erzsébet körút 2 for its big burgers, steaks and Tex-Mex dishes any more, but the salad bar – the best in town – and the draft beer brewed on the premises remain an attraction. Chicago is open from noon till midnight (later at weekends). Moderate. If you crave things like pancakes (yes, with maple syrup), Cajun chicken and big salads, the *Orchidea* at VIII Rákóczi út 29 can accommodate (sort of). It is open every day from 8 am till 11 pm. Moderate to expensive.

For steaks, spare ribs and Caesar salad, the best choice would be *Leroy's Country Pub* (☎ 270 3202) at XIII Visegrádi utca 50/a. It's small and very popular, so make sure you call ahead. Leroy's is open every night to 2 or 3 am.

Asian A very inexpensive place for a fix of noodles or fried rice is the *Miyako Ramen House* café-restaurant at XIII Visegrádi utca. It's open daily from noon to midnight (1 pm to 10 pm on Sunday).

The *Kilenc Sárkány* (Nine Dragons; ☎ 342 7120) at Dózsa György út 56 is the most authentic and frequented by Chinese expatriates who can read the menu. It's open daily from 11.30 am to midnight. Chinese restaurants can be expensive in Budapest, so if the budget is tight, try *Xi Hu* at Nádor utca 5. It's open from noon to midnight.

Tourists flock to the cavernous *Tian Tan* (☎ 118 6444) at V Duna utca 1 near Elizabeth Bridge, but much, much better is the *Hong Kong Pearl Garden* (☎ 212 3131), II Margit körút 2. Try the Peking duck, Sichuan eggplant or the Singapore noodles. It's open for lunch and dinner till 11.30 pm Monday to Saturday, and Sunday from noon till 10 pm. Very expensive.

The standards at *Chan-Chan* (☎ 118 0452), V Váci utca 69 (enter on Pintér utca), have fallen considerably over the past few years, but the food does retain a Thai taste. It's also become very expensive for what it is; stick to the tom yam gung. Chan-Chan is open for lunch and dinner daily to 11 pm. Expensive.

Japán (☎ 114 3427), VIII Luthur utca 4-6, once the only place for sukiyaki and sushi in the capital and very popular with well-heeled Japanese expatriates, is now competing with the new *Sushi* restaurant next to the British Embassy at V Harmincad utca 2, where a mixed sushi plate is 1800 Ft. Both are open for lunch and dinner every day till 10.30 or 11 pm.

Seoul House (☎ 201 7452), I Fő utca 8, is the better of Budapest's two Korean restaurants and the food here is arguably the most authentically Asian in the capital. Lunch and dinner is available every day till midnight. Expensive.

For Indian food, you might try the flashy *Bombay Palace* (☎ 131 3787) at VI Andrássy út 44, but for the genuine taste of masala dosa, head for *Laksmi* at VII Király utca 69 or *Govinda* (see Vegetarian) instead.

The Polynesian restaurant known both as the *Luau* and the *Tiki* (☎ 131 4352) at V Zoltán utca 16 has 'rain' cascading down the windows and 'lightning' flashing at intervals during the course of a meal. It may not suggest the ultimate Budapest experience, but it's fun. The Luau/Tiki is open every day from noon till midnight. Moderate to expensive.

Vegetarian One of the healthiest and least expensive places to eat in the city at is the *Falafel Faloda* (also called *No 1 Falafel*), VI Paulay Ede utca 53. It's strictly vegetarian, and you pay a fixed price to stuff a piece of pitta bread or fill a plastic container yourself from the great assortment of salad bar options. The bright, modern décor attracts a young crowd (open weekdays from 10 am to 8 pm only).

The *Vegetárium* (☎ 267 0322), V Cukor utca 3 just off Ferenciek tere, has main courses from 690 Ft and generous macrobiotic plates for 850 Ft, but also serves 'poultries and fishes'. It opens from noon till 10.30 pm. Moderate. More strictly vegetarian is the *Govinda*, an Indian vegetarian restaurant at V Belgrád rakpart 18. Over in Buda, a decent vegetarian place is *Életház Biocentrum* at XII Böszörményi út 13-15 with a choice of three dishes in three sizes.

Kosher Budapest's only kosher restaurant, *Hannah*, in an old school behind the Orthodox Synagogue at VII Dob utca 35 opens weekdays from 11.30 am to 4 pm only. There are kosher bakeries, butchers and a delicatessen in the area; see Walking Tour 10 for details. A branch of the *Rothschild* supermarket chain at VII Nyár utca 1 sells kosher products only.

Late-Night In Buda, hearty Hungarian meals are served round the clock at *Söröző a Szent Jupáthoz* at II Retek utca 16, which is a block north of Moszkva tér. Nearby, the *Nagyi Palacsintázója* (Granny's Palacsinta Place) at I Hattyú utca 16 has as many varieties of Hungarian pancakes as you care to count. It's also open 24 hours.

In Pest, the *Stop* restaurant near Fővám tér at V Váci utca 86 is another all-night place offering a good variety of fish and meat dishes plus several vegetarian selections. Prices are reasonable, and the menu is in many languages. The *Grill 99* diner at VIII Dohány utca 52 is a popular place for late, late meals or a very early morning breakfast (as young expatriates on the go all know). *Talk Talk*, V Magyar utca 12-14, is a nonstop café also popular with after-club crowds. It has pretty good breakfasts.

Cafés

Like Vienna, Budapest is famous for its cafés and cake shops and the most famous of the famous is the *Gerbeaud*, on the west side of V Vörösmarty tér, a fashionable meeting place for the city's elite since 1870. But, sorry to say, in recent years this place has become pretentious and overpriced. The service remains abominable. Although the surrounds lack atmosphere, the *Bécsi Kávéház* at the Forum hotel, V Apáczai Csere János utca 12-14, has the best cakes in town.

The *Művész*, VI Andrássy út 29, almost opposite the State Opera House, is a more interesting place to people-watch than Gerbeaud and has a better selection of cakes at lower prices. It is now open 24 hours a day.

The *New York Café*, VII Erzsébet körút 9-11, has been a Budapest institution since 1895. The elegant turn-of-the-century décor glitters around the literati who still meet here. For the best cherry strudel in the capital head for *Szalai* at V Balassi Bálint utca 7. It's open from 9 am till 7 pm daily except Monday and Tuesday.

The perfect place for coffee and cakes up in the Castle District is the crowded *Ruszwurm*, I Szentháromság utca 7 near Matthias Church. Two more good cafés on the Buda side are *Angelika*, I Batthyány tér 7, and the untouristy *Caffè Déryné* at I Krisztina tér 3.

ENTERTAINMENT

For a city its size, Budapest has a huge choice of things to do and places to go after dark – from opera and folk dancing to jazz and meat-market discos. It's almost never difficult getting tickets or getting in; the hard part is deciding what to do.

Your best sources of general information in the city are Tourinform and the free bilingual publications *Programme in Ungarn/in Hungary* and *Budapest Panorama*. If you can manage a bit of Hungarian, pick up a copy of the weekly *Pesti Műsor* (Budapest Programme). The monthly *Koncert Kalen-drium* lists concerts, opera and dance in Hungarian.

The busiest theatrical ticket agency is the Színházak Központi Jegyiroda (☎ 112 0000), VI Andrássy út 18 (metro: Opera), open weekdays from 9 am till 6 pm. They have tickets there to numerous theatres and events, although the best are gone a couple of days in advance. It's open weekdays from 9 am to 6 pm. For opera or ballet tickets, go to the office next door at No 20. It is open weekdays from 10 am to 5.30 pm.

For concert tickets try the Nemzeti Filharmónia Jegyiroda (☎ 117 6222), V Vörösmarty tér 1 (metro: Vörösmarty tér). It's open weekdays from 10 am to 6 pm, to 2 pm on Saturday.

Music Mix (☎ 138 2237), V Váci utca 33 (metro: Ferenciek tere), has tickets to special events such as rock spectaculars, appearances by foreign superstars etc. It's open daily from 10 am to 6 pm and Saturday from 9 am to 2 pm.

Cinemas

A couple of dozen movie houses show English-language films with Hungarian subtitles. Consult the listings in the *Budapest Week* or *Budapest Sun* newspapers. See anything at the fantastic *Uránia Cinema*, VIII Rákóczi út 21, in an old music hall built in 1893, or the renovated *Corvin* at VIII Corvin köz 1, which saw a lot of action during the 1956 Uprising.

The *Örökmozgó*, part of the Hungarian Film Institute at VII Erzsébet körút 39, shows an excellent assortment of foreign and classic films in their original languages.

Discos & Clubs

One of Budapest's top discos is *Bahnhof* at VI Váci út 1; it attracts a twenty-something crowd. *Trocadero* (also called *Franklin Trocadero*), VI Szent István körút 15, plays great canned Latin (salsa and meringue), with live acts usually from Wednesday to Sunday.

A massive place and the biggest meat market in town is the *Hully Gully* at XII Apor Vilmos tér 9 (tram No 59 five stops from

Moszkva tér). The laser show, go-go girls and late hours (it closes at 5 or 6 am) attract large crowds. A younger Hungarian crowd goes to *Highlife* at III Kalap utca 15 north of Óbuda. It's huge and glitzy and has dancing women in cages – trash city. Take bus No 6 from Nyugati tér or bus No 86 from Batthyány tér.

Less throbbing (maybe) places for a bop are the *Guillotine Live Music Club* at IX Üllői út 45-47 with two dance floors and lots of techno, and the *Black Horse* at VIII Dohány utca 39, with hip-hop/club/house. Not a place to wear stockings or tights, I'm told. Every one moves over to the Grill 99 (see Late Night under Places to Eat) afterwards.

The very chichi *Fortuna*, on Castle Hill at I Hess András tér 4, hosts a disco on Wednesday, Friday and Saturday nights. It's huge, expensive and attracts lots of models and Austrians in plum and lime-coloured suits. In fact, Wednesday is models' night.

Gay & Lesbian Venues

There are no women-only clubs in Budapest, but lesbians frequent the *Capella Café*, V Belgrád rakpart 23, and even *Angel*, VII Szövetség utca 33, two gay venues that are becoming increasingly mixed. *Mystery Bar*, V Nagysándor József utca 3, is a quiet gay bar, a good place to take a date, while the name of the *Action Bar*, V Magyar utca 42, says it all. Take the usual precautions. Another gay club called *No Limit*, V Vitkovics Mihály utca 11-13 on the corner with Semmelweiss utca, has a pretty descriptive name, too, but in more of a voyeuristic sense.

Like everywhere, gay clubs come and go in Budapest. You can always get the latest information from one of your fellow bathers at the *Király* baths (especially on Friday afternoons), the *Rác* baths on Saturday afternoons or the *Gellért* baths on Sunday mornings. If you prefer to meet friends en plein air, the Duna korzó walkway between Elizabeth and Chain bridges in Pest is notoriously cruisy after dark (AYOR).

The only gay publication in Hungary,

Mások (Others), is available at the bars and newsstands in the inner town.

Theatre

If you want to brave a play in Hungarian, go to the *József Katona Theatre* at V Petőfi Sándor utca 6 for the best acting in the city, or the *János Arany Theatre* at VI Paulay Ede utca 35 for the amazing Art Deco theatre itself.

You won't have to understand Hungarian to enjoy the *Budapest Puppet Theatre*, VI Andrássy út 69 (metro: Vörösmarty utca). It presents shows designed for children during the day and occasional evening programmes for adults. The kids' shows are generally held at 3 pm Monday to Thursday and at 10.30 am and 4 pm Friday to Sunday. Tickets are 100 to 200 Ft, and the theatre is closed all summer.

Classical Music

The *Koncert Kalendárium* lists all concerts in Budapest each month, and most nights you'll have several to choose from. The motto of the Budapest Spring Festival in late March is '10 days, 100 venues, 1000 events' and you'll have a huge selection of musical events each night. Budapest's main concert halls are the stunning *Liszt Academy of Music* at VI Liszt Ferenc tér 8 (metro: Oktogon) and the modern *Budapest Congress Centre* at XII Jagelló út 1-3 in Buda. The *Pesti Vigadó*, V Vigadó tér 2, has light classical music.

There are many places where chamber music is played, but those with the best atmosphere are the concert halls at the *Liszt Memorial Museum*, VI Vörösmarty utca 35; the *Béla Bartók Memorial House*, II Csalán utca 29; and the *Music History Museum*, I Táncsics Mihály utca 7. Organ recitals are best heard in the city's churches, including *Matthias Church* on Castle Hill, *St Stephen's Basilica* on V Szent István tér, the *Inner Town Parish Church* on V Március tér, and the *Great Synagogue* on Dohány utca.

Opera

You should pay at least one visit to the *State*

Opera House, VI Andrássy út 22 (metro: Opera), to hear a concert and to see the frescos and incredibly rich decoration inside. The box office is on the left-hand side of the building behind the tour office (closed on Saturday and Monday).

Budapest has a second opera house, the modern (and ugly) *Erkel Theatre* at VIII Köztársaság tér 30 near Keleti train station. Tickets are sold just inside the main door (Tuesday to Saturday from 11 am to 7 pm, Sunday from 10 am to 1 pm and 4 to 7 pm).

Operettas – always a riot, especially one like the campy *Queen of the Csárdás* by Imre Kálmán – are presented at the *City Operetta Theatre* at VI Nagymező utca 17. Tickets are sold at the box office at No 19 on the same street, and it's worth checking here in summer as there are often special programmes.

Rock & Pop

The *Petőfi Csarnok* (☎ 343 4327) at XIV Zichy Mihály utca 14 in the City Park is the main place for rock concerts in Budapest. It's great if you get tickets as the hall is small enough to get really close to the performers. The Petőfi Csarnok produces a monthly programme available at the information counter. You can reach the Petőfi Csarnok most easily on trolley bus No 72 or 74 or take the metro to Széchenyi Fürdő.

The *Laser Theatre* (☎ 263 0871) at the Planetarium in the Népliget (People's Park) in district X has a mixed bag of video concerts with laser and canned music featuring the likes of Pink Floyd, Queen, U2, Led Zeppelin and Dire Straits. There are usually shows held from Monday to Saturday at 7 and 8.30 pm, which cost 990 Ft. You can get to Népliget on the blue metro or via trolley bus No 75 from Heroes' Square.

Places with live rock bands and/or decent canned music include the *Viking Rock Club*, XIII Kerekes utca 6; the *Park Café*, a Hard Rock Café wannabe on the shores of Buda's 'Bottomless Lake' at XI Kosztolányi Dezső tér 2; and *Rocktogon*, VI Mozsár utca 9, with funky metal.

Jazz & Blues

The *Merlin Jazz Club*, V Gerlóczy utca 4, around the corner from Károly körút 28 (metro: Deák tér), has live music nightly from 10 pm. The *Jazz Café* in a cellar at V Balassi Bálint 25 is flooded in blue light that makes the smoky air seem even denser; the music starts at 8 pm on Monday, Wednesday, Friday and Saturday. From Tuesday to Saturday night, the *Made Inn Club*, VI Andrássy út 112 (metro: Bajza utca), presents live Latin American music, acoustic, pop or blues. You can socialise in the outside courtyard in summer.

Hades, at VI Vörösmarty utca 31, is actually a 'jazztaurant', but most come here just for the music. *Fat Mo's Speakeasy* plays the blues nightly till 4 am at V Nyáry Pál utca 9. Another good place is the *Fél Tíz Jazz Club*, with an eclectic mix at VIII Baross utca 30.

More relaxed places for jazz and blues are the *Nothing But the Blues Club* at VIII Krúdy utca 6, with quiet music and an artsy crowd, and sporadically at the *Közgáz* at the Economics University, IX Fővám tér 8.

Folk Music & Dance

Authentic folk-music workshops (*táncház* or 'dance house') are held at least once a week at several locations around the city, including the *Municipal Cultural House* (Fővárosi Művelődési Ház) at XI Fehérvári út 47 in Buda; the *Kalamajka Táncház* at V Molnár utca 9; and the *Marczibányi Művelődési Ház*, II Marczibányi tér 5/a, where the popular folk group Muzsikás usually jams on Thursday at 8 pm. The táncház evenings at the *Petőfi Csarnok*, XIV Zichy Mihály utca 14, give you the opportunity to learn folk dancing. Ask about the Sirtos Greek dancing on Sunday evenings as this attracts lots of young people who form massive circles and dance to the lively Greek folk music.

Many people come to táncház evenings to learn the folk dances that go with the music (and of course you can dance too). These workshops have nothing to do with tourism and are a great opportunity to hear musicians practising and get involved in a local scene at next to no expense. You become part of the programme instead of merely watching others perform.

Every Monday, Friday and Saturday from May to mid-October at 8.30 pm, the more touristy Folklór Centrum presents a programme of Hungarian dancing accompanied by a Gypsy orchestra at the Municipal Cultural House. This performance is one of the best of its kind in Budapest.

Also in summer, the 40 dancers of the Hungarian State Folk Ensemble perform at the *Budai Vigadó*, I Corvin tér 8 (metro: Batthyány tér). The 1½-hour programmes begin at 8 pm daily, except Friday and Saturday, from April to October. On the same nights at 8 pm most of the year you can see Hungarian folk dancing at the stately *Duna Palota*, V Zrínyi utca 5 just off Roosevelt tér in Pest. All three shows cost 2500/1900 Ft for adults/students.

Budapest's two ballet companies are based at the Opera House.

Pubs & Bars

Budapest is loaded with pubs and bars and there are enough to satisfy all tastes. A popular place in Pest to start an evening on the town is *Morrison's Music Pub*, an English-style pub and disco at VI Révay utca 25 next to the Opera House. The first 'English' pub in Budapest and now a local Hungarian hangout is the *Fregatt* at V Molnár utca 26.

For Irish-style pubs (and music), head for *Becketts*, V Bajcsy-Zsilinszky út 72, or *Irish Cat* at V Múzeum körút 41, which has Guinness and Kilkenny on tap, a whisky bar and the fiercest bouncers outside a gorilla cage.

Pertu Station at Váci utca 41/a is a pubby place with décor reminiscent of the little yellow metro. It also does good salads and sandwiches; the service is funny and cheeky. Less expatty but more interesting for that is *Portside* at VII Dohány utca 7. It has pool tables and is open till 2 am on weekdays and to 4 am at the weekend.

Janis Pub at V Királyi Pál utca 8 near Ferenciek tere is usually a stop for a quick few on the way to somewhere else, but some people linger here for the great chilli.

Picasso Point at VI Hajós utca 31 is a very popular club attracting a friendly, arty crowd. *Café Noir* just opposite is a popular pool pub.

Paris Texas at Ráday utca 22 near Kálvin tér has a coffeehouse feel to it and pool tables; *Big Mambo* in a cellar bar at VIII Mária utca 48 has a bohemian crowd and great pizza.

Champions Sports Bar at VII Alsó Erdősor utca 1 just off Rákóczi út shows sports (mostly American) on 10 big-screen TVs. It's open daily till 1 or 2 am.

More subdued places for a drink are *Café Incognito* and *Café Mediterán* opposite one another at Liszt Ferenc tér 3 and 10 respectively. The *Balloon Bar* in the Atrium Hyatt hotel, V Roosevelt tér 2, has a sleazy 1970s feel to it – and the best views of the river and Castle Hill. On Castle Hill itself, the *Café Pierrot* piano bar is a pricey but comfortable spot for a drink or a coffee at I Fortuna utca 14.

Circus

The *Grand Circus*, XIV Állatkerti körút 7 (metro: Széchenyi Fürdő), has performances on Saturday and Sunday at 10 am; Wednesday, Thursday, Friday and Saturday at 3 pm; and Wednesday, Friday, Saturday and Sunday at 7 pm (closed in summer). Although the matinées are occasionally booked out by school groups, there's almost always space in the evening. Advance tickets (250 to 420 Ft) are sold at the circus itself.

SPECTATOR SPORT
Horse Racing

The descendants of the nomadic Magyars are keen about horse racing. For trotting, go to the *Kerepesi Ügetőpálya* at VIII Kerepesi út 9, about 10 minutes south of Keleti train station via bus No 95. About 10 races are held on Saturday from 3 pm and on Wednesday from 5 pm. Admission is 100 Ft.

The *Galopp Lóversenytér* has flat racing from 2 pm on Thursday and Sunday between April and November. It's in Kincsem Park at X Albertirsai út 2, about a 15-minute walk

BUDAPEST

(follow the signs) south of the Pillangó utca red metro stop. Admission here is also 100 Ft.

THINGS TO BUY

Before you do any shopping for handicrafts at street markets, have a look in the Folkart Centrum, V Váci utca 14, a large store where prices are clearly marked. It's open daily from 9.30 am till very late.

Frankly, though, most of the stuff for sale at folk-art shops (*népművészeti bolt*) in Hungary is junk; seek the real thing from the women from Transylvania who sometimes congregate on Váci utca (now rarely), Moszkva tér or at the market on the corner of Fehérvári út and Schönherz utca in Buda's district XI.

In the far back corner upstairs in the Central Market Hall on Fővám tér (metro: Kálvin tér) are a group of stalls where vendors sell Hungarian folk costumes, dolls, painted eggs, embroidered tablecloths etc. Holló Atelier at V Vitkovics Mihály utca 12, near Váci utca, has attractive folk art with a modern look.

For fine porcelain, there's a Herend outlet at V József nádor tér 11 and a Zsolnay one at V Kigyó utca 4, near Váci utca. Haas & Czjek at VI Bajcsy-Zsilinszky út 23, just off Deák tér, sell Hollóháza and Alföldi porcelain.

If you don't have time to head all the way out to the Ecseri market (see the following Flea Market section), check the antique shops on XIII Falk Miksa utca and V Vitkovics Mihály utca in Pest and II Frankel Leó út in Buda.

Báv is essentially a chain of pawn shops with branches around town. Try VI Andrássy út 43 for old jewellery, V Bécsi utca 1-1 for knick-knacks and glassware, and XIII Szent István körút 3 for chinaware and textiles.

The Zeneszalon on the Danube side of V Vörösmarty tér has compact discs of Hungarian folk music, including a few by the excellent Gypsy band Kalyi Jag and Muzsikás, the popular Hungarian folk group. For locally produced classical CDs and tapes (500 to 2000 Ft), try the Liszt Ferenc Zeneműbolt at VI Andrássy út 45.

There's an excellent selection of Hungarian wines at the Boutique des Vins (V József Attila utca 12 – entrance on Hild tér). Ask the staff to recommend a label if you feel lost. Demi John (V Cukor utca 4) also stocks many of the best labels; it's open weekdays from 10 am till 8 pm and Saturday till 4 pm.

Feather or goose-down products like pillows or duvets (comforters) are of excellent quality at Ruti Butik, V Irányi utca 18. Down pillows start at 3500 Ft and duvets at 12,000 Ft.

The Derby shop at V Irányi utca 7 sells everything and anything you might need to kit you and a horse out for riding. The tackle shop at V Váci utca 46 can do the same if you're going fishing.

Flea Market

Ecseri (often just called 'the piac', or 'market'), on Nagykőrösi út in the far-flung XIXth district, is one of the biggest and best flea markets in Eastern Europe, selling everything from antique jewellery and Soviet army watches to old musical instruments and Fred Astaire-style top hats. It's open weekdays till about 4 pm and Saturday till 1 pm (the best day to go). To get there, take bus No 54 from Boráros tér near the Petőfi Bridge or, better, the red express bus No 54 from the Határ utca stop on the blue metro line and get off when you see the crowds.

GETTING THERE & AWAY
Air

Malév Hungarian Airlines has its main ticket office (☎ 266 5616) near Vörösmarty tér at V Dorottya utca 2 and another office (☎ 266 5627) at Apáczai Csere János utca 19. Other major carriers and their locations include:

Aeroflot
    V Váci utca 4 (☎ 118 5892)
British Airways
    VIII Rákóczi út 1-3 (☎ 118 3299)
Delta
    V Apáczai Csere János utca 4 (☎ 266 1400)

Lauda
V Aranykéz utca 4-6 (☎ 266 3169)
Lufthansa
V Váci utca 19-21 (☎ 266 4511)
LOT
V Vigadó tér 3 (☎ 266 4772)
SAS
V Bajcsy-Zsilinszky út 12 (☎ 266 2633)
Swissair
V Kristóf tér 7-8 (☎ 267 2500)

See also The Airport in the following Getting Around section.

Bus

There are three important bus stations in Budapest. Most buses to Western Europe as well as to Prague, Bratislava, Slovenia and Croatia and destinations in Hungary south and west of Budapest leave from the station at V Erzsébet tér (☎ 117 2966 or ☎ 118 2122; metro: Deák tér). There's a left-luggage office inside the station open daily from 6 am to 6 pm.

Some buses for Eastern Europe as well as Turkey and Sweden and destinations east of the Danube leave from the bus station at Népstadion (☎ 252 4496 or ☎ 252 1896) at XIV Hungária körút 48-52 (metro: Népstadion). The left-luggage office here keeps the same hours as the one at Erzsébet tér.

Buses to the Danube Bend leave from the Árpád Bridge station (☎ 129 1450; metro: Árpád híd). A small station at Széna tér next to Moszkva tér in Buda handles buses to and from the Pilis Hills and towns north-west of the capital, including a few departures to Esztergom, as an alternative to the Árpád Bridge station. For details of international bus services, see the introductory Getting There & Away chapter.

Train

Budapest also has three main train stations. Keleti train station at Baross tér (☎ 113 6835; metro: Keleti pályaudvar) handles domestic trains to and from the north and north-east. Trains for the Great Plain and the Danube Bend arrive and depart from Nyugati train station (☎ 149 0115; metro: Nyugati pályaudvar). For trains bound for

Transdanubia and Lake Balaton, go to Déli train station (☎ 175 6293; metro: Déli pályaudvar).

The handful of secondary stations are of little importance to long-distance travellers. Very occasionally, though, a through train in summer will stop only at Kőbánya-Kispest train station (the terminus of the blue metro line) or even at Kelenföld train station in Buda.

The stations are pretty dismal places, with unsavoury-looking characters hanging about day and night, but they all have some amenities. Keleti and Nyugati stations have left-luggage sections, post offices and grocery stores that are open late or even round the clock. Déli has coin-operated lockers and a 24-hour convenience store nearby on Alkotás utca.

All the stations are on metro lines, but if you need to take a taxi, avoid the sharks hovering around. At Déli, cross over to Alkotás utca and hail one there. At Keleti station, get into one of the legal cabs at the rank on Kerepesi út, south of the terminal. Nyugati tér is a major intersection, so you'll have no problem finding a legitimate taxi.

You can buy tickets and seat reservations directly at all three stations, but the queues are often long, passengers are in a hurry and salespeople are not the most patient in the city. Many of the travel agencies listed in this chapter will get you train tickets, and you can buy advance tickets for express trains at the main MÁV ticket office (☎ 322 9035) at VI Andrássy út 35.

For information about international train travel, see the Getting There & Away chapter earlier in this book.

Car & Motorcycle

Prices at the big international car-rental firms in Budapest are very high. An Opel Corsa from Avis (☎ 118 4240), V Szervita tér 8, for example, costs US$240 a week plus US$0.40 per km or US$100 a day unlimited km (US$165 for a weekend). The 25% ÁFA (value-added tax) doesn't apply to foreigners who sign an affidavit saying they do not intend staying in Hungary more than 180 days.

One of the cheapest outfits in Budapest for renting cars is Inka (☎ 117 2150) at V Bajcsy-Zsilinszky út 16. Its least expensive car – a Suzuki Swift – costs 13,860 Ft a week without ÁFA plus 22 Ft per km or 5500 Ft a week unlimited km (14,380 for a weekend). Insurance is 1200 Ft a day extra. Though more expensive than Inka, Americana Rent-a-Car (☎ 120 8287), in the Ibis Hotel Volga at XIII Dózsa György út 65, is reliable and has US cars with automatic transmissions. A Suzuki Swift here costs US$55 a day or $110 for a three-day weekend.

Hitching

There's a service in Budapest called Kenguru (☎ 266 5857), VIII Kőfaragó út 15 (metro: Blaha Lujza tér), that matches up drivers and riders for a fee – mostly to points abroad. Kenguru gets 1.40 Ft per km and the driver 4.40 Ft. Sample one-way costs are: Amsterdam 8300 Ft, London 9700 Ft, Munich 4150 Ft, Paris 8850 Ft, Prague 3100 Ft and Vienna 1600 Ft. They give out a free booklet listing other ride-share centres in Europe and North America. The office is open weekdays from 8 am till 6 pm and Saturday from 10 am to 2 pm.

Boat

Mahart ferries and hydrofoils to Vienna depart from the International Ferry Pier (Nemzetközi hajóállomás) on Belgrád rakpart, just north of Szabadság Bridge on the Pest side in district V. For details of schedules and fares, see the introductory Getting There & Away chapter.

Mahart river ferries and, in summer, hydrofoils link Budapest with the towns on the Danube Bend; see that chapter for fares and schedules. In the capital the boats leave from below Vigadó tér (metro: Vörösmarty tér) on the Pest side. The first stop is usually Batthyány tér on the Buda side.

GETTING AROUND
The Airport

There are two terminals about five km apart at Budapest's Ferihegy airport, which is 16 km south-east of the capital. Malév, Delta, Lufthansa, Alitalia and Air France flights arrive and depart from Terminal 2; all other airlines use the older Terminal 1. Be sure to ask the airline representative or travel agent which terminal you're departing from when confirming your flight.

With three much cheaper options for getting to/from Ferihegy, it would be senseless to take a taxi and risk a major rip-off. If the driver doesn't fiddle with the meter, you will at least be asked to pay the return fare. But if you must take a taxi, the fares posted at the airport are 2900/3300/3900 Ft to Pest/Buda/Buda Hills. Expect to pay about 1800 Ft if transferring between the terminals. The Tele 5 taxi company (☎ 155 5555) was advertising a flat fare of 1955 Ft to the airport from anywhere in Budapest at the time of writing.

The Airport Minibus Service (☎ 296 6283) picks up passengers wherever they're staying – be it hotel, hostel or private home. But there are drawbacks: you have to book 24 hours in advance and, as the van seats about half a dozen people, it can be a time-consuming process (and nerve-wracking if you're running late). The fare is 1000 Ft per person. Tickets into the city are available in the airport arrival halls.

An easier way to go is with the Centrum Bus (☎ 296 8555), which links Erzsébet tér with both Ferihegy terminals. Vans run every half-hour between 5.30 am and 9.30 pm. The fare is 500 Ft, and they advise you to count on 30 minutes to Terminal 1 and 40 minutes to Terminal 2.

The cheapest way to go in either direction is to take the blue metro to the end of the line (the Kőbánya-Kispest stop) and board bus No 93. Note that both the red express and black No 93 are good for Ferihegy 1; only the red one carries on to Ferihegy 2. The total cost is 100 Ft.

The general flight information phone number at the airport is ☎ 296 9696.

Public Transport

Budapest has an ageing but safe, inexpensive and efficient transport system that will never have you waiting more than five or 10 minutes. There are four types of vehicles in use: metro trains, blue buses, yellow trams and red trolley buses.

Public transport in Budapest runs from 4.30 am till shortly after 11 pm. There are also about 15 night buses and trams (marked with an 'É' after the designated number) running every half-hour or so on the main routes. After 8 pm, you must board buses from the front entrance and show the driver your ticket or pass. Eating is strictly taboo on buses, and your fellow passengers will lose no time in pointing this out.

Fares & Transit Passes

To use public transport you must buy tickets at a kiosk, newsstand or metro entrance. To travel on trams, trolleybuses, regular buses and the HÉV (as far as the city limits, which is the Békásmegyer stop) the fare is a flat 50 Ft. In July 1996 the fare structure for the metro changed. The basic fare is 50 Ft, allowing you to travel as far as you want on the same metro line; it drops to 35 Ft if you are just going three stops within 30 minutes. Five stops with a change (transfer) at Deák tér to another metro line costs 55 Ft. Unlimited stops travelled with one change within one hour is 80 Ft. You must always travel in one continuous direction on a metro ticket; return trips are not allowed.

You can get passes valid on all trams, buses, trolleybuses, HÉV (to the city limits) and metro lines for a day (400 Ft), three days (800 Ft) or 10/20 trips (450/850 Ft). None of these require a photograph. Passes good for a week (975 Ft), a fortnight (1300 Ft) or a month (1950 Ft) require a mug shot. All but the monthly passes are valid from midnight to midnight, so buy them in advance and specify the date(s) you want. The most central places to get them are at the Deák tér metro station (near the entrance to the Underground Museum) and the Nyugati tér metro concourse.

Travelling 'black' (ticketless) is more risky than ever in Budapest; with increased surveillance (including a big crackdown in the metro), there's a good chance you'll get caught. Tickets are always checked on the HÉV. The on-the-spot fine is 600 Ft, which rises to 1500 Ft if you pay later at the BKV office, VII Akácfa utca 22. It's your call, but if you do get nabbed, do us all a favour: shut up and pay up. The inspectors – and your fellow passengers – hear the same stories every day of the year.

Bus, Tram & Trolley Bus

There's an extensive network of tram, trolleybus and bus services run by the BKV city transport company (☎ 322 4416); you'll seldom wait more than a few minutes for any of them. On certain bus lines the same numbered bus may have a black or a red number. In this case, the red-numbered bus is the express, which makes limited stops. An invaluable transit map detailing all services is available at most metro ticket booths.

Buses and trams are much of a muchness, though the latter are often faster and generally more pleasant for sightseeing. Trolley buses go along cross-streets in central Pest and are of little use to visitors, with the exception of the ones to the City and Népliget parks.

The most important tram lines are:

- Nos 2 and 2/a, which travel along the Pest side of the Danube as far as Jászai Mari tér
- Nos 4 and 6, which start at Fehérvári út and Móricz Zsigmond körtér in district XI (Buda) respectively and follow the entire length of the Big Ring Road in Pest before crossing back to Moszkva tér
- No 18, which runs from southern Buda along Bartók Béla út through the Tabán to Moszkva tér
- No 19, which covers part of the same route but then runs along the Buda side of the Danube to Batthyány tér
- Nos 47 and 49 linking Deák tér in Pest with points in southern Buda
- No 61 connecting Móricz Zsigmond tér with Déli station and Moszkva tér

Buses you might take are:

- the black No 4, which runs from northern Pest via Heroes' Square to Deák tér (the red No 4 follows the same route but crosses over Chain Bridge into central Buda)

- No 7, which cuts across a large swathe of central Pest and southern Buda from Bosnyák tér and down Rákóczi út to Kelenföld station in southern Buda
- No 86, which runs the length of Buda from Kosztolányi Dezső tér to Óbuda
- No 105 from Heroes' Square to Deák tér

Metro Budapest has three underground metro lines intersecting (only) at Deák tér: M1, the little yellow line from Vörösmarty tér to Mexikoi út; M2, the red line from Déli train station to Örs vezér tere; and M3, the blue line from Újpest-Központ to Kőbánya-Kispest. A possible source of confusion on the yellow line (no one says the 'M1') is that one stop is called Vörösmarty tér and another is Vörösmarty utca. The metro is the fastest (but obviously the least scenic) way to go. Though it only has three stops in Buda, the green HÉV suburban railway functions almost like a fourth metro line. It has four lines, but only one is of real use to most travellers: from Batthyány tér in Buda via Óbuda and Aquincum to Szentendre.

Car & Motorcycle

Though it's not so bad at night, driving in Budapest during the day is a nightmare: road works reduce traffic to a snail's crawl; there are more serious accidents than fender-bender ones; and parking spots are very difficult to find. There are covered parking areas in Szervita tér and at the Corvinus Kempinski and Duna Marriott hotels in the inner city. The public transport system is good and cheap. Use it – at least in the city.

For assistance if you break down, or if you're trying to trace a towed vehicle, ring ☎ 252 8000.

Taxi

Taxis aren't as cheap as they once were in Budapest and, considering the excellent public transport network, you won't really have to use them much. We've heard from several readers who were grossly overcharged and even threatened by taxi drivers in Budapest, so taking a taxi in this city should be approached with caution.

Not all taxi meters are set at the same rates,

and some are much more expensive than others. The taxis with no name on the door and only a removable taxi sign on the roof are the most likely to cheat you. Never get into a taxi that does not have a yellow licence plate (required by law), the logo of one of the reputable taxi firms listed below on the side doors and a table of fares posted on the dashboard inside.

The following are the telephone numbers of reliable taxi firms in Budapest – in order of preference. You can call them from anywhere (the dispatchers usually speak English), and they'll arrive in a matter of minutes. Make sure you know the number of the phone you're using, as that's how they establish your address.

City	☎ 211 1111
Tele 5	☎ 155 5555
Fő	☎ 122 2222
Rádió	☎ 177 7777
Volán	☎ 166 6666
Buda	☎ 233 3333

Bicycle

The main roads in the city might be a bit too busy and nerve-wracking to allow enjoyable cycling, but there are quite a few areas where a bike would be ideal. See Cycling under the previous Activities section for ideas on where to cycle, and information on where to rent bikes.

Boat

BKV runs passenger ferries from Boráros tér, beside Petőfi Bridge, to Rómaifürdő, with many stops along the way, between late May and mid-September some four to six times daily from Thursday to Sunday. Tickets (200/100 Ft for adults/children) are usually sold on board. The ferry stop closest to Castle Hill is Batthyány tér, and Petőfi tér is not far from Vörösmarty tér, a convenient place to pick up the boat on the Pest side.

Private boats at the foot of Margaret Bridge on the Pest side will take you to Rómaifürdő from Thursday to Sunday, but you'll have to negotiate your own deal. You can return to Budapest on the HÉV from there.

See the previous Organised Tours section for information about river cruises.

Around Budapest

Let's face it: an awful lot in Hungary is 'around Budapest' and many of the towns and cities in the Danube Bend, Transdanubia, Northern Uplands and even the Great Plain could be day trips from the capital. You can be in Szentendre in half an hour, for example, and Gyöngyös in the Mátra foothills is only 80 km to the east.

SZOBOR PARK

A truly mind-blowing experience is a visit to Szobor Park (Statue Park) in district XXII, home to almost four dozen busts and statues of Lenin, Marx, Béla Kun and heroic workers that have ended up on trash heaps in other Eastern European countries. It's Eastern Europe's first such theme park. Ogle at the socialist realism and try to imagine that at least four of these monstrous monuments were erected as recently as the late 1980s; many were still in place when I first moved to Budapest in early 1992.

Szobor Park is on XXII Szabadkai út and Balatoni út, just off the old route No 70 towards Lake Balaton. It can be reached on the yellow bus to Érd, which can be boarded from bay No 6 at the little station on the southern side of Kosztolányi Dezső tér in Buda. The park is open daily from 10 am to 6 pm and admission costs 100 Ft.

RÁCKEVE
• pop 8467

This town is on the south-east end of Csepelsziget, the long island in the Danube south of Budapest. Csepel is often dismissed as an industrial dump, but it becomes very rural as you move away from the city. Ráckeve's lures are its pretty riverside park and beach, a Gothic Serbian Orthodox church (rác is the old Hungarian word for 'Serb') and, if you've got the dosh, a hotel located in the former Savoy Mansion.

Savoy Mansion

From the HÉV station in Ráckeve, walk south along Kossuth Lajos utca to the Savoy Mansion hotel at No 95, which faces the Ráckeve-Danube River branch. The domed manse with two wings was built in 1702 for Prince Eugene of Savoy by an Austrian architect who would later design the Schönbrunn Palace in Vienna. The mansion was completely renovated and turned into a pricey hotel and conference centre in 1982.

Serbian Orthodox Church

As you carry on south toward the centre of town, you can't miss the blue belfry of the Serbian Orthodox church to the west. The church is at Viola utca 1 and opens Tuesday to Saturday from 10 am till noon and 2 till 5 pm (afternoon only on Sunday). The church was originally built in 1487 by Serbs who fled their town of Keve ahead of the invading Turks. It was enlarged in the following century. The free-standing clock tower was added in 1758. It used to have Cyrillic letters instead of numbers to show the time, but these seem to have disappeared.

The walls and ceiling of the church interior are covered with colourful murals painted by a Serbian master from Albania in the mid-18th century. They depict scenes from the Old and New Testaments and were meant to teach illiterate parishioners the Bible. The first section of the nave is reserved for women; the part beyond the separating wall is for men. Only the priest and his servers enter the sanctuary beyond the iconostasis, the richly carved and gilded gate festooned with icons.

Places to Stay & Eat

The top choice for accommodation is naturally the 28-room Savoy Mansion hotel (☎ 385 253). Singles/doubles are DM80/100 with private bath and breakfast. You can have a look around the hotel by visiting the vaulted Pince restaurant in the cellar.

The ugly Kerámia hotel (☎ 24-385 753),

across the Árpád Bridge at Szitakötő utca 2, is a very distant second choice, but has doubles for half the price of those at the Savoy Mansion. *Hídláb Camping* (☎ 24-385 501) on the same side at Dömsödi utca 4 is open from May to mid-September.

The *Fekete Holló* restaurant and cellar bar, in a renovated 16th-century townhouse in the centre on Kossuth Lajos utca, stays open till 11 pm.

Getting There & Away

The easiest way to reach Ráckeve, about 40 km south of Budapest, is on the HÉV suburban train departing from the Közvágóhíd terminus in district IX on the Buda side. You can get to that station on tram No 2 or from Keleti train station on tram Nos 23 and 24. The HÉV trip takes 75 minutes.

The last HÉV train back to Budapest leaves Ráckeve at 11 pm.

Danube Bend

The Danube (Hungarian: Duna), the second-longest river in Europe after the Volga, rises in the Black Forest in the south-west of Germany and flows in an easterly direction until it reaches a point about 40 km north of Budapest. Here the Börzsöny Hills on the left bank and the Pilis Hills on the right force it to bend sharply southward through Budapest and the rest of Hungary for some 400 km before it again resumes its easterly flow, finally emptying into the Black Sea in Romania.

The Danube 'Bend' is, strictly speaking, the S-curve that begins just below Esztergom and twists for 20 km past Visegrád to where it splits in two, forming long, skinny Szentendre Island. But the name has come to describe the entire region of peaks, resorts and river towns to the north and north-west of the capital. The Bend is the most beautiful stretch of the Danube along its entire course of almost 3000 km and should not be missed.

The right bank (that is, the area south and west of the river) has the lion's share of historical towns and parkland. This was the northernmost region of the Roman colonies; Esztergom was the first seat of the Magyar kings and has been the centre of Roman Catholicism in Hungary for more than 1000 years.

Visegrád was central Europe's 'Camelot' during Hungary's brief flirtation with the Renaissance in the 15th century, when the powerful royal family was based here. Szentendre, which has its origins in Serbian culture, is an important art centre. And then there's the Pilis Park Forest, once a royal hunting ground and now a popular recreational area of hills, gorges and trails.

The left bank (north and east of the Danube) is far less developed, though the ancient town of Vác and the woods of the Börzsöny Protected Area on have much to offer visitors.

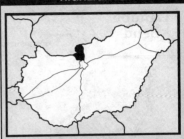

HIGHLIGHTS

- the medieval hilltop citadel at Visegrád and the wonderful views of the Danube
- a trip via Mahart ferry from Budapest to Szentendre, Visegrád or even Esztergom
- the splendid Gothic altarpieces and paintings at the Christian Museum in Esztergom
- the Margit Kovács Museum of ceramic art in Szentendre
- a visit to the arboretum at Vácrátót on a warm spring afternoon
- any of a number of hikes in the Börzsöny Hills from 12th-century Nográd Castle

SZENTENDRE
- *pop 19,000*
- *area code ☎ 26*

A mere 19 km north of Budapest, Szentendre (translated as 'St Andrew') is the southern gateway to the Danube Bend but has none of the imperial history or drama of Visegrád or Esztergom. As an art colony turned lucrative tourist centre easily accessible from Budapest, Szentendre strikes many travellers as a little too 'cute', and the town is crowded and relatively expensive most of the year. Still, it's an easy train trip from the capital, and the town's dozens of art museums, galleries and churches are well worth the trip. Just try to avoid it at weekends in summer.

Like most towns along the Danube Bend, Szentendre was home first to the Celts and

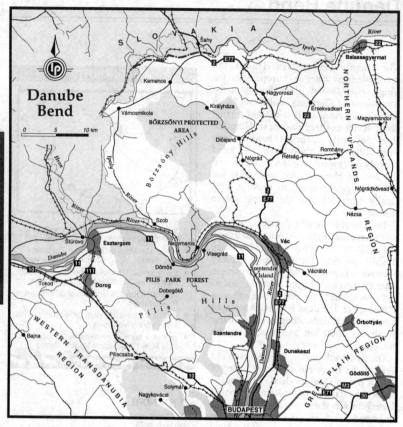

then the Romans, who built an important border fortress here called Ulcisia Castra (Wolf's Castle). The area was overrun by a succession of tribes during the Great Migrations until the Magyars arrived late in the 9th century and established a colony here. By the 14th century, Szentendre was a prosperous estate under the supervision of the royal castle at Visegrád.

It was about this time that the first wave of a people who would build most of Szentendre's churches and give the town its unique Balkan feel, the Serbian Orthodox Christians, came from the south in advance

of the Turks. They settled here, and many were employed as boatmen and border soldiers by Matthias Corvinus, Hungary's beloved Renaissance king. But the Turkish occupation of Hungary brought this peaceful coexistence to an end, and by the end of the 17th century Szentendre was deserted.

Though Hungary was liberated from the Ottomans not long afterward, fighting continued in the Balkans and a second wave of Serbs, Greeks, Dalmatians and others – as many as 8000, in fact – fled to Szentendre. Believing they would eventually return home, but enjoying complete religious freedom under the relatively benevolent rule of the Habsburgs (a right denied Hungary's Protestants around the same time), a half-dozen Orthodox clans each built their own wooden churches.

The refugees prospered as merchants, tanners and vintners, and Szentendre became an important market town, rivalling Leipzig in Germany and Polish Kraków. It was also the centre of Serbian culture, commerce and religion in Hungary, and most of the churches and houses were rebuilt in stone in the baroque style at this time. But a series of natural catastrophes in the late 19th century – including the arrival of the phylloxera lice that wiped out the vineyards – drove most of the settlers away. Today Szentendre has some of the most important relics of Serbian culture in Hungary, but only a few descendants of the artisans and builders who actually produced them remain.

Szentendre's delightful location on the west bank of the Danube within full view of the Visegrád and Pilis hills began to attract day-trippers and painters from Budapest early this century; an artists' colony was established here in the 1920s. It has been known for its art and artists ever since.

Orientation

The HÉV suburban commuter train and bus stations lie side by side south of the town centre at the start of Dunakanyar körút (Danube Bend Ring Road). From here walk through the subway and north along Kossuth Lajos utca and Dumtsa Jenő utca to Fő tér, the heart of Szentendre. The Duna korzó promenade along the Danube and the ferry to Szentendre Island are a few minutes' walk east and north-east of Fő tér. The Mahart ferry pier is about a km north on Czóbel Béla sétány, which branches off from Duna korzó, and the camping ground on Pap Island about a km beyond that.

Information

Tourinform (☎ 317 965), Dumtsa Jenő utca 22, has brochures and information on Szentendre as well as other parts of the Bend. It is open weekdays from 10 am to 4 pm, to 2 pm on Saturday and Sunday. Dunatours (☎ 311 311) is at Bogdányi utca 1 and Ibusz (☎ 310 181) at No 15 of the same street. Visitors should note that between November and March much of Szentendre shuts down during the week.

There's an OTP bank at Dumtsa Jenő utca 6, just off Fő tér, and a K&H Bank at Bogdányi utca 11 with an ATM. Ibusz is open longer hours than the banks and gives a rate only about 2% lower for travellers' cheques. You'll find the main post office at Kossuth Lajos utca 23-25 across from the HÉV and bus stations.

Things to See

If you begin visiting sights on arrival, you won't want to miss **Požarevačka Church** at Kossuth Lajos utca 1 just before you cross the narrow Bükkös Stream. This Serbian Orthodox church was dedicated in 1763; the lovely iconostasis inside (1742) graced a wooden church that stood earlier on the site and is the oldest in Szentendre. The church is usually open to visitors at the weekend only.

The **SS Peter & Paul Church** at Péter-Pál utca 6 off Dumtsa Jenő utca began life as the Čiprovačka Orthodox Church in 1753, but was later taken over by Dalmatian Catholics. The **Barcsay Museum** at Dumtsa Jenő utca 10 contains the work of one of the founders of Szentendre's art colony.

Fő tér is the colourful centre of Szentendre and much of interest is nearby. The museums, all in splendid 18th and 19th-century burghers' houses, are open daily between 10 am and 6 pm from April to October (excluding Monday). In winter, the hours are from 10 am to 4 pm, often on Friday, Saturday and Sunday only.

In the centre of Fő tér stands the **Plague Cross** (1763), not the usual sandstone pillar raised by the grateful faithful in squares throughout Hungary but an iron cross on a marble base decorated with icons. The **Kmetty Museum** on the south-west side of Fő tér displays the work of János Kmetty (1889-1975), a Cubist.

For a little less rational thought, go across

DANUBE BEND

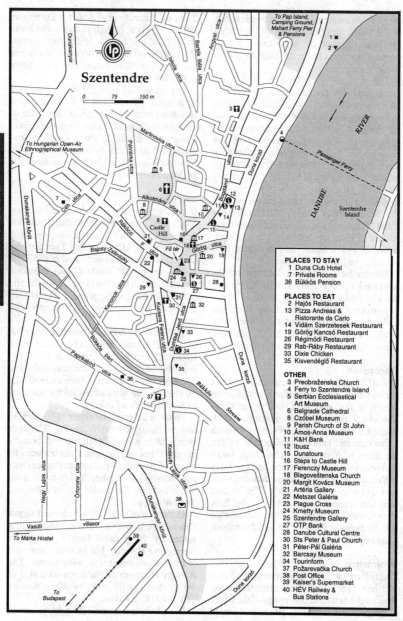

Szentendre

0   75   150 m

To Pap Island,
Camping Ground,
Mahart Ferry Pier
& Pensions

To Hungarian Open-Air
Ethnographical Museum

RIVER

Passenger Ferry

DANUBE

Szentendre
Island

To Márka Hostel

Vasúti

villasor

To
Budapest

PLACES TO STAY
1 Duna Club Hotel
7 Private Rooms
36 Bükkös Pension

PLACES TO EAT
2 Hajós Restaurant
13 Pizza Andreas &
    Ristorante da Carlo
14 Vidám Szerzetesek Restaurant
19 Görög Kancsó Restaurant
26 Régimódi Restaurant
29 Rab-Ráby Restaurant
33 Dixie Chicken
35 Kisvendéglő Restaurant

OTHER
3 Preobraženska Church
4 Ferry to Szentendre Island
5 Serbian Ecclesiastical
    Art Museum
6 Belgrade Cathedral
8 Czóbel Museum
9 Parish Church of St John
10 Ámos-Anna Museum
11 K&H Bank
12 Ibusz
15 Dunatours
16 Steps to Castle Hill
17 Ferenczy Museum
18 Blagoveštenska Church
20 Margit Kovács Museum
21 Artéria Gallery
22 Metszet Galéria
23 Plague Cross
24 Kmetty Museum
25 Szentendre Gallery
27 OTP Bank
28 Danube Cultural Centre
30 Sts Peter & Paul Church
31 Péter-Pál Galéria
32 Barcsay Museum
34 Tourinform
37 Požarevačka Church
38 Post Office
39 Kaiser's Supermarket
40 HÉV Railway &
    Bus Stations

the square to **Blagoveštenska Church**, built in 1754. The church, with fine baroque and rococo elements, hardly looks 'Eastern' from the outside (it was designed by the baroque architect András Mayerhoffer), but once you are inside, the ornate iconostasis, elaborate 18th-century furnishings and canned Slavonic church music give the game away. It's interesting to examine the icons; though painted only half a century after the ones in Požarevačka Church, they are much more realistic and have lost that other-world spirituality.

If you descend Görög utca and turn right on to Vastagh György utca, you'll reach the entrance to the **Margit Kovács Museum** in an 18th-century salt house at No 1. The museum is Szentendre's biggest crowd-pleaser and one of the few open all year. Kovács (1902-77) was a ceramicist who combined Hungarian folk, religious and modern themes to create elongated, Gothic-like figures. Some of her works are overly sentimental but many are very powerful, especially the later ones in which she became obsessed with mortality and death. Keep an eye out for *Old Shepherd*, the glorious *Stove with Wedding Scenes* and *Mourning II*.

The **Ferenczy Museum** next to the Blagoveštenska Church at Fő tér 6 is devoted to Károly Ferenczy, the father of *plein air* painting in Hungary, and his twin son and daughter, who sculpted and wove wonderful tapestries respectively.

Bogdányi utca, Szentendre's busiest street, leads north from here to the excellent **Ámos-Anna Museum** displaying the symbolist paintings of the husband-and-wife team Margit Anna and Imre Ámos at No 12. But to avoid the crowds, slip up Váralja lépcső, the narrow steps between Fő tér 8 and 9.

Castle Hill (Vár-domb) was the site of a fortress in the Middle Ages, but all that's left of it is the walled **Parish Church of St John** in Templom tér, from where you get splendid views of the town. In the warmer months, a weekend folk-craft market is held in the square. St John's was originally built in the late 13th century but reconstructed several times over the centuries. The entrance to the church – the only one in town that has always been Catholic – is early Gothic; the frescos in the sanctuary were painted by members of the artists' colony in the 1930s. West of the church at Templom tér 1, the **Czóbel Museum** contains the works of the impressionist Béla Czóbel (1883-1976), a friend of Pablo Picasso and student of Henri Matisse.

The red tower of **Belgrade Cathedral** (1764) on Alkotmány utca rises from within a leafy, walled courtyard north of the parish church. It is the seat of the Serbian Orthodox bishop in Hungary. One of the church buildings beside it (entrance from Pátriárka utca 5) now contains the **Serbian Ecclesiastical Art Museum**, a treasure trove of icons, vestments and other sacred objects in precious metals. A 14th-century glass painting of the crucifixion is the oldest item on display; a 'cotton icon' of the life of Christ from the 18th century is unusual. Take a look at the defaced portrait of Christ upstairs on the right-hand wall. The story goes that a drunken Kuruc mercenary slashed it and, told what he had done next morning, drowned himself in the Danube.

Hungarian Open-Air Ethnographical Museum (Magyar Szabadtéri Néprajzi Múzeum) This collection of buildings, about three km north-west of the centre on Sztaravodai út, is not Hungary's largest *skanzen* (open-air or village museum), but it certainly is the most ambitious. Situated on a 46-hectare tract of rolling land, the museum was opened in the 1970s to introduce Hungarians and tourists to traditional Magyar culture by bringing bits and pieces of villages to one site. The plans call for some 300 farmhouses, churches, bell towers, mills and so on to be set up in 10 regional units. So far four are complete: the units for the Upper Tisza area of North-East Hungary and the Kisalföld and Őrség regions of Western Transdanubia give full impressions of their regions while the one representing the Great Plain is disappointing.

The houses and other buildings have been carefully reassembled and are all in good condition; highlights include the Calvinist church and 'skirted' belfry from the Erdőhát of the North-East, the German 'long house' from Harka outside Sopron, and the curious heart-shaped gravestones from the Buda Hills. Craftspeople and artisans do their thing in the warmer months. The museum is open April to October only, every day except Monday from 9 am to 5 pm.

Activities

Pap Island (Pap-sziget), two km north of the centre, is Szentendre's playground and has a grassy strand for sunbathing, a swimming pool (open May to September, 8 am to 7 pm), tennis courts and rowing boats for hire.

You can rent bicycles from the Holdas Udvar at Kossuth Lajos utca 19; take the hourly ferry across to Szentendre Island and you'll have km of uncrowded cycling ahead of you. The Hajós restaurant on the boat moored next to the posh Duna Club hotel, located north of the centre, rents boats and jet skis.

Places to Stay

Szentendre is so close to Budapest that there's no point in spending the night here unless you want to continue on to other towns on the Danube Bend without returning to the capital. Be warned, though, that most accommodation is a fair way north or west of Fő tér, and what little there is in the centre of town can be expensive in season.

Camping Two km north of Szentendre on Pap Island near the Danube River boat landing is *Pap-sziget Camping* (☎ 310 697). Camping is 1090 Ft for two persons with a tent, and there are 14 bungalows with bath at 2690 Ft for one or two people. The 20 motel rooms with shared bath are 1490 Ft. The overnight fee includes admission to the swimming pool next door; other facilities include a small supermarket, a snack bar and a restaurant. Pap-sziget Camping is open from May to September.

Private Rooms & Hostel Both Ibusz and Dunatours organise private rooms in town

for 1500 to 2000 Ft a double, but a cheaper place is the *Márka* (☎ 312 788) a workers' hostel five minutes west of the bus and train stations at Szabadkäi utca 9. The charge is 1000 Ft per person in spartan multi-bed rooms. Readers have recommended the private rooms let by *Tibor Jászai* (☎ 310 657), north-west of Fő tér at Céh utca 3.

Pensions There are quite a few of these around town, but all are relatively expensive. The most central is *Bükkös* (☎ 312 021), a 16-room pension halfway between the stations and Fő tér at Bükkös part 16. Singles/doubles with bath are 5000/5800 Ft.

The *Villa Apollo* (☎ 310 909), just off the ring road at Méhész utca 3, has six double rooms with shower for DM35 to DM40. The nearby *Coca-Cola* (☎ 310 410), with 12 terraced rooms at Dunakanyar körút 50, charges from 3800 Ft for a double. The eight-room *Villa Castra* (☎ 311 240), farther north at Ady Endre út 54, is a clean, comfortable place with doubles (including bath) priced at 4000 Ft.

Hotel By far the poshest place on the Danube Bend is the 29-room *Duna Club* (☎ 314 102) in a park by the river at Duna korzó 5. It has a fancy restaurant, an outside grill in summer, a huge swimming pool, tennis courts and a separate health club with gym, sauna and hot tub. Of course all this costs: singles are from DM80 to DM160 and doubles from DM95 to DM185, depending on the season.

Places to Eat

There are a couple of *food stalls* at the bus and HÉV stations – very convenient if you're going directly on to the open-air museum, where the choice is limited. A cheap Hungarian restaurant close by is the *Kisvendéglő* over the Bükkös Stream bridge on Jókai Mór tér.

Dixie Chicken, Dumtsa Jenő utca 16, is your standard Hungarian local fast-food joint, but they do have a salad bar and you can sit in the back courtyard. Check out the *lángos stall*, halfway up Váralja lépcső, the narrow steps between Fő tér 8 and 9. It's closed Monday and in winter opens only at the weekend.

The *Régimódi*, on the corner of Fő tér and Futó utca just down from the Margit Kovács Museum, occupies an old Szentendre house. Another old stand-by is the *Rab-Ráby* at Kucsera Ferenc utca 1.

There are a couple of Italian places on Duna korzó: the *Ristorante da Carlo* at No 6-8 is a relatively expensive restaurant with tables outside in summer, while *Pizza Andreas* at No 5/a is a more simple affair. Avoid the misnamed *Görög Kancsó* (Greek Jug) nearby at Görög utca 1. There's not a souvlakia in sight and its standard Hungarian fare is way overpriced.

The *Vidám Szerzetesek* (Merry Monks) restaurant at Bogdányi utca 3-5 is pretty touristy, but it has outside tables in summer and you're sure to make yourself understood: the menu is written in more than a dozen languages.

There's a big *Kaiser's* supermarket next to the HÉV station.

Entertainment

Tourinform or the staff at the *Danube Cultural Centre* at Duna korzó 11/a (☎ 312 657) can tell you what's on in Szentendre. Annual events to watch out for include the Spring Days art festival in late March, the Serbian Festival on 19 August in front of the Preobraženska Church on Bogdányi utca, the Szentendre Open-Air Theatre performances in Fő tér in July and August, and the fairs in Templom tér on summer weekends.

Things to Buy

Szentendre is a shopper's town – from souvenir embroidery to the latest fashions – and although prices are at Budapest levels, not everything you see is available in the capital. For glassware and ceramics, try the Péter-Pál Galéria on Péter-Pál utca. The Metszet Galéria at Fő tér 14 has wonderful old engravings, maps and prints. For fine art, try the Szentendre Gallery at Fő tér 20, or the Artéria Gallery, which is a few steps to the west at Városháza tér 1.

Getting There & Away

Bus Buses from Budapest's Árpád Bridge bus station, which is on the blue metro line, run to Szentendre at least once an hour. Onward service to Visegrád (45 minutes, 134 Ft) and Esztergom (1½ hours, 268 Ft) is good.

Train The easiest way to reach Szentendre from Budapest is to catch the HÉV suburban train from Batthyány tér in Buda, which takes just 40 minutes. You'll never wait longer than 20 minutes (half that in rush hour), and the last train leaves Szentendre for Budapest at 11.30 pm. Remember that a yellow city bus/metro ticket is good only as far as the Békásmegyer stop on the way up and you'll have to pay extra for Szentendre. Also, some HÉV trains run only as far as Békásmegyer, where you must cross the platform to board the train for Szentendre.

Boat From late May to mid-September, three daily Mahart river boats between Budapest (at 7.30 and 10 am and 2 pm) and Visegrád stop at Szentendre. From April to late May and late September till seasonal shutdown, only one boat a day operates (10 am). The one-way fare is 320/220/160 Ft for adults/students/children.

Getting Around

Any bus heading north on route No 11 to Visegrád and Esztergom will stop near most of the pensions, hotels and camp site mentioned earlier. For Pap Island, ring the bell after you pass the Danubius hotel at Ady Endre utca 28.

Some 10 buses on weekdays and seven on Saturday and Sunday leave bus stop No 8 for the skanzen (43 Ft).

You can call a taxi on ☎ 314 314.

VÁC
- *pop 34,500*
- *area code* ☎ 27

Vác lies 34 km north of Budapest on the left (ie east) bank of the Danube opposite Szentendre Island. To the north-west and stretching as far as Slovakia are the Börzsöny

DANUBE BEND

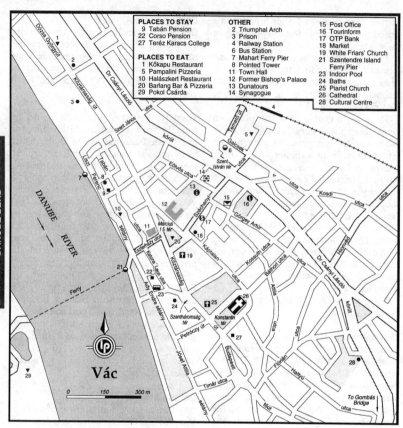

PLACES TO STAY
9 Tabán Pension
22 Corso Pension
27 Teréz Karacs College

PLACES TO EAT
1 Kőkapu Restaurant
5 Pampalini Pizzeria
10 Halászkert Restaurant
20 Barlang Bar & Pizzeria
29 Pokol Csárda

OTHER
2 Triumphal Arch
3 Prison
4 Railway Station
6 Bus Station
7 Mahart Ferry Pier
8 Pointed Tower
11 Town Hall
12 Former Bishop's Palace
13 Dunatours
14 Synagogue

15 Post Office
16 Tourinform
17 OTP Bank
18 Market
19 White Friars' Church
21 Szentendre Island
    Ferry Pier
23 Indoor Pool
24 Baths
25 Piarist Church
26 Cathedral
28 Cultural Centre

DANUBE RIVER

Ferry

Vác

0   150   300 m

To Gombás
Bridge

DANUBE BEND

Hills, the start of Hungary's mountainous northern region. The Cserhát Hills are to the east.

Unlike most Hungarian towns, Vác can prove its ancient origins without putting a spade into the ground: Uvcenum – the town's Latin name – is mentioned by Ptolemy in his 2nd-century *Geographia* as a river-crossing on an important road. King Stephen established an episcopal seat here in the 11th century, and within 300 years Vác was rich and powerful enough for its silver mark to become the realm's legal tender. The town's medieval centre and Gothic cathedral were destroyed during the Turkish occupation; the reconstruction of Vác under several bishops in the 18th century gave it its present baroque appearance.

Though no more than a sleepy provincial centre in the middle of the last century, Vác (German: Wartzen) was the first Hungarian town to be linked with Pest by train (1846), but development didn't really come until after WWII. Sadly, for many older Hungarians the name Vác conjures up a single frightening image: the notorious prison on Köztársaság út, where political prisoners were incarcerated and tortured both before the war under the rightist regime of Miklós Horthy and in the 1950s under the Communists.

Today you'd scarcely know about that as you enjoy the breezes along the embankment of the Danube, a more prominent feature here than in other towns on the Bend. Vác is also less touristed than Szentendre, Visegrád or Esztergom – perhaps the strongest recommendation for stopping over.

Orientation

The train station is at the northern end of Széchenyi utca, the bus station a few steps south-west on Galcsek utca. Following Széchenyi utca toward the river for about half a km will bring you across the ring road (Dr Csányi László körút) and down to the main square (Március 15 tér). The Mahart ferry pier is at the northern end of Liszt Ferenc sétány; the car and passenger ferry to Szentendre Island arrives and departs from the dock just south of it.

Information

There's a Tourinform office (☎ 16 160) at Dr Csányi László körút 45, and Dunatours (☎ 10 950) is at Széchenyi utca 14. Both are open from 8 am to 4 pm on weekdays; Dunatours works till noon on Saturday.

There's an OTP bank with an ATM at Széchenyi utca 8. The main post office is in Posta Park off Görgey Artúr utca.

Things to See

Március 15 (or Fő) tér has the most colourful buildings in Vác. The Dominican **White Friars' church** on the south-west side is 18th-century baroque; there's a lively **market** just behind to the north-east. The seals held by the two figures on the front of the magnificent baroque **town hall** (1764) at No 11 are those of Hungary and Bishop Kristóf Migazzi, the driving force behind Vác's reconstruction 200 years ago. The building next door at No 7-9 has been a hospital since the 18th century. Opposite at Március 15 tér 6, the former **Bishop's Palace**, parts of which belong to the oldest

building in Vác, is now an institute for the deaf and dumb.

If you walk north along Köztársaság út to No 62-64, you'll see the enormous 18th-century school that was turned into the town's infamous **prison** in the last century. It's still in use, as you'll gather from the armed guard staring from the glassed-in tower. The Communist commemorative plaque to the victims of the Horthy regime is now gone, but ghosts abound – don't tarry (and ignore the funeral parlour across the street).

A little farther north on Dózsa György út is the **Triumphal Arch**, the only one in Hungary. The arch was built by Bishop Migazzi in honour of a visit by Empress Maria Theresa and her husband Francis of Lorraine (both pictured in the arch's oval reliefs) in 1764. Migazzi, who was later named archbishop of Vienna, also planned to put up theatrical hoardings along Köztársaság út to prevent the Habsburg royal couple from seeing the town's poor housing, but he dropped the idea.

From Köztársaság út, dip down one of the narrow side streets (eg Molnár utca) to the west for a stroll along the Danube. The **old city walls** and Gothic **Pointed Tower** are near Liszt Ferenc sétány 12.

If you climb up Fürdő utca near the pool complex, you'll reach tiny Szentháromság tér and its central **Trinity Statue** (1755). The **Piarist church** (1745), with a stark white interior and marble altar, is to the east across the square.

Tree-lined Konstantin tér to the south-east is dominated by **Vác Cathedral** (1775), one of the first examples of neoclassical architecture to appear in Hungary. This imposing grey church designed by the French architect Isidore Canevale is not to everybody's liking, but the frescos on the vaulted dome and the altarpiece by Franz Anton Maulbertsch are worth a look inside. There's a display of stone fragments from the medieval cathedral in the crypt.

If you continue walking south along Budapesti főút, you'll reach the small stone **Gombás Bridge** lined with the statues of seven saints (1757) – Vác's modest answer to Charles Bridge in Prague!

The old **synagogue** at Eötvös utca 5 off Széchenyi utca was designed by an Italian architect in the Romantic style in 1864. It barely still stands.

Activities

The Vác Strandfürdő behind the Trinity statue at Szentháromság tér 1 has outdoor pools open in summer from 9 or 10 am to 7 pm. The indoor pool on the southern edge of the 'beach', is open all year and is accessible from Ady Endre sétány 16.

Places to Stay

Vác is an easy day trip from Budapest and Szentendre, and that's how most visitors see it. Accommodation is very limited – Vác is one of the few places of its size in Hungary without a real hotel.

Dunatours offers *private rooms* for 1000 Ft (double), and the *Teréz Karacs College* on Budapesti főút opposite Migazzi tér sometimes lets out dormitory rooms in July and August.

The *Tabán* (☎ 315 607), an attractive five-room pension just up from Liszt Ferenc sétány at Dombay utca 11, charges 3500 Ft for a double. The *Corso* pension (☎ 310 608), farther south along the embankment at Ady Endre sétány 6/a, couldn't be more different. Its four rooms with shared shower are above a smoky bar and cost 1000 Ft per person.

Places to Eat

Pampalini Pizzeria at Széchenyi utca 38 is convenient to the bus and train stations. A more interesting place for a pizza, though, is the *Barlang Bar* in a medieval wine cellar below Március 15 tér (entrance in the centre of the square).

Kőkapu near the Triumphal Arch at Dózsa György út 5 is one of the more established restaurants in Vác with solid Hungarian fare on offer. The *Halászkert* at Liszt Ferenc sétány 9 is a fine place for fish soup in summer, when you can sit outside and watch the ferries cross over to Szentendre Island.

On the island itself, the *Pokol Csárda* (Hell's Inn) is a popular place with locals waiting for the ferry. It's open from mid-March to mid-September.

Entertainment

The circular *Imre Madách Cultural Centre* (☎ 316 411) at Dr Csányi László körút 63 can help you with what's on in Vác and has a few exhibits of its own (one on its namesake, the 19th-century playwright, another on bookbinding). Concerts are sometimes held in Vác Cathedral and White Friars' church. Don't miss the chance to hear the Vox Humana, Vác's award-winning mixed choir.

Getting There & Away

Bus Buses depart for Árpád Bridge station in Budapest every half-hour; they are slightly less frequent to the bus station at Népstadion in Budapest. Count on at least a dozen daily buses to Balassagyarmat, Nógrád, Rétság and Vácrátót. You can also reach the county capital, Salgótarján, four times a day. Two buses a week (on Wednesday and Saturday at 7.35 am) leave for the Polish ski resort of Zakopane in the Tatra Mountains.

Train Trains depart Budapest-Nyugati station almost every half-hour for Szob via Vác, and a total of six continue along the eastern bank of the Danube to Štúrovo in Slovakia (across the river from Esztergom). Slow trains north to Balassagyarmat (five a day) from Vác stop at Diósjenő and Nógrád in the Börzsöny Hills.

From May to September MÁV runs a vintage steam train *(nosztalgiavonat)* from Budapest-Nyugati (departing at 9.50 am) to Szob via Vác and returning from Szob at 4.30 pm (Vác at 5.19 pm). But verify this service and schedule with MÁV before making plans.

Car & Motorcycle Car ferries cross over to Szentendre Island hourly from 6 am to 8 pm; a bridge connects the island's west bank with the mainland at Tahitótfalu. From there hourly buses run to Szentendre, about 10 km south.

Boat From late May to mid-September, one daily Mahart river boat sails between Budapest's Vigadó tér (at 8 am) and Vác. The same boat continues on to Visegrád and Esztergom at 10.20 am. From April to late May and late September till winter closing, the boat leaves Budapest at 7.45 am and departs Vác at 10.05 am.

AROUND VÁC
Vácrátót
You can make an easy excursion by bus to this village, 11 km south-east of Vác, celebrated for its 28-hectare **arboretum** (☎ 360 122). It was established in the late 19th century by Count Sándor Vigyázó, who later bequeathed it to the Hungarian Academy of Science (MTA). The MTA now maintains a research centre here. The arboretum contains tens of thousands of flowers, shrubs and trees, many of them, such as the Japanese cork, the Turkish hazelnut and the swamp cypress, quite rare. With its ponds, streams and little waterfall, it's a pleasant place to find yourself in spring or on a hot summer afternoon. The arboretum is open from 7 am to 6 pm April to September, to 5 pm in October and to 4 pm the rest of the year. The bus will drop you off at the entrance at Alkotmány utca 2-6. There are snack stands nearby, and the *Botanika* restaurant is just across the street at Alkotmány utca 9. You can also reach Vácrátót from Vác or Budapest-Nyugati by slow train, but the station there is about four km from the arboretum and there's not always a connecting bus.

Börzsöny Hills
These hills begin the series of six ranges that make up Hungary's Northern Uplands, and Vác is the best starting point for a visit. Surprisingly, this protected region sees few visitors, which perhaps is why birds and deer continue to be attracted by the area in such large numbers. There's very good hiking, but make sure you get hold of a copy of Cartograhia's 1:40,000 *A Börzsöny* (No 8).

Nógrád, with the ruins of a hilltop castle dating back to the 12th century, could be considered the gateway to the Börzsöny, and there's a *camp site* (☎ 35-364 134) with four-bed bungalows (1900 Ft) six km north at Diósjenő. From here you can strike out west along marked trails to 864m **Nagy Hideg** or 739m **Magas-Tax**. The Börzsöny's highest peak, 938m **Csóványos**, lies to the west of Diósjenő and is a much more difficult climb.

If you're under your own steam, take the beautiful restricted road (a small fee is charged) from Diósjenő to Kemence via Királyháza (where you'll find the 10-room *Mathias* riding pension, ☎ 27-365 139). The road follows the Kemence Stream almost the entire way – a great place for a cool dip or a picnic in summer. Just before you reach Kemence, there's a turn south into the **Fekete-völgy**, the beautiful 'Black Valley' and the 18-room *Fekete-völgy* pension (☎ 27-365 153).

An easy and excellent excursion is the five-km walk south-west from Nógrád to **Királyrét**, the royal hunting grounds of King Matthias Corvinus. Here a **narrow-gauge train** runs 10 km south to Kismaros, where you can catch a train back to Vác, Budapest or even Štúrovo in Slovakia across the Danube from Esztergom.

VISEGRÁD
• *pop 2100*
• *area code* ☎ *26*
Situated on the Danube's abrupt loop, Visegrád and its 'high castle' (the meaning of its Slavic name) is the most beautiful section and the very symbol of the Bend. As you approach Visegrád from Szentendre, 23 km to the south, keep your eyes open for a glimpse of the citadel high up on Castle Hill. Together with the palace at the base, it was once the royal centre of Hungary.

The Romans built a border fortress on Sibrik Hill just north of the present castle in the 4th century, and it was still being used by Slovak settlers 600 years later. After the Mongol invasion in 1242, King Béla IV began work on a lower castle by the river and then on the hill-top citadel. Less than a

DANUBE BEND

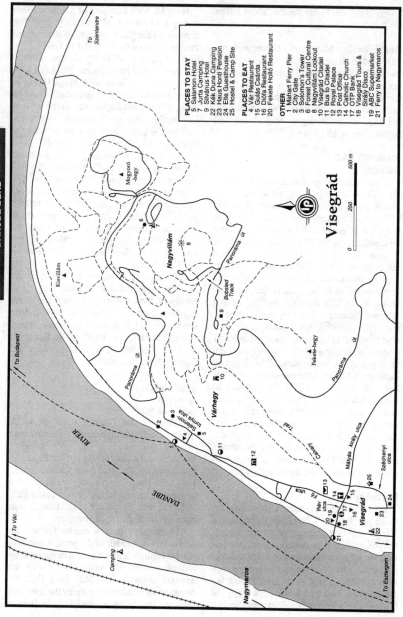

Visegrád

PLACES TO STAY
5 Salamon Hotel
7 Jurta Camping
9 Silvánus Hotel
22 Kék Duna Camping
23 Haus Honti Pension
24 Elte Guesthouse
25 Hostel & Camp Site

PLACES TO EAT
4 Vár Restaurant
15 Gulás Csárda
16 Dóra Restaurant
20 Fekete Holló Restaurant

OTHER
1 Mahart Ferry Pier
2 City Gate
3 Solomon's Tower
6 Forest Cultural Centre
10 Nagyvillám Lookout
11 Visegrád Citadel
12 Bus to Citadel
12 Royal Palace
13 Post Office
14 Catholic Church
17 OTP Bank
18 Visegrád Tours &
    Sirály Disco
19 ABC Supermarket
21 Ferry to Nagymaros

0   250   500 m

To Szentendre

To Budapest

To Vác

DANUBE

RIVER

To Esztergom

Nagymaros

Camping

Mogyoró-hegy

Kisvillám

Nagyvillám

Fekete-hegy

Bobsled Track

Várhegy

Panoráma út

Panoráma út

Salamon-torony utca

Calvary

Trail

Mátyás király utca

Rév utca

Fő utca

Széchenyi utca

century later, King Charles Robert of Anjou, whose claim to the local throne was being fiercely contested in Buda, moved the royal household to Visegrád and had the lower castle converted to a palace.

For almost 200 years, Visegrád was Hungary's 'other' (often summer) capital and an important diplomatic centre. Indeed, in 1335 King Charles Robert met the Polish and Czech kings, as well as princes from Saxony and Bavaria, to discuss territorial disputes and an east-west trade route that would bypass Vienna. But Visegrád's real golden age came during the reign of King Matthias Corvinus (ruled 1458-90) and Queen Beatrice, who had Italian Renaissance craftsmen rebuild the Gothic palace. The sheer size of the residence, its stonework, fountains and hanging gardens were the talk of the 15th century.

The destruction of Visegrád came with the Turks and later in 1702 when the Habsburgs blew up the citadel to prevent Hungarian independence fighters from using it as a base. All trace of the palace was lost until the 1930s when archaeologists, following descriptions in literary sources, uncovered the ruins that you can visit today.

Orientation & Information

The Mahart ferry pier on route No 11, just south of the city gate and the 13th-century Water Bastion (Vízibástya), is where the bus from Szentendre or Budapest will drop you off. Across the street are steps to Salamontorony utca, which leads to the lower castle and the citadel. If you were to continue south on Fő utca for just over a km, you'd reach the village centre and the car ferry to Nagymaros.

The only place for information is Visegrád Tours (☎ 398 160) at Rév utca 15 near the Nagymaros ferry pier. There's a small OTP bank branch at No 9 of the same street. The post office is at Fő tér 77.

Things to See

The first thing you'll see as you walk north up Salamon-torony utca is 13th-century **Solomon's Tower**, a stocky, hexagonal

keep with walls up to eight metres thick. Once used to control river traffic, it now houses many of the precious objects unearthed at the royal palace. Watch out for the celebrated Lion Fountain and the red marble Visegrád Madonna relief. The tower is open every day except Monday from 9 am to 4 or 4.30 pm.

North of the tower, a trail marked 'Fellegvár' turns south-east at a fork and leads up to **Visegrád Citadel** (1259), sitting atop a 350m hill and surrounded by moats hewn from solid rock. This was the repository for the Hungarian crown jewels until 1440, when Elizabeth of Luxembourg, the daughter of King Sigismund, stole them with the help of her lady-in-waiting and hurried off to Székesfehérvár to have her infant son László crowned king. (The crown was returned to the citadel in 1464 and held here – under a much stronger lock, no doubt – until the Turks arrived.)

There's a small pictorial exhibit in the residential rooms on the west side of the citadel and two smaller displays near the east gate: one on hunting and falconry, the other on traditional occupations in the region (stone-cutting, charcoal-burning, beekeeping and fishing). Restoration work on the three defensive levels of the citadel will continue for many years, but it's great fun just walking along the ramparts of this eyrie, admiring the views of the Börzsöny Hills and the Danube. Across the Danube from Visegrád lies Nagymaros and the abandoned site of what was to have been Hungary's section of the Gabčíkovo-Nagymaros dam project (see aside). The citadel is open from April to mid-November.

You can also reach the citadel by half-hourly buses from the King Matthias statue (where Fő utca and Salamon-torony utca meet). If you're walking from the village centre, Kálvária sétány (Calvary Trail) from behind the 18th-century Catholic church on Fő tér is less steep than the trail from Solomon's Tower.

The **Visegrád Royal Palace** at Fő utca 29, the 15th-century seat of King Matthias, once had 350 rooms and was said to be

DANUBE BEND

The Antediluvian Dam

In 1977 the Communist regimes of Hungary and Czechoslovakia agreed – without public or parliamentary debate – to build a canal system and power station along the Danube River. The project would produce cheap electricity and be financed by energy-hungry Austria. It wasn't long before environmentalists foresaw the damage the dam would cause, and the public outcry was loud and unmitigated. In 1989 Hungary's last reform government under Communism caved in to the pressure and halted all work on its part of the project across from Visegrád at Nagymaros.

Efforts to convince newly democratic Czechoslovakia to do the same with its much larger Gabčikovo Canal upstream near Bratislava dragged on without much success. As Czechoslovakia came closer to dividing, the Czechs turned a blind eye on work continued by the Slovaks, and in October 1992 the river was diverted into the canal. Energy gains were minor as the project depended on the Hungarian dam at Nagymaros, which has now been demolished. Both Hungary and Slovakia have cases pending before the International Court in The Hague. ■

unrivalled in Europe in splendour and size. Everything you see at the terraced palace today – the Court of Honour with its Renaissance Hercules Fountain in the centre, the arcaded Gothic hallways, the Lion Fountain and the foundations of St George's Chapel (1366) – are reconstructions or replicas. The palace is open from 9 am to 4.30 pm (closed Monday) from May to October, from 8 am to 4 pm the rest of the year.

Activities

There are some easy walks and hikes in the immediate vicinity of Visegrád Citadel – to the 377m Nagy Villám Lookout, for example. Across from the Jurta camp site is the sod and wood Forest Cultural Centre designed by Imre Makovecz. It contains a small wildlife exhibit.

A 'bobsled' track, on which you wend your way down a metal chute sitting on a hessian sheet, is on the hillside below the lookout; rides are available in warm weather.

There are tennis courts for hire daily from 7 am to 9 pm near the Royal Palace at Fő utca 41.

About three km south of Visegrád on route No 11 to Esztergom is the *Tekla* guest house (☎ 397 051) at Gizella-major, which has a horse-riding school with some of the finest stock in Hungary.

Places to Stay

Camping Up on Mogyoró-hegy (Hazelnut Hill), about two km north-east of the citadel, *Jurta Camping* (☎ 398 217) has relatively expensive bungalows and camping (360/240/120 Ft per tent/person/car). It's nicely situated but far from the centre, and buses only run there between June and August. Motorists may prefer *Kék Duna Camping* (☎ 398 102), by the highway just south of the Nagymaros ferry. Camping space is 240 Ft per person and 75 to 300 Ft per tent (depending on size), but there are no bungalows. Both sites are open May to September.

Hostel The *tourist hostel* (☎ 398 158) at Széchenyi utca 7 near the centre of the village is pretty basic, but dorm beds are only 550 Ft per person, while camping is about 500 Ft. This quiet, uncrowded site should be the first place you check, but it is closed from October to April.

Private Rooms & Pensions Many houses along Fő utca have signs advertising 'Zimmer frei' or 'szoba kiadó'. *Haus Honti* (☎ 398 120), a friendly, seven-room pension at Fő utca 66 next to a picturesque little stream, has singles/doubles with shower for 1500/3000 Ft. Nearby at Fő utca 117 is the *Elte* (☎ 398 165), a four-storey guesthouse with 33 rooms at 1600/2000 Ft for singles/doubles. Most of the rooms have terraces, and there's a great sun deck on the room overlooking the river.

Hotels The 28-room *Salamon* hotel (☎ 398 278), in a decaying old building with gardens at Salamon-torony utca 1, has bathless singles/doubles for about 1200/2400 Ft. The *Silvánus* (☎ 398 311), a 70-room hotel on

Fekete-hegy (Black Hill) a few minutes' walk east of the citadel, has a great location, terrace restaurant, bar and 10-pin bowling. But it's expensive: singles with bath and breakfast are DM70 to DM80, doubles DM90 to DM108, depending on the season.

Places to Eat

The *Vár* at Fő utca 13 is a nothing-special, Hungarian-style restaurant, but it's cheap and convenient to the Mahart ferry pier. In the village, try the *Diófa* at Fő utca 48 or the *Fekete Holló*, a somewhat touristy fish restaurant opposite the Nagymaros ferry at Rév utca 12. The best place in town is the *Gulás Csárda* at the start of Mátyás király utca.

There's an *ABC* supermarket opposite the OTP bank on Rév utca.

Entertainment

Enquire at Visegrád Tours about the medieval pageants and horse tournaments held during the Visegrád Palace Pageant in July. The *Sirály* restaurant and disco at Rév utca 7 is about the only place open at night.

Getting There & Away

Bus & Train Buses are very frequent to/from Budapest's Árpád Bridge station, the Szentendre HÉV suburban train station and Esztergom.

No railway line reaches Visegrád, but you can take one of two dozen daily trains to Szob from Budapest-Nyugati. Get off at Nagymaros-Visegrád, and hop on the ferry across to Visegrád.

Boat Between late May and mid-September, daily Mahart ferries link Visegrád with Esztergom (360/250/180 for adults/students/children) at 11.20 am and 1.20 pm and 5.30 pm. They depart for Szentendre and Budapest at 11.20 am, and 5 and 6.30 pm. From April to late May and from late September to as long as the weather holds up, there's a ferry to Esztergom at 11.20 am on Saturday and public holidays and one daily to Szentendre and Budapest at 4.30 pm (4 pm on Saturday and holidays). From late May to early September a Mahart hydrofoil links

Budapest and Esztergom via Visegrád twice a day (8 am and 2.10 pm) on Saturday and holidays; from late June to early September these ferries run on Friday as well.

Hourly ferries cross the Danube to Nagymaros. Don't panic if the large car ferry closes down early for the night as a smaller passenger launch usually takes its place. The Nagymaros-Visegrád ferry operates all year except when the Danube freezes over (which seldom happens), but service is also suspended when fog descends, a common occurrence in winter. From Nagymaros train station, just inland from the ferry pier, there are trains to Budapest-Nyugati about every hour.

There's another ferry at the Dömösi átkelés train stop (two more down the line), which is good for the Dömös camp site and the entrance to the Pilis Park Forest (see the following section).

AROUND VISEGRÁD
Pilis Hills

If you want to explore the protected forest in the Pilis, the limestone and dolomite hills south-west of Visegrád, take the Esztergom bus for six km to Dömös, where there is an excellent beach and a *camp site* (☎ 33-371 163) with cabins along the Danube open from May to mid-September.

If you follow Duna utca across from the camp for three km, you'll reach the entrance to the 32,000-hectare **Pilis Park Forest**, where Matthias once hunted and Hungary's first hiking trails were laid in 1869. Marked ones lead to **Prédikálószék** (Pulpit Seat), a 639m crag for experienced hikers and climbers only, and to **Dobogókő**, a much easier ascent of about three hours via the Rámszakadék (Rám Precipice). There are sweeping views of the river and mountains through openings in the forest along the way.

At Dobogókő there's an excursion centre with further trails mapped out, or you can catch a bus to Esztergom (there are five a day) or to the HÉV station in Pomáz, one stop before Szentendre.

Alternatively, you can take a small ferry across the Danube from Dömös to Dömösi átkelés, then climb to the caves that are visible on the hillside and hike back into the hills behind Nagymaros. Cartographia's 1:40,000 *A Pilis és a Visegrádi-helység* (The Pilis and Visegrád Hills) map (No 16) outlines the many hiking possibilities in this area. Some of the best bird-watching in western Hungary is in the Pilis Hills.

ESZTERGOM
- *pop 32,000*
- *area code* ☎ *33*

Esztergom, 25 km from Visegrád and 66 km from Budapest via route No 11, is one of Hungary's most historical and sacred cities. For more than 1000 years it has been the seat of Roman Catholicism (the archbishop of Esztergom is the primate of Hungary). The country's first king, St Stephen, was born here in 975, and it was a royal seat from the late 10th to mid-13th centuries. For these and other reasons, Esztergom has both great spiritual and temporal significance for most Hungarians.

Esztergom lies on a high point above a slight curve of the Danube across from the Slovakian city of Štúrovo (Hungarian: Párkány), which can now be reached by ferry. Vár-hegy (Castle Hill) was the site of the Roman settlement of Solva Mansio in the 1st century, and it is thought that emperor-to-be Marcus Aurelius finished his *Meditations* in a camp nearby during the second half of the 2nd century.

Prince Géza chose Esztergom as his capital, and his son Stephen (or Vajk as he was known before his baptism) was crowned king here in 1000. Stephen founded one of the country's two archbishoprics and a basilica at Esztergom, bits of which can be seen in the palace.

Esztergom (German: Gran) lost its political significance when King Béla IV moved the capital to Buda following Mongol invasion. It remained an important trading centre and the ecclesiastical seat, however, vying with the royal court for power and influence. Esztergom's capture by the Turks in 1543 interrupted the church's activities, and the archbishop fled to Nagyszombat (now Trnava in Slovakia).

The church did not re-establish its base here – the 'Hungarian Rome' – until the early 19th century. It was then that Esztergom went on a building spree that transformed it into a city of late baroque and (in particular) neoclassical buildings. The city's biggest boost in the present decade was the opening by Suzuki of Hungary's first automobile-assembly plant.

Orientation
The modern centre of Esztergom is Rákóczi tér, a few steps east of the Kis Duna (Little Danube), the tributary that branches off to form Prímás-sziget (Primate Island). To the north-west up Bajcsy-Zsilinszky utca is Castle Hill. To the south-west of Rákóczi tér is Széchenyi tér, the town centre in the Middle Ages and site of the rococo town hall.

Esztergom's bus station is near the market on Simor János utca south-east of Rákóczi tér. The train station is another 15 minutes farther south on Bem József tér. Mahart ferries dock at the pier just south of the 'broken bridge' on Primate Island.

Information
Three tourist information offices in Esztergom are Komturist (☎ 312 082), Lörincz utca 6; Gran Tours (☎ 313 756), Széchenyi tér 25; and Express (☎ 313 113), Széchenyi tér 7. Gran Tours is the visitors' centre run by the city and is very helpful. They are open from 8 am to 6 pm weekdays and till noon on Saturday.

There's an OTP bank on Rákóczi tér in the centre of town and a K&H branch with an ATM diagonally across the square. The newly renovated post office is at Arany János utca 2 just off Széchenyi tér.

Esztergom Cathedral
The centre of Hungarian Catholicism and the largest church in the country is in Szent István tér on Castle Hill. Indeed, its 72m central dome can be seen soaring up for km around. The present neoclassical church was begun in 1822 on the site of a 12th-century

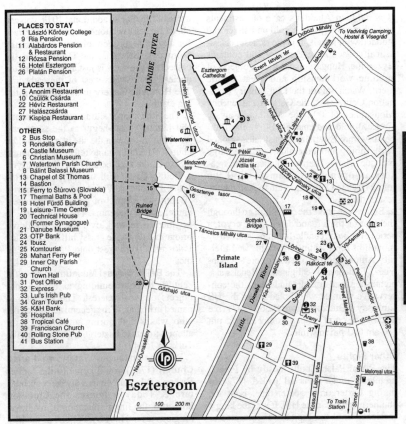

PLACES TO STAY
1 László Kőrösy College
9 Ria Pension
11 Alabárdos Pension & Restaurant
12 Rózsa Pension
16 Hotel Esztergom
26 Platán Pension

PLACES TO EAT
5 Anonim Restaurant
10 Csülök Csárda
22 Hévíz Restaurant
27 Halászcsárda
37 Kispipa Restaurant

OTHER
2 Bus Stop
3 Rondella Gallery
4 Castle Museum
6 Christian Museum
7 Watertown Parish Church
8 Bálint Balassi Museum
14 Chapel of St Thomas
15 Ferry to Štúrovo (Slovakia)
17 Thermal Baths & Pool
18 Hotel Fürdő Building
19 Leisure-Time Centre
20 Technical House (Former Synagogue)
21 Danube Museum
23 OTP Bank
24 Ibusz
25 Komtourist
28 Mahart Ferry Pier
29 Inner City Parish Church
30 Town Hall
31 Post Office
32 Express
33 Lui's Irish Pub
34 Gran Tours
35 K&H Bank
36 Hospital
38 Tropical Café
39 Franciscan Church
40 Rolling Stone Pub
41 Bus Station

Esztergom

0   100   200 m

DANUBE BEND

one destroyed by the Turks. József Hild, who designed the cathedral at Eger, was involved in the final stages, and the basilica was consecrated in 1856 with a Mass composed by Franz Liszt.

The grey church is colossal (118m long and 40m wide) and rather bleak inside, but the white and red marble **Bakócz Chapel** on the south side is a splendid example of Tuscan Renaissance stone-carving and sculpture. It was commissioned by Archbishop Tamás Bakócz who, failing in his bid for the papacy, launched a crusade that turned into the peasant uprising under

György Dózsa in 1514 (see the History section in the Facts about the Country chapter). The chapel escaped most (though not all) of the Turks' axes, was dismantled into 1600 separate pieces and then reassembled in its present location in 1823. The copy of Titian's *Assumption* over the main altar is said to be the largest painting on a single canvas in the world.

On the north-west side of the church, to the left of the macabre relics of three priests martyred in Košice early in the 17th century and canonised as saints by Pope John Paul II in 1995, lies the entrance to the **treasury** (kincstár), an Aladdin's cave of vestments and religious objects in gold and silver and studded with jewels. It is the richest ecclesiastical collection in Hungary and contains Byzantine, Hungarian and Italian objects of sublime workmanship and great artistic merit. Watch out for the 13th-century Coronation Oath Cross, the Garamszentbenedek Monstrance (1500), the Matthias Calvary Cross of gold and enamel (1469), the 18th-century Imre Esterházy Monstrance studded with rubies and emeralds, and the large baroque Maria Theresa Chalice. The treasury is open from 9 am to 4.30 pm mid-March to October, 11 am to 3.30 pm the rest of the year.

Before you leave the cathedral, go through the door on the left and down to the **crypt**, a series of spooky, candle-lit tombs guarded by monoliths representing Mourning and Eternity. Among those at rest down here are János Vitéz, Esztergom's enlightened Renaissance archbishop, and József Mindszenty, the conservative primate who holed up in the US Embassy in Budapest from 1956 to 1971 (see aside). The crypt is open from 9 am to 5 pm (10 am to 3 pm in winter).

Other Sights

The Royal Palace, built mostly by French architects under Béla III (ruled 1172-96) during Esztergom's golden age, is at the southern end of Castle Hill. It was the king's residence until the capital was relocated to Buda – at which time the archbishop moved in. Most of the palace was destroyed and covered with earth for defensive purposes under the Turks; it did not see the light of day again until excavations in the 1930s.

The palace's dozen or so restored rooms house the **Castle Museum**, which traces the history of the fortress and city and is open from 9 am to 4.30 pm (shorter hours in winter). Among the most interesting rooms are: the vaulted 12th-century room marked No 5 and said to be the oldest 'living room' in Hungary; the study of János Vitéz, with 15th-century wall paintings of the Virtues (No 8); and the 12th-century chapel (No 11), with a rose window and frescos of lions and

a tree of life. For an additional 10 Ft, you can climb the narrow stone steps to the terrace for a windswept view of the palace, dingy Štúrovo in Slovakia, the Danube and the cathedral. The view is just as good from the ancient castle walls west of the cathedral. The **Rondella Gallery** to the east has rotating exhibits.

The little chapel sitting atop **St Thomas Hill** (Szent Tamás-hegy) to the south-east was built in 1823 on the site of a much older church. The hill's name refers to St Thomas à Becket, the 12th-century English martyr.

Below Castle Hill on the banks of the Little Danube is **Víziváros**, the colourful 'Watertown' district of pastel town houses, churches and museums. The easiest way to get there is to walk over the palace drawbridge and down the grassy hill to Batthyány Lajos utca. Turn west onto Pázmány Péter utca.

The **Bálint Balassi Museum**, in an 18th-century baroque building at No 13, has objects of local interest. The museum is named in honour of the general and lyric poet who was killed during an unsuccessful attempt to retake Esztergom Castle from the Turks in 1594.

Past the Italianate **Watertown Parish Church** (1738) you'll come to the former Bishop's Palace at Mindszenty hercegprímás tere 2. Today it houses the **Christian Museum**, the finest collection of medieval religious art in Hungary and one of the best museums in the country. Established by Archbishop János Simor in 1875, it contains Hungarian Gothic triptychs and altarpieces, later works by German, Dutch and Italian masters, tapestries, and what is arguably the most beautiful object anywhere in Hungary: the **Holy Sepulchre of Garamszentbenedek** (1480). It's a sort of wheeled cart in the shape of a cathedral with richly carved figures of the 12 Apostles (above) and Roman soldiers (below) guarding Christ's tomb. It was used at Easter Week processions and was painstakingly restored in the 1970s.

Be sure to see Tamás Kolozsvári's *Calvary* altar panel (1427), which was influenced by Italian art, the late Gothic *Christ's*

Cardinal Mindszenty

Born near Szombathely in 1892, József Pehm Mindszenty was politically active from the time of his ordination in 1915. Imprisoned under the short-lived regime of Béla Kun in 1919 and again when the fascist Iron Cross came to power in 1944, Mindszenty was made archbishop of Esztergom (and thus primate of Hungary) in 1945 and cardinal the following year.

When the new cardinal refused to secularise Hungary's Roman Catholic schools under the new Communist regime in 1948, he was arrested, tortured and sentenced to life imprisonment for treason. Released during the 1956 Uprising, Mindszenty took refuge in the US Embassy on Szabadság tér when the Communists returned to power. There he would remain until 1971.

As relations between the Kádár regime and the Holy See began to thaw in the late 1960s, the Vatican made several requests for the cardinal to leave Hungary, which he refused. Following the intervention of US President Richard Nixon, Mindszenty left for Vienna where he continued to criticise the Vatican's relations with the regime in Hungary. He retired in 1974 and died the following year. But as he had vowed not to return to Esztergom until the last Soviet soldier had left Hungarian soil, Mindszenty's remains were not returned until May 1991 – several weeks before that actually occurred. ■

Passion by 'Master M S', the gruesome *Martyrdom of the Three Apostles* (1490) by the so-called Master of the Martyr Apostles, and the *Temptation of St Anthony* (1530) by Jan Wellens de Cock with its drug-like visions of devils and temptresses. The museum's displays are labelled in five languages, and a guided tour in English can be booked by ringing the museum (☎ 313 880) in advance.

If you cross the little Kossuth Bridge, past the pier where ferries head for Štúrovo in Slovakia, and on to Primate Island, you can't help noticing the ruins of **Mária Valéria Bridge**, with the jagged spans on both sides of the river failing to meet in the middle. The bridge was destroyed during WWII and was never rebuilt. The island is a pleasant place for a walk along the river on a warm summer's evening, with dramatic views of the palace and cathedral.

The gaudy salmon and grey **Technical House** (1888) at Imaház utca 4 once served as a synagogue for Esztergom's Jewish community, the oldest in Hungary. It was designed in 'Moorish Romantic' style by Lipót Baumhorn, the master architect who also engineered the synagogues in Szeged, Szolnok and Gyöngyös.

The **Danube Museum** at Kölcsey Ferenc utca 2 (closed Tuesday), just south of the Technical House, has exhibits on all aspects of the history and use of Hungary's mightiest river. Its photos and mock-ups are quite interesting, but the captions are mostly in Hungarian.

Activities

Between the old Fürdő hotel and the Little Danube at Bajcsy-Zsilinszky utca 14-18, there are outdoor thermal pools open May to September from 9 am to 6 pm. You can use the indoor pool the rest of the year from 6 am to 6 pm (9 am to noon or 1 pm at the weekend). The Romans took the waters here, and the first public baths in Hungary opened on this spot in the 12th century.

Places to Stay

Camping There are no camp sites in Esztergom itself. *Gyopár Camping* (☎ 311 401) is on Sípoló Hill three km to the east along winding Vaskapui út (bus No 1), and *Vadvirág Camping* (☎ 312 234) is at Bánomi dűlő, three km on the way to Visegrád (bus No 6). The sites are open from late April or May to late September or mid-October.

Private Rooms & Hostel See Gran Tours for private rooms (1300 Ft) or apartments (4000 Ft). In summer, Express can help with summertime dormitory rooms for 600 to 700 Ft at the *trade school* (☎ 311 746) near the train station at Budai Nagy Antal utca 38 or the *László Kőrösy College* (☎ 312 813) at Szent István tér 16.

The Hostelling International-affiliated *Youth Sport Centre* hostel (☎ 313 735) is in Búbánat-völgy, five km east of Esztergom's centre, on route No 11; take any of the buses bound for Visegrád and Szentendre. The hostel has 20 doubles in bungalows and dormitory rooms and is open from mid-April to mid-October.

Pensions *Platán* pension (☎ 311 355), Kis Duna sétány 11, is like a small hotel with excellent prices: 900 Ft for a single with shared bath, 2300 Ft for a double with bath. The entrance is to the right as you walk into the courtyard.

Another cheap place to stay is the 16-room *Rózsa* pension (☎ 313 581) above Bajcsy-Zsilinszky utca at Török Ignác utca 11. It has older singles/doubles with shared bath for 1800/2000 Ft and new doubles/triples with shower for 3000/4000 Ft. Nearby are two nicer, but much more expensive, places: the 12-room *Alabárdos* (☎ 312 640) down the hill and around the corner at Bajcsy-Zsilinszky utca 49 with singles/doubles from 3500/5000 Ft, and the *Ria* pension (☎ 313

115) with singles/doubles in both a new and an older building for 4500/6000 Ft.

Hotels The 36-room *Esztergom* (☎ 312 883) is a modern block hotel on Nagy Duna sétány on Primate Island, with singles from DM40 to DM69 and doubles from DM67 to DM97, depending on the season. There's a rather fancy restaurant, a roof terrace and a sport centre with a tennis court and canoes for rent.

The run-down but central *Fürdő* hotel at Bajcsy-Zsilinszky utca 14 was getting a much needed face-lift during my last visit to Esztergom and may have reopened by now.

Places to Eat

The *Hévíz* in the Bástya shopping centre above Rákóczi tér is the cheapest place in town for a meal – and looks, smells and feels it. Go instead to the charming *Csülök Csárda* at Batthyány utca 9. It has very good home cooking and huge main courses from 500 Ft.

The *Anonim*, in a historical town house at Berényi Zsigmond utca 4, is convenient to the museums in Watertown but closes at 9 pm. The *Halászcsárda*, a fish restaurant on Primate Island just across Bottyán Bridge at Gesztenye fasor 14, is open noon to midnight daily except Monday. A popular old-style place is *Kispipa* at Kossuth Lajos utca 21 east of Széchenyi tér.

Entertainment

Pilgrims flock to Esztergom from all over Hungary on major feast days dedicated to the Virgin Mary, such as Assumption Day (15 August). In summer, organ concerts are held in the cathedral, and the Esztergom Chroniclers sometimes perform ancient Hungarian music at the palace; check with Gran Tours or any of the other agencies for more information. The *Leisure-time Centre* (Szabadidő-központ) on Bajcsy-Zsilinszky utca down from the old Fürdő hotel has a cinema and rotating exhibits. It's open from 8 am to 9 pm on weekdays, 8 am to 1 pm and 2 to 5 pm on Saturday and 8 am to noon on Sunday.

A miniature strip of activity after dark is the market street of Simor János utca, which continues south from Bajcsy-Zsilinszky utca. The *Tropical Café* at No 44 is popular with students from the nearby trade school; the *Rolling Stone* at No 64 attracts a more mature crowd and plays decent canned music. *Lui's Irish Pub* at Széchenyi tér 18 is the place for a pint of Guinness or Kilkenny.

Getting There & Away

Bus Buses from Budapest's Árpád Bridge station run about every half-hour from 5 am to 8 pm. They may go via Dorog (75 minutes) or via Visegrád and Szentendre (two hours). Buses from Esztergom to Visegrád and Szentendre depart hourly between 6 am and 8.40 pm and to Sopron and Győr twice daily. Other important destinations served are limited: Balatonfüred (one); Dobogókő (five); Komárom (two), Pilisszentlélek (five); Sopron (two), Tatabánya (three); and Veszprém (two).

Train Trains to Esztergom depart from Budapest-Nyugati train station up to a dozen times a day. To get to Western Transdanubia from Esztergom, take one of the three daily trains to Komárom, where you can change for Győr, Székesfehérvár, Vienna and Bratislava (via Komárno on the Slovakian side).

Boat Mahart river boats travel to/from Budapest (400/280/200 Ft for adults/students/children) two or three times a day from late May to late September, but you must change at Visegrád and it's a very slow trip (upwards of five hours). From April to late May and late September to seasonal shutdown, there's only one boat a day on Saturday and holidays. From late May to early September a Mahart high-speed hydrofoil links Budapest and Esztergom via Visegrád twice a day (8 am and 2.10 pm) on Saturday and holidays; from late June to early September these run on Friday as well.

A ferry crosses the Danube from Esztergom to Štúrovo in Slovakia 13 times a day from 7.20 am to 7.20 pm. Adults/children pay 80/40 Ft, and it costs another 240/100 Ft to take a car/bicycle along.

Car & Motorcycle If you're driving to/from Budapest, you can follow route No 11 along the river the entire way or take the shorter (46 km) route No 10 – the so-called Panorama Highway – through the Pilis Hills, turning north on route No 111 at Dorog.

Western Transdanubia

As its name suggests, Western Transdanubia (Nyugati Dunántúl) lies 'across the Danube' from Budapest, stretching west and southwest to the borders with Austria and Slovenia. It is a region of hills and plains with some of the most historically important towns, castles, churches and monuments in Hungary. As the nation's 'window on the West', it has always been the richest and most developed area and popular with Austrian day-trippers in search of cut-rate services and goods. In the westernmost towns, you would almost think you had crossed the border from all the Alpine architecture and the preponderance of German spoken.

The Danube River was the limit of Roman expansion in what is now Hungary, and most of Western Transdanubia formed the province of Upper Pannonia. The Romans built some of their most important military and civil towns here – Arrabona (Győr), Scarbantia (Sopron), Savaria (Szombathely), Adflexum (Mosonmagyaróvár) and Brigetio (Komárom). Because of their positions on the trade route from northern Europe to the Adriatic and Byzantium, and the influx of Germans, Slovaks and other ethnic groups, these towns prospered in the Middle Ages. Bishoprics were established, castles were built and many of the towns were granted special royal privileges.

A large part of Western Transdanubia remained in the hands of the Habsburgs during the Turkish occupation, and it was thus spared the ruination suffered in the south or on the Great Plain. As a result, some of the best examples of Romanesque and Gothic architecture can be found here. Because the influence of Vienna continued throughout the 16th and 17th centuries, Western Transdanubia received Hungary's first baroque churches and public buildings.

That domination by Austria continued, with parts of the region changing hands several times over the following centuries.

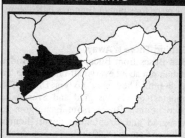

HIGHLIGHTS

- the Imre Patkó Collection of Asian and African art and the Herm of László reliquary at the cathedral in Győr
- colourful Jurisics tér in Kőszeg
- the opulent Esterházy Palace at Fertőd
- the neoclassical Széchenyi Mansion at Nagycenk
- Sopron's Storno Collection of Romanesque and Gothic furnishings and the city's unusual Bakery Museum
- the restored Romanesque Abbey Church at Ják
- the massive Benedictine abbey complex at Pannonhalma and its treasures
- the lake-side öregvár (Old Castle) and ancient mills of Tata
- the Őrség region in westernmost Transdanubia
- Zalaegerszeg's stunning former synagogue (now concert hall)

Western Transdanubia took a pounding during WWII, and though many of the town centres were spared, the outlying districts were demolished. As a result, they have distinctly similar appearances: a medieval or baroque core ringed with concrete housing blocks, factories and sometimes farmland. The region was industrialised after the war, especially around Tatabánya and Győr (there were plans to transform the latter into a 'Hungarian Ruhr Valley'), and it is also an

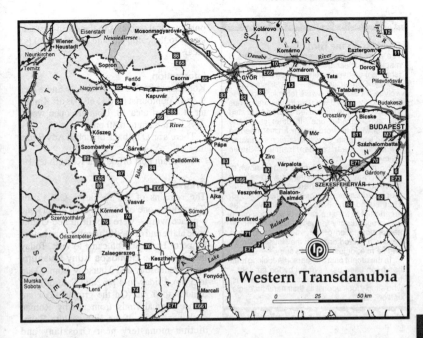

important source of such raw materials as bauxite, coal and oil. Agriculture here is less important, though Sopron and Mór are important wine centres.

If you're entering Hungary from Vienna, your first impression of Western Transdanubia will not be a favourable one; the view from the train or along the M1 motorway is monotonous and sometimes depressing. But the many sights you can't see from the train or car window – Győr's lovely Inner Town, the lakeside castle at Tata, Pannonhalma's historic abbey – are just minutes away behind the gloom.

TATA
- *pop 25,500*
- *area code* ☎ 34

Tata (not to be confused with Tatabánya) is a pleasant town situated west of the Gerecse Hills and not far from the Vértes range. Tatabánya is a heavily industrial city 14 km to the south-east whose only real claim to

fame is a giant statue of the symbolic *turul* (see aside). While Tatabánya is large and mostly new, Tata (Totis in German) is a small town of springs, canals and lakes, a castle and a lot of history.

Much of the action has focused in and around the 14th-century Öregvár (Old Castle) perched on a rock at the northern end of a large lake. It was a favourite residence of King Sigismund, who added a palace in the 15th century; his daughter, Elizabeth of Luxembourg, tarried here in 1440 with the purloined crown of St Stephen en route to Székesfehérvár where her newly born son would be crowned king. King Matthias Corvinus turned Tata into a royal hunting reserve attached to Visegrád, and his successor, Vladislav (Úlászló) II, convened the Diet here to avoid plague-ravaged Buda. Tata Castle was badly damaged by the Turks in 1683, and the town did not begin its recovery until it was acquired by a branch of the aristocratic Esterházy family in the 18th

Blame it on the Bird

The ancient Magyars were strong believers in magic and celestial intervention, and the *táltos* (shaman) enjoyed an elevated position in their society. Certain animals – bears, stags and wolves, for example – were totemic, and it was taboo to mention them directly by name. Thus the wolf was 'the long-tailed one' and the stag the 'large-antlered one'. In other cases the original Magyar word for an animal deemed sacred was replaced with a foreign loan word: *medve* for 'bear' comes from the Slavic *medved*.

No other totemic animal is better known to modern Hungarians than the *turul*, an eagle or hawk-like bird that had supposedly impregnated Emese, the grandmother of Árpád. That legend can be viewed in many ways: as an attempt to foster a sense of common origin and group identity in the ethnically heterogeneous population of the time; as an effort to bestow a sacred origin on the House of Árpád and its rule; or just as a nice story.

In the recent past the fearsome-looking turul has been used as a symbol by the far right – much to the distress of average Hungarians, who simply look upon it as their heraldic 'eagle' or 'lion'. ■

century. They retained the services of a Moravian-born architect named Jakab Fellner, who designed most of Tata's fine baroque buildings.

Tata is as much a town of recreation as of history. Tata's two lakes offer ample opportunities for sport, and there's a spa complex to the north. Tata is also a convenient gateway to other Western Transdanubian towns from Budapest and the Danube Bend.

Orientation

Tata's busy main street, a section of route No 100 called Ady Endre utca here, separates the bigger Öreg-tó (Old Lake) from Cseke-tó (Tiny Lake). Tata's other 'centre' is up on Kossuth tér, west of Öreg-tó.

The bus station is north-west of the castle on Május 1 út. There are two train stations. The main one is a couple of km north of the city centre and about the same distance from the Fényes spa complex and camp site. The second station, Tóvároskert, which is used only by local trains, is to the south-east and closer to the camp site and hostel on Fáklya utca.

Information

Komtourist (☎ 383 211) is at Ady Endre utca 9, and Cooptourist (☎ 381 602) is off Kodály tér at Tópart utca 18. Both are open weekdays from 8 am to 6.30 pm.

There's an OTP bank branch at Ady Endre utca 17.

The main post office is at Kossuth tér 19.

Öregvár

The remains of the medieval Old Castle (Öregvár) – one of four original towers and a palace wing – were rebuilt in neo-Gothic style at the end of the 19th century just before Emperor Franz Joseph came to visit. Today they house the **Domokos Kuny Museum**, open Wednesday and Thursday from 10 am to 3 pm, Friday to 4 pm, and Saturday and Sunday to 5 pm. On the ground floor are archaeological finds from nearby Roman settlements, bits of the 12th-century Benedictine monastery near Oroszlány and contemporary drawings of the castle in its heyday. The exhibit on the 1st floor entitled 'Life in the Old Castle' is pretty interesting; don't miss the cathedral-like Gothic stove that takes pride of place in the **Knights' Hall**. Material on the 2nd floor examines the work of a dozen 18th-century artisans, including Kuny, a master ceramist. Tata porcelain was well known for centuries (the lobster or crayfish was a common decoration here) and the craft indirectly led to the foundation of the porcelain factory at Herend near Vezprém. The castle's neoclassical **chapel** (1822) is also open to the public.

Mills

Öregvár, attractively reflected in the lake, is surrounded by a moat, and a system of locks and sluices regulates the flow of water into nearby canals. Tata made good use of this water power; it was once known as the 'town of mills'. The shell of the 16th-century **Cifra Mill**, east of the castle at Bartók Béla utca 3, is interesting only for its red marble window

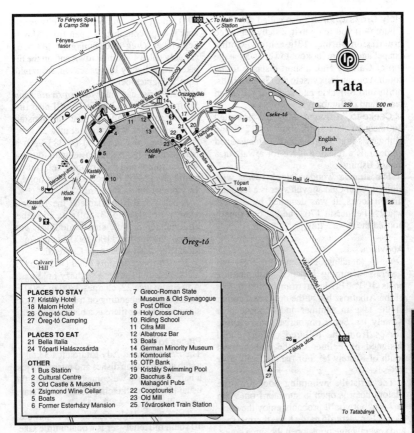

Tata

0   250   500 m

Cseke-tó

English
Park

Öreg-tó

Calvary
Hill

PLACES TO STAY
17 Kristály Hotel
18 Malom Hotel
26 Öreg-tó Club
27 Öreg-tó Camping

PLACES TO EAT
21 Bella Italia
24 Tóparti Halászcsárda

OTHER
1 Bus Station
2 Cultural Centre
3 Old Castle & Museum
4 Zsigmond Wine Cellar
5 Boats
6 Former Esterházy Mansion

7 Greco-Roman State
   Museum & Old Synagogue
8 Post Office
9 Holy Cross Church
10 Riding School
11 Cifra Mill
12 Albatrosz Bar
13 Boats
14 German Minority Museum
15 Komtourist
16 OTP Bank
19 Kristály Swimming Pool
20 Bacchus &
   Mahagóni Pubs
22 Cooptourist
23 Old Mill
25 Tóvároskert Train Station

To Tatabánya

frames and five water wheels, but the magnificently restored **Nepomucenus Mill** (1758), a bit farther on at Alkotmány utca 2, now houses the **German Minority Museum**. Like Pécs and Székesfehérvár, Tata was predominantly German-speaking for several centuries, and all aspects of the German experience in Hungary are explored here. The collections of festive clothing and musical instruments are in very good condition.

Other Things to See
Walking south-west from the castle for a few minutes through leafy Kastély tér to Hősök

tere, you'll pass the Zopf-style former **Esterházy Mansion** designed by Jakab Fellner in 1764; today part of it serves as a hospital and doctors' surgeries. At Hősök tere 3, in the old Romantic-period synagogue, the weird **Greco-Roman Statue Museum** displays plaster copies of stone sculptures that lined the walkways of Cseke-tó in the 19th century. At Bercsényi utca 1, just before you enter Kossuth tér, stands the birthplace of Mór Farkasházi Fischer, founder of the Herend porcelain factory and Tata's most famous son. Dominating the square is another of Fellner's works, the 18th-century

Holy Cross Church (also called the Great Church). If you're up to it, a sadly neglected crucifixion shrine, 13th-century Gothic chapel and a 45m lookout tower await at the top of **Calvary Hill**, a short distance to the south. You can look east to the Gerecse Hills, north into Slovakia and south to the urban wasteland of Tatabánya.

Cseke-tó, surrounded by the protected 200-hectare Angolpark, built in 1780 and Hungary's first 'English park' (a landscaped garden), is a relaxing place for a walk or a day of fishing.

The strange wooden **clock tower** with eight sides in Országgyűlés tér is a lot older than it looks. It was designed by – guess who? – Fellner in 1763, and at one time it housed the town's tiny prison.

Activities

Öreg-tó (a nature conservation area) has several swimming beaches, and pleasure boats (100/50 Ft) depart from the pier in front of the Albatrosz bar at the north-east corner of the lake in summer and opposite near Kastély tér. See Komtourist about renting horses from the pillared riding school designed by Fellner on the embankment south of Kastély tér. For fishing, walk over to Cseke-tó.

The Kristály swimming pool near the Malom hotel is open in summer from 9 am to 7 pm, but you'll probably enjoy the complex at Fényesfürdő more. It has thermal spas and several huge pools open the same hours.

As odd as it may seem with a main highway only 100m away, Öreg-tó attracts a considerable number and variety of waterfowl; between 20,000 and 40,000 bean and white-fronted geese pass through in February alone. The best spot for bird-watching is the southern end of the lake in winter where a warm spring prevents that part of the lake from freezing over. And go at dawn or dusk – during other times the birds are busy pecking at stubble in the nearby fields.

Places to Stay

There are two camp sites in Tata, both with bungalows. *Fényesfürdő Camping* (☎ 381 591), about two km north of the city centre near the spa complex, is open from May to September. *Öreg-tó Camping* (☎ 383 496), at Fáklya utca 1 south of town and on the big lake, has a slightly longer season: from mid-April to September.

Komtourist can find you a *private room* for from 1000 to 1300 Ft. You'll also find private rooms available near the Kristály swimming pool at Hattyúliget utca 2.

The *Öreg-tó Club* hotel (☎ 383 960) at Fáklya utca 4 has both a hostel with four and six-bed rooms and a 22-room hotel. But the hostel charges by the room and the hotel is very pricey for its standard.

A better deal is available at the 15-room *Malom* hotel (☎ 383 530) at Erzsébet királyné tér 8 with singles/doubles with shared shower for 1100/1600 Ft. It's on a quiet, tree-lined street near Cseke-tó.

The 26-room *Kristály* hotel (☎ 383 577), a 200-year-old former Esterházy holding at Ady Endre utca 22, charges 3800 to 5600 Ft for a double, depending on the season, room size and whether there is a bath or shower.

Places to Eat

The *Bella Italia* at Ady Endre utca 33 takes a stab at real Italian dishes and misses by just a hair. Still, it's a welcome change from the usual Hungarian 'ketchup pizza' and it stays open till 2 am.

The *Tóparti Halászcsárda* on Tópart utca 10 south of Kodály tér is a quaint little lakeside eatery serving fish from Öreg-tó. Try the Baja fish soup. The *Múzeum Presszó* in the castle has snacks and drinks.

Entertainment

The *Zoltán Magyary Cultural Centre* (☎ 380 811), between the castle and the bus station at Váralja utca 4, will provide you with up-to-date information on what's going on in this culturally aware town. The Tata Summer concert cycle from June to August is the main event of the year and the Mini-Marathon, which circles the lake, is run in August. Venues include the atmospheric but cramped *Knights' Hall* in the castle and the *Holy Cross*

Church. Jazz and rock concerts are usually held at the amphitheatre in English Park.

The *Albatrosz* bar in an attractive old house at Tópart utca 3 near the castle attracts a lively young crowd till midnight. The *Zsigmond* cellar at the castle is a great place for a glass of wine. It's open daily till midnight (to 2 am Friday and Saturday).

On Ady Endre utca, the 18th-century Miklós Mill at No 26 has been put to good use as a wine bar, called the *Bacchus*. Even more attractive is the *Mahagóni* pub in a townhouse next door at No 28.

Getting There & Away

Buses leave very frequently for Tatabánya, Komárom, Esztergom and Oroszlány, the gateway to the Vértes Hills. There are at least half a dozen daily departures to Duna-szentmiklós and four to Tarján in the Gerecse Hills. Budapest buses depart three or four times a day.

Tata is on the train line linking Budapest-Déli with Győr and Vienna. A few daily trains go directly to Sopron and Szombathely via Tata, but you usually have to change at Győr. If you're travelling by train to Esztergom, change at Almásfüzitő. To cross into Slovakia, take the train to Komárom and walk across.

Getting Around

Bus No 1 links the main train station with the bus station and Kossuth tér. Bus No 3 will take you to Fényesfürdő; No 5 goes to Tóvároskert train station and Fáklya utca.

You can also order a local taxi on ☎ 381 808 or ☎ 380 080.

AROUND TATA

The **Gerecse Hills**, while not the Alps (the highest point is 633m), are east of Tata and tailor-made for hiking. Though you can start from Tata, you should get a head start by taking a bus to Tardosbánya (the closest village to Mt Gerecse), Tarján or Duna-szentmiklós. Cartographia publishes a tourist map (1:40,000) of the area with clear trail markings called *A Gerecse Turistatérképe* (No 10).

ÁROM

* *pop 19,800*
* *area code* ☎ 34

Komárom is the gateway to Hungary for visitors arriving from Komárno in Slovakia. Until 1920 these two towns were one. In antiquity the Romans had a military post called Brigetio here and the Habsburgs also fortified the area, though their castles ended up being used against them by Hungarian rebels during the 1848-49 Independence War. Komárom's position is the only thing that makes it of interest to travellers. There's a good camping ground next to the public thermal baths within walking distance of the train station and border crossing, and a couple of inexpensive hotels should you arrive late in the afternoon and want to spend the night. But you'll be gone in the morning, no doubt about it.

Orientation & Information

The train station is very close to the highway bridge over to Slovakia; the bus station is 100m to the south. The train station in Komárno is two km to the north of the bridge.

Komturist (☎ 341 767) is at Mártírok útja 19/a in the centre of town (open weekdays from 8 am to 3.30 pm). Walk south from the bridge down Igmándi út to Jókai Mór tér, and you'll find it a block to the east on the right-hand side.

OTP has a bank branch next to Komturist at Mártírok útja 21. The post office is near the Béke hotel on the corner of Kállai Tivadar utca and József Atilla utca.

Things to See & Do

Among the sights of Komárom are two large 19th-century fortifications that were built by the Habsburgs. **Csillagvár** (Star Castle) is near the river just north-east of the Thermál hotel. You can see it from the train as you arrive from Budapest. The **Igmándi-erőd** (Igmánd Fortress) is on the south side of town.

Right next to the Thermál hotel are the **thermal baths** (open all year, 180 Ft). To get to the baths from the bridge, go south for two blocks and then turn east on Táncsics Mihály utca. Sauna and massage are available in addition to the big thermal pool.

Places to Stay

Komturist should have *private rooms* for about 1000 Ft per person, but they're usually fully booked.

The closest hotel to the Danube bridge is the *Béke* (☎ 340 333), Bajcsy-Zsilinszky út 8, a renovated two-storey building with over-priced rooms with shared bath at 3000 Ft per single/double.

The 39 rooms with bath at the *Thermál* hotel (☎ 342 447), Táncsics Mihály utca 38, cost 2600 to 3600 Ft for one and 4100 to 5000 Ft for two, depending on the season. Prices include admission to the thermal baths. Next to this resort hotel is a *camping ground* that is open throughout the year. Motel-style units here are 1800 Ft for up to three people without bath, but they're only available from mid-April to mid-October. It costs from 280 to 500 Ft to pitch a tent.

The newer and more luxurious *Karát* hotel (☎ 342 222), two blocks west of the baths at Czuczor Gergely utca 54, is 3500/4000 Ft for a single/double in the low season and 4000/6000 Ft in summer.

Getting There & Away

Though there are hourly runs to Tata, bus service from Komárom is generally limited. Count on only two a day to Budapest, four to Esztergom, three to Győr, one to Sopron and, on weekdays only, five to Komárno in Slovakia, where you can catch a local train to Bratislava.

On the other hand, train services from Komárom to Budapest, Győr and Sopron are fairly frequent. Most trains on this line depart from Budapest-Keleti but a few use Budapest-Déli. For the Danube Bend, catch a train to Esztergom (three daily), and for Lake Balaton go via Székesfehérvár (nine daily).

GYŐR

• *pop 130,000*
• *area code* ☎ 96

Most travellers see no more of Győr

(German: Raab) than what's visible in the distance from the highway as they whiz between Vienna and Budapest. It's usually pegged as 'that big industrial city with the funny name' (it's pronounced something like 'jyeur') and, well, neither can be denied. An important producer of trucks, rolling stock and textiles, Győr is the nation's third-largest industrial centre.

But Győr is also a historical city; in fact, after Budapest and Sopron, no place in the country can boast as many important buildings and monuments. Stroll 100m up pedestrian Baross Gábor utca, and you'll enter a world that has changed little since the 17th and 18th centuries.

Situated in the heart of the so-called Little Plain (Kisalföld) at the meeting point of the Mosoni-Duna and Rába rivers, Győr was settled by the Celts and later the Romans who called it Arrabona. The Avars came here too and built a circular fort (called *gyűrű* from which the town took its name) before the arrival of the Magyars in the 10th century.

King Stephen established a bishopric at Győr in the 11th century, and 200 years later the town was granted a royal charter, allowing it to levy taxes on goods passing through it. Later, the shipping and trading of grain along the rivers would bring even greater wealth.

A castle was built here in the 16th century and, being surrounded by water, was an easily defended outpost between Turkish-held Hungary and the seat of the Habsburg Empire, Vienna, until late in the century. When the Ottomans did manage to take Győr, they were able to hold on for only four years and were evicted in 1598 (though not without blowing up much of the cathedral first). For that reason Győr has been praised as the 'dear guard', watching over the nation through the centuries.

Orientation

Győr's train station lies south of Honvéd liget (Soldier Park) and the large neo-baroque city hall on Városháza tér. Reach the bus station on the other side of the railway line through the underpass east of the main

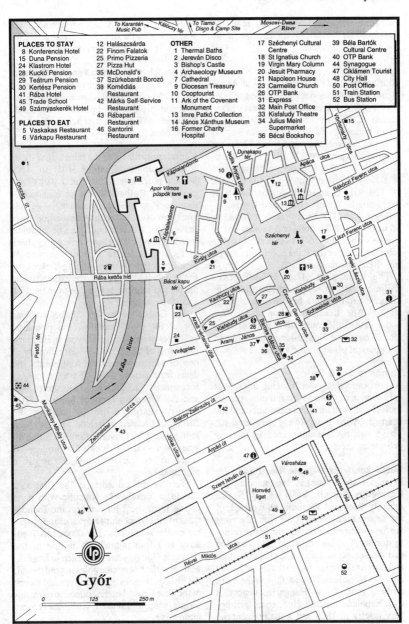

PLACES TO STAY
8 Konferencia Hotel
15 Duna Pension
24 Klastrom Hotel
28 Kuckó Pension
29 Teátrum Pension
30 Kertész Pension
41 Rába Hotel
45 Trade School
49 Szárnyaskerék Hotel

PLACES TO EAT
5 Vaskakas Restaurant
6 Várkapu Restaurant

12 Halászcsárda
22 Finom Falatok
25 Primo Pizzeria
27 Pizza Hut
35 McDonald's
37 Szürkebarát Borozó
38 Komédiás
   Restaurant
42 Márka Self-Service
   Restaurant
43 Rábaparti
   Restaurant
46 Santorini
   Restaurant

OTHER
1 Thermal Baths
2 Jereván Disco
3 Bishop's Castle
4 Archaeology Museum
9 Cathedral
9 Diocesan Treasury
10 Cooptourist
11 Ark of the Covenant
   Monument
13 Imre Patkó Collection
14 János Xánthus Museum
16 Former Charity
   Hospital

17 Széchenyi Cultural
   Centre
18 St Ignatius Church
19 Virgin Mary Column
20 Jesuit Pharmacy
21 Napoleon House
23 Carmelite Church
26 OTP Bank
31 Express
32 Main Post Office
33 Kisfaludy Theatre
34 Julius Meinl
   Supermarket
36 Bécsi Bookshop

39 Béla Bartók
   Cultural Centre
40 OTP Bank
44 Synagogue
47 Ciklámen Tourist
48 City Hall
50 Post Office
51 Train Station
52 Bus Station

Győr

WESTERN TRANSDANUBIA

entrance. Baross Gábor utca leads to Belváros, the historic Inner Town, and the river runs to the north.

Information

Tourinform (☎ 317 709) is based at Árpád utca 32, but its services are limited to telephone and written enquiries for some strange reason. Ciklámen Tourist (☎ 311 557) at Aradi Vértanúk útja 22 is open from 8 am to 4.30 pm on weekdays and to 12.30 pm on Saturday. Express (☎ 328 833), open weekdays only from 8 am to 3.45 pm, has an office at Bajcsy-Zsilinszky utca 41. Cooptourist (☎ 320 801) is at Jedlik Ányos utca 8. It keeps similar hours to Ciklámen Tourist.

There's an OTP bank branch at Árpad út 36 next to the Rába hotel and another one at Baross Gábor utca 16. If both are closed, the reception desk at the Rába hotel will change travellers' cheques and cash.

The main post office is at Bajcsy-Zsilinszky út 46, opposite the Kisfaludy Theatre, and there is a branch near the train station. The Bécsi bookshop and coffee house in the little courtyard at Baross Gábor utca 18 has some foreign-language stock and is a pleasant place to sit and read.

Things to See & Do

Almost everything worth seeing in Győr is in or around three areas just minutes apart on foot: Bécsi kapu tér, Káptalandomb, and the heart of Győr's Inner Town, Széchenyi tér. These squares are connected by narrow pedestrian streets.

Bécsi kapu tér Baroque Bécsi kapu tér (Vienna Gate Square) is dominated by the **Carmelite church**, built in 1725 and recently renovated. On the north-west side of the square and cutting it off from the river are the fortifications built in the 16th century to stop the Turkish onslaught, and a bastion that has served as a prison, a chapel, a store and now a restaurant. Just to the east at Király utca 4 is **Napoleon House**. One of the more unusual footnotes in Hungarian history is that Napoleon entered Hungarian territory very briefly in 1809 and actually spent the night of 31 August in this house since Győr was near a battle site. An inscription on the Arc de Triomphe in Paris recalls 'la bataille de Raab'.

A branch of the **János Xánthus Museum** – an archaeology museum of cellars containing a rich collection of Roman and medieval bits and pieces – is housed in the castle casemates at Bécsi kapu tér 5. It is open April to October.

Káptalandomb From the museum, walk up Káptalandomb (Chapter Hill) to Apor Vilmos püspök tere, the oldest part of the city. **Győr Cathedral**, whose foundations date back to the 11th century, is an odd amalgam of styles, with Romanesque apses (have a look from the outside), a neoclassical façade and a Gothic chapel riding piggyback on the south side. But most of what you see inside, including the stunning frescos by Franz Anton Maulbertsch, the main altar and the bishop's throne, is baroque from the 17th and 18th centuries.

The Gothic **Héderváry Chapel** contains one of the most beautiful (and priceless) examples of medieval gold work in Hungary, the **Herm of László**. It's a bust reliquary of one of Hungary's earliest king-saints and dates from around 1400. If you're looking for miracles, though, move to the north aisle and the **Weeping Icon of Mary**, a 17th-century altarpiece brought here by the Bishop of Clonfert in Ireland who had been sent packing by Oliver Cromwell. Some 40 years later – on St Patrick's Day no less – it began to cry tears of blood and is still a pilgrimage site.

West of the cathedral is the **Bishop's Castle**, a fortress-like structure with parts dating from the 13th century; the foundations of an 11th-century Romanesque chapel are on the south side. The **Diocesan Treasury** at Káptalandomb 26 is one of the richest in Hungary and is labelled in English. Marvel at the heavy chasubles in gold thread, the bishops' crooks of solid silver and pieces of the True Cross, but the collection of manuscripts (some illuminated) is ultimately more impressive.

Széchenyi tér A couple of blocks south-east of Káptalandomb is Széchenyi tér, a large square in the heart of Győr and the market in the Middle Ages. Along the way, at the bottom of the hill on Jedlik Ányos utca, you'll pass the outstanding **Ark of the Covenant**, a large statue dating from 1731. Local tradition has it that the king erected the city's finest baroque monument to appease the angry people of Győr after one of his soldiers accidentally knocked the Eucharist out of a priest's hands during a Corpus Christi procession.

The **Column of the Virgin Mary** in Széchenyi tér was raised in 1686 to honour the recapture of Buda Castle from the Turks. The Jesuit and later Benedictine **Church of St Ignatius**, the city's finest, dates from 1641. The 17th-century white-stucco side chapels and the ceiling frescos painted by the Viennese artist Paul Troger in 1744 are worth a look. The **pharmacy** next door at Széchenyi tér 9, established by the Jesuits in 1667, is a fully operational baroque institution. You can inspect the rococo vaulted ceiling and the frescos with religious and herbal themes during opening hours (from 8 am to 6.30 pm on weekdays; from 10 am to 6.30 pm on Wednesday).

If time is limited, skip the main branch of the **János Xánthus Museum** across the square at Széchenyi tér 5 (Győr history, stamps and coins, antique furniture, natural history) and head for the **Imre Patkó Collection** in the 17th-century **Iron Stump House** (Vastuskós Ház) at No 4, which still sports the log into which itinerant artisans would drive a nail to mark their visit. The museum, one of the best of its size anywhere in Hungary, has an excellent collection of 20th-century fine art on the first two floors; the 3rd floor is given over to objects collected by the journalist and art historian Imre Patkó during his travels in India, Tibet, Vietnam and West Africa.

Other Things to See

One of the nicest things about Győr is its atmospheric old streets. Take a stroll down Bástya utca, Apáca utca, Rákóczi Ferenc utca, Liszt Ferenc utca and Király utca (east and north-east of Széchenyi tér), where you'll see many fine buildings. The late Renaissance **palace** at Rákóczi Ferenc utca 6 was once a charity hospital. Go inside to see the courtyards.

The richly decorated octagonal cupola, galleries and tabernacle of the city's **synagogue** (1869), across the river at Kossuth Lajos utca 5, are well worth a look if you can get into the decrepit old building. Try at the entrance to the music academy (formerly a Jewish school) next door.

A colourful open-air **market** unfolds on Dunakapu tér, by the river and north of Széchenyi tér. Have a look, too, at the colourful **flower market** on Virágpiac south of Bécsi kapu tér.

Activities

On the left bank of the Rába River are Győr's well maintained **thermal baths**. To get there, cross Rába kettős híd (Rába Double Bridge) over the little island and walk north to Ország út 4. The covered pool is open all year from 6 am to 8 pm weekdays, 7 am to 6 pm at weekends. The strand pools are open between May and September.

Places to Stay

Camping *Kiskút Camping* (☎ 318 986), near the stadium some three km north-east of town, has a motel open all year (2100/3000 Ft doubles/triples) and horrid little bungalows for up to four people (2500 Ft) open between mid-April and mid-October.

Private Rooms & Hostels Private rooms are available from about 1600 Ft a double from Ciklámen Tourist. Singles are scarce. In summer, dormitory accommodation may be available in the huge *college* at Ságvári Endre utca 3 north of the Mosoni-Duna or the one west of the old town on the corner of Erkel Ferenc utca and Kossuth Lajos utca opposite the old synagogue.

Pensions Győr is full of small private pensions and, while not the cheapest places to stay, they are usually very central and in some

WESTERN TRANSDANUBIA

of the city's most colourful old buildings. The *Kuckó* (☎ 316 260), in an old townhouse at Arany János utca 33, has eight doubles with bath for 3600/4200 Ft singles/doubles. The smaller *Kertész* (☎ 317 461) to the east at Iskola utca 11 has rooms for 3800/4700 Ft. The picks of the crop, though, and under the same management, are the 10-room *Teátrum* (☎ 310 640) at No 7 of pedestrian Schweidel utca and the Regency-blue *Duna* (☎ 329 084), with 14 rooms and antique furniture at Vörösmarty utca 5. Singles/doubles/triples at both are 3800/4700/5600 Ft.

Hotels The four-storey, 30-room *Szárny-askerék* hotel (☎ 314 629), at Révai Miklós utca 5 opposite the train station, charges 2350 Ft for double with washbasin and 3650 Ft for one with bath.

The *Rába* hotel (☎ 315 533), a 175-room colossus with old and new wings between Árpád utca and busy Szent István út, charges DM100 to DM110 for singles, DM140 to DM150 for doubles. It has lots of outlets and facilities and is central, but if you don't mind paying that kind of money, book into the three-star *Klastrom* hotel (☎ 315 611) south of Bécsi kapu tér at Zehmeister utca 1. It has 42 rooms with bath (DM100/155 doubles/triples) in a 250-year-old Carmelite convent and boasts a sauna, a solarium, a pub with a vaulted ceiling, and a rather cramped restaurant. Though the views of the square and the river are lovely, the best rooms face the inner courtyard.

The modern carbuncle on Apor Vilmos püspök tere next to the cathedral – how do architects get planning permission for these monstrosities? – is the 20-room *Konferencia* hotel (☎ 314 011), once a company guesthouse and now Győr's most expensive (and pretentious) accommodation. Singles/doubles are a budget-destroying DM165/210. So classy is this place that they can't seem to manage any language other than Hungarian.

Places to Eat

For a cheap self-service meal, try the *Márka* at Bajcsy-Zsilinszky út 30, which is open weekdays from 7.30 am to 4.30 pm, weekends from 7 am to 2.30 pm. Another inexpensive place is *Finom Falatok* at Kazinczy utca 12, east of Bécsi kapu tér. There's a *Pizza Hut* at No 13 and *McDonald's* at No 21 of Baross Gábor utca.

A decent wine cellar is the *Szürkebarát Borozó*, Arany János utca 20 (closed Sunday). A stairway in the courtyard leads down into this vaulted restaurant. Only cold dishes are available at lunch. For lighter fare and a younger crowd, the *Primo Pizzeria* at Aradi vértanúk útja 3 can be recommended.

The *Rábaparti*, Zehmeister utca 15, serves tasty Hungarian fare in an unpretentious (though rather gloomy) restaurant at very reasonable prices. The cellar-like *Vaskakas* restaurant, in the former castle casemates near the Rába River at Bécsi kapu tér 2, has loads of atmosphere as long as you don't mind long tables of German-speaking pensioners to your left and right. Instead, try the charming little *Várkapu* at Bécsi kapu tér 7, overlooking the Carmelite church. It lists its dishes on a blackboard outside.

A typical inn with fish dishes near the market is the *Halászcsárda*, Apáca utca 4. More expensive places include *Santorini*, a Greek/Mediterranean restaurant at Munkácsy Mihály utca 6 with mains from 650 Ft, and *Komédiás*, an eatery decorated in postmodern greys and blacks and opposite the cultural centre at Czuczor Gergely utca 30.

Entertainment

The celebrated Győr Ballet and the city's opera company and philharmonic orchestra all perform at the modern *Kisfaludy Theatre*, Czuczor Gergely utca 7, a technically advanced though unattractive structure covered in op art tiles by Victor Vasarely (the ticket office is at Kisfaludy utca 25). The *Béla Bartók Cultural Centre*, which stages less-highbrow performances like folk dances and rock operas, is at Czuczor Gergely utca 17. Győr Summer is a month-long festival of music, opera, theatre and dance from late June to late July. The Győr Baroque festival takes place in March.

The *Jereván* on Radó sétány in the middle of the island in the Rába River and the *Tiamo* on Héderváry utca north of the centre are Győr's most popular discos. A good music venue is the *Karantén Music Pub* at Káloczy tér 6.

Getting There & Away

Bus The bus service is very good from Győr, and the posted timetable is one of the most user-friendly in the land. There are at least a dozen departures a day to Budapest, Kapuvár, Pannonhalma, Pápa and Veszprém, and half as many go to Balatonfüred, Mosonmagyaróvár and Székesfehérvár. Other destinations include: Dunaújváros (four buses daily), Esztergom (two), Hévíz (two), Keszthely (five), Lébény (from eight to 12), Pécs (two), Szombathely (three to five), Tata (two), Tapolca (three) and Zalaegerszeg (five). Four buses run to Vienna daily, and there's a daily one to Bratislava at 9.15 am.

Train Győr is the main rail junction after Budapest and has convenient connections with both Budapest-Keleti and Budapest-Déli stations and Vienna via Hegyeshalom. Trains into Austria via Sopron, which are run by a private concern called GySEV and not part of the MÁV system, are not as frequent. From Győr, you can also reach Szombathely by train via Pápa and the gateway to the Balaton region, Veszprém, via Pannonhalma. If you're heading for Slovakia, change at Komárom.

Getting Around

You can reach the Kiskút camp site on bus No 8 from in front of city hall on Városháza tér.

Local taxis can be ordered on ☎ 312 222.

AROUND GYŐR

Lébény

• *pop 3200*

This village, about 15 km north-west of Győr, contains the most important example of Romanesque architecture still standing in Hungary: the Benedictine **Abbey Church of St James**. Though not as intimate or evoca-

tive of medieval Hungary as the Abbey Church at Ják near Szombathely, it is nonetheless worth a visit for its sheer size and superb condition.

The church was begun by two Győr noblemen in 1199 and consecrated in 1212 under the authority of Pannonhalma Abbey. Though the Lébény church managed to escape destruction during the Mongol invasion, it was set aflame twice by the Turks. The abbey hired Italian stonemasons to raze the structure in 1563, but apparently they were so impressed with it that they refused to carry out the task. In the 17th century the church passed into the hands of the Jesuits, who renovated it in the baroque style 100 years later. In the late 19th century, when neo-Romanesque and neo-Gothic architecture was all the rage in Transdanubia, the church was restored by a German architect.

Take a close look at the carved-stone west portal and the south entrance portal; they're in excellent condition. The fresco fragment of the Three Magis above the west portal dates from the mid-17th century.

There's not much else of interest in this hard-scrabble village which, judging from the smells, devotes much of its time and energy to pig farming. If you get hungry, there's a rough-looking *esztresszó* on the square in front of the church and the *Kisvendéglő* restaurant at Fő út 62 in a former monastery.

Between eight and 12 buses make the run every day from Győr. The bus stop is on Fő utca, a two-minute walk east of the church.

PANNONHALMA

• *pop 3500*

• *area code ☎ 96*

Since late in the 10th century, this small village 21 km south-east of Győr has been the site of a Benedictine abbey, which even managed to continue functioning during the darkest days of Stalinism. Its secondary school, attended by some 360 students, is tops in the nation; oddly, the only other Hungarian Benedictine monastery in operation today is in the Brazilian city of São Paolo.

The abbey celebrated its millennium to great fanfare in 1996. It is expected to be added to UNESCO's World Heritage List soon.

The monastery was founded by monks from Venice and Prague with the assistance of Prince Géza. The Benedictines were considered a militant order, and Géza's son King Stephen made use of the order to help Christianise Hungary.

The abbey and associated buildings have been razed, rebuilt and restored many times over the centuries. Under the Turks, the basilica did not sustain as much damage as it could have for the simple reason that it faced east and was turned into a mosque. As a result the complex is a crazy patchwork of architectural styles.

Pannonhalma is an easy day trip from Győr, but the area is so quiet and the monastery so timeless that you may want to stay a while. The village is also conveniently situated for those heading for Veszprém and Lake Balaton.

Orientation & Information

The village is dominated by the 282m Castle Hill (Várhegy) and the abbey. The bus from Győr stops in the centre of the village; from here, follow Váralja up to the abbey. Some buses continue up the eastern side of the hill and stop at the abbey's main entrance.

The train station is a couple of km southwest of the village off Petőfi utca in the direction of route No 82.

Pax Tourist (☎ 470 191), the only agency here, is just south of the abbey's main entrance at Vár utca 1.

Pannonhalma Abbey

The abbey was spruced up for its 1000th birthday (and Pope John Paul II's visit) in 1996 and is now one of the most impressive historical complexes in Hungary. You'll begin your guided tour in the central courtyard, with its statue of the first abbot, Asztrik, who brought the crown of King Stephen to Hungary from Rome, and a relief of King Stephen presenting his son Imre to

The 13th-Century seal of Pannonhalma Abbey

the tutor Bishop Gellért. To the north there are dramatic views over the Kisalföld while looming behind you are the abbey's modern wings and neoclassical clocktower built in the early 19th century.

The entrance to **St Martin's Basilica**, built early in the 12th century, is through the **Porta Speciosa**. This is an arched doorway in red limestone that was recarved in the mid-19th century by the Stornos, a controversial family of restorers who imposed 19th-century Romantic notions of Romanesque and Gothic architecture on ancient buildings. It is beautiful despite the butchery. The fresco above the doorway by Ferenc Storno depicts the church's patron, St Martin of Tours, giving half his cloak to a crouching beggar. Look down to the right below the columns and you'll see what is perhaps the oldest graffiti in Hungary: 'Benedict Padary was here in 1578' it reads in Latin.

The interior of the long and sombre church contains more of the Stornos' handiwork, including the neo-Gothic pulpit and raised marble altar. The Romanesque niche in the wall of the 13th-century crypt is called the Seat of St Stephen; legend says that it contains the saint-king's throne.

As you walk along the cloister arcade (or ambulatory), notice the little faces carved in stone on the wall. They represent human emotions and vices such as wrath, greed and conceit. In the cloister garden a Gothic sundial offers a sobering thought: 'Una Vestrum, Ultima Mea' ('One of you will be my last').

The most beautiful part of the monastery is the neoclassical **library** built in 1836 by János Packh, who helped design the cathedral at Esztergom. It contains some 300,000 volumes – many of them priceless historical records – making it the largest private library in Hungary. But the rarest and most important document is in the **abbey archives**. It is the *Deed of Foundation* of Tihany Abbey and dates from 1055. Though in Latin, it contains about 50 Hungarian place names and is the earliest surviving example of written Hungarian. The library's interior may look like marble, but it is made entirely of wood. An ingenious system of mirrors within the skylights reflect and direct natural light throughout the room.

The **gallery** off the library contains works by Dutch, Italian and Austrian masters from the 16th to 18th centuries. The oldest work, however, goes back to 1350. The most valuable piece is the 17th-century *Dead Christ* by Teniers the Younger. Below the library are the new **millennium exhibition rooms** tracing the development of the abbey in Hungarian, German and English as well as liturgical objects from the abbey treasury.

Because it is a working monastery, the abbey must be visited with a guide, available (in Hungarian) between six and nine times a day and in English, Italian, German, French and Russian on request. For foreign languages you must pay 300 Ft above the usual 100 Ft entry fee, but the tour is well worth it. The complex is open every day from Tuesday to Saturday from 8.30 am to 4.30 or 5 pm and on Sunday from 11.30 am.

Places to Stay & Eat

Panoráma Camping (☎ 471 240) to the east of Castle Hill at Fenyvesalja utca 4/a has a couple of bungalows sleeping four people (2500 Ft), a small büfé and a salad bar. Camping costs 500 Ft for a tent and 300/150 Ft per adult/child. Open from mid-April to mid-October, the camp site is in a good location for visiting the abbey – just go through the gate in the back and climb the hill to the car park.

There are two small pensions in town: the six-room *Família* (☎ 470 192) at Béke utca 61 as you enter town from the north on route No 82, and the seven-room *Pannon* (☎ 470 041) at Hunyadi utca 7/c on the way up to the abbey.

The *Pax* (☎ 470 006 at Dózsa György utca 2 is a 25-room hotel with the kinds of facilities you'd expect to find in Budapest, not in a little place like Pannonhalma. Singles with bath are 4000 to 5000 Ft, doubles 5000 to 6500 Ft, depending on the season.

In the village, the *Pannonhalma* restaurant on Szabadság tér near Dózsa György utca may do in a pinch, but the *István* at Szabadság tér 24 is a better choice. It's only open till 10 pm, though. You might also try the *Café Picasso* on the corner of Hunyadi utca and Szabadság tér.

The *Szent Márton* complex below the abbey near the car park has a snack bar, restaurant, pub and gift shop.

Entertainment

There are a half-dozen organ and choral concerts scheduled between April and December in the basilica. There appears to be no rhyme or reason behind the dates, so check with Pax Tourist.

Getting There & Away

Buses to/from Győr are frequent with at least a dozen passing through every day. Six trains a day stop at Pannonhalma on their way to Veszprém from Győr.

SOPRON
- *pop 56,600*
- *area code ☎ 99*

Sopron, at the foot of the Lővér Hills and just six km from the Austrian border, is the most charming medieval city in Hungary. With its preponderance of Gothic and early baroque architecture, Sopron is the closest thing the country has to Prague. Exploring the backstreets and courtyards of the thumb-shaped Inner Town is a step back in time, and you

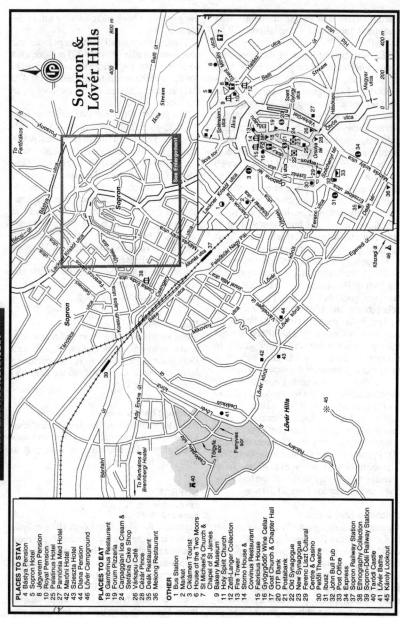

Sopron & Lővér Hills

PLACES TO STAY
4 Bástya Pension
5 Sopron Hotel
8 Jégverem Pension
10 Royal Pension
25 Palatinus Hotel
27 Pannónia Med Hotel
42 Maróni Hotel
43 Szieszta Hotel
44 Diana Pension
46 Lővér Campground

PLACES TO EAT
18 Gambrinus Restaurant
19 Forum Pizzeria
24 Carpaggiani Ice Cream &
   Stefánia Cake Shop
26 Várkapu Café
28 Cézár Pince
35 Deák Restaurant
36 Mekong Restaurant

OTHER
1 Bus Station
2 Market
3 Ciklámen Tourist
6 House of the Two Moors
7 St Michael's Church &
   Chapel of St James
9 Bakery Museum
11 Holy Spirit Church
12 Zettl-Langer Collection
13 Fire Tower
14 Storno House &
   Corvinus Restaurant
15 Fabricius House
16 Gyógygödör Wine Cellar
17 Goat Church & Chapter Hall
20 OTP Bank
21 Postabank
22 Old Synagogue
23 New Synagogue
29 Ferenc Liszt Cultural
   Centre & Casino
30 Petőfi Theatre
31 Ibusz
32 John Bull Pub
33 Post Office
34 Express
37 Sopron Railway Station
38 Ethnography Collection
39 Sopron-Déli Railway Station
40 Taródi Castle
41 Lővér Baths
45 Károly Lookout

almost expect knights in armour or damsels in wimples to emerge from the narrow Gothic doorways and courtyards.

Sopron (German: Ödenburg) has had a long and tumultuous past with more wars and decisions thrust upon its population than most cities. Indeed, as recently as 1921 the citizens of Sopron had to vote whether to stay in Austria's Bürgenland as a result of the Trianon Treaty or be re-annexed by Hungary. They resoundingly chose the latter, and that explains the little knot of Hungarian territory that juts into Austria.

The Celts arrived in the area first and then came the Romans, who lived in a settlement called Scarbantia (now Sopron's inner town) between the 1st and 4th centuries. The Germans, Avars, Slavs and finally the Magyars followed. In medieval times, Sopron was ideally situated for trade along the so-called Amber Route from the Baltic Sea to the Adriatic and Byzantium. By the 1300s, after a century of struggle for hegemony over the city between the Hungarians and the Austrians, Sopron had been made a royal free town – its mixed population able to pursue their trades without pressure from feudal landlords. Thus a strong middle class of artisans and merchants emerged here, and their wealth contributed to making Sopron a centre of science and education.

Neither the Mongols nor the Turks were able to penetrate the heart of Sopron, which is why so many old buildings still stand. But damage during WWII was severe, and restoration work continued apace in the 1960s under the direction of Endre Csatkai (1896-1970) who, as a memorial plaque near the Előkapu (front gate) explains, 'worked ceaselessly for 50 years to preserve and protect the city'. Sopron was awarded the Europa Prize for the Protection of Monuments in 1975.

Sopron is an anomaly in Hungary – a city with a Gothic heart and a modern mind. It's true that it attracts enormous amounts of tourists, but most of the visitors who flock the streets on a Saturday are Austrians in search of cut-rate haircuts, dental work and enough sausage to open their own delicatessens. Come nightfall, the city is once again in the hands of the loyal citizens of Sopron.

Orientation

The medieval Belváros (Inner Town) contains almost everything of interest in Sopron, though there are a few worthy sights across the Ikva Stream to the north-east just beyond the city walls. The Lővér Hills are about four km south-west of the city.

Sopron's main train station is on Állomás utca south of the inner town. Walk north along Mátyás király utca and past Széchenyi tér to reach Várkerület and Hátsókapu (Back Gate), one of the few entrances to the inner town. Várkerület and Ógabona tér beyond it form a ring around the inner town, roughly following the city's Roman and medieval walls. Sopron-Déli station, through which trains to/from Szombathely also pass, is to the north-west. The bus station is north-west of the inner town on Lackner Kristóf utca.

Information

Ciklámen Tourist (☎ 312 040) at Ógabona tér 8 is open from 8 am to 4.30 pm on weekdays and on Saturday to 1 pm. Express (☎ 312 024), between the Inner Town and the train station at Mátyás király utca 7, can help with dormitory accommodation and is open weekdays only from 8 am to 3 pm.

There's an OTP bank at Várkerület 96 and a Postabank with an ATM at Új utca 8 in the Inner Town. Ciklámen Tourist will change travellers' cheques, but they give a mediocre rate. The main post office is at Széchenyi tér 7-10.

Inner Town

The best place to begin a tour of Sopron is to climb the narrow circular staircase to the top of the 60m **fire tower** at the northern end of Fő tér. The tower affords excellent views over the city, the Lővér Hills to the south-west and the Austrian Alps to the west. Below you are Fő tér and the four narrow streets that make up the inner town.

The fire tower, from which trumpeters would warn of fire, mark the hour (now done by chimes) and greet visitors to the city in the Middle Ages, is a true architectural hybrid. The two-metre thick square base, built on a Roman gate, dates from the 12th century, and the cylindrical middle and arcaded balcony from the 16th century. The baroque spire was added in 1681. **Fidelity Gate** at the bottom of the tower pictures Hungary receiving the *civitas fidelissima* (from the Latin meaning the 'most loyal citizenry') of Sopron. It was erected in 1922 after that crucial referendum.

Though virtually every building in the inner town is of interest, Sopron has relatively few specific monuments of importance. Fő tér contains the lion's share of what there is and most of the museums. The choice is great and each charges a separate admission fee, so choose carefully. In general, the museums are open from 10 am to 5 pm between March and October and 10 am and 2 pm the rest of the year. Most close on Monday.

The focal points of this graceful square are the **Holy Trinity Column** (1701), the best example of a 'plague pillar' in Hungary, and on the south side of the square the old **Goat Church**, whose name comes from the heraldic animal of its chief benefactor. The church was originally built in the late 13th century, but many additions and improvements were made over the centuries. The interior is mostly baroque, the red marble pulpit in the centre of the south aisle dates from the 15th century and there is a lovely little Gothic domed tabernacle. Beneath the Goat Church is **Chapter Hall**, part of a 14th-century Franciscan monastery with frescos and stone carvings.

The **Pharmacy Museum** is at Fő tér 2 in a Gothic building beside the church. Across to the north are **Fabricius House** at No 6 and **Storno House** at No 8; both contain several exhibits.

Fabricius House is a comprehensive historical museum with rooms devoted to domestic life in Sopron in the 17th and 18th centuries on the upper floors. There are a few kitchen mock-ups and exhibits explaining how people made their beds and did their washing-up in those days, but the highlights

are the rooms facing the square, which are crammed with priceless antique furniture. You can follow the exhibits with a photocopied fact-sheet at your leisure while old women 'guides' sit by the window, making lace in the afternoon sunlight. Scarbantia-era statues reconstructed from fragments found in the area, including enormous ones of Juno, Jupiter and Minerva, guard the cellar, once a Gothic chapel, with vaulted ceilings 15m high.

On the 2nd floor of Storno House, originally built in 1417, is the wonderful **Storno Collection**, which belonged to a 19th-century Swiss-Italian family of restorers whose recarving of Romanesque and Gothic monuments throughout Transdanubia is frowned upon today. To their credit, the much maligned Stornos did rescue many altarpieces and church furnishings from oblivion, and their house is a Gothic treasure trove. Highlights include the beautiful enclosed balcony with leaded windows and frescos, leather chairs with designs depicting Mephisto and his dragons, and door frames made from pews taken from 15th-century St George's Church on Szent György utca.

If you walk down Új utca – known as Zsidó utca (Jewish Street) until the Jews were evicted from Sopron in 1526 – you'll reach the **Old Synagogue** at No 22 and the **New Synagogue** across the street at No 11. Both were built in the 14th century and are among the greatest Jewish Gothic monuments in Europe and unique in Hungary. The Old Synagogue is now a museum and can be visited between 10 am and 5 pm on Monday, Wednesday and Sunday from March to September only. The New Synagogue forms part of a private house, though you can see the exterior quite clearly by entering the courtyard at Szent György utca 12. The Old Synagogue contains two rooms, one for each sex (note the women's windows along the west wall). The main room contains a medieval 'holy of holies' with geometric designs and trees carved in stone, and some ugly new stained-glass windows. The inscriptions on the walls date from 1490. There's a reconstructed *mikvah* (ritual bath) in the courtyard.

Other Things to See

Sopron's sights are not entirely confined to the inner town. Walk back to Fő tér, past the old Roman walls, under Előkapu and over a small bridge leading to Ikva, once the district of merchants and artisans. At Balfi út 11 is the excellent **Zettl-Langer Private Collection** of ceramics, paintings and furniture, open only from 10 am to noon from Tuesday to Sunday.

To the north on Dorfmeister utca is the 15th-century **Church of the Holy Spirit**. Farther north at Szent Mihály utca 9 is the **House of the Two Moors**. It was fashioned from two 17th-century peasant houses and is guarded by two large and very black statues.

At the top of the hill is **St Michael's Church**, built between the 13th and 15th centuries, and behind it the Romanesque-Gothic **Chapel of St James**, the oldest structure in Sopron. Not much escaped the Stornos' knives when they 'renovated' St Michael's (they also added the spire). See what you think of their work.

If you return to the House of the Two Moors and walk west along Fövényverem utca, you'll soon reach Bécsi út and the **Bakery Museum** at No 5, the second-best museum in Sopron. It's actually the completely restored home, bakery and shop of a successful 19th-century bread and pastry maker named Weissbeck and contains some interesting gadgets and work-saving devices. It's open Wednesday, Friday and Sunday from 10 am to 2 pm, and Tuesday, Thursday and Saturday from 2 to 6 pm.

The city museum's **Ethnography Collection**, with an interesting array of implements used in wine-making, baking and weaving is at Deák tér 2.

Places to Stay

Camping *Lővér Camping* (☎ 311 715), at Pócsi-domb on Kőszegi út about five km south of the city centre, has more than 100 bungalows available between mid-April and mid-October. Doubles with shared bath are 1500 to 2400 Ft and camping costs 300/400 Ft per person/tent.

Hostels The *Brennbergi* hostel (☎ 313 116) on Brennbergi út is pretty far to the west of the city centre, but a bed is under 600 Ft a night. There's also a pension here. It's open from mid-April to mid-October. You can also stay at *Taródi Castle* (see Lővér Hills in the Around Sopron section).

Private Rooms Ciklámen Tourist has private rooms for about 2000 Ft a double. Rooms are sometimes full in summer, and singles may have to pay for a double.

You can also find quite a few private rooms by taking bus No 1 from the train station to the Szieszta hotel, Lővér körút 37, then walking back down the hill looking for houses with 'Zimmer frei' signs.

Pensions Most of the pensions in Sopron are pretty expensive, but there are a couple of exceptions. The 16-room *Bástya* (☎ 325 325) at Patak utca 40, a 10-minute walk north of the Inner Town up Szélmalom utca, charges 3000/4600 Ft for singles/doubles, while the more central *Jégverem* (☎ 312 004), with five rooms in an 18th-century ice cellar at Jégverem utca 1 in the Ikva district, charges almost the same rates. The seven-room *Royal* (☎ 314 481) in a renovated old townhouse at nearby Sas tér 13 has singles/doubles for 2500/5000 Ft.

You could also stay at the *Diana* in the Lővér Hills; see the following Around Sopron section.

Hotels The 30-room *Palatinus* (☎ 311 395) at Új utca 23 couldn't be more central, but it's in a badly renovated building that doesn't fit in well with its surrounds. Small, rather dark singles/doubles are DM75/110. Sopron's grand old hotel is the 100-year-old *Pannónia Med* hotel (☎ 312 180) at Várkerület 75. A complete renovation has pushed prices out of sight for most: DM100 for a single, DM130 for double.

Up on Coronation Hill with views of the city and the Lővér Hills is the sprawling 112-room *Sopron* resort hotel (☎ 314 254) at Fövényverem utca 7, with bars, a restaurant, clay tennis courts and an outdoor swimming pool. Of course all this will cost you: from DM120/160 for a single/double.

There are also several hotels in the Lővér Hills; see the following Around Sopron section.

Places to Eat

The best place in Sopron for an inexpensive lunch or light meal is the *Cézár Pince* in a medieval cellar at Hátsókapu 2 off Orsolya tér (open till 9.30 pm). The platter of sausages and salad for only 250 Ft attracts locals; chase it with a glass of Soproni Kékfrankos (a red) or the young white Zöldveltelini (230 Ft a litre). There's a *McDonald's* next to the Pannónia Med hotel at Várkerület 73.

The *Corvinus*, with its café tables on Fő tér, is a great place for a pizza in the warmer months. For something more substantial, try the *Gambrinus*, across the square at No 3 and open till 10 pm. The *Forum* at Szent György utca 3 also does decent pizza.

The *Deák*, Erzsébet utca 20 on the corner of Deák tér, specialises in game dishes like wild boar or venison, though fish is also on the menu. In the evening there's live music, and the place is popular with Austrian border-jumpers. The *Mekong*, a short distance to the south-east at Deák tér 46, has passable Chinese (main courses from 380 Ft) and opens nightly till midnight.

You'll find good ice cream in an unusual place – at *Carpaggiani* in the medieval courtyard off Szent György utca 12 backed by the New Synagogue. Check the ancient Gothic windows above you as you sit and lick your tutti-frutti. For cakes, try *Stefánia* next door, or head for the wonderful *Várkapu Café* on the corner of Hátsókapu and Várkerület.

Entertainment

Sopron is a musical town – the child prodigy Franz Liszt gave concerts here in 1820 – and the highlights of the season are the Spring Days in March, the Ancient Music Days in June and the Sopron Festival Weeks from mid-June to mid-July. Tickets to the various events are available from the box office (☎ 338 673) at Széchenyi tér 17-18.

During the rest of the year, the *Ferenc Liszt Cultural Centre* (☎ 314 170) off Széchenyi tér at Liszt Ferenc tér 1 is the place to go for music and other events. The beautiful *Petőfi Theatre* is around the corner on Petőfi tér. Those who want to take a chance should head for the *Sopron Casino* next to the cultural centre.

The Sopron region is noted for red wines like Kékfrankos and Merlot. They're pretty cheap even in restaurants but particularly high in acid and tannin, so watch your intake if you don't want a massive *macskajaj* ('cat's wail' – the Hungarian term for a hangover) the next day. A good place to sample them is in the *Gyógygődőr*, a deep, deep cellar at Fő tér 4. The *John Bull* chain has an up-market pub on Széchenyi tér.

Getting There & Away

Bus The bus service is good to/from Sopron. Up to 20 buses a day head for Fertőd, Fertőrákos, Fertőszentmiklós, Győr, Kapuvár and Nagycenk, and departures are frequent to Kőszeg (eight a day) and Szombathely (nine). Other destinations include: Baja (one bus daily), Balatonfüred (two), Budapest (five), Esztergom (two), Lake Fertő (eight), Hévíz and Keszthely (three), Kaposvár (two), Keszthely (three), Komárom (two), Nagykanizsa (two), Pécs (one), Sárvár (three), Székesfehérvár (two), Tapolca (one), Tatabánya (two), Veszprém (five) and Zalaegerszeg (two).

There's a daily bus to Vienna at 8 am and another on Monday, Thursday and Friday at 9.20 am. A bus also leaves for Munich and Stuttgart on Sunday at 9.05 pm.

Train Express trains en route to Vienna's Südbahnhof pass through Sopron three times a day, though local services to Ebenfurth and Wiener Neustadt (where you can transfer for Vienna) are much more frequent. There are four express trains a day to Budapest-Keleti via Győr and Komárom, and eight to 10 local trains to Szombathely.

Getting Around

Bus No 12 from both the bus and train stations stops directly in front of Lővér Camping. If you take bus No 1 from the bus station or No 2 from the train station, get off at Citadella Park and walk down Sarudi utca to Kőszegi utca. The camp site is just south. For the Brennbergi hostel take bus No 3 or 10 from the bus station.

Local taxis can be ordered on ☎ 312 222 or ☎ 333 333.

AROUND SOPRON
Lővér Hills
This range, 300 and 400m foothills of the Austrian Alps some five km south and south-west of the city centre, makes up Sopron's playground. It's a great place for hiking and walks, but is not without bitter memories, for it was here that partisans and Jews were executed by Nazis and the fascist Hungarian Arrow Cross during WWII. You can climb to the top of **Károly Lookout** on the 394m hill west of the Lővér hotel, or visit the Lővér Baths at Lővér körút 82, with outside pools open in summer and a covered pool, sauna and solarium open every day all year from 8 am to 8 pm.

You can't miss **Taródi Vár** at Csalogány köz 8, a 'self-built private castle' owned by the obsessed Taródi family. It's a bizarre place – not unlike Bory's Castle in Székesfehérvár – with the same half-baked, neo-Gothic, crazed feel to it. To get to the castle, take bus No 1 from the station and get off at the Lővér Baths. Follow Fenyves sor and Tölgyfa sor north for three blocks and turn left (west) on Csalogány köz. The castle is on your right up the hill.

Places to Stay Taródi Castle has three dormitory rooms where you can stay for 400 Ft a night and doubles for 1600 Ft. It is open from May to September. The *Diana* (☎ 329 013) at Lővér körút 64 is a nine-room pension run by a charming family with doubles for 3800 Ft.

There are several big hotels mostly catering to Austrians in the Lővér Hills, including the 180-room *Maróni* (☎ 312 549) at Lővér körút 74, which has doubles from DM 31 to DM50, and the *Szieszta* (☎ 314 260), a huge former trade-union holiday house and now a 288-room hotel at No 37, with doubles from DM56 to DM67. These two hotels can be reached on bus No 1 from the bus station and bus No 2 from the train station.

Fertőrákos
The **quarries** (*kőfejtő*) in Fertőrákos, a village of 2000 people some nine km northeast of Sopron, were worked by the Romans, and the pliable limestone was later used to decorate many of the buildings around the Ring in Vienna, including the Votivkirche. Today, the quarry's enormous 12m chambers – reminiscent of the Egyptian temples in Cecil B De Mille's epic films – are open to the public year round from 9 am to between 4 and 7 pm depending on the season, but they probably won't hold your interest for very long. From late June to late August concerts and operas are performed in the acoustically perfect **Cave Theatre**.

From the walkway around the rim of the quarry you can gaze across the plateau to the Austrian Alps and **Lake Fertő**, a shallow and brackish lake that lies mostly in Austria (and is called Neusiedlersee there). The lake is known for its waterfowl (herons, spoonbills, storks and egrets). It's national parkland, and you must seek permission to visit the reed beds from the park directorate (☎ 370 919) in Sarród (Rév-Kócsagvár).

The other big sight in Fertőrákos (German: Kroisbach) is the **Bishop's Palace** at Fő utca 153, built by the episcopate of Győr in 1743. The palace, east of the quarry, now contains a small museum of furniture, a heavily decorated dining hall, a small chapel with lovely frescos and the simple Kastély hotel.

Places to Stay & Eat The 14-room *Kastély* (☎ 355 040) in the former Bishop's Palace has doubles without bath for 1400 Ft. If it is full or closed (often the case out of season), check the cheap *Vízimalom* hostel (☎ 355 034) in an 18th-century mill at Fő utca 141. Accommodation is in 10 multi-bed rooms or in a couple of doubles with shared baths. You'll find the manager at Fő utca 135 if no one's at the hostel. The nine-room *Horváth Ház* (☎ 355 368) is a pricey pension at Fő utca 194-196.

For something to eat, try the *Melody Café* in a beautifully renovated farmhouse at Fő utca 142.

FERTŐD

- *pop 2800*
- *area code* ☎ 99

Fertőd, 27 km east of Sopron, has been associated with the aristocratic Esterházy family since the mid-18th century when Miklós Esterházy, proclaiming that 'Anything the (Habsburg) emperor can afford, I can afford too' began construction of the largest and most opulent summer palace in central Europe. When completed in 1766, it boasted 126 rooms, a separate opera house, a hermitage (complete with cranky old man in a sack cloth who wanted to be left alone), temples to Diana and Venus, a Chinese dance house, a puppet theatre and a 250-hectare garden laid out in the French manner. Fertőd – or Esterháza as it was known until the middle of this century – was on the map.

Much has been written about the Esterházy Palace and many hyperbolic monikers bestowed on it (the 'Hungarian Versailles' is the most common). But the fact remains that this baroque and rococo structure – its architects unknown except for the Austrian Melchior Hefele – is the most beautiful and best preserved palace in Hungary. While the rooms are mostly bare, history is very much alive here: in the Concert Hall, where many of the works of composer Franz Joseph Haydn, a 30-year resident of the palace, were first performed, including the *Farewell Symphony*; in the Chinoiserie Rooms, where Empress Maria Theresa attended a masked ball in 1773; and in the French Garden, where Miklós 'the Splendour Lover' threw some of the greatest parties of all times for friends like Goethe, complete with fireworks and tens of thousands of Chinese lanterns.

After a century and a half of neglect (it was used as a stables in the 19th century and a hospital during WWII), the palace has been partially restored to its former glory. It is among the top 10 sights in Hungary and an easy day trip from Sopron. Don't miss it.

Orientation & Information

The palace and its gardens on Bartók Béla utca dominate the town; the bus will let you off almost in front of the main gate. The town centre is a few minutes' walk to the west. The closest train station (it's on the Sopron-Győr line) is at Fertőszentmiklós, four km to the south.

The staff at the palace ticket office can answer any questions you have about the palace or the town of Fertőd.

An OTP bank branch can be found on Fő utca across from the Esterházy pension. The post office is at No 6 diagonally opposite the Music House.

Esterházy Palace

Some 26 renovated rooms at the horseshoe-shaped Esterházy Palace are open to the public; the rest of the complex houses a hotel, a secondary school and a horticultural research centre.

As you approach the main entrance to the so-called **Courtyard of Honour**, notice the ornamental wrought-iron gate, a rococo masterpiece. You can only tour the palace with a guide, but armed with a fact sheet in English available from the ticket office, lag behind and explore the rooms away from the crowds.

On the ground floor of the palace you'll pass through several rooms done up in mock Chinese style (all the rage in the late 18th century); the pillared **Sala Terrena**, with its floor of glimmering marble and Miklós Esterházy's initials in floral frescos on the ceiling; and the Prince's Bed Chamber, with frescos of Amor. On the 1st floor are more sumptuous baroque and rococo salons as well as the lavish **Concert** and **Ceremonial halls**, which give on to each other. Take a close look here at the statues of the four seasons with their campy headgear, and the *Triumph of Apollo*, a striking fresco by Johann Basilius Grundemann that looks at you from all sides. There's also an exhibit dedicated to the life and times of Haydn.

Excluding Monday, the palace is open from 9 am to 5 pm from mid-April to mid-October. It closes an hour earlier the rest of the year.

The apartment where Haydn lived off and on from 1761 to 1790 in the baroque **Music House**, south-west of the palace at Madach sétány 1, has been turned into a temple to the great composer. The **Esterháza Gallery** in the same building displays contemporary works and has some interesting antiques and curios for sale.

Places to Stay

Don't miss the chance to stay at the 19-room *Kastély* hotel (☎ 370 971) in the east wing of the palace. You won't be sleeping in anything like the Prince's Bed Chamber but, for a palace, the price is right: 1700/2000/2300 Ft for doubles/triples/quads with shared bath. The truly romantic (or flush) will choose to stay at the *Bagatelle*, a separate pavilion in the garden with two apartments.

If you arrive to find the Kastély full, don't let yourself be talked into staying at the Esterházy pension nearby at Fő utca 20. It's an overpriced place with most unpleasant management and full of drunks. One reader wrote to say she actually had a camera stolen from a locked room there! Instead, see if the hostel in the *Udvaros-ház* (☎ 345 971), an outbuilding of the palace at Fő utca 1, has a bed.

Places to Eat

The *Gránátos* café in Grenadier House, the former living quarters of the grenadier guards directly across from the palace's main entrance, is pleasant enough, and in summer *food stalls* dispensing lángos and wirsli fill the nearby car park.

The *Haydn* restaurant in Udvaros-ház has standard Hungarian favourites and garden seating in summer. It's open till 9 pm. A better choice might be the *Árkád* restaurant opposite the Gránátos café on Bartók Béla utca.

Entertainment

Fertőd has been a music centre since Miklós Esterházy first engaged Haydn as court conductor. From May to August there are piano and string quartets performing in the palace *Concert Hall* on most Saturdays at 6 pm and some Sundays at 11 am or 7 pm.

The Fertőd Music Festival in August is usually booked out months in advance, but try your luck at the ticket counter or at Ciklámen Tourist in Sopron.

Getting There & Away

About 30 buses a day link Sopron with Fertőd on weekdays (between a dozen and 18 on Saturday and Sunday). There are also buses to Győr and Kapuvár. Nine trains a day link Sopron and Győr with Fertőszentmiklós to the south.

NAGYCENK

- *pop 1600*
- *area code ☎ 99*

Only 14 km west of Fertőd and the Esterházy Palace, but light-years away in spirit, lies Nagycenk, site of the ancestral mansion of the Széchenyi clan. No two houses – or families – could have been more different than these. While the privileged, often frivolous Esterházys held court in their imperial palace, the Széchenyis – democrats and reformers all – went about their work in a sombre neoclassical manor house that aptly reflected their temperament and sense of purpose. The mansion has been completely renovated and turned into a three-star hotel and a superb museum dedicated to the Széchenyis.

The family's public-spiritedness started with Ferenc Széchenyi, who donated his entire collection of books and *objets d'art* to the state in 1802, laying the foundations for the National Library named in his honour. But it was his son, István (1791-1860), who made the greatest impact of any Hungarian on the economic and cultural development of the nation (see The Greatest Hungarian aside).

Orientation & Information

The train station is near the centre of Nagycenk, not far from neo-Romanesque St Stephen's Church designed by Miklós Ybl

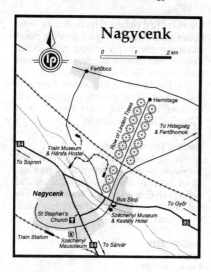

(1864) and the Széchenyi family's mausoleum. The bus from Sopron stops at the mansion's main gate.

Széchenyi Mansion

The entrance to the **István Széchenyi Memorial Museum** in the mansion is through the Sala Terrena – almost austere compared with the one at the Esterházy Palace in Fertőd. Guided tours on cassette are available in several languages (including English) from the ticket office for 300 Ft. You would do well to rent one: as excellent as this museum is, the labels are only in Hungarian.

The rooms on the ground floor of the museum, with furniture contemporary with the times, deal with the history of the Széchenyi family and their political development, from typical baroque aristocrats in the 18th century to key players in the 1848 War of Independence and István's involvement in the government of Lajos Batthyány. A sweeping baroque staircase leads to the exhibits on the 1st floor – a veritable temple to the István's accomplishments – from Budapest's Chain Bridge and the Danube and Tisza river engineering works to steamboat and rail transport. The museum is open

April to September daily except Monday from 10 am to 6 pm and to 2 pm the rest of the year.

It is fitting that the mansion of a railway developer like István Széchenyi lies near an open-air **Train Museum**, with steam engines that were still in use on main lines as late as 1950. You can actually ride a 100-year-old **narrow-gauge steam train** for 3.5 km to Fertőboz and back for 140/70 Ft adults/children. Departures between mid-April and late September from the Kastély station at Nagycenk are at 10.05 and 11.30 am and 3.25 and 6.15 pm. All but the last one turn around at Fertőboz for the return trip to Kastély.

A 2.5-km **row of linden trees** opposite the mansion and planted by István's grandmother in 1754 leads to a **hermitage**. Like the Esterházys, the Széchenyi family had a resident loner who, in this case, was expected to earn his keep by ringing the chapel bell and tending the garden.

The **Széchenyi Mausoleum**, the final resting place of István and other family members, is in the village cemetery across the road from St Stephen's Church.

Cross-country riding and coach tours are available at the 200-year-old Nagycenk Stud Farm (☎ 360 026), which has 60 horses. You can also rent horses at the Nemet Riding School (☎ 360 196) in the village.

Places to Stay & Eat

Cheap accommodation is available at the tiny *Hársfa* (☎ 360 105), a six-room hostel behind the train museum at Kiscenki utca 1. Doubles with shared bath are 1200 Ft. The Hársfa is open from May to October.

The *Kastély* hotel (☎ 360 061), in the west wing of the mansion at Kiscenki utca 3, is a beautifully appointed 19-room inn, but it may exceed your budget: singles are DM88 to DM144 and doubles DM110 to DM158, depending on the season and room type. If you can afford between DM116 and DM194, opt for No 106, a large suite with period furniture and restful views of the six-hectare garden.

The Greatest Hungarian

The contributions of Count István Széchenyi to Hungarian society were enormous and extremely varied. In his seminal 1830 work *Hitel* (meaning 'credit' and based on *hit*, or 'trust'), he advocated sweeping economic reforms and the abolition of serfdom (he himself had distributed the bulk of his property to landless peasants two years earlier). The Chain Bridge, the design of which Széchenyi helped push through Parliament, was the first link between Buda and Pest and for the first time everyone, nobles included, had to pay a toll. Széchenyi was instrumental in straightening the serpentine Tisza River, which rescued half of Hungary's arable land from flooding and erosion, and his work made the Danube navigable as far as the Iron Gates in Romania. He arranged the financing for Hungary's first railway lines (from Budapest north and east to Vác and Szolnok and west to what is now Wiener Neustadt in Austria) and launched the first steam transport on the Danube and Lake Balaton. A lover of all things English, Széchenyi got the upper classes interested in horse racing with the express purpose of improving breeding stock for farming. A large financial contribution made by Széchenyi led to the establishment of the nation's prestigious Academy of Science.

Széchenyi joined Lajos Batthyány's revolutionary government in 1848, but political squabbling and open conflict with Vienna caused him to lose control and he suffered a nervous breakdown. Despite a decade of convalescence in an asylum, Széchenyi never fully recovered and tragically he took his own life in 1860.

For all his accomplishments, Széchenyi's contemporary and fellow reformer, Lajos Kossuth, called him 'the greatest Hungarian'. This dynamic but troubled visionary retains that accolade to this day. ■

The splendid dining room at the *Kastély* hotel is the place for lunch if you don't mind eating elbow-to-elbow with crowds of Austrian day-trippers. The *Pálya* restaurant in the renovated little train station near the Train Museum is cheaper and will be almost as crowded at weekends with local tourists. If you can't get a seat, snack at the *Park* or any of the other food stalls in the car park. The café just outside the Kastély hotel restaurant serves excellent cakes and ice cream.

Getting There & Away

Nagycenk is accessible from Sopron by bus every half-hour. The village is on the railway line linking Sopron and Szombathely, and some eight trains arrive and depart each day.

If you time it right, you can reach Nagycenk by the toy train. Take the bus from Sopron to Fertőboz and board the train for Kastély station at 10.50 am, 12.30 or 4.10 pm.

SZOMBATHELY

- *pop 86,600*
- *area code* ☎ *94*

Szombathely (German: Steinamanger) is a major crossroads in western Hungary. Its name (pronounced roughly as 'som-bot-hay') translates as 'Saturday place' and refers to the important weekend markets held here in the Middle Ages. For many Austrians who cross the border in search of cheap edibles and services, it remains just that.

Szombathely had an early start. In 43 AD the Romans established a trade settlement called Savaria here on the all-important Amber Route. By the start of the 2nd century it was important enough to become the capital of Upper Pannonia. Over the next few centuries, Savaria prospered and Christianity arrived; Martin of Tours, the patron saint of France, was born here in 316. But attacks by Huns, Longobards and Avars weakened its defences. It was destroyed by an earthquake in 455.

Szombathely began to develop in the early Middle Ages, but the Mongols, then the Turks and the Habsburgs, put a stop to that. It wasn't until 1777, when János Szily was appointed Szombathely's first bishop, that the city really began to flourish economically and culturally. The building of the railway line to Graz brought further trade. In 1945 Allied bombers levelled much of the town, which has since been rebuilt (not very successfully in many parts). Szombathely is an important industrial city and the capital of Vas County.

Orientation

Szombathely is made up of narrow streets and squares with the centre at leafy Fő tér,

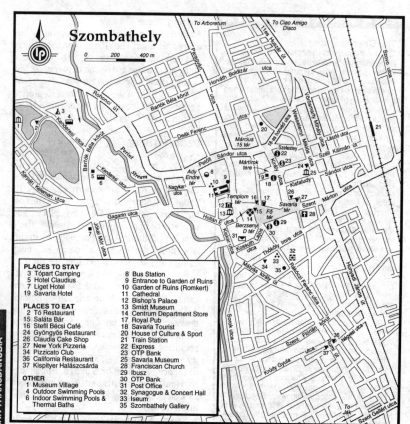

Szombathely

0   200   400 m

PLACES TO STAY
3 Tópart Camping
5 Hotel Claudius
7 Liget Hotel
19 Savaria Hotel

PLACES TO EAT
2 Tó Restaurant
15 Saláta Bár
16 Steffl Bécsi Café
24 Gyöngyös Restaurant
26 Claudia Cake Shop
27 New York Pizzeria
34 Pizzicato Club
36 California Restaurant
37 Kispityer Halászcsárda

OTHER
1 Museum Village
4 Outdoor Swimming Pools
6 Indoor Swimming Pools &
   Thermal Baths

8 Bus Station
9 Entrance to Garden of Ruins
10 Garden of Ruins (Romkert)
11 Cathedral
12 Bishop's Palace
13 Smidt Museum
14 Centrum Department Store
17 Royal Pub
18 Savaria Tourist
20 House of Culture & Sport
21 Train Station
22 Express
23 OTP Bank
25 Savaria Museum
28 Franciscan Church
29 Ibusz
30 OTP Bank
31 Post Office
32 Synagogue & Concert Hall
33 Iseum
35 Szombathely Gallery

one of the largest squares in Hungary. To the
west are Berzsenyi Dániel tér and Templom
tér, the administrative and ecclesiastical
centres of town. The train station is on Éhen
Gyula tér, five blocks east of Mártírok tere at
the end of Széll Kálmán út. The bus station
is on Petőfi Sándor utca, north-west of the
cathedral.

Information

Two agencies are just a block apart from one
another: Savaria Tourist (☎ 312 348) at
Mártírok tere 1 and Express (☎ 311 230) at
Király utca 12. Ibusz (☎ 314 141) is at Fő tér

44. All are open from 8 am to 4.30 or 5 pm
weekdays, to noon Saturday.

There's an OTP bank branch diagonally
opposite Savaria Tourist at Király utca 10
and another branch on the corner of Fő tér
and Bejczy István utca. The main post office
is at Kossuth Lajos utca 2.

Things to See

Allied bombing in the final days of WWII
did not spare the Zopf-style **Szombathely
Cathedral** (1797) on Templom tér – as the
before-and-after photographs in the porch
confirm. Designed by Melchior Hefele for

Bishop Szily in 1791, the cathedral was once covered in stucco work and frescos by Franz Anton Maulbertsch and supported by grand marble columns. They're now gone, of course, though a couple of Maulbertsch originals and a glorious red and white marble pulpit remain, breaking the monotony of this sterile place.

Maulbertsch frescos in the upstairs Reception Hall at the **Bishop's Palace** (Hefele, 1783) south of the cathedral at Berzsenyi Dániel tér 3 miraculously survived the air raids, but these are not usually open to the public. You can, however, admire the frescos of Roman ruins and gods (1784) by István Dorffmeister in the Sala Terrena on the ground floor. Other rooms contain more prewar photographs of the cathedral and items taken from the Episcopal Treasury, including missals and Bibles from the 14th to 18th centuries, Gothic vestments and a beautiful 15th-century monstrance from Kőszeg. The palace is open from Tuesday to Friday and on Sunday from 9.30 am to 3.30 pm and on Saturday to 11.30 am.

The **Smidt Museum**, in a baroque mansion behind the Bishop's Palace at Hollán Ernő utca 2, contains the private collection of one Lajos Smidt, a pack-rat physician who spent most of this century squirreling away antique weapons, furniture, fans, pipes, clocks, Roman coins and so on. None of it looks like it's worth very much, but the volume and zaniness of it all makes the museum worth a visit. (Keep an eye open for Franz Liszt's pocket watch.)

Szombathely has some of the most important Roman ruins in Hungary, and many of them are on display. The **Garden of Ruins** (Romkert) behind the cathedral and accessible from Templom tér contains a wealth of Savaria relics excavated here since 1938 and is open from 10 am to 6 pm April to October (to 4 pm in winter). You can't miss the beautiful mosaics of plants and geometrical designs set in concrete(!) on the floor of what was **St Quirinus Church** in the 4th century, and there are also remains of Roman road markers, a customs house, shops and the medieval castle walls.

The **Iseum**, south of Fő tér on Rákóczi utca (same hours as the Garden of Ruins), is part of a grand 2nd-century complex of two temples dedicated to the Egyptian goddess Isis by Roman legionnaires. When the smaller temple was excavated in the 1950s, the city decided to reconstruct it – with cement blocks. The result is grotesque and should be removed. The frieze on the sacrificial altar depicts Isis riding the dog Sirius; it's spoiled by the location. Frankly, after the Iseum, the medieval-looking sculpture entitled *Holiday March* (1980) by Károly Majtenyi outside on the corner of Rákóczi utca and Thököly Imre utca seems a masterpiece.

The **Szombathely Gallery** overlooking the temple at Rákóczi utca 12 is one of the best modern art galleries in Hungary (closed Monday and Tuesday). The lovely twin-towered Moorish building across the street at No 3 is the former **synagogue** designed in 1881 by the Viennese architect Ludwig Schöne. Today it houses a music school and the **Bartók Concert Hall**. A plaque points out the spot from which '4228 of our Jewish brothers and sisters were deported to Auschwitz on 4 July 1944'.

The **Savaria Museum**, fronting a little park at Kisfaludy Sándor utca 9 east of Mártírok tere, is worth a short look around. The ground floor is devoted to highly decorative but practical items carved by 19th-century shepherds to while away the hours; the cellar is full of Roman altars, stone torsos and blue-glass vials found at Savaria excavation sites. There's a local history exhibit on the 1st floor.

The **Vas County Museum Village**, on the western bank of the fishing lake at Árpád utca 30, is a *skanzen* (open-air museum) with a dozen 18th and 19th-century *porták* (farmhouses) moved from various villages in the Őrség region. They are arranged around a semicircular street, as was usual on the western border. The most interesting of these are the Croatian (No 2), German (No 8) and 'fenced' (No 12) houses. Nettles from a strange plant called *kővirózsa* (the 'stone rose') growing on the thatch were used to pierce little girls' ears.

Three km north-east along Szent Imre herceg útja at No 102 is the rich **Kámoni Arboretum** established in the 19th century with some 3000 species of trees and shrubs. It's dazzling in spring when the magnolias are in bloom.

Activities

The rowing and fishing lakes north-west of the centre along Kenderesi utca cover an area of 12 hectares and make up Szombathely's playground; boats can be hired. There's a huge outdoor swimming pool on the east bank open to the public in summer. The city's indoor pools and thermal baths are next to the Claudius hotel.

The city's famed horse-riding school (☎ 313 461) lies south-west of the Liget hotel on Középhegyi út.

Places to Stay

Camping From May to September you can stay at *Tópart Camping* (☎ 314 766) at Kenderesi utca 4 by the lakes north-west of town. From the bus stop (bus No 7) walk along the causeway between the lakes. Bungalows for two with shared shower are 2400 Ft, and for four people with shower, they're 6000 Ft. Camping costs 300 Ft per person and 200 Ft for a tent. The big outdoor public swimming pool is nearby.

Private Rooms & Hostels Private rooms (2000 to 2500 Ft a double) are assigned by staff at Savaria Tourist and Ibusz. In summer, ask Express about dormitory rooms at the *student hostels* (600 to 700 Ft a bed) on Ady Endre tér and Nagykar utca 1-3.

Hotels The 38-room *Liget* hotel (☎ 314 168), west of the centre at Szent István park 15, has singles/doubles with shower for 2350/2700 Ft. It's effectively a motel but convenient to the lakes, the museum village and the riding school.

Szombathely's nicest hotel is the *Savaria* (☎ 311 440) at Mártírok tere 4 in the very centre of town. It's a 90-room Art Nouveau gem built in 1917 and, while the rooms are somewhat dark and unexceptional, its res-

taurant with antique *kocsma* (saloon) furniture and Winter Garden function room are easy places to conjure up ghosts of a more elegant past. Depending on the size of the room and what facilities are in them, singles range from 4000 to 8350 Ft, doubles from 4500 to 8850 Ft. Room No 318 with bath and views of the square is the best.

The 102-room *Claudius* (☎ 313 760) is a three-star hotel near the lakes at Bartók Béla körút 39 with five-star prices: DM80/95 for singles/doubles with bath.

If you're driving north-west to Kőszeg, check the *Kastély* hotel (☎ 360 960) at Rákóczi utca 1 in Bozsok, about 20 km north-west of Szombathely. The 12-room hotel, housed in a 17th-century manor house and set amid a lovely park, has doubles for about 3600 Ft, a tennis court and sauna.

Places to Eat

The *New York* at Savaria tér 1/c has pizza, but the selection is better at the *Pizzicato Club* at Thököly utca 14. The *Saláta Bár* at the end of tiny pedestrian Belsikátor utca connecting Berzsenyi Dániel tér with Fő tér is a good place for a cheap lunch.

The *Gyöngyös*, Széll Kálmán út 8, has an inexpensive set menu at lunchtime, and the food and service are always good. It's closed on Monday. The *Kispityer Halászcsárda*, 1500m south-west of Fő tér at Rumi út 18, is worth the trip if you're in search of fish. Carnivores can cross the street to the *California* at No 21, an almost authentic American steakhouse with a very real salad bar.

If you're messing around in boats on the lake or visiting the museum village and get hungry, head for the *Tó* restaurant on the narrow isthmus (Rajki sétány) separating the two lakes and get a table on the terrace.

The *Claudia* on Savaria tér has decent cakes and ice cream.

Entertainment

Szombathely has devoted a lot of attention to music since Bishop Szily engaged the services of full-time musicians to perform at church functions – not services. Today many of the cultural events staged during March's

Spring Festival take place in the *Bartók Concert Hall*, Rákóczi Ferenc utca 3, where the Savaria Symphony Orchestra also performs throughout the year. The International Bartók Festival late in July is actually a music seminar with 'workshop' concerts. Another venue is the ugly 1960s *House of Culture & Sport* (☎ 312 666) at Március 15 tér 5.

For a less mannered evening, start at the *Royal*, a pub with sidewalk tables on the northern side of Fő tér. The *Steffl Bécsi* café opposite is also good. The House of Culture & Sport has a weekend disco called *Club Mylos*. Another popular night spot is *Ciao Amigo* out at the edge of town on 11es Huszár út.

Getting There & Away
Bus The bus service is not so good to/from Szombathely, though up to 20 buses leave every day for Ják and about 10 go to Kőszeg, Sárvár and Velem. Other destinations include Baja (one departure daily), Budapest (two), Győr (six), Kaposvár (two), Keszthely via Hévíz (three), Nagykanizsa (seven), Pécs (two), Sopron (six), Szentgotthárd (one) and Zalaegerszeg (six). One bus a week departs for Graz (Friday at 7 am) and Vienna (Wednesday at 6.40 am) in Austria.

Train Express trains to Budapest-Déli go via Veszprém and Székesfehérvár. Other express trains run to Győr via Celldömölk. There are frequent local trains to Kőszeg and Sopron and an early morning express train to/from Pécs.

Szombathely is only 13 km from the Austrian border, and there are direct trains to/from Graz. Some of the Graz services involve a change of trains at Szentgotthárd on the border.

Getting Around
Szombathely is simple to negotiate on foot, but bus No 7 will take you from the train station to the museum village, lakes, camp site and the Liget hotel. No 2 is good for the Kámoni Arboretum.

You can order a taxi on ☎ 312 222 or ☎ 326 666.

AROUND SZOMBATHELY
Ják
• *pop 2100*
Try to visit Ják, 12 km south of Szombathely and an easy half-day trip by bus. This sleepy village boasts the Benedictine **Abbey Church**, one of the finest examples of Romanesque architecture in Hungary. Its main feature, a magnificent portal carved in geometric patterns 12 layers deep and featuring carved stone statues of Christ and his Apostles on the west side, was renovated for the Millecentenary in 1996. The decorative sculptures on the outside wall of the sanctuary and the church's interior are also worth a look.

The two-towered structure was begun as a family church in 1214 by Márton Nagy and dedicated to St George four decades later in 1256. Somehow the partially completed church managed to escape destruction during the Mongol invasion, but it was badly damaged during the Turkish occupation. The church has had many restorations, the most important being in the mid-17th century, between 1896 and 1904 (when most of the statues in the portal were recut or replaced, rose windows added and earlier baroque additions removed) and 1992-96.

Enter through the south door, once used only by the monks based here. The interior, with its single nave and three aisles, has a much more graceful and personal feel than most later Hungarian Gothic churches. To the west and below the towers is a gallery reserved for the benefactor and his family. The faded rose and blue frescos on the wall between the vaulting and the arches below could very well be of Márton Nagy and his progeny. If you slip 50 Ft into the machine nearby, you'll illuminate the church, transforming the cold grey stone to soft yellow.

To the west of the Romanesque church is the tiny clover-leaf **Chapel of St James** topped with an onion dome. It was built around 1260 as a parish church since the main church was monastic. Note the paschal

WESTERN TRANSDANUBIA

lamb (symbolising Christ) over the main entrance, and the baroque altar and frescos inside.

The Abbey Church is open daily April to October from 8 am to 6 pm. If you miss Ják, take comfort in the fact that you can visit a model of the church (complete with carved stone portal) at the Vajdahunyad Castle in Budapest's City Park. It was erected for the Millenary Exhibition in 1896.

Ják has no accommodation but there's a snack bar at the ticket office, and the simple *Falatozó* restaurant is on Szabadság utca as you walk up (or down) the hill.

Buses from Szombathely are very frequent and will drop you off at the bottom of the hill a few minutes' walk from the church. From Ják you can return to Szombathely on one of up to 20 daily buses or continue on to Szentpéterfa (15 a day), Körmend (four) or Szentgotthárd (one).

SÁRVÁR

- *pop 16,000*
- *area code ☎ 95*

Some 27 km east of Szombathely on the Rába River, the quiet town of 'Mud Castle' has experienced some good and some very bad times. During the Reformation, Sárvár's fortified castle was a centre of Calvinist culture and scholarship, and its owners, the Nádasdy family, a respected dynasty in statecraft and military leadership. In 1537, Tamás Nádasdy set up a press that published the first two printed books in Hungarian – a Magyar grammar in Latin and a translation of the New Testament. Ferenc Nádasdy II, the so-called Black Captain, fought heroically against the Turks, and his grandson Ferenc III, a lord chief justice, established one of the greatest libraries and private art collections in central Europe.

But everything began to sour at the start of the 17th century. It seems that while the Black Captain was away at war, his wife Erzsébet Báthory, as mad as a hatter and blood-thirsty to boot, began torturing and murdering servant girls. (The 'Blood Countess' would later be banished to a castle in Transylvania where she would die in 1614, and she is believed to have been partly the model for Bram Stoker's *Dracula*.) Then Ferenc III's involvement in a plot led by Ferenc Wesselényi to overthrow the Habsburgs was exposed. He was beheaded in Vienna in 1671.

Sárvár is not all history and blood-letting. It is equally well known for its 44°C thermal waters, discovered in the 1960s during experimental drilling for oil.

Orientation & Information

The train station is on Selyemgyár utca. To reach the town centre, walk south along Hunyadi János utca and turn east on Batthyány Lajos utca, which leads to Kossuth tér and the castle. The bus station is on the western end of Batthyány Lajos utca.

Savaria Tourist (☎ 320 578), almost opposite the castle entrance at Várkerület 33, is open on weekdays from 9 am to 4.30 pm and on Saturday to 12.30 pm.

There's an OTP bank branch at Batthyány Lajos utca 2 and a K&H Bank with an ATM and foreign currency exchange machine at Kossuth tér 1. The main post office is at Várkerület 32.

Nádasdy Castle & Museum

The entrance to the **Ferenc Nádasdy Museum** in the pentagonal castle is across a brick footbridge from Kossuth tér and through the gate of a 14th-century tower. Though parts of the castle date from the 13th century, most of it is in 16th-century Renaissance style and in remarkably good condition despite Erzsébet Báthory's shenanigans and all the plundering by the Habsburgs. As punishment for their involvement in the rebellion of 1670, the Nádasdy estate was confiscated by the Austrian crown and the castle's contents – including much of the library – were carted off to Vienna. As a result, many of the furnishings, tapestries and *objets d'art* you see today in the museum's three wings were collected from other sources.

What the Habsburgs could not take away were the magnificent ceiling frescos in the **Knight's Hall** (Lovag Terme) picturing

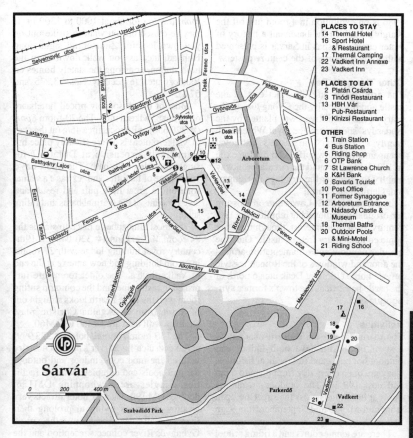

PLACES TO STAY
14 Thermál Hotel
16 Sport Hotel
& Restaurant
17 Thermál Camping
22 Vadkert Inn Annexe
23 Vadkert Inn

PLACES TO EAT
2 Platán Csárda
3 Tinódi Restaurant
13 HBH Vár
Pub-Restaurant
19 Kinizsi Restaurant

OTHER
1 Train Station
4 Bus Station
5 Riding Shop
6 OTP Bank
7 St Lawrence Church
8 K&H Bank
9 Savaria Tourist
10 Post Office
11 Former Synagogue
12 Arboretum Entrance
15 Nádasdy Castle &
Museum
18 Thermal Baths
20 Outdoor Pools
& Mini-Motel
21 Riding School

Sárvár

WESTERN TRANSDANUBIA

Hungarians – the Black Captain included – doing battle with the Turks at Tata, Székesfehérvár, Buda and Győr. They were painted by Hans Rudolf Miller in the mid-17th century. The biblical scenes (1769) on the walls, depicting Samson and Delilah, David and Goliath, Mordechai and Esther and so on, are by István Dorffmeister. There's a particularly beautiful 16th-century cabinet of gilded wood and marble to the right of the hall as you enter.

The Nádasdy Museum contains one of the finest collections of weapons and armour in Hungary, and almost an entire wing is given over to the Hussars, a regiment of which was named after the family. The uniforms, all buttons and ribbons and fancy epaulets, would do any Gilbert & Sullivan operetta proud. Among the exhibits about the castle and Sárvár is the printing press established here and some of the then inflammatory Calvinist tracts it published. One Hungarian work, entitled *The Pope Is Not the Pope – That's That* and dated 1603, was later vandalised by a Counter-Reformist who wrote 'Lutheran scandal' across it in Latin.

A superb collection of 60 antique Hungarian maps donated by an expatriate Magyar in

1986 is on exhibition in a room just off the Knight's Hall. In the basement a history of water cures and spas in Sárvár is presented with some fine turn-of-the-century posters.

Other Things to See
The **arboretum** on Várkerület east of the castle and bisected by the Gyöngyös, a tributary of the Rába River, was planted by the Nádasdys' successors, the royal Wittelsbach family of Bavaria (the castle's last royal occupant was Ludwig III, who died in exile in 1921). Stroll around the circular walkway and try to decipher the tree tags in Hungarian, German and Latin.

The **Church of St Lawrence** on Kossuth tér, originally medieval but rebuilt in the 19th century, is of little interest, though there are some contemporary frescos inside. Only the circular window and ornamentation around the door and windows of the Romantic-style private home (1850) at Deák utca 6 north of the castle betray it as the town's former **synagogue**.

Activities
The thermal baths on Vadkerti utca southeast of the castle have both indoor and outdoor hot pools and full medical facilities. They are open every day from 8 am to 6 pm and cost 190 Ft. The outdoor swimming pools at the strand across the street are open from mid-May to mid-September from 9 am to 7 pm.

There are tennis courts and a riding school (☎ 320 045) at the end of Vadkerti utca. Ask the staff at the Vadkert inn about rentals (1200 Ft an hour and 5000 Ft for a coach seating four). The Riding Shop (Lovas Bolt) behind the church at Széchenyi utca 3 has all the gear if you feel you must kit yourself out.

Places to Stay
You can pitch a tent at *Thermál Camping*, Vadkerti utca 1, for 350/400 Ft per tent/person, but there are no bungalows. They do run a less-than-salubrious *mini-motel* opposite on Vadkerti utca in the warmer months and charge 1600 Ft per room.

Savaria Tourist can organise a *private room* for you for about 1000 to 1300 Ft. If they're closed or you want to strike out on your own, look for 'Zimmer frei' signs along Hunyadi utca as you walk down from the train station, or among the stately homes on Rákóczi utca (especially Nos 23, 25 and 57/a).

Most of the reasonably priced hotels are on or near Vadkerti utca. The 20-room *Sport* (☎ 320 656) at Rákóczi utca 46/a (at the start of Vadkerti utca) is a very friendly place but surprisingly expensive at DM50/77 for singles/doubles with bath. The Sport has a wide range of facilities and 'extras': a sauna/solarium, a great little pub and restaurant, and discounts at the thermal baths and riding school.

The most atmospheric place to stay is the 24-room *Vadkert* inn (☎ 320 045), a 19th-century royal hunting lodge with 27 rooms in an old building and new annexe at the end of Vadkerti utca. The older rooms are furnished in rustic pine, and the common sitting room with the large hearth looks straight out of a set from an Agatha Christie play. Doubles with bath are DM50 to DM60.

The 136-room *Thermál* hotel (☎ 323 999) at Rákóczi utca 1 is Sárvár's poshest hostelry with all the mod cons, indoor and outdoor thermal pools and complete curative facilities. Singles are a whopping DM136, doubles DM 190. Thus the hotel attracts very wealthy Austrians trying to prolong their lives. A small covered bridge over the narrow Gyöngyös River connects reception and the Nádor restaurant with the main building, and there's a statue outside of the Black Captain holding a spear that doubles as a sundial.

Places to Eat
The *Platán* is a csárda (and pension) in a renovated neoclassical building at Hunyadi utca 23 between the train station and the town centre. It's open till midnight. The *Tinódi*, a block away at No 11, is cheaper but not so pleasant and closes at 10 pm. The *HBH Vár* pub-restaurant on Rákóczi utca just before the Thermál hotel is open daily to midnight. The *Kinizsi* restaurant next to the thermal baths is there if you're hungry after

a soak, but the health-conscious will head for the *Sport* hotel restaurant, which serves salads and a couple of vegetarian dishes.

Entertainment
Concerts are occasionally held in the Knight's Hall at the castle; check with Savaria Tourist or the *Lajos Kossuth Cultural Centre* at the castle for dates. Sárvár's main event is the International Folklore Festival held in mid-August under the spreading chestnut trees in the castle courtyard.

Getting There & Away
Destinations served by bus to/from Sárvár and their daily frequencies include Bük (seven buses a day), Celldömölk (nine), Győr (two), Keszthely (two), Pápa (two), Sitke (12), Sopron (two), Sümeg (three), Szombathely (eight to 10), Veszprém (one) and Zalaegerszeg (three).

Sárvár is on the railway line linking Szombathely with Veszprém, Székesfehérvár and Budapest-Déli (and sometimes Budapest-Keleti). You can expect up to two-dozen trains a day to Szombathely, from where several continue on to Graz in Austria via Szentgotthárd. Between 10 and 12 trains reach the other three cities every day.

KŐSZEG
• *pop 13,700*
• *area code* ☎ *94*

The tranquil little town of Kőszeg (German: Güns) is sometimes called 'the nation's jewellery box', and as you pass under the pseudo-Gothic Heroes' Gate into Jurisics tér, you'll understand why. What opens up before you is a treasure trove of colourful Gothic, Renaissance and baroque buildings that together make up one of the most delightful squares in Hungary.

In the shadow of Mt Írottkő – at 882m, the highest point in Transdanubia – and just three km from the Austrian border, Kőszeg has switched its nationality on several occasions and played pivotal roles in the nation's defence. The best known story is the storming of the town's castle by Suleiman the Magnificent's troops in August 1532, which

sounds all too familiar but has a surprise ending. Miklós Jurisics' 'army' of fewer than 50 soldiers and the town militia held the fortress for 25 days against 100,000 Turks. An accord was reached when Jurisics allowed the Turks to run up their flag over the castle in a symbolic declaration of victory provided they then left town immediately thereafter. The Turks kept their part of the bargain (packing their bags at 11 am on 30 August), and Vienna was spared the treatment that would befall Buda nine years later. To this day church bells in Kőszeg peal an hour before noon to mark the withdrawal.

Orientation
Kőszeg's heel-shaped historic district, the Belváros (Inner Town), is ringed by the Várkör, which follows the old castle walls. The city's bus 'station' is a half-dozen stops on Liszt Ferenc utca a few minutes' walk to the south-east. The train station is about 1.5 km to the south-east on Alsó körút.

Information
Kőszeg is an easy destination for Austrians, so the town has an abundance of tourist offices, including Savaria Tourist (☎ 360 238) at Várkör 69, Express (☎ 360 247) around the corner at Városház utca 5 and Ibusz (☎ 360 376) at Várkör 35-37. All are open from 8 am to about 4 or 5 pm on weekdays and to noon on Saturday.

There's an OTP bank branch with an ATM and a foreign currency exchange machine at Kossuth Lajos utca 8. The main post office is next to Savaria Tourist on Várkör. The Városkapu bookshop at Jurisics tér 5 has a decent English-language section.

The telephone code for Kőszeg is ☎ 94.

Things to See
Heroes' Gate (Hősök kapu) leading into Jurisics tér was erected in 1932 (when these nostalgic portals were all the rage in Hungary) to mark the 400th anniversary of Suleiman's departure. The tower above is open to visitors and offers wonderful views (and photographs) of the square. The **General's House**, next to the gate at Jurisics

WESTERN TRANSDANUBIA

Kőszeg

0   150   300 m

tér 4-6, contains a branch of the **Miklós Jurisics Museum** with exhibits on the folk art, trades and crafts and the natural history of the area.

Almost all of the buildings on Jurisics tér are interesting. The red and yellow **town hall** at No 8, a mixture of Gothic, Renaissance, baroque and neoclassical styles, has oval paintings on its façade of worldly and heavenly worthies. The Renaissance house at No 7, built in 1668, is adorned with graffiti etched into the stucco. No 11 is the **Golden Unicorn Pharmacy** (Arany Egyszarvú Patikaház) – one of two pharmacy museums

in little Kőszeg. For those of you who can't get enough of controlled substances behind glass, the other, the **Black Moor Pharmacy** (Fekete Szerecsen Patikaház), is at Rákóczi utca 3.

A statue of the Virgin Mary (1739) and the town fountain (1766) in the middle of the square adjoin two fine churches. The Gothic **Church of St James** (1407) to the north contains very faded 15th-century frescos on the east wall of a giant St Christopher carrying the Christ Child, Mary Misericordia sheltering supplicants under a massive cloak and the Three Magi with their gifts. The altars and pews are masterpieces of baroque woodcarving, and Miklós Jurisics and two of his children are buried in the crypt. The baroque **Church of St Imre** with the tall steeple has two art treasures: frescos of the church's patron by István Dorffmeister and an altarpiece of Mary visiting her cousin Elizabeth by Franz Anton Maulbertsch.

Just off Rajnis József utca to the north-west is a path leading to **Jurisics Castle**. Originally built in the mid-13th century, but reconstructed again and again (most recently in 1962), the four-towered castle is now a hotchpotch of Renaissance arcades, Gothic windows and baroque interiors. The **Castle Museum** on the 1st floor has exhibits on the history of Kőszeg (with the events of 1532 taking up most of the space) and on local wine production. Among the latter is the curious *Arrival of the Grape* book, a kind of gardener's log of grape-bud sketches begun in 1740 and updated every year on the same day (St George's Day – 23 April). You can climb two of the towers, from which a brass ensemble entertained the townspeople in the Middle Ages.

Walking south along narrow Chernel utca with its elegant baroque façades and saw-toothed rooftops (which allowed the defenders a better shot at the enemy), you'll pass the remains of the **old castle walls** and the **Old Tower** (Öreg Zwinger) at No 16, an 11th-century corner bastion.

The neo-Gothic **Church of the Sacred Heart** (1894) in Fő tér is unexceptionable save for its refreshingly different geometric frescos and those 'midday' bells at 11 am. The circular **synagogue** (1859) with its strange neo-Gothic towers once served one of the oldest Jewish communities in Hungary, but now sits abandoned and in decay on Várkör to the north-east.

Activities

Walking up to the baroque chapel on 393m Kálvária-hegy (Calvary Hill) north-west of the town centre or into the vineyards of Király-völgy (King's Valley) west of the castle is a pleasant way to spend a few hours, or you can follow Temető utca south-west

and south up to Szabó-hegy (Tailor's Hill). A copy of Cartographia's *A Kőszegi-hegység* 1:40,000 tourist map (No 13) will prove useful if you plan to do more adventurous hiking.

The pool and 'beach' on Strand sétány near the camp site is open mid-June to August from 10 am to 6 pm. To get there, walk east along Kiss János utca and turn south after crossing the footbridge over the Gyöngyös River.

The little willow-lined rowing lake, a 15-minute walk north from the castle along Sziget utca, offers boating and fishing. It's a great spot for a picnic, too.

Special Events

Events to watch out for include the Arrival of the Grape festival in April; Kőszeg Summer, a festival of chamber music, theatre and opera in the castle courtyard in June; the Castle Theatre Festival in July; and the Vintage Days wine festival in September.

Places to Stay

Camping *Camping West* (☎ 360 981), next to a public swimming pool at Strand sétány 1, is one of the nicest places around to camp. Two people with a tent pay 600 Ft and accommodation in the 44-bed dormitory is the same price. Camping West is open from mid-April to October.

Private Rooms & Hostel Savaria Tourist can arrange private rooms for about 1500 to 1800 Ft per double. The nine-room *Jurisics Castle* hostel (☎ 360 227), in a small building near the entrance to the castle at Rajnis József utca 9, is pretty decrepit, but the location and price make it attractive: 1500 Ft a double or 600 Ft a head in multi-bed rooms. Check-in time is 5 pm, check out at 8 am.

Pension The *Várkör* (☎ 360 972) is a spotlessly clean 10-room pension at Hunyadi János utca 19 west of the old town. Rooms with bath are 2000 to 3000 Ft for singles and 2800 to 4000 Ft for doubles. The smaller rooms on the top with shared shower are 2000/2800 Ft singles/doubles.

Hotel One of the best places to stay in Kőszeg is at the 18-room *Aranystrucc* hotel (☎ 360 323) in an 18th-century building at Várkör 124. Singles/doubles with bath at the 'Golden Ostrich' are 2000/2800 Ft (3800 Ft for larger rooms with antique furnishings). Room No 7 on the corner with views over the square is the biggest and best.

The nearby *Írottkő* (☎ 360 373) at Fő tér 4 is Kőszeg's main hotel but, with an uninspiring restaurant, ugly concrete galleries and a dental clinic for visiting Austrians, it has little to recommend itself. Singles are 2458 Ft, doubles 3900 Ft.

Places to Eat

The *Bécsikapu* at Rajnis József utca 5, almost opposite St James Church, is a pleasant little place close to the castle; the *Kulacs* at Várkör 12 is more convenient to the bus stops. Other options include the *Szarvas*, in an attractive salmon-pink 19th-century house at Rákóczi utca 12, with main courses from 500 Ft, and the *Betérő az Aranykoszorúhoz* at Temető utca 59 (the name looks quite a mouthful but just means 'Visitor at the Sign of the Golden Wreath'). It has excellent food but closes at 9 pm and all day Monday.

For coffee and cakes you can't beat the *Korona Eszpresszó*, Várkör 18, open daily 8 am to 6 pm.

Entertainment

The city's *cultural centre* (☎ 360 046) is in the castle.

The *pub* in the castle is fun for a beer. It's open until midnight daily except Monday year round. The huge *beer garden* where Schneller István utca meets the northern end of Várkör is great in warm weather. For wine (mostly common Sopron vintages), go to the old *wine cellar* at Rajnis József utca 10 with vaulted ceilings and high Gothic windows (complete with extractor fan).

Getting There & Away

At least half a dozen daily buses a day run to Sopron, Szombathely and Velem, but there's only two a day to Nagykanizsa and one a day to Baja and Keszthely. Two buses a week (on Friday at 8.10 am and Wednesday at 7.05 am) head for Oberpullendorf and Vienna in Austria.

Kőszeg is at the end of an 18-km railway spur from Szombathely; there are 15 arrivals/departures each day.

KÖRMEND
* *pop 13,000*
* *area code ☎ 94*

Though certainly not worth a detour, this town 25 km south of Szombathely is considered the gateway to the Őrség, a region on the border with Austria and Slovenia that retains many of its folk traditions and characteristics to this day. Körmend was for many years the seat of the Batthyány family, an aristocratic clan that once owned much of the Őrség and would later change its spots to support the independence struggles of the mid-19th century.

Orientation & Information

Körmend's bus and train stations are five minutes apart just north of the town centre on Vasútmellék utca. Walk south on Deák Ferenc utca or Kossuth Lajos utca to reach the main thoroughfare, Rákóczi utca. The shopping area and centre of town is Szabadság tér (also called Fő tér) to the south.

Savaria Tourist (☎ 410 161) is at Rákóczi utca 11. Its opening hours are from 8.30 am to 5 pm on weekdays and till noon on Saturday. There's an OTP bank branch at Vída utca 6 and a K&H Bank at Olcsai tér 3. The new post office is at Dr Batthyány-Strattmann utca 3.

The telephone code for Körmend is ☎ 94.

Things to See

The **Batthyány Manor**, east of Szabadság tér and buffered by an arboretum (Várkert), is a typically Hungarian mix of medieval, baroque and neoclassical elements that together form a strong, very pleasing edifice. It houses a student dormitory and the **Rába Historical Collection**. The exhibition enti-

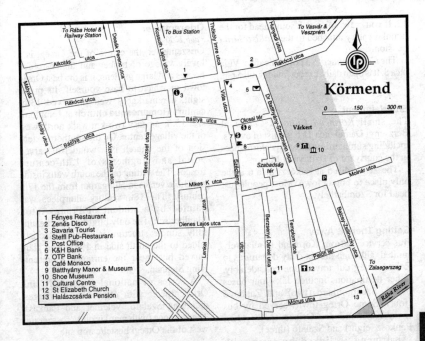

1 Fényes Restaurant
2 Zenés Disco
3 Savaria Tourist
4 Steffi Pub-Restaurant
5 Post Office
6 K&H Bank
7 OTP Bank
8 Café Monaco
9 Batthyány Manor & Museum
10 Shoe Museum
11 Cultural Centre
12 St Elizabeth Church
13 Halászcsárda Pension

Körmend

0   150   300 m

tled 'Pictures from Körmend's Past' focuses on town history through old photographs (the splendid synagogue was bombed to bits in WWII), the successes of local sons and daughters and the work of local artisans, including clockmakers, metalworkers and indigo-dyers. The interesting **Shoe Museum** in the manor's 18th-century archives building looks exclusively at the cobbler's trade. In summer, the museum is open from 9 am to noon and 1 to 5 pm every day except Monday; winter hours are from 10 am to 3 pm on Saturday and Sunday only.

The late-Gothic and baroque **Church of St Elizabeth** on Petőfi tér has contemporary ceiling frescos, but is really notable only for its memorial in the porch to László Batthyány-Strattmann (1870-1931), Körmend's much revered 'Doctor of the Poor' who restored the sight of many peasants. Inspect the gruesome, bloodshot eyeball rising above his grateful patients in the memorial portrait.

Places to Stay & Eat

In summer, Savaria Tourist can organise dormitory accommodation at the *hostel* in Batthyány Manor for under 500 Ft per head. *Private rooms* average about 1000 Ft per person with two-bed *apartments* starting at 3500 Ft. Private rooms are also available at Mátyás király utca 3 and 44.

The 21-room *Rába* hotel (☎ 410 089), in an interesting neoclassical building at Bercsényi utca 24, is convenient to the bus and train stations if you're headed for the Őrség and want to break for the night. Singles/doubles are 1650/2900 Ft. The *Halászcsárda* pension (☎ 410 069) at Bajcsy-Zsilinszky utca 20 has nine doubles for 2700 Ft. The back rooms have restful views of the Rába River.

The *Steffl* pub-restaurant on the corner of Rákóczi utca and Vída utca won't win any awards for originality, but it's convenient, inexpensive and open to 11 pm. A similar place is the *Fényes* restaurant at Rákóczi utca

12. If you crave spicy fish soup, head for the popular eatery attached to the *Halászcsárda* pension.

The *Café Monaco* is a popular café at Vída utca 8. It is open daily, except Sunday, till 5 pm.

Entertainment

The small *Körmend Cultural Centre* at Berzsenyi Dániel utca 11 has a list of events, including summertime theatre performances in the courtyard of Batthyány Manor.

The *Zenés* disco at Rákóczi utca 6 is the only place to bop in town. Most people just head for Szombathely.

Getting There & Away

Bus service to/from Körmend is relatively limited, although the six daily departures to Zalaegerszeg cut travel time considerably. Other destinations include Ják (four buses daily), Szentgotthárd (two) and Zalalövő (four). Some Őrség towns served by bus from Körmend are Őriszentpéter (12), Pankasz (eight) and Szalafő (three).

Körmend is linked by train with Szombathely and Szentgotthárd, from where you can continue on to Graz in Austria on one of seven trains a day. To reach Zalaegerszeg by train, you must change at Zalalövő.

ŐRSÉG REGION

• *area code* ☎ 94

This westernmost region, where Hungary, Austria and Slovenia come together, has for centuries been the nation's 'sentry' (*őrség*), and its houses and villages, spaced unusually far apart on the crests and in the valleys of the Zala foothills, once served as the national frontier. For their service as sentries, the inhabitants of the region were given special privileges by the king, which they were able to retain until the arrival of the Batthyány family. There are several villages worth visiting in this hilly, protected area. Őriszentpéter and nearby Szalafő are the easiest to reach and the most interesting.

Őriszentpéter

• *pop 1200*

Őriszentpéter, the centre of the Őrség, is a lovely village of timber and thatch-roofed houses and large gardens; it is the best Őrség town in which to base yourself. Its prime sight, a remarkably well preserved 13th-century **Romanesque church** at Templomszer 15, is an easy two-km walk north-west of the village centre. On the southern extension of the church is a wonderful carved portal and fragments of 15th-century frescos. The writing on the south walls inside are Bible verses in Hungarian from the 17th century. The 18th-century altarpiece was painted by a student of Franz Anton Maulbertsch. The only blight on this beautifully simple structure is an ugly sacristy added to the north side in 1981. The giant carved bust near the entrance represents King Stephen.

A series of national park trails link Őriszentpéter with other Őrség villages, including Szalafő, Velemér and Pankasz. The entrance (with map) is on Városszer just west of the Őrségi hostel/camp site.

Szalafő

• *pop 300*

Energetic travellers may want to continue along Templomszer for another four km, past arcaded old peasant houses, abandoned crank wells (and a 'kangaroo crossing' sign nailed to a telephone pole south of the church) to Szalafő, the oldest settlement in the Őrség. In Szalafő-Pityerszer, two km west of the village, is a mini-skanzen of three **folk compounds** unique to the Őrség. Built around a central courtyard, the houses have large overhangs allowing neighbours to chat when it rained – a frequent occurrence in this very wet area. The **Calvinist church** in the village centre has murals from the 16th century.

Places to Stay & Eat

The cheapest accommodation in Őriszentpéter is at the simple *Őrségi* (☎ 428 046), a tourist hostel with five rooms and a camping ground just around the corner from the bus station at Városszer 57 open from mid-April to mid-October. Doubles are 1400 to 1600 Ft, and it costs 400/300 Ft per person/tent to camp. The manager, who also serves as a rep for Savaria Tourist, can also book you a *private room* for 1000 Ft, or accommodation at one of the *peasant houses* for four people in Szalafő (4000 Ft). During off-hours you can find her at Kovácsszer 16.

The *Domino* (☎ 428 115), a five-room motel at Siskaszer 5 (opposite the turn for Szalafő), charges 1000 Ft per person or 3900 Ft for a small holiday house. It is open all year.

The *Bognár* at Kovácsszer 96, Őriszentpéter's only real restaurant, is about 500m up the hill south of the bus station. The *Pitvar Presszó* at Városszer 101 in the centre of the village serves snacks and drinks.

Getting There & Away

Őriszentpéter and Szalafő can be reached by bus from Körmend and Zalaegerszeg via Zalalövő. Some six daily buses leave Őriszentpéter for Szalafő.

ZALAEGERSZEG
• *pop 62,400*
• *area code* ☎ 92

Zala (as the locals gratefully call their city with the long name) is an oil town, and the Zala fields to the south have contributed enormously to this county seat's development since the 1930s, bringing with it such modern eyesores as the ever-present TV tower and an expensive sport centre.

However, the other part of Zalaegerszeg's name speaks of a very different world: *éger* are the moisture-loving alder trees of the Göcsej Hills to the west, where until recently peasants toiled away like their forebears in an area that gets the most rainfall and has some of the worst soil in Hungary. Lying side by side, the city's two open-air museums (one devoted to oil, the other to traditional village life) illustrate all too well the dichotomy that is Zalaegerszeg.

Orientation & Information

The bus station is a few minutes' walk east of Széchenyi tér, across from the Balaton hotel. The train station is about 1.5 km south at the end of Zrínyi Miklós utca on Bajcsy-Zsilinszky tér.

All the big agencies are represented in Zalaegerszeg, including Zalatour (☎ 311 389) at Kovács Károly tér 1, Express (☎ 314 144) at Dísz tér 3 and Ibusz (☎ 311 458) at Kölcsey utca 2. All are open on weekdays from 8 am to 4 or 5 pm; Zalatour and Ibusz stay open till noon on Saturday.

There's a Budapest Bank branch at Kossuth Lajos utca 2 and a K&H bank a bit farther south on Dísz tér. The main post office is on Berzsenyi Dániel utca south-east of Széchenyi tér.

Things to See & Do

The rose-coloured **synagogue** (1903) at Ady Endre utca 14, with its enormous Torah-shaped organ and stained-glass rose windows, now serves as a concert hall and gallery. On Szabadság tér there's an interesting baroque **Catholic church**, built near the ruins of a 15th-century chapel, with lovely frescos by the Austrian painter Johannes Cymbal.

Zalaegerszeg is best known for its museums. The **Göcsej Museum** at Batthyány Lajos utca 2 north of Szabadság tér is divided into three parts. The first examines the work of painter-sculptor Zsigmond Kisfaludi Strobl, who moved away from portraits and busts of Somerset Maugham, the Duke of Kent and other social-set personalities of the 1920s and 1930s to socialist themes after the war. He also designed the striking statue *Independence* atop Gellért Hill in Budapest – but for Admiral Miklós Horthy's son during WWII.

After the war, when heroic monuments were in short supply, Kisfaludi Strobl passed it off as a memorial to the Soviets. He very much deserves his nickname, the 'Side-Stepper'. The next section of the museum concerns local history and folk art and is very well presented; the Roman finds from nearby Zalalövő are especially interesting, but labelled only in Hungarian. The last series of rooms contain exhibits about the oil industry

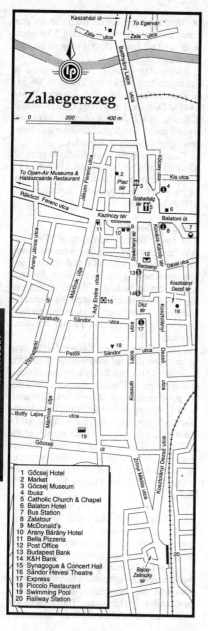

1 Göcsej Hotel
2 Market
3 Göcsej Museum
4 Ibusz
5 Catholic Church & Chapel
6 Balaton Hotel
7 Bus Station
8 Zalatour
9 McDonald's
10 Arany Bárány Hotel
11 Bella Pizzeria
12 Post Office
13 Budapest Bank
14 K&H Bank
15 Synagogue & Concert Hall
16 Sándor Hevesi Theatre
17 Express
18 Piccolo Restaurant
19 Swimming Pool
20 Railway Station

in Zala County that presumably wouldn't last in the rain at the outdoor village museum.

The **Göcsej Village Museum**, defined by a backwater of the Zala River off Ola utca north-west of the centre, is the oldest skanzen in Hungary and it shows; of the three dozen structures, a good one-third are shut tight or rotting into oblivion. Still, the museum offers a realistic view of a turn-of-the-century Göcsej traditional village, with its unique U-shaped farmhouses that lead to a central courtyard *(kerített házak)*, pálinka stills and smokehouses. Don't miss the five carved and painted house façades: they date from the late 19th century and have been called 'the most monumental creation of Hungarian folk art'. The museum is open daily except Monday from 10 am to 6 pm April to October. The open-air **Oil Industry Museum**, open the same hours, is a few steps to the west.

Zalaegerszeg's lively **market** for produce and clothes is on Piac tér west of Szabadság tér. The indoor pool and sauna between Mártírok útja and Ady Endre utca is open every day except Monday until 7 pm.

Places to Stay & Eat

Ask Zalatour about *private rooms*, which should cost from 2000 to 2500 Ft per double. They can also book you into old *peasant houses* accommodating between three and five people at Gombosszeg in the Göcsej Hills south-west of Zalaegerszeg for about 4000 Ft, but you'll have to be travelling under your own steam to get here.

Zalatour also runs a *hostel* (☎ 364 015) at the romantic 18th-century Várkastély (Castle Palace) on Vár utca in Egervár, 10 km north of Zalaegerszeg. There is a regular bus service (see Getting There & Away following). A bed in its six dormitory rooms is 800 Ft; doubles with shower are 2500 Ft.

The 22-room *Göcsej* hotel (☎ 311 580) at Kaszaházi utca 2 is not very conveniently located and no bargain at 3500 Ft for a double.

The 52-room *Arany Bárány* hotel (☎ 314 100) at Széchenyi tér 1 has both a new and an old wing (1898) and singles/doubles for 4600/5500 Ft.

A decent place for a meal is the homy *Piccolo* restaurant at Petőfi Sándor utca 16. The *Belvárosi* pub at Kossuth Lajos utca 1 (for snacks and drinks) is open till 1 am. There's a *McDonald's* on one side of the Arany Barany hotel.

The *Bella Pizzeria* at Kazinczy tér 11 makes for a nice change from gulyás and stays open till midnight. If you're looking for lunch near the Village and Oil museums, you couldn't do better than at the *Halászcsárda* fish restaurant at Rákóczi utca 47, with garden seating in summer.

Entertainment

The *Sándor Hevesi Theatre* (☎ 314 405) at Kosztolányi Dezső tér 1 is well known for its drama and musical productions (though they will be in Hungarian). The city's symphony orchestra may be playing here or at the *concert hall* in the former synagogue.

The most popular disco in town is the *Street Dance House* on Zrínyi Miklós utca. It's open most nights from 10 pm to 5 am.

Getting There & Away

More than a dozen buses a day head for Egervár, Keszthely, Lenti and Nagykanizsa. Other destinations include Balatonfüred (four a day), Budapest (five), Győr (five), Kaposvár (three), Körmend (six), Pécs (five), Sárvár (three), Sopron (two), Székesfehérvár (three), Szombathely (six to eight), Tapolca (five) and Veszprém (three).

Zalaegerszeg was bypassed during railway construction in the 19th century; today few places of any interest are serviced by trains from here. A couple of trains a day leave for Szombathely, but generally you'll have to change at Zalaszentiván. If you want to reach Budapest-Déli without any changes, expect only three trains a day.

Getting Around

Bus Nos 1/a and 1/y run from the train station to Széchenyi tér and then west along Rákóczi utca and Ola utca to the open-air museums. To reach the Göcsej hotel, take bus No 3 or 3/y.

You can order a local taxi on ☎ 333 666.

WESTERN TRANSDANUBIA

Balaton Region

Hungary may not have majestic mountains or sweeping ocean beaches but it does have Lake Balaton, the largest freshwater body of water in Europe outside Scandinavia. This oblong-shaped lake is 77 km long, 14 km across at its widest point and covers an area of almost 600 sq km.

Lake Balaton has been called 'Hungary's inland sea' and 'the nation's playground'. It is bounded by hills to the north, gentle slopes to the south and its surface seems to change colour with the seasons and the time of day. The lake has been eulogised in songs, poems and paintings for centuries, and the surrounding region produces some of Hungary's best wines.

But Lake Balaton, often simply referred to as the Balaton, is not to everyone's taste. The resorts are overrun in summer – though nowhere near as crowded as they were before 1989, when the lake was one of the few places where East and West Germans could meet and relax together on neutral turf. The Balaton is shallow, and on the southern shore you'll paddle for a km before the water gets above your waist. The water is silty and alkaline – almost oily – and not very refreshing, averaging 33°C in summer and 26°C in winter. Then there are reed beds, especially on the western and north-western shores, which suggest a swampy marsh. Indeed, the lake's name could come from the Slavic root word *blatna*, which means just that.

Lake Balaton lies in central Transdanubia, about 100 km from Budapest. It is fed by about 40 canals and streams, but its main source is the Zala River to the south-west. The lake's only outflow is the Sió Canal, which connects it at Siófok with the Danube River east of Szekszárd.

History

The area around Lake Balaton was settled as early as the Iron Age, and the Romans, who

HIGHLIGHTS

- the Bishop's Palace and the Hungarian Art Nouveau Petőfi Theatre at Veszprém
- Tihany's Abbey Church
- a hot summer's night out on the town in Siófok
- the Festetics Palace at Keszthely
- a meal or a drink at the Kisfaludy House restaurant overlooking Lake Balaton at Badacsony
- a dip in the Gyógy-tó (Thermal Lake) at Hévíz
- Franz Anton Maulbertsch's wonderful frescos at the Church of the Ascension in Sümeg
- a concert in the gardens of Brunswick Mansion at Martonvásár

called the lake Pelso, built a fort at Valcum (now Fenékpuszta), south of Keszthely, in the 2nd century AD. Throughout the Great Migrations, Lake Balaton was a reliable source of water, fish, reeds for thatch and ice in winter. The early Magyars found the lake a natural defence line, and many churches, monasteries and villages were built in the vicinity. In the 16th century the Balaton served as the divide between the Turks, who occupied the southern shore, and the Habsburgs to the north-west, but before the Ottomans were pushed back they had already crossed the lake and razed many of the towns and border castles in the northern hills. Croats, Germans and Slovaks resettled the area in the 18th century, and the subsequent building booms gave towns like Sümeg, Veszprém and Keszthely their baroque appearance.

Balatonfüred and Hévíz developed early as resorts for the wealthy, but it wasn't until the late 19th century that landowners, their vines destroyed by phylloxera lice, began building summer homes to rent out to the burgeoning middle classes. The arrival of the southern railway in 1861 and the northern line in 1909 increased the tourist influx, and by the 1920s resorts on both shores welcomed some 50,000 holiday-makers each summer. Just before the outbreak of WWII, that number had increased fourfold. After the war, the Communist government expropriated private villas and built new holiday homes for trade unions. In recent years, many of these have been turned into hotels, greatly increasing the accommodation possibilities.

Orientation

The two shores of Lake Balaton are as different as chalk and cheese. The southern coast is essentially one long resort: from Siófok to Fonyód, there are high-rise hotels, concrete embankments to prevent flooding, and minuscule grassy 'beaches' packed with lobster-red bodies in summer. Here the water is at its shallowest and safest for children, and the beaches are not reedy as they are on the northern shore.

Things get much better as you round the bend from Keszthely, a pretty town hugging the westernmost corner of the lake, to the northern shore. The north has many more historical towns and sights, mountain trails and better wine. The resorts at Badacsony, Tihany and Balatonfüred have more grace and atmosphere and are far less commercial than, say, Siófok or Balatonboglár to the south.

Activities

The main pursuits for visitors on Lake Balaton – apart from swimming, of course – are boating and fishing. Motorboats are banned entirely (the only water-skiing is by means of a tow at Balatonfüred) so 'boating' here means sailing, rowing and windsurfing. Fishing is good – the indigenous *fogas* (pike-perch) and its young, *süllő*, being the prized catch – and edible *harcsa* (catfish) and *ponty* (carp) are in abundance. *Angolna* (eels), whose numbers increased dramatically during an outbreak of filarial worms, threatened to take over the lake in the early 1990s, and hundreds of tonnes of them were removed.

You can get a fishing licence from Siotour in Siófok (see the Siófok Information section), or from the national angling association, Mohosz (☎ 1-131 3199), at VI Ó utca 3 in Budapest. One of the big events of the year at the lake is the Cross-Balaton Swimming Race from Révfülöp to Balatonboglár in late July.

Lake Balaton is not doing as well as it once did, especially on the southern shore, and has been one of the biggest 'victims' of the political changes since 1989. East and West Germans no longer need a neutral meeting place, and Austrians and the Hungarians themselves have discovered that a package tour in the Canary Islands or Greece doesn't cost much more than a week on the lake. But they still come in fairly large numbers, and the Balaton is one of the few places where Hungarians really do let their hair (and most everything else) down.

If you can get into the swing of it, the lake is a good place to meet people. Bear in mind, though, that during the off season (roughly late October to early April) virtually all the hotels, restaurants, museums and recreational facilities here shut down.

Getting There & Away

Trains to Lake Balaton leave from Budapest-Déli train station and buses leave from the bus station at Erzsébet tér. If you're travelling north or south from the lake to towns in western or southern Transdanubia, buses are usually preferable to trains.

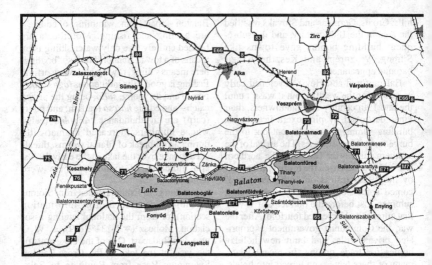

Getting Around

Railway service on both the northern and southern sides of the lake is fairly frequent. A better way to see Lake Balaton up close, though, is on a Mahart passenger ferry. Ferries operate on the route between Siófok, Balatonfüred, Tihany and Tihanyi-rév and Balatonföldvár from late March to late October, with more frequent sailings in July and August. During the main summer season, which is from June to early September, ferries ply the entire length of the lake from Balatonkenese to Keszthely (five hours) with frequent stops on both shores. There are also car ferries across the lake between Tihanyi-rév and Szántódi-rév (from early March to late November), and Badacsony and Fonyód (from late March to late October). There are no passenger services on the lake in winter.

Fares are cheap. Adults pay 150 Ft for distances of one to 10 km; 300 Ft for 11 to 40 km, and 400 Ft for 41 to 70 km. Children pay half-price, and return fares are always double the one-way fare. It costs 120 Ft to transport a bicycle. The short-hop car ferries charge 100/100/200/400 Ft per person/ bicycle/motorcycle/car.

SIÓFOK

- *pop 23,700*
- *area code ☎ 84*

Siófok, 106 km south-west of Budapest, typifies the resorts of the southern shore: it's loud, brash and crowded. The dedicated pursuits here are eating, drinking, sunbathing and swimming – and whatever comes in between. It is the largest of the lake's resorts and is always jammed in the height of summer.

Siófok didn't start out this way. In the 19th century it was every bit as elegant as Balatonfüred, and the lovely villas on Batthyány Lajos utca near Jókai Park and the lakeside promenade recall those days. But late in the last century, after the southern railway line had reached Siófok, more and more people began to holiday here. Today many of the villas have been converted to hotels or offices, and the promenade, with its mock gas lamps, has been paved. Tourism on a mass scale is now the business of Siófok.

Orientation

Greater Siófok stretches for a dozen km, almost as far as the resort of Balatonvilágos to the east (once reserved exclusively for

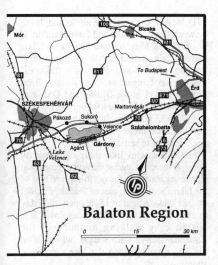

Balaton Region

0   15   30 km

Communist honchos) and Balatonszéplak to the west. The dividing line between the so-called Gold Coast (Aranypart) in the east and the Silver Coast (Ezüstpart) to the west is the Sió Canal, which runs south-east to the Danube. Boatspeople use the canal to get their vessels from Budapest to the lake. The Gold Coast is the older, more posh resort section of Siófok, and all the big hotels are here. The Silver Coast has several resorts, but overall it's far less developed.

Szabadság tér, the centre of Siófok, is to the east of the canal, about one km south-east of the ferry pier. The bus station and *fin-de-siècle* train station are on Váradi Adolf tér just off Fő utca, the main drag.

Information

Tourinform (☎ 315 355), the best source of information for Siófok and the lake's southern shore, has an office at the base of the old water tower on Szabadság tér. It is open weekdays from 9 am to 4 pm (daily from 8 am to 6 pm from June to August). All the main tourist agencies have branches in Siófok, including Siotour (☎ 310 900) at Szabadság tér 6; Ibusz (☎ 311 481) at Fő utca

174; and Cooptourist (☎ 312 643) at Mikes Kelemen utca 6. Generally they're open from 8 am to 4 pm Monday to Friday, but they close as late as 8 pm in summer and are open on Saturday then, too.

There's an OTP bank branch with an ATM and currency-exchange machine near the stations at Fő utca 188, but you'll find exchange offices everywhere in town. The main post office is just west of the OTP at Fő utca 186.

Things to See

There's not a whole lot to see of cultural or historical importance in a place where the baser instincts tend to rule, but if you must do something educational or want to see what Siófok looked like in the old days, visit the **József Beszédes Water-Management Museum** at Sió utca 2 by the canal. Beszédes (1757-1852) was the engineer who drained the nearby marshes and regulated the Sió Canal, which had been partly built by the Romans in 292 AD and used extensively by the Turks in the 16th and 17th centuries. The museum deals with the hydro-engineering of the lake and canal and has an interesting collection of old photographs. It's open from mid-April to mid-October from 10 am till noon and 1 to 6 pm.

The canal's **lock system** can be seen from Krúdy sétány, the walkway near the ferry pier, or Baross Bridge to the south. Nearby is the headquarters of the Hungarian navy. Siófok was the seemingly unlikely centre of command under Miklós Horthy – himself an admiral – during the suppression of the Communist Republic of Councils in 1919. The excellent covered **market** is across the canal from the museum.

The wooden **water tower** on Szabadság tér dates from 1912. If you walk north on narrow Hock köz, you'll reach the **Imre Kálmán Memorial House** at Kálmán Imre sétány 5. It is devoted to the life and works of the composer of popular operettas who was born in Siófok in 1882. East of Szabadság tér in Oulu Park, Hungary's maverick architect Imre Makovecz strikes again with

BALATON REGION

his winged and 'masked' **Evangelist Lutheran church**, which bears a strong resemblance to an Indonesian garuda.

The tower on the western tip of the canal entrance is the National Meteorological Weather Observatory. Believe it or not, Balaton can actually get quite rough when the wind picks up, and there's a system of warning signals. East of the observatory and just north of Petőfi sétány is Nagy Strand, the city's 'big' public beach. There are many more 'managed' swimming areas along the Gold and Silver coasts. Entry generally costs 120/60 Ft for adults/children.

Activities

There are rowing boats and sailing boats for rent at various locations along the lake, including Nagy Strand. You can hire bicycles and motorcycles from the Móló stand (☎ 314 692) on the corner of Vitorlás utca and Horgony utca on the canal's western bank from mid-May to mid-September. Bicycles cost 300/1500 Ft per hour/day, and motorcycles 800/8000 Ft.

LRI (☎ 322 655) at the air strip in Balatonkiliti, five km south of Siófok and accessible by bus, offers sightseeing flights in summer. For horse riding, see the following Around Siófok section.

Places to Stay

Siófok is one of the few places on the lake where you might have trouble finding accommodation. Though it's not attracting the numbers it once did, Siófok gets very crowded in summer (especially in late July and August) and all but closes down between late October and early April.

Camping There are some two dozen camping grounds along the Balaton's southern shore, and Siófok has a couple with bungalows open from April to September. *Aranypart* (☎ 352 801) has its own beach at Szent László utca 183-185, four km east of town; if you're coming from Budapest by train, get off at Balatonszabadi-Fürdő station, one stop before Siófok. *Ifjúság* is on Pusztatorony tér in Siófok-Sóstó (☎ 352

571), seven km east of Siófok and lying between tiny Salt Lake and Lake Balaton. It is open mid-May to mid-September. The correct train station for this camp site is Balatonszabadi-Sóstó. Prices for the sites' four-person bungalows vary widely, from lows of DM31 at the Ifjúság and DM48 at the Aranypart in May to a whopping DM132 and DM183 respectively in August. It will pay to check these prices with one of the agencies before setting out.

For those who like their camping *au naturel*, there's a nudist camping ground at Balatonakarattya at the north-eastern end of the lake about 12 km east of Siófok. *Piroska* (☎ 381 084), Aligai út 15, is open mid-May to early September and has bungalows. It is within easy walking distance of the Balatonakarattya train station, which is on the line running along the lake's northern shore.

Hostels From mid-June to August, a hostel with multi-bed rooms (650 Ft per person) operates in the *Trade School Holiday Home* (☎ 310 131) at Erkel Ferenc utca 46. The huge *Ezüstpart* hotel (see Hotels) on Liszt Ferenc sétány also has hostel rooms available in summer.

Private Rooms The agencies can find you a private room (from 800 to 900 Ft per person), but singles are rare and overnighters generally unwelcome. If you want to do it alone, check the '*Zimmer frei*' signs along Erkel Ferenc utca on the Silver Coast and Petőfi sétány and Beszédes József sétány on the Gold Coast.

Pension One of the nicest places to stay in Siófok for atmosphere is the lovely old *Tengerszem* pension (☎ 310 146) at Karinthy Frigyes utca 4. Singles are 2450 to 4250 Ft, doubles 3200 to 5300 Ft, depending on the season. The Tengerszem is open all year.

Hotels Four Pannonia-chain hotels line Petőfi sétány – Nos 9 to 17 – and a narrow beach at the start of the Gold Coast: the

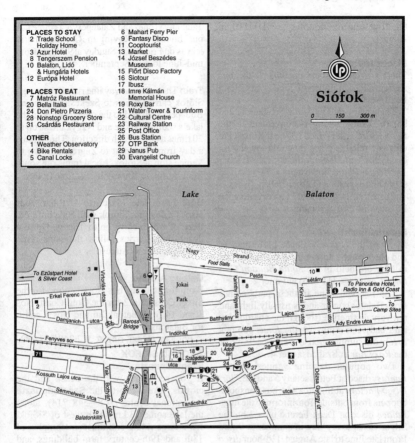

PLACES TO STAY
2 Trade School
   Holiday Home
3 Azur Hotel
8 Tengerszem Pension
10 Balaton, Lidó
   & Hungária Hotels
12 Európa Hotel

PLACES TO EAT
7 Matróz Restaurant
20 Bella Italia
24 Don Pietro Pizzeria
28 Nonstop Grocery Store
31 Csárdás Restaurant

OTHER
1 Weather Observatory
4 Bike Rentals
5 Canal Locks

6 Mahart Ferry Pier
9 Fantasy Disco
11 Cooptourist
13 Market
14 József Beszédes
   Museum
15 Flört Disco Factory
16 Siotour
17 Ibusz
18 Imre Kálmán
   Memorial House
19 Roxy Bar
21 Water Tower & Tourinform
22 Cultural Centre
23 Railway Station
25 Post Office
26 Bus Station
27 OTP Bank
29 Janus Pub
30 Evangelist Church

Siófok

0   150   300 m

Lake   Balaton

Nagy   Strand
Food Stalls

Jokai
Park

Balaton (☎ 310 655); *Lidó* (☎ 310 633); *Hungária* (☎ 310 677); and the high-rise *Európa* (☎ 313 411). All are three-star standard and each has about 130 rooms. Doubles cost from DM73 to DM93.

A better deal can be had at the former trade-union holiday homes farther along on Beszédes József sétány. The 60-room *Radio Inn* (☎ 311 634) at No 77 charges 3400 to 5000 Ft for a double with bath, depending on the season.

The 164-room *Panoráma* (☎ 311 637) at No 80 is more expensive, with singles from

3980 to 4960 Ft and doubles from 5408 to 6512 Ft.

Though it's not in the nicest part of Siófok, the *Azur* hotel (☎ 312 419) at Vitorlás utca 11 on the western side of the canal mouth is friendly and reasonably priced. It has 400 rooms in four buildings; singles are DM29 to DM40 and doubles DM60 to DM82, depending on the season. The main building (No 4) is the nicest one. Further down at Liszt Ferenc sétány 2-4 is the enormous *Ezüstpart* hotel (☎ 350 622) with more than 900 rooms in three buildings. Singles start at DM39 in the low season; doubles are DM110 in August.

Places to Eat

There's a cheap stand-up *büfé* at the bus station and a number of *food stalls* along Petőfi sétány.

The canary-yellow *Matróz* restaurant and bar on Krúdy sétány is convenient to the ferry. *Csárdás* at Fő utca 105 near Kinizsi Pál utca is a reliable place in an old townhouse open till 11 pm. *Bella Italia* at Szabadság tér 1 and *Don Pietro* downstairs at Fő utca 178 serve pizza, pasta and other Italian dishes.

There's a 24-hour *ABC* grocery store on Fő utca just east of the bus station.

Entertainment

Many of the concerts, dance performances and plays staged during the Balaton Festival in May are held in the *South Balaton Cultural Centre* (☎ 311 855) at Fő tér 2.

The regional wine in these parts comes from Balatonboglár and is usually light and not very distinctive (though the chardonnay isn't bad). For a pint, try the *Janus* pub in a lovely old summer house at Fő utca 93-95 or the *Roxy Bar* at Szabadság tér 4.

Two popular dancing venues are the *Fantasy* disco at Petőfi sétány 5 and the *Flőrt Disco Factory* at Sió utca 4. A bus transports boppers from outside Tourinform to the huge *Palace* disco at Deák Ferenc utca 2 on the Silver Coast every day in summer at 9 pm. From late June to late August, 1½-hour *disco cruises* depart from the Mahart ferry pier at 9.30 pm (8 pm during the last week in August).

Getting There & Away

Bus Buses serve a lot of destinations from Siófok, but compared with the excellent train connections, they're not very frequent. The exceptions are to Budapest (eight a day), Fonyód (10), Kaposvár (12), Nagyberény (15), Szekszárd (six) and Veszprém (12). Other destinations include: Gyula (one a day), Győr (two), Harkány (one), Hévíz and Keszthely (four), Kecskemét (one), Pécs (four), Szeged (one), Tapolca (one),

Tatabánya (one) and Zalaegerszeg (three). A bus bound for Rovinj in Croatian Istria leaves on Friday and Sunday at 9.30 pm from mid-June to mid-September.

Train The main railway line running through Siófok carries trains to Székesfehérvár and Budapest-Déli and to the other resorts on the lake's southern shore and Nagykanizsa up to 20 times a day in each direction. Three trains a day from Budapest to Zagreb and two to Venice stop at Siófok. Local trains run south from Siófok to Kaposvár four times a day.

Boat From late March to October, four ferries a day link Siófok with Balatonfüred, three of which carry on to Tihany. Up to a dozen daily ferries follow the same route from late June to August.

Getting Around

From the stations, bus No 1 is good for the Silver Coast, No 2 for the Gold Coast, Nos 4 and 14 for Balatonkiliti and Nos 5 and 6 for Balatonszéplak.

For a local taxi, ring ☎ 312 240/312 222.

AROUND SIÓFOK
Szántódpuszta

If you get bored with the beach and the crowds, take a trip to the **Szántódpuszta** recreational centre (☎ 84-348 714), along the lake some 13 km south-west of Siófok. It's a large riding and museum complex of 18th and 19th-century farm buildings, and the stables, barns, workshops, dwellings and baroque **St Christopher's Chapel** (1735) are all perfectly preserved. Horse riding starts at 1800 Ft, there are coach tours for about 1500 Ft per person and a couple of *csárdás* if you should get hungry. Horse shows take place daily between mid-June and mid-September. Opening hours for the complex change according to the season, but you can visit Szántódpuszta at least till 5 pm every day (excluding Monday). The main summer event is the Equestrian and Horse-herd Days in late July.

The bus bound for Balatonföldvár or Fonyód will drop you off here; the correct train station is Szantód-Kőröshegy, about two km west of the complex.

The town of **Kőröshegy** four km south of the station has a 15th-century **Franciscan church** (József Attila utca 1) with a Gothic rose window and a magnificently restored organ. Concerts are held here in summer.

If you're driving on the main road from Siófok to Szántódpuszta, stop at the *Kocsi Csárda* near the Zamardi felső train station, six km east of Szántódpuszta. It's a touristy but extremely attractive inn with exposed rafters, Gypsy music and working stables. Coach tours and horse riding are available here, too.

KESZTHELY

* *pop 23,000*
* *area code ☎ 83*

Keszthely, at the western end of Lake Balaton about 70 km from Balatonfüred, is really the only town on the lake not entirely dependent on tourism. As a result, Keszthely does not have that melancholy, ghost-town feel to it that Siófok or Badacsony do in the off season.

The Romans built a fort at Valcum (now Fenékpuszta) five km to the south, and their road north to the colonies at Sopron and Szombathely is today's Kossuth Lajos utca running straight through Keszthely. The town's fortified monastery and church on Fő tér were strong enough to repel the Turks in the 16th century.

In the middle of the 18th century, Keszthely and its surrounds (including Hévíz) came into the possession of the Festetics family, progressives and reformers very much in the tradition of the Széchenyi family. In fact, Count György Festetics (1755-1819), who founded Europe's first agricultural college, the Georgikon, here in 1797, was an uncle of István Széchenyi.

Today, Keszthely is a pleasant town of grand houses, trees, cafés and enough to see and do to keep you here for a spell. It has a unique view of both the northern and southern shores of Lake Balaton, and the large student population contributes to the town's nightlife.

Orientation
The centre of town is Fő tér, from which Kossuth Lajos utca, lined with colourful old houses, runs to the north (pedestrian only) and south. The bus and train stations stand side by side near the lake at the end of Mártírok útja. From the stations, follow Mártírok útja up the hill, then turn right onto Kossuth Lajos utca into town. The ferry docks at a stone pier within sight of the old Hullám hotel. From here, follow the path past the hotel; Erzsébet királyné utca, which flanks Helikon Park, leads to Fő tér.

Information
Tourinform (☎ 314 144) at Kossuth Lajos utca 28 is an excellent source of information on the whole Balaton area. Four other agencies can be found on Kossuth Lajos utca so you'll be spoiled for choice: Express (☎ 312 032) at No 22; Keszthely Tourist (☎ 314 288) at No 25; Ibusz (☎ 314 320) at No 27; and Zalatour (☎ 312 560) at No 1. All of the agencies are open on weekdays till 4 or 5 pm; Tourinform and Zalatour open on Saturday morning as well.

There's an OTP bank branch at Kossuth Lajos utca 3 and a Budapest Bank at Pethő Ferenc utca 1. The main post office is to the north-west at Georgikon utca 23. The Frida & Frida bookshop at Kossuth Lajos utca 8 has a good selection of maps and some titles in English.

Things to See
The **Festetics Palace**, in the large 'English garden' on Kastély utca, contains 100 rooms in two sprawling wings. The 19th-century northern wing contains a music school, city library and conference centre; the **Helikon Castle Museum** and the palace's greatest treasure, the **Helikon Library**, are in the baroque southern wing. The entrance fee is an outrageous 500/200 Ft for adults/students though Hungarians pay only 150/50 Ft. Ask for your ticket convincingly in magyarul and you'll pay the local price.

The museum's rooms (about 12 in all, each in a different colour scheme) are full of portraits, bric-a-brac and furniture, much of

Lehel utca
Pál utca
Kastély utca
Tapolcai út
Rákóczi tér
Szalasztó utca
To Hévíz & Zalaegerszeg
Georgikon
Pethő Ferenc utca
Bakacs utca
Lovassy
Ady utca
Endre utca
Városház utca
Széchenyi
Bem József
Rákóczi utca
Sándor
Móra Ferenc utca
Fő tér
Erzsébet királyné utca
Vaszary Kolos utca
Kossuth Lajos
Deák Ferenc utca
Vak Bottyán utca
Bercsényi Miklós utca
Gagarin utca
Fodor
Balaton utca
Hunyadi utca
Apád utca
Helikon Park
Eötvös utca
Csók István utca
Park utca
Kossuth Lajos utca
Mártírok utca
Kazinczy
Rózsa utca
Szent Miklós
Imre
Madách utca
Festetics György út
Honvéd
Rómal
Lake Balaton
City Beach
Szendreytelepi út
Ferenk út
Csárda utca
To Fenékpuszta
Helikon Beach
Ernő Géza sétány

Keszthely

0   150   300 m

PLACES TO STAY
2 Georgikon Hotel
5 Amazon Hotel
17 Pannon Agricultural University
26 Helikon Hotel
27 Phoenix Hotel
29 Hullám Hotel
33 Forrás Pension
34 Sport Camping
36 Ferenc Pethe College
37 Zalatour Camping

PLACES TO EAT
9 Oászis Restaurant
16 Pizzeria da Marcello
19 Hungária Gösser Pub-Restaurant
24 Golf Restaurant
25 Béke Restaurant
35 Halászcsárda Fish Restaurant

OTHER
1 Festetics Palace & Museum

3 Georgikon Farm Museum
4 Post Office
6 Zalatour
7 OTP Bank
8 Frida & Frida Bookshop
10 Bus to Badacsony
11 Express
12 Tourinform & Goldmark Cultural Centre
13 Keszthely Tourist & Ibusz
14 Budapest Bank
15 Piccolo Bar
18 Dick Turpin's Pub
20 Town Hall
21 Bus Stops
22 Catholic Church
23 Kolibri Bar & Easy Rider Club
28 Mahart Ferry Pier
30 Railway Station
31 Bus Station
32 Balaton Museum

Top: Siklós Castle, Siklós, Southern Transdanubia
Bottom: Garden at Széchenyi Memorial Museum, Nagycenk, Western Transdanubia

STEVE FALLON

STEVE FALLON

BERTHOLD DAUM

Top: Gypsy horse market in Debrecen
Left: Sundial on the former Franciscan Church, Máriagyűd, Southern Transdanubia
Right: Horse trainer on the *puszta*

it brought from England by one Mary Hamilton, a duchess who married one of the Festetics men in the 1860s. The library is renowned for its 90,000-volume collection, ranging from medieval codices to the more mundane *Driving Lessons* and *Hungarian Myths for Children* in English. But just as impressive is the golden oak shelving and furniture carved by local craftsman János Kerbl in 1801. Also worth noting are the Louis XIV Salon with its stunning marquetry, the rococo Music Room and the private chapel (1804). Other exhibits in the museum include weapons spanning 10 centuries and a collection of grisly African and Asian hunting trophies presented to the palace by Ferenc-József Windisch-Grätz, an expatriate Austro-Hungarian aristocrat who lived in Nairobi for 30 years after WWII.

The **Farm Museum** at Bercsényi Miklós utca 67 is housed in several early 19th-century buildings of what was the Georgikon's experimental farm. It contains exhibits on the history of the college and the later Pannon Agricultural University (now a few blocks to the south-east on the corner of Széchenyi utca and Deák Ferenc utca), viniculture in the Balaton region and traditional farm trades such as those performed by wagon builders, wheelwrights, coopers and blacksmiths. The stables are crammed with old farming and transport equipment, including some antique sledges (sleighs) for travel across the frozen lake. The museum is open from April to October daily except Monday from 10 am to 5 pm (6 pm on Sunday).

Fő tér is a colourful square with some lovely buildings, including the late baroque **town hall** on the northern side, the **Trinity Column** (1770) in the centre and the Catholic **Church of Our Lady** in the park to the south. The church was originally built in the 14th century for Franciscan monks in the Gothic style, but many alterations were made in subsequent centuries. The Gothic rose window above the porch remains, though, as do some faded 15th-century frescos in the sanctuary and on the southern wall. Count György and other Festetics family members are buried in the crypt below.

The **Balaton Museum** on the corner of Mártírok útja and Kossuth Lajos utca was purpose-built in 1928 and, with all the plants decorating the central court, it is a cool oasis on a hot day. There's much here on the Roman fort at Valcum and traditional life around Lake Balaton, but most interesting is the history of navigation on the lake and the photographs of summer frolickers at the turn of the century.

Activities

Keszthely has two beaches: City Beach (Városi Strand), close to the ferry pier, and reedy Helikon Beach farther south. There's a windsurfing school at City Beach in summer and another one at Vonyarcvas-hegy Strand across the bay in the eastern suburb of Gyenesdias. You can use the indoor pool at the Helikon hotel for 1000 Ft.

There are a couple of horse-riding schools north-east of Keszthely in Sömögyei dűlő – Musztáng (☎ 312 289) and No 1 János (☎ 312 534) – but more convenient is the Pferd (☎ 312 408) on Szendreytelepi út south-west of the centre.

There's a bird-watching camp with very knowledgeable guides in Fenékpuszta near the delta of the Zala River south of Keszthely. It's just one stop on the train heading for Balatonszentgyörgy; if you're driving, the exit is at the 111-km stone on route No 71. A vintage steam train serves Keszthely daily in summer (see the following Getting There & Away section).

Places to Stay

Camping There are several camping grounds near the lake, all of which have bungalows and are open from May to September. As you leave the train station, head south across the tracks and you'll soon reach *Sport Camping* (☎ 313 777) at Csárda utca. However, wedged between the railway tracks and a road, it's noisy and not very clean. Carry on south for 20 minutes to *Zalatour Camping* (☎ 312 998), a much bigger place with large bungalows for four people from DM50 to DM70 and smaller holiday houses for DM18 to DM24. There are tennis courts, and the site has access to Helikon Beach. *Castrum Camping* (☎ 312 120), north of the stations at Móra Ferenc utca 48, has its own beach but is really for caravans.

Hostels In July and August you can stay in the student dormitory at *Ferenc Pethe College* (☎ 311 290), Festetics György út 5, for about 800 Ft per person. Ask Express about dormitory rooms at the more central *Pannon Agricultural University* on the corner of Széchenyi utca and Deák Ferenc utca in summer.

Private Rooms Private rooms are available from Ibusz, Zalatour and Keszthely Tourist for about 1500 Ft per double. Ask around, though, as prices differ.

If you're only staying one night, some of the agencies levy heavy surcharges, making it worthwhile to forgo their services and go directly to houses with 'szoba kiadó' or 'Zimmer frei' signs, where you may be able to bargain with the owners.

Pension The 39-room *Forrás* (☎ 311 418), close to the lake at Római utca 1, has doubles for 3600 Ft and is open all year.

Hotels The *Amazon* hotel (☎ 314 213) in a decrepit 18th-century townhouse at Kastély utca 11 is not the bargain it used to be: singles/doubles without bath are 2400/2900 Ft, with bath 3400/3900 Ft. Still, its location at the top of Kossuth Lajos utca, a minute from the palace, is excellent. The *Georgikon* apartment hotel (☎ 315 730), housed in one of the agricultural college's original buildings at Georgikon utca 20, has 14 suites with cooking facilities and all the mod cons. Singles/doubles with bath are 4000/5500 Ft; there's a huge family suite for five people for 12,500 Ft. If you can afford it and don't want to stay right on the lake, this is Keszthely's best place.

The three hotels on the lake are expensive, but they're among the most attractive and best equipped resort facilities in Hungary. The most charming is the renovated 50-room

Hullám (☎ 312 644), straight up from the ferry pier and built in 1892. Singles are from DM64 to DM114 and doubles from DM84 to DM134. The 78-room *Phoenix* (☎ 312 630) in the park behind it has more of a woodsy feel and is much cheaper, but mosquitoes might be a problem. Singles are from DM38 to DM70, doubles DM48 to DM86. Both hotels are closed from November to March.

The *Helikon* (☎ 311 330), by far the biggest hotel in Keszthely with 224 rooms, is a few minutes walk north-east through the park. The Helikon has its own island for swimming, an indoor swimming and sports centre with covered clay tennis courts and anything else you could imagine. Singles are DM53 to DM128, doubles DM84 to DM168, depending on the season.

Places to Eat

The *Hungária Gösser* pub-restaurant, in a historical building with stained-glass windows at Kossuth Lajos utca 35 (the corner of Fő tér), has pizza, Hungarian dishes and a salad bar (250 Ft). The renovated *Béke*, Kossuth Lajos utca 50, is open all year and has a reasonable menu including several fish dishes; it also has a decent café. A good place for a simple (and cheap) Hungarian meal is the *Golf* restaurant almost opposite the Béke at Kossuth Lajos utca 95.

The *Pizzeria da Marcello*, in a cellar with rustic furniture at Városház utca 4, serves made-to-order pizzas and salads till 11 pm. The *Oászis*, a 'reform' restaurant east of the palace at Rákóczi tér 3, serves vegetarian dishes from 11 am to 4 pm.

The *Halászcsárda* fish restaurant is convenient to Helikon Beach and stays open till 11 pm.

Entertainment

On Sunday at 8.30 pm from July to mid-August you can see Hungarian folk dancing in the courtyard of the *Károly Goldmark Cultural Centre* (☎ 314 286), Kossuth Lajos utca 28. Concerts are often held in the Music Room of the *Festetics Palace* in summer; check with the staff at the Cultural Centre or

Tourinform. Most of the events staged during May's Balaton Festival take place in Keszthely.

There are several interesting places for a drink along Kossuth Lajos utca. *Easy Rider* at No 79 draws the local young bloods, while the *Kolibri* cocktail bar at No 81 is for an older crowd. *Dick Turpin's Pub* at Városház utca 2 plays the coolest music while the *Piccolo* at No 9 of the same street is a small pub with Czech beer that attracts friendly students and soldiers (Keszthely is a garrison town).

Getting There & Away

Bus The only important destinations with more than 10 daily bus departures from Keszthely are Hévíz, Zalaegerszeg and Veszprém; there are about six to Nagykanizsa, Sümeg, Szombathely and Tapolca. Other towns served by bus include Baja (one trip daily), Budapest (one), Győr (one), Pápa (three), Pécs (one), Sopron (two) and Székesfehérvár (one). Some of these buses – including those to Budapest, Zalaegerszeg, Nagykanizsa and Sümeg – can be boarded at the bus stops in front of the Church of Our Lady on Fő tér. Buses to Hévíz from stand No 4 are frequent.

Train Keszthely is on a branch line linking Tapolca and Balatonszentgyörgy, from where half a dozen daily trains continue along the southern shore to Székesfehérvár and Budapest-Déli. To reach Szombathely or towns along Lake Balaton's northern shore by train, you must change at Tapolca and sometimes at Celldömölk too, but the connections are quick. For Pécs take a train to Kaposvár, then change to a bus.

In July and August, MÁV runs a *nosztalgiavonat* (vintage steam train) from Keszthely (departing at 9.55 am) to Révfülöp via Tapolca, returning from Révfülöp at 3.20 pm. Check with MÁV to make sure the service is still running and the times are accurate.

Boat Mahart ferries sail to/from Badacsony between June and early September. In July

and much of August these boats also link Keszthely with Siófok.

Getting Around

Bus Nos 1 and 2 run from the train and bus stations to the church on Fő tér, but unless there's one waiting upon your arrival, it's just as easy to walk.

You can order a taxi on ☎ 333 666 or ☎ 312 222.

HÉVÍZ
• *pop 6000*
• *area code* ☎ *83*

If you enjoy visiting spas and taking the waters, you'll love Hévíz, site of Europe's largest thermal lake, Gyógy-tó. The people of this town seven km north-west of Keszthely have made use of the warm mineral water for centuries, first in a tannery in the Middle Ages and later for curative purposes. The lake was developed as a private resort by Count György Festetics of Keszthely in 1795, but it really only became popular at the end of the 19th century.

Orientation & Information

The centre of Hévíz is really Parkerdő, the large 'Park Forest' and the thermal lake. The bus station is on Deák tér a few steps from one of the entrances to the lake; the commercial centre – such as it is – lies to the west of the station. Kossuth Lajos utca, where most of the big hotels are located, forms the western boundary of Parkerdő.

There are two tourist agencies north-west of the bus station almost side by side along Rákóczi utca: Hévíz Tourist (☎ 341 348) at No 4, and Zalatour (☎ 341 048) at No 8.

An OTP bank branch is near the bus station at Erzsébet királynő utca 7. The post office is at Kossuth Lajos utca 4.

Gyógy-tó

The thermal lake is an astonishing sight: a surface of almost five hectares in the Parkerdő covered for most of the year in pink and white lotuses. The source is a spring spouting from a crater some 40m deep that disgorges up to 80 million litres of warm

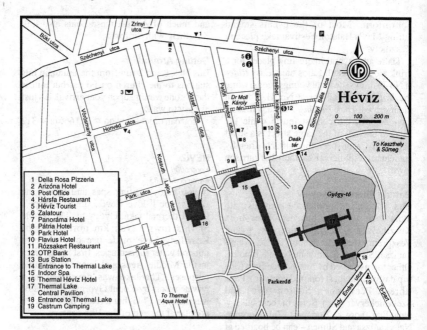

Map legend:
1 Della Rosa Pizzeria
2 Arizóna Hotel
3 Post Office
4 Hársfa Restaurant
5 Hévíz Tourist
6 Zalatour
7 Panoráma Hotel
8 Pátria Hotel
9 Park Hotel
10 Flavius Hotel
11 Rózsakert Restaurant
12 OTP Bank
13 Bus Station
14 Entrance to Thermal Lake
15 Indoor Spa
16 Thermal Hévíz Hotel
17 Thermal Lake
   Central Pavilion
18 Entrance to Thermal Lake
19 Castrum Camping

water a day, renewing itself every two days or so. The surface temperature averages 33°C and never drops below 26°C in winter, allowing bathing throughout the year. In winter, it's quite an experience to float along comfortably when there's ice on the nearby fir trees.

The water and the mud on the bottom are slightly radioactive and recommended for various medical conditions, especially loco-motor and nervous ailments. It's probably not a good idea to stay in the water for more than an hour at a time, but wrinkled skin will no doubt drive you out before you start to glow in the dark.

A covered bridge leads to the lake's *fin-de-siècle* central pavilion, from where catwalks and piers fan out. You can swim protected beneath these or make your way to the small rafts and 'anchors' farther out in the lake. There's a couple of piers along the shore for sunbathing as well.

The lake is open in summer from 8 am to 6 pm, in winter from 9 am to 5 pm, and there is an entrance fee of 280 Ft for three hours or 560 Ft for the whole day. The indoor spa at the entrance to the park is open year-round from 7 am to 4 or 5 pm.

Places to Stay

Finding accommodation is no problem in Hévíz; paying the prices might be. Most of the big hotels in Hévíz cater to Austrians on short trips who can afford to pay premium prices, or to people on packaged health tours, though a lot of the former trade-union holiday homes have been transformed into hotels offering better deals. Remember that many of these places close in the off season.

Camping *Castrum Camping* (☎ 343 198), on the southern end of the lake at the start of Tó-part, is the only camping ground in town. It is a relatively expensive place (400/600/400 Ft per tent/adult/child) and has no bun-galows.

Private Rooms Zalatour and Hévíz Tourist can find you a private room for 3500 Ft per double, though things could be tight in summer. You'll see a lot of 'Zimmer frei' and 'szoba kiadó' signs on Kossuth Lajos utca and Zrínyi utca, where you can make your own deal for less.

Holiday Homes The best deals in town are at the 86-room *Flavius* (☎ 343 463) at Rákóczi utca 11-13, and the 46-room *Pátria* (☎ 343 281), one street over at Petőfi Sándor utca 11. Both charge 1200/1800 Ft for singles/doubles with shared bath. The 13-storey *Panoráma* (☎ 341 074) with 208 rooms in two buildings at Petőfi Sándor utca 9 is more expensive: singles are 1500 to 2300 Ft and doubles 2300 to 3500 Ft, depending on the season. Another former union house, the 86-room *Arizóna* (☎ 340 482), at Széchenyi utca 23, has singles/doubles without bath for 2500/3500 Ft and ones with bath for 4000/6000 Ft.

Hotels The 30-room *Park* (☎ 341 193), in elegant Kató Villa (1927) at Petőfi Sándor utca 26, is the loveliest hotel in Hévíz and just a few steps up from the Parkerdő. The Park's singles are DM60 to DM94, doubles DM80 to DM120, depending on the season. Guests can use the indoor and outdoor pools, sauna, solarium, gym and tennis courts at the nearby *Thermal Hévíz* hotel (☎ 341 180) at Kossuth Lajos utca 9-11. The 203-room Thermal and its sister hotel, the 230-room *Thermal Aqua* (☎ 341 090) farther south along Kossuth Lajos utca at No 13-15, are the most expensive places in town: singles are DM78 to DM142 and doubles DM128 to DM204.

Places to Eat
The best place for a quick bite is Deák tér near the bus station, which has cafés (including the *Grill Garten)* and *food stalls* selling lángos, sausages and fish. For a proper meal, try the nearby *Rózsakert* with a huge beer garden at Rákóczi utca 3, the *Hársfa* restaurant and wine bar just up from Kossuth Lajos utca at Honvéd utca 13, or the *Della Rosa*, a

pizzeria on Széchenyi utca open daily until 9 pm.

If you're driving to Sümeg, stop for a meal or a drink at the *Gyöngyösi Betyár Csárda*, about five km north of Hévíz. Though tacky imitations abound throughout the country, this is the real thing: an 18th-century highwayman's inn.

Getting There & Away
Hévíz isn't on a railway line, but buses travel the seven km east to Keszthely almost every half-hour from stand No 3. There are at least a dozen daily departures to Sümeg and Zalaegerszeg and half as many to Badacsony, Balatonfüred, Nagykanizsa and Veszprém. Other destinations include: Baja (one departure daily), Budapest (five), Győr (three), Kaposvár (three), Kecskemét (one), Pápa (five), Pécs (two), Sopron (three), Székesfehérvár (three), Szekszárd (two) and Szombathely (four).

BADACSONY
• *area code* ☎ 87

The Badacsony region is named after the 400m basalt massif that rises like a bread loaf from the Tapolca Basin along the north-western shore of Lake Balaton. There are four towns in the area: Badacsonylábdihegy, Badacsonyörs, Badacsonytördemic and Badacsonytomaj. But when Hungarians say Badacsony, they usually mean the little resort at the Badacsony train station, near the ferry pier south of Badacsonytomaj.

Badacsony has been thrice-blessed. Not only does it have the lake for swimming and the mountains for wonderful walks and hikes, but it has produced wine – lots of it – since the Middle Ages. Badacsony was one of the last places on Balaton's northern shore to be developed and has more of a country feel to it than most resorts. It vies only with Tihany in beauty (both places are nature preserves), and you might stop here for a day or two to relax.

Orientation
Route No 71, the main road along the Balaton's northern shore, runs through

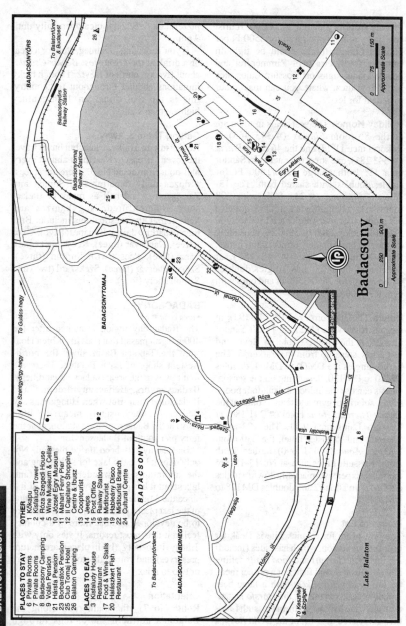

Badacsony

PLACES TO STAY
6 Private Rooms
7 Private Rooms
8 Badacsony Camping
9 Volán Pension
9 Hársfa Pension
23 Bobátok Pension
25 Club Tomaj Hotel
26 Balaton Camping

PLACES TO EAT
3 Kisfaludy House
17 Restaurant
18 Food & Wine Stalls
20 Halászkert Fish
   Restaurant

OTHER
1 Kökapu
2 Kisfaludy Tower
4 Róza Szegedi House
5 Wine Museum & Cellar
10 József Egry Museum
11 Mahart Ferry Pier
12 Il Capitano Shopping
   Centre & Ibusz
13 Cooptourist
14 Jeeps
15 Post Office
16 Railway Station
19 Midtourist
19 Habléány Disco
22 Midtourist Branch
24 Cultural Centre

Badacsony, where it is called Balatoni út. The ferry pier is on the southern side of this road; almost everything else – hotels, restaurants, the train station and 437m Badacsony Hill – is north. Above the village, several pensions and houses with private accommodation ring the base of the hill on Római út, which debouches into Balatoni út at Badacsonytomaj, a few km to the north-east. Szegedi Róza utca branches off to the north from Római út through the vineyards to the Kisfaludy House restaurant.

Information

Miditourist (☎ 431 028) is in the centre of the village at Park utca 6, and Cooptourist (☎ 431 134) is hidden behind some food stalls nearby at Egry sétány 1. Balatontourist (☎ 431 249) is in the Il Capitano shopping centre below Balatoni út near the ferry pier. These agencies are open only in season from May to August or September. At other times, check with Miditourist's branch at Park utca 53 (☎ 431 028).

The post office is on Park utca, opposite the line of 4WDs that transport passengers up to Badacsony Hill. You can change money at the post office and at most of the travel agencies.

Things to See & Do

The **József Egry Museum** at Egry sétány 52 in town is devoted to the Balaton region's leading painter (1883-1951) and is open from May to October.

The slopes and the vineyards above the town are sprinkled with little wine-press houses and 'folk baroque' cottages. One of these is the **Róza Szegedi House** (1790), which belonged to the actress wife of the poet Sándor Kisfaludy from Sümeg. It contains a literary museum. A press house (1798) belonging to the Kisfaludy family is now the Kisfaludy House restaurant.

If you follow the cobbled road (Hegyalja utca) west from below the Róza Szegedi House, you'll come to the **Wine Museum** up on a bluff with great views of the lake. It's open daily from 10 am to 4 pm (excluding Monday) between mid-May and mid-

October and has a wine cellar for tasting beneath it. Try a glass of Szürkebarát (Pinot Gris) or Kéknyelű (Blue Stalk), Badacsony's premier white wines.

The flat-topped forested massif overlooking the lake is just the place to escape the tipsy herds. If you'd like to get a running start on your hike, catch one of the open 4WDs marked 'Badacsony-hegyi járat', which depart from opposite the post office between May and September from 9 am to 7 or 8 pm whenever at least six paying passengers climb aboard (300 Ft per person). The driver will drop you off at the Kisfaludy House restaurant, where a large map outlining the marked trails is posted by the parking lot. Or you might arm yourself in advance with a copy of *A Balaton* (No 41), Cartographia's 1:40,000 topographical map available at bookshops for 350 Ft.

Several paths lead to lookouts (**Kisfaludy Tower** is the highest), and to neighbouring hills like **Gulács-hegy** (393m) to the north-east and **Szentgyörgy-hegy** (415m) to the north. The landscape includes abandoned quarries and large basalt towers that resemble organ pipes; of these, **Kőkapu** (Stone Gate) is the most dramatic. Several of the trails take you past **Rózsakő** (Rose Rock). A 100-year-old plaque explains an unusual tradition: 'If a lad and a lass sit here together with their backs to the lake, they will be married in a year.' Good luck – or regrets (as the case may be).

The postage-stamp-size **beach** is reedy and not among Lake Balaton's best; you would do better to head a few km north-east to Badacsonytomaj or Badacsonyörs for a swim. The Badacsony beach does have changing rooms and showers, though.

Places to Stay

Camping The closest camping ground is *Badacsony Camping* (☎ 431 091) at the water's edge about 1.5 km west of the ferry pier. It's a casual place, but be sure to bring mosquito repellent. It costs between 390 and 500 Ft for a tent and the same per person. *Balaton Camping* (☎ 331 253), which is a bit cheaper, is in Badacsonyörs, north-east of

Badacsony village on route No 71. Both sites are open from late May to early September.

Private Rooms Private rooms are available from all the agencies. Balatontourist charges 2000 to 4000 Ft for a double, depending on the season, while Cooptourist's cheapest accommodation is a house for four people for 4500 Ft. Singles are usually not available, and most of the houses with rental signs prefer not to accept guests for less than three or four days. The private house near the wine-bottling plant at Muskotály utca 4 has a few cheap doubles. Another house at Szegedi Róza utca 83 (☎ 431 192) has fantastic views of the lake and is within easy walking distance of the trails up to Badacsony Hill. Doubles are 3000 Ft.

Pensions There are several small pensions among the vineyards on the road above the railway line, a 10-minute walk from the station, including the *Hársfa* (☎ 431 293), north of Miditourist on Római út, and the *Volán* (☎ 431 013) at Római út 168. But they close from October to April. In Badacsonytomaj, the *Borbarátok* (Friends of Wine) pension (☎ 471 597) at Római út 78 has a dozen modern, very comfortable rooms and only closes the first three months of the year. Doubles are 2500 to 3000 Ft, depending on the season.

Hotel The 50-room *Club Tomaj* resort hotel (☎ 471 040) at Balatoni út 14 on the shore is the biggest and most expensive place around. It has tennis courts, 10-pin bowling, sauna and a private beach. Singles are DM34 to DM72, doubles DM48 to DM90, depending on the season.

Places to Eat
There are *food stalls* with picnic tables dispensing sausage, fish soup and lángos as well as *wine stalls* (20 Ft a glass, 250 Ft a litre) between the train station and Park utca. The *Halászkert* restaurant at Park utca 5 is crowded and touristy, but the fish dishes are excellent. *Pizzeria Il Capitano* is in the shopping centre by the ferry pier. The bar and restaurant at the *Borbarátok* (see Pensions) is very lively.

The best place for a meal or a drink in Badacsony is the alfresco terrace at the *Kisfaludy House* restaurant, Szegedi Róza utca 87, perched on the hill overlooking the vineyards and the lake. To the west is Szigliget Bay, the loveliest on the lake, and directly across to the south lie the two 'breasts' of Fonyód: the Sípos and Sándor hills. If you can't afford the prices – and the Kisfaludy House is relatively expensive – you can eat a picnic lunch at the tables between the restaurant and the car park.

Entertainment
Badacsony Vintage is a two-day long wine-guzzling binge in September featuring a fair, a parade and a ball where a lot of people probably fall down and hurt themselves. The *József Egry Cultural Centre* is opposite the Borbarátok pension on Római út. *Il Capitano* is a big nightclub and disco at the beach that heaves in summertime. The *Hableány* restaurant at Park utca 12 also has a weekend disco then.

Getting There & Away
Three buses a day head for Balatonfüred, Veszprém and Székesfehérvár. Other destinations include: Budapest (one trip daily), Hévíz (two), Keszthely (one), Nagykanizsa (one), Révfülöp (three), Tapolca (three) and Zalaegerszeg (four). Badacsony is on the rail line linking all the towns on Lake Balaton's northern shore with Budapest-Déli and Tapolca. To get to Keszthely you must change at Tapolca, but there's often an immediate connection.

Ferries between Badacsony and Fonyód are fairly frequent between late March and late October; in Fonyód you can get a connection to Southern Transdanubia by taking a train direct to Kaposvár.

A boat ride to Badacsony from Siófok or Balatonfüred is the best way to get the feel of Lake Balaton. Boats operate from June to early September. Ferries also travel on to Keszthely at this time.

SÜMEG
• *pop 7200*
• *area code* ☎ 87

This small town, some 30 km north of Keszthely between the Bakony and Keszthely hills, has a few pleasant surprises. Sümeg was on the map as early as the 13th century, when an important border fortress was built by King Béla IV in the aftermath of the Mongol invasion. The castle was strengthened several times during the next three centuries, repelling the Turks but falling to the Habsburg forces, who torched it in 1713.

Sümeg's golden age came later in the 18th century when the all-powerful bishops of Veszprém took up residence here and commissioned some of the town's fine baroque buildings. Sümeg declined afterwards, but those glory days live on in its fine architecture. It remains one of the most pleasant small towns in the region and is well worth a visit.

Orientation & Information
Kossuth Lajos utca is the main street running north-south through Sümeg. The bus station is on Flórián tér, a continuation of Kossuth Lajos utca south of the town centre. The train station is a 10-minute walk north-west, at the end of Darnay Kálmán utca.

Tourinform (☎ 352 481) has an office in the old Kisfaludy hotel at Kossuth Lajos utca 13 and can provide information about Sümeg, the Balaton and central Transdanubia. There's an OTP bank in a renovated townhouse at Kossuth Lajos utca 17 (corner of Kisfaludy tér). The post office is at No 1 of the same street, opposite the bus station.

Sümeg Castle
The imposing castle sits on a 270m cone of limestone above the town – a rare substance in this region of basalt. You can reach it by climbing Vak Bottyán utca, which is lined with lovely baroque *kúriák* (mansions), from Szent István tér and then taking Bem utca and Vároldal utca past the castle stables at No 5, which now house a rather specialised **Saddle and Harness Museum**. The castle

is also accessible from the north-east via route No 84.

Sümeg Castle fell into ruin after the Austrians abandoned it early in the 18th century, but it was restored in the 1960s. Today it is the largest and best preserved castle in Transdanubia and well worth the climb for the views east to the Bakony Hills and south to the Keszthely Hills. There's a small **Castle Museum** of weapons, armour and castle furnishings in the 13th-century **Old Tower** open from mid-March to mid-October, pony rides and archery in the castle courtyard for children, a snack bar and a wine cellar. You can still see bits of the old town walls below the castle at the northern end of Kossuth Lajos utca (Nos 13 to 33). A 16th-century tower is now the living room of the house at No 31.

Church of the Ascension
The castle may dominate the town, but for many people it is not Sümeg's most important sight. That distinction goes to the Church of the Ascension on Széchenyi György utca, west of Kossuth Lajos utca and just off Deák Ferenc utca. You would never know it from the outside; architecturally, the building (1757) is unexceptional. But step inside and marvel at what has been called the 'Sistine Chapel of the rococo'.

That's perhaps an overstatement, but it's true that Franz Anton Maulbertsch's frescos are the most beautiful baroque ones in Hungary and by far the prolific painter's best work. The frescos, whose subjects are taken from the Old and New Testaments, are brilliant expressions of light and shadow, but you should pay special attention to the Crucifixion scene in *Golgotha* on the northern wall in the nave, the *Adoration of the Three Kings* with its caricature of a Moor opposite across the aisle, the *Gate of Hell* under the organ loft on the western side under the porch, and the altarpiece of Christ ascending airily to the clouds. Maulbertsch managed to include himself in a couple of his works, most clearly among the shepherds in the first fresco on the southern wall (he's the one holding the round cheeses and hamming it up for the audience). The commissioner of

BALATON REGION

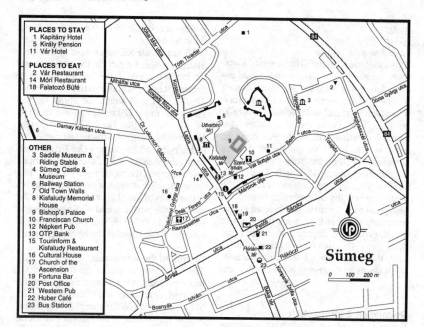

PLACES TO STAY
1 Kapitány Hotel
5 Király Pension
11 Vár Hotel

PLACES TO EAT
2 Vár Restaurant
14 Móri Restaurant
18 Falatozó Büfé

OTHER
3 Saddle Museum & Riding Stable
4 Sümeg Castle & Museum
6 Railway Station
7 Old Town Walls
8 Kisfaludy Memorial House
9 Bishop's Palace
10 Franciscan Church
12 Népkert Pub
13 OTP Bank
15 Tourinform & Kisfaludy Restaurant
16 Cultural House
17 Church of the Ascension
19 Fortuna Bar
20 Post Office
21 Western Pub
22 Huber Café
23 Bus Station

Sümeg

0   100   200 m

the frescos, Márton Padányi Bíró, bishop of Veszprém, is shown on the western wall near the organ. Drop 40 Ft in the machine to illuminate the frescos and view them at their best.

Town Centre

The **Church of the Ascension** steals the limelight from the 17th-century **Franciscan church** at Szent István tér, which has naive frescos, a beautifully carved baroque altar, and a Pietà that has attracted pilgrims for 300 years. Don't miss the ornate pulpit with the eerie thing-like hand grasping a crucifix.

The former **Bishop's Palace** at No 8-10 on the square was a grand residence when completed in 1755. It is now in an advanced state of decay, but you can still admire the two Atlases holding up the balcony at the entrance, and the copper rain spouts in the shape of sea (or perhaps lake) monsters.

The **Kisfaludy Memorial House** at Kisfaludy tér 3 is the birthplace of Sándor

Kisfaludy (1772-1844), the Romantic 'poet of the Balaton'. Together with a history of his life and work, the museum (open mid-April to mid-October) contains further exhibits on Sümeg Castle and the area's geology. Outside along a wall is the **Sümeg Pantheon** of local sons and daughters who made good.

Activities

There is some excellent hiking east of Sümeg into the Bakony Hills (known as 'Hungary's Sherwood Forest'), but get yourself a copy of *A Bakony Turistatérképe – Déli Rész* (No 3; Bakony Tourist Map – Southern Part). If you want to go horse riding, visit the stable (☎ 352 367) at the Saddle and Harness Museum, Vároldal 5.

Places to Stay

The 32-room *Vár* hotel (☎ 352 414), a spruced-up hostel at Vak Bottyán utca 2, is a very central place to stay, with singles/doubles without bath for 1200 Ft and 2000 Ft for those with one. The Vár is on the way to the castle, and the staff are friendly and knowledgeable. The rooms on the 1st floor are bigger and more modern than those at ground level – request any of Nos 205 to 208.

The *Király* (☎ 352 605) is a seven-room, family-run pension in an old farmhouse behind the Kisfaludy Memorial House on Szent István tér at Udvarbíró tér 5. Doubles with showers are 3000 Ft. Parts of the building date back to the 15th century, so the rooms are small, but there's a sauna, fitness room and wine cellar.

A new up-market place is the 29-room *Kapitány* hotel (☎ 352 598), north of the castle at Tóth Tivadar utca 19. Doubles are 3000 to 3900 Ft, depending on the season.

Places to Eat

The *Falatozó* is a cheap stand-up büfé at Kossuth Lajos utca 9 open most days to 5 pm. The restaurant and café at the former *Kisfaludy* hotel, Kossuth Lajos utca 13, remain open, and the former is one of the few places in town where you can have a sit-down meal. It's open till 11 pm. Another option is the old-style *Móri* at Kossuth Lajos utca 22, which is open till 9 or 10 pm.

Up by the castle on the eastern side, the *Vár* restaurant specialises in game. The restaurant at the *Kapitány* hotel is the new kid in town and popular for that.

Entertainment

The *Kisfaludy Cultural House*, near the Church of the Ascension at Széchenyi György utca 9-11, or Tourinform will let you know what's on in Sümeg. The Sümeg Festival at the castle in mid-August features medieval games, horse shows and lots of wine.

For a town its size, Sümeg has a surprising number of lively watering holes, including the *Fortuna* bar at Kossuth Lajos utca 3, open till 11 pm, the sawdust-and-spit *Népkert* pub on Szent István tér, and the *Huber* café at Flórián tér 8. The supposedly 24-hour *Western Pub* is yet another one of those generic Hungarian bars with saloon

doors, split-log tables and Marlboro Country music. It attracts a young crowd.

Getting There & Away

At least a dozen buses a day leave Sümeg for Hévíz, Keszthely, Tapolca and Veszprém; departures to Pápa and Zalaegerszeg are also frequent. Other destinations include Budapest (three or four buses daily), Győr (six), Kaposváǔ (one), Nagykanizsa (two), Sopron (three), Pécs (one), Szombathely (two) and, on the border with Slovenia, Lenti (two).

Sümeg is on the railway line linking Tapolca and Celldömölk, from where four daily trains continue on to Szombathely. For Budapest and other points to the east and west along the northern shore of Lake Balaton, change at Tapolca.

NAGYVÁZSONY

* *pop 1700*
* *area code* ☎ 88

When you grow tired of the Balaton hubbub, take an easy excursion north to Nagy-vázsony, a sleepy little market town in the southern Bakony Hills. The drive from Badacsony or from Tihany, 15 km to the south-east, takes you through some of the prettiest countryside in central Transdanubia, and the town has an important 15th-century castle. To the south-west lies the **Káli Basin** and such picturesque towns as **Mind-szentkálla** and **Szenbékkálla**, with Romanesque church ruins, gentle landscapes and bountiful vineyards. Mindszentkálla also has an ostrich farm (☎ 348 171), which can be visited.

Orientation & Information

The four bus stops and an OTP bank branch are in the centre of town on Kinizsi utca. Opposite at Kinizsi utca 59 is the post office. The staff at the Kastély hotel (☎ 364 109) act as reps for Balatontourist and can provide information.

Vázsonykő Castle

This castle, on a gentle slope north of the tiny town centre at the end of Vár utca, was begun early in the 15th century by the Vezsenyi family, but was presented to Pál Kinizsi by King Matthias Corvinus in 1462 in gratitude for the brave general's military successes against the Turks. It became an important border fortress during the occupation and was used as a prison in the 1700s.

The castle is essentially a rectangle with a horseshoe-shaped barbican. The 30m, six-storey keep is reached via a bridge over the dry moat. A large crack runs from the top of the tower to the bottom, but it must be secure enough: the upper rooms contain the **Kinizsi Castle Museum**, open May to September. Part of General Kinizsi's red-marble sarcophagus sits in the centre of the restored chapel, and there's a collection of archaeological finds in the crypt.

Other Things to See
The **Post Office Museum** is behind the castle at Temető utca 3. Nagyvázsony was an important stop along the post road between Budapest and Graz in the 19th century, and horses were changed here. The museum is a lot more interesting than it sounds, particularly the section on the history of the telephone in Hungary beginning with the installation of the first switchboard in Budapest in 1890. It's open from 10 am to 6 pm from March to October and until 2 pm in other months.

Nearby at Bercsényi utca 21 is a small **Folk Museum** in a farmhouse dating from 1825. It was once the home of a coppersmith, and his workshop remains. It is open daily May to October from 10 am to 6 pm (Monday excluded). The **Church of St Stephen** in the centre of town on Rákóczi utca was built by Kinizsi in 1481 on the site of an earlier chapel. Most of the interior, including the richly carved main altar, is baroque.

You can ride horses at the school next to the Kastély hotel for between 1500 and 2000 Ft an hour. Horse-drawn coaches seating three people cost DM40/150 per hour/day.

Places to Stay
The *Kinizsi* hostel (☎ 364 318), with six eight-bed rooms at Vár utca 9 opposite the castle, is the cheapest place in Nagyvázsony

but opens from May to September only. Between April and November, try the seven-room *Vázsonykő* pension (☎ 364 344) at Sörház utca 2. Doubles are DM40.

The worn-out *Kastély* hotel north-east of the centre at Kossuth utca 12 (☎ 364 109) has 20 rooms in an 18th-century mansion on six hectares of parkland that once belonged to the aristocratic Zichy family. Singles/doubles with bath are DM40/65. The cheaper *Lótel* (that translates as 'Horse-tel') in an outbuilding on the same grounds costs DM21/35 for singles/doubles with shared shower. Both the Kastély and the Lótel are closed between December and March.

Places to Eat
The thatched *Vár Csárda* overlooking the castle at Temető utca 5 is open in summer only. Try the good home cooking at the *Vázsonykő* pension at other times. The *Vázsony* is a divey büfé at Kinizsi utca 84 near the bus stops. The *Malomkő* at No 49 of the same street has decent cakes.

Entertainment
The main events on Nagyvázsony's calendar are the Kinizsi Days in early August and the Knights' Tournament (Lovagi Turna), a medieval-style equestrian pageant held in mid-August on the grounds of the Kastély hotel.

Getting There & Away
Some 15 buses a day link Nagyvázsony and Veszprém, 23 km to the north-east, and eight to 10 run to Tapolca to the south-west. You can also reach Balatonfüred (via Tótvázsony) and Keszthely on two or three direct buses a day.

TIHANY
• *pop 1750*
• *area code* ☎ 87
Although Veszprém has more monuments than any town in the Balaton region, the place with the greatest historical significance on the lake is Tihany, 11 km south-west of Balatonfüred. Tihany village is on a peninsula of the same name that juts five km into

Lake Balaton, almost linking the lake's northern and southern shores. The entire peninsula is a nature reserve of hills and marshy meadows; it has an isolated, almost wild, feel to it that is unknown around the rest of the lake. The village, on a hill top on the eastern side of the peninsula, is one of the most charming in the Balaton region.

There was a Roman settlement in the area, but Tihany only appeared on the map in 1055, when King Andrew I (ruled 1046-60), a son of King Stephen's great nemesis, Vászoly, founded a Benedictine monastery here. The *Deed of Foundation* of the Abbey of Tihany, now in the archives of the Benedictine abbey at Pannonhalma south of Győr, is the first document bearing any Hungarian words – some 50 place names within a mostly Latin document. It's a linguistic treasure in a country where the vernacular in its written form was spurned – particularly in education – in favour of the more 'cultured' Latin and German until the 19th century.

In 1267 a fortress was built around the church and was able to keep the Turks at bay when they arrived 300 years later. But the castle was demolished by Habsburg forces in 1702, and all you'll see today are ruins.

Tihany Peninsula is a popular recreational area with beaches on its eastern and western coasts and a big resort complex on its southern tip. The waters of the so-called Tihany Well off the southern end of the peninsula are the deepest – and coldest – in the lake, reaching an unprecedented 12m in some parts.

Orientation

Tihany village, perched on an 80m plateau along the peninsula's eastern coast, is accessible by two roads when you turn south off route No 71. The Inner Harbour (Belső Kikötő), where ferries to/from Balatonfüred and Siófok dock, is below the village. Tihanyi-rév (Tihany Port), to the south-west at the tip of the peninsula, is Tihany's recreational area. From here, car ferries run to Szántódi-rév and passenger ferries to Balatonföldvár. Two inland basins are fed by rain and ground water: the Inner Lake (Belső-tó), almost in the centre of the penin-

sula and visible from the village, and the Outer Lake (Külső-tó) to the north-west, which has almost completely dried up and is now a tangle of reeds. Both attract bird life.

Information

The bus from Balatonfüred stops on Kossuth Lajos utca below the Abbey Church and next to Balatontourist (☎ 448 519) at No 20 (open from May to August). Tihany Tourist (☎ 448 481), open from April to October, is at Kossuth Lajos utca 11.

There's an OTP bank branch next to Balatontourist on I András tér. The post office is across the street at Kossuth Lajos utca 37.

Abbey Church

This twin-spired, ochre-coloured church was built in 1754 on the site of King Andrew's church and contains fantastic altars, pulpits and screens carved between 1753 and 1779 by an Austrian lay brother named Sebastian Stuhlhof. They are baroque-rococo masterpieces and all are richly symbolic.

With your back to the sumptuous main altar (the saint with the broken chalice and snake is Benedict, the founder of Western monasticism) and the Abbot's Throne, look right to the side altar dedicated to Mary. The large angel kneeling on the right is said to represent Stuhlhof's fiancée, a fisherman's daughter who died in her youth. On the Altar of the Sacred Heart across the aisle, a pelican (Christ) nurtures its young (the Christian faithful) with its own blood. The besotted figures atop the pulpit beside it are four doctors of the Roman Catholic Church: SS Ambrose, Gregory, Jerome and Augustine. The next two altars on the right and left sides are dedicated to Benedict and his twin sister, Scholastica; the last pair, a baptismal font and the Lourdes Altar, are from the 20th century.

Stuhlhof also carved the magnificent choir rail above the porch and the organ with all the cherubs. The frescos on the ceilings by Bertalan Székely, Lajos Deák-Ébner and Károly Lotz were painted in 1889, when the church was restored.

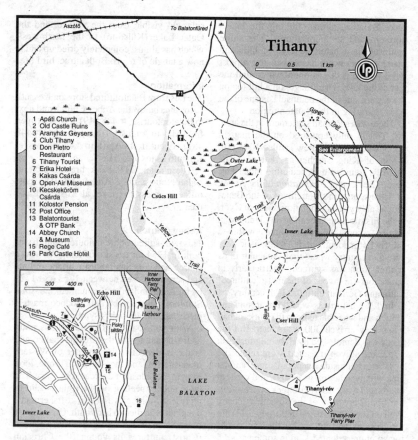

The remains of King Andrew lie under a limestone sarcophagus in the Romanesque **crypt**. The spiral sword-like cross on the cover is similar to ones used by 11th-century Hungarian kings. The Abbey Church is open every day from 9 am to 5.30 pm.

The **Abbey Museum** next door in the former Benedictine monastery, which can be entered to the right of the main altar in the Abbey Church, contains exhibits related to Lake Balaton, liturgical vestments, a library of manuscripts and a bedroom where the deposed Habsburg Emperor Charles IV and his wife Zita spent a week in October 1921.

('They filled the house with their sacred presence,' reads the plaque). In the cellar, there's a small museum of Roman statues and ghastly modern sculptures. It's open from 9 am to 5 pm every day (except Monday) from May to September.

North of Abbey Church

Pisky sétány, a promenade running along the ridge north from the church to Echo Hill, passes a cluster of folk houses which have now been turned into a small **Open-Air Folk Museum** (same hours as the Abbey Museum).

You'll find **Echo Hill** at the end of Pisky sétány. At one time, up to a dozen syllables of anything shouted in the direction of the Abbey Church would bounce back but, alas, because of more building in the area and perhaps climatic changes, you'll be lucky to get three nowadays. From Echo Hill you can descend Garay utca and Váralja utca to the Inner Harbour and a small beach, or continue on to the hiking trails that pass this way.

Hiking

Walking is one of Tihany's main attractions; there's a good map outlining the trails near the front of the Abbey Church. Following the green trail north-east of the church for an hour will bring you to the **Russian Well** (Oroszkút) and the ruins of the **Old Castle** (Óvár), where Russian Orthodox monks brought to Tihany by Andrew hollowed out cells in the soft basalt walls.

The 232m **Csúcs Hill**, with panoramic views of Lake Balaton, is about two hours west of the church via the red trail. From here you can join up with the yellow trail originating in Tihanyi-rév, which will lead you north to the 13th-century **Apáti Church** and route No 71. The blue trail takes you south to the **Inner Lake** and **Aranyház**, a series of geyser cones formed by warm-water springs. Though the trails are poorly marked, you're unlikely to get lost.

Places to Stay

Accommodation is limited and expensive in Tihany; you should consider making it a day trip from Balatonfüred by bus, which takes only 20 minutes. Also, most of the hotels and restaurants listed below are closed between mid-October or November and March or April.

Private Rooms Tihany Tourist has private rooms for 3000 to 4000 Ft per double in the low season and 4000 to 5000 Ft in the high season. Many houses along Kossuth Lajos utca and on the little streets north of the Abbey Church have 'Zimmer frei' signs, so in the off season you could try there.

Hotels The swish *Erika* hotel (☎ 448 644) at Batthyány utca 6, on the hill around the corner, charges from DM80 to DM100 per double with bath and all the mod cons. It has a small swimming pool. The inferior but more expensive *Kolostor* (☎ 448 408) is an eight-room pension at Kossuth Lajos utca 14 with doubles priced at DM100.

The *Park Castle* hotel (☎ 448 611) at Fürdőtelepi út 1 on the Inner Harbour has 26 rooms in a former Habsburg summer mansion (the Castle) and 44 more in an ugly modern wing (the Park). Singles in the Castle with bath and balcony are DM69 to DM119, doubles DM89 to DM139; the Park rooms are DM59 to DM89 for singles and DM79 to DM109 for doubles. The hotel has a five-hectare garden and its own beach.

The *Club Tihany* (☎ 448 088) at Rév utca 3, just up from the car-ferry pier at Tihanyi-rév, is a 13-hectare resort with every sporting, munching and quaffing possibility. It's difficult imagining anyone wanting to stay here, but bungalows for two start at DM70 in the low season and reach as high as DM220 in summer. Singles with lake views in the high-rise hotel are DM50 to DM112, doubles DM70 to DM146.

Places to Eat

The *Rege Café* in the former monastery stables next to the church and museum serves light meals and cakes and offers a panoramic view from its terrace, but you would do better to eat at the atmospheric *Kecskeköröm Csárda*, Kossuth Lajos utca 13, a few hundred metres north-west on the main road, or at the *Kakas Csárda*, in a rambling basalt house almost opposite at Batthyány utca 1.

The restaurant at the *Kolostor* pension has German-Hungarian pub grub and makes its own beer on the premises. In Tihanyi-rév, the *Don Pietro* is reliable for pizzas and pastas.

Entertainment

Organ concerts are held in the floodlit *Abbey Church* in summer; check with the staff at Balatontourist or Tihany Tourist for dates and times. Vintage Days is a wine festival held in mid-September on I András tér. The wine to try here is Tihanyi Merlot.

Getting There & Away

Buses cover the 11 km from Balatonfüred's train station to and from Tihany about 20 times a day. The bus stops at both ferry landings before climbing to Tihany village.

The Balaton passenger ferries stop at Tihany from late March to late October. Catch them at the pier below the abbey or at Tihanyi-rév. From early March to late November the car ferry crosses the narrow stretch of water between Tihanyi-rév and Szántódi-rév about every 40 minutes.

BALATONFÜRED

• *pop 15,100*
• *area code ☎ 87*

Balatonfüred is the oldest and most popular resort on the northern shore of Lake Balaton. It has none of the frenzy or brashness of Siófok, partly because of its aristocratic origins and partly because the thermal waters of its world-famous heart hospital attract a much older crowd. You can see them all year long taking the 'drinking cure' from the warm-water spring in Gyógy tér or shuffling along the lakeside promenade.

The thermal water here, rich in carbonic acid, had been used as a cure for stomach ailments for centuries, but its other curative properties were only discovered by scientific analysis in the late 18th century. Balatonfüred was immediately declared a spa with its own chief physician in residence.

Balatonfüred's golden age was in the 19th century, especially the first half, when political and cultural leaders of the Reform Era (roughly 1825-48) gathered here in summer. The town became a writers' colony of sorts, and in 1831 the poet Sándor Kisfaludy established Transdanubia's first Hungarian-language theatre here, emblazoned with a banner proclaiming 'Patriotism Towards Our Nationality'. (Until then German had been the language of the stage.) Balatonfüred was also the site chosen by István Széchenyi to launch the lake's first steamship in 1846.

By 1900, Balatonfüred was a popular place for increasingly wealthy middle-class families to escape the heat of the city. Wives would base themselves here all summer long with their children while husbands would board the 'bull trains' in Budapest for the lake at the weekend. The splendid promenade and a large wooden bath (now dismantled) were built on the lake to accommodate the increasing crowds.

Orientation

Balatonfüred has two distinct districts: the resort area on the lake and the commercial centre in the older part of town around Szent István tér to the north-west. Almost everything to see and do is by the water.

The train and bus stations are on Dobó István utca. The quickest way to get to the lake from either is to walk east on Horváth Mihály utca and then south on Jókai Mór utca. The ferry pier is at the end of a jetty off Vitorlás tér.

Information

Balatontourist (☎ 343 471) has moved from Blaha Lujza utca 5 to Tagore sétány 1 near the ferry pier, the same building housing the Vitorlás restaurant. It is open from 9 am to 6.30 pm and, in season, on Saturday to 6 pm and Sunday to 1 pm. Ibusz (☎ 342 028) is at Garay János utca 1 while Cooptourist (☎ 342 677) is at Jókai Mór utca 23.

There's an OTP bank branch next to a large supermarket at Jókai Mór utca 15. The post office is at Zsigmond utca 14.

Things to See

The **Mór Jókai Memorial Museum** is housed in the prolific writer's summer villa on the corner of Jókai Mór utca and Honvéd utca just north of Vitorlás tér. In his study here, Jókai churned out many of his 200 novels under the stern gaze of his wife, the actress Róza Laborfalvi. A member of parliament for 30 years, Jókai was only able to write – so the explanatory notes tell us – in 'purple ink on minister's paper'. The museum is open daily except Monday from May to October from 10 am to 6 pm.

Across the street at Blaha Lujza utca 1 is

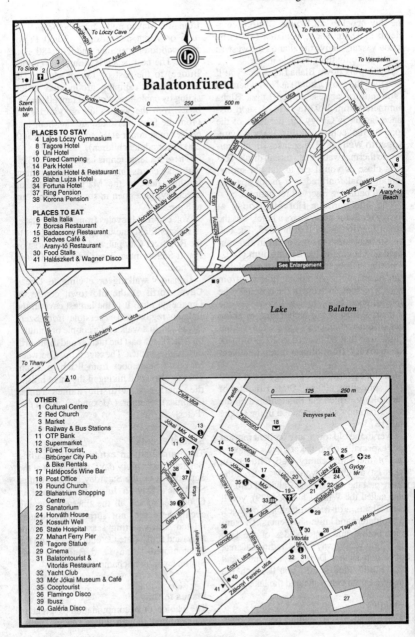

Balatonfüred

0   250   500 m

PLACES TO STAY
4 Lajos Lóczy Gymnasium
8 Tagore Hotel
9 Uni Hotel
10 Füred Camping
14 Park Hotel
16 Astoria Hotel & Restaurant
20 Blaha Lujza Hotel
34 Fortuna Hotel
37 Ring Pension
38 Korona Pension

PLACES TO EAT
6 Bella Italia
7 Borcsa Restaurant
15 Badacsony Restaurant
21 Kedves Café &
   Arany-tó Restaurant
30 Food Stalls
41 Halászkert & Wagner Disco

Lake   Balaton

OTHER
1 Cultural Centre
2 Red Church
3 Market
5 Railway & Bus Stations
11 OTP Bank
12 Supermarket
13 Füred Tourist,
   Bitbürger City Pub
   & Bike Rentals
17 Hátlépcsős Wine Bar
18 Post Office
19 Round Church
22 Blahatrium Shopping
   Centre
23 Sanatorium
24 Horváth House
25 Kossuth Well
26 State Hospital
27 Mahart Ferry Pier
28 Tagore Statue
29 Cinema
31 Balatontourist &
   Vitorlás Restaurant
32 Yacht Club
33 Mór Jókai Museum & Café
35 Cooptourist
36 Flamingo Disco
39 Ibusz
40 Galéria Disco

0   125   250 m

Fenyves park

Gyógy tér

Vitorlás tér

the tiny neoclassical **Round Church** completed in 1846. The *Crucifixion* (1891) by János Vaszary above the altar on the western wall is the only thing notable inside.

If you walk down Blaha Lujza utca you'll pass the villa (now a hotel) at No 4 where the 19th-century actress-singer Lujza Blaha summered from 1893 to 1916. A short distance farther is Gyógy tér, the heart of the spa. In the centre of this leafy square, **Kossuth Well** (1853) dispenses slightly sulphuric thermal water that you can drink. This is as close as you'll get to the hot spring; although Balatonfüred is a major spa, the mineral baths are reserved for patients.

The late baroque **Horváth House** at Gyógy tér 3, for many years a hotel, was the site of the first Anna Ball in 1825. The ball has since become the big event in Balatonfüred and is held in the **Sanatorium** (1802) opposite in July. Next to it is the **Balaton Pantheon**, with memorial plaques from those who took the cure at the hospital. The Bengali poet Rabindranath Tagore was one of them. A bust of this Nobel Prize-winning man of letters stands on Tagore sétány before a lime tree that he planted in 1926 to mark his recovery from illness after treatment here.

On the eastern side of Gyógy tér at No 2 is the sprawling, 600-bed **State Hospital of Cardiology**, which put Balatonfüred on the map. Kisfaludy's theatre stood in the square until 1873.

Over in the old town, an excellent **market** with especially good bakery stalls is northeast of the 18th-century **Red Church** on Szent István tér. By walking west from the square past the neoclassical **Calvinist church** (also called the White Church; 1829), you'll reach **Siske**, a district of thatched cottages, embroiderers and knife-sharpeners. The sunburnt bodies and water slides of the lake seem light years away in this traditional area, but if you follow Dózsa György utca and then Fürdő utca south, you'll reach the massive Füred camp site and the lake.

Activities

Balatonfüred has six public beaches open from mid-May to mid-September from 9 am to 6 or 7 pm and costing 130/80 Ft for adults/children per day and 780/480 Ft a week. The best beach is Aranyhíd (Golden Bridge) to the east of Tagore sétány. The beach at the camping ground has waterskiing by cable-tow. You can rent all sorts of boats from the yacht club on Vitorlás tér. From the ferry pier there are one-hour lake cruises in summer at 11 am and 2 pm (300/200 Ft for adults/children).

There's a large tennis centre (☎ 342 335) with clay courts, instruction and equipment for hire next to the Margaréta hotel on Széchenyi utca open in summer from 7 am to 8 pm.

You can rent bicycles from several places in Balatonfüred, including the stand next to the Bitbürger City pub and Füred Tourist on Petőfi Sándor utca. They cost 120/1000 Ft per hour/day.

Consider walking or cycling to **Lóczy Cave**, north of the old town centre on Öreghegyi utca. It is the largest cave in the Balaton region and accessible from Szent István tér. Just walk east a couple of minutes on Arácsi utca past the market and then north on Öreghegyi utca. The cave is open between May and September from 9 am to 5 pm. There's also good hiking in the three hills to the north-east with the names Tamás (Thomas), Sándor (Alexander) and Péter (Peter).

Special Events

The Anna Ball, an extravaganza recalling Balatonfüred's glory days, takes place at the Sanatorium on the Saturday before or after St Anne's Day (6 July); hang around in Gyógy tér to see all the finery. Other big events here are, not surprisingly, water-related: the yachting season's start (mid-May) and finish (late October) races, and the Balatonfüred-Tihany and Balatonfüred-Siófok swimming championships.

Places to Stay

The choice of accommodation is great in Balatonfüred though things can get pretty tight in the very high season (most of July and August). Remember that many hotels close down between October or November and late March or April.

Camping There's only one camping ground at Balatonfüred, but it can accommodate 3500 people. *Füred Camping* (☎ 342 872), Széchenyi utca 24, is beside the Marina hotel on the lake, about 1.5 km south-east of the train station. Three-person bungalows here start at DM100 from mid-June to August, DM70 from May to mid-June and in early September, and DM40 in April and from mid-September to mid-October. Camping (April to mid-October) for three people with a tent or caravan costs from DM18 to DM28. To get a bungalow you have to arrive during reception office hours (8 am to 1 pm and 3 to 7 pm daily). The camping ground, open from April to mid-October, has tennis courts, 10-pin bowling and the only water-skiing on Lake Balaton.

Private Rooms & Hostels As elsewhere around Lake Balaton, private room prices are rather inflated. The staff at Balatontourist and Cooptourist have them from 1500 Ft per person while those from Füred Tourist (☎ 342 237) at Petőfi Sándor utca 2 are more expensive: from 3000 to 5000 Ft for a double. There are lots of houses with rooms for rent on the streets north of Aranyhíd Beach.

The *Lajos Lóczy Gymnasium* on Ady Endre utca near the stations, and the far-flung *Ferenc Széchenyi College* on Iskola utca, three km to the north-east of the resort, charge 400 to 600 Ft a night for dormitory rooms in summer.

Pensions The 12-room *Ring Pension* (☎ 342 884) at Petőfi Sándor utca 6/a is so-named because the owner was a champion boxer and not a jeweller. Neat, clean singles with shared bath cost DM30 to DM45, doubles DM50 to DM90. The nearby *Korona* (☎ 343 278), with 18 rooms at

Vörösmarty Mihály utca 4, costs about the same.

Hotels The most central place in town is the cosy *Blaha Lujza* hotel (☎ 343 703), with 19 rooms at Blaha Lujza utca 4, the former summer home of the much loved 19th-century actress-singer. Singles are 1500 to 2000 Ft, doubles 3000 to 4000 Ft, depending on the season.

Once a retreat for burnt-out school teachers, the up-market *Fortuna* (☎ 343 037) on a hill at Huray utca 6 has 34 rooms and charges 2850 to 4500 Ft for singles and 4000 to 6000 Ft for doubles with bath.

The run-down *Tagore* (☎ 343 173), with 36 rooms at Deák Ferenc utca 56 by Arany-híd Beach, charges 2300 to 2600 Ft for singles and 3500 to 5000 Ft for doubles with shower.

Of the dozen or so high-rise hotels lining the lake in Balatonfüred, one of the best (and surprisingly the cheapest) is the 45-room *Uni* (☎ 342 239) at Széchenyi utca 10, with singles from 2300 to 6500 Ft and doubles from 2900 to 7700 Ft, depending on the season. The poshest place in town is the old world *Park* hotel (☎ 343 203), with 32 rooms at Jókai Mor utca 24. Singles are DM47 to DM84; doubles DM60 to DM100.

Places to Eat

The *food stalls* on the north-eastern side of Vitorlás tér are great for something fast and cheap, especially the large pieces of fried carp and catfish sold by weight. The nearby *Vitorlás* restaurant, with its central location, is expensive and touristy; walk west on Zákonyi Ferenc utca to the *Halászkert*, which serves some of the best korhely halászlé (drunkard's fish soup) in Hungary.

The eastern end of Tagore sétány is now a strip of pleasant bars and terraced restaurants including *Bella Italia*, with good pizza, pastas and a wonderful terrace facing the lake, and the *Borcsa* restaurant, very popular with local residents.

Jókai Mór utca is another good hunting ground for restaurants. The *Badacsony* at

No 26 has a multilingual menu and is popular with young tourists. The opulent restaurant at the *Astoria* hotel in a restored 19th-century villa next door is for the very well heeled indeed. The restaurant at the *Blaha Lujza* hotel is a lovely place for an affordable sit-down meal.

The *Kedves* coffee house – where Lujza Blaha herself took cha – is at Blaha Lujza utca 7. There's a Chinese restaurant upstairs called the *Arany-tó* (Golden Lake).

Entertainment

The *cultural centre* (☎ 343 633) is near Szent István tér at Kossuth Lajos utca 3.

The *Jókai* is a fun coffee house and bar sacrilegiously located in the back of the Mór Jókai Museum and open till 2 am. To sample one of Balatonfüred's famous rieslings, visit the *Hátlépcsős* (Back Steps) wine bar at Jókai Mór utca 30. If you prefer a beer, carry on north to the big *Bitbürger City* pub at Petőfi Sándor utca 2 or the popular *Fregatt Irish Pub* in the new Blahatrium shopping centre at Blaha Lujza utca 19.

There are discos all over town in summer, including two side by side: the *Wagner* at the Halászkert restaurant and the *Galéria* opposite. Another hot spot is the *Flamingo* at Honvéd utca 3, open till 4 am.

Getting There & Away

Bus Buses for Tihany and Veszprém leave continually throughout the day. Other daily departures are to Budapest (four), Esztergom (one), Győr (seven), Hévíz (seven), Kecskemét (one), Nagykanizsa (one), Nagyvázsony (three), Sopron (two), Székesfehérvár (two), Tapolca (three), Tatabánya (one) and Zalaegerszeg (five).

Train Frequent express and local trains travel north-east to Székesfehérvár and Budapest-Déli and south-west to Tapolca and lake-side towns as far as Badacsony.

Boat From late March to late October several Mahart ferries a day link Balatonfüred with Siófok and Tihany. Up to 10 ferries a day serve the same ports from June

to mid-September; one ferry just before 9 am goes on to various ports, terminating at Badacsony.

Getting Around

You can reach Vitorlás tér and the lake from the train and bus stations on bus Nos 1, 1/a and 2; bus No 1 continues on to the camp site.

Local taxis can be ordered by calling ☎ 342 844.

VESZPRÉM
* *pop 72,000*
* *area code ☎ 88*

Spreading over five hills between the northern and southern ranges of the Bakony Hills, Veszprém has one of the most dramatic locations in central Transdanubia. The walled castle district atop a plateau is a living museum of baroque art and architecture. Though not as rich as, say, Sopron in sights or historical buildings, what Veszprém has is generally in better condition, and it's a delight to stroll through the windy Castle Hill district's single street, admiring the embarrassment of fine churches. As the townspeople say, 'Either the wind is blowing or the bells are ringing in Veszprém.'

The Romans did not settle in what is now Veszprém but eight km to the south-east at Balácapuszta, where important archaeological finds have been made. Prince Géza, King Stephen's father, founded a bishopric in Veszprém late in the 10th century, and the city grew as a religious, administrative and educational centre (the university was established in the 13th century). It also became a favourite residence of Hungary's queens.

The castle at Veszprém was blown up by the Habsburgs in 1702, and it lost most of its medieval buildings during the Rákóczi independence war shortly thereafter. But this cleared the way for Veszprém's golden age, when the city's bishops, rich landlords all, constructed most of what you see today. The church's iron grip on Veszprém prevented it from developing commercially, however, and it was bypassed by the main railway line in the 19th century.

Although considered a Balaton town – merchants here rejoice when it rains since that's when holiday-makers house-bound on the lake come to Veszprém to do some shopping and sightseeing – the city seems a lot farther away than 16 km. As a result this centre of art, culture and education has a life that, happily, carries on all year.

Orientation

The bus station is on Piac tér, a few minutes walk north-east from Kossuth Lajos utca, a busy pedestrian street of shops, restaurants and travel agencies. If you turn north at the end of Kossuth Lajos utca at Szabadság tér, you'll soon reach Óváros tér, the entrance to Castle Hill.

The train station is three km north of the bus station at the end of Jutasi út.

Information

Balatontourist (☎ 429 630) at Kossuth Lajos utca 21 between the bus station and the castle can provide information and a map. Express (☎ 424 508) is upstairs at No 6 of the same street. Cooptourist (☎ 422 313) is closer to the Castle Hill district at Óváros tér 2. All are open daily from 8 or 8.30 am to 4 pm and in summer on Saturday to noon.

You can change money at the OTP bank branch at Óváros tér 25; there's a large post office at Kossuth Lajos utca 19. Bibliofil opposite the post office is a bookshop with English-language titles, and a decent map selection.

Óváros tér

You should begin any tour of Veszprém in Óváros tér, the medieval market place. Of the many fine 18th-century buildings here, the most interesting is the late baroque **Pósa House** (1793) with an iron balcony at No 3. The buildings at Nos 7 and 9 are the former **customs house** and the **town hall**.

Overlooking the square to the north-west is the **fire tower**; like the one in Sopron, it is an architectural hybrid of medieval, baroque and neoclassical styles. The chimes heard on the hour throughout Veszprém emanate from here, and you can climb to the top for excel-

lent views of the rocky hill and the Bakony Hills. The entrance to the tower is at Vár utca 17 (open 9 am to 8 pm in season).

Castle Hill

As you begin to ascend Castle Hill and its sole street, Vár utca, you'll pass through **Heroes' Gate**, an ominous-looking entrance way built in 1936 from the stones of a 15th-century castle gate. The tower to the right houses the **Castle Museum** dealing with the history of Veszprém, local folk culture and minerals. It's open daily (except Monday and Wednesday) from 9 am to 5 pm from May to September.

The extremely rich **Piarist church** at Vár utca 12 was built in 1836. The red marble **altar stone** (1467) diagonally opposite outside house No 27 is the oldest piece of Renaissance stonework in Hungary.

The U-shaped **Bishop's Palace**, Vár utca 16, where the queen's residence stood in the Middle Ages, is in Szentháromság tér, named for the **Trinity Column** (1751) in the centre. The palace, designed by Jakab Fellner of Tata in 1765, is now open to the public and the interior is richly decorated. The huge salon upstairs looks just as it probably did when the Habsburg Emperor Franz Joseph slept here in 1908; portraits of Veszprém's bishops (who were crowned on the shoulder in deference to the Archbishop of Esztergom, who got it right on the head) gaze down on you. The salon's anteroom contains original 18th-century frescos and carved oak doors; the halls are crammed with liturgical objects. The palace dining hall has beautiful **ceiling frescos** of the four seasons (1772) by Johannes Cymbal, and the unusual one in the chapel is of the Holy Trinity symbolised by the seasons and at various stages of life. The views east to the Buhim Valley from the terrace are excellent. The palace is open daily from May to September from 9 am to 5 pm. The 200/100 Ft admission for adults/children also gets you into the **Queen Gizella Museum** of religious art at Vár utca 35.

Next to the Bishop's Palace is the early Gothic **Gizella Chapel**, named after the wife of King Stephen, who was crowned near here

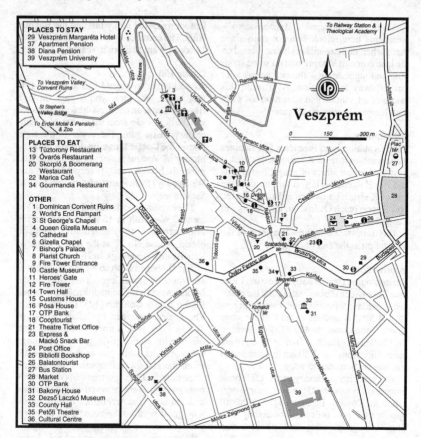

PLACES TO STAY
29 Veszprém Margaréta Hotel
37 Apartment Pension
38 Diana Pension
39 Veszprém University

PLACES TO EAT
13 Tüztorony Restaurant
19 Óváros Restaurant
20 Skorpió & Boomerang Westaurant
22 Marica Café
34 Gourmandia Restaurant

OTHER
1 Dominican Convent Ruins
2 World's End Rampart
3 St George's Chapel
4 Queen Gizella Museum
5 Cathedral
6 Gizella Chapel
7 Bishop's Palace
8 Piarist Church
9 Fire Tower Entrance
10 Castle Museum
11 Heroes' Gate
12 Fire Tower
14 Town Hall
15 Customs House
16 Pósa House
17 OTP Bank
21 Theatre Ticket Office
23 Express & Mackó Snack Bar
24 Post Office
25 Bibliofil Bookshop
26 Balatontourist
27 Bus Station
28 Market
30 OTP Bank
31 Bakony House
32 Dezső Laczkó Museum
33 County Hall
35 Petőfi Theatre
36 Cultural Centre

To Veszprém Valley Convent Ruins

St Stephen's Valley Bridge

To Érdei Motel & Pension & Zoo

To Railway Station & Theological Academy

Veszprém

0   150   300 m

early in the 11th century. The chapel was discovered when the Bishop's Palace was being built in the mid-18th century. Inside the chapel are Byzantine-influenced 13th-century frescos of the Apostles.

Parts of the **Cathedral of St Michael**, site of the first bishop's palace, date from the beginning of the 11th century, but the cathedral has been rebuilt many times since then. Restorers in the early part of this century tried to return it to its original Romanesque style – and not very successfully. The early Gothic crypt is original, though. Beside the cathedral, the octagonal foundation of the

Chapel of St George (1230) sits under a glass dome.

From the rampart known as **World's End** at the end of Vár utca, you can gaze north to craggy Benedict Hill (Benedek-hegy) and the Séd Stream and west to the concrete viaduct (now St Stephen's Valley Bridge) over the Betekints Valley. It is a source of local pride but, sadly, it has been the preferred spot for Veszprém's suicides since it was completed in 1938. Below you, in Margit tér, are the ruins of the medieval **Dominican Convent of St Catherine** and to the west what little remains of the 11th-

3

Prose## Reach Out

247

Balaton Region – Veszprém 247

Reach Out & Touch

It could have been a chapter from a macabre Mills & Boone. The year was 1996 and the Millecentenary celebrations honouring the arrival of the Magyars in the Carpathian Basin in 896 were under way. People were in the mood to mark dates and one of those people was the archbishop of Veszprém.

He knew that it had been in Veszprém that the future king, Stephen (István), and Gisella (Gizella), a Bavarian princess, were married in 996. Just suppose, he thought, that the bishop of the Bavarian city of Passau, where Gisella's remains had been resting these 900-odd years, agreed to send part of her right hand to Hungary: the Holy Dexter, St Stephen's revered right hand, could be brought down from the Basilica in Budapest and they could... Well, the mind boggled.

All parties agreed (the bishop of Passau even threw in Gisella's arm bone) and the date was set. On 4 May, in the small square in front of the Cathedral of St Michael, the hands were laid together and – 1000 years to the day – coyly touched in marital bliss once again.

The world did not end as we know it that fine spring morning; the No 2 tram raced along the Danube in Budapest; Mr Kovács dished out steaming lángos from his stall somewhere along Lake Balaton; schoolchildren in Sárospatak recited their *ábécé*. But most Magyars deep in their hearts knew all was right with the world. ■

century **Veszprém Valley Convent,** whose erstwhile cloistered residents are said to have stitched Stephen's crimson silk coronation robe in 1031. The vestment is now in the National Museum in Budapest. The **statues of King Stephen and Queen Gizella** at World's End were erected in 1938 to mark the 900th anniversary of Stephen's death. The 1000th anniversary of the royal couple's wedding was marked in a strange and – shall we say? – somewhat 'touching' fashion (see aside).

Dezső Laczkó Museum

This museum (sometimes known as the Bakony Museum), at Erzsébet sétány 1 south of Megyeház tér, has archaeological exhibits (the emphasis is on the Roman settlement at Balácapuszta), a large collection of Hungarian, German and Slovak folk costumes and superb wood carvings, including objects made by the famed outlaws of the Bakony Hills in the 18th and 19th centuries.

Next to the main museum is **Bakony House,** a copy of an 18th-century peasant dwelling in the Bakony village of Öcs, southwest of Veszprém. It has the usual three rooms found in Hungarian peasant homes, and in the *kamra* the complete workshop of a flask maker has been set up.

The museum is open from 10 am to 6 pm every day (except Monday) between mid-March and mid-October (to 2 pm the rest of the year).

Petőfi Theatre

Take a peek inside this theatre at Óváry Ferenc utca 2, even if you're not attending a performance. It's a pink and cream gem of Hungarian Art Nouveau architecture and decoration designed by István Medgyaszay in 1908. It's also important structurally; it was the first building in Hungary to be made entirely of reinforced concrete. The large round stained-glass window entitled *The Magic of Folk Art* by Sándor Nagy is exceptional.

Places to Stay

Hostels Veszprém has few places to stay as

BALATON REGION

most people tend to make it a day trip from Lake Balaton. Ask Balatontourist or Express about dormitory rooms (600 to 800 Ft) at *Veszprém University* south of Megyeház tér at Egyetem utca 12. The *Theological Academy* (Hittudomány Akadémia; ☎ 426 116), formerly the Jutas hotel and convenient to the train station at Jutasi utca 18, accepts travellers in summer only. Doubles with bath are 2200 Ft.

Private Rooms Balatontourist can help with private rooms (1500 Ft for a double) and flats (from 3000 Ft).

Pensions There are two pensions in attractive villas on József Attila utca south-west of the centre: the *Apartment* (☎ 320 097) at No 25 and the *Diana* (☎ 421 061) across the street at No 22. Both charge 4000 to 5000 Ft for a double.

The *Erdei* motel/pension (☎ 425 458) near the city zoo at Kittenberger utca 12 is one of the cheapest places to stay in Veszprém, with rooms with shared shower for 810 Ft per person. It's open between mid-April and mid-October.

Hotel The 76-room *Vesprém Margaréta* hotel (☎ 424 876) at Budapest út 6 has the most central location, though it's not a particularly nice place to stay. Doubles (no singles) are 4400 Ft. Be sure to choose a room facing the quiet square off Kossuth Lajos utca and not noisy Budapest út.

Places to Eat
The cheapest place in town for a bite is the self-service *Mackó*, which serves up little pizzas, salads and cakes at Kossuth Lajos utca 6. The *Gourmandia* remains seriously misnamed, but it's central at Megyeház tér 2.

There are relatively few places to eat in the protected Castle Hill district, but the *Tűztorony* Chinese restaurant between the Fire Tower and Heroes' Gate at Vár utca 1 is open daily to 11 pm. Restaurants around Szabadság tér include the *Óváros* in a lovely baroque building at Szabadság tér 14 and, side by side, the *Skorpió* grill restaurant and

Boomerang Westaurant, both with steaks, on Virág Benedek utca.

The *Vadásztanya* restaurant at the Diana pension gets rave reviews from local people. If you've got a car, there's a wonderful 18th-century csárda called the *Betyár* (Outlaw) at Nemesvámos about four km south-west of Veszprém. It's on the road to Nagyvázsony and Tapolca.

The *Marica* café at Kossuth Lajos utca 5 near Szabadság tér is a decent place for cakes and a popular student hang-out.

Entertainment
The *Veszprém Cultural Centre* (☎ 429 693), headquarters of the city's symphony orchestra, is at Dózsa György utca 2. The magnificent *Petőfi Theatre* (☎ 424 064) stages both plays and concerts; tickets are available from the box office (☎ 422 440) at Szabadság tér 7. Concerts are often held in July and August in front of the *Bishop's Palace* on Szentháromság tér, which is said to have perfect acoustics, and from time to time at the *Piarist church*.

Getting There & Away
Bus Connections are excellent from Veszprém, with at least a dozen a day running to Budapest (both express and via Székesfehérvár), Herend, Sümeg, Tapolca, Pápa, Nagyvázsony, Keszthely and towns on Lake Balaton's northern shore, including Balatonfüred. Eight buses a day also run to Siófok. Other important destinations include Esztergom (three buses daily), Győr (eight), Kaposvár (two), Kecskemét (two or three), Nagykanizsa (three), Pécs (two), Sopron (three), Szeged (two), Szekszárd (two), Szombathely (two) and Zalaegerszeg (three).

Train Three railway lines meet at Veszprém. The first connects Veszprém with Szombathely and Budapest-Déli station via Székesfehérvár (up to eight a day in each direction). The second line carries up to six daily trains north to Pannonhalma and Győr, where you can transfer for Vienna. The third, south to Lepsény, links Veszprém with the railway lines on the northern and southern shore of Lake Balaton.

Getting Around

Bus Nos 1, 2 and 9 run from the train and bus stations to Szabadság tér. Bus Nos 1 and 2, which you can also board outside the Veszprém hotel, also go to the zoo and Erdei pension.

For a local taxi, ring ☎ 444 444.

AROUND VESZPRÉM
Herend
• *pop 3000*

The porcelain factory at Herend, 13 km west of Veszprém, has been producing Hungary's finest hand-painted chinaware for over a century and a half. There's not a lot to see in this dusty one-horse village, and prices at the outlet don't seem any cheaper than elsewhere in Hungary, but the **Porcelain Museum**, displaying the most prized pieces, is definitely worth a trip. It's at Kossuth Lajos utca 140, a five-minute walk from the bus station, and is open Monday to Saturday from 8.30 am to 4 pm. Labels are in four languages including English, which makes it easy to follow the developments and changes in patterns and tastes (see aside).

Across from the museum is an outlet with expensive china, and at Kossuth Lajos utca 122 the *Lila Akác* restaurant. If you're driving from Veszprém, make sure to stop for a meal at the *Udvarház* at Petőfi Sándor utca 2 in Bánd, a couple of km south-east of Herend. It's a lovely csárda with Swabian specialities.

Getting There & Away You can reach Herend by bus from Veszprém at least every 30 minutes, and six local trains run through Herend every day on their way to Ajka. Change there for Szombathely.

SZÉKESFEHÉRVÁR
• *pop 113,000*
• *area code* ☎ 22

Székesfehérvár may look like just another big city on the M7 between Budapest and Lake Balaton, 35 km to the south-west. But

---

Herend Porcelain

A terracotta factory set up at Herend in 1826 began producing porcelain 13 years later under one Mór Farkasházi Fischer of Tata in Western Transdanubia. Initially he specialised in copying and replacing the nobles' broken imports from Asia, and you'll see some pretty kooky 19th-century interpretations of Japanese art and Chinese faces on display in the museum here. But the factory soon began producing its own patterns; many, like the Rothschild bird and *petites roses*, were inspired by Meissen and Sèvres designs from Germany and France. The Victoria pattern of butterflies and wild flowers of the Bakony was designed for Queen Victoria after she admired a display of Herend pieces at the Great Exhibition in London in 1851.

To avoid bankruptcy in the 1870s, the Herend factory began mass production; tastes ran from kitschy pastoral and hunting scenes to the ever-popular animal sculptures with the distinctive scale-like triangle patterns. In 1992, the factory was purchased from the state by its 1500 workers and became one of the first companies in Hungary privatised through an employee stock-ownership plan. ■

Székesfehérvár (Stuhlweissenburg in German) is traditionally known as the place where the Magyar chieftain Árpád first set up camp, making this the oldest town in Hungary. It is the most important city in central Transdanubia and the capital of Fejér County.

Although Székesfehérvár is not on Lake Balaton, everyone travelling between Budapest and the lake passes this way so it's included here for convenience. Székesfehérvár can also be seen as a day trip from Budapest. Close to the city is Lake Velence, a much smaller and more subdued version of Balaton.

History

As early as the 1st century, the Romans had a settlement at Gorsium near Tác, 17 km to the south. When Árpád arrived late in the 9th century, the surrounding marshes and the Sárvíz River offered protection – the same reason Prince Géza built his castle here less than 100 years later. But it was Géza's son, King Stephen, who raised the status of Székesfehérvár by building a fortified basilica in what he called Alba Regia. Hungary's kings (and some of its queens) would be crowned and buried here for the next 500 years. It fact, the city's seemingly unpronounceable name ('Saykesh-fehair-vahr') means 'Seat of the White Castle', as it was the royal capital and white was the king's colour.

With Visegrád, Esztergom and Buda, Székesfehérvár served as an alternative royal capital for centuries, and it was here in 1222 that King Andrew II was forced by his *servientes* (mercenaries) to sign the *Golden Bull*, an early bill of rights (if not exactly the *Magna Carta* that Hungarian history books suggest it was). The Turks captured Székesfehérvár in 1543 and used Stephen's basilica to store gunpowder. It exploded during a siege in 1601; when the Turks left in 1688, the town, the basilica and the royal tombs were in ruins. Only the foundations of the basilica can now be seen amidst all the excavation work in the so-called Garden of Ruins.

Stephen – much less Árpád – would hardly recognise today's Székesfehérvár. The stones from his basilica were used to construct the Bishop's Palace in 1801; several decades later, the marshland was drained and the Sárvíz River diverted. The city had been at a crossroads since the 11th century, when crusaders on a budget from Western Europe passed through Székesfehérvár on their way to the Adriatic (even then Hungary was cheaper than Italy to travel through). The arrival of the railway in the 1860s turned the city into a transport hub.

In March 1945 the Germans launched their last big counteroffensive of WWII near Székesfehérvár. Though the fighting razed the city's outskirts (the historic centre was left more or less intact), it opened the way for postwar industrial development.

Orientation

Városház tér and Koronázó tér together form the core of the old town; pedestrian Fő utca runs north from here. The train station is a 15-minute walk south-east in Béke tér; reach it via József Attila utca and then Deák Ferenc utca. The bus station is in Piac tér near the market, just outside the old town's western wall.

Information

Tourinform (☎ 313 818) has an office in the town hall at Városház tér 1. Other tourist agencies represented here include: Albatours (☎ 312 494), in the Udvárház shopping centre at Kossuth Lajos utca 14/a; Ibusz (☎ 329 393), south of Koronázó tér at Vasvári Pál utca 3; and Express (☎ 312 510), a few minutes walk to the north-east at Rákóczi utca 4. All are open from 8 or 8.30 am to 4 or 4.30 pm on weekdays only.

There's an OTP bank branch with an ATM at Fő utca 7 and a foreign currency exchange machine in the entrance to the Udvárház shopping centre on Kossuth Lajos utca. The main post office is at Kossuth Lajos utca 16 near Szent István tér.

St Stephen's Cathedral

The cathedral on Géza nagyfejedelem tér at the northern end of Arany János utca was constructed in 1470 and originally dedicated to SS Peter and Paul. But what you see is essentially an 18th-century baroque church. The ceiling frescos inside were painted by Johannes Cymbal in 1768. On the paving stones in front of the cathedral are foundation outlines of an earlier (perhaps 10th-century) church. The striking wooden crucifix on the cathedral's northern wall is dedicated to the victims of the 1956 Uprising.

Just north of the cathedral is **St Anne's Chapel** built around the same time, with additions (the tower, for example) made some centuries later. The Turks used the chapel as a place of worship; you can still see the remains of a painting from that era.

Around Városház tér & Koronázó tér

Arany János utca debouches into what was until 1992 Szabadság tér but has now been given two names: Városház tér to the west and Koronázó tér to the east. The single-storey block of the **town hall** on Városház

Székesfehérvár
PLACES TO STAY
2 Magyar Király Hotel
23 Alba Regia Hotel
28 Rév Hotel
PLACES TO EAT
11 Korzó Pub
17 Ősfehérvár Restaurant
24 Főnix Restaurant
26 Faló Büfé
27 Kaiser Pub
37 McDonald's
OTHER
1 Public Swimming Pool
3 Vörösmarty Theatre
4 OTP Bank
5 King Stephen Museum (Branch)
6 King Stephen Museum
7 Cistercian Church
8 Black Eagle Pharmacy
9 Theatre Ticket Office
10 István Csók Gallery
12 Franciscan Church
13 Tourinform & Town Hall
14 St Anne's Chapel
15 St Stephen's Cathedral
16 Ibusz
18 Bishop's Palace
19 Garden of Ruins
20 Express
21 Cooptourist
22 Skála Department Store & Kaiser's Supermarket
25 Cinema
29 Royal Darts Pub
30 Post Office
31 Udvárház Shopping Centre & Albatours
32 John Bull Pub
33 Carmelite Church
34 St Stephen Monument
35 Bus Station
36 Market
To Bory Castle & Két Góbé Pension
To Railway Station
Deák Ferenc utca
Mészöly Géza utca
Zichy liget
Dózsa György utca
Berényi út
körút
Mátyás király
Szabadságharcos utca
Dr Koch László utca
Fő utca
Országzászló tér
Ady Endre utca
Mátyás király körút
Oskola
Jókai
Koronázó tér
Városház tér
Kossuth Lajos
Arany
Megyeház
János
Rákóczi utca
József Attila utca
Várkörút
Kégl György utca
Távirda utca
Petőfi utca
Budai út
Károly János utca
Prohászka Ottokár
Gyümölcs utca
Palotai út
Halász utca
Selyem utca
Piac tér
Szent István tér
0 200 400 m

tér dates from 1690; the larger northern wing was formerly the Zichy Palace built in the 18th century. Opposite is the austere **Franciscan church** (1745). The stone ball with the crown in the centre of the square is the **National Orb** (or 'apple' in Hungarian) dedicated to King Stephen. The monument that looks like a broken bell (1995) lying on its side is dedicated to the victims of WWII. Don't miss the lovely salmon-coloured Hungarian Art Nouveau house at Kossuth Lajos utca 10 to the south.

The most imposing building on Koronázó tér is the Zopf-style **Bishop's Palace** built with the rubble from the medieval basilica and royal burial chapels. They stood to the east, in what is now the **Garden of Ruins** (Romkert). The site is particularly sacred to Hungarians – some three dozen of their kings and queens were crowned and 15 buried here. The doleful-looking white-marble sarcophagus in the chamber to the right as you enter the main gate is thought to contain the remains of Géza, Stephen or his young son, Prince Imre; the frescos are early 20th century. Decorative stonework from the basilica and royal tombs lines the walls of the loggia, and in the garden are the foundations of the cathedral and the Coronation Church. Excavation of the site continues. The Garden of Ruins is open from 10 am to 6 pm from April to October, but you get to see most of it from the street.

Around Fő utca

Lying to the north of the town centre, the **Black Eagle** (Fekete Sas) at Fő utca 5 is a pharmacy set up by the Jesuits in 1758, with beautiful rococo furnishings. Across the street on the corner of Ady Endre utca is an unusual monument to the Renaissance King Matthias Corvinus, erected in 1990 to mark the 500th anniversary of his death. A few steps down Oskola utca in the bizarre cultural centre at Bartók Béla tér 1, the **István Csók Gallery** has a good collection of 19th and 20th-century Hungarian art.

The **King Stephen Museum** (István Király Múzeum) at Fő utca 6 has a large collection of Roman pottery (some of it from Gorsium), an interesting folk-carving display and an exhibit covering 1000 years of Székesfehérvár history. The museum's branch at Országzászló tér 3 has temporary exhibits.

Bory Castle

Bory Vár, to the north-east of the city centre at Máriavölgy utca 54, is the weirdest sight in Székesfehérvár. It's a neo-Gothic/Romanesque/Scottish-style castle built over a period of 40 years by an obsessed sculptor and architect called Jenő Bory (1879-1959) as a virtual shrine to his wife, Ilona Komócsin. She's in the paintings on the walls, the statues in the gardens and is the subject of poems inscribed on marble tablets. The castle's towers, courtyard and gardens are open every day from 9 am to 5 pm from March to November, but visitors are only allowed into the art studio and other rooms at weekends from 10 am to noon and 3 to 5 pm.

Places to Stay

Private Rooms & Hostels Express may know about accommodation in college dormitories in July and August. Private rooms are available from Albatours and Ibusz.

Pension The *Két Góbé* (☎ 327 578) is a 23-room pension at Gugásvölgyi út 4 northeast of the city centre. Facing busy route No 8, it's noisy, but the price is right: from 2000 Ft for a double.

Hotels The 63-room *Rév* hotel (☎ 327 015), József Attila utca 42, is a workers' residence that also accepts tourists. Here you pay 1500 Ft for a spartan but clean single or double with washbasin and 1700 Ft for a triple. Showers and toilets are down the hall.

If you're feeling flush, the 150-year-old *Magyar Király* hotel (☎ 311 262), Fő utca 10, has 58 rooms with baths at 5400/5800 Ft for a single/double.

The *Alba Regia* (☎ 313 484), a stone's throw from the Garden of Ruins at Rákóczi utca 1, is a modern, multistorey hotel with 104 rooms and expensive outlets. Singles/doubles start at 7600/8000 Ft.

Places to Eat

The *Faló Büfé* at Távírda utca 19 south-east of the Alba Regia hotel is a cheap place to eat. *McDonald's* has an outlet on Piac tér across from the market.

The *Korzó* pub on Fő utca is a decent place for breakfast or dinner. Also good (and surprisingly cheap) is the *Ősfehérvár* restaurant (closed Sunday) on Koronázó tér, opposite the Garden of Ruins. The *Főnix* in the small Ferenc shopping mall at Távírda utca 15 has decent salads. The *Kaiser* at Távírda utca 14 is a good place for a pub lunch or pizza.

The wine to try in these parts is Ezerjó (literally 'a thousand good things') from Mór, 27 km to the north-west in the Vértes Hills. It's a sweet, greenish-white tipple that is light and fairly pleasant.

Entertainment

You can buy tickets to cultural performances at the *Vörösmarty Theatre*, next to the Magyar Király hotel, from the box office at Fő utca 3. It's open weekdays from 9 am to 6 pm.

The *Kaiser* pub on Távírda utca is always a good place for a drink (it has a couple of pool tables in an adjoining room) as is the *Royal Darts* at Budai út 18, a student hangout not far from the Rév hotel. There's a *casino* in the Magyar Király hotel. The *John Bull* chain has opened one of its cookie-cutter pubs at Petőfi utca 14. Ask Tourinform about the new location of the *Bahnhof*, the city's hottest disco.

Getting There & Away

Bus The bus service to/from Székesfehérvár is excellent. Buses depart for Budapest's Erzsébet tér station, Veszprém and the vineyards near Mór at least once every 30 minutes, and you can reach Lake Velence towns like Pákozd, Sukoró, Velence and Gárdony (via Agárd) frequently throughout the day.

Other destinations include Baja (two buses daily), Balatonfüred (five), Esztergom (two), Győr (eight), Hévíz (four), Kalocsa (two), Kecskemét (four), Kaposvár (two), Keszthely (one), Pécs (two), Siófok (seven), Sopron (two), Sümeg (five), Szeged (five), Szekszárd (five), Tapolca (four), Tata (two) and Zalaegerszeg (two).

Train Székesfehérvár is an important rail junction, and you can reach most destinations in Transdanubia from here. One line splits at Szabadbattyán some 10 km to the south, leading to Lake Balaton's northern shore and Tapolca in one direction and to the southern shore and Nagykanizsa in the other. Trains every half-hour link Székesfehérvár with Budapest-Déli; another eight a day run to Szombathely via Veszprém. A local train runs north six to nine times a day to Mór and Komárom, where you cross over to Slovakia.

Getting Around

Bus No 26/a will take you from the bus station to Bory Castle. Local taxis can be ordered on ☎ 333 333/343 343.

AROUND SZÉKESFEHÉRVÁR
Lake Velence

If you don't have the time (or inclination) to visit Lake Balaton, you might make an excursion by bus or train to Velence, a 26-sq-km lake about 10 km east of Székesfehérvár. The surrounding countryside is hilly and quite pretty, the lake shallow and warm and it's a great place for boating and windsurfing. Cartographia's 1:20,000 *A Velencei-tó és környékének* (No 19; Velence Lake and Surrounds) is the map to buy if you're serious about hiking here.

As at Lake Balaton, the southern shore of Lake Velence is more developed, especially around the towns of Gárdony and Agárd, where there is a slew of hotels and other accommodation. Places like Pákozd and Sukoró in the north don't get much business: they are cut off from Velence by the busy M7. The south-western edge is a reedy protected area that attracts waterfowl in summer and autumn. Perhaps the best choice is the town of Velence at the lake's north-eastern end.

Places to Stay & Eat There are a half-dozen camp sites in Velence including the huge *Panoráma* (☎ 472 043) at the northern end of the town. It has no bungalows, but there are canoes, bikes and windsurfing equipment for rent. It's open from mid-April to mid-October.

There are lots of 'Zimmer frei' signs on Tópart utca, which runs north along the lake from Velence town's train and bus stations, and Albatours in Székesfehérvár can book you cottages for up to four people for about 4000 Ft.

The *Helios* hotel (☎ 472 941) at Tópart utca 34 has 15 rooms and charges 3500 to 5500 Ft for singles, 5500 to 7500 Ft for doubles. Its sister hotel, the modern *Juventus* (☎ 472 159) at No 6/a, has 35 rooms and is closer to the water. Singles there are 4500 to 6500 Ft and doubles 7000 to 8500 Ft, depending on the season.

The shocking pink *Lidó* restaurant, across the tracks at Balatoni út 2 and facing route No 70, is fine for a casual meal, but if you're looking for something a bit more up-market, try the *Vitorlás* restaurant at the Juventus hotel. Should you make it across the lake to Sukoró, there's a nice little csárda called the

Boglya at Fő utca 31. Just bring plenty of insect repellent.

MARTONVÁSÁR
• *pop 4300*

Lying almost exactly halfway between Székesfehérvár and Budapest and easily accessible by train, Martonvásár is the site of **Brunswick Mansion**, one of the loveliest summertime concert venues in Hungary. The mansion was built in 1775 for Count Antal Brunswick (or Brunszvik), patriarch of a family of liberal reformers and patrons of the arts (Teréz Brunszvik established Hungary's first nursery school in Pest in 1828).

Beethoven was a frequent visitor to the manse, and it is believed that Jozefin, Teréz's sister, was the inspiration behind the *Appassionata* and *Moonlight* sonatas, which the great Ludwig van composed here.

Brunswick Mansion, which was rebuilt in neo-Gothic style in 1875 and restored to its ivory and sky-blue glory a century later, now houses the Agricultural Research Institute of the Academy of Sciences. But you can see at least part of the mansion by visiting the small **Beethoven Museum** to the left of the main entrance. It is open Tuesday to Friday from 10 am to noon and 2 to 4 pm (from 10 am to 4 pm at weekends from mid-April to mid-October).

A walk around the grounds – one of Hungary's first 'English parks' to be laid out when these were all the rage in the early 19th century – is a pleasant way to spend a warm summer's afternoon. It's open every day from 8 am to 4 pm. Concerts are held on the small island in the middle of the lake (reached by a wooden footbridge) during the Martonvásár Summer festival from May to October. The climax is the 10-day Martonvásár Days festival in late July. For information contact Tourinform in Székesfehérvár.

The baroque **Catholic church**, attached to the mansion but accessible from outside the grounds, has frescos by Johannes Cymbal. There's also a small **Nursery Museum** in the park.

Places to Stay & Eat
The six-room *Macska* (Cat) pension (☎ 460 127) at Budai út 21, with singles/doubles for 2000/4000 Ft, is crawling with felines – definitely not the place for hyperallergenics. The Macska's restaurant serves the standard Hungarian csárda dishes and has a good wine cellar. The *Postakocsi* restaurant at Fehérvári utca 1 is a convenient place for lunch.

Getting There & Away
Dozens of trains between Budapest-Déli and Székesfehérvár stop at Martonvásár every day and, if you attend a concert, you can easily make your way back to Velence town and Székesfehérvár or on to Budapest on the last trains (11.18 pm and 11.32 pm respectively). The station is a 10-minute walk along Brunszvik utca, north-west of the main entrance to the mansion.

Southern Transdanubia

Southern Transdanubia (Déli Dunántúl) is bordered by the Danube to the east, the Dráva River and Croatia to the south and west, and Lake Balaton to the north. It is generally flatter than Western and Central Transdanubia, with the Mecsek and Villány hills rising in isolation from the plain, and is considerably wetter. The rains are heavy in the Zala Hills north-west of Nagykanizsa, and the Kapos, Sió, Rinya and Zala rivers crisscross the region from all directions.

Although there are some large towns here, Southern Transdanubia is not nearly as important industrially as Western Transdanubia. In general it is thickly settled with villages, mostly small in population. Agriculture is still the mainstay – from the fruit orchards of the Zselic region south of Kaposvár and the almonds of Pécs to the wines of Szekszárd and the Villány-Siklós region. The pleasant, almost Mediterranean climate helps: spring arrives early, summer is long, winter is mild.

Southern Transdanubia was settled by the Celts and then the Romans, who built important towns at Alisca (Szekszárd) and Sophianae (Pécs) and introduced grape-growing. The north-south trade route passed through here, and many of the settlements prospered during the Middle Ages.

The region was a focal point of the Turkish occupation. The battle that led to the Ottoman domination of Hungary for more than a century and a half was fought at Mohács in 1526, and one of the most heroic stands taken by the Hungarians against the invaders took place at Szigetvár some 40 years later. Pécs was an important political and cultural centre under the Turks.

Late in the 17th century, the abandoned towns of Southern Transdanubia were resettled by Swabian Germans and Southern Slavs, and after WWII ethnic Hungarians came from Slovakia and Bukovina in Romania as did Saxon Germans. They left a mark that can still be seen today in local architecture,

HIGHLIGHTS

- the Zsolnay and Csontváry museums and the old synagogue in Pécs
- the wines of Villány
- a ride on the narrow-gauge train through the Gemenc Forest in the Sárköz region
- the Castle Museum's collection of gloves, fans and umbrellas at Siklós
- a performance at Kaposvár's splendid Gergely Csiky Theatre
- the outdoor folk village museum at Szenna

food and certain traditions. Also, the isolation of areas like the Sárköz near Szekszárd and the Ormánság region south of Szigetvár helped preserve some folk customs.

This part of Transdanubia has a lot to offer travellers – from the art museums of Pécs and the castles of Siklós and Szigetvár to the thermal spas of Harkány and Zalakaros. Driving through the countryside is like stepping back in time: whitewashed farmhouses with thatched roofs and long colonnaded porticoes decorated with floral patterns and plaster work haven't changed in centuries.

SZEKSZÁRD

- *pop 38,000*
- *area code ☎ 74*

The wine-producing city of Szekszárd lies south of the Sió River, which links Lake

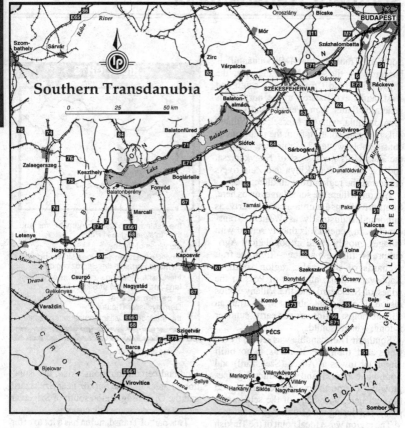

Balaton with the Danube, among seven of the Szekszárd Hills. It is the capital of Tolna County and the centre of the Sárköz folk region, but more than anything else Szekszárd is the gateway to Southern Transdanubia. In fact, you can actually see the region start in the town's main square (Garay tér), where the Great Plain, having crossed the Danube, rises slowly, transforming into the Szekszárd Hills. The Tolna, Mecsek and Somogy hills follow to the west and southwest.

Szekszárd was a Celtic and later a Roman settlement called Alisca. The sixth Hungarian king, Béla I, conferred royal status on Szekszárd and founded a Benedictine abbey here in 1061, the third-largest after the ones at Tihany and Pécsvárad.

The Turkish occupation left Szekszárd deserted and in ruins, but the area was repopulated late in the 17th century by immigrant Swabians from Germany, and the economy was revitalised in the next century by wheat cultivation and viticulture.

Mild winters and warm, dry summers combined with favourable soil help Szekszárd produce some of the best red wines in Hungary. The premier grape is the Kadarka,

STEVE FALLON

BERTHOLD DAUM

Top: Riding stables, Máta, near Hortobágy, Great Plain
Bottom: Costumed *csikósok* (cowboys) on Nonius steeds

STEVE FALLON

STEVE FALLON

Top: Hollókő Castle, Hollókő, Northern Uplands
Bottom: Minorite Church, Eger, Northern Uplands

a late-ripening and vulnerable varietal that is produced in limited quantities. Franz Schubert is said to have been inspired to write his *Trout Quintet* after a glass or two, and Franz Liszt, a frequent visitor to Szekszárd in the 1840s, preferred to 'drink it until his death' some 40 years later. Sadly, today you're more likely to be offered Kékfrankos or Óvörös, drinkable but vastly inferior wines, though Kadarka is sometimes used as a blend in locally produced Bikavér (bull's blood).

Orientation

The bus and train stations are side by side on Pollack Mihály utca. From here, follow pedestrian Bajcsy-Zsilinszky utca west through the park to the city centre. Garay tér ascends to the old castle district, today's Béla tér. Munkácsy Mihály utca runs south-west from Béla tér to Kálvária utca and Calvary Hill.

Information

Both Tolna Tourist (☎ 312 144) at Széchenyi utca 38 and Ibusz (☎ 319 822) at Arany János utca 6 are open on weekdays from 8 am to 4.30 pm and on Saturday to noon. Express (☎ 312 934) and Coop-tourist (☎ 316 323) are at Kölcsey lakótelep 1, in a housing and shopping complex north of the modern cultural centre.

There's an OTP bank at Mártírok tere 5-7 and a K&H bank opposite at Széchenyi utca 34. The main post office is at Széchenyi utca 11-13.

Things to See

You can get a good overview of Szekszárd by following Kálvária utca from outside the Alisca hotel and up the grassy steps to 205m **Calvary Hill**. The hill's name recalls the crucifixion scene and chapel erected here by grief-stricken parents who had lost their son in the 18th century (still remembered thanks to a famous poem by Mihály Babits, a son of Szekszárd). The Danube and the Great Plain are visible to the east, the Sárköz region beyond the hills to the south, the Szekszárd

Hills to the west and, on a clear day, you can just see the nuclear power station at Paks, 30 km to the north.

The hill itself is dominated by another sculpture, done by István Kiss for the city's 925th anniversary. On the surface it looked fine when unveiled in 1986 – a modernistic bunch of grapes representing Szekszárd's wine, sheaves for its wheat and a large bell for Béla's 11th-century abbey. But on closer inspection, the inscriptions on the grape leaves revealed not just the names of Hungarian heroes and literary greats but those of local Communist officials. The townspeople were not amused, though the monument and some of the leaves in question remain.

The little village – the so-called Upper Town (Felsőváros) – in the valley to the west is full of vineyards, private cellars and free-range chickens; it's about 100 years away from Garay tér. Walk along Remete utca to **Remete Chapel** (1778) at the end, an important pilgrimage site on any day connected with the Virgin Mary (but especially on her birthday, 8 September), and return via Bocskai utca to the north of Szekszárd Stream.

The neoclassical **old county hall** in Béla tér, designed by Mihály Pollack in 1828, sits on the site of Béla's abbey and an earlier Christian chapel. You can see the excavated foundations in the central courtyard. On the upper floor of the building, there is the **Franz Liszt Exhibition** and across the hall the **Eszter Mattioni Gallery**, whose works in striking mosaics of marble, glass and mother-of-pearl invoke peasant themes with a twist. The cellar houses the **Wine Museum** (open daily from 11 am to 7 pm), an unimpressive collection of ancient wine growers' tools and 16th-century quotations ('We bury sorrow deep when we drink wine'). Still, you can enjoy a glass of local plonk at the bar here, and the woodcuts of medieval drunken bashes are amusing. The square's baroque yellow **Inner City Catholic Church** (1805) is the largest single-nave church in Hungary.

The **Mór Wosinszky Museum** at Mártírok tere 26 was purpose-built in 1895 and is now named after a local priest and

SOUTHERN TRANSDANUBIA

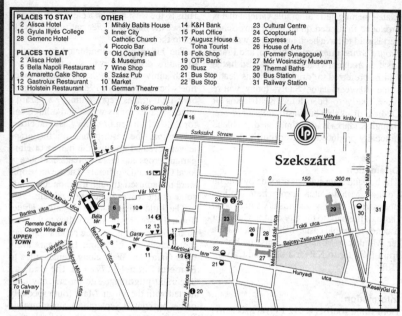

PLACES TO STAY
2 Alisca Hotel
16 Gyula Illyés College
28 Gemenc Hotel

PLACES TO EAT
2 Alisca Hotel
5 Bella Napoli Restaurant
9 Amaretto Cake Shop
12 Gastrolux Restaurant
13 Holstein Restaurant

OTHER
1 Mihály Babits House
3 Inner City
   Catholic Church
4 Piccolo Bar
6 Old County Hall
   & Museums
7 Wine Shop
8 Szász Pub
10 Market
11 German Theatre

14 K&H Bank
15 Post Office
17 Augusz House &
   Tolna Tourist
18 Folk Shop
19 OTP Bank
20 Ibusz
21 Bus Stop
22 Bus Stop

23 Cultural Centre
24 Cooptourist
25 Express
26 House of Arts
   (Former Synagogue)
27 Mór Wosinszky Museum
29 Thermal Baths
30 Bus Station
31 Railway Station

archaeologist who discovered the remains of a Neolithic culture at the town of Lengyel to the north-west. The finds, artefacts left by various peoples who passed through the Danube Basin ahead of the Magyars, are among the best anywhere (don't miss the fine Celtic and Avar jewellery), as is the large folk collection of Serbian, Swabian and Sárköz artefacts. Three period rooms – that of a well-to-do Sárköz farming family and their coveted spotted-poplar furniture, another from the estate of the aristocratic Apponyi family of Lengyel (who contributed generously to the museum), and a poor gooseherd's hut – illustrate very clearly the different economic brackets that existed side by side in the region a century ago. Also interesting are the exhibits relating to the silk factory that was started in Szekszárd in the 19th century with Italian help and employed so many of the region's young women.

The Moorish flourishes of the **House of Arts** next door at Mártírok tere 20 reveal its former life as a synagogue. It is now used as a gallery and concert hall. Four of its original iron pillars have been brought outside and enclosed in an arch, suggesting a tablet, and there's a striking 'tree of life' monument nearby to the 'heroes and victims of WWII'.

Liszt performed several times at the eye-catching, chocolate-coloured **Augusz House** at Széchenyi utca 36-40; today it houses a music school and Tolna Tourist.

Szekszárd produced two of Hungary's most celebrated poets: Mihály Babits (1883-1941) and the lesser-known János Garay. Babits' birthplace at Babits Mihály utca 13 has become the **Mihály Babits Memorial House** and, while the poet's avant-garde, deeply philosophical verse may be obscure even in Hungarian, it's a good chance to see how a middle-class family lived in 19th-century provincial Hungary.

There's a large **market** in Piac tér along Vár köz just down the steps from Béla tér.

Activities

The covered thermal baths and outdoor pools are near the train and bus stations at Toldi utca 6. The pools are open daily from 9 am to 5 pm in summer; the baths from 6 am to 8 pm (2 to 8 pm on Monday) all year.

The centre for horse riding in Tolna County is really Tamási, 50 km to the north-west on the way to Siófok; contact the Lov-Ker Riding School (☎ 471 339) there at Dózsa György út 96. The Gemenc forest, however, is closer (see the following Around Szekszárd section). To book a sightseeing flight over the city and Gemenc, contact Agro Air (☎ 319 303), Rákóczi utca 132, or Tolna Tourist.

Special Events

Among the big events staged annually in Szekszárd are the Raven Days Contemporary Arts Festival in spring, choral gatherings in May and September, the Alisca Wine Days in mid-June and the Danube Folklore Festival, held in conjunction with Tolna and Baja in July.

Places to Stay

Accommodation in Szekszárd is limited. Sió Camping (☎ 312 458), about five km north of the city centre on Rákóczi utca near route No 6, has an 18-room motel (open from April to October) with bathless doubles costing 1240 Ft. The 20 yurt-like wooden 'apartments' for four to six people, available all year, are 4360 Ft. There's a 24-hour grocery store and csárda near the entrance.

There may be dormitory rooms available in summer at the Gyula Illyés College (☎ 412 133), Mátyás király utca 3, and both Tolna Tourist and Ibusz have private rooms available for around 1000 Ft per person.

The 19-room Alisca hotel (☎ 312 228) at Kálvária utca 1 has singles/doubles/triples with bath for 5520/7360/9669 Ft. It's a pleasant place up in the hills, with almost a country feel, but a bit far from what little action there is.

The modern 87-room Gemenc hotel (☎ 311 722) at Mészáros Lázár utca 1 has all the usual outlets and facilities; singles/

doubles are DM60/80. It's an ugly block but central to everything.

Places to Eat

The Gastrolux on Garay tér and the Holstein next door at Széchenyi utca 29-31 have similar menus, but the former is cheaper. Both stay open till midnight. The Bella Napoli in a small shopping centre on Szent László utca is decent for pasta and pizzas.

The restaurant at the Alisca hotel has a lovely outside terrace open in the warmer months, with views of the city. The Sió Csárda is convenient to the camping ground and a favourite stop with truckers.

Try the ice cream at the Amaretto cake shop at Garay tér 6; it's the best in town.

Entertainment

The modern Mihály Babits Cultural Centre (☎ 316 722), next to the old synagogue at Mártírok tere 10, has information about concerts and other cultural events taking place in the former county hall courtyard, the New City Church on Pazmány tér and the House of Arts.

Unlike the wine-producing towns of Eger, Tokaj and even little Villány, Szekszárd has few places in which to sample the local vintage. The Wine Museum closes at 7 pm, but you might try the Csurgó at Kápolna tér 12 in Felsőváros – the closest bar to the vineyards.

For a quiet drink, choose the Piccolo on Fürdőház utca 3 or, better yet, the Szász (Saxon) beer hall at Garay tér 20. A short distance to the east is the Deutsche Bühne or Német Színház in Hungarian), a German theatre dating from early this century and still in use.

Things to Buy

The Wine Museum has an outlet on Garay tér, opposite the Szász pub, with some of Szekszárd's best wines. For pottery, try the gift shop at the Folk Art House in Decs (see the following section on the Sárköz Region), though you probably won't find any examples of the unique írókázás fazékok, the inscribed pots made usually as wedding gifts. It also sells weavings and some embroidery. The folk-art shop in the complex at Augusz Imre utca 13 also sells some handmade Sárköz articles.

Getting There & Away

Bus The bus service to/from Szekszárd is good. There are a dozen or more daily departures to Budapest, Baja, Dombóvár, Paks and Pécs, and more than six buses leave every day for Decs, Tamási, Siófok, Mohács and Harkány (via Pécs). From Szekszárd you can also reach Székesfehérvár (four buses a day), Kaposvár (three), Szeged (three), Győr (two) and Veszprém (four). Many of these buses can be boarded on Mártírok tere south of the cultural centre.

Buses bound for Keselyűs (six to eight a day) will drop you off near the Gemenc Excursion Centre in Bárányfok.

Train Only four direct trains leave Budapest-Déli station every day for Szekszárd. Otherwise, take the Pécs-bound train from the same station and change at Sárbogárd. To travel east (eg to Baja), west (to Kaposvár) or south (to Pécs), you must change trains at Bátaszék, 20 km to the south. Ócsény and Decs, four and eight km to the south respectively, are on this line.

Getting Around

Bus No 1 goes from the stations through the centre of town to Béla tér and then on to the Upper Town as far as Remete Chapel. For the camp site and motel north of town, take bus No 11.

Local taxis can be ordered on ☎ 316 033/ 411 111.

AROUND SZEKSZÁRD
The Gemenc Forest

The Gemenc, a protected 20,000-hectare flood forest of poplars and willows 12 km east of Szekszárd, was the favourite hunting ground of former Communist leaders including the late János Kádár, who shot 'whatever and whenever he chose', as they say here. Until engineers removed some 60 curves in the Danube in the mid-19th century, the

Gemenc would flood to such a degree that the women of the Sárköz region would come to the market in Szekszárd by boat.

Today the backwaters, lakes and ponds beyond the earthen dams, which were built by wealthy landowners to protect their farms, offer sanctuary to deer, boar, black storks, herons and woodpeckers. Hunting is restricted to certain areas, and you can visit the forest all year, but not on foot. In fact, there are almost no trails in this wilderness.

The main entrance is at the **Gemenc Excursion Centre** in Bárányfok, about halfway down Keselyűsi út between Szekszárd and the forest. Keselyűsi út was once the longest stretch of covered highway in the Austro-Hungarian Empire, and in the late 19th century mulberry trees were planted along it to feed the worms at the silk factory in Szekszárd. At the centre you can choose from one of three modes of transport allowed in the forest: narrow-gauge train, horse or pleasure boat. There's an information office (☎ 312 552) at the centre open daily from 10 am to 5 pm.

The **narrow-gauge train**, which once carried wood out of the forest, is the most fun – and difficult – way to go. It sometimes runs from Bárányfok to Pörböly some 30 km to the south (see the Around Baja section in the Great Plain chapter), but often covers just the seven-km stretch to Lassi before turning around. Trains depart at 10.30 am daily and also at 4 pm on Saturday and Sunday and cost 240/160 Ft for adults/children. The abridged trip in itself is worthwhile, weaving and looping around the Danube's remaining bends, but make sure you double-check the times with Tolna Tourist in Szekszárd or with the train station at Pörböly (☎ 491 483) before you set out.

Boats usually sail along the Sió River from the excursion centre to the Danube and back four times a day (at 10 am, noon and 2 and 4 pm) from late July through August. Horses as well as carriages for riding along the earthen dams can be hired at the riding school next to the **Trophy Museum**, an ornate wooden hall built without a nail for Archduke Franz Ferdinand to house his hunting trophies 100 years ago. It was exhibited at the 1896 Millenary Exhibition in Budapest and is now in its fourth location – most recently reassembled from Mártírok tere in Szekszárd by Polish labourers who (this is not a Polish joke) foolishly used nails. It's a museum of weapons, dead fauna and furniture made of spotted poplar, an indigenous golden-hued wood. The *Trófea* is a csárda-style restaurant near the entrance to the centre and opens daily till 10 pm. See the Szekszárd Getting There & Away section for information on transport.

Sárköz Region

The folkloric region of Sárköz, consisting of five towns south-east of Szekszárd between route No 56 and the Danube, is the centre of folk weaving in Hungary. **Őcsény** is the largest town but, for the visitor, the most interesting is **Decs**, with its high-walled cottages, late-Gothic Calvinist church and folk houses.

The Sárköz became a very rich area after flooding was brought under control. In a bid to protect their wealth and land, most families limited themselves to one child and, judging from the displays at the **Gemenc Folk Art House** at Kossuth utca 34-36 in Decs, they spent a lot of their money on lavish interior decoration and some of the most ornate (and Balkan-looking) embroidered folk clothing in Hungary. Other items on display here include native pottery (most often coloured brown and decorated with birds), the distinctive black and red striped woven fabric even used as mosquito netting, and an ingenious porcelain 'stove with eyes' (concave circles) to radiate more heat. The house was built in 1836 of earth and woven twigs so that when the floods came only the mud had to be replaced. The museum is open from 9 am to 4 pm every day except Monday.

The *Göründ Presszó* on the museum grounds, which serves drinks, sandwiches and snacks, closes at 10 pm. The church nearby has inscriptions dating from 1516. In August mock Sárköz-style weddings are staged at the Village House on Ady Endre

utca. See the Szekszárd Getting There & Away section for information on transport.

MOHÁCS
- *pop 21,000*
- *area code ☎ 69*

The defeat of the Hungarian army by the Turks here in 1526 was a watershed in the nation's history. With it came partition and foreign domination that would last almost five centuries. It is not hyperbole to say that the effects of the battle at Mohács can still be felt in Hungary today.

Mohács is a sleepy little port on the Danube that wakes up only during the annual Busójárás festival, a pre-Lenten free-for-all late in February or March. The town is also a convenient gateway to Croatia and the beaches of the Adriatic, with the border crossing at Udvar 11 km to the south now open round the clock.

Orientation

The centre of Mohács lies on the west bank of the Danube; residential New Mohács (Újmohács) is on the opposite side. Szabadság utca, the main street, runs west from the river, beginning and ending with large war memorials in dubious condition.

The bus station is on Rákóczi utca, south of leafy Deák tér. Catch trains about 1.5 km north of the city centre near the Strandfürdő at the end of Bajcsy-Zsilinszky utca.

Information

Mecsek Tours (☎ 311 961) is at Szentháromság tér 2, and is open from 8 am to 4.30 pm on weekdays, till noon on Saturday. Ibusz (☎ 311 531) is at Szabadság utca 3 and keeps the same weekday hours.

You'll find an OTP bank branch across from the former Korona hotel at Jókai Mór utca 1 and a K&H bank on the corner of Szabadság utca and Rákóczi utca. The post office is in the southern wing of the town hall at Széchenyi tér 2.

Mohács Battle Historical Site

This memorial, west of route No 56 at

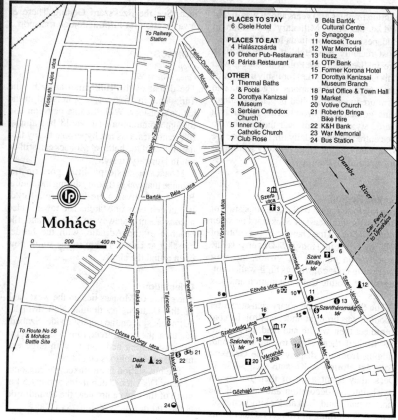

PLACES TO STAY
6 Csele Hotel

PLACES TO EAT
4 Halászcsárda
10 Dreher Pub-Restaurant
16 Párizs Restaurant

OTHER
1 Thermal Baths
  & Pools
2 Dorottya Kanizsai
  Museum
3 Serbian Orthodox
  Church
5 Inner City
  Catholic Church
7 Club Rose
8 Béla Bartók
  Cultural Centre
9 Synagogue
11 Mecsek Tours
12 War Memorial
13 Ibusz
14 OTP Bank
15 Former Korona Hotel
17 Dorottya Kanizsai
   Museum Branch
18 Post Office & Town Hall
19 Market
20 Votive Church
21 Roberto Bringa
   Bike Hire
22 K&H Bank
23 War Memorial
24 Bus Station

Mohács

Sátorhely (literally 'encampment') about six
km south-west of Mohács, was opened in
1976 to mark the 450th anniversary of the
battle. It's a fitting memorial to the dead:
over 100 carved wooden markers in the
shape of bows, arrows, lances and heads lean
this way and that over a common grave that
was only discovered in the early 1970s.
Above the entrance, a carved sign proclaims:
'Here began the deterioration of a strong
Hungary.' The memorial is open April to
October from 8 or 9 am to 5 pm. Avoid
visiting on 29 August, the day the battle took
place.

Dorottya Kanizsai Museum

This museum, named after the heroic noble-
woman from Siklós who presided over the
burial of the dead after the battle at Mohács,
has two branches. A small one at Szerb utca
2 next to the Serbian Orthodox church is
devoted entirely to the 1526 battle and is a
well balanced exhibit, with both the Turks
and the Hungarians getting the chance to tell
their side of the story. Follow the displays
with a typed explanation in English available
at the entrance.

The museum's other branch, behind the
town hall at Városház utca 1, has a large

collection of costumes worn by the Sokác, Slovenes, Serbs, Croats, Bosnians and Swabians who repopulated this devastated area in the 17th century. (You only need to look at the public notices in Hungarian, German and Serbo-Croatian in the Moorish town hall on Széchenyi tér to realise how heterogeneous the local population still is.) The distinctive (and, to some, ugly) grey-black pottery of Mohács and the various devil's or ram's-head masks worn at the Busójárás carnival are also on display. The museums are open daily except Monday from 10 am to 4 or 5 pm with an hour lunch break at the weekend.

Other Things to See
The city's other sights amount to a handful of churches. The Byzantine-style **Votive Church** on Széchenyi tér was erected in 1926 for the 400th anniversary of the battle and looks not unlike a mosque. It has some contemporary frescos of the event and unusual modern stained-glass windows in its large dome, but otherwise it's unremarkable – even sterile.

The pulpit in the baroque **Inner City Catholic Church** (1776) near the Csele hotel on Szent Mihály tér is interesting, and from here it's a short walk north up Szentháromság utca to the **Orthodox church** (1732), which until WWI served a very large local congregation of Serbs. The church's icons and ceiling frescos date from the 18th century, as the priest-guide-turnkey will explain.

In the courtyard of the old **synagogue** at Eötvös utca 1, a large monument featuring stars of David, menorahs and tablets honours the Jewish victims of fascism.

The **market** is in a courtyard just west of Jókai Mór utca.

Activities
The ferry company (☎ 322 228) near the Csele hotel offers boat excursions on the Danube, and there's a beach and swimming pools at the Strandfürdő north of the city centre on Indóház utca near the train station.

You can rent horses at the Schmidt gödör riding school, on the road to the battle memo-

rial, for 300 Ft an hour. Another place with horses is Geihauer school at Liszt Ferenc utca 2/c.

Bicycles are available for hire from a shop called Roberto Bringa at Szabadság utca 23.

Special Events
The Busójárás festival on the last Sunday before Lent is one of the rare times when Hungarians go wild in public. Originally a South Slav spring rite, the festival is now a fancy-dress mummery directed at the erstwhile enemy, the Turks. Thus the horrifying masks and blazing torches...

Places to Stay
There's not much choice in the way of accommodation in Mohács now that the old Korona hotel on Jókai Mór utca 2 has closed. See Mecsek Tours or Ibusz about *private rooms* or head for the only hotel in town: the modern, 49-room *Csele* (☎ 311 825) on the river at Szent Mihály tér 6-7. Singles here are DM67 to DM75, doubles DM75 to DM85, depending on the season. All rooms have bath; choose one of the riverside ones with a balcony on the 2nd floor.

Places to Eat
The *Dreher* pub-restaurant at Szentháromság utca 7 is a cheap place for a meal and stays open till 11 pm. The *Párizs*, an ordinary Hungarian restaurant at Szabadság utca 20, stands out only for its night-time music. Try the more up-market *Halászcsárda* next to the Csele hotel at Szent Mihály tér 5. It has a beautiful terrace overlooking the Danube, Gypsy music some nights and a dozen different fish dishes on the menu.

Entertainment
Staff at the *Béla Bartók Cultural Centre* (☎ 311 828) at Vörösmarty utca 3 north of Széchenyi tér can tell you what's on offer in Mohács.

The *Club Rose*, around the corner from the Dreher pub on Eötvös utca, is one of the very few late-night spots in town.

Getting There & Away

At least a dozen buses head for Pécs every day, and there are frequent departures to Villány, Siklós, the spa at Harkány and Bátaszék. Other destinations include: Baja (up to 10 buses a day), Békéscsaba (one), Budapest (three), Kaposvár (one), Kalocsa (one at the weekend), Kecskemét via Baja (two), Szeged (eight), Szekszárd (six) and Székesfehérvár (one).

Mohács is linked by rail with Villány and Pécs (seven departures a day), but to get anywhere else, the bus is the best – indeed, often the only – option.

Getting Around

Buses headed for the towns of Nagynyárád (five a day), Majs (12), Lippó (eight), Bezedek and Magyarbóly (six apiece) will let you off at the Mohács Battle Historical Site.

A year-round car ferry links Szent Mihály tér south of the Csele hotel with residential New Mohács – and the start of the Great Plain – across the Danube to the east. The trip takes only a few minutes.

Local taxis can be ordered on ☎ 322 323.

SIKLÓS

• *pop 11,000*
• *area code* ☎ 72

Until very recently, the medieval fortress in Siklós, Hungary's southernmost town, was the longest continuously inhabited castle in the country. But Siklós hardly needs superlatives to delight. Protected from the north, east and west by the Villány Hills, Siklós has been making wine since the Romans settled here at a place they called Seres. Siklós is also close to Villány (in competition with Szekszárd for producing Hungary's best red wines) and the spa centre at Harkány.

Orientation & Information

The town centre of Siklós runs from the bus station on Szent István tér along Felszabadulás utca – a pre-1989 name meaning 'Liberation Street' – to Kossuth tér. Siklós Castle stands watch over the town from the hill to the west. The main train station is

north-east of Kossuth tér at the end of Táncsics Mihály utca. The town's other train station, Siklósi-szőlők, north-west of the centre on the road to Máriagyűd, is more convenient to the bus station.

Mecsek Tours (☎ 479 399) has an office near the bus station at Felszabadulás utca 63. There's an OTP bank branch at Felszabadulás utca 42 and a K&H bank at No 46-48 of the same street. The post office is at Flórián tér 1.

Siklós Castle

Though the original foundations of Siklós Castle date from the mid-13th century, what you see when you look up from the town is an 18th-century baroque palace girdled by 15th-century walls and bastions. The castle has changed hands many times since it was built by the Siklósi family. Its most famous occupant was the reformer Count Kázmér Batthyány (1807-54), among the first of the nobility to free his serfs. He joined the independence struggle of 1848 and was named foreign minister by Lajos Kossuth at Debrecen.

Walk to the castle either from Kossuth tér via Batthyány Kázmér utca or up Váralja from Szent István tér near the bus station. The drawbridge leads to the entrance at the barbican, which is topped with loopholes and a circular lookout. You can also explore the castle and enjoy some fine views of the Villány Hills from along the promenade linking the four mostly derelict towers.

The three-storey palace in the central courtyard housed a hotel and a hostel in three of its wings until 1993; the **Castle Museum** is in the south wing. To the right as you enter the main door is an unusual exhibit devoted to the manufacture and changing styles of gloves, fans and umbrellas since the Middle Ages, with much emphasis on the Hamerli and Hunor factories at Pécs, which produced some of Europe's finest kid gloves in the 19th century. The **cellar** contains barely recognisable stone fragments from Roman, Gothic and Renaissance times. Most of the 1st floor is now a modern art gallery, but don't miss the wonderful **Zsigmond Hall** with its Renaissance fireplace and star-vaulted, enclosed balcony. On the 2nd floor is an exhibition of the work of István Gádor, an award-winning ceramicist.

To the right of the museum entrance, two doors lead to the dark and spooky **cells** – a real dungeon if ever there was one. The walls are several metres thick, and up to five grilles on the window slits discouraged would-be escapers. Woodcuts on the walls of the upper dungeon explain how various torture devices were put to use. After this, the Gothic **chapel** is a little bit of heaven itself, with its brilliant arched windows behind the altar, web vaulting on the ceiling and 15th-century frescoed niches.

Other Things to See

The **Franciscan church** south of the castle on Vajda János tér is 15th-century Gothic, but you'd hardly know it from the outside. Its cloister at No 4 is now the **City Gallery** with revolving exhibits, mostly dealing with ceramics. At No 6 of the same square, the small **City Museum**, which may remain closed for a spell, usually contains exhibits on the history of Siklós, folk art and agriculture.

If you walk down Batthyány Kázmér utca past the little statue of the heroic Dorottya Kanizsai (see the Mohács section), you'll come to the 16th-century **Malkocs Bej Mosque** at Kossuth tér 16. Now beautifully restored, it houses temporary exhibits and is one of the very few Turkish legacies you'll find in this area.

The busy **market** is south of Dózsa György utca behind the Spar supermarket on Mária utca.

Activities

The pools at the Strandfürdő at Baross Gábor utca 2 are open from early June to August from 10 am to 6 pm. You can hire a tennis court at the Gold Fassl pub-restaurant on Gordisai út south-west of the bus station.

Places to Stay & Eat

With the closure of the combination hotel/hostel in the castle in 1993 and more recently the Központi guesthouse on Kossuth Lajos tér, Siklós can claim the dubious distinction of being one of the few towns in Hungary with no accommodation. Make it a side trip from Harkány, six km to the west, or book a private room in Siklós through one of the agencies there.

Places for a quick bite include the basic *Finom Falatok* at Felszabadulás 16 and *O Sole Mio*, with pizzas and simple pastas, at Dósza György utca 2/d (or Felszabadulás utca 44 from the other side).

The *Sport* is a working-class restaurant with working-class prices and dishes (fish soup, tripe pörkölt and sausages) at Felszabadulás 74 near the bus station. It stays open till 9.30 pm. The *Központi* restaurant at Kossuth tér 5 is a little more expensive, and then there's *Pinocchio* at Felszabadulás út 65/a, a small csárda with pleasant service that stays open till 10 pm. The *Fehérház* restaurant is convenient to the market.

Entertainment

You should really save the wine tasting for Villány and the cellars at Villánykövesd, but if you want to sample a glass here, try the little *borozó* (wine bar) in the castle courtyard, the divey *Gilde* at Felszabadulás utca 7 near Kossuth tér (till midnight), or the *Fehérholló* north of the market at Szabadság utca 7 (till 10 pm).

The *Központi* restaurant hosts a corny disco with live music at weekends for the mature set. The *Madison*, halfway between Siklós and Harkány, about three km west of Siklós, is a more popular disco.

Getting There & Away

Generally you won't wait more than 30 or 40 minutes for buses to Pécs or Harkány (either can go via Máriagyűd), Máriagyűd, Villány and Mohács. Other destinations include Budapest and Székesfehérvár (one bus each daily), Szigetvár and Szekszárd (two each), and Sellye (three).

Trains link Siklós with Villány (change here for Mohács or Pécs), Máriagyűd, Harkány, Sellye and Barcs. But trains are

SOUTHERN TRANSDANUBIA

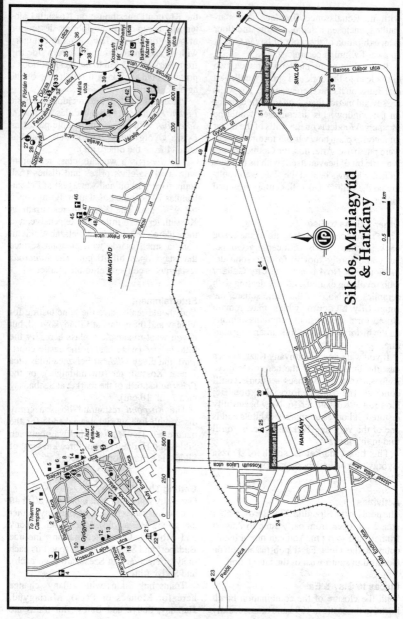

Siklós, Máriagyűd
& Harkány

SIKLÓS

MÁRIAGYŰD

HARKÁNY

PLACES TO STAY
1 Dráva Hotel
5 Napsugár Hotel/Ibusz
6 Bosna Hotel & Restaurant
8 Baranya Hotel
10 Siesta Club Hotel
14 Balkon Viking Hotel
25 Thermál Camping
26 Platán Hotel

PLACES TO EAT
2 Charlie's Grill
13 Robinson Restaurant
15 Food Stalls
18 Éden Pizzeria
29 Sport Restaurant
32 O Sole Mio Restaurant
35 Spar Supermarket
37 Fehérház Restaurant
38 Finom Falatok
41 Központi Restaurant
48 Kukurikú Restaurant
51 Pinocchio Restaurant

52 Gold Fassl Pub-Restaurant

OTHER
3 Harkány Post Office
4 Calvinist Church
7 Mecsek Tours & Main Entrance to Baths
9 K&H Bank
11 Thermal Baths & Pools
12 Entrance to Baths
16 OTP Bank (Seasonal)
17 Entrance to Baths
19 Open-Air Theatre
20 Harkány Bus Station
21 Former Bulgarian Museum
22 Harkány Cultural House
23 Táltos Pension (Horse Riding)
24 Harkány Railway Station
27 Mecsek Tours

28 Siklós Bus Station
30 Siklós Post Office
31 K&H Bank
33 OTP Bank
34 Fehérholló Wine Bar
36 Market
39 Gilde Wine Bar
40 Siklós Castle & Museums
42 Siklós City Museum
43 Malkocs Bej Mosque
44 Franciscan Church
45 Former Franciscan Church
46 Calvary Chapel
47 Wine Cellar
49 Siklósi-szőlők Railway Station
50 Siklós Main Railway Station
53 Strand Pools
54 Madison Disco

infrequent (a maximum of six a day), and not all of them run the full line.

AROUND SIKLÓS
Máriagyűd

The **former Franciscan church** in this village at the foot of 408m Mt Tenkes northwest of Siklós has been a place of pilgrimage for 800 years, and you can make your own by walking (or hopping on a Máriagyűd or Pécs-bound bus) for about three km along Gyűdi út and Pécsi út and turning north on Járó Péter utca when the church's two towers come into view. The chance to sample some of Siklós' white wines here is also an attraction.

Máriagyűd was on the old trade route between Pécs and Eszék (now Osijek in Croatia), and a church has stood here since the mid-12th century. Today's is a large 18th-century affair with modern frescos, baroque painted altars and some beautifully carved pews, but the treat is to arrive here on Sunday or on a búcsú (a patron's festival – the Virgin Mary has lots of them) when merchants set up their stalls beside the church (see aside). Mass is conducted in Hungarian in the church, but at the outdoor altar above it, just as many people attend German-language services complete with oompah band. Large stations of the Cross in Zsolnay porcelain line the way to the Zopf-style Calvary Chapel, a short distance up Mt Tenkes.

There's a restaurant called the *Kukurikú* (that's 'cock-a-doodle-doo' in Hungarian) in the old rectory at the bottom of the church steps (try the Stifolder sausage, a Swabian speciality of Southern Transdanubia) and an old *wine cellar* opposite with tastings. From the square here, you can start a six-km hike up and around Mt Tenkes.

HARKÁNY
• *pop 3200*
• *area code ☎ 72*

It's a wonder that no statue stands in honour of János Pogány in this spa town six km west of Siklós and 26 km south of Pécs. He was the poor peasant from Máriagyűd who cured himself of swollen joints early in the 19th century by soaking in a hot spring he had discovered here. The Batthyány family recognised the potential almost immediately, erecting bathing huts in 1824 near the 62°C spring, which has the richest sulfuric content

Farewell to All That

The word *búcsú* (church festival) derives from the ancient Turkish for 'absolution' or 'the forgiveness of sins'. From medieval times it has taken on the additional meaning of 'pilgrimage' in Hungarian.

Búcsúk were usually linked with an icon or statue in a particular church, such as the Black Madonnas at Andocs in Southern Transdanubia or Máriapócs near Nyírbátor in the North-East. They could also honour the name of a church's patron saint. People would march, often for days, to the holy place carrying banners and singing. Local people would accommodate and feed the pilgrims for little or nothing; often the faithful would spend the night in the church itself, believing that in sleep, the absolution – or the cure or miracle – was more likely to occur.

Over the centuries búcsúk took on a more secular tone. Merchants would set up their stalls around the church, selling not only relics and religious articles but clothing, food and drinks. Showmen, buskers and musicians entertained the crowds and, in some places, there was even a 'bride market' with hopeful young women appearing with their full dowries. While the old and infirm congregated in the church to touch and venerate the holy picture or statue, the young remained outside for the entertainment.

As it happens, búcsú has yet another meaning in Hungarian: 'farewell'. Thus the Búcsú festival in Budapest every June marking the departure of the last Soviet soldier from Hungarian soil in 1991 has a double meaning: it is both a raving rock-music party and a 'goodbye' to the last of the much despised occupiers. ∎

in Hungary. Today, aside from Pécs, no town in Baranya County brings in as much money as Harkány. The town owes Mr Pogány at least a plaque.

Of course, all that means crowds (well over 100,000 Hungarian, Austrian, Croatian and Yugoslavian visitors in the high season), *lángos* stalls in spades and an all-pervasive stench of rotten eggs. But you might like it. People come to Harkány to socialise – it's not as brash as Hajdúszoboszló on the Great Plain – and the town is on the western edge of the Villány-Siklós region, so there is plenty of wine about.

Orientation

Harkány is essentially the Gyógyfürdő, a 12-hectare green square filled with pools, fountains and walkways, and bordered by hotels and holiday homes of every description. The four streets defining the thermal complex are Bartók Béla utca to the north, Ady Endre to the south, Bajcsy-Zsilinszky utca with most of the hotels to the east, and Kossuth Lajos utca, with several restaurants, to the west. The bus station is on Bajcsy-Zsilinszky utca at the south-east corner of the park. The train station is to the north-west on Petőfi utca, which branches off from Kossuth Lajos utca.

Information

Mecsek Tours (☎ 480 322) has an office at the main entrance to the baths at Bajcsy-Zsilinszky utca 4, north of the bus station, while Ibusz (☎ 480 068) is in the Napsugár hotel diagonally opposite at No 7. In summer, these offices are open on weekdays from 8 am to 5 pm and on Saturday till noon. In winter, they are open till 4 pm on weekdays only.

K&H bank has an exchange office at the main entrance to the spa. The OTP bank has a kiosk between the bus station and the baths on Bajcsy-Zsilinszky utca, open May to September only. The post office is at Kossuth Lajos utca 57.

Things to See & Do

The main entrance to the **thermal baths** and **pools**, which are meant to cure just about everything, is on Bajcsy-Zsilinszky utca. The complex is open from 8 am to 11 pm mid-June to August; during the rest of the year it keeps regular office hours – 9 am to 5 pm. Services range from drinking cures and mud massage to the enticing 'wine foam bath', but it's a treat just to swim in the 38°C outdoor pool, especially in cool weather. Entrance to the regular pools is 210/120 Ft for adults/children and 540/340 Ft for the thermal baths.

One of the town's few 'sights' – the Bulgarian Museum on Kossuth Lajos utca honouring that nation's contribution to

Hungary's liberation in WWII – is still 'closed indefinitely for technical reasons'. If you must see something, sober up at the Zopf-style **Calvinist church** (1802) at Kossuth Lajos utca 66.

You can ride horses or hire a coach at the Táltos pension north-west of the centre at Széchenyi tér 30/d, off Petőfi utca. There's another riding school (☎ 480 228) nearby at Vasút utca 6. Radius at Thermál Camping hires out bicycles daily in summer from 8 am to 7 pm for 200 Ft an hour (plus 5000 Ft deposit).

Special Events

During the Harkány Spa Festival in mid-July and Harkány Summer from June to August, performances are staged at the open-air theatre on Zsigmond sétány in the spa park.

Places to Stay

Camping *Thermál Camping* (☎ 480 117), Bajcsy-Zsilinszky utca 6, has a 20-room motel (DM20 to DM22 per double), a hotel with 26 rooms (DM31 to DM36) and two dozen bungalows with two double rooms and kitchen from DM48 to DM65. All are open between mid-April and mid-September.

Private Rooms Both Mecsek Tours and Ibusz rent private rooms for about 1000 Ft per person, but for a one-night stay you may be better off going to a hotel or investigating the possibilities yourself by strolling east on Bartók Béla utca, where *Zimmer frei* signs proliferate. A two to four-room apartment in one of the former holiday homes lining that street starts at about DM50.

Hotels Harkány has an incredible array of hotels and pensions to suit all budgets. The cheapest is the 41-room *Napsugár* hotel (☎ 480 300) at Bajcsy-Zsilinszky utca 7, which has singles/doubles with shower for 2000/2600 Ft in the low season and 2400/3500 Ft in summer. The upstairs rooms can get very warm in summer.

The rather rough *Baranya* hotel (☎ 480 160), nearby at Bajcsy-Zsilinszky utca 5 and opposite the baths entrance, has doubles for 4700 Ft.

The *Dráva* (☎ 480 434), with a total of 71 rooms in two buildings, is in a pretty park just short of the camp site at Bartók Béla utca 3. Doubles are DM50 to DM70, depending on the month and whether you've chosen building B or the superior building A. The *Platán* (☎ 480 411), a former trade-union holiday home at Bartók Béla utca 15, has been converted into a modern 60-room hotel. Singles are 4000 to 4900 Ft, doubles 5900 to 7000 Ft.

The 54-room *Balkon Viking* (☎ 480 049) at Bajcsy-Zsilinszky utca 2 is housed in an Art Deco sanatorium once used by Communist Party honchos. It has lots of atmosphere and lovely grounds, but the clientele is composed almost entirely of retired Austrians and Germans on health cures. Singles are DM36 to DM38 and doubles are DM58 to DM64.

The fanciest place to stay in town is the 79-room *Siesta Club* (☎ 480 611) to the west of the spa at Kossuth Lajos utca 17. Doubles with bath are from DM50 to DM85, depending on the season.

Places to Eat

You're not going to starve in this town of sausage stands and wine counters, but if you want to sit down while eating, try the *Robinson*, with pizza and other dishes, at Kossuth Lajos utca 7. *Éden*, in a beautiful pink Eclectic building across the street at No 12, makes pizzas every day except Monday till 11 pm.

Two places are recommended for South Slav-style grills like čevapčiči and pleskavici: the terrace of the *Bosna* hotel between the Baranya and Napsugár hotels on Bajcsy-Zsilinszky utca, and *Charlie's Grill* on Bartók Béla utca.

Entertainment

The *Harkány Cultural House* (☎ 480 459) is at Kossuth Lajos utca 2/a, but don't expect too much in the way of high-brow entertainment here.

Getting There & Away

Bus While buses depart frequently for Siklós and Pécs, other destinations are not so well served, with only one bus a day to Baja, Kecskemét, Kalocsa, Sellye, Veszprém, Szeged and Székesfehérvár. Other destinations include Budapest (two buses a day), Szekszárd (two), Szigetvár (two or three), Mohács (four) and Drávafok.

Four buses a day link Harkány with Croatia: two to Osijek (at 12.30 and 5.30 pm) and one each to Našice (weekdays at 10 am) and Slavonski Brod (5.15 pm). In summer, buses to Stuttgart leave Harkány on Sunday at 2.30 pm and arrive in the German city at 7 am on Monday.

Train By rail from Harkány, you can reach Sellye and Barcs to the west (four to five a day) and Siklós and Villány to the east (five or six). Change at Villány for Mohács or Pécs.

Getting Around

For a local taxi, ring ☎ 480 123.

VILLÁNY

- *pop 2900*
- *area code ☎ 72*

Some 13 km north-east of Siklós and dominated by cone-shaped Mt Szársomlyó (422m) to the west, Villány is a village of vineyards, vineyards and more vineyards. It was the site in 1687 of what has become known as the 'second battle of Mohács', a ferocious confrontation in which the Turks got their comeuppance and were driven southward by the Hungarians into the Dráva marshes and slaughtered unmercifully. After liberation, Serbs and Swabians moved in (Villány is known as Wieland in German) and viticulture resumed. Today, Villány is one of Hungary's principal producers of wine, noted especially for its red Oportó, Cabernet Sauvignon, Merlot and Nagyburgundi wines.

You might consider visiting Villány during the September harvest, when the town is a beehive of activity: human chains pass buckets of almost black grapes from trucks to big machines that chew off the vines, reduce the fruit to a soggy mass and pump the must – the grape juice – into enormous casks. However, you run the risk of not getting a drop to taste: everyone's too busy and the cellars and restaurants will be closed.

Orientation & Information

Villány is essentially just one main street, Baross Gábor utca, and the bus stops in the centre of the village near the ABC supermarket. The train station is about 1200m to the north on Ady Endre fasor en route to Villánykövesd.

There's an OTP bank at Baross Gábor utca 27, and the post office is at No 35 of the same street next to the Oportó restaurant.

Wine Museum & Tasting

The **Wine Museum**, housed in a 200-year-old tithe cellar at Bem József utca 3, has a collection of 19th-century wine-producing equipment, such as barrels, presses and hand corkers. Downstairs in the sand-covered cellars, Villány's celebrated wines age in enormous casks, and vintage bottles dating from 1895 to 1971 are kept in safes. There's a small shop at the entrance selling Villány and Siklós wines, some of them vintage and among the best labels available in Hungary. You can sample wines at the museum (500 to 1000 Ft per person), in a few **cellars** on Baross Gábor utca (Nos 44, 71 and 87) and in Diófás tér on Friday evenings from June to August.

But the best place for tasting is in the cellars cut into the loess soil at **Villánykövesd** (German: Growisch), about 3.5 km north-west of town along the road to Pécs. Cellars line the main street (Petőfi út) and the narrow lane (Pincesor) above it. Along the former, try the Polgár at No 51 (with a deep cellar) or the house at 27/a. On Pincesor, Nos 15 and 18 are cute but my favourite is No 5. The cellars keep difficult hours, so it's a hit-or-miss proposition; the Polgár Pince, for example, is open Thursday to Sunday, May to October, from 3 pm to 9 pm.

Among Villány's red wines, try the Oportó (also called Kékoportó or Blue Portuguese), a light, young wine, or the more substantial Cabernet or Cabernet Sauvignon. The Merlot is good but somewhat sweet.

Among the whites (from both Villány and Siklós), sample the Olaszrizling or the Hárslevelű, which some maintain is better than the original from the village of Debrő in the Mátra foothills.

Places to Stay & Eat

There are plenty of signs advertising *private rooms* in Villány, but don't miss the chance to stay at the eight-room *Gere* pension (☎ 492 195) at Diófás tér 4, with doubles for 3500 Ft. The pension's restaurant (open to guests only) serves its own wine, one of the best labels in Hungary. The manager at the Gere pension can help organise horse riding through the vineyards and up into the hills.

The *Oportó* at Baross Gábor utca 33 is a large, pleasant restaurant with a terrace near the town centre close to where the bus lets you off. The *Julia*, a little csárda near the Wine Museum at Baross Gábor utca 43, serves some of the best veal pörkölt in Hungary.

The *Fülemüle Csárda* (Nightingale Inn), a couple of hundred metres past the train station on Ady Endre fasor, is a good place to stop for a bite on your way to or from Villánykövesd.

Getting There & Away

There are infrequent buses to Pécs, Siklós, Harkány, Budapest, Mohács and Villány-kövesd (five to six a day), but for most destinations, you must go to Siklós first. Trains run east to Mohács, west to Siklós and Harkány and north to Pécs.

ORMÁNSÁG REGION

About 30 km west of Harkány, this plain was prone to flooding by the nearby Dráva River for centuries. That and the area's isolation – 'somewhere behind the back of God,' as the Hungarians call it – is reflected in its unusual architecture, folk ways and distinct dialect. Couples in the Ormánság usually limited themselves to only one child since, under the land-tenure system here, peasants were not allowed to enlarge their holdings. That's not the only reason why the area's *talpás házak* are so small: these 'soled' or 'footed' houses were built on rollers so that they could be dragged to dry land in the event of flooding.

Sellye
• *pop 300*

In Sellye, the 'capital' of and most interesting town in the Ormánság region, a representative footed house of mortar, lime and a wooden frame sits behind the **Ormánság Museum** at Köztársaság tér 6. (Mátyás király utca, the main drag, is south-west of the bus station, and the train station is to the south-east on Vasút utca.) The house has the typical three rooms and some big differences: the parlour was actually lived in; the front room was a 'smoke kitchen' without a chimney; and to keep mosquitoes at bay, what few windows the house had were kept very small.

The museum's rich collection contains Ormánság costumes and artefacts, including brocaded skirts, 'butterfly' head-dresses, mirror holders, shaving kits and staffs carved from horn and wood by shepherds. The oaken trousseau chests decorated with geometrical shapes are unique and superior to the 'tulip chests' usually found in prosperous peasant houses throughout Hungary.

There's an **arboretum** with rare trees and plants surrounding the Draskovich family mansion (now a school) behind the museum, and a couple of restaurants on Mátyás király utca, including the little *Borostyán* at No 56 and the *Ormánság* at No 72 near the museum.

Other Ormánság Villages

The Calvinist church at **Drávaiványi**, with a colourful panelled ceiling and choir loft dating from the late 18th century, is five km south-west of Sellye and can be reached by bus. **Vajszló**, another Ormánság village 11 km south-east of Sellye with several footed houses, is on the same train line as Sellye. Buses travel eastward from Vajszló to **Kórós**, whose folk-decorated Calvinist church (1795) is among the most beautiful in the region.

Getting There & Away

Harkány is the easiest starting point for any excursion into the Ormánság, but the area is also accessible by public transport from Szigetvár – in fact, it is actually closer to that city. But the infrequent milk-run buses from Szigetvár take almost two hours to cover 25 km (admittedly passing through some very attractive little villages), and if you catch the train, you must change at Szentlőrinc. The train from Harkány to Sellye and Vajszló (five departures a day) involves no change and takes only about an hour. See Getting There & Away in the Harkány section for more information.

PÉCS

• *pop 179,000*
• *area code* ☎ *72*

Blessed with a mild climate, an illustrious past and a number of fine museums and monuments, Pécs is one of the most pleasant and interesting cities to visit in Hungary. For those reasons and more (a handful of universities, the nearby Mecsek Hills, a lively nightlife scene), many travellers put it second to Budapest on their 'must-see' list. You too should spend some time here.

Lying equidistant from the Danube to the east and the Dráva to the south on a plain sheltered from northern winds by the Mecsek Hills, Pécs enjoys an extended summer and is ideal for viticulture fruit and nut growing, especially almonds. The Romans may have settled here for the region's weather, fertile soil and abundant water, but more likely they were sold by the protection offered by those hills.

They called their settlement Sophianae (a name most readily recognised today as Hungary's top brand of cigarettes), and it quickly grew into the commercial and administrative centre of Lower Pannonia. The Romans brought Christianity with them, and reminders of it can be seen in the early clover-shaped chapels unearthed at several locations around Pécs.

Pécs' importance grew in the Middle Ages, when it was known as Quinque Ecclesiae after the five steeples dotting the town; it is still called Fünfkirchen (Five Churches) in German. King Stephen founded a bishopric here in 1009, and the town was a major stop along the trade route to Byzantium. Pécs developed as an intellectual and humanist centre with the founding of a university – Hungary's first – in 1367. The 15th-century bishop Janus Pannonius, who wrote some of Europe's most celebrated Renaissance poetry in Latin, was based in Pécs.

The city was fortified with walls – a large portion of which still stand – after the Mongol invasion of the early 13th century, but they were in such poor condition by 1543 that the Turks took the city with virtually no resistance. The Turks moved the local populace outside the walls and turned Pécs into their own administrative and cultural centre. When they were expelled almost 150 years later, Pécs was virtually abandoned, but still standing were monumental souvenirs that now count as the most important Turkish structures in the nation. The resumption of wine production by German and Bohemian immigrants and the discovery of coal in the 18th century spurred Pécs' development. The manufacture of luxury goods (gloves, Zsolnay porcelain, Pannonvin sparkling wine, Angster organs) as well as uranium mining would come later.

For the visitor, the capital of Baranya County is more than anything else a 'town of art', beating Szentendre on the Danube Bend hands down. Of course, the housing blocks ringing the city, the massive tanneries and the mines in the hills to the north-east don't contribute to this perception, but they seem very much in the background as you gaze over the Mediterranean-like tiled roofs during a warm *indián nyár* (indian summer), when the light seems to take on a special quality.

Orientation

The oval-shaped inner town has as its heart Széchenyi tér, where a dozen streets converge. One of these is Király utca, a pedestrian promenade of restored shops, pubs and restaurants to the east. To the north-west lies Pécs' other important square, Dóm tér. Here you'll find the cathedral, early Christian chapels and the end of Káptalan utca, the 'street of museums'.

Pécs' train station is in Indóház tér; from the station, follow Jókai Mór utca north to the inner town. The bus station is close to the big market, which is on Zólyom utca. Walk north along Bajcsy-Zsilinszky utca and Irgalmasok utcája to the centre.

Information

Tourinform (☎ 213 315), Széchenyi tér 9, has copious information on Pécs and Baranya County and is open weekdays from 8 am to 4 pm (to 6 pm weekdays and on Saturday and Sunday from 9 am to 2 pm from mid-June to August). Mecsek Tours (☎ 212 044) at Széchenyi tér 1 is another excellent and helpful source of information. It is open weekdays from 9 am to 5 pm and Saturday to 1 pm all year. South of Széchenyi tér at Irgalmasok utcája 22 is Cooptourist (☎ 213 407); Express (☎ 313 900) is closer to the bus station and market at Bajcsy-Zsilinszky utca 6.

The main OTP bank is on Rákóczi út and there's a branch opposite the Pécs National Theatre at Király utca 11. M&M Exchange at Király utca 16 offers a decent rate and opens daily from 8 am to 2.30 pm and 3.30 to 10 pm.

The main post office is in a beautiful Art Nouveau building dating from 1904 (note the angels in relief writing, mailing and delivering the post) at Jókai Mór utca 10.

The Corvina Art Bookshop, in the House of Artists at Széchenyi tér 7-8, has one of the best selections of English-language books and world-music CDs and tapes in Hungary.

Széchenyi tér

Széchenyi tér, a lovely square of mostly baroque buildings backed by the Mecsek Hills, is where you should start a walking tour of Pécs. Dominating the square – indeed, the symbol of the city – is the former Pasha Gazi Kassim Mosque. Today it's the inner town Parish Church but more commonly known as the **Mosque Church**. It is the largest building from the Turkish occupation still standing in Hungary.

The square mosque with a green copper dome was built with the stones of the ruined medieval church of St Bertalan in the mid-16th century; after the expulsion of the Turks, the Catholic Church took possession again. The northern semicircular part was added this century. The Islamic elements on the south side are easy to spot: windows with distinctive Turkish ogee arches; the prayer niche *(mihrab)* carved into the south-east wall inside; faded verses from the Koran to the south-west; lovely geometric frescos on the corners. The mosque's minaret was pulled down in 1753 and replaced by a tower. The Mosque Church can be visited Monday to Saturday from 10 am to 4 pm and on Sunday from 11.30 am to 4 pm.

The **Archaeology Museum** (Régészeti Múzeum), behind the Mosque Church at Széchenyi tér 12 in the 17th-century home of a janissary commander, traces the history of Baranya County up to the time of Árpád and contains much Roman stonework from Pannonia, a model of St Bertalan's Church and medieval porcelain.

The **Trinity Column** in the lower part of Széchenyi tér is the third one to grace the spot and dates from 1908. The **porcelain fountain** with a lustrous glaze to the south-east in front of the rather gloomy **Church of the Good Samaritan** was donated to the city by the Zsolnay factory in 1892.

Kossuth tér

Kossuth tér, a square south-east of Széchenyi tér, has two important buildings: the Eclectic **town hall** (1891) to the north and the restored **synagogue** to the east. The synagogue (open daily except Saturday from 10 to 11.30 am and noon to 4 pm May to October) was built in the Romantic style in 1869 and is one of Pécs' finest monuments. Fact sheets in a dozen languages are available, and you should spend a few moments looking at the carved oak galleries and pews,

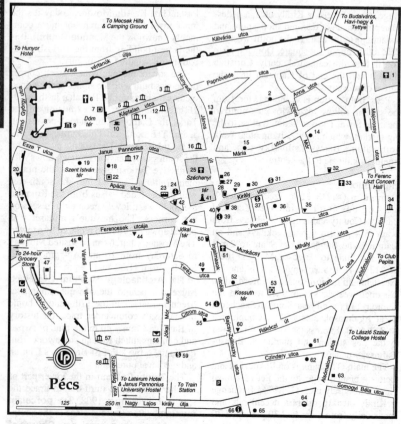

Pécs

the ceiling paintings, the magnificent Angster organ and the ornate Ark of the Covenant in the sanctuary. Shortly after the fascist Hungarian government set up the Pécs ghetto in May 1944 – just a year before the end of the war in Europe – most of the city's 3000 Jews were deported to German death camps. Only 300 survived.

Around Dóm tér

The foundations of the four-towered **Basilica of St Peter** on Dóm tér date back to the 11th century and the side chapels are from the 1300s. But most of what you see today

of the neo-Romanesque structure is the result of renovations carried out in 1881. Another controversial 'renovation' occurred in 1991 when the basilica was given a scrub for Pope John Paul II's first visit to Hungary. But the towers were thought to be too fragile for such treatment, and the church now has a somewhat strange two-tone appearance.

The basilica is very ornate inside; the elevated central altar is a reproduction of a medieval one. The most interesting parts of the basilica are the four chapels under the towers and the crypt, the oldest part of the structure. The **Chapel of Mary** on the north-

PLACES TO STAY
13 Főnix Hotel
30 Palatinus Hotel
47 Pátria Hotel
63 Gastrium Pension

PLACES TO EAT
20 Barbakán Restaurant
21 Santa Maria
    Restaurant
29 Dóm Restaurant
35 Apolló Takeaway
    Restaurant
40 McDonald's
44 Görög Taverna
46 Minaret Restaurant
49 Aranykacsa
    Restaurant
60 Pizza Hut

OTHER
1 St Augustine Church
2 Croatian Theatre
3 Zsolnay Porcelain
   Museum
4 Modern Hungarian Art
   Gallery I
5 Ferenc Martyn
   Museum

6 Basilica of St Peter
7 Jug Mausoleum
8 Barbican
9 Bishop's Palace
10 Kioszk Café
11 Endre Nemes Museum
12 Vasarely Museum
14 Puppet Theatre
15 Jazz Café
16 Archaeology Museum
17 Csontváry Museum
18 Pannonvin
    Champagne
    Factory
19 Tomb Chapel
22 Roman Tomb Site
23 Lajos Nagy Swimming
    Pool
24 Tourinform
25 Mosque Church
26 Nádor Hotel Building
27 Mecsek Cake Shop
28 Royal Pub
31 OTP Bank
32 Liceum Pub
33 Church of St Stephen
34 City History Museum
36 Pécs National Theatre
37 M&M Exchange
38 John Bull Pub

39 Mecsek Tours
41 Trinity Column
42 Nothing But the Blues
    Club
43 House of Artists &
    Corvina Art
    Bookshop
45 Memi Pasha Baths
48 Hassan Jakovali
    Mosque
50 Áfium Bar &
    Restaurant
51 Church of the Good
    Samaritan
52 Town Hall
53 Synagogue
54 Cooptourist
55 Dani Wine Bar
56 Main Post Office
57 Ethnology Museum
58 Modern Hungarian Art
    Gallery II
59 Main OTP Bank
61 A Gyár Disco
62 West Disco
64 Bus Station
65 Market
66 Express

west side and the **Chapel of the Sacred Heart** to the north-east contain works by the 19th-century painters Bertalan Székely and Károly Lotz. The **Mór Chapel** to the south-east has more works by Székely and some magnificent pews. The **Corpus Christi Chapel** on the south-west side (enter from the outside) boasts a 16th-century tabernacle in the same lovely red marble used to decorate the Bakócz Chapel in Esztergom Cathe-dral. It is one of the finest examples of Renaissance stonework in the country. On the steps leading to the simple crypt are reproductions of 12th-century friezes depicting scenes from the New Testament, bloody battles and everyday life (cathedral building, a blind man being led by a child). The basilica is open every day from 9 am to 5 pm (with a one-hour lunch break) and on Sunday afternoon.

The **Bishop's Palace** (1770) to the south-west is not generally open to the public, but have a look at the strange **Franz Liszt statue** (Imre Varga, 1983) peering over from a balcony. On the southern side of the baroque Ecclesiastical Archives is the entrance to the **Jug Mausoleum** (Korsós Sírkamra), a 4th-century Roman tomb whose name comes from a painting of a large drinking vessel with vines found here. The **early Christian tomb chapel** (Ókeresztény Sírkápolna) across Janus Pannonius utca in Szent István tér dates from about 350 AD and has frescos of Adam and Eve, and Daniel in the lion's den. There's another later **Roman tomb site** containing 110 graves a little farther south at Apáca utca 14.

The **Csontváry Museum** at Janus Pannonius utca 11 exhibits the major works of Tivadar Csontváry (1853-1919), a unique symbolist painter whose tragic life is sometimes compared with that of Vincent van Gogh (who was born in the same year). Many of Csontváry's oversized canvases are masterpieces, especially *Storm on the Great Hortobágy* (1903), *Solitary Cedar* (1907) and *Baalbeck*, an artistic search for a larger identity through religious and historical themes that has to be seen.

To the west and north of Dóm tér is a long stretch of the **old city wall** that enclosed an area far too large to defend properly. The circular **barbican**, the only stone bastion to survive, dates from the late 15th century and was restored in the 1970s. You can stroll along the catwalk running just below the loopholes.

Káptalan utca

Káptalan utca, running east from Dóm tér, contains half a dozen art museums, all of them in listed buildings. There's so much to see here that you'd better be selective.

The **Ferenc Martyn Museum** at Káptalan utca 6 displays works by the Pécs-born painter and sculptor (1899-1986) and sponsors special exhibits of local interest. The house at No 5 is devoted to paintings by **Endre Nemes**. In a separate pavilion behind it is Erzsébet Schaár's *Utca* (or *'Street'*), a complete artistic environment in which the sculptor has set her whole life in stone. The **Modern Hungarian Art Gallery I** at No 4 is the best place for an overview of art in Hungary between 1850 and 1950; pay special attention to the works of Simon Hollósy, József Rippl-Rónai and Ödön Márffy. The **Péter Székely Gallery** behind the museum has large stone and wood sculptures.

The two most interesting museums are at the eastern end of the street: the **Vasarely Museum** at No 3 and the **Zsolnay Porcelain Museum** at No 2. Victor Vasarely was the father of op art and, although some of the works on exhibit by him and his disciples are dated, most are evocative, very tactile and just plain fun. (Remember that Vasarely was producing this stuff long before it became the darling of the art world and *de rigueur* for 1960s album covers.) To my mind, the most striking of Vasarely's works here is *Vega-Sakk* (1969). It's a red, blue and orange weaving of an orb that grows into a distended belly as you stare at it.

The Zsolnay porcelain factory was established in Pécs in 1851 and was at the forefront of art and design in Europe for more than half a century. Many of its majolica tiles were used to decorate buildings throughout the country and contributed to establishing a new pan-Hungarian style of architecture. Zsolnay's darkest period came when the postwar Communist government turned it into a plant for making ceramic electrical insulators. It's producing art again, but contemporary Zsolnay can't hold a candle to the chinoiserie pieces from the late 19th century and the later Art Nouveau and Art Deco designs done in the lustrous eosin glaze. The museum, housed in a residence dating from the Middle Ages, was the home of the Zsolnay family and contains many of their furnishings and personal effects.

Other Things to See

The **Modern Hungarian Art Gallery II**, south-west of the inner town at Szabadság utca 2, picks up where Gallery I on Káptalan utca leaves off; there's a lot of abstract and constructionist art here from the 1960s and 1970s. Watch out for the names András Mengyár, Tamás Hencze and Gábor Dienes.

A short distance to the north-west opposite the Pátria hotel at Rákóczi út 2 is the **Hassan Jakovali Mosque**, wedged between a trade school and a hospital. Complete with minaret, the 16th-century mosque is the most intact of any Turkish structure in Hungary and contains a small museum of Ottoman *objets d'art*.

After seeing the mosque, follow Pécs' most enjoyable pedestrian malls, Ferencesek utcája and Király utca, east across the city. You'll pass the ruins of the 16th-century **Memi Pasha Baths** (Ferencesek utcája 35), three beautiful old churches and the neo-rococo **Pécs National Theatre** on Király utca. Just beyond the **Church of St Stephen** (1741), on Király utca 44/a, turn south (right) to Felsőmalom utca 9, where you'll find the excellent **City History Museum**.

The suburb of Budaiváros to the north-east of the town centre is where most Hungarians settled after the Turks banned them from living within the city walls. The centre of this community was the **All Saints' Church** just off Tettye utca. Originally built in the 12th century and reconstructed in Gothic style 200 years later, it was the only

Christian church allowed in Pécs during the occupation and was shared by three sects – who fought bitterly for every square cm. It was the Turks who had to keep the peace among the Christians.

To the north-east up on a hill is **Havi-hegy Chapel**, built in 1691 by the faithful after the town was spared the plague. The church is an important city landmark and offers wonderful views of the inner town and the narrow streets and old houses of the Tettye Valley. A short distance to the north is a striking bronze **crucifix** with a painfully contorted body of Christ by Sándor Rétfalvi.

Pécs' fruit and vegetable **market** is near the bus station on Zólyom utca. The Sunday **flea market** at Vásártér, about three km south-west of the inner town on Megyeri út, attracts people from the countryside, especially on the first Sunday of the month.

You can get a taste of the Mecsek Hills by walking north-east from the centre of Pécs to Tettye and the **Garden of Ruins** – what's left of a bishop's summer residence built early in the 16th century and later used by Turkish dervishes as a monastery. To the north-west, up Fenyves sor and past the **zoo** (open every day from 9 am to 4 or 5 pm), a winding road leads to 535m **Misina Peak** and a **TV tower**, an impressive 194m structure with a viewing platform, coffee shop and restaurant. But these are just the foothills; from here, trails lead to the lovely towns of **Orfű** and **Abaliget**, on a plateau some 15 to 20 km to the north-west, and to Southern Transdanubia's highest peak, 682m **Mt Zengő**. See the following Mecsek Hills section for more details.

Activities

The outdoor Lajos Nagy Swimming Pool, up a few steps from Cisztercei köz, off Apaca utca, is open in summer from 9 am to 6 pm; there's a great little pub called the Fontana attached. The Koncz Tennis Team (☎ 326 860), west of the inner town at Közép-Makár dűlő 4, has courts and gives lessons from 7 am to dusk. The Baranya Flying and Parachuting Club (☎ 450 619), based at the city's small airport at Pogányi some 12 km to the

south, has sightseeing flights and skydiving lessons.

The Mecsek Hills are great for hiking and walking. See the separate Mecsek Hills section for details.

Special Events

The big annual events are the International Music Festival in late June/early July and Pécs Days in September, a month-long festival of dance and music with a couple of alcohol-related events thrown in for good measure.

Places to Stay

Camping *Mandulás Camping* (☎ 315 981), up in the Mecsek Hills near the zoo at Ángyán János utca 2, has 28 bungalows with shared shower from DM35 and a 20-room hotel with doubles (including bath) from DM45.

Hostels In July and August, both the *Janus Pannonius University* (☎ 251 203), west of the centre at Szánto Kovács János utca 1/c, and the *László Szalay College* (☎ 324 473), at Universitas út 2 east of the centre, accommodate travellers in three-bed dorm rooms for 400 Ft per person. You can ask Express to book you in or go directly there.

Private Rooms Mecsek Tours and Cooptourist can arrange private rooms from 1100/1800 Ft for singles/doubles; apartments range from 2000 to 3400 Ft. Unless you stay more than three nights there's a 30% surcharge on the first night.

Pensions As in Budapest, most of the pensions in Pécs are sprinkled in the surrounding hills and rather difficult to get to without your own transport. The eight-room *Toboz* (☎ 325 232) is on tree-lined Fenyves sor at No 5 just south of the zoo. The rate is about 1500 Ft per head, regardless of occupancy. The *Avar* (☎ 321 924) at Fenyves sor 2, with seven cramped rooms (2500 Ft for a double) and a unkempt garden, is a distant second choice.

One central exception is the *Gastrium*

pension (☎ 326 495) opposite the bus station at Somogyi Béla utca 1. It charges 2200 to 2500 Ft for a double with shower. There are only five rooms, but if you arrive by bus it only takes a few minutes to try for one.

Hotels A very central yet affordable place is the 15-room *Főnix* hotel (☎ 311 680), a stone's throw from the Mosque Church at Hunyadi János út 2. Singles/doubles with shower cost from 2790/3890 Ft.

An excellent (though far-flung) place to stay is the *Laterum* hotel (☎ 255 829) on the far west side of town at Hajnóczy utca 37-39. Prices range from 600 to 1800 Ft per head depending on whether you sleep in a dorm room, a room with shared bath or one with private bath, and there's an inexpensive self-service restaurant just off the hotel lobby.

The *Hunyor* (☎ 315 677), in the Mecsek foothills at Jurisics Miklós utca 16, is a bit out of the way, but has excellent views of the city and almost a resort feel. There's a pleasant restaurant attached and all 53 rooms have TVs, telephones and baths. Singles are DM55 to DM68 and doubles DM77 to DM95, depending on the season.

Farther into the hills near the TV tower is the *Kikelet* hotel (☎ 310 777), a former trade-union resort at Károlyi Mihály utca 1. Its 34 rooms without/with bath are 2000/3000 Ft per person, a good bet if you're alone. The 18-room, two-star *Fenyves* hotel (☎ 315 996), south of the Kikelet at Szőlő utca 64, has a great view of the city (doubles with bath are 4000 Ft).

Pécs' old-world hotel is the 88-room *Palatinus* (☎ 233 022), at Király utca 5, where singles range from DM81 to DM98 and doubles are from DM87 to DM104. Avoid the Palatinus' wicked (but cheaper) stepsister, the *Pátria* (☎ 213 322), an ugly 113-room block at Rákóczi út 3.

Places to Eat

The *Apolló* is a small takeaway place at Perczel Mór utca 23 serving Middle Eastern specialities like gyros and felafel. There are several fast-food places around town like *McDonald's* at Király utca 2 and *Pizza Hut*

on the corner of Rákóczi utca and Bajcsy-Zsilinszky utca.

One of the nicest places in town is the *Minaret*, Ferencesek utcája 35, which serves inexpensive Hungarian and Chinese meals in the pleasant courtyard of an old Franciscan cloister (1738). The *Görög Taverna*, a bit farther east on Ferencesek utcája, has excellent home-made Greek dishes like dolmades, pastitsio and moussaka.

Two excellent bets are the *Aranykacsa*, Teréz utca 4 south of Széchenyi tér, which has a salad bar, and the *Dóm*, a small loft restaurant in the courtyard at Király utca 3. The latter has wonderful *fin-de-siècle* paintings and stained-glass windows and is open till 11 pm.

Two restaurants on the pricey side are built into the western city wall along Klimó György utca. At No 18, the *Barbakán*, a wine cellar with Gypsy music, serves great platters of Stifolder sausage and 'Mecsek Lad's Soup' (open till 2 am). The *Santa Maria* at No 12 is a classy place done up like one of Columbus' Spanish galleons and open till midnight. It specialises in seafood.

The best place in Pécs for cake and ice cream is the *Mecsek* at Széchenyi tér 16 near the old Nádor hotel. There's a 24-hour grocery store at Hungária utca 18 west of Kórház tér.

Entertainment

The *House of Artists* (☎ 315 388) at Széchenyi tér 7-8 advertises its many programmes outside. This is the place to ask about classical music concerts. Other musical venues include the *Ferenc Liszt Concert Hall* east of the centre at Király utca 83 and the *Basilica of St Peter*, where organ concerts frequently take place on Friday at 8 pm.

Pécs is also renowned for its opera company and the Sophianae Ballet. If you're told that tickets to the *Pécs National Theatre* on Király utca are sold out, try for a cancellation at the box office an hour before the performance. This theatre is closed all summer so ask Tourinform about concerts and other events elsewhere.

Other stages are the *Chamber Theatre*

next door to the National Theatre and the *Croatian Theatre* at Anna utca 17.

Pécs is a big university town (one of the three here was moved from Bratislava when that city was ceded to Czechoslovakia after WWII), and that is reflected in the city's nightlife. Some of Pécs' most popular discos are *Club Pepita* on 48-as tér near the university east of the centre; *A Gyár* (The Factory), an 'alternative culture and rock music club', which is open from Tuesday to Saturday from 8 pm to 4 am at Czindery utca 3-5; and the *West Disco* opposite A Gyár at Czindery utca 12. It's open Friday and Saturday till 5 am.

There are pubs and bars almost the entire length of Király utca, many of them with outside tables in summer. The *Royal* at No 1, the *John Bull* at No 4, the *Dóm* at No 5 and the *Liceum* in the courtyard at No 35 are all good bets. The *Nothing but the Blues* club at Apáca utca 2 has live music most nights, while the *Áfium* restaurant and bar, at Irgalmasok utcája 2, is popular with students. The *Jazz Café* at Mária utca 9 has both live acts and canned music. The most spectacular place for a drink is the *TV Torony* bar and restaurant atop the TV tower on Misina Peak.

There's a nice little wine bar called *Dani* in a courtyard off Citrom utca south of Széchenyi tér. The wine to try here is the white Cirfandli, a speciality of the Mecsek Hills.

While visiting the cathedral or the museums along Káptalan utca, stop in for a drink or a coffee at the *Kioszk* in the little park between Káptalan utca and Janus Pannonius utca. It's probably the only chance you'll ever have to drink in what was once a baptistery.

Things to Buy

Pécs has been renowned for its leatherwork since Turkish times, and you can pick up a few bargains in several shops around the city. Try Blázek at Teréz utca 1. There's a Zsolnay outlet at Jókai tér 2.

Getting There & Away

Bus Pécs is a major hub for bus travel, and there are few places you can't reach from here. Departures are frequent to Siklós,

Pécsvárád Fortress, near Pécs

Mohács, Harkány, Kaposvár, Vajszló, Szigetvár and Szekszárd. You can also reach Budapest on five buses a day, Győr (two), Hévíz (two), Kecskemét (two), Sellye (up to five), Siófok (three), Székesfehérvár (two), Sopron (one), Szeged (six), Veszprém (two), Villány (two) and Zalaegerszeg (two).

There are some two dozen daily departures in summer to Abaliget and Orfű in the Mecsek Hills, but only eight or so in winter.

Buses run about five times a day from Barcs to Zagreb, and there are also two afternoon buses a day from Pécs to Osijek.

Train Some 10 trains a day connect Pécs with Budapest-Déli station. You can reach Nagykanizsa and other points north-west via a rather circuitous but scenic line along the Dráva River. From Nagykanizsa, three or four trains a day continue on to Szombathely. One early morning express (at 5.40 am) follows this route from Pécs all the way to Szombathely.

For Croatia, a daily train runs between Pécs and Zagreb, leaving Pécs in the very early morning and Zagreb in the late afternoon.

Getting Around

To get to the Hunyor hotel, take bus No 32 from the train station or the No 36 from opposite the Mosque Church. Bus Nos 34 and 35 run direct to the Kikelet and Fenyves hotels from the train station. Bus No 34 goes on to the camping ground, while bus No 35 continues to the TV tower. For the Laterum hotel, take bus No 4 from the train station or the market near the bus station to the end of the line at Uránváros. Bus Nos 3 and 50 from the train station are good for the flea market on Vásártér.

You can order a local taxi on ☎ 233 333/ 333 333.

MECSEK HILLS

Buses from Pécs reach most towns in the Mecsek Hills, but if you plan to do a lot of hiking, get a copy of Cartographia's 1:40,000 *A Mecsek Turistatérképe* (No 15) before setting out.

Orfű

• *pop 580*
• *area code* ☎ 72

The most accessible of the Mecsek resorts and the one with the most recreational facilities is Orfű, a series of settlements on four artificial lakes where you can swim, row, canoe and fish. There's a riding school called Eldorádó at Petőfi utca 3 in nearby Tekeres. From Széchenyi tér you can walk south along tiny Lake Orfű to the Mill Museum, a series of old pump houses open from 10 am to 6 pm in summer.

Places to Stay & Eat Orfű's main places to stay are the Mecsek Tours-run *hostel* (☎ 378 501) at Petőfi utca 6 in Tekeres at the northern end of Lake Pécs (600 Ft); the cheap four-room *Vaskakas* pension (☎ 378 529) at Mecsekárosi utca 29 on the lake's eastern shore; the nine-room *Molnár* pension (☎ 378 563) at Széchenyi tér 18/a; and *Panoráma Camping* (☎ 378 501) at Dollár utca 1 above the large public beach in the lake's southwestern corner and open mid-April to mid-October. Bungalows here are 2400 to 4100 Ft, depending on the season, and there are dinghies, sailboards and bicycles for rent.

The *Muskátli* is a pleasant little restaurant

in Széchenyi tér near Molnár pension. The *Hegyalja* is a cheap büfé on a hill above Lake Orfű, open to 10 pm.

Abaliget

• *pop 650*
• *area code* ☎ 72

Abaliget, three km north-west of Orfű and accessible by bus or on foot via a trail up and over the hill behind Panoráma Camping, is quieter but not as attractive. There are lots of *private rooms* for rent along the main street (Kossuth Lajos utca), but the only standard accommodation in town is at *Barlang Camping* (☎ 378 530) on the town's tiny lake and near the cave. The site also has a nine-room *inn* and a *motel* with doubles for 3000 Ft. There's a small horse-riding school here, the 450m **Abaliget Cave** to explore and the large *Aranyszarvas* restaurant at Kossuth utca 78.

KAPOSVÁR

• *pop 74,000*
• *area code* ☎ 82

Somogy County is usually associated with Lake Balaton and rightly so: it 'owns' the entire money-spinning southern shore of the lake from Siófok to Balatonberény. Kaposvár, the county seat 55 km to the south, does not generally spring to mind.

It's not an unattractive place, situated in the Zselic foothills along the valley of the Kapos River. But don't come to 'Kapos Castle' looking for a fortress like the one at Siklós or Szigetvár; the Turks and then the Habsburgs dispatched that long ago. In fact, so heavy and constant was the fighting here over the centuries that few buildings date from before 1900. Instead, visit Kaposvár for its art (the city is associated with three great painters: the postimpressionists József Rippl-Rónai and János Vaszary, as well as Aurél Bernáth) and its theatre, among the best in provincial Hungary.

Kaposvár now gets marked on the world map because of the village of Taszár, eight km to the east. This is the site of NATO's first operating military base in the former Eastern

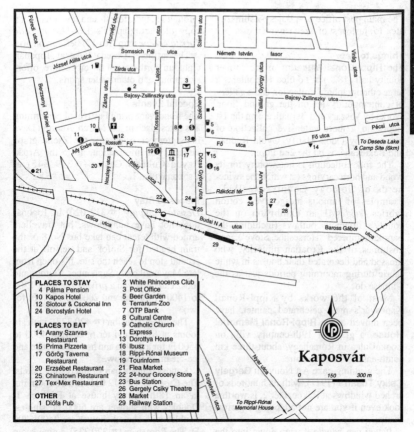

Kaposvár

0   150   300 m

PLACES TO STAY
4 Pálma Pension
10 Kapos Hotel
12 Siotour & Csokonai Inn
24 Borostyán Hotel

PLACES TO EAT
14 Arany Szarvas Restaurant
15 Prima Pizzeria
17 Görög Taverna Restaurant
20 Erzsébet Restaurant
25 Chinatown Restaurant
27 Tex-Mex Restaurant

OTHER
1 Diófa Pub
2 White Rhinoceros Club
3 Post Office
5 Beer Garden
6 Terrarium-Zoo
7 OTP Bank
8 Cultural Centre
9 Catholic Church
11 Express
13 Dorottya House
16 Ibusz
18 Rippl-Rónai Museum
19 Tourinform
21 Flea Market
22 24-hour Grocery Store
23 Bus Station
26 Gergely Csiky Theatre
28 Market
29 Railway Station

bloc and, since December 1995, Taszár has been the main logistical centre for troops and supplies funnelling into the US-run northern zone of the peacekeeping operation in Bosnia. Some 2000 GIs are garrisoned here (with another 20,000 troops irregularly passing through), but you won't see many in town – there are sharp limits on their fraternising with the locals.

Orientation & Information

The train and bus stations are a block apart south of the city centre. From here, walk up

Teleki utca to Fő utca, a lovely pedestrian street where most of the action is.

For information about Kaposvár and surrounds, see Tourinform (☎ 320 404) at Fő utca 8. It is open weekdays from 9 am to 5 pm and Saturday to noon (an hour later in summer). Siotour (☎ 320 537), in the same building as the Csokonai inn at Fő utca 1, is open weekdays from 8 am to 4.30 pm and to noon on Saturday.

There's an Express office (☎ 318 416) at Ady Endre utca 8, and Ibusz (☎ 315 477) is at Dózsa György utca 5.

OTP bank has a branch at Széchenyi tér 2.

The main post office is at Bajcsy-Zsilinszky utca 15, just west of Széchenyi tér.

Things to See

The **Rippl-Rónai Museum** in the former county hall (1820) at Fő utca 10 contains a large ethnographical collection and a gallery of contemporary art on the ground floor. Works by Vaszary and Bernáth are on the 1st floor and a more extensive collection of paintings by Ödön Márffy, Gyula Rudnay and Béla Kádár is on the 2nd floor.

The folk collection is noteworthy for its wood and horn carvings (at which the swineherds of Somogy County excelled), examples of famous indigo-dyed cotton fabrics (*kékfestő*), an exhibition on the county's infamous outlaws (including the paprika-tempered 'Horseshoe Steve'), and costumes of the Croatian minority, who dressed and decorated their houses in white fabric during mourning periods just as the Chinese do.

Most of the works by Rippl-Rónai, Kaposvár's most celebrated painter, have been moved to the **Rippl-Rónai Memorial House**, a graceful 19th-century villa on Lonkai utca in Rómahegy, about three km south-east of the city centre.

The wedding-cake Art Nouveau **Gergely Csiky Theatre** (1911), with its hundreds of arched windows at Rákóczi tér 2, is worth a look even if you are not attending a performance.

If you can handle it, step down into the **Terrarium-Zoo** in a humid cellar at Fő utca 31. Cobras, caymans, boas and a python as thick as a stevedore's forearm are all there to greet you from 9 am to 5 pm weekdays, till noon on Saturday and from 2 to 5 pm on Sunday.

The fruit and vegetable **market** is east of Rákóczi tér on Baross Gábor utca. There's a small daily **flea market** at Vásárteri út west of the bus station.

Activities

The Zselic region south of Kaposvár, a large part of which is under a nature-conservation order, is webbed with trails for easy hikes through villages, forests and low hills. Get a copy of Cartographia's 1:60,000 *A Zelic Turistatérképe* map (No 17) before you go.

The artificial Deseda Lake at Toponár, eight km north-east of the city centre, offers swimming and other water sports.

Special Events

The Kaposvár Spring Festival of performing arts takes place in late March. Autumn Days in September celebrates the Zselic grape vintage. For information, go to the Árpád Együd Cultural Centre (☎ 319 845) at Csokonai utca 1.

Places to Stay

Deseda Camping (☎ 312 020) in Toponár does not have bungalows, but travellers armed with a tent can take bus No 8 or the train headed for Siófok and get off at the second stop to reach the site. It's open from late May until early September. Siotour and Ibusz can book you a *private room* for 1200 to 1400 Ft for one and 2000 to 2500 Ft for two.

The *Pálma* pension (☎ 420 227), with six rooms at Széchenyi tér 6, charges 4300 to 4500 Ft for a double and has a great cake and ice-cream shop below.

Kaposvár has a pair of interesting hotels. The *Csokonai* (☎ 312 011) is a 21-room inn in an 18th-century house at Fő utca 1. Doubles with shower are 6600 Ft, singles/doubles with shared shower are 2400/5700 Ft. The *Borostyán* (☎ 320 735), a nine-room Art Nouveau extravaganza at Rákóczi tér 3, is one of provincial Hungary's most interesting hotels. Singles/doubles are 5300/5800 Ft.

The 49-room *Kapos* hotel (☎ 316 022) is an unattractive, modern affair at Ady Endre utca 2. Singles range from 4500 to 5500 Ft and doubles from 5900 to 6700 Ft, depending on the room category.

If you want to do some horse riding, consider the 50-room *Castle* hotel (☎ 370 801) at Gálosfa in the Red Apple Hills 20 km south-east of Kaposvár. Tennis, fishing, sauna, horses – it has the works. Singles are about 5000 Ft, doubles are from 6500 Ft.

Places to Eat

Prima Pizzeria at Dósza György utca 1/a is a cheap and fast place, but the pizzas are better (and the surrounds more relaxed) at the *Erzsébet*, in a gorgeous robin's-egg-blue old house at Noszlopy Gáspár utca 4. The *Bianco Nano* coffee shop at the Kapos hotel has pizza as well as a salad bar.

Kaposvár has seen a plethora of ethnic restaurants spring up recently – could it be all those hungry GIs? The *Görög Taverna* on the corner of Fő utca and Irányi Dániel utca serves passable Greek food daily until midnight. The food at the *Chinatown* across from the Gergely Csiky Theatre at Rákóczi tér 1 is almost American-Chinese (and not half bad). And of course there has to be a place for tacos and burritos – in this case, the *Tex-Mex* restaurant on the opposite side of Rákóczi tér at No 17.

The *Arany Szarvas* at Fő utca 46 is a typical, middle-range Hungarian restaurant with game specialities. The restaurant at the *Csokonai* hotel has seating both in a charming courtyard and a rather cramped cellar. One of the fanciest places in town is the dining room at the *Borostyán* hotel (open daily except Sunday to 11 pm).

There's a 24-hour *grocery store* across from the bus station on Budai Nagy Antal utca.

Entertainment

Aside from being a masterpiece of Art Nouveau (or Secessionist) architecture, the yellow and white *Gergely Csiky Theatre* at Rákóczi tér 2 has a high reputation and was at the forefront of artistic innovation under Gábor Zsámbeki in the 1970s. Tickets can be purchased at the booking office (☎ 311 113) at Fő utca 8.

Kaposvár is known for its choral groups, and concerts are given in venues around the city, including the *Catholic church* facing Kossuth tér.

The *Sörkert* (beer garden) on Széchenyi tér next to Dorottya House, where most of the action in playwright Mihály Csokonai Vitéz's comic epic *Dorottya* (1804) takes place, is a good spot for a beer, as is the *Diófa*

pub at Zárda utca 39 north of Kossuth tér. If you're looking for something a bit more frisky, head for the *White Rhinoceros* (Fehér Orrszarvú) club in a big old house at Bajcsy-Zsilinszky utca 1/c or the *Arizona Disco* on Fő utca (open daily except Sunday from 9 pm to 2 or 4 am).

Getting There & Away

Bus At least eight buses leave every day for Barcs, Pécs, Siófok, Gálosfa and Nagykanizsa. Other destinations include: Baja (one bus a day), Budapest (three), Győr (two), Hévíz (two), the thermal spa at Igal (five), Mohács (two), Sopron (one), Szeged (one), Szekszárd (two), Szenna (four), Szigetvár (four), Szombathely (one) and Tapolca (one).

Train You can reach Kaposvár by train from both the eastern (Siófok) and western (Fonyód) ends of Lake Balaton's southern shore. Another line links Kaposvár with Budapest (via Dombóvár) to the north-east four times a day and, to the west, with Gyékényes, from where international trains depart for Zagreb (three a day).

Getting Around

Bus No 8 terminates near the lake and the camp site in Toponár. For the Rippl-Rónai Memorial House in Rómahegy, take bus No 15.

Local taxis are available on ☎ 310 333.

AROUND KAPOSVÁR

Szenna

• *pop 650*

This village nine km south-west of Kaposvár and accessible by bus has Hungary's smallest and arguably its best **skanzen**. What makes it unique is that the large 18th-century **Calvinist church**, with its 'crowned' pulpit, coffered and painted ceiling, loft and pews, still functions as a house of worship for villagers.

Half a dozen *porták* (farmhouses with outbuildings) from central Somogy County and the Zselic region surround the 'folk baroque' church – as they would in a real village – and

Zrínyi's Big Sally

For more than a month in late 1566 at Szigetvár, Captain Miklós Zrínyi and the 2500 Hungarian and Croatian soldiers under his command held out against Turkish forces numbering up to 80,000. The leader of the Turkish forces was Sultan Suleiman I, who was making his seventh attempt to march on Vienna and was determined to take what he derisively called 'this molehill'. When the defenders' water and food supplies were exhausted – and reinforcements from Győr under Habsburg Emperor Maximilian II were refused – Zrínyi could see no other solution but a suicidal sally. As the moated castle burned behind them, the opponents fought hand to hand, and most of the soldiers on the Hungarian side, including Zrínyi himself, were killed. An estimated one-quarter of the Turkish forces died in the siege; Suleiman suffered a heart attack and died and his corpse was propped up on a chair during the fighting to inspire his troops and avoid a power struggle until his son could take command.

More than any other heroes in Hungarian history, Zrínyi and his soldiers are remembered for their self-sacrifice in the cause of the nation and for saving Vienna (and thereby Europe) from Turkish domination. *Peril at Sziget*, a 17th-century epic poem by Zrínyi's great-grandson and namesake (and himself a brilliant general), immortalises the siege and is still widely read in Hungary. ■

the caretaker will point out the most interesting details: 'smoke' kitchens with stable (Dutch) doors; the woven-wall construction of the stables and barns; lumps of sugar suspended from the ceiling to soothe irritable children (bread soaked in pálinka was given to those who were particularly pesky); a coop atop the pigsty to keep the chickens warm in winter; and ingenious wooden locks 'so secure that even God couldn't get in'.

The skanzen, at Rákóczi utca 2 and across from the main bus stop, is open daily except Monday from 10 am to 6 pm April to October, and 11 am to 3 pm the rest of the year.

SZIGETVÁR

• *pop 12,500*
• *area code* ☎ 73

Szigetvár, 33 km west of Pécs and 40 km south of Kaposvár, was a Celtic settlement and then a Roman one called Limosa before the Magyar conquest. The strategic importance of the town was recognised early on, and in 1420 a fortress was built on a small island (Szigetvár means 'island castle') in the marshy areas of the Almás River. But Szigetvár would be indistinguishable today from other Southern Transdanubian towns had the events of September 1566 not taken place (see aside).

Today you can visit what remains of the town's famous castle, and there are a handful of Turkish-era monuments to gawk at. The town's popular thermal spa has re-opened after a long hiatus, and work on architect Imre Makovecz's stunning cultural and civic centre has finished. Szigetvár in the late 1990s has come back to life after almost withering on the vine five years ago.

Orientation & Information

The bus and train stations are next to one another a short distance south of the town centre. Follow Rákóczi utca north into lovely Zrínyi tér. Vár utca on the north side of the square leads to the castle.

Mecsek Tours (☎ 310 116), open from 7.30 am to 4 pm on weekdays, is in the lobby of the Oroszlán hotel at Zrínyi tér 2. There's a K&H bank at Széchenyi István utca 4 and a branch of OTP with an ATM at Vár utca 4. The main post office is at József Attila utca 27-31.

Zrínyi Castle

Our hero Miklós Zrínyi would probably not recognise the four-cornered castle he so valiantly fought to save more than 400 years ago. The Turks strengthened the bastions and added buildings; the Hungarians rebuilt it again in the 18th century. Today there are only a few elements of historical interest left: walls from three to six metres thick linked by the four bastions; the **Baroque Tower** crowning the southern wall; the 16th-century **Sultan Suleiman Mosque** with a shortened minaret; and a summer mansion built by Count Andrássy in 1930, which now houses the **Castle Museum**.

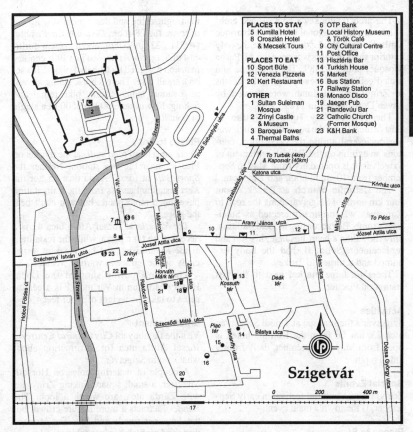

PLACES TO STAY
5 Kumilla Hotel
8 Oroszlán Hotel & Mecsek Tours

PLACES TO EAT
10 Sport Büfe
12 Venezia Pizzeria
20 Kert Restaurant

OTHER
1 Sultan Suleiman Mosque
2 Zrínyi Castle & Museum
3 Baroque Tower
4 Thermal Baths
6 OTP Bank
7 Local History Museum & Török Café
9 City Cultural Centre
11 Post Office
13 Hisztéria Bar
14 Turkish House
15 Market
16 Bus Station
17 Railway Station
18 Monaco Disco
19 Jaeger Pub
21 Randevúu Bar
22 Catholic Church (Former Mosque)
23 K&H Bank

Szigetvár

Naturally, the museum's exhibits focus on the siege and its key players. Zrínyi's praises are sung throughout, there's a detailed account of how Suleiman built a bridge over the Dráva in 16 days to attack Szigetvár, and the miniatures of Hungarian soldiers being captured, chopped up and burned are still quite horrifying. Sebestyén Tinódi, the beloved 16th-century poet and wandering minstrel who was born in Szigetvár, also rates an altar of worship. The mosque next door, completed in the year of the siege, contains an art gallery of debatable interest,

but the arches, prayer niches and Arabic inscriptions on the walls are worth a look. From April to September the museum is open daily (except Monday) from 8 am to 6 pm; the rest of the year from 10 am to 3 pm.

Other Things to See

The tiny **Local History Museum** at Vár utca 1 is a hotchpotch of folk carvings, embroidery and valuables from local churches, but it displays a great collection of 18th and 19th-century shop signs as well as locks and keys from the castle.

The arched 'donkey's back' (ogee arch) windows and hexagonal roof of the baroque **Catholic church** at Zrínyi tér 9 are the only exterior signs that this was once the Ali Pasha Mosque, built in 1589. The altarpiece and muted ceiling frescoes depicting the deaths of Zrínyi and Suleiman were painted by István Dorffmeister in 1789.

The 16th-century **Turkish House** at Bástya utca 3 near the bus station, which was a caravanserai during the occupation, contains an exhibit on the Turkish settlement of Szigetvár. It is open daily from May to September from 10 am to noon and 2 to 4 pm.

The **Catholic church** at Turbék, about four km north of Szigetvár along the road to Kaposvár, was originally erected as Suleiman's tomb. But according to local tradition, only the sultan's heart lies here; his son and replacement, Selim II, had the body exhumed and returned to Turkey.

There's a large **market** next to the bus station on Piac tér.

Activities

Szigetvár's thermal spa at Tinódi Sebestyén utca 23, not far from the Kumilla hotel, is open from May to September, daily from 9 am to 6 pm.

Special Events

Zrínyi Days, a cultural festival in early September, is the town's main event.

Places to Stay

Mecsek Tours can organise *private rooms* for between 2000 and 2400 Ft for two people.

The *Oroszlán* (☎ 331 0116) at Zrínyi tér 2 has 34 purely functional rooms (singles/doubles 3100/4600 Ft), but the hotel is central to everything and the staff are very helpful.

An old music school at Olay Lajos utca 6 is now the 32-room *Kumilla* hotel (☎ 310 150), which takes its name from the beloved daughter of Suleiman and his Russian wife. Singles/doubles with showers are DM45/60. Some of the rooms have interesting old furniture.

If you're more interested in recreation

than sightseeing and don't mind staying out of town, the 28-room *Domolos Castle* hotel (☎ 311 222) in Zsibót, about six km northeast of Szigetvár, is housed in a 19th-century mansion designed by Mihály Pollack. It's set on a small lake. There's horse riding as well as a sauna, tennis courts, bike rental and fishing. Rooms are 3000 to 3500 Ft a single or double.

Places to Eat

There are a lot of *food stalls* at the market on Piac tér near the bus station. Neither the *Sport Büfe* at József Attila utca 15 nor the *Kert* restaurant across from the train station have much atmosphere, but you can't beat the prices.

The *Venezia* at József Attila utca 41 is a decent place for a pizza, while the restaurant at the *Kumilla* is quiet but pleasant, especially on the terrace in warmer weather.

The *Török* coffee shop at the Local History Museum at Vár utca 1 is a central place to take the weight off your feet.

Entertainment

Visit the flamboyant *City Cultural Centre* on József Attila utca for information about what's on in Szigetvár.

A couple of watering holes on Horváth Márk tér, a small square linking Zrínyi tér with Zárda utca, are worth a look. The *Randevú* attracts a more mature crowd, but the *Jaeger* is rowdy and fun. The *Monaco* disco and nightclub is just behind the Jaeger; enter from Zárda utca. The enticingly named *Hisztéria* bar at Kossuth Lajos tér 12 has pool tables and is open to 1 am (4 am at weekends).

Getting There & Away

Bus Each day up to 10 buses depart Szigetvár for Pécs, while four a day run to Kaposvár. Otherwise, there are three daily departures to Barcs, two to Mohács, one or two to Szentlőrinc, three or four to Zalaegerszeg and a couple to Nagykanizsa and Siklós. From Barcs, on the border with Croatia 32 km to the south-west, buses head for Zagreb.

The Ormánság folk region is accessible

from Szigetvár, but there is only one very slow bus at 12.40 pm on weekdays (12.20 pm on Saturday). By train, you must travel east for 15 km and change at Szentlőrinc.

Train Szigetvár is on a rail line linking Pécs and Nagykanizsa. The 84-km stretch from Barcs to Nagykanizsa follows the course of the Dráva River and is very scenic, especially around Vízvár and Bélavár. If you're trying to leave Hungary from here, get off at Murakeresztúr (two stops before Nagykanizsa), through which trains pass en route to Zagreb, Ljubljana and the Adriatic Coast, including Trieste and Venice.

NAGYKANIZSA

• *pop 55,300*
• *area code* ☎ *93*

Lying on a canal linking the Zala River to the north with the Mura River on the Croatian border, Nagykanizsa hosted a succession of settlers, including Celts, Romans, Avars and Slavs, before the arrival of the Magyars. Early in the 14th century, Charles Robert, the first Anjou king of Hungary, ceded the area to the Kanizsay family, who built a castle in the marshes of the canal west of today's town centre. The castle was fortified after the fall of Szigetvár in 1566 but, despite the heroics of one Captain György Thury, it too was taken by the Turks and remained an important district seat for 90 years under their rule. Development didn't really begin until a few centuries later with the construction of the Budapest-Adriatic railway line through the town and the discovery of the Zala oil fields to the west.

Nagykanizsa is not especially noted for its sights (nothing remains of the castle that was blown to smithereens by the Habsburgs in the 18th century); the town's almost totally focused on drilling for oil, making light bulbs and furniture, and brewing beer for the rest of the country. But if you think of it as a convenient stepping stone, you'll literally be on the right track. From Nagykanizsa you can easily reach Western Transdanubia, both

shores of Lake Balaton, Croatia and the beaches of the Adriatic.

Orientation & Information

The train station is south of the city centre. Walk north along Ady Endre utca for about 1200m, and you'll be on Fő út, the main street. The bus station is in the centre on the west side of Erzsébet tér.

Zalatour (☎ 311 185) is at Fő út 13 while Ibusz is at Rozgonyi utca 3. The former opens between 8 am and 5 pm on weekdays and till noon on Saturday; the latter keeps weekday hours only. Express ☎ 314 375) has an office at Deák Ferenc tér 1.

OTP bank has a branch in Deák tér on the corner of Sugár út. The main post office is at Ady Endre utca 10 close to the market.

The excellent Zrínyi bookshop in the courtyard behind Fő út 8 has a selection of foreign-language publications. It is open from 9 am to 5 pm weekdays and till noon on Saturday.

Things to See

The **György Thury Museum** at Fő út 5 has a surprisingly interesting standing exhibit called 'The Forest and the People in Zala'; absolutely nothing connected with wood, the woods and forestry is overlooked – from antique saws and charcoal-burning equipment to household utensils made of bark and exquisite hunting knives and rifles. The contemporary illustrations of Kanizsa Castle are fascinating, especially the idealised Turkish one from 1664 showing 14 minarets within the castle walls. The museum is open from 10 am to 6 pm Tuesday to Saturday.

The **City Art Gallery** is in the 18th-century Iron Man House (Vasemberház) at Erzsébet tér 1, named after the suit of armour on the façade that once advertised an ironmonger's. Enter from Ady Endre utca. The gallery exhibits small sculptures and other work by local artists on Wednesday and Thursday from 10 am to 2 pm and Friday to Sunday from 2 to 6 pm.

The neoclassical **synagogue**, built in 1810 in a courtyard behind Fő út 6 (once a

SOUTHERN TRANSDANUBIA

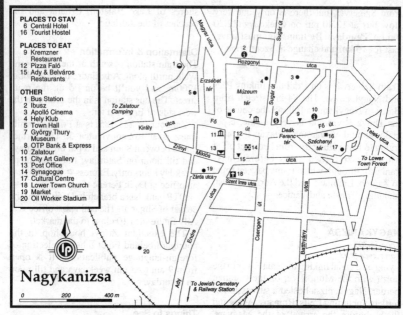

PLACES TO STAY
6 Centrál Hotel
16 Tourist Hostel

PLACES TO EAT
9 Kremzner
   Restaurant
12 Pizza Faló
15 Ady & Belváros
    Restaurants

OTHER
1 Bus Station
2 Ibusz
3 Apolló Cinema
4 Hely Klub
5 Town Hall
7 György Thury
   Museum
8 OTP Bank & Express
10 Zalatour
11 City Art Gallery
13 Post Office
14 Synagogue
17 Cultural Centre
18 Lower Town Church
19 Market
20 Oil Worker Stadium

Nagykanizsa

0   200   400 m

Jewish school), is in appalling condition, having most recently served as a storeroom for the Thury Museum. Outside the western entrance a cenotaph remembers the 2700 Jews who were rounded up here in late April 1944 and deported to death camps in Germany. The condition of the **Jewish cemetery** and mortuary on Ady Endre utca near the train station is just as bad.

On Szent Imre utca, the Franciscan **Lower Town Church**, begun in 1702 but not completed for 100 years, has some ornate stucco work and a rococo pulpit, but you can't miss the holy-water font, carved from the burial stone of a Turkish general named Mustafa.

Even if you're not going to see a film, have a look at the **Apolló** cinema (formerly the Municipal Theatre), in a small garden south of Rozgonyi utca. It's a unique example of Art Nouveau and Hungarian folk architecture designed by István Medgyaszay in 1926. He also did the exquisite Petőfi Theatre in Veszprém.

The main **market** is on Zárda utca.

Activities

The so-called Lower Town Forest, six km east of the town centre, has a large rowing lake with boats available from May to October.

If you want to swim, though, you'll have to go to the spa at Zalakaros, 18 km to the north-east near the Little Balaton (Kis Balaton). The Zalakaros spring, which gushes out of the ground at an incredible 92°C, was discovered by workers drilling for oil in the early 1960s, and now a half-dozen hotels surround it. Thermal Tours (☎ 340 412) at Gyógyfürdő tér 3 can book you into the 66-room *Termál-Liget* hotel (☎ 340 105), Gyógyfürdő tér 6, for about 3500 Ft for a double with shower.

Special Events

Olajbányász (Oil Worker) Stadium off Ady Endre utca is the venue for the Kanizsai Summer festival in June and Kanizsai Days, a three or four-day cultural, sport and beer gala held in June and again in early September.

Places to Stay

Zalatour Camping (☎ 319 119), at Vár utca 1 west of the city centre, has tiny two-person cabins available from May to September.

Zalatour can organise *private rooms* for under 1000 Ft. In summer, ask Express about *dormitory rooms* at the agricultural or trade schools. If they're closed, try the *tourist hostel* (☎ 312 340) at Fő út 24, which has triples (only) with shared shower for 680 Ft per person.

The 36-room *Centrál* hotel (☎ 314 000) at Erzsébet tér 23, built in 1912, has little old-world charm but its name describes it well. Singles/doubles with bath are 7200/9500 Ft and 5500/7100 Ft without.

Places to Eat

There are a number of good places on Ady Endre utca, including *Pizza Faló* at No 3, the *Ady* at No 5 and the *Belváros* at No 7. The *Kremzner* restaurant at Deák Ferenc tér 11 is a clean, modern place with a Germanic twist.

Entertainment

The city's symphony orchestra performs at the *Sándor Hevesi Cultural Centre* (☎ 311 468) at Széchenyi tér 5-9, and there's a theatre and youth centre there as well.

The local Kanizsai beer flows as freely throughout the year as it does at the Kanizsai Days festival. The *Pepita az Oroszlánhoz* (which effectively means the 'Chequered Banner at the Sign of the Lion') pub at the Centrál hotel is as good a place as any to try it. There's also a popular *disco* at the hotel on Friday and Saturday from 9 pm to 4 am. The *Hely Klub* at Sugár utca 13 is a studenty place that is alcohol and tobacco-free.

Getting There & Away

There's a bus every 30 minutes to the Zalakaros spa and at least half a dozen a day to Zalaegerszeg, Keszthely, Kaposvár and Balatonmagyaród on the Little Balaton. Otherwise, there are between five and six daily departures to Budapest, two to Sopron, seven to Szeged, two or three to Pápa and five each to Pécs and Szombathely.

From Nagykanizsa, six trains head north for Szombathely and other points in Western Transdanubia including Sopron, and south to Zagreb, Ljubljana and the Adriatic Coast, including Trieste and Venice. Trains run direct to Budapest-Déli (at 220 km, one of the longest train trips in Hungary) and the resorts on the southern shore of Lake Balaton, but if you're headed for the western or northern sides (such as Keszthely or Balatonfüred), you must change at Balatonszentgyörgy.

Getting Around

Nagykanizsa is an easy walking city, but you may prefer to wait and ride. From the train station, bus No 19 goes to the bus station and city centre, and No 21 runs to the camp site. Bus No 15 terminates near the rowing lake in the Lower Town Forest, or you can take the Budapest-bound local train and get off at the first stop (Nagyrécse).

Local taxis are available on ☎ 333 333/ 333 111.

Great Plain

The Great Plain (Nagyalföld) is Hungary's 'Midwest', an enormous prairie that stretches for hundreds of km east and southeast of Budapest. It covers nearly half of the nation's territory – some 45,000 sq km – but only about a third of all Hungarians live here.

After Budapest and Lake Balaton, no area is so well known outside Hungary as the Great Plain, also called the *puszta*. Like Australians and their Outback, many Hungarians tend to view the Great Plain romantically as a region of hardy shepherds fighting the wind and the snow in winter and trying not to go stir-crazy in summer as the notorious *délibáb* (mirages) rise off the baking soil, leading them, their mop-like *puli* dogs and flocks astray. This mythology of the Great Plain can be credited to 19th-century paintings like *Storm on the Puszta* and *The Woebegone Highwayman* by Mihály Munkácsy, and the nationalist poet Sándor Petőfi, who described the Plain as 'My world and home... The Alföld, the open sea'.

But that's just a part of the story of the Great Plain; like the USA's Midwest, it defies such an easy categorisation. Grassland abounds in the east but much of the south is given over to agriculture, and there's industry in the centre. The graceful architecture of Szeged and Kecskemét, the recreational areas along the Tisza River, the spas of the Hajdúság region, the paprika fields around Kalocsa – all are as much a part of the Great Plain as the whip-cracking *csikós* (cowboy).

Five hundred years ago the region was not a steppe but forest land – and at the constant mercy of the flooding Tisza and Danube rivers. The Turks chopped down most of the trees, destroying the protective cover and releasing the topsoil to the winds; villagers fled north or to the market and *khas* towns under the sultan's jurisdiction. The region had become the puszta (from *pusztít*, 'to devastate' or 'destroy') and it was the home to shepherds, fisherfolk, runaway serfs and outlaws. The regulation of the rivers in the

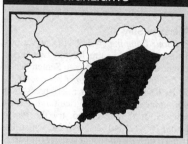

HIGHLIGHTS

- Kecskemét's wonderful Art Nouveau architecture and Museum of Naive Artists
- the Ferenc Móra Museum, Art Nouveau synagogue and *szegedi halászlé* (spicy fish soup) of Szeged
- bird-watching in the Hortobágy region
- horse riding in Máta
- canoeing on the Tisza River
- Debrecen's colourful flea market and Gypsy horse market
- the black pottery of Ferenc Fazekas at Nádudvar
- the horse show at Kiskunság National Park
- the incredibly rich Archbishop's Treasury at Kalocsa Cathedral
- enormous Szentháromság tér, Baja's main square beside the Danube
- the restored 360° panorama painting entitled *The Arrival of the Hungarians* at Ópusztaszer
- Gyula's Ladics House museum and the Százéves cake shop and museum next door

19th century dried up the marshes and allowed for methodical irrigation, paving the way for intensive agriculture, particularly on the Southern Plain.

Hungarians generally divide the Great Plain in two: the area 'between the Danube and the Tisza rivers', stretching from the foothills of the Northern Uplands to the border with Yugoslavia, and the land

290

'beyond the Tisza' (Tiszántúl) from below Hungary's North-East region to Romania. But this does not really reflect the lie of the land, the routes that travellers usually take or, frankly, what's of interest. Instead, it can be divided into the Central Plain, the Eastern Plain and the Southern Plain.

Central Plain

The Central Plain, stretching east from Budapest and including Szolnok, Jászberény and the Tisza River, is the smallest of the Plain's divisions. Though it offers the least of the three areas to travellers, that does not mean there's nothing here: the spas and Tisza resorts attract foreign and domestic visitors by the busload every year. But the Central Plain is usually crossed without a second glance en route to 'richer' areas.

Though it had been a crossroads since Neolithic times, the Central Plain only came into its own after the Mongol invasion of the early 13th century, which left it almost completely depopulated. In a bid to strengthen his position, King Béla IV (ruled 1235-70) settled the area with Jász, or Jazygians, an obscure pastoral people of Persian origin whose name still appears in towns throughout the region, and Kun (Cumans) from western Siberia, known for their horse-riding skills.

The area suffered under the Turks and during the independence wars of the 18th and 19th centuries. But Transylvanian salt and timber from the Carpathians had brought commerce to the region and, with the construction of the Budapest-Szolnok railway line (1847) and river drainage, industry developed.

SZOLNOK
- *pop 81,000*
- *area code ☎ 56*

A 'deed of gift' issued by King Géza I makes mention of Szolnok (then called Zounok) as early as 1075, and it has remained the most important settlement in the Central Plain

since that time. Szolnok has had its own share of troubles; it was laid to waste more than a dozen times over the centuries. The last disaster came in 1944, when Allied bombing all but flattened the city and the retreating German troops blew up the bridge over the Tisza. The appearance of present-day Szolnok is postwar, but a few old monuments, the city's thermal spas and the Tisza (a river Daniel Defoe once described as 'three parts water and two parts fish') give it a calm, almost laid-back feel.

Orientation
Szolnok is situated on the confluence of the Tisza and the narrow Zagyva rivers. Its main street, Kossuth Lajos út, runs roughly west-east a few blocks north of the Tisza. Across the Tisza Bridge (rebuilt in 1963) to the south is the city's recreational area, Tisza-liget (Tisza Park), with a hotel and hostel as well as swimming pools. A backwater of the Tisza (Alcsi-Holt-Tisza) lies south-east of the park.

The city's busy train station is on Jubileumi tér a couple of km west of the city centre at the end of Baross Gábor út (the continuation of Kossuth Lajos út). The bus station is a few minutes walk north of Kossuth Lajos út.

Information
Tourinform (☎ 424 803) is at Ságvári körút 4, around the corner from the bus station. Express (☎ 421 502) is on the corner of Szapáry utca and Kossuth Lajos út, while Ibusz (☎ 420 039) is farther south at Szapáry utca 24. All are open on weekdays from 8 am to 4 or 5 pm; Tourinform opens on Saturday morning in summer.

There's an OTP bank at Szapáry utca 31 and an MKB bank with an ATM on the corner of Baross Gábor út and Sütő utca. The main post office is at Baross Gábor út 1.

Things to See
Like so many fortresses on the Great Plain, Szolnok Castle was blown to bits by the Habsburgs in 1710, and the rubble was later used to rebuild the city centre. What little is

GREAT PLAIN

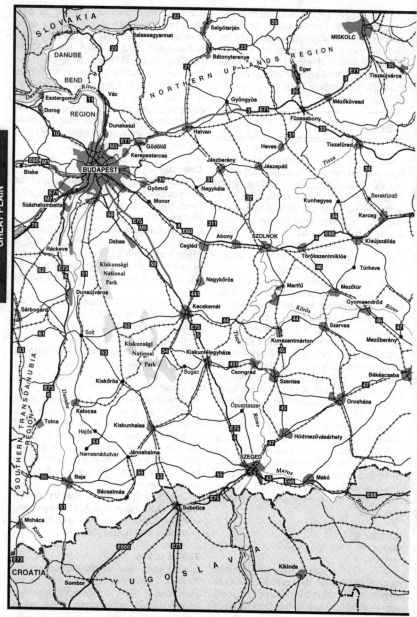

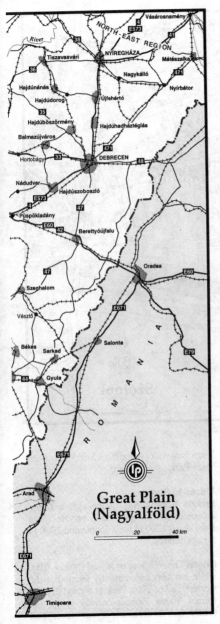

Great Plain
(Nagyalföld)

0   20   40 km

left of the **castle ruins** – just a bit of wall – can be seen near Gutenberg tér across the Zagyva. Gutenberg tér is also the site of Hungary's most famous **artists' colony** (*művésztelep*), founded in 1902 and once counting among its members the realist painters Adolf Fényes, István Nagy and László Mednyánszky.

Fronting the Zagyva north-east of Szabadság tér is the **Tabán district** with the last remaining peasant houses in Szolnok. Once scorned, the Tabán has become a desirable neighbourhood to live in, and nouveau peasant houses with all the mod cons mingle with older thatch-roofed cottages and a few housing blocks.

The **János Damjanich Museum** at Kossuth tér 4, with artefacts relating to the history of the city and county as well as archaeological finds, has been undergoing extensive renovations for several years now. One of these days... Damjanich, a great hero during the siege of Szolnok in 1849, was executed by the Austrians along with 12 other Hungarian generals later that year in Arad (now in Romania).

The **Szolnok Gallery** at Templom utca 2 shows works by contemporary artists, but they're disappointing for this arty town. The primary reason for visiting the gallery is to see the building itself – a Romantic-style **synagogue** designed by Lipót Baumhorn in 1898. (Baumhorn also did the glorious temples in Szeged and Gyöngyös.) West of the gallery at No 8 is the baroque **Franciscan church** and **monastery** completed in 1757 – today the city's oldest standing buildings. Opposite Templom utca is an unusual folk-baroque statue of a seated Christ under glass.

Architecture buffs should walk up Szapáry utca from the Szolnok Gallery to No 19 for a look at one of the finest Hungarian Art Nouveau buildings in the country. Today it houses a few small businesses and a coffee shop.

Activities

Szolnok is a spa town and has several places where you can 'take the waters'. The Tisza

GREAT PLAIN

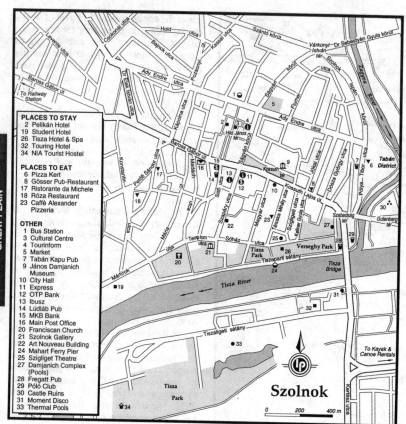

PLACES TO STAY
2 Pelikán Hotel
19 Student Hotel
26 Tisza Hotel & Spa
32 Touring Hotel
34 NIA Tourist Hostel

PLACES TO EAT
6 Pizza Kert
8 Gösser Pub-Restaurant
17 Ristorante da Michele
18 Róza Restaurant
23 Caffè Alexander
   Pizzeria

OTHER
1 Bus Station
3 Cultural Centre
4 Tourinform
5 Market
7 Tabán Kapu Pub
9 János Damjanich
   Museum
10 City Hall
11 Express
12 OTP Bank
13 Ibusz
14 Lúdláb Pub
15 MKB Bank
16 Main Post Office
20 Franciscan Church
21 Szolnok Gallery
22 Art Nouveau Building
24 Mahart Ferry Pier
25 Szigliget Theatre
27 Damjanich Complex
   (Pools)
28 Fregatt Pub
29 Póló Club
30 Castle Ruins
31 Moment Disco
33 Thermal Pools

Szolnok

0   200   400 m

Park thermal pools across the river on Tiszaligeti sétány are open only in summer. There's a small rowing lake behind.

Closer to town, west of Tisza Bridge at Damjanich utca 7, the Damjanich complex has an indoor and outdoor thermal pool (from May to September) and a large sunbathing area. The more serious thermal baths, those at the Tisza hotel, are mock Turkish with a bit of Art Deco thrown in and are a great place to laze away an afternoon. They're open weekdays from 7.30 am to 4 pm.

You can rent kayaks and canoes on the

Tisza backwater (almost a lake) not far from Tisza Park.

Places to Stay

Private Rooms Any of the agencies (see Information) can get you a private room from about 1200 Ft for a double and 2000 Ft for apartments.

Hostel The *NIA Tourist Hostel* (☎ 424 705), while not very conveniently located at the western end of Tisza Park, is a good deal. A former Young Pioneer holiday camp, the centre has double, triple and multi-bed rooms in 21 bungalows for about 800 Ft per person. The eight little cottages with six beds (600 Ft per person) are available May to mid-September. The complex has a restaurant and büfé, and guests can use rowing boats and kayaks free of charge.

Hotels By the entrance to Tisza Park close to the bridge, the *Touring* hotel (☎ 379 805) has 32 rooms from 3800 Ft for singles and 5500 Ft for doubles, all with shower or bath.

On the opposite bank and closer to the centre of town, the *Student* hotel (☎ 421 688) at Mártírok útja 12-14 has 22 rooms with showers available all year at 2200/2350 Ft for singles/doubles. From late June to late August, another 160 beds become available. This is the best place to stay in Szolnok if you're looking for company; the small bar is a congenial meeting spot.

Also on the river's right bank, the *Tisza* (☎ 371 155) at Verseghy Park 2 is Szolnok's old-world hotel built in 1928 over a thermal spring. It has 35 rooms, an attached spa, decent pub and restaurant and loads of atmosphere. Singles are 4500 to 5500 Ft, doubles 6000 to 8000 Ft, depending on the season. Room Nos 108 to 111 overlooking the garden and river are the best in the house; the rooms on the 3rd floor with dormer windows are the cheapest.

The *Pelikán* hotel (☎ 423 855), in the centre of town at Jászkürt utca 1, is a good example of what happened to Hungarian hotel design in the 1960s and 70s. It's a big cement block sitting on a podium with 96 rooms, indifferent restaurant and bar, billiard club and casino. Singles/doubles are DM45/70.

Places to Eat
For pizza, the most popular place in town is the *Caffè Alexander* at Táncsics Mihály utca 15 near the Szigliget Theatre. It's open till midnight (to 1 am on Friday and Saturday). Or try the *Pizza Kert* on Pólya Tibor utca 35 in the Tabán district. The *Gösser*, a pub-restaurant at Kossuth Lajos út 9, has Germano-Hungarian dishes at affordable prices.

The *Róza* restaurant at Konstantin utca 36 is a bit out of the way but serves Hungarian dishes that are better than average. It closes at 10 pm (4 pm on Sunday). Perhaps a better choice, though, is the more upscale *Ristorante da Michele* nearby at Petőfi Sándor utca 6. It has decent pastas and salads among other things and is largely no-smoking.

The garden of the *Tisza* restaurant at the Tisza hotel is the most pleasant spot in town for a meal on a warm summer night, watching the crowds stroll along the river walk. At other times, eat at the small *Kistisza* pub-restaurant on the hotel's south side.

Entertainment
The *City Cultural Centre* (☎ 344 899) on Hild János tér 1 across from the Pelikán hotel can tell you whether there are concerts on at the Franciscan church or whether Szolnok's celebrated symphony orchestra or Béla Bartók Chamber Choir are performing. Szolnok hosts a classical music festival in May and a week-long jazz festival in August.

The *Szigliget Theatre*, across from the Tisza hotel at Sóház utca and one of the most attractive theatres in provincial Hungary, was at the forefront of drama in Hungary in the 1970s and 80s, when Gábor Székely, who went on to head the influential József Katona theatre company in Budapest, breathed new life into its troupe. The theatre was the first in Eastern Europe to stage *Dr Zhivago* (1988), which at the time was pretty daring.

Demographically, Szolnok is one of the youngest cities in Hungary and the nightlife ain't half bad. The northern end of Sütő utca off Baross Gábor utca is something of a 'strip', with several clubs, a popular bar called *Lúdláb* and a cinema.

Two pubs that attract students by the dozen – the *Fregatt* and the *Póló Club* – are below and on opposite sides of Tisza Bridge. The *Tabán Kapu* garden pub at Pólya Tibor utca 14 is another good choice. The *Moment* disco near the Touring hotel and the *Matróz* disco at Tiszaparti sétány 7 rage till the wee hours at weekends.

Getting There & Away
Bus connections to/from Szolnok are just

GREAT PLAIN

adequate. There are eight daily departures to Kecskemét, at least a dozen to Kunszent-márton, eight to Szeged, seven to Gyöngyös, five to Eger and four to Tiszafüred and Karcag.

On the other hand, Szolnok has excellent rail service; you can travel to/from Budapest, Debrecen, Nyíregyháza, Békéscsaba, Warsaw, Bucharest and dozens of points in between without changing. (For Miskolc, change at Hatvan; Hódmezővásárhely is where you transfer for Szeged.)

Between April and October you may be able to link up with one of the charter boats making the 90-km run south to Csongrád. Check with Tourinform.

Getting Around
From the train station, bus No 6, 7 or 8 will take you to Kossuth tér. If heading for the NIA Tourist Hostel or other accommodation in Tisza Park, take bus No 15. For a local taxi, dial ☎ 427 333.

JÁSZBERÉNY
• pop 30,000
• area code ☎ 57

Jászberény was the main political, administrative and economic centre of the Jász settlements as early as the 13th century but developed slowly as the group began to die out.

The town's biggest draw has always been the Lehel Horn, which was the symbol of power of the Jazygian chiefs for centuries. Nowadays, say 'Lehel' and most Hungarians will think of the country's largest refrigerator and air-conditioner manufacturer, located several km west of the city.

Orientation
Jászberény's main street is actually a long 'square' (Lehel vezér tér), which runs almost parallel to the narrow 'city branch' of the Zagyva River. The bus station is a couple of blocks to the west across the Zagyva on Petőfi tér. The train station is another 1.5 km west at the end of Rákóczi út.

Information
Tourinform (☎ 411 976) has an office in the Deryné Cultural Centre at Lehel vezér tér 33. It is open weekdays from 9 am to 4.30 pm and on Saturday till noon in summer. Ibusz (☎ 412 143) is to the south-west at Szövetkezet utca 7.

There's an OTP bank at Lehel vezér tér 28. The main post office is to the north on the same street at No 7-8.

Things to See & Do
The **Jász Museum**, housed in what was once Jazygian military headquarters at Táncsics Mihály utca 5, runs the gamut of Jász culture and life – from costumes and woodcarving to language. (Impress your Hungarian friends with your knowledge of a few now very dead Jazygian words: *daban hoaz* is 'hello', *dan* is 'water', *hah* is 'horse' and *sana* is 'wine'.) But all aisles lead to the **Lehel Horn**, an 8th-century Byzantine work carved in ivory. Legend has it that a Magyar leader called Lehel (or Lél) fell captive during the Battle of Augsburg against the united German armies in 955 and, just before he was executed, struck the king on the head with the horn. The alleged murder weapon, richly carved with birds, battle scenes and anatomically correct satyrs, doesn't seem to have suffered any serious damage from the blow to the royal noggin.

The museum also spotlights local sons and daughters who made good, including the watercolourist András Sáros and the 19th-century actress Róza Széppataki Déryné. You've seen Mrs Déry before, though you may not know it. She is forever immortalised in that irritating Herend porcelain figurine you see in antique shops everywhere in Hungary of a woman in a wide organza skirt playing her *lant* (lute) and kissing the wind.

Have a look at the ceiling frescos inside the **Roman Catholic parish church** on Szentháromság tér; the nave was designed in 1774 by András Mayerhoffer and József Jung, two masters of baroque architecture. The **Franciscan church and monastery** on Ferencesek tere off Hatvani út to the north-

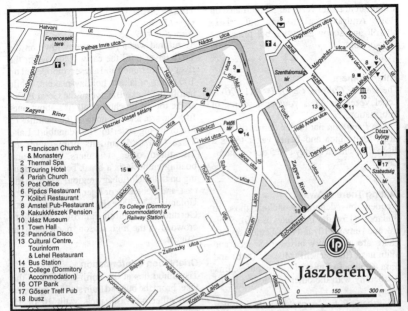

1 Franciscan Church
   & Monastery
2 Thermal Spa
3 Touring Hotel
4 Parish Church
5 Post Office
6 Pipács Restaurant
7 Kolibri Restaurant
8 Amstel Pub-Restaurant
9 Kakukkfészek Pension
10 Jász Museum
11 Town Hall
12 Pannónia Disco
13 Cultural Centre,
   Tourinform
   & Lehel Restaurant
14 Bus Station
15 College (Dormitory
   Accommodation)
16 OTP Bank
17 Gösser Treff Pub
18 Ibusz

Jászberény

west date from late in the 15th century but were heavily baroqued 250 years later.

The **thermal spa** at Hatvani út 5 is open all year Tuesday to Sunday from 9 am to 7 pm. The outdoor strand pools are open from 9 am to 6 pm from May to mid-September.

Special Events

If you're in Jászberény in early August, ask about the annual four-day Csángó Festival, which highlights traditional Hungarian folk music from Transylvania. This is followed by the 10-day Jászberény Summer folklore festival with groups from all over Europe.

Places to Stay

Ibusz can arrange *private rooms* from a list of about 40. In summer, ask about the availability of dormitory rooms in the *colleges* at Rákóczi út 15 and 55 on the way to the train station.

The 25-room *Touring* hotel (☎ 412 051), near the tiny Zagyva branch at Serház utca

3, is a clean and central place but overpriced at 3000/4000/5000 Ft for singles/doubles/triples.

The *Kakukkfészek* pension (☎ 412 345), with nine rooms at Táncsics Mihály utca 8, is convenient to the museum and town centre.

Places to Eat

Táncsics Mihály utca near the Jász Museum is your best hunting ground. The *Kolibri*, serving pizza, pasta and assorted green stuff at No 7, is open till 9 pm on weekdays and 2 am on weekends; *Pipács* at No 10 is a more traditional Hungarian restaurant. The *Amstel* pub-restaurant on the corner of Táncsics Mihály utca and Rév utca has a much more interesting menu.

The *Gösser Treff* on Dózsa György út has pub-style food in relatively up-market surrounds. It shuts at 11 pm during the week and at 1 am on Friday and Saturday. The *Lehel* is an 'old-style' (pre-1989) Hungarian

298 Central Plain – Tiszafüred

restaurant at Lehel vezér tér 34 (entrance on Holló András utca) dishing out gristly pörkölt and soapy galuszka, but prices are rock-bottom.

Entertainment

The *Déryné Cultural Centre* (☎ 411 976) at Lehel vezér tér 33 is your best source of information.

The *Pannónia* bar on the corner of Táncsics Mihály utca and Lehel vezér tér is a disco till 2 am on Friday and 5 am on Saturday.

Getting There & Away

Frequent bus departures include those to Budapest (15 a day), Gyöngyös (10), Szolnok and Hatvan (10) and Kecskemét (seven). There are also daily buses to Szeged and Mátraháza (three each), Miskolc (two) and Baja (one). Dozens of daily buses link Jászberény with the other Jász towns in the area.

Jászberény lies approximately halfway between Hatvan and Szolnok on the railway line. These two cities are on Hungary's two main trunks, and virtually all main cities in the east are accessible from one or the other. Both Hatvan and Szolnok have direct links to Budapest.

Getting Around

Bus Nos 2 and 4 connect the train station and bus terminus, from where you can walk to the centre of town.

TISZAFÜRED
• *pop 15,700*
• *area code ☎ 59*

Tiszafüred was a rather sleepy town on the Tisza River until the early 1980s when the river was dammed and a reservoir opened up 100 sq km of lake to holiday-makers. While hardly the 'Lake Balaton of the Great Plain' as the tourist brochures call it (it's about one-fifth the size and has none of the facilities or life of its big sister in Transdanubia), Lake Tisza (Tisza-tó) and its primary resort, Tiszafüred, offer swimmers, anglers and boating enthusiasts a break before continuing on to the Hortobágy region, 30 km to the east, and Debrecen, or Eger and the Northern Uplands. The lake is very popular with German and Dutch families, and gets crowded in the high season, particularly in August.

Orientation & Information

Tiszafüred lies at the north-east end of the lake. From the bus and train stations opposite each other on Vasút utca, walk 10 or 15 minutes west to the beach and camp sites. To reach the centre of town, follow Baross Gábor utca and then Fő út south for about one km.

The helpful Tourinform office (☎ 353 000) is at Húszöles út 21/a, not far from the thermal spa. It's open weekdays from 8 am to 4 pm, and from May to September daily from 8 am to 7 pm. Kormorán Info (☎ 352 896), another agency at Ady Endre utca 27, can help with fishing licences and boat rentals.

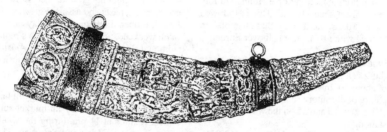

The Lehel Horn at the Jász Museum in Jászberény

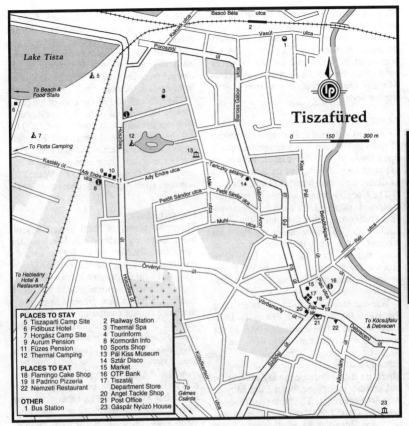

Tiszafüred

0   150   300 m

GREAT PLAIN

PLACES TO STAY
5 Tiszaparti Camp Site
6 Fidibusz Hotel
7 Horgász Camp Site
9 Aurum Pension
11 Füzes Pension
12 Thermal Camping

PLACES TO EAT
18 Flamingo Cake Shop
19 Il Padrino Pizzeria
22 Nemzeti Restaurant

OTHER
1 Bus Station

2 Railway Station
3 Thermal Spa
4 Tourinform
8 Kormorán Info
10 Sports Shop
13 Pál Kiss Museum
14 Sztár Disco
15 Market
16 OTP Bank
17 Tiszatáj
     Department Store
20 Angel Tackle Shop
21 Post Office
23 Gáspár Nyúzó House

There's an OTP bank behind Fő út at Piac utca 3. The post office is on the corner of Fő út and Szőlősi út.

Things to See

Tiszafüred is essentially a resort town, but there are a couple of interesting sights. The **Pál Kiss Museum** is in a beautiful old manor house (1840) south of the city's thermal baths at Tariczky sétány 6. Most of the collection is given over to the everyday lives of Tisza fisherfolk and the work of local potters. It is open daily except Monday from 9 am till noon and 1 to 5 pm and closes in December and January.

The area south of Szőlősi út is chock full of traditional houses with thatched roofs and orderly little flower and vegetable gardens – a nice respite from the hubbub of the beach. One of them, the **Gáspár Nyúzó House** at Malom utca 12 (you can get the key from No 9), is a former potter's residence and contains antique potting wheels, drying racks, furniture and plates in the light primary colours and patterns of stars, and birds and flowers unique to the region. The house is open daily except Monday from 10 am to 4 pm from

May to October. Several potters still live and work in the surrounding area.

There's an interesting **Csárda Museum** on Széghalom utca in Kócsújfalu, 14 km south-east of Tiszafüred on the Debrecen road (route No 33). It is open daily except Monday from 9 am to 6 pm from May to September.

Activities

Tiszafüred's thermal spa, at the northern end of town by the lake, has four open-air pools open from May to September, as well as sauna and a wide range of medical services available from mid-March to November.

The Horgász camp site rents bicycles and mountain bikes (600 Ft a day). If you want to get out onto – rather than into – the water, contact the Fidibusz hotel on the boat moored by the public beach for information about cruises. Its little cruiser sails three times a day in season and costs 300 Ft per person. Kormorán Info also does 2½-hour boat tours for four people for 4900 Ft.

You can rent bikes and motorboats from the Hableány hotel (see Places to Eat). There's horse riding available (1000 Ft per hour) at the Gulyás farm (☎ 351 814) nearby.

Places to Stay

There are half a dozen camping grounds in and around Tiszafüred, open from May or June to September. The four-star *Thermal Camping* (☎ 352 911), unattractively located on busy Húszöles út south-west of the thermal spa, has bungalows for four people (3700 to 4700 Ft) and clay tennis courts.

The lakeside *Horgász* camp site (☎ 351 220) has snack stalls, a restaurant, recreational facilities (including tennis) and two holiday homes (from 1600 to 2000 Ft a double with shared showers). The public beach is a short distance to the north. *Tisza-parti* (☎ 351 132), a few minutes east along the shore and past the reed beds, is for visitors with tents and caravans only. *Flotta Camping* (☎ 352 424) to the south-west is suitable only for those with their own transport. Bungalows for four people start at 1500 Ft. Flotta also rents both bicycles and boats.

In summer, the *Lajos Kossuth College* (☎ 352 932) at Baross Gábor utca 36 has dormitory beds for 500 Ft per person.

The 10-room *Fidibusz* hotel (☎ 351 818), on a ship moored near the public beach, charges from 2000 Ft for doubles. It is open from April to October.

The *Füzes* (☎ 351 854), south of the camp sites at Húszöles út 31/b, is a comfortable 10-room pension with doubles for 2800 Ft. All the rooms have showers and TVs, and there's a popular restaurant and busy local bar in the cellar. The newer *Aurum* (☎ 351 338), almost next door at Ady Endre utca 29, is more expensive, with doubles at 3500 Ft.

Places to Eat

There are plenty of food outlets (gyros, pizza, lángos etc) at the public beach and the camp sites. The *Nemzeti* at Fő út 8 is a smoky restaurant just beyond the central square (Piac tér) with Gypsy music occasionally at night. A better choice would be the *Il Padrino*, a bright new pizzeria in the little shopping complex opposite the post office on Fő út. It is open till 10 pm daily. The food at the *Füzes* pension's restaurant is particularly good. In summer, find a spot on the breezy terrace.

According to local people, the best restaurant in Tiszafüred is the one at the *Hableány* hotel, but you'll need to have your own wheels: it's at Hunyadi utca 2 in Tiszaörvény, about four km to the south-west. Another good choice – but also far – is the *Gémes*, a csárda at Húszöles út 80/a.

Flamingo, a combination 'cukrászda and bronzárium' on Fő út opposite the start of Szőlősi utca has excellent cakes and ice cream.

Entertainment

The open-air bar on top of the *Fidibusz* 'boatel' is a great place for a sundowner and the pub in the basement of the *Aurum* pension is a popular local meeting place. The *Sztár* disco on the corner of Tariczky sétány and Gábor Áron út is open till 5 am at weekends.

Things to Buy

Tiszafüred abounds in shops selling fishing gear, including the Angel shop on Szőlősi utca, the Tiszatáj department store on Fő út, and the sports shop at Ady Endre utca 27.

Getting There & Away

Some 10 buses a day link Tiszafüred with Abádszalók, another popular lake resort to the south. Other destinations served daily include: Budapest's Népstadion bus station (four buses a day); Szolnok, Karcag and Eger (four each); Szeged and Jászberény (two); Miskolc and Debrecen (three); and Hajdúszoboszló (one).

Tiszafüred is on the railway line linking Karcag (the transfer point from Szolnok) and Füzesabony, from where you can carry on to Eger or Miskolc. The train going east to Debrecen passes through the Hortobágy region.

KARCAG

- *pop 24,000*
- *area code* ☎ *59*

If you're travelling from Szolnok to Tiszafüred by train, you must change at Karcag, 45 km to the south of Tiszafüred. During the stopover, have a look around this historical town, once the seat of Kun chiefs, or check out its spa 12 km to the north-west at Berekfürdő, which is also on the train line to Tiszafüred (see below).

Karcag is known throughout the country for its burns hospital and its highly regarded schools of science and medicine. Its sights are within easy walking distance of the train station, south-east of town at the end of Vasút utca, and the bus terminus, just north-west of Kossuth tér.

There's a K&H bank opposite the **Calvinist church** (1745) on Kossuth tér.

The **István Győrffy Nagykun Museum** at Kálvin utca 4 has a good collection of folk art, including pottery and Karcag's distinctive woven rugs, but most interesting is the exhibit of decorative wrought iron fashioned by local artisans. The nearby **Sándor Kántor Pottery House** at Erkel Ferenc utca 1 dis-

plays the work of the city's most famous potter and, a few blocks away at Jókai utca 16, there's a **Village House** furnished in the traditional style of the Nagykun region. Karcag has several interesting buildings, including a lovely Hungarian Art Nouveau townhouse at Horváth Ferenc utca 1 near the bus station.

The *Fehér Holló* (White Raven) pension (☎ 313 555) at Püspökladány út 3 has accommodation (from 3500 Ft) and a decent – if expensive – pizzeria. The *Kunsági* restaurant on Dózsa György út just north of Kossuth tér has 'Cuman specialities' (raw meat?); the *Kaiser* is a pub-restaurant in a small shopping area just north.

See the people at the *Déryné Cultural Centre* (☎ 311 222), Dózsa György út, for information about what's on. The Nagykunság Cultural Days in mid-August is Karcag's main event.

If you miss your train, you can reach the following cities and towns from Karcag by bus: Berekfürdő (hourly); Békéscsaba (one a day); Debrecen (three); Gyöngyös (two); Hajdúszoboszló (three); Hódmezővásárhely (two); Jászberény (one); Kecskemét (one); Miskolc (two); Szarvas (three); Szeged (two); Szolnok (four); and Tiszafüred (four).

AROUND KARCAG
Berekfürdő

Some people claim that Berekfürdő is the prettiest spa in the county, but it's difficult to see how it differs much from most others in Hungary, with mums floating their babies in the wading pools while dads and local young bloods demolish the contents of the lángos and beer stands. Still, the waters are supposed to be as beneficial as those at Hajdúszoboszló, so if you've got a problem or you just want to soak, the indoor spa is open all year, the strand pools in summer only.

Fürdő Camping (☎ 319 162) at Tűzoltó utca 1 has bungalows from 1400 to 1600 Ft for two people and pension-style accommodation for the same price. The *Touring* hotel (☎ 319 226) almost next door at Berek tér 13

GREAT PLAIN

charges 1500 to 2500 Ft for singles and 2500 to 3600 Ft for doubles, depending on the season. This 24-room hotel is connected to the spa and pool complex by a covered walkway.

Eastern Plain

The Eastern Plain includes Debrecen, the towns of the Hajdúság and Bihar regions, and the Hortobágy, the birthplace of the puszta legend. This part of the Great Plain was important for centuries as it was on the Salt Road – the route taken by traders in that precious commodity, from Transylvania via the Tisza River and across the Eastern Plain by bullock cart to the wealthy city of Debrecen. When the trees were chopped down and the river was regulated, the water in the soil evaporated, turning the region into a vast, saline grassland suitable only for grazing. The myth of the lonely *pásztor* (shepherd) in billowy trousers, the wayside *csárdas* and Gypsy violinists was born, and was kept alive in literature, fine art and the imagination of the Hungarian people.

DEBRECEN

• *pop 214,800*
• *area code ☎ 52*

Debrecen is Hungary's second-largest city (though Miskolc is close on its heels) and has been synonymous with wealth and conservatism since the 16th century. That may not be immediately apparent on Piac utca on a Saturday night as you collide with drunks and panhandlers, but you don't have to go far to find either.

The area around Debrecen had been settled since earliest times, and when the Magyars arrived late in the 9th century they found a colony of Slovaks here who called the region Dobre Zliem for its 'good soil'. Debrecen's wealth, based on salt, the fur trade and cattle-raising, grew steadily through the Middle Ages and increased during the Turkish occupation; the city kept all sides happy by paying tribute to the Otto-

mans, the Habsburgs and Transylvanian princes at the same time.

Most of the large estates on the Eastern Plain were owned by Debrecen's independent-minded burghers, who had converted to Protestantism in the mid-16th century. These *civis* (from the Latin word for 'citizen') lived in the city while the peasants raised horses and cattle in the Hortobágy. Hajdúk (from *hajt*, 'drive') – landless peasants who would later play an important role in the wars with the Habsburgs as Heyduck mercenaries (see aside) – drove the animals on the hoof westward to markets as far as France. In the 1500s, Debrecen was already one of the largest and wealthiest towns in Hungary, exporting up to 75,000 head of livestock a year.

Debrecen played a pivotal role in the 1848-49 War of Independence and, late in the 19th century and early in the 20th, it experienced a major building boom. Today it is the capital of Hajdú-Bihar County and is an important university city. It is also renowned for its summer language school for foreigners (see Language Courses in the Facts for the Visitor chapter).

Orientation

Debrecen is an easy city to negotiate. A ring road, built on the city's original earthen walls, encloses the inner town, the Belváros. This is bisected by Piac utca, which runs northward from the train station at Petőfi tér to Kálvin tér, site of the Great Church and Debrecen's centre. With the exception of Nagyerdei Park, the recreational 'Big Forest Park' some three km farther north, all of Debrecen's attractions are within easy walking distance of Kálvin tér.

The bus station is on Külső-Vásártér, the 'outer marketplace' at the western end of Széchenyi utca.

Information

The helpful Tourinform office (☎ 412 250) is in the town hall at Piac utca 20. It is open daily from 8 am to 8 pm from June to August, weekdays only from 8.30 am to 4.30 pm the

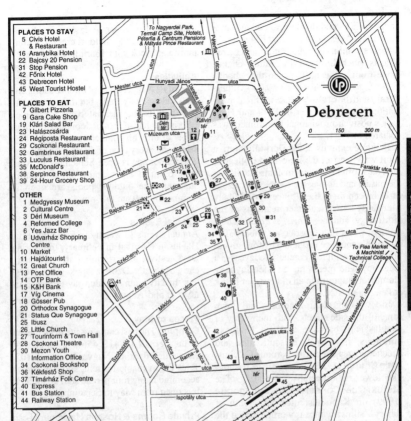

PLACES TO STAY
5 Civis Hotel
   & Restaurant
16 Aranybika Hotel
22 Bajcsy 20 Pension
31 Stop Pension
42 Fõnix Hotel
43 Debrecen Hotel
45 West Tourist Hostel

PLACES TO EAT
7 Gilbert Pizzeria
9 Gara Cake Shop
19 Klári Salad Bar
23 Halászcsárda
24 Régiposta Restaurant
29 Csokonai Restaurant
32 Gambrinus Restaurant
33 Luculus Restaurant
35 McDonald's
38 Serpince Restaurant
39 24-Hour Grocery Shop

OTHER
1 Medgyessy Museum
2 Cultural Centre
3 Déri Museum
4 Reformed College
6 Yes Jazz Bar
8 Udvarház Shopping
   Centre
10 Market
11 Hajdútourist
12 Great Church
13 Post Office
14 OTP Bank
15 K&H Bank
17 Víg Cinema
18 Gösser Pub
20 Orthodox Synagogue
21 Status Que Synagogue
25 Ibusz
26 Little Church
27 Tourinform & Town Hall
28 Csokonai Theatre
30 Mezon Youth
   Information Office
34 Csokonai Bookshop
36 Kékfestõ Shop
37 Tímárház Folk Centre
40 Express
41 Bus Station
44 Railway Station

Debrecen

0   150   300 m

GREAT PLAIN

rest of the year. Hajdútourist (☎ 415 588) is at Kálvin tér 2/a in the Udvarház shopping mall across from the Great Church. It's open from 8 am to 4.30 pm on weekdays and till 12.30 pm on Saturday. Ibusz (☎ 415 555), near the Little Church at Révész tér 2, and Express (☎ 418 332), at Piac utca 77, keep similar hours.

There's an OTP bank with an ATM on Hatvan utca, opposite the main post office, at No 5-9. The K&H bank is on Piac utca next to the Aranybika hotel. The Csokonai Bookshop at Piac utca 45 has a fairly good foreign-language and map selection.

Things to See

The yellow neoclassical **Great Church** (1821) has become so synonymous with Debrecen that mirages of its twin clock towers were reportedly seen on the Great Plain early this century. Accommodating some 3000 people, the Nagytemplom is Hungary's largest Protestant church, and it was here that Lajos Kossuth read the Declaration of Independence from Austria on 14 April 1849. Don't miss the magnificent organ in the loft behind the pulpit.

North of the church stands the **Reformed College** (1816), the site of a prestigious secondary school and theological college since the Middle Ages. Downstairs at Kálvin tér 16 there are exhibits on religious art and sacred objects (including a 17th-century chalice made from a coconut) and on the school's history; go up to visit the 650,000-volume **library** and the **oratory** where the breakaway National Assembly met in 1849 and Hungary's postwar provisional government was declared in 1944.

Folklore exhibits at the **Déri Museum**, a short walk west of the Reformed College at Déri tér 1, offer excellent insights into life on the puszta and among the bourgeois citizens of Debrecen up to the 19th century. Mihály Munkácsy's mythical interpretations of the Hortobágy and his *Christ's Passion* take pride of place in a separate art gallery. The museum's entrance is flanked by four superb bronzes by sculptor Ferenc Medgyessy, a local boy who merits his own **Medgyessy Memorial Museum** in an old burgher house at Péterfia utca 28.

Just walking along Piac utca and down some of the side streets, with their array of neoclassical, baroque and Art Nouveau buildings, is a treat. Kossuth utca and Széchenyi utca, where the baroque Calvinist **Little Church** (1726) stands with its bastion-like tower, is especially interesting. The **Status Que Conservative Synagogue** (1909) on Kápolnási utca just south of Bajcsy-Zsilinszky utca is worth a look if the caretaker will let you in. The derelict **Orthodox Synagogue** is across the street at Pászti utca 6.

Tímárház is a new folk-craft centre and workshop at Nagy Gál István utca 6, where embroiderers, basket weavers, carvers and so on do their stuff in rotation. It's an excellent place to visit and well worth the detour.

There's a covered **market** for fruit, vegetables and other supplies every day on Csapó utca, but much more colourful is the **flea market** near the large sports complex on Vágóhíd utca, served by bus Nos 30 and 30/a from the train station. In the morning it attracts a motley group of Ukrainians, Poles, Romanians, Gypsies and Hungarians from Transylvania who hawk everything from

used shoes to caviar. A fascinating **horse market** is usually held there on Friday morning; check with Tourinform.

Activities

The city's Nagyerdei Park offers boating and walks along leafy trails, but the main attraction here is the thermal bath, a complex offering a half-dozen indoor and open-air pools of brownish mineral and fresh water, sauna and every type of therapy imaginable. The indoor spa is open September to April from 6 am to 7 pm, and 8 am to 4 pm in summer. The outdoor pools are open in summer from 9 am to 7 pm.

Special Events

Annual events to watch out for include the Hajdúság Carnival in February, the Spring Days festival of performing arts in March, early August's Dzsessznapok (Jazz Days) and the city's famous four-day Flower Carnival in mid-August.

Places to Stay

Camping The best camping site in Debrecen is the *Termál* (☎ 412 456), north-east of Nagyerdei Park at Nagyerdei körút 102. Tents are available for rent, and bungalows accommodating four people start at 3000 Ft. It is open from May to September.

Private Rooms & Hostels Hajdútourist can arrange *private rooms* for 900/1500 Ft in singles/doubles, and apartments for four people from 2200 to 3900 Ft. With so many universities and colleges in town, there's plenty of *dormitory accommodation* in summer costing from 500 to 600 Ft per person. Book through Hajdútourist or Express. Dormitories at the *Új Kollégium III* (☎ 316 666) in Nagyerdei Park or the at *Machinist Technical College*, at Bokányi Dezső utca 84 past the flea market, take independent travellers all year if there's space. The *West* (☎ 420 891) is a tourist hostel near the train station at Wesselényi utca 4. Room prices are 600 to 1000 Ft.

Pensions The *Péterfia* pension (☎ 423 582)

has nine rooms in a charming row house at Péterfia utca 37/b. Doubles are 2500 Ft with shower. The *Centrum* (☎ 416 193), just next door at No 37/a, is flashier and more expensive: from 3000 to 3500 Ft, depending on whether you're in the old or new wing.

A more central pension is the 12-room *Stop* (☎ 420 301), a friendly place in a courtyard at Batthyány utca 18 with doubles for 2200 Ft. Another central, though dingier, alternative is the *Bajcsy 20* pension (☎ 343 321) on Bajcsy-Zsilinszky utca 20. Doubles start at 1900 Ft.

Hotels The 86-room *Debrecen* (☎ 413 942), opposite the train station at Petőfi tér 9 and popular with Russian and Ukrainian 'beesneesmen', charges 1700 Ft for a double room with shower on the hall and 3000 Ft for a room with shower. It's pretty run-down and noisy. A better choice would be the *Főnix* (☎ 413 355) with 52 rooms at Barna utca 17, a relatively quiet side street off Petőfi tér. Doubles with shower are 4000 Ft, while singles/doubles with shared shower cost 1300/2400 Ft.

The *Térmal* (☎ 411 888) at Nagyerdei körút 9-11 in Nagyerdei Park has 26 rooms from 3050 Ft, entry to the baths included. The *Nagyerdő* spa hotel (☎ 410 588) at Pallagi út 5 is much larger (107 rooms) and more costly (from 3300 Ft).

The landmark Art Nouveau *Aranybika* (☎ 416 777), with 250 very different rooms at Piac utca 11-15, is still the place to stay, despite the advent of the flashier *Civis* (☎ 418 522) at 4 Kálvin tér. Singles/doubles at the Aranybika start at DM120/150 or DM80/100, depending on whether you stay in the charming old wing or garish new building. Rooms at the Civis start at 8500 Ft.

Places to Eat

For a cheap, quick lunch, head for the lobby of the *Aranybika* hotel where there is a sandwich/salad bar and cake shop set up at lunch time. There's a *McDonald's* on the corner of Arany János utca and Piac utca.

Debreceners flock to the *Serpince a Flaskához* at Miklós utca 2, a cellar restaurant with excellent regional specialities including stuffed cabbage, which originated in Debrecen. Walk through the shingled 'bottle' *(flaska)* and down the stairs. You'll have to line up for the pizza and pasta at *Gilbert* pizzeria in the Udvarház mall on Kálvin tér.

A popular meeting place for students is the *Mátyás Pince*, a restaurant and bar open till late in a historical cellar north of Kálvin tér at Ajtó utca 1. Another restaurant attracting a young crowd is the *Csokonai* at Kossuth utca 21.

The *Halászcsárda* (also called the *Civis Bisztro*) at Simonffy utca 4 serves basic, inexpensive fish dishes until 9 pm. Vegetarians are catered for at the *Klári Salátabár* next to the Gösser pub on Bajcsy-Zsilinszky utca. Romantics will enjoy the *Régiposta*, a 17th-century inn with Gypsy music at Széchenyi 6, though service is – in a word – appalling.

Two restaurants that get top marks from local people for a night out are the *Civis* hotel restaurant at Kálvin tér 4 and the *Luculus*, a cellar restaurant at Piac utca 41.

The *Gara Cukrászda* gets my vote for having the best cakes and ice cream (made with real fruit) outside Budapest. It's open daily from 9 am to 6 pm. There's a 24-hour *grocery shop* at Piac utca 75.

Entertainment

Debrecen prides itself on its cultural life; check with the *Csokonai Theatre* (☎ 417 811) at Kossuth Lajos utca 10 or the *Kölcsey Cultural Centre* (☎ 417 848), behind the Déri Museum at Hunyadi János utca 1-3, for event schedules. Ask about concerts in the Bartók Room of the Aranybika hotel or at the Great Church. The Mezon youth information office (☎ 415 498), Batthyány utca 2/b, can fill you in on the popular music scene. It's open weekdays from noon to 6 pm and on Saturday from 10 am to 1 pm.

The *Híradó* cinema in Petőfi tér near the train station shows imported films six times a day, but there are better choices at the *Víg*, an elaborate building just behind the Aranybika hotel.

Discos rage to the wee hours on weekends

GREAT PLAIN

at the *El Dorado* in Nagyerdei Park, the *Pálma* at Simonyi út 44 and the *Flamingo Club*, north-west of the city centre on Füredi utca. The *Yes Jazz Bar* at Kálvin tér 8 has live blues and jazz sets every second night. It opens at 3 pm on weekdays and at 5 pm on Saturday and Sunday.

Things to Buy
You can't leave the city without buying – or at least trying – some of the famous Debrecen sausage available at butcher shops (eg on Kossuth utca) and grocery stores everywhere.

The Kékfestő shop on Szent Anna utca sells folk articles made from the distinctive blue-dyed homespun called *kékfestő*, which is enjoying something of a revival in Hungary these days.

Getting There & Away
Because Debrecen is so well served by trains, bus service inevitably suffers. Still, from Debrecen you can catch a direct bus to any of the following cities and towns: Bánk (three a day); Békéscsaba (10); Berettyóújfalu (hourly); Eger (three); Fehérgyarmat (one); Gyöngyös (three); Gyula (seven); Hajdúböszörmény (half-hourly); Hajdúnánás (10); Hajdúszoboszló (half-hourly); Hódmezővásárhely and Szeged (two); Kecskemét (one); Mátészalka (three); Miskolc (hourly); Nádudvar (12); Nyírbátor and Nyíregyháza (three each); Sátoraljaújhely (two); Szarvas (two); and Tokaj (two).

Debrecen is served by some two dozen trains a day from Budapest-Nyugati via Szolnok, including five 2½-hour expresses. Daily international departures from Debrecen reach Košice in Slovakia; Kraków and Warsaw in Poland; Satu Mare and Baia Mare in Romania; Lvov in Ukraine; and Moscow. Hungarian cities to the north and north-west – Nyíregyháza, Tokaj and Miskolc – can be reached most effectively by train. For Eger, take the train to Füzesabony and change. For points south, use the bus or a bus/train combination.

Getting Around
Tram No 1 – the only line in town – is ideal both for transport and sightseeing. From the train station, it runs north along Piac utca to Kálvin tér and then carries on to Nagyerdei Park, where it loops around for the same trip southward.

Most other city transport can be caught at the southern end of Petőfi tér. Bus Nos 12 and 19 and the No 2 trolleybus link the train and bus stations. Ticket inspectors are a regular sight in Debrecen, and riding 'black' – particularly on bus No 30 or 30/a to the flea market – is risky. They show no mercy: you'll be fined on the spot.

For a local taxi, ring ☎ 444 444.

AROUND DEBRECEN
The Erdőpuszta
The so-called Wooded Plain, a protected area of pine and acacia forests, lakes and trails a few km to the east and south-east of Debrecen, is an excellent breakaway from the city. **Bánk** has a splendid arboretum with a small village museum at Fancsika utca 93/a. At **Vekeri Lake** there's rowing and the Víg-Kend Major, a zoo/farm with horses for hire (700 Ft). The *Paripa* is a popular csárda and the *Dorcas Center* camp site (☎ 441 119) at Vekeri has bungalows for two at 1500 Ft and three-person apartments for 3400 Ft.

For Bánk, take one of three daily buses from Debrecen or one headed for Vértes or Létavértes (hourly). Most buses going to Hosszúpályi (hourly) also stop at Vekeri. An excellent map for the area is Cartographia's 1:40,000 *Debrecen Környékének* (No 9; Environs of Debrecen).

HORTOBÁGY
• *pop 1700*
• *area code* ☎ 52
This village, some 40 km west of Debrecen, is the centre of the Hortobágy region, once celebrated for its sturdy cowboys, inns and Gypsy bands. But you'll want to come here to explore the 70,000-hectare Hortobágy National Park and wildlife preserve – home to hundreds of birds as well as plant species that are usually found only by the sea.

It's true that the Hortobágy has been milked by the Hungarian tourism industry for everything it's worth, and the stage-managed horse shows, costumed *csikósok* and tacky gewgaws on sale are all over the top. Still, dark clouds appearing out of nowhere to cover a blazing sun and the possibility of spotting a mirage may have you dreaming of a different Hortobágy – the mythical one that only ever existed in paintings, poems and people's imaginations.

Orientation & Information

Buses – as few as there are – stop on the main road (route No 33) near the village centre; the train station is at the northern end of Kossuth utca. Tourinform (☎ 369 119) has an office in the Herder Museum; it is open weekdays from 9 am to 5 pm from April to October only. Hajdútourist (☎ 369 039), open from 8 am to 6.30 pm weekdays and till 1 pm on Saturday, is around the corner from the Hortobágy Csárda and on the other side of the Hortobágy Gallery at Petőfi tér 4. The post office, where you can change money, is opposite the Hortobágy Inn at Kossuth utca 2.

Hortobágy National Park

With its varied terrain and water sources, the park offers some of the best bird-watching in Europe. Indeed, some 260 species (of the continent's total 410) have been spotted here in the past 20 years, including many types of grebes, herons, egrets, spoonbills, storks, kites, shrikes, warblers and eagles. The great bustard, one of the world's largest birds, standing a metre high and weighing in at 20 kg, has its own reserve with limited access to two-legged mammals.

To see the best parts of the park – the closed areas north of route No 33 and the saline swamplands south of it – you must have a guide and travel by horse, carriage or special 4WD. Contact Aquila (☎ 386 348) at PO Box 8, 4015 Debrecen, a private company with specialised bird-watching tours. The price is 1000 Ft per hour plus 13 Ft per km. The Hungarian Ornithological and Nature Conservation Society (MME) offers a similar programme. Tourinform has details.

The national park office in the Round Theatre offers a two-hour coach tour of the park for 1000 Ft. Buses leave from the museum for the starting points at the 79-km and 86-km stones on route No 33 at 11 am, noon, 2 and 4 pm every day from April to October.

Other Things to See

The **Nine-Hole Bridge** (1833) spanning the marshy Hortobágy River is the longest stone bridge (and certainly the most sketched, painted and photographed bridge) in Hungary. Just before it, at Petőfi tér 2, stands the **Hortobágyi Csárda**, one of the original eating houses (1781) used by salt traders on their way from the Tisza River to Debrecen. The going was rough along the muddy trails, and bullock carts could only cover about 12 km a day. That's why you'll still find inns spaced at those intervals today at, for example, Látókép, Nagyhegyes and Hortobágy. The inns provided itinerant Gypsy fiddlers with employment, though they did not originally live in this part of Hungary. Gypsy music and csárdas have been synonymous ever since.

The **Hortobágy Gallery**, just behind the restaurant, has a potpourri of art styles and media with a Hortobágy theme, some of them saccharine-sweet, others quite evocative. Check the big skies in some of the works by László Holló or Arthur Tölgyessy and see if they don't match the real one. The gallery is open from 9 am to 5 pm with slightly shorter hours in winter, and it is always closed Monday.

The **Herder Museum** (Pásztormúzeum), housed in an 18th-century carriage house across Petőfi tér from the csárda, has good exhibits on how riders, cowherds, shepherds and swineherds fed and clothed themselves and played their music. Spare some time for a close look at the finely embroidered jackets and elaborate long capes (*szűr*) they wore. The Herder Museum is open daily from 9 am

GREAT PLAIN

GREAT PLAIN

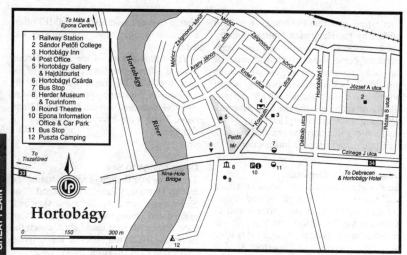

Hortobágy

0   150   300 m

Legend:
1 Railway Station
2 Sándor Petőfi College
3 Hortobágy Inn
4 Post Office
5 Hortobágy Gallery & Hajdútourist
6 Hortobágyi Csárda
7 Bus Stop
8 Herder Museum & Tourinform
9 Round Theatre
10 Epona Information Office & Car Park
11 Bus Stop
12 Puszta Camping

to noon and 1 to 6 pm from April to October only. The thatch-roofed **Round Theatre** (Körszín) opposite, open the same hours and operated by the national park, is devoted to the ecology of the Hortobágy. It puts on a good slide show of the region in English, French and German.

Máta, about two km north of Hortobágy village, is the centre of the Hortobágy horse industry, and Hungary's mighty Nonius breed is raised here. State-owned until the early 1990s, the horses, carriages, herds of grey Hungarian cattle and the *racka* sheep with their corkscrew horns have been taken over by a German-Hungarian riding and hotel company called Epona. But even if you don't ride and aren't interested in staged 'rodeos', it's worth a walk over for a look at the stables, the horses and the fine old carriages.

Activities
Horse Riding At Máta, the Epona Riding Village (☎ 369 092) offers any number of horse-related activities: riding and roping displays by the csikósok, with a two-hour tour of the puszta by carriage to see the cattle, sheep and perhaps something a little wilder

(1200 Ft); horse riding (800 to 1000 Ft, depending on location); and riding lessons for 1500 Ft an hour. Epona has an information booth in the car park near the Herder Museum.

Other Activities
You can rent rowing boats on the Hortobágy River in summer for 600 Ft per hour and, between mid-May and September, there are hourly motorboat tours between 9 am and 8 pm. The one-hour tour costs 600/300 Ft for adults/children.

A company called Poszméh Air offers sightseeing flights of the region from 10 am to 6 pm from April to November. Prices vary considerably but expect to pay 6000 Ft for a five-minute flight around the Hortobágy for up to three people; 9000 Ft for an eight-minute 'Puszta Panorama' flight and 15,000 Ft for a 12-minute 'Puszta Safari'. Planes take off from the airfield at Macskatelek west of the village at the 70-km stone.

The Puszta camp site rents bicycles for 400 Ft a day.

Special Events
The area is busiest in late June when Máta

hosts the Hortobágy Equestrian Days and during the Bridge Fair on 19 and 20 August, an attempt to recreate the old 'outlaw' fairs held here in the last century.

Places to Stay

Accommodation is at a premium here in summer, so be prepared to carry on to Debrecen or Tiszafüred, where the choices are greater. *Puszta Camping* (☎ 369 300), about 300m from the Csárda, has bungalows (1500 Ft) and tents available from May to September. Hajdútourist can help with *private rooms* for 2400 Ft for two, or try the houses at Kossuth utca 23 or Czinege János utca 28. The *Sándor Petőfi College* (☎ 369 128) at József Attila utca 1 has four-bed dormitory rooms available in summer for 500 Ft per person.

The most central place is the *Hortobágyi Fogadó* (Hortobágy Inn; ☎ 369 137), at Kossuth utca 1, which has singles/doubles for 1200/2000 Ft with showers in the hall. It's a basic but pleasant place with friendly staff. If there's no room at the inn but you're determined to stay in the village, check the *Hortobágy* hotel (☎ 369 071), a concrete shoe box at Borsós two km east, with expensive doubles (3000 Ft).

Two other possibilities are a bit far out, but each has its own attractions. The nine-room *Vadászház* (☎ 369 442), by the Hortobágyi halastó (Hortobágy Fish Pond) seven km north-west of the village, is an excellent spot for some informal bird-watching. It charges 4500 Ft for a double. The *Tájház* (Country House) (☎ 354 217) is a traditional Hortobágy-style cottage at Nagyiván, just within the national park borders 25 km to the south-west. Doubles are 3500 Ft.

The new *Epona* resort hotel (☎ 369 092) in Máta, with its 58 deluxe rooms, 20 houses (complete with private stables), swimming pool, fitness centre and two restaurants, is a world apart. The prices are out of this world too: DM120/160 or DM130/190 for singles/doubles, depending on the season.

Places to Eat

It's touristy and a little pricey, but you've got to have a meal at the *Hortobágyi Csárda*, Hungary's most celebrated roadside inn. Order a duck dish, relax to the Gypsy standards and admire the Hortobágy kitsch taking up every square cm of wall space. And count your change carefully after your meal.

There ain't much else around. The *Hortobágy Inn* has a small, rather rough restaurant and there is a simple *büfé* across from it on Kossuth utca. Over in Máta, the Epona complex has a couple of restaurants (the *Csárda* and the *Hajdú*). The *Nyerges Presszó* near the paddocks and stables is pleasant for a drink if the wind is in your favour.

Getting There & Away

A daily bus between Debrecen and Eger stops at Hortobágy, and there are two daily buses to/from Hajdúszoboszló between mid-June and August.

Hortobágy is on the railway line linking Debrecen and Füzesabony and is served by up to six trains a day, depending on the season, with the last train leaving for Debrecen about 6.15 pm. Trains headed for Füzesabony also stop at Hortobágyi halastó station near the Vadászház inn.

HAJDÚSÁG REGION

The Hajdúság region is a loess (silt) area of the Eastern Plain west of Debrecen that was settled by the Heyducks, a medieval community of drovers and outlaws turned mercenaries and renowned for their skill in battle (see aside).

The Hajdúság continued as a special administrative district until the late 19th century but lost its importance after that. Today it is one of the most sparsely populated areas of Hungary.

Hajdúszoboszló

• *pop 24,000*
• *area code* ☎ 52

Hajdúszoboszló, 20 km south-west of Debrecen, was a typical town in the Hajdúság until 1925, when springs were discovered during drilling for oil and natural gas. Today, with its huge spa complex, park, pools, grassy 'beaches' and other recreational facil-

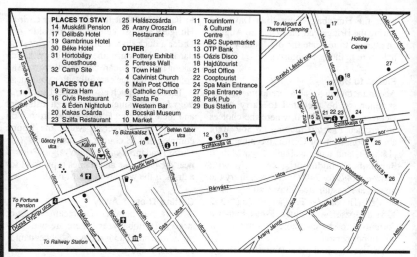

PLACES TO STAY	25 Halászcsárda	11 Tourinform
14 Muskátli Pension	26 Arany Oroszlán	& Cultural
17 Délibáb Hotel	Restaurant	Centre
19 Gambrinus Hotel		12 ABC Supermarket
30 Béke Hotel	OTHER	13 OTP Bank
31 Hortobágy	1 Pottery Exhibit	15 Oázis Disco
Guesthouse	2 Fortress Wall	18 Hajdútourist
32 Camp Site	3 Town Hall	21 Post Office
	4 Calvinist Church	22 Cooptourist
PLACES TO EAT	5 Main Post Office	24 Spa Main Entrance
9 Pizza Ham	6 Catholic Church	27 Spa Entrance
16 Civis Restaurant	7 Santa Fe	28 Park Pub
& Éden Nightclub	Western Bar	29 Bus Station
20 Kakas Csárda	8 Bocskai Museum	
23 Szilfa Restaurant	10 Market	

ities, it is Hungary's Coney Island, Blackpool and Bondi Beach all rolled into one – for better or for worse.

It may indeed be the 'poor man's Balaton', as one holiday-maker told me, but Hajdúszoboszló has its serious side too. A large percentage of the hundreds of thousands of visitors who flock here every year are in search of a cure from its therapeutic waters. Indeed, some people call the place 'Reumások Mekkája' ('Rheumatics Mecca').

Orientation Almost everything you'll want or need can be found on the broad street (route No 4) running through town and changing names four times: Debreceni útfél, Szilfákalja út, Hősök tere and Dózsa György utca. The thermal baths and park, lumped together as the 'Holiday Centre', occupy the north-eastern portion of Hajdúszoboszló. Hősök tere – the town centre – lies to the south-west.

The bus station is on Fürdő utca, just north of Debreceni útfél. The train station lies about three km south on Déli sor. Reach Hősök tere by walking north-west along Rákóczi utca. To get to the Holiday Centre,

follow Rákóczi utca north for three blocks and then head north-east on Hőforrás utca.

Information The Tourinform office (☎ 361 612), one of the least helpful in Hungary, is in the cultural centre building at Szilfákalja út 2. It is open weekdays from 8.30 am to 5 pm and till noon on Saturday. Head instead for Hajdútourist (☎ 362 966) at József Attila utca 2, just up from the spa's main entrance. It's open from 7.45 am to 5.30 pm and on Saturday from 8 am to 2 pm. Cooptourist (☎ 362 041) is around the corner at Szilfákalja út 44/b next to the post office branch at No 44. The main post office is in Kálvin tér. There's a large OTP bank next to the ABC supermarket at Szilfákalja út 10.

Things to See & Do The main attraction in Hajdúszoboszló is the **thermal baths** complex of a dozen mineral and freshwater pools, saunas, solarium and treatment centre. With the exception of the summer-only outdoor pools, the centre is open every day from 8 am to 6 pm. Admission costs 200/100 Ft for adults/children.

Near the **Calvinist church** (1717) on Hősök tere stands all that remains of a 15th-

The Heyducks

The Hajdúság region was settled predominantly by the Hajdúk (Heyducks), a medieval community of Magyar and Slav drovers and outlaws turned mercenaries and renowned for their skill in battle. When the Heyducks helped István Bocskai (1557-1606), prince of Transylvania and the Tiszántúl's biggest landowner, rout the Habsburg forces at Álmosd south-east of Debrecen in 1604, they were raised to the rank of nobility, and some 10,000 were granted land – as much to keep the ferocious brigands in check as to reward them.

The Heyducks built seven towns with walled fortresses around the region. Many of the streets in today's Hajdú towns trace the concentric circles of these walls, the outermost forming ring roads. The Hajdúság continued as a special administrative district until 1876, when it was incorporated into Hajdú-Bihar County and the Heyducks privileges were terminated. ∎

century Gothic **fortress** destroyed by the Turks in 1660: about 20m of wall and a small tower. Across Hősök tere a statue of István Bocskai stands not so proud – a pint-sized prince out of all proportion to his enormous snorting stallion and great deeds.

Down Bocskai utca, past the 18th-century baroque **Catholic church** (Pope John Paul II prayed here as Karol Wojtyla, bishop of Kraków, in the early 1970s), is the **Bocskai Museum** at No 12, a temple to the memory of Prince István and his Heyduck helpers. Among the saddles, pistols and swords hangs Bocskai's banner, the standard of the Heyduck cavalry, picturing the prince doing battle with a leopard (which mysteriously changes into a lion in later versions). There are also exhibits of the city's cultural achievements and of the development of the thermal baths, with some curious Art Deco spa posters and medical instruments that could have come from a medieval dungeon. It's open daily, except Monday, from 9 am to 1 pm and 3 to 6 pm.

A lovely thatched cottage at Ady Endre utca 2 houses the **István Fazekas Pottery Exhibit**, featuring the distinctive black pottery produced in the neighbouring town

of Nádudvar (see the following section). But unless you're in Hajdúszoboszló on a Monday between 8 am and 4 pm, you'll miss it; those are the only hours it keeps.

Tennis equipment is available at the Gázláng court on Szép Ernő utca north-east of the Holiday Centre. The Aero Club (☎ 362 673), based at the small airport at the end of József Attila utca, offers sightseeing flights over Hajdúszoboszló and Debrecen.

Places to Stay The choice of accommodation in this tourist-oriented town is enormous, and prices vary considerably from season to season.

Hajdútourist manages the unnamed *camping ground* (☎ 362 427) in the park along the noisy motorway to Debrecen. There are cabins accommodating four people for 2200 to 3200 Ft as well as hotel rooms (2000 to 2800 Ft) available from mid-April to mid-October. There's another camping ground – *Thermal Camping* (☎ 365 991) – north-east of the Holiday Centre at Böszörményi út 35/a.

Virtually every third household in Hajdúszoboszló lets out *private rooms* in the high season, and 'szoba kiadó' signs sprout like mushrooms after a rain along the city's quiet backstreets, especially Wesselényi utca and Bessenyei utca south of route No 4. If you're not in a do-it-yourself mood, have Hajdútourist or Cooptourist make the arrangements for you from about 1000 Ft. Apartments start at 2500 Ft, and you can get a whole house for six people starting at 5000 Ft.

Among the many pensions in town, the most central is the *Muskátli* (☎ 361 027) at Daru zug 5. It has a dozen large and small doubles from 4000 to 4500 Ft, and a pleasant restaurant with outside seating in front. The *Fortuna* (☎ 362 126), on the outskirts of the city at Dózsa György utca 11, charges 2500 Ft for its nine doubles, breakfast included.

The 47-room *Gambrinus* hotel (☎ 362 054), opposite Hajdútourist at József Attila utca 3, is very run-down but the price is right: doubles are 1500 Ft with shower, 1000 Ft without. A better deal, though, is at the *Hortobágy* (☎ 362 357), a complex of four guesthouses near the baths at Mátyás király sétány 3 with rooms from 1500 Ft.

Among the larger spa hotels (many of which offer one and two-week 'cure packages'), the 252-room *Délibáb* (☎ 360 366) at József Attila utca 4 has singles from DM45 to DM59 and doubles from DM55 to DM89 in its cheapest wing. Prices at the *Béke* (☎ 361 411), with 198 rooms, are higher: singles are DM50 to DM58 and doubles DM82 to DM96. It can be found in the park to the east of the thermal baths at Mátyás király sétány 10.

Places to Eat There are plenty of sausage, lángos and ice-cream stalls along Szilfákalja út and in the park. The supposedly 24-hour *Kakas Csárda* next to the Gambrinus hotel on József Attila utca is a cheap büfé and restaurant. *Pizza Ham* at Hősök tere 19 is open weekdays to 11 pm and Friday and Saturday till 2 am.

The *Szilfa* is a pleasant enough little eatery upstairs at Szilfákalja út 48. The *Civis* restaurant at Szilfákalja út 54 serves the usual Hungarian dishes until 11.30 pm. A better

alternative is the *Arany Oroszlán* at Bessenyei utca 14. The *Halászcsárda* at Jókai sor 12-14 serves inexpensive fish dishes till midnight daily.

Entertainment The *City Cultural Centre* (☎ 361 031), Szilfákalja út 2, can offer advice on what's on in Hajdúszoboszló, including organ and choral concerts in the Calvinist church. The main events here are the Szoboszló Summer Festival in mid-July and the Hajdúszoboszló Horse-Riding Days in early August.

After a long day soaking in steamy brown mineral water, you'll find a lot of prowling going on at the *Oázis* disco, Szilfákalja út 40. It's open Wednesday to Saturday from 9 pm to 4 am. The *Éden* is a topless nightclub in the same building as the Civis restaurant at Szilfákalja út 54.

The *Park* pub serves the cheapest beer in town, al fresco on the corner of Fürdő utca and Mátyás király sétány. The *Santa Fe Western Bar* on the corner of Hősök tere and Kossuth utca is an interesting place for a pint.

Getting There & Away Buses from Hajdúszoboszló depart for Miskolc three times a day and Eger (via Hortobágy) and Szeged once daily. There's direct twice-daily service to Hortobágy from mid-June to August. International destinations served by bus include Satu Mare (Friday at 5 am) and Oradea (Thursday at 6 am) in Romania; and, in Slovakia, Košice (Tuesday at 6.20 am).

Trains headed for Szolnok and Budapest from Debrecen stop at Hajdúszoboszló a couple of times an hour throughout the day.

Getting Around Bus Nos 1, 4 and 6 connect the train and bus stations. There's a large taxi rank on Hősök tere.

Nádudvar
• *pop 8600*
• *area code* ☎ *54*
This tidy town, 18 km west of Hajdúszoboszló and easily reached by one of five daily buses, is the centre of the black-pottery cottage industry.

From the bus station on Kossuth Lajos tér, turn left onto Fő utca and walk 800m in a westerly direction past the neoclassical **Catholic church**, some well maintained graves of Soviet soldiers killed in WWII, and a huge modern cultural centre, to No 152, where Ferenc Fazekas maintains his **pottery workshop**. The potter's clay, rich in iron, is gathered and stored for a year before it is turned on a wheel into vases, jugs, pitchers and candlesticks, then decorated, smoked in a kiln and polished, giving the objects their distinctive black glossy appearance. Ferenc is usually on hand to give visitors a demonstration, and his wares are available in the small shop next door. There is also a small **museum** containing 18th-century pottery made by the Fazekas family and an old foot-operated potter's wheel.

The old *Csillag* restaurant on Kossuth Lajos tér serves decent Hungarian dishes, and the *Korona Presszó* at Fő utca 128 is fine for snacks and drinks. With Hajdúszoboszló and Debrecen so close, there is no point in staying overnight in Nádudvar. But should you miss the last bus, *private rooms* are available at Fő utca 106, and there are expensive doubles and suites at the posh *Trófea Vadászház* (☎ 480 704), in a wood on the eastern edge of town.

Hajdúböszörmény

* *pop 31,000*
* *area code ☎ 52*

Hajdúböszörmény, about 20 km north-west of Debrecen, was the original capital of the Hajdúság region. It has a typical Heyduck arrangement: houses ring the circular old town and are backed by the outer protective walls. Though admittedly frayed around the edges, Hajdúböszörmény is the most historical of all the Heyduck settlements. And the imposing 18th and 19th-century buildings on Bocskai tér lend it a grandeur seldom seen in smaller towns on the Eastern Plain.

Orientation & Information Hajdúböszörmény is dominated by two squares – Bocskai tér and Kálvin tér – which are the inner cores in a town of circles. Kálvin tér is where you

catch long-distance buses; the train station is about one km east at the end of Rákóczi utca.

Hajdútourist (☎ 371 416), open from 8 am to 4 pm on weekdays, is south-east of Bocskai tér at Kossuth Lajos utca 17 and there's an OTP bank almost opposite at No 16. The main post office is at Kálvin tér 1.

Things to See The enormous **Calvinist church** on Kálvin tér is more impressive for its size than its history (it was built in the last century). Instead, have a look at the originally Gothic **Calvinist church** on the west side of Bocskai tér. You can get the keys from the church office at Benedek János utca 2.

Bocskai tér contains a number of impressive buildings, including the huge pink **town hall** on the east side, but the most interesting is the baroque building on the south side housing the **Hajdúság Museum**, with exhibits devoted to archaeology and Heyduck history, and a lovely courtyard that predates the rest of the 18th-century building. The ancient oak trees in the square outside formed a natural defence when this building served as Heyduck headquarters. In the middle of Bocskai tér is a statue of a fearsome group of Heyducks on the warpath, and a more subdued likeness of their boss, István Bocskai.

About seven km south-east of town in Józsa en route to Debrecen on route No 35 stands the **Zelemér Broken Tower**, all that remains of a 14th-century church.

Places to Stay & Eat *Káplár Camping* (☎ 371 388) has several lovely old peasant houses for hire at Polgári út 92-100, but they are about four km north-west of Bocskai tér and bus service is infrequent. Ask Hajdútourist about *private rooms* for about 1000 Ft. There are no hotels in Hajdúböszörmény.

The *Petőfi* restaurant at Petőfi Sándor utca 6 is a big and pleasant place just east of Bocskai tér. The *Délibáb Halászcsárda* is a bare-bones fish place with a certain amount of local colour at Kassa utca 36.

Entertainment Check the *Múzeum Presszó* next to the Hajdúság Museum on Bocskai tér

GREAT PLAIN

for drinks and live music most nights, or the *Kaktusz Bár* at Mester utca 2, which attracts a young crowd. Something might be happening at the *Youth Club* at Kassa utca 24 (you can't miss it from the sign at the entrance that reads: 'Hajdú You Do?'). If not, the people at the modern *Gábor Sillye Cultural Centre* (☎ 371 799) behind the Calvinist church at Bocskai tér 4 are sure to know where something is happening.

Getting There & Away Buses to Debrecen are very frequent, departing every 15 minutes or so. Other destinations include Hajdúnánás via Hajdúdorog (12 buses a day), Hajdúszoboszló (six), Miskolc (12) and Nyíregyháza (one).

Six trains leave Debrecen every day for Tiszalök in western Szabolcs-Szatmár-Bereg County, stopping at Hajdúböszörmény about 40 minutes later. They also call at Hajdúdorog and Hajdúnánás.

Hajdúnánás
• *pop 18,400*
• *area code ☎ 52*

This town, 22 km north-west of Hajdúböszörmény, is the northernmost of the Hajdú settlements and about as far off the beaten track as you'll get in these parts. Today 'Nánás' is a market town serving northern Hajdú-Bihar County, but the main draw here is the spa, popular with tourists from Poland and Slovakia. It also has the distinction of being the site of Hungary's first ostrich farm (there's a newer one at Mindszentkálla north of Lake Balaton).

Orientation & Information The centre of town is Köztársaság tér; intercity buses stop a few blocks north of here at Kossuth utca and Nyíregyházi utca. The train station is 1.5 km due south of the square at the end of tree-lined Bocskai utca. The spa complex is west of the train station on Fürdő utca.

There's an OTP bank on the east side of Köztársaság tér; the post office is a few steps north at Kossuth utca 1.

Things to See & Do The **Calvinist church** (1687) on Köztársaság tér and the neoclassical **Catholic church** farther south on Bocskai utca are listed monuments, but they're not worth more than a cursory look. The rebuilt **medieval wall** with a turret from the 16th century in front of the Calvinist church contains a memorial plaque to the 'martyrs of Hajdúnánás', 900 of them Jews, who were brutally murdered in Nazi concentration camps.

The **Tájház** (Village House), an 18th-century Heyduck home and smithy at Hunyadi utca 21 and open on Monday from 2 to 4 pm and Friday from 10 am till noon, offers an interesting look at a typical Heyduck abode. Check the old tools in the yard used for making wine.

There's a colourful **market** off Kossuth utca, across from the clothing factory – now run by the Dutch – that seems to dominate Hajdúnánás.

Most visitors are drawn to Hajdúnánás by the town's **Strandfürdő**, a large complex of five outdoor swimming pools with fresh and mineral water on Fürdő utca. While not of the same calibre as the baths at Hajdúszoboszló or Debrecen, the surrounds are a welcome 'green lung' on a hot summer's day.

The Hajdú Strucc **ostrich farm** (☎ 381 616) is south of Fürdő utca beyond the old cemetery and can be visited.

Places to Stay & Eat There are two camping grounds on Fürdő utca near the spa complex: the three-star *Thermalbad* (☎ 381 858) at No 7 and the one-star *Termál* (☎ 381 802) farther west at No 22. Neither has bungalows, though. The only hotel in Hajdúnánás is the eight-room *Béke* (☎ 382 218), a decrepit little place but centrally located just off the main square at Bocskai utca 2-4. Doubles are under 1000 Ft.

The *Hajdú* restaurant next to the Béke inn is open daily to 1 am but the *Strucc* at Kossuth Lajos utca 13 is a much nicer place. The *Cabrio* at Dorogi utca 10 is a big pizzeria open till 11 pm (2 am on Friday and Saturday).

Entertainment You could try the *Halidó*, at Dorogi utca 9-11, which bills itself as a restaurant, bar, disco and casino, but the *cultural centre* (☎ 382 400) at Köztársaság tér 6 may come up with some better ideas. The *Lucky Luke Saloon*, just before the Tájház at Hunyadi utca 13, is a fun place to drop in.

Getting There & Away There are about a dozen daily buses to Debrecen via Hajdúdorog. Hajdúnánás and Hajdúdorog are on the railway line linking Debrecen and Hajdúböszörmény with Tiszalök and are served by half a dozen trains a day.

Hajdúdorog
• *pop 9300*
This bishopric and site of a beautiful 18th-century **Greek Catholic church** (Tokaji utca 2) is a mere six km south-east of Hajdúnánás. If you take the bus, you'll be dropped off virtually in front of the church at Petőfi tér. From the train station, it's a two-km walk along Vasút utca and Böszörményi út. Ask someone at the presbytery behind to open the church door for you; otherwise you'll have to be content with admiring the vaulted ceilings and the magnificent **iconostasis** from the porch.

The **Calvinist church** through the churchyard on the main road to Hajdúnánás is in itself not noteworthy, but its simple interior – white with no ornamentation whatsoever – stands in stark contrast to the ornate Greek Catholic church.

There are several places along Böszörményi út for light refreshment, including the *Pagoda* cake shop at No 9, the *Hajdú Presszó* at No 16 and the dumpy *Jäger* pub next to the post office at No 32.

BIHAR REGION
The Bihar region, the southern reaches of the Eastern Plain, is quite different topographically from the Hajdúság. Drained by canals and artificial lakes, much of the land is marshy.

Berettyóújfalu
• *pop 17,000*
• *area code ☎ 54*
Berettyóújfalu is not worth a stop on its own, but if you're heading for Bucharest or Oradea in Romania, it's a more pleasant place to spend the night than Püspökladány, 38 km to the north-west, with its horrid housing projects and busy motorways.

Orientation & Information The centre of town is Kálvin tér, with smaller Szent István tér to the south-west. The bus station is just off Szent István tér on Eötvös utca, while the train station is about one km to the south-west at the end of Ady Endre utca.

There being no tourist office here, your best bet for information is to visit the town's cultural centre at the end of Bajcsy-Zsilinszky utca north-east of Kálvin tér.

You can change money at the OTP bank at Dózsa György utca 5. The post office is on the southern side of Kálvin tér.

Things to See & Do The baroque **Calvinist church** and the neoclassical **town hall** under reconstruction on Kálvin tér are listed buildings, but it would be more interesting to continue along Kossuth utca to No 36, where the **Bihar Museum** displays folk art peculiar to the region.

The **market**, at the corner of Dózsa György utca and Kádár Vitéz utca behind the enormous water tank, is a colourful place full of Ukrainian, Polish, Romanian and Gypsy hawkers. There's not much to buy, but the atmosphere is lively. On the eastern side of the market is a new swimming pool and bath complex.

About two km east of Berettyóújfalu on the road to Biharkeresztes and Romania stands the town's main sight: the ruins of the 13th-century **Herpály Church**, one of the very few examples of Romanesque architecture left in eastern Hungary. To get there on foot, walk east along Bajcsy-Zsilinszky utca (which becomes Tardy út) until you reach Biharkeresztesi út (route No 42). The ruins are across the road atop a small bluff. Pack a

GREAT PLAIN

picnic lunch or stop at the small *presszó* nearby for some light refreshment.

Places to Stay & Eat *Private rooms* may be available at the top of Kossuth utca (Nos 87 and 93). It's a cool, green neighbourhood – if not very central. Just west, where Kossuth utca meets route No 42, there's the small *Tranzit Camping* (☎ 402 341), with bungalows. It is open from June to September.

The tiny *Fatour* inn (☎ 401 419), northeast of Kálvin tér at Móricz Zsigmond utca 3, has three rooms costing from 1600 to 3500 Ft. The *Angéla* pension (☎ 404 040), north of Kálvin tér at Kossuth utca 51, is flashier but a lot more expensive: its 18 double rooms with baths start at 5500 Ft.

The *Bakonszegi Finom Falatok* at Dózsa György utca 9 is a cheap lunch place and centrally located. For a more substantial meal, try the *Hullám* fish restaurant at Kádár Vitéz utca 13 near the little canal. For pizza, there's the *Mandula* on Bocskai utca opposite Kádár Vitéz utca. *Barbie*, at Kádár Vitéz utca 10, is a pleasant place for ice cream on a warm summer's day.

Getting There & Away Berettyóújfalu is well served by buses from Debrecen – there are two or three an hour – and from Békéscsaba via Szeghalom or Gyula. Two daily buses from Hajdúszoboszló also stop here before continuing on to Szeged. Other destinations include Furta and Zsáka (10 a day), Nádudvar (six) and Szarvas (one). Buses to the Romanian city of Oradea depart on Tuesday and Thursday at 7.25 pm.

Berettyóújfalu is on the railway line connecting Püspökladány with Romania. International trains headed for various cities in Romania (Bucharest, Tirgu Mureş, Cluj-Napoca, Braşov) stop here four times a day.

Around Berettyóújfalu
The towns of **Furta** and **Zsáka**, almost side by side about 10 km south of Berettyóújfalu, have maintained some of their folk traditions. Furta has a small museum devoted to local embroidery; Zsáka, prettier with more

traditional cottages, has a couple of fine 18th-century churches.

Southern Plain

The Southern Plain spans the lower regions of the Danube and Tisza rivers and contains many of the most interesting towns and cities of the Great Plain. Even so, at times the plain seems even more endless here, with large farms and the occasional *tanya* (homestead) breaking the monotony. The Southern Plain was even less protected than the rest of the region, and its destruction by the Turks was complete. With little precipitation and frequent drought, the area is the hottest part of the Great Plain and summer lasts well into October.

KECSKEMÉT
• *pop 103,000*
• *area code ☎ 76*

Lying halfway between the Danube and the Tisza rivers in the heart of the Southern Plain, Kecskemét is ringed with vineyards and orchards that somehow don't stop at the limits of this 'garden city'. Colourful architecture, fine museums, apricot groves and the region's excellent *barackpálinka* (apricot brandy) beckon, and the Kiskunság National Park, the puszta of the Southern Plain, is right at the back door.

History has been kind to Kecskemét, now the capital of Hungary's largest county (Bács-Kiskun). While other towns on the Ottoman-occupied Great Plain were administered by the dreaded *spahis*, who had to pay their own way and took what they wanted when they wanted it, Kecskemét – like Szeged farther south – was a khas town, under the direct rule and protection of the sultan. In the 19th century the peasants in the region planted vineyards and orchards to bind the poor, sandy soil. When phylloxera struck in 1880, devastating vineyards throughout Hungary, Kecskemét's vines

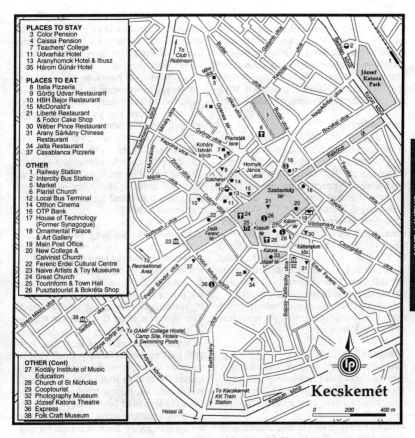

Kecskemét

PLACES TO STAY
3 Color Pension
4 Caissa Pension
7 Teachers' College
11 Udvarház Hotel
13 Aranyhomok Hotel & Ibusz
35 Három Gúnár Hotel

PLACES TO EAT
8 Italia Pizzeria
9 Görög Udvar Restaurant
10 HBH Bajor Restaurant
15 McDonald's
21 Liberté Restaurant
& Fodor Cake Shop
30 Wéber Pince Restaurant
31 Arany Sárkány Chinese
Restaurant
34 Jalta Restaurant
37 Casablanca Pizzeria

OTHER
1 Railway Station
2 Intercity Bus Station
5 Market
6 Piarist Church
12 Local Bus Terminal
14 Otthon Cinema
16 OTP Bank
17 House of Technology
(Former Synagogue)
18 Ornamental Palace
& Art Gallery
19 Main Post Office
20 New College &
Calvinist Church
22 Ferenc Erdei Cultural Centre
23 Naive Artists & Toy Museums
24 Great Church
25 Tourinform & Town Hall
26 Pusztatourist & Bokréta Shop

OTHER (Cont)
27 Kodály Institute of Music
Education
28 Church of St Nicholas
29 Cooptourist
32 Photography Museum
33 József Katona Theatre
36 Express
38 Folk Craft Museum

GREAT PLAIN

proved immune: apparently the dreaded lice didn't like the sand. Today the region is responsible for a third of Hungary's total wine output, though it must be said that this thin, rather undistinguished 'sand wine' is not the best. It's also a major producer of *foie gras*, and the large goose farms – some of them with tens of thousands of the cranky creatures – have increased the Plain's fox population substantially.

Kecskemét's agricultural wealth was used wisely – it was able to redeem all its debts in cash in 1832 – and today the city can boast some of the most spectacular architecture in the country. Art Nouveau and the so-called Historical Eclectic (or Hungarian Romantic) style predominate, giving the city a turn-of-the-century feel. It also was – and still is – an important cultural centre: an artists' colony was established here in 1912, and the composer Zoltán Kodály chose Kecskemét as the site for his world-famous Institute of Music Education. Two other local boys who made good include László Kelemen, who formed Hungary's first provincial travelling theatre here late in the 18th century, and József Katona (1791-1830), the father of modern Hungarian drama.

Orientation

Kecskemét is a city of multiple squares that run into one another without warning and can be a little confusing at first. The bus and main train stations are opposite one another near József Katona Park. A 10-minute walk south-west along Nagykőrösi utca will bring you to the first of the squares, Szabadság tér.

Information

Tourinform (☎ 481 065) is on the west side of the town hall at Kossuth Lajos tér 1. It is open weekdays from 8 am to 5 pm and Saturday from 9 am to 1 pm. In summer, it stays open till 6 pm and keeps Sunday hours as well. Pusztatourist (☎ 483 493), at Szabadság tér 2, and Ibusz (☎ 486 955) at the Aranyhomok hotel (Széchenyi tér 2) are open from 8 am to 4.30 pm on weekdays, to noon on Saturday in summer. Express (☎ 329 236), out of the way above Dobó István körút 11, has similar weekday hours but does not open Saturday. Cooptourist (☎ 481 472) is at Kéttemplom köz 9-11.

OTP bank has a branch at Szabadság tér 5 next to the former synagogue. The main post office is at Kálvin tér 10.

Things to See

Kecskemét is chock-a-block with museums, churches and other interesting buildings. Though most of the sights are within a relatively compact area, choose carefully.

Around Kossuth tér On the eastern side of Kossuth tér is the **Franciscan Church of St Nicholas**, dating in parts from the late 13th century; the **Kodály Institute of Music Education** occupies the baroque monastery behind it at Kéttemplom köz 1. But the main building in the square is the sandy-pink **town hall**, a lovely turn-of-the-century building designed by Ödön Lechner, who mixed Art Nouveau with folkloric elements to produce a unique 'Hungarian' style. (Another beautiful example of this style is the restored Otthon Cinema on Széchenyi tér.) The town hall's carillon chimes out strains of works by Ferenc Erkel, Kodály, Mozart, Handel and Beethoven several times during the day, and

groups are allowed into the spectacular **Council Chamber** (call ☎ 483 683 to arrange a tour). The floral ceilings and the frescos of Hungarian heroes and historical scenes were painted by Bertalan Székely, who tended to romanticise the past. Just outside and half-covered by a rhododendron bush, the **József Katona Memorial** marks the spot where the young playwright dropped dead of a heart attack in 1830.

You can't miss the tall tower of the Catholic **Great Church** (1806) – sometimes called the Old Church – next to the town hall. The big tablets on the front honour citizens who died in the 1848-49 War of Independence and a mounted regiment of Hussars that served in WWI.

Szabadság tér Walking north-east into Szabadság tér, you'll pass the 17th-century **Calvinist church** and **New College** (1912), a later version of the Hungarian Romantic style that looks like a Transylvanian castle and is now a music school. Two other buildings in the square are among the city's finest. The Art Nouveau **Ornamental Palace** (Cifrapalota), dating from 1902 and covered in multicoloured majolica tiles, now contains the **Kecskemét Gallery**. Don't go in so much for the art; climb the steps to the aptly named **Decorative Hall** to see the amazing stucco peacock, bizarre windows and more tiles. The **House of Technology** (1871), the Moorish structure across Rákóczi út, was once a synagogue. Today it is used for conferences and exhibitions.

Museums The **Museum of Naive Artists**, arguably the city's finest museum and the only one of its kind in Europe outside Paris, is in the Stork House (1730), surrounded by a high white wall on Gáspár András utca just off Petőfi Sándor utca. Lots of predictable themes here, but the warmth and craft of Rozália Albert Juhászné's work, the druglike visions of Dezső Mokry-Mészáros and the paintings of András Süli (Hungary's answer to Henri Rousseau) will hold your attention.

The **Toy Museum** next door has a small

collection of 19th and early 20th-century dolls, wooden trains, board games and so on dumped haphazardly in glass cases. But the museum spends most of its time and money on organising events and classes for kids. Much is made of Ernő Rubik, the Hungarian inventor of that infuriating Rubik cube from the 1970s.

The granddaddy of all museums in Kecskemét – the **Hungarian Folk Craft Museum** – is farther south-west at Serfőző utca 19, a block in from Dózsa György út. Nine rooms of an old farm complex are crammed with embroidery, woodcarving, furniture, agricultural tools and textiles, so don't try to see everything.

The **Hungarian Photography Museum**, in part of an Art Deco Orthodox synagogue at Katona József tér 12, is not very impressive but it is the only one in the country. It's open Wednesday to Sunday from 10 am to 5 pm. The rest of the synagogue is still used on high holidays by the city's tiny congregation of Orthodox Jews.

The **Musical Instrument Museum**, Zimay utca 6/a, traces the development of music-making over the centuries and has a decent collection of instruments from five continents. It is open Monday to Saturday from 9 am to 5 pm.

Markets Kecskemét's **market** is behind the Piarist Church on Jókai utca, north of Szabadság tér. The lively **flea market** is south-east of the city on Külső Szegedi út.

Activities

Kecskemét has an abundance of thermal water, and in summer the four Szék-tó pools on Izsáki út, the continuation of Dózsa György út, or the lake in 'Leisure Time Park' to the north of them are a treat. There's a large indoor swimming pool at Izsáki út 1 open every day throughout the year between 6 am and 9 pm.

Special Events

Special events in Kecskemét include a jazz festival in March; the cultural Spring Days and Crafts Fair, both in March/April; the Kodály International Music Festival in July; and the Agricultural & Folk Fair held in September in even-numbered years.

Places to Stay

Camping *Autós Camping* (☎ 329 398) is on Sport utca, on the south-western side of Kecskemét, nearly five km from the train station and crammed with German and Dutch tourists in caravans. If you must, the site also has bungalows for two for 3200 Ft and bicycles for rent. It is open from mid-April to mid-October.

Hostels About three blocks from the camping ground is Kecskemét's hostel at the *GAMF College* (☎ 321 916), Izsáki út 10. A bed in a four-bed room here is about 600 Ft, singles/doubles are 1000/1500 Ft. Officially it's only open from mid-June to August, but you can sometimes get a bed in other months.

In July and August you may be able to get a room in the *Teachers' College* (☎ 321 977), Piaristák tere 4, for about 1200 Ft. In fact, it's worth trying this 100-room dormitory right in the centre of town any time – you could get lucky.

Private Rooms Pusztatourist charges from 900 Ft per person for a private room. Cooptourist is about the same but usually has only doubles.

Farm Accommodation If you want a quiet break, have your own transport and can stay put in one place for a minimum of three nights, a farmhouse stay is a great option. The area outside Kecskemét is called the *tanya világ* (or 'farm world') and is very picturesque, with isolated thatch-roofed farmhouses and distinctive sweep-pole wells *(gémeskút)* set amid orchards and mustard fields. Pusztatourist has dozens for rent throughout the county, priced between 7000 and 8000 Ft a night, but many are within a 30-km radius of Kecskemét at Bugac, in the Helvécia vineyards to the south-west, and at Lajosmizse, a horse-riding centre to the north-west.

GREAT PLAIN

Pensions *Color* (☎ 483 246), Jókai utca 26, is a small pension with eight rooms at 2800 Ft a double (no singles). *Caissa* (☎ 481 685), Gyenes tér 18, has 11 rooms for 2400 to 2600 Ft. Two larger rooms for up to five people are also available. Caissa's location is excellent so it's always worth a try.

Hotels The *Aranyhomok* (☎ 486 286) at Széchenyi tér 2 is the city's largest and ugliest hotel, with 113 rooms and a slew of outlets. Singles/doubles with bath are DM87/93. For something smaller and far more charming, try the *Három Gúnár* (☎ 483 611), a small hotel formed by cobbling four old townhouses together at Batthyány utca 1-7 (the hotel name means 'three ganders'). Its 45 smallish rooms (the best are Nos 306 to 308) cost 5300/6300 Ft for singles/doubles. The hotel has a so-so restaurant, a popular bar with an outside terrace, and tenpin bowling in the basement.

Farther afield, the dumpy but clean *Sport* hotel (☎ 323 090) at Izsáki út 15/a has 15 cramped double rooms for 1800 Ft. The 38-room *Sauna* (☎ 481 859) at Sport utca 3 is a vast, modern place in a quiet location next to the thermal spa. Rooms start at 3200 Ft and it has a restaurant, a gym and, naturally enough, a sauna. The newest up-market hotel in Kecskemét is the *Udvarház* (☎ 413 912), tucked away in a courtyard at Csányi utca 1-3.

Places to Eat

The pizza at the *Italia* on Koháry István körút has improved in recent years, but you can opt instead for black olives and feta cheese by crossing the street to the *Görög Udvar* (Greek Court) restaurant. The *Arany Sárkány* is a Chinese place at Erkel Ferenc utca 1/a, south-east of Katona József tér. There's a *McDonald's* at Kossuth tér 6-7.

For well-prepared Germano-Hungarian food, try the *HBH Bajor* in a sheltered courtyard at Csányi utca 4 behind the cultural centre. A better choice for similar food is the *Wéber Pince* at Csongrádi utca 2. The *Casablanca* is a popular hang-out with decent

pizza, and a large terrace overlooking Deák Ferenc tér at Dobó István 1.

The *Jalta*, Batthyány utca 2, opposite the Három Gúnár hotel, is a rather homely wine cellar with a menu in English and German. Their speciality is grilled South Slav dishes. If you want to splurge, you couldn't do better than the *Liberté*, in a historical building next to Pusztatourist on Szabadság tér, one of my favourite restaurants in provincial Hungary. The best ice cream and cakes in Kecskemét are at *Fodor*, in the same building.

To or from Bugac (see the following Kiskunság National Park section), you might stop at the *Szélmalom Csárda* at Városföld utca 167, a 'windmill restaurant' a few km south-east of town along route No 5.

Entertainment

Kecskemét is a city of music and theatre; you'd be crazy not to see at least one performance here. Head first for the *Ferenc Erdei Cultural Centre* (☎ 484 594) at Deák Ferenc tér 1, which sponsors some events and is a good source of information. The 19th-century *József Katona Theatre* on Katona József tér stages dramatic works as well as operettas and concerts by the Kecskemét Symphony Orchestra; the ticket office (☎ 481 064) there is open Tuesday to Friday from 10 am to 1 pm and 3 to 6 pm.

Club Robinson, Akadémia körút 2 (closed Monday and Tuesday) is a large, popular disco.

Things to Buy

You can buy folk art peculiar to the Southern Plain at Bokréta, a shop on Kossuth tér next to Pusztatourist. The Hungarian Museum of Naive Artists has an interesting gallery in its cellar where for reasonable prices you can purchase original paintings almost as good as those on display upstairs.

Getting There & Away

Bus It's not surprising, given its central location, that Kecskemét is well serviced by buses, with frequent departures for the most far-flung destinations. There are almost hourly buses to Budapest, buses every couple of hours to Szeged and two a day to Pécs. Buses also run to Arad in Romania about four times a week and to Subotica in Yugoslavia at least once a day, but check this information before making plans.

Train Kecskemét is on the railway line linking Budapest-Nyugati with Szeged, from where trains cross the border to Subotica and Belgrade. To get to Debrecen and other towns on the Eastern Plain, you must change at Cegléd. A very slow narrow-gauge train leaves Kecskemét KK train station south of the city centre four times a day for Kiskőrös. Transfer there for Kalocsa. Kecskemét KK is also the station from which trains leave for Bugac (see the following section on Kiskunság National Park).

Getting Around

Bus Nos 1, 5 and 11 link the bus and train stations with the local bus terminus behind the Aranyhomok hotel. From Kecskemét KK station, catch the No 2 or 13 to the centre. For the pools, hotels and camp site on Sport utca, bus Nos 1, 11 and 22 are good. The No 13 goes past the flea market.

Local taxis can be ordered on ☎ 481 481 or ☎ 484 848.

KISKUNSÁG NATIONAL PARK

Kiskunság National Park consists of half a dozen 'islands' of land totalling 35,000 sq hectares. Much of the park's alkaline ponds, dunes and grassy 'deserts' are off-limits to casual visitors, but you can get a close look at this environmentally fragile area – and see the famous horse herds go through their paces to boot – at **Bugac** on a sandy steppe 30 km south-west of Kecskemét.

The easiest but most pricey way to see the sights of Bugac is to join a tour in Kecskemét with Pusztatourist or Bugac Tours (☎ 76-481 643; Szabadság tér 1/a). For about 3500 Ft, they'll bus you to the park, take you by carriage past costumed shepherds and carefully 'planted' racka sheep and grey cattle to the horse show, and serve you lunch at a touristy csárda.

But if you've had enough of geriatric Germans, take the 8.15 am narrow-gauge train from Kecskemét KK station – not the main train station in Kecskemét. Kecskemét KK is on Halasi út, which is the southern continuation of Batthyány utca; you can walk from the centre of Kecskemét or hop aboard bus No 2 or 13 from the local bus terminus behind the Aranyhomok hotel. Make sure you get off at the Bugac felső station (31 km; 1¼ hours) and not the Bugacpuszta or Bugac train stations, which come before it.

From the Bugac felső station, walk north for 15 minutes to the Bugaci Karikás Csárda and the park entrance (650/325 Ft adults/children). There you can board a horse-driven carriage for 1300 Ft or walk another three km along the sandy track to the **Herder Museum**, a circular structure designed to look like a horse-driven dry mill that is filled with stuffed fauna and pressed flora of the Kiskunság, as well as branding irons, carved wooden pipes, embroidered fur coats and a tobacco pouch made from a gnarled ram's scrotum. It's open daily (except Monday) from April to September.

There will still be plenty of time to inspect the stables before the **horse show** at 1 pm (this can vary slightly so ask at the park entrance). Outside, you may come across a couple of noble Nonius steeds being made to perform tricks that most dogs would be disinclined to do (sit, play dead, roll over). The real reason for coming, though, is to see the horseherds crack their whips, race one another bareback and ride 'five-in-hand', a breathtaking performance in which one csikós gallops five horses around the field at full speed while standing on the backs of the last two.

The *Bugaci Karikás Csárda*, with its gulyás and folk-music ensemble, is a lot more fun than first appears, and they have horses for riding (1300 Ft per hour) and a *camp site* (☎ 76-372 688) for 60 people (250 Ft per person). Bugac Tours, with a branch office at the park entrance, has rustic *cottages* for rent nearby for DM60 for two people.

Unless you entertain yourself with bird-

GREAT PLAIN

watching or drinking apricot pálinka under the trees at the csárda, you've got a lot of time to kill between the end of the show and the next little train at 6 pm. If a group has chartered the 4 pm steam train, try to hitch a ride, or catch one of four buses back to Kecskemét from the main highway (route No 54). You can also reach Kiskunfélegyháza, 18 km to the east, from where buses depart more regularly for Kecskemét.

KALOCSA
• *pop 20,000*
• *area code* ☎ *78*

It is doubtful that Pál Tomori, the 16th-century archbishop of Kalocsa and military commander at the fateful battle of Mohács, would recognise his town today. When he last saw it before galloping off to fight the Turks, Kalocsa was a Gothic town on the Danube with a magnificent 14th-century cathedral. Today an 18th-century baroque church stands in its place and the river is six km to the west, the result of 19th-century regulation.

With Esztergom, Kalocsa was one of the two archbishoprics founded by King Stephen in 1009 from the country's 10 dioceses. The town had its heyday in the 15th century when, fortified and surrounded by swamps and the river, it could be easily protected. But Kalocsa was burned to the ground during the Turkish occupation and was not rebuilt until the 18th century.

While never as significant as Esztergom, Kalocsa played an important role after the 1956 Uprising. For 15 years, while the ultra-conservative József Mindszenty, archbishop of Esztergom and thus primate of Hungary, took refuge in the US Embassy in Budapest (see aside in the Danube Bend chapter), the prelate of Kalocsa was forced to play a juggling game with the government to ensure the church's position – and, indeed, existence – in a nominally atheistic Communist state.

Today Kalocsa is a quiet town, as celebrated for its paprika and folk art as for its turbulent history.

Orientation & Information

The streets of Kalocsa fan out from Szent-háromság tér, site of Kalocsa Cathedral and the Archbishop's Palace. The bus station lies at the southern end of the main avenue, Szent István király út. The train station is to the north-east on Mártírok tere, a 20-minute walk from the centre along Kossuth Lajos utca.

Ibusz (☎ 462 102) is at Szent István király út 23, and there's another agency, Korona Tours (☎ 462 186), in the Paprika Museum on the same street at No 6. Both are open weekdays from 8 am to 6 pm; Ibusz also opens on Saturday morning.

There's an OTP bank branch with an ATM at Szent István király út 43-45 and a K&H bank at No 28. The post office is on the

Hungary's Red Gold

Paprika, the 'red gold' (*piros arany*) so essential in Hungarian cuisine, is cultivated primarily around Szeged and Kalocsa. About 10,000 tonnes of the spice is produced annually, 55% of which is exported. Opinions vary on how and when the *Capsicum annum* plant first arrived in Hungary – from India via Turkey and the Balkans or from the New World – but mention of it is made in documents dating from the 16th century.

There are many types of fresh or dried paprika available in Hungarian markets and shops, including the rose, apple and king's varieties. But as a ground spice it is most commonly sold as *csipős* or *erős* ('hot' or 'strong') paprika and *édes* ('sweet') paprika.

Capsicum annum is richer in vitamin C than citrus fruits, and it was during experimentation with the plant that Dr Albert Szent-Györgyi of Szeged first isolated the vitamin. He was awarded the Nobel prize for medicine in 1937.

The Hungarian government suspended the sale of all paprika in late 1994 when traces of lead oxide were found in a third of all paprika samples tested. Unscrupulous dealers, it turned out, had been cutting poor quality paprika with red paint and flour and earning significant profits. Everything is back to normal now – with Hungarians continuing to consume about half a kg of the stuff per capita every year. ■

corner of Szent István király út and Ady
Endre utca.

Kalocsa Cathedral

Almost everything of interest in Kalocsa is
on or near Szent István király út, beginning
at Szentháromság tér, where the **Trinity
Column** (1786) is corroding into sand.
Kalocsa Cathedral, the fourth church to stand
on the site, was completed in 1754 by András
Mayerhoffer and is a baroque masterpiece,
with a dazzling pink and gold interior full of
stucco and reliefs. Some believe that the
sepulchre in the crypt is that of the first
archbishop of Kalocsa, Asztrik, who brought
King Stephen the gift of a crown from Pope
Sylvester II, thereby legitimising the Christian convert's control over Hungary.

The **Archbishop's Treasury** in the back
of the cathedral up a set of winding steps
(open daily except Monday from 9 am to 5
pm from May to October) is a trove of gold
and bejewelled objects and vestments. In
case you were wondering, the large bust of
St Stephen was cast for the millenary exhibition in 1896 and contains 48 kg of silver
and two kg of gold. Among the other valuable objects is a 16th-century reliquary of St
Anne, and a gold and crystal baroque monstrance.

Archbishop's Palace

The Great Hall and the chapel of the Archbishop's Palace (1766) contain magnificent
frescos by Franz Anton Maulbertsch, but
you won't get to see these unless there's a
concert on. The **Episcopal Library**, however,
is open to visitors in groups of less than 10
from April to October daily except Monday
from 9 am till noon and 2 to 5 pm. The library
contains more than 100,000 volumes,
including 13th-century codices, a Bible belonging to Martin Luther and annotated in
the reformer's hand, illuminated manuscripts, and verses cut into palm fronds from
what is now Sri Lanka.

Museums

With Szeged, Kalocsa is the largest producer
of paprika, the 'red gold' (*piros arany*) so

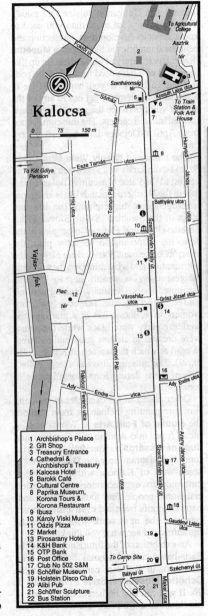

Kalocsa

0   75   150 m

1 Archbishop's Palace
2 Gift Shop
3 Treasury Entrance
4 Cathedral &
   Archbishop's Treasury
5 Kalocsa Hotel
6 Barokk Café
7 Cultural Centre
8 Paprika Museum,
   Korona Tours &
   Korona Restaurant
9 Ibusz
10 Károly Viski Museum
11 Oázis Pizza
12 Market
13 Pirosarany Hotel
14 K&H Bank
15 OTP Bank
16 Post Office
17 Club No 502 S&M
18 Schöffer Museum
19 Holstein Disco Club
20 Alibi Pub
21 Schöffer Sculpture
22 Bus Station

GREAT PLAIN

important in Hungarian cuisine (see aside). You can learn a lot more than you need to know about its development, production and beneficial qualities at the **Paprika Museum** (Szent István király út 6), which is set up like the inside of a barn used for drying the pods in long garlands. If you happen to be in Kalocsa in September, get out to any of the nearby villages to see the green fields transformed into red carpets. The museum is open from April to October daily from 10 am to 5 pm.

The renovated **Károly Viski Museum** at Szent István király út 25 is as rich in folklore and art as the Palóc Museum in Balassagyarmat in the Northern Uplands but is also more heterogeneous, highlighting the life and ways of the Swabian (Sváb), Slovak (Tót), Serbian (Rác) and Hungarian peoples of the area. It's surprising to see how plain the interiors of peasant houses were early in the 19th century and what rainbows they became 50 years later as wealth increased: walls, furniture, doors – virtually nothing was left undecorated by the famous 'painting women' of Kalocsa. Yet at a marriage the wedding party wore black while the guests were dressed in clothes gaily embroidered, (a craft at which the women of Kalocsa also excel). The museum also has a large collection of coins dating from Roman times to today.

Other places to see examples of wall and furniture painting include the **train station**, the **House of Folk Arts** at Tompa Mihály utca 7 (open mid-April to mid-October), and **Juca néni csárdája** (Aunt Judy's Csárda), a touristy restaurant near the Danube six km south-west of Kalocsa with 'performing' embroiderers, egg decorators and wall painters. Some people find today's flower-and-paprika motifs twee and even a little garish; compare the new work with that in the museums and see what you think.

An exhibition of the futuristic work of the Paris-based artist Nicholas Schöffer, who was born in Kalocsa, can be seen at the **Schöffer Museum** at Szent István király út 76. If you can't be bothered, have a look at his 'kinematic sculpture' *Chronos 8* (1982)

near the bus station – a Meccano-set creation of steel beams, flashing lights and spinning mirrors that is supposed to portend the art of the 21st century. Let's hope not.

Places to Stay

Duna Camping (☎ 462 534), about five km south-west of town on Meszesi út, operates between mid-May and mid-September. Ibusz has *private rooms* in Kalocsa and vicinity and may be able to get you a dormitory room at the *Agricultural College* on Asztrik tér during the summer.

The 22-room *Pirosarany* hotel (☎ 462 220) at Szent István király utca 37 has been tarted up in recent years but is still a bargain with rooms for 1990/3400 Ft without/with shower. The *Két Gólya* inn (☎ 462 259), across the little Vajas stream at Móra Ferenc utca 4, charges 3000 Ft for its six doubles with shared shower.

The *Kalocsa* hotel (☎ 461 244) at Szentháromság tér 4, housed in beautifully restored episcopal offices built in 1780, has 30 rooms in a main building and courtyard annexe. Singles are DM69 to DM84 and doubles DM72 to DM89, depending on the season.

Places to Eat

For pizza, try the *Oázis* at Szent István király út 31 or the oddly named *Club No 502 S&M* at No 64.

The *Korona* restaurant at Szent István király út 6 has a cellar dating from the Middle Ages and tables in a lovely courtyard in summer. The restaurant at the *Kalocsa* hotel is no great shakes and a bit pricey.

If you happen to be heading for the Danube ferry crossing over to Gerjen southwest of Kalocsa or staying at the camping ground, the *Juca néni csárdája* (see the previous Museums section) is in the vicinity.

Entertainment

The *Kalocsa Cultural Centre* (☎ 462 200) is housed in an 18th-century baroque seminary at Szent István király út 2-4. See if any concerts are scheduled in the Great Hall of the Archbishop's Palace or in the cathedral.

The *Barokk* café in the same building and facing Szentháromság tér has pool tables and attracts the town's many students.

The Danube Folklore Festival, held in conjunction with Baja and, across the river, Szekszárd and Tolna, takes place in July.

Several popular bars can be found along Szent István király út in the direction of the bus station, including: the cellar of the *Alibi Pub* at No 89; the *Holstein Disco Club* at No 87; and the *Club No 502 S&M* at No 64. The most popular disco in the area is the *Fekete Horgony*, four km west of Kalocsa in Foktő.

Things to Buy

Tacky Kalocsa folk souvenirs are churned out by the cooperative at Tomori Pál utca 13 and shipped to every *népművészeti bolt* (folk art shop) in the land; there's no point in looking for anything special here. If you must, the small shop at Szentháromság tér 3 has the best selection. You can buy gift packets of Kalocsa paprika at the Paprika Museum.

Getting There & Away

There are frequent buses to/from Budapest, Baja (mostly via Hajós) and Solt. There are also buses to Kiskunhalas (six daily), Szeged (five), Székesfehérvár (three) and Nagykőrös (four). You can catch a daily bus to Arad in Romania at 5.45 am.

Kalocsa is at the end of a rail spur to Kiskőrös, the birthplace of Hungary's greatest poet, Sándor Petőfi (1823-49); there are six departures a day. From Kiskőrös you can make connections to Budapest and over the border to Subotica and Belgrade. A very slow (2¼-hour) narrow-gauge train links Kiskőrös with the smaller of Kecskemét's train stations, Kecskemét KK.

AROUND KALOCSA

If you're travelling by bus between Kalocsa and Baja, you may pass through **Nemesnádudvar** and **Hajós**, two Swabian villages settled by Maria Theresa in the 18th century.

Both towns appear to consist of nothing but wine cellars cut into the loess soil; there are some 1200 in Hajós alone. If you have time, stop in at the *Judit* pension at Borbíró sor 1 (or any of the cellars that look open) for a glass of Hajósi Cabernet, one of the best red wines produced on the Great Plain.

To get to Kecskemét from Kalocsa by bus, you may have to change at **Solt**, a horse-breeding centre with many riding and carriage-driving opportunities. The *Teleki Castle* hotel (☎ 60-389 502) is at Kálimajor utca 1 (doubles from DM65). Solt produces a good, semi-dry Merlot.

BAJA

• *pop 40,300*
• *area code ☎ 79*

On the Danube about 45 km south of Kalocsa, Baja was a fortified town during the Turkish occupation but suffered greatly and had to be repopulated with Germans and Serbians in the 18th century. Today it is an important commercial centre and river port, but it is perhaps best known as a holiday and sports centre – the perfect place to relax for a spell before heading on.

Baja has one of the loveliest locations of any town on the Southern Plain. One of its main squares (Szentháromság tér) gives on to a branch of the Danube, and just across are two recreational islands with beaches and flood-bank forests. The bridge across the river to the north is an important one. There's only one other crossing between here and Budapest (at Dunaföldvár, 78 km to the north), and the Baja bridge serves as a gateway to Transdanubia.

Orientation

A pedestrian street links Baja's three main squares – Vörösmarty tér, Szent Imre tér and Szentháromság tér. The last one lies on the Kamarás-Duna (or Sugovica as it is known locally), a branch of the Danube River that cuts Petőfi and Nagy Pandúr islands off from the mainland before emptying into the main river downstream. The bus station is on

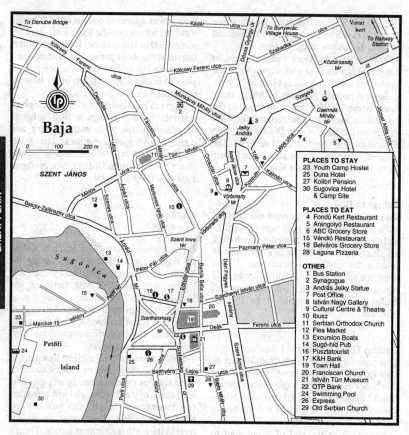

Baja

SZENT JÁNOS

Sugovica

Szent Imre tér

Petőfi

Island

PLACES TO STAY
23 Youth Camp Hostel
25 Duna Hotel
27 Kolibri Pension
30 Sugovica Hotel & Camp Site

PLACES TO EAT
4 Fondü Kert Restaurant
5 Arangolyó Restaurant
6 ABC Grocery Store
15 Véndió Restaurant
18 Belváros Grocery Store
28 Laguna Pizzeria

OTHER
1 Bus Station
2 Synagogue
3 András Jelky Statue
7 Post Office
8 István Nagy Gallery
9 Cultural Centre & Theatre
10 Ibusz
11 Serbian Orthodox Church
12 Flea Market
13 Excursion Boats
14 Sugó-híd Pub
16 Pusztatourist
17 K&H Bank
19 Town Hall
20 Franciscan Church
21 István Türr Museum
22 OTP Bank
24 Swimming Pool
26 Express
29 Old Serbian Church

Csermák Mihály tér; the train station is a few minutes to the north across Vonat kert (Train Garden).

Information

Pusztatourist (☎ 321 237) and Express (☎ 322 191) are on Szentháromság tér, at Nos 8 and 5 respectively. Ibusz (☎ 321 644) is at Táncsics Mihály utca 5. All are open on weekdays only from 8.30 am to 4 or 5 pm.

There's a K&H bank branch with an ATM and currency exchange machine at Szentháromság tér 10 and an OTP bank on the corner of Szentháromság tér and Deák Ferenc

utca. The post office is on Arany János utca south of Jelky András tér.

Things to See

The enormous **Szentháromság tér**, a colourful square of baroque and neoclassical buildings marred only by all the parked cars, is dominated on the east side by the renovated **town hall** and its 'widow's walk' looking out to the Danube.

South of the town hall at Deák Ferenc utca 1 stands the **István Türr Museum**, named after a local hero who fought in the 1848-49 War of Independence and alongside Garibaldi in southern Italy in 1860. The museum's prime exhibit, entitled 'Life on the Danube', covers wildlife, fishing methods and boat building. Another deals with the folk groups of Baja and its surrounds: the Magyars, Germans, South Slavs (Bunyevác, Sokac) and – surprisingly for Hungary – Gypsies; all have lived together in this region for several centuries. The rarely seen Gypsy woodcarving is good, but don't miss the exquisite South Slav black lace, the gold work for which Baja was once nationally famous, and the weavings from Nagybaracska to the south.

The museum couldn't possibly ignore the city's famous sons, including Türr, the painter István Nagy and András Jelky (1738-83), an apprentice tailor who set out for Paris in the mid-18th century but ended up wandering around China, Japan, Ceylon and Java for 10 years before returning to Hungary to write his memoirs. You'll find a statue of this unusual Hungarian dressed in his Chinese best on Jelky András tér.

The **István Nagy Gallery** at Arany János utca 1 – once the mansion of the Vojnich family and an artists' colony after the war – is named after the leading painter of what is known as the Alföld School. Other members are featured, including Gyula Rudnay, as well as 'outsiders' like the cubist Béla Kádár and sculptor Ferenc Medgyessy.

Buildings of architectural note include the **Franciscan church** (1728) behind the town hall on Bartók Béla utca, which has a fantastic baroque organ; and the late baroque **Serbian Orthodox church** in a quiet square at Táncsics Mihály utca 21. The iconostasis is definitely worth a detour.

But the neoclassical **synagogue** (1845) at Munkácsy Mihály utca 7-9 beats them both. Now a public library, it can be visited on weekdays till 6 pm and on Saturday till noon. On the right as you enter the gate, you'll pass a sheltered memorial to the victims of fascism. Above the columns on the synagogue's tympanum (the façade below the roof) on the west side, the Hebrew inscription reads: 'This is none other than the house of God and the gate to heaven.' The taberna-

cle inside, with its Corinthian pilasters, is topped with two lions holding a crown while four doves pull back a blue and burgundy curtain.

The **Bunyevác Village House** displays South Slav furniture, clothing, decorative items and tools in an old cottage at Pandúr utca 51 in Baja-Szentistván, a half-hour walk from the city centre.

One of the liveliest **flea markets** in Hungary, full of Serbs, Romanians and Hungarians from Transylvania, is north of Árpád tér just beyond the bridge over to Petőfi Island.

Activities
The Sugovica resort on Petőfi Island has fishing, boating, mini-golf and tennis on offer to anyone willing to pay, and there's a covered swimming pool – the Baja Sports Pool – across the walkway open weekdays (except Wednesday) from 6 am to 7.30 pm, Saturday and Sunday from 8 am to 7.30 pm. The Youth Camp hostel (see Places to Stay) has kayaks and canoes for rent (200 Ft per hour).

Avoid the public beaches on Petőfi Island in favour of the less crowded ones on the mainland in Szent János or on Nagy Pandúr Island. But be prepared to swim to the latter or face a long walk to the southern suburb of Homokváros, across the bridge to Nagy Pandúr Island and then north to the beach.

Places to Stay
The *Youth Camp* hostel (☎ 324 022), in a block at the northern end of Petőfi Island and HI-affiliated, has seven doubles for 2000 Ft (2500 Ft with shower) and 14 multi-bed rooms for 700 Ft per head. It's open from May to September.

Bungalows at the nearby *Sugovica Camping* (☎ 321 755) to the south are expensive, but they are in a relatively attractive camp site. There are 19 in all, with doubles costing from 2270 to 2760 Ft, according to the season. The two most 'remote' bungalows are those designated R9 and R10, though they're not directly on the water.

The agencies can book you into a *private room* from 1000 Ft.

The five rooms at the *Kolibri* pension (☎ 321 628) at Batthyány utca 18 are small but cheap enough at 1500 Ft for doubles with shared shower. The pension is just south-east of Szentháromság tér.

The 49-room *Duna* (☎ 323 224) at Szentháromság tér 6 has had a coat of green paint slapped on it, but that's done nothing to spoil the atmosphere of this wonderfully tired old place. Hard by the Danube (many rooms have river views), the hotel has singles with shower for 2800 Ft and doubles with/without shower for 3400/3000 Ft. If there are four of you (or money is no problem), stay in No 118, a two-room suite with a beautiful roof terrace overlooking the river, for 4800 Ft. Other good rooms are Nos 111, 239 and 246.

The 34-room *Sugovica* (☎ 321 755) on Petőfi Island is Baja's most expensive hotel, with singles from 6800 Ft, doubles from 8000 Ft. All rooms have bathroom, TV, minibar and a balcony looking onto the park or river. There's even a private mooring and winching for guests arriving by boat.

Places to Eat

Neither the *Duna* hotel's restaurant nor pub (open till midnight) is very agreeable, but the terrace café out the front on the square is a great place to sit in warmer months. For outside seating, though, nothing beats the *Véndió* restaurant, a few minutes across the bridge at the northern end of Petőfi Island.

Melted cheese is not a major player in Hungarian cuisine, but the *Fondü Kert*, a fun little place in a courtyard at Kossuth Lajos utca 19, does a roaring trade every day till 11 pm. A pot of fondue and a salad will keep you going all day. The *Laguna Pizzeria*, south of the Kolibri pension on Babits Mihály utca, attracts a young crowd, both inside and out in the parking lot.

An inexpensive place beside the bus station at Csermák Mihály tér 9 is the *Aranygolyó*, but it closes at weekends.

The *ABC grocery store* on Tóth Kálmán utca next to the modern telephone exchange building that looks like a beached Noah's Ark – complete with crow's nest – is open daily till 10 pm. A more central grocery store keeping the same hours is the *Belváros* opposite the north-east corner of Szentháromság tér.

Entertainment

The *József Attila Cultural Centre & Theatre* at Oroszlán utca 3 is your source for information about what's going on in Baja. Ask about concerts in the old Serbian church (now a music school and hall) on Batthyány utca.

Baja usually joins forces with Kalocsa, Szekszárd and Tolna for the large Danube Folklore Festival in July.

There are discos at the cultural centre some weekends and, in summer, nightly till 2 am at the *Youth Camp* hostel bar. The *Sugóhíd* pub on the river opposite the Véndió restaurant is a nice place for a quiet drink.

Getting There & Away

Bus Buses to Kalocsa, Szeged and Mohács number about 15 a day; there are at least 10 daily departures to Szekszárd, Pécs, Kecskemét and Budapest. Other daily destinations include: Békéscsaba and Csongrád (two each), Hévíz (one), Jászberény (one), Kaposvár (two), Orosháza (two) and Szolnok (one). International buses depart for Timişoara in Romania on Friday at 2.30 pm and Sunday at 6 am and for Subotica and Sombor in Yugoslavia on Friday at 7.20 am.

Train Baja is not particularly convenient for train travel. The rail line here links Bátaszék and Kiskunhalas; you must change at the former for Budapest, Szekszárd, Pécs and other points in Southern Transdanubia. From Kiskunhalas, it's impossible to get anywhere of importance without at least another change (the one exception is the fast train to Budapest).

AROUND BAJA
Gemenc Forest

From May to October, a narrow-gauge train runs from Pörböly, 13 km west of Baja, along some stunning hairpin turns of the Danube to the protected Gemenc Forest near Szekszárd. The reserve is incredibly beautiful and a rich hunting ground. From the terminus at Bárányfok, you can carry on to Szekszárd and other points in Southern Transdanubia.

The best way to schedule such a trip is to take the 7 am train from Baja to Pörböly, from where you'll catch the little train at 7.30 am. At the Szomfova Delta (11 km and 1¼ hours later), you can either return to Pörböly at 9 am or wait for the 12.15 pm train, which will take you another 19 km to Bárányfok. From here there are buses the last seven km to Szekszárd. However, the trains do not always run to schedule and some may be seasonal. Check times and dates at the Baja train station before you set out, or call the information service in Pörböly on ☎ 74-491 483; you don't want to be marooned in the Gemenc with a lot of crazy hunters running wild.

For more information on the Gemenc Forest, see the Around Szekszárd section in the Southern Transdanubia chapter.

SZEGED
• *pop 185,500*
• *area code* ☎ *62*

Szeged – a corruption of the Hungarian word *sziget* (or 'island') – is the largest and most important city on the Southern Plain and lies just west of where the Tisza and Maros rivers converge. In fact, some would argue that in terms of culture and sophistication, Szeged (German: Segedin) vies with Debrecen as the 'capital' of the Great Plain as a whole.

Remnants of the Körös culture suggest that these goddess-worshipping people lived in the Szeged area 4000 or 5000 years ago, and one of the earliest Magyar settlements in Hungary was at Ópusztaszer to the north. By the 13th century, the city was an important trading centre, helped along by the royal monopoly it held on the salt being shipped in via the Maros River from Transylvania. Under the Turks, Szeged was afforded some protection since the sultan's estates lay in the area, and it continued to prosper in the 18th and 19th centuries as a free royal town.

But disaster struck in March 1879, when the Tisza swelled its banks and almost washed the city off the map. All but 300 houses were destroyed, and Szeged, under the direction of engineer Lajos Tisza, was rebuilt with foreign assistance between 1880 and 1883. As a result, the city has an architectural uniformity unknown in most other Hungarian cities, and the leafy, broad avenues that ring the city in an almost perfect circle were named after the European cities that helped bring Szeged back to life. (The Moscow and Odessa sections appeared after the war for political reasons and the latter has since been changed to Temesvári körút in honour of Timişoara, where the Romanian revolution of 1989 began.)

Since WWII, Szeged has been an important university town – students marched here in 1956 before their classmates in Budapest did – and a cultural centre. Theatre, opera and all types of classical and popular music performances abound, culminating in the Szeged Open-Air Festival in summer. But the city is just as famed for its edibles: Szeged paprika, which mates so wonderfully with fish from the Tisza River in *szegedi halászlé* (spicy fish soup), and Pick, Hungary's finest salami. Its other claim to fame is the unusual Szeged accent in Hungarian (eg 'e' is pronounced as 'ö'), which sounds strange in a country with so few dialectical differences.

Orientation
The Tisza River, joined by the Maros, flows west and then turns abruptly south through the centre of Szeged, splitting the city in two as cleanly as the Danube bisects Budapest. But comparison of the two cities and their rivers stops there. The Tisza is a rather undignified muddy channel here, and the other side of Szeged is not the city's throbbing commercial heart like Pest but a large park given over to sunbathing, swimming and other hedonistic pursuits.

Szeged's many squares and ring roads make the city confusing for some, but virtually every square in the city has a large signpost with detailed plans and a legend in

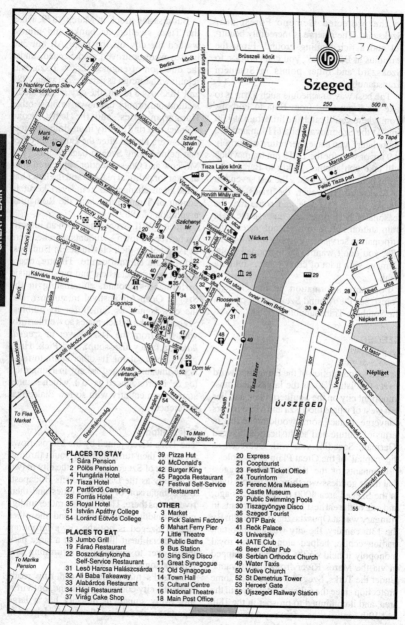

Szeged

0   250   500 m

PLACES TO STAY
1 Sára Pension
2 Pölös Pension
4 Hungária Hotel
17 Tisza Hotel
27 Partfördö Camping
28 Forrás Hotel
35 Royal Hotel
51 István Apáthy College
54 Loránd Eötvös College

PLACES TO EAT
13 Jumbo Grill
19 Fáraó Restaurant
22 Boszorkánykonyha
   Self-Service Restaurant
31 Lesö Harcsa Halászcsárda
32 Ali Baba Takeaway
33 Alabárdos Restaurant
34 Hági Restaurant
37 Virág Cake Shop

39 Pizza Hut
40 McDonald's
42 Burger King
45 Pagoda Restaurant
47 Festival Self-Service
   Restaurant

OTHER
3 Market
5 Pick Salami Factory
6 Mahart Ferry Pier
7 Little Theatre
8 Public Baths
9 Bus Station
10 Sing Sing Disco
11 Great Synagogue
12 Old Synagogue
14 Town Hall
15 Cultural Centre
16 National Theatre
18 Main Post Office

20 Express
21 Cooptourist
23 Festival Ticket Office
24 Tourinform
25 Ferenc Móra Museum
26 Castle Museum
29 Public Swimming Pools
30 Tiszagyöngye Disco
36 Szeged Tourist
38 OTP Bank
41 Reök Palace
43 University
44 JATE Club
46 Beer Cellar Pub
48 Serbian Orthodox Church
49 Water Taxis
50 Votive Church
52 St Demetrius Tower
53 Heroes' Gate
55 Újszeged Railway Station

GREAT PLAIN

several languages. The main train station is south of the city centre on Indóház tér; tram No 1 connects the station with the town. The bus station, to the west of the centre on Mars tér, is within easy walking distance via pedestrian Mikszáth Kálmán utca.

Information

The best source of information is Tourinform (☎ 311 711) at Victor Hugo utca 1. Szeged Tourist (☎ 321 800) is at Klauzál tér 7. Both are open from 9 am to 5 pm and on Saturday to 1 pm. Express (☎ 481 411) is at Kígyó utca 3 and Cooptourist (☎ 312 158) is nearby at Kis Menyhért utca 2.

There's an OTP bank branch with an ATM at Klauzál tér 2, the building where the revolutionary hero Lajos Kossuth gave his last speech before going into exile in Turkey in 1849. The main post office is at Széchenyi tér 1.

Things to See

Begin an easy walking tour of Szeged in Széchenyi tér, a square so large it almost feels like a park. The neobaroque **town hall**, with its graceful tower and colourful tiled roof, dominates the square, while statues of Lajos Tisza, István Széchenyi and the navvies who helped regulate the Tisza River take pride of place under the chestnut trees.

Pedestrian Kárász utca leads south through Klauzál tér. Turn west on Kölcsey utca and walk for about 100m to the **Reök Palace** (1907), a mind-blowing green and lilac Art Nouveau structure that looks like a knick-knack on the bottom of an aquarium. It's a bank nowadays.

Farther south, Kárász utca meets Dugonics tér, site of the **Attila József Science University** (abbreviated JATE), named after its most famous alumnus. József (1905-37), a much loved poet, was actually expelled from here in 1924 for writing the verse 'I have no father and I have no mother/I have no God and I have no country' during the ultra-conservative rule of Admiral Miklós Horthy.

From the south-east corner of Dugonics tér, walk along Jókai utca into Aradi vértanúk

tere. **Heroes' Gate** to the south was erected in 1936 in honour of Horthy's White Guards, who were responsible for 'cleansing' the nation of 'Reds' after the ill-fated Republic of Councils in 1919. The fascistic murals have disappeared (replaced with some 'nice' but amateurish ones) and the Art Deco-ish lighting fixtures are broken, but the brutish sculptures will send a chill down your spine.

Dóm tér, a few paces to the north-east, contains Szeged's most important monuments and is the centre of events during the annual summer festival (as you'll guess from the unsightly viewing stands that are permanently in place there). The **National Pantheon** – statues and reliefs of 80 notables running along an arcade around the square – is a crash course in Hungarian art, literature, culture and history. Even the Scotsman Adam Clark, who supervised the building of Budapest's Chain Bridge, wins accolades, but you'll look forever for any sign of a woman.

The Romanesque **St Demetrius Tower**, the city's oldest structure, is all that remains of a church erected here in the 12th century. In its place stands the twin-towered **Votive Church**, a disproportionate brown brick monstrosity that was pledged after the flood but not completed until 1930. About the only things worth seeing in the church are the organ, with more than 11,500 pipes, the dome covered with frescos and the choir. Instead, peek inside the **Serbian Orthodox church** (1779) to the north-east for a look at the fantastic iconostasis: a central gold 'tree' with 60 icons hanging off its 'branches'.

Oskola utca, one of the city's oldest streets, leads from Dóm tér to Roosevelt tér and the Palace of Education (1896), which now houses the **Ferenc Móra Museum**. The museum's strength lies in its collection of folk art from Csongrád County, bearing intelligent descriptions in several languages. That and the unique exhibit of 7th-century Avar finds done up to look like a clan yurt put this light years ahead of most other museums in Hungary. The park north of Roosevelt tér – Várkert – contains ruins of what was **Szeged Castle**. It served as a

GREAT PLAIN

prison in the 18th century before being pulled down after the flood. The casemates now contain the very informative **Castle Museum**.

For many people, Szeged's most compelling sight is the Hungarian Art Nouveau **Great Synagogue**, Gutenberg utca 13, which was designed by Lipót Baumhorn in 1903. It is the most beautiful Jewish house of worship in Hungary and still very much in use. If the grace and enormity of the exterior don't impress you, the blue and gold interior will. The cupola, decorated with stars and flowers (representing Infinity and Faith), appears to float skyward, and the tabernacle of carved acacia wood and metal fittings is a masterpiece. The synagogue is open every day except Saturday from 9 am to noon and 2 to 5 pm. There are a few other buildings of interest in this area, the former Jewish quarter, including the neoclassical **Old Synagogue** (1843) at Hajnóczy utca 12.

If you'd like to know more about the making of Szeged's famed salami – from hoof to shrink-wrap – the **Pick Salami Factory** at Felső Tisza part 10 (since 1869) can oblige, but you must call in advance on ☎ 483 283 to arrange a time. Don't bother trekking out to the **Paprika Museum**, a sad little collection of dusty seed-pods in the cultural centre at Kapisztrán út 42 in Szentmihály, a suburb to the south-west. Instead wait for the much better Paprika Museum in Kalocsa.

Szeged has two big fruit and vegetable **markets**, one on Mars tér, site of the notorious Star Prison for political prisoners early in the 1950s, and the other north-west of Széchenyi tér on Szent István tér. The **flea market** is near Vám tér at the start of Szabadkai út south-west of the centre.

Activities

Across the Tisza River, the parkland of Újszeged (New Szeged) has swimming pools and a thermal spa on Partfürdő utca, as well as beaches along the river. But the best place for swimming is in the suburb of Sziksósfürdő, about 10 km to the west of town at Kiskundorozsma. Along with a con-

ventional strand, swimming pool and rowing boats, this thermal 'Soda Salt Lake' also has a nudist beach.

Szeged is a good place for bike riding and has an excellent system of bicycle lanes; the Csongrád County government produces a useful little brochure with a few itineraries called *Hobby*. One of the camp sites may rent you a bicycle, or try the Marika pension (☎ 313 861) at Nyíl utca 45.

Special Events

The Szeged Open-Air Festival (mid-July to late August) unfolds on Dóm tér with the two towers of the Votive Church as a backdrop. The outdoor theatre here seats some 6000 people. Main events include an opera, an operetta, a play, folk dancing, classical music, ballet and a rock opera. Festival tickets and information are available from the ticket office (☎ 471 411) at Deák Ferenc utca 28-30 (open weekdays from 10 am to 5 pm, to 3 pm in summer). But Szeged isn't all highbrow; others might prefer the annual International Trucker Country Meeting in mid-July when lorry drivers gather and, well, schmooze.

Places to Stay

Camping Szeged has several camping grounds, all of which operate between May and September and have bungalows. *Partfürdő* (☎ 430 843) is on Közép-kikötő sor in New Szeged along the river opposite the city centre. Camping is 350 Ft per person and per tent, and there are 26 hotel rooms at 1800 to 2200 Ft per double. Guests have free use of the swimming and thermal pools nearby.

A second (and much less attractive) site convenient to the city is *Napfény Camping* (☎ 421 800), Dorozsmai út 4, across a large bridge near the western terminus of tram No 1. Bungalows for two are 2850 Ft.

There a couple of camping grounds by Sziksósfürdő in Kiskundorozsma, including *Sziksós Camping* (☎ 361 029) and *Naturista Camping* (☎ 361 488), an *au naturel* site by the lake's beach.

Hostels Plenty of student dormitories in Szeged open their doors to travellers in July and August, including those at the central *István Apáthy College* (☎ 323 155) at Eötvös utca 4 next to the Votive Church. *Loránd Eötvös College* (☎ 310 641), Tisza Lajos körút 103, charges less than 500 Ft a head. Go directly to the colleges or ask Express for information.

Private Rooms Your best bet for a private room is Szeged Tourist, which charges 1800 to 2500 Ft for a double; flats are 2600 to 4000 Ft. Aktiv Tourist (☎ 323 290) at Dáni János utca 7 also has private rooms.

Pensions If you arrive by bus you'll be within walking distance of the five-room *Sára* pension (☎ 314 920), Zákány utca 13, where singles/doubles are 2800/3800 Ft. If it's full there's the larger *Pölös* pension (☎ 327 974) opposite at Pacsirta utca 17/a. Most of the other pensions are over in New Szeged, including the seven-room *Fortuna* (☎ 431 585) at Pécskai utca 8.

Hotels The fine old two-star *Tisza* hotel (☎ 478 278), Wesselényi utca 1 just off Széchenyi tér, is an excellent deal for budget travellers: singles/doubles without bath cost 1600/2700 Ft; those with bath are 3900/4300 Ft. The rooms are large, bright and airy.

Napfény (see Camping) has a 130-room motel open from May to September and a year-round hotel with 42 rooms. Doubles at the motel cost 1600 Ft, while the hotel's singles/doubles, all with showers, are 3700/4700 Ft.

The most central of Szeged's up-market hotels is the *Royal* (☎ 475 275) at Kölcsey utca 1-3, with 110 rooms in renovated old and new wings. Singles/doubles with bath are 9100/10,700 Ft.

The biggest hotels in town are the boxy, 135-room *Hungária* (☎ 480 580), near a noisy stretch of road at Maros utca 1 but with good views of the river (doubles from DM72 to DM82), and the *Forrás* spa hotel (☎ 430 130) with 179 rooms at Szent-Györgyi

Albert utca 16-24 in New Szeged. Singles/doubles here are DM69/89, though the ones in the attic are cheaper: DM47/59.

Places to Eat

The *Boszorkánykonyha*, Híd utca 8, just off Széchenyi tér, is an unappetising, but very cheap, self-service place. Better yet try the *Festival* self-service in the modern building on Oskola utca across the street from the entrance to the Votive Church. There's also *Jumbo Grill*, Mikszáth Kálmán utca 4, which serves almost real salads and excellent grilled chicken. *Ali Baba* at Oskola utca 3 is a Middle Eastern takeaway place.

Szeged is loaded with fast-food places (all those students on the go, no doubt) including: *McDonald's* at Kárász utca 11; *Pizza Hut* at Kárász utca 10; and *Burger King* at Árpád tér 1.

The *Hági*, an old Szeged standby at Kelemen utca 3 in the centre, serves reliable and reasonably priced Hungarian and South Slav dishes. Another possibility serving similar food is *Fáraó* in an old cellar at Nagy Jenő utca 1 near Széchenyi tér.

The *Pagoda* at Zrínyi utca 5 serves mock Chinese food amid faded vermilion, but it's a nice change and has a smoke-free room. The *Leső Harcsa Halászcsárda* – that's the 'Eager Catfish Fishermen's Inn' – at Roosevelt tér 14 is a Szeged institution and serves up szegedi halászlé by the cauldron.

Szeged's 'silver-service' eatery is the *Alabárdos* at Oskola utca 13, where posy waiters and a supercilious maître d' fawn over German tourists who have come to see 'Segedin'.

Check out the *Virág* on Klauzál tér, one of the nicest cake and coffee shops in Hungary. The outlet at No 8 is for stand-up service and takeaway; No 1 has tables inside and on the square. The Herend coffee machines in the latter are museum-quality.

Entertainment

Your best sources of information in this culturally active city are Tourinform or the *Gyula Juhász Cultural Centre* (☎ 312 060)

GREAT PLAIN

Lamp post from Szeged's National Theatre

at Vörösmarty utca 3. The *National Theatre* (1886) on the same street has always been the centre of cultural life in Szeged and usually stages operas and ballet. For plays, go to the *Little Theatre* (Kisszínház) at Horváth Mihály utca 3.

There's a vast array of bars, clubs and other night spots in this student town, especially around Dugonics tér. The *JATE Club* at Toldy utca 1 is the best place to meet students on their own turf; in summer there's a disco on Thursday, Friday and Saturday to 4 am. Or try the *Beer Cellar* pub at No 2. The huge *Tiszagyöngye Disco* on Közép-kikötő sor in New Szeged is open at summer weekends till 4 am. *Sing Sing Disco* occupies a huge pavilion at Mars tér and Dr Baross József utca near the bus station. It's open Wednesday, Friday and Saturday from 10 pm to 4 am.

Things to Buy

The Pick Salami Factory outlet at Felső Tisza part 10 and delicatessens throughout Szeged have everything a carnivore could hope for. Szeged paprika is sold in gift packs everywhere; it's much better than the stuff from Kalocsa.

Getting There & Away

Bus Bus service is very good from Szeged, with frequent departures to Békéscsaba, Csongrád, Ópusztaszer, Makó and Hódmezővásárhely. Other destinations include Budapest (seven buses daily), Debrecen (two), Eger (two), Gyöngyös (two), Győr (two), Gyula (five), Kecskemét (eight), Mohács (seven), Pécs (six), Siófok (two), Székesfehérvár (five), Tiszafüred (two) and Veszprém (two). Buses also cross the Romanian border for Arad daily from Tuesday to Saturday at 6.30 am and for Timişoara twice a week (Tuesday and Friday at 6.30 am). Buses run to Senta in Yugoslavia two times daily and to Subotica Tuesday to Saturday at 6 am and 12.30 pm.

Train Szeged is on a main railway line to Budapest-Nyugati. Another line connects the city with Hódmezővásárhely and Békéscsaba, where you can change trains for Gyula or Romania. Southbound local trains leave Szeged for Subotica in Yugoslavia five times a day.

Boat From June to late August, on Saturday and holidays only, a Mahart riverboat (☎ 313 834) plies the Tisza River for 70 km between Szeged and Csongrád, leaving Szeged at 7 am and Csongrád at 4 pm. Though it's a pleasant way to travel, the 4½-hour trip is more than twice as long as the bus trip, with half a dozen stops along the way.

Getting Around

The No 1 tram from the train station will take you north to Széchenyi tér. It turns west on Kossuth Lajos sugárút and goes as far as Izabella Bridge, where it turns around. Alight there for the Napfény complex.

You can get closer to the Napfény on bus

No 78, which stops directly opposite the complex on Kossuth Lajos sugárút. Get off just after you cross the bridge over the railway tracks. The correct bus to Szentmihály and the flea market is the No 76; you can also take tram No 4. For Sziksósfürdő, take bus No 2/t or No 7/t from the main bus station.

Local taxis can be ordered on ☎ 470 470 or ☎ 488 888. You can hire a water taxi (☎ 484 386) near the Inner Town Bridge on the Tisza's right bank.

ÓPUSZTASZER

- *pop 2100*
- *area code ☎ 362*

About 28 km north of Szeged, the **National Historical Memorial Park** in Ópusztaszer commemorates the single most important event in Hungarian history: the *honfoglalás*, or conquest, of the Carpathian Basin by the Magyars in 896. Contrary to what many people – Hungarians included – think, the park does not mark the spot where Árpád, mounted on his white charger, first entered 'Hungary'. That was actually the Munkács Valley, Hungarian territory until after WWI and now in Ukraine.

But according to the 12th-century chronicler known as Anonymous, it was at this place called Szer that Árpád and the six clan chieftains who had sworn a blood oath of fidelity to him held their first assembly, and so it was decided that a **Millennium Monument** would be erected here in 1896. (Scholars had actually determined the date of the conquest to be between 893 and 895, but the government at the time was not ready to mark the 1000-year anniversary until 1896.) Ópusztaszer was also symbolically chosen for the redistribution of land by the coalition government after WWII.

Situated atop a slight rise in the Great Plain about one km from the Szeged road, the park is an attractive though sombre place. Besides the neoclassical monument with Árpád taking pride of place, there are ruins of an 11th-century **Romanesque church** and **monastery** still being excavated, and an excellent **open-air museum** with a farm-house, windmills, an old post office, a schoolhouse and cottages moved from villages around south-east Hungary. In one, the home of a rather prosperous and smug onion grower from Makó, a sampler admonishes potential gossips: 'Neighbour lady, away you go/If it's gossip you want to know' (or words to that effect).

To the west of the park beside the little lake, a museum reminiscent of a Magyar chieftain's tent houses a huge **panorama painting** entitled *The Arrival of the Hungarians*. Completed by Árpád Feszty for the millenary exhibition in Budapest in 1896, the enormous work, which measures 15 by 120m, was badly damaged during WWII and was restored by a Polish team in time for the 1100th anniversary of the conquest in 1996.

The park is open daily all year from 9 am to 5 pm (to 7 pm April to October). Admission is 100 Ft for just the park and 500/300 Ft for adults/students and children to view the Feszty painting.

Szeri Camping (☎ 375 123) at Árpád liget 111 has 14 bungalows (from 1500 Ft for a double with shared shower; open mid-April to mid-October), and you can go horse riding across the street for about 400 Ft an hour. The *Szeri Csárda* next door serves a decent gulyás.

FEHÉR-TÓ

About six km out of Szeged on the way to or from Ópusztaszer, you'll pass the eastern edge of Fehér-tó (White Lake), a conservation area crisscrossed by embankments. The lake is home to aquatic and other birds; some 250 species have been spotted here. Entrance to the area is restricted; without permission (see Tourinform in Szeged) you'll have to be content with peering from the viewing platform at Szatymaz Cemetery Hill on the western shore of the lake.

HÓDMEZŐVÁSÁRHELY

- *pop 54,000*
- *area code ☎ 62*

Sitting on the dried-up bed of what was once Lake Hód 25 km north-east of Szeged, the city of 'Hód Field Marketplace' was no more

GREAT PLAIN

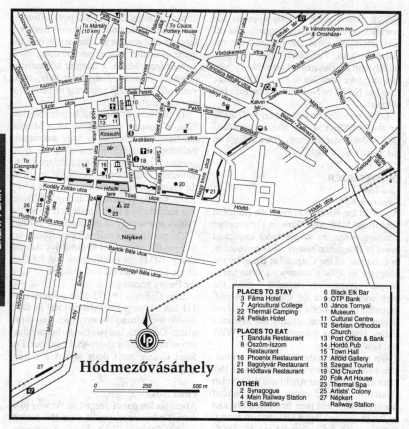

Hódmezővásárhely

0   250   500 m

PLACES TO STAY		6	Black Elk Bar
3	Fáma Hotel	9	OTP Bank
7	Agricultural College	10	János Tornyai
22	Thermál Camping		Museum
24	Pelikán Hotel	11	Cultural Centre
		12	Serbian Orthodox
PLACES TO EAT			Church
1	Bandula Restaurant	13	Post Office & Bank
8	Őszöm-Iszom	14	Hordó Pub
	Restaurant	15	Town Hall
16	Phoenix Restaurant	17	Alföld Gallery
21	Bagolyvár Restaurant	18	Szeged Tourist
26	Hódtava Restaurant	19	Old Church
		20	Folk Art House
OTHER		23	Thermal Spa
2	Synagogue	25	Artists' Colony
4	Main Railway Station	27	Népkert
5	Bus Station		Railway Station

than a collection of disparate communities until the Turkish invasions, when much of the population was dispersed and the town's centre razed. The peasants of Hódmezővásárhely returned to subsistence farming in the 17th century. But the abolition of serfdom in the mid-19th century without the redistribution of land only increased their isolation and helped bring about an agrarian revolt led by János Kovács Szántó in 1894, an event the townspeople are justly proud of – and which the Communist regime trumpeted for decades.

Folk art, particularly pottery, has a rich tradition in Hódmezővásárhely; some 400 independent artisans working here in the mid-1800s made it the largest pottery centre in Hungary. Today you won't see much more pottery outside the town's museums than you would elsewhere, but the influence of the dynamic artists' colony here is felt well beyond Kohán György utca – from the galleries and Autumn Art Festival to the ceramic and bronze street signs by eminent artists.

Orientation

At more than 48,000 sq hectares, greater Hódmezővásárhely is Hungary's second-largest city in area – though that shouldn't make much difference to travellers as almost everything of interest is right in the centre. The bus station is just off Andrássy utca on Bocskai utca, about a 10-minute walk north-east from Kossuth tér, the city centre. There are two train stations: Hódmezővásárhely and Hódmezővásárhelyi Népkert. The first is south-east of the city centre at the end of Mérleg utca, the second due south at the end of Ady Endre utca.

Information

Szeged Tourist (☎ 341 432) is housed in an old granary next to the Old Church at Szőnyi utca 1. It is open from 8 am to 5 pm weekdays and till noon on Saturday in summer.

OTP bank has a branch with an ATM at Andrássy utca 1. The main post office is on the north-west corner of Kossuth tér at Hódi Pál utca 2.

Museums & Galleries

The **János Tornyai Museum** at Szántó Kovács János utca 16-18, named after a leading member of the Alföld School of painting, displays some early archaeological finds, but its *raison d'être* is to show off the folk art of Hódmezővásárhely – the painted furniture, 'hairy' embroidery done with yarn-like thread, and pottery unique to the region. The collection of jugs, pitchers and plates, most of them made as wedding gifts, is the finest of all and represents the many types once made here and named after city districts, including Csúcs (white and blue), Tabán (brown) and Újváros (yellow and green).

More pottery is on display at the **Csúcs Pottery House**, once the home of master potter Sándor Vékony, at Rákóczi utca 101 (open from 1 to 5 pm Tuesday to Sunday), and at the **Folk Art House**, two old thatched farmhouses standing self-consciously in the middle of a housing estate at Árpád utca 21 and open Tuesday to Friday from 1 to 5 pm. Enter from Nagy Imre utca.

Outsiders are not allowed into the **artists' colony** on Kohán György utca, founded in the early part of this century, but you can

view selected members' work at the **Alföld Gallery**, across from Szeged Tourist in a neoclassical former Calvinist school at Kossuth tér 8. Naturally the Alföld School dominates; you might go a little crazy looking at horses and sweep wells and cowboys on the Great Plain in every season through the eyes of Tornyai, István Nagy and József Koszta. But there are other things to enjoy such as the frog-like women of painter Menyhért Tóth and the work of the impressionist János Vaszary.

Other Things to See

It was said that the peasants of Hódmezővásárhely were so poor that they only found comfort in God. Judging from the number of places of worship in town (about a dozen representing half as many religions or sects), they didn't have two pennies to rub together. Few of them are outstanding monuments, but check the Calvinist folk baroque **Old Church** dating from the early 1700s next to Szeged Tourist; the **Serbian Orthodox church** (1792) at Szántó Kovács János utca 9; and the **synagogue** (1857), an old pile with a later Art Nouveau façade on Szeremlei utca north of Kálvin tér. It has a wonderful stained-glass rose window.

You may wonder about the long stone wall that stretches from the bus station westward for almost four km. It's a **flood barrier** built in 1881, just two years after Szeged was inundated. The Hódtó Canal south of Népkert park may not look very threatening, but that's probably just what Szegeders were saying about the tranquil Tisza River before 1879.

Activities

The thermal spa in the Népkert south of Kossuth tér at Ady Endre utca 2 has hot and cold pools open every day from 8 am to 8 pm, but Mártély, about 10 km to the north-west on a backwater of the Tisza, is the city's real recreational centre, with boating, fishing and swimming available.

The Vándorsólyom inn, about four km north-east of the city on route No 47 (Kutasi út) en route to Orosháza, has horses for cross-country riding and carriage driving. See Places to Stay for more information.

Special Events
If you're in the area in October, check the dates for the Autumn Art Festival, a nationally attended event. The city's other big festival is the Agricultural & Sheep Fair in April.

Places to Stay
There are a handful of rather uncomfortable (but convenient) bungalows for four people at *Thermál Camping* (☎ 345 033) in the Népkert at Ady Endre utca 1; they cost 1600 Ft (2000 Ft with shower). *Tisza-part Camping* (☎ 342 753) in Mártély has bungalows from 800 Ft per person and permanent tents for 300 Ft. It's open from May to September.

Szeged Tourist has *private rooms* for about 600 Ft per person. In summer, beds in dormitory rooms in the *Agricultural College* east of Kossuth tér at Andrássy utca 15 are available for 400 Ft per person.

The 18-room *Fáma* hotel (☎ 344 292), Szeremlei utca 7, a few minutes from the bus station on a street lined with cherry trees, charges 3500 Ft for a double with bath, 3200 Ft without. The *Pelikán* (☎ 345 072), with 18 rooms at Ady Endre utca 1 next to the spa, charges 3000/4500 Ft for singles/doubles.

The nine-room *Vándorsólyom* (☎ 341 900) is the obvious place to stay if you're a horse lover (see Activities). Doubles at this inn are 2270 to 2970 Ft, depending on room size. There's a small restaurant and a bar.

Places to Eat
One of the cheapest places for a meal in Hódmezővásárhely is the *Hódtava* at Hóvirág utca 2/b, open at the weekend only. Don't be surprised if your fellow diners are splattered with paint or have clay under their fingernails: the artists' colony is just around the corner. Two other decent choices any time are the *Bandula* on the corner of Szántó Kovács János utca and Pálffy utca; and the *Öszöm-Iszom* (that's 'I Eat-I Drink' in Szeged dialect) at Szent Antal utca 8.

The *Phoenix*, next to the town hall building overlooking Hősök tere, is a rather pricey restaurant and pizzeria. The *Bagolyvár* at Nagy Imre utca 31 south of Andrássy utca is the best restaurant in town, though still very reasonable. In warm weather, the terrace is a pleasant place to while away an hour or two.

Entertainment
The *Petőfi Cultural Centre* (☎ 341 750) is at Szántó Kovács János utca 7.

There are several good pubs along Szántó Kovács János utca; the *Hordó* pub on Városház utca is also fine for a glass. The *Black Elk Bar* at Petőfi út 37 attracts a motley crowd.

Getting There & Away
Buses to Szeged, Békéscsaba, Makó, Szentes, Csongrád and the holiday area of Mártély are very frequent; there is a minimum of three daily departures to Szolnok, Jászberény, Budapest, Orosháza and Szeghalom. One or two buses a day head for Baja, Parádfürdő, Tiszafüred, Miskolc, Debrecen, Hajdúszoboszló, Gyöngyös and Pécs.

Two railway lines pass through Hódmezővásárhely, and all trains serve both train stations, which are two km apart. The more important of the two lines connects Szeged with Békéscsaba. The smaller line links Makó, Hungary's onion capital and the birthplace of Joseph Pulitzer, with Szolnok.

CSONGRÁD
• pop 20,800
• area code ☎ 63
The 13th century did not treat the town of Csongrád (from the Slavic name Černigrad, meaning 'Black Castle') very well. Once the royal capital of Csongrád County, the town and its fortress were so badly damaged when the Mongols overran it that Béla IV transferred the seat to Szeged in 1247.

Csongrád never really recovered from the invasion, and development was slow; until the 1920s it was not even a town. As a result, the Öregvár – the Old Castle district to the east – looks pretty much the way it did in the

17th century: a quiet fishing village of thatched cottages and narrow streets on the bank of the Tisza.

Orientation

Csongrád lies on the left bank of the Tisza, close to where it is joined by the Körös River, some 58 km north of Szeged. A backwater (Holt-Tisza) south of town is used for recreation. The bus station is on Hunyadi tér, five minutes from the main street, Fő utca. The train station lies to the south-west at the end of Vasút utca.

Information

Szeged Tourist (☎ 383 069) at Fő utca 14 is open from 9 am to 5 pm on weekdays. An OTP bank branch can be found on Szentháromság tér next to the Kossuth Cultural Centre (☎ 383 414) at No 8. The main post office is north of the bus station on Dózsa György tér.

Things to See & Do

The **László Tari Museum** at Iskola utca 2 is dedicated to the thousands of *kubikosok* (navvies) who left Csongrád and vicinity in the 19th century to work on projects regulating rivers and building canals. Some travelled to sites as far away as Istanbul and Warsaw and were virtual slaves, working from 5 am to 8 pm with meatless meals and the occasional 'smoke' break. The museum also contains the grisly contents of a couple of 8th-century Avar graves found in nearby Felgyő and some superb woodcarving (roof frames, lintels, doors) by Csongrád's fisherfolk. The museum is open Tuesday to Friday from 1 to 5 pm, on Saturday from 9 am to noon and on Sunday from 9 am to 5 pm.

Walking eastward from the museum to the Öregvár district, you'll pass the baroque **Church of Our Lady** (1769) and the beautiful Hungarian Art Nouveau **János Batsányi College** on Kossuth tér and, farther on, **St Rókus Church**, built in 1722 on the site of a Turkish mosque. Don't bother looking for

Suicide: A Dubious Distinction

Hungary has Europe's highest rate of suicide – 39 per 100,000 people, well ahead of Russia, which ranks second with 26 per 100,000. Psychologists are still out to lunch on why Hungary should have such a high incidence. Some say that Hungarians' inclination to gloom leads to the ultimate act of despair. Others link it to a phenomenon not uncommon late in the 19th century. As the Hungarian aristocracy withered away, the *kis nemesek* (minor nobles), some of them no better off than the local peasantry, would do themselves in to 'save their name and honour'. As a result, suicide was – and is – not looked upon dishonourably, victims may be buried in hallowed ground and the euphemistic sentence used in obituaries is: 'Mr/Mrs X died suddenly and tragically'. About 60% of suicides are by hanging. ■

the much ballyhooed ceiling frescos of navvies, fisherfolk and Csongrád scenes here: they've been wiped clean. The **City Gallery** is at Kossuth tér 9-11 and the tiny **Tisza Gallery** at Dózsa György tér 4 by the bus station.

The cobblestone streets of the protected Öregvár district begin at a little roundabout three blocks east of St Rókus Church. Most of the district is made up of private homes or holiday houses, but the **Village Museum** at Gyökér utca 1 is open to all and gives a good idea of how the simple fisherfolk and navvies of Csongrád lived until not so long ago. It's housed in two old cottages connected by a long thatched roof and contains period furniture, household items and lots of fish nets and traps. The museum is open from 1 to 5 pm from Wednesday to Sunday, May to September.

The **thermal spa**, fed by a spring with water that reaches 46°C, is in a large park at Dob utca 3-5 and open on weekdays (usually from 7 am to 7 pm). The outdoor pools and strand are open from 10 am to 7 pm in summer.

Szeged Tourist can arrange fishing and boating trips from the Körös-toroki camp site as well as bike rentals.

GREAT PLAIN

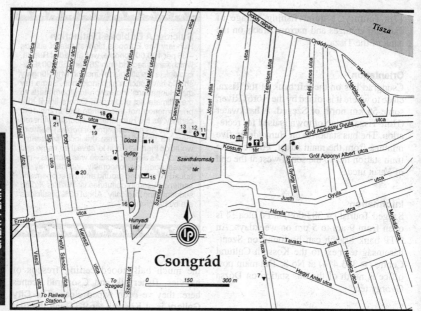

Csongrád

Places to Stay

Körös-toroki Camping (☎ 383 631), on the beach near where the Körös River flows into the Tisza a couple of km east of the town centre, has bungalows (mercifully on stilts – the area floods in heavy rain and the mosquitoes are unbearable) costing 850 Ft (2500 Ft with shower) and a rather ugly five-room holiday house costing 3700 Ft for a double. The site is open from mid-May to mid-September.

Szeged Tourist has *private rooms* and *apartments* costing 2200 to 3400 Ft for two people, but from June to mid-October they'll almost certainly try to book you into one of their more expensive *fishing cottages* in the Öregvár. If you're feeling flush, this is the most atmospheric place to stay. Prices for these 200-year-old houses, some of which have kitchens and living rooms, run from 5500 to 9900 Ft, with the average about 8500 Ft. The nicest ones are at Öregvár utca 49, 57/b and 58. If Szeged Tourist is closed, try

renting a room from the blacksmith at Baross Gábor rakpart 35 across from the Mahart ferry pier.

The *Erzsébet* (☎ 383 960) is an old 13-room hotel, minutes from the bus station at Fő utca 3. Singles/doubles with shower start at 1700/2200 Ft; doubles without bath are from 1600 Ft. To the west, the modern 15-room *Tisza* hotel (☎ 383 594) at Fő utca 23 charges 3500 to 4500 Ft for a double with shower.

Places to Eat

The obvious choice in the Öregvár for a meal is the *Kemence*, an attractive csárda at Öregvár 54. There are no fish dishes on the menu – surprising in a fishing town – but whatever you have, try a glass of Csongrádi Kadarka along with it. It's the spicy, ruby-red local wine.

The *Tulipán* is a simple café-restaurant at Szentháromság tér 2. The *Pompeii* serves pizza and South Slav specialities in a renovated old house at Kis Tisza utca 6.

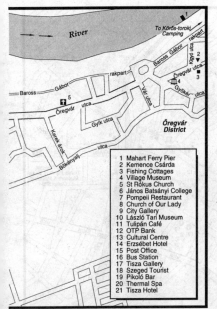

1 Mahart Ferry Pier
2 Kemence Csárda
3 Fishing Cottages
4 Village Museum
5 St Rókus Church
6 János Batsányi College
7 Pompeii Restaurant
8 Church of Our Lady
9 City Gallery
10 László Tari Museum
11 Tulipán Café
12 OTP Bank
13 Cultural Centre
14 Erzsébet Hotel
15 Post Office
16 Bus Station
17 Tisza Gallery
18 Szeged Tourist
19 Pikoló Bar
20 Thermal Spa
21 Tisza Hotel

The *Erzsébet* hotel has a bar serving light meals and snacks. In summer, it turns into a street café. The *Pikoló*, opposite Szeged Tourist at Fő utca 13, is a similar place.

Getting There & Away

Bus From Csongrád buses run to Baja (two daily), Békéscsaba (three), Budapest (eight), Eger (two), Gyula (one), Hódmezővásárhely and Kecskemét (12 each), Kiskunfélegyháza (every half-hour), Lajosmizse (five), Orosháza (seven), Szentes (every 15 minutes) and Szolnok (three). The 10 daily buses to Szeged go via Ópusztaszer.

There's a daily departure for Arad in Romania at 5.30 am.

Train Csongrád is on the 80-km secondary railway line linking Szentes to the east with Kiskunfélegyháza to the west. But you can't get very far from either of those places; buses are always a faster, more frequent option.

Boat If you're travelling to Szeged from Csongrád in summer, consider the Mahart ferry, which makes the 70-km run from down the Tisza River. From June to late August, boats leave the ferry pier on Baross Gábor rakpart at 4 pm on Saturday and holidays. Be warned, though, that the trip takes 4½ hours – double the bus time – and stops at Szentes, Csanytelek, Mindszent, Algyő and a csárda before reaching Szeged. Between April and October, you may be able to hook up with one of the charters making the 90-km run north to Szolnok.

BÉKÉSCSABA

- *pop 70,700*
- *area code ☎ 66*

When most Hungarians hear mention of Békéscsaba, they usually think of two very disparate things: fatty sausage and bloody riots. Csabai, a sausage not unlike Portuguese *chorizo*, is manufactured here, and Békéscsaba was the centre of the Vihar Sarok, the 'Stormy Corner' where violent riots broke out among day labourers and harvesters in 1890. Ironically, the city is now the capital of Békés (or 'Peaceful') County.

Békéscsaba was an important fortified settlement as early as the 14th century, but it was razed and its population scattered under Turkish rule. Early in the 18th century, a Habsburg emissary named János György Harruckern invited Rhinelanders and Slovaks to resettle the area, and it soon became a Lutheran stronghold. The influence of the Slovaks in particular can be felt to this day – in the city's bilingual street signs and the Slovak-language schools and social clubs – and there is no shortage of ethnic Serbs, Romanians and Gypsies living here as well.

Development began to reach Békéscsaba in the 19th century when the railway passed through the city (1858). In 1906, in response to the earlier agrarian movements, András Áchim founded his radical Peasants' Party here, an important political force in Hungary for many years. By 1950, Békéscsaba had surpassed nearby Gyula in importance and the county seat was moved here – something

GREAT PLAIN

PLACES TO STAY
15 Fiume Hotel

PLACES TO EAT
6 Iparosok Háza
   Restaurant
20 Márvány Cake Shop
22 Halbisztró
23 Halászcsárda
27 Market

OTHER
1 Peasant Houses
2 Slovak Village House
3 Peasant Houses
4 Small Church
5 Great Church
7 'Stingray' Building
8 Csabai Mill
9 Mihály Munkácsy
   Museum
10 Ibusz
11 Town Hall
12 Cultural Centre
13 Phaedra Cinema
   & Western Pub
14 Jókai Theatre
16 OTP Bank &
   Club Narancs
17 Post Office
18 Cooptourist
19 Békés Tourist
21 Express
24 Thermal Baths
25 Greek Orthodox Church
26 Liberation Arch
28 Railway Station
29 Bus Station

Békéscsaba

0   250   500 m

for which Gyula has yet to forgive her sister city.

Relying essentially on agriculture (wheat, rice, cattle) and food-processing, Békés County has been in the economic doldrums for some time, with unemployment among the nation's highest and the population sharply decreasing. That may not sound like much of an incentive to visit Békéscsaba, but it is a pleasant, friendly place to tarry on the way to the spas at Gyula or perhaps to Romania.

Orientation

Békéscsaba's train and bus stations stand

side by side at the south-west end of Andrássy út, the main drag. A long stretch of this street, from Petőfi utca and Jókai utca to Szent István tér, is a pedestrian walkway, and just beyond it lies the Élővíz-csatorna, the 'Live Water Canal' that links Békéscsaba with Békés to the north, Gyula to the east, and the Körös River. To the east and north of the canal lies Parkerdő, the city's playground. Árpád sor along the canal's east bank is a cool and quiet place for a stroll on a warm afternoon.

Information

The staff at Békés Tourist (☎ 323 448) at

Andrássy út 10 are well informed and helpful. The office is open on weekdays from 8 am to 4 pm. Cooptourist (☎ 326 856), which stays open to 6 pm, and Express (☎ 324 201) are on the same street at Nos 6 and 29 respectively. Ibusz (☎ 328 428) is next to the town hall at Szent István tér 5.

There's an OTP bank at Szent István tér 3. The main post office is on Andrássy út opposite the Fiume hotel.

Things to See & Do

The **Mihály Munkácsy Museum** at Széchenyi utca 9 has exhibits devoted to the wildlife and ecology of the Great Plain as well as to the folk culture of the region, but it's essentially a temple to the painter Munkácsy (1844-1900). Some may find his depictions of the Great Plain and its denizens a little sugar-coated, but as a chronicler of that place and time (real or imagined) he is unsurpassed in Hungarian fine art. The demure young couple pictured in *Novices* and *A Village Reading* are particular favourites. An ethnographic exhibit traces the history of the Romanian, Slovak, German and Hungarian ethnic groups of the region. Don't miss the fine Slovak embroidery and the Hungarian painted furniture. Opposite the museum on Széchenyi utca is the structure that gets my vote for the ugliest building in Hungary: a 1960s-style youth centre and auditorium shaped like a beached stingray.

Present or future farmers might be interested in the **Grain Museum** on Gyulai út 65, housed in several old thatched barns and crammed with traditional tools and implements. The 19th-century windmill is one of the best examples surviving in Hungary. See Békés Tourist about gaining entry.

The **Slovakian Village House** at Garay utca 21 is a wonderful Slovakian farmhouse built in 1865 and full of folk furniture and ornamentation. It is open daily, except Monday, from 10 am till noon and 2 to 6 pm. A lot of other typical peasant houses can be found in the neighbourhood, especially on Szigetvári utca and Sárkantyú utca.

Don't miss the 19th-century **István Csabai**

Mill, a bizarre grey-brick colossus from the turn of the century on Gőzmalom tér and best viewed from the small canal bridge near the Mihály Munkácsy Museum. It was the first steam mill built in Hungary and is still in operation. It contains museum-quality flour sifters and shakers.

The Lutheran **Great Church** (1824) and the 18th-century **Small Church** (1745) facing each other across Kossuth tér attest to the city's deeply rooted Protestantism. The baroque **Greek Orthodox church** (1838) at Bartók Béla utca 51-53 could easily be mistaken for yet another Lutheran church from the outside.

The splendid **town hall**, with a façade (1873) designed by the overworked Budapest architect Miklós Ybl, is at Szent István tér 7. Walk east on József Attila utca to the canal and Árpád sor, which is lined with busts of Hungarian literary, artistic and musical greats and some wonderful turn-of-the-century mansions. Farther north there's a Transylvanian-style carved 'totem' to the Arad Martyrs, 13 generals executed in 1848 by the Habsburgs in what is now Romania.

The **Árpád thermal baths** and indoor and outdoor **swimming pools** are near the Halászcsárda fish restaurant at Árpád sor 2.

Places to Stay

Any of the agencies in Békéscsaba can book you a *private room* from 1500 Ft for a double. Express may be able to help with *dormitory rooms* at the technical schools and colleges near the Parkerdő or you can try the *Garzon* hostel (☎ 457 377) south-east of the park in the Ifjusági-tábor (Youth Camp).

The 14 rooms of the *Sport* hostel (☎ 449 449) ring the inside of the ghastly stadium across from the Parkerdő on Gyulai út. Doubles are 2200 to 4000 Ft, and all rooms have showers and TV. Sporting events and concerts are held in the huge auditorium across from the rooms, so don't expect much sleep if a rock band or a basketball game is on. Still, you couldn't ask for better seats.

The *Troféa* (☎ 441 066) is a 10-room pension at Gyulai út 61. It's comfortable but a bit far out. Singles/doubles are 4000/4500 Ft.

Békéscsaba's premier hotel and one of the nicest in Hungary is the restored *Fiume* (☎ 443 243) at Szent István tér 2, which bears the old name of the Croatian port of Rijeka. The 39-room hotel has a top-class restaurant, a popular pub-restaurant and a cake shop. Singles are 4700 Ft, doubles 6600 Ft.

Places to Eat
For a very inexpensive lunch, try the restaurant at the *Iparosok Háza* at Kossuth tér 10, which serves hearty Hungarian specialities till 10 pm. The stand-up *Halbisztró* at Andrássy út 31 serves several varieties of fish.

The *HB Pub* at the Fiume hotel makes its own beer and serves some of the best food in town in clean, bright surroundings. But on a warm evening, all that meat won't do. Cross the canal and head for the *Halászcsárda* fish restaurant near the spa on Árpád sor.

You can satisfy your sweet tooth at the *Márvány*, a cake and pastry shop at Andrássy út 21. It has outside seating on a pretty square and stays open till 10 pm.

There's a big food *market* just north of Andrássy út on Szabó Dezső utca; market days are Wednesday and Saturday.

Entertainment
The beautifully restored *Jókai Theatre* (1875) at Andrássy út 1 and the *Great Church* are the main cultural venues in Békéscsaba. Ask the staff at Békés Tourist or the *County Cultural Centre* (☎ 442 122), Luther utca 16, for dates and times.

The best place in town for a pint is the *Club Narancs*, a meeting place for students in a cellar with vaulted ceilings, cold beer and occasional live music. It's at Szent István tér 1 across from the Fiume hotel. Try to see a film at the Art Deco *Phaedra* movie house on the corner of Irány utca and Csaba utca. You'll feel like you're attending a 1930s film premiere. The *Western Pub* next door to the Phaedra on Irány utca is a popular place for pool and pints.

Getting There & Away
For points north like Debrecen, take one of half a dozen buses departing every day. Buses leave from Gyula and Békés every half-hour and for Szarvas once an hour. Eight buses a day go to Szeged and two to Budapest. Other destinations and their daily departure frequencies include Baja (two), Berettyóújfalu (10), Eger (two), Hajdúszoboszló (one), Hódmezővásárhely (eight), Karcag (one), Kecskemét (seven), Miskolc (two), Pécs (one), Szeghalom (12), Szolnok (one) and Vésztő via Gyula (two) and via Mezőberény (one). There's a bus twice a week to Subotica in Yugoslavia (Wednesday and Saturday at 5.25 am).

A dozen daily trains – most of them expresses – link Békéscsaba with Szolnok and Budapest-Keleti. Trains are frequent (about 15 a day) to Gyula, and most of them continue on to Vésztő. Nine trains a day depart Békéscsaba for Szeged. Three international trains leave Békéscsaba daily for Bucharest via Arad and Brașov.

Getting Around
Transport within Békéscsaba is not good, even though it is not a particularly small place – the walk from the train or bus stations up Andrássy út to Szent István tér takes a good 20 minutes at a brisk pace. From the bus station catch bus No 5 to Szabadság tér. Bus Nos 9 and 19 (or the bus headed for Gyula) pass through the square on their way past the stadium, Grain Museum, Troféa pension and colleges near the Parkerdő.

There's a big taxi rank on Justh Gyula utca north of the Fiume hotel or you can order one on ☎ 444 111/777.

VÉSZTŐ
• *pop 7800*

The **Vésztő-Mágor National Historical Monument**, four km north-west of this village, contains two burial mounds of a type found in Hungary and as far east as Korea. Such mounds are not all that rare on the Great Plain, but these are particularly rich in archaeological finds. The first is a veritable layer cake of cult and everyday objects, shrines and graves dating from the 4th century BC onward. The second contains a 10th-century church and monastery. The site is open every day (except Monday) from 10 am to 4 pm from April to November, to 6 pm between May and September. It is in the centre of the patchwork 925-hectare **Körös-Maros Conservation Area**, which is very rich in aquatic vegetation and wildlife.

Two reasonably priced places for a meal are the *Réti Csárda* at Békési út 8 as you enter Vésztő from the south, and the *Monostor* restaurant, which is closer to the village centre at Kossuth Lajos utca 54. There's a small *büfé* at the Vésztő-Mágor site.

Vésztő is 45 km north-east of Békéscsaba and there are a couple of buses a day via Gyula. From the village you can walk for four km to the site or catch the bus bound for Szeghalom, which will drop you off just outside. Eight trains a day leave Békéscsaba for Vésztő, but be warned that they follow a circuitous route by way of Gyula and take two hours to cover a mere 64 km.

SZARVAS
- *pop 19,200*
- *area code ☎ 66*

Szarvas is a pretty, very green town 45 km north-west of Békéscsaba on a backwater of the Körös River (Holt-Körös). Szarvas was a market town that also suffered decimation under the Turks; Slovaks came here in large numbers late in the 18th century. But the best thing that ever happened to Szarvas was the arrival of Sámuel Tessedik, a Lutheran minister and pioneering scientist who es-tablished one of Europe's first agricultural institutes here in 1770. This Renaissance man, who is also considered the father of Hungarian ethnography for his seminal *The Peasant in Hungary: What He Is and What He Could Become* (1786), also rebuilt the devastated town in an organised, chessboard-like fashion that can still be seen today.

Szarvas' big draws are water sports on the Holt-Körös, and the town's arboretum, easily the best in Hungary.

Orientation
Szabadság út, the main street, bisects the town and leads west to the Holt-Körös and the arboretum. On either side of Szabadság út are dozens of small squares full of gardens and even small orchards.

The train station is in the eastern part of town at the end of Vasút utca, while the bus station is in the centre at Szabadság út near Bocskai István utca.

Information
Szarvas Tours (☎ 313 522), a commercial travel agency at Kossuth Lajos utca 60, may be able to help with information. Its opening hours are 8 am to 6 pm on weekdays, till noon on Saturday.

OTP has a bank branch next to the Árpád hotel on Szabadság út while the main post office is a few steps west and on the other side of the street at No 5-9.

Things to See & Do
The **Szarvas Arboretum**, with some 30,000 individual plants not native to the Great Plain, is Hungary's finest. On 85 hectares it contains some 1100 species of rare trees, bushes and grasses, including mammoth pine, ginkgo, swamp cedar, Spanish pine and pampas grass. Boats can be rented at the river pier in the arboretum in season. The arboretum is open from 8 am to 6 pm from mid-March to mid-November and to 3 pm in winter.

The **Sámuel Tessedik Museum** at Vajda Péter utca 1 has some interesting Neolithic exhibits from the goddess-worshipping Körös culture taken from burial mounds on the Great Plain, and much on Slovakian and Magyar ethnic dress and folk art. The section devoted to Tessedik and his work in making Szarvas bloom is interesting but unfortunately only in Hungarian. It's open every day but Monday from 10 am to 4 pm. The **birthplace of Endre Bajcsy-Zsilinszky**, the resistance leader murdered by Hungarian fascists in 1944, is on the same street four blocks to the north.

The neoclassical **Bolza Mansion** (1810)

GREAT PLAIN

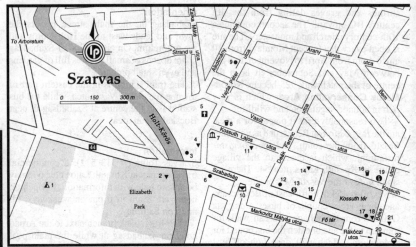

facing the Holt-Körös at Szabadság út 2 was the homestead of the landowners of that name who founded the arboretum. Today it is part of the Tessedik Agricultural College but the grounds can be visited. On the steps leading down to the river stands a statue of Romulus and Remus, revealing the Bolza family's Roman origins.

The horse-driven **dry mill** *(szárazmalom)*, dating from the early 19th century at Ady Endre utca 1, is the best preserved in Hungary. It was still operating until the 1920s and is 100% original. Ask the guide to explain how the two horses actually got into the mill to work and how the miller was paid his tithe of anything ground here. It's open from 1 to 5 pm daily except Monday from April to October.

The **Slovakian Village House** nearby at Hoffmann utca 1 has three rooms filled with handworked textiles and articles from everyday life. It's open from 1 to 5 pm on Tuesday and Friday and from 10 am to noon on Saturday from April to October.

Places to Stay
Szarvas Tours can organise *private rooms* and the *Tessedik Agricultural College*

(☎ 313 311) on Szabadság út has dormitory rooms available in summer. *Liget Camping* (☎ 311 954), with an eight-room pension, is across the river and beyond Elizabeth Park.

Much more central – and expensive – is the new *Lux* pension (☎ 311 068) near the bus station at Szabadság út 35. Doubles are 4000 Ft. The 20-room *Árpád* (☎ 312 120), a 19th-century old world hotel at Szabadság út 32, was undergoing a major renovation during my last visit to Szarvas and may be ready by now. Check out the grandiose Great Hall function room to see if they've retained all the gypsum moulding and *fin-de-siècle* bits and pieces.

Places to Eat
The *Csobolyó*, at Szabadság út 38 and open till midnight, is a nice little restaurant with Hungarian specialities. For pizza, try the *Belváros* at Kossuth Lajos utca 23 or the *Primó* on Vajda Péter utca near the museum. The latter has a salad bar. The *Aroma* teahouse at Kossuth Lajos utca 15 serves some vegetarian dishes weekdays till 8 pm (2 pm on Saturday).

The best place for a meal in Szarvas is the

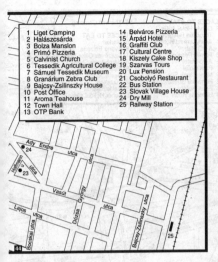

1	Liget Camping	14	Belváros Pizzeria
2	Halászcsárda	15	Árpád Hotel
3	Bolza Manslon	16	Graffiti Club
4	Primó Pizzeria	17	Cultural Centre
5	Calvinist Church	18	Kiszely Cake Shop
6	Tessedik Agricultural College	19	Szarvas Tours
7	Sámuel Tessedik Museum	20	Lux Pension
8	Granárium Zebra Club	21	Csobolyó Restaurant
9	Bajcsy-Zsilinszky House	22	Bus Station
10	Post Office	23	Slovak Village House
11	Aroma Teahouse	24	Dry Mill
12	Town Hall	25	Railway Station
13	OTP Bank		

Halászcsárda fish restaurant in the northeast corner of Elizabeth Park just over the bridge west of town. It's open till 11 pm and has tables on a terrace by the river.

The *Kiszely* is a great cukrászda near the bus station, on the corner of Szabadság út and Béke utca.

Entertainment

The *Péter Vajda Cultural Centre* on Szabadság út near Béke utca has updates on what might be on in Szarvas. Szarvas has a couple of excellent music clubs with live acts most weekends: the *Graffiti Club* at Kossuth Lajos utca 50 and the *Granárium Zebra Club*, in a splendid old townhouse at Kossuth Lajos utca 2. Both are open till late and nonstop at the weekend.

Getting There & Away

Szarvas can be reached by bus from Békéscsaba (at least hourly), Debrecen (two a day), Gyula (four), Kecskemét (12), Orosháza (four) and Szolnok (one). The town is on the train line linking Orosháza with Mezőtúr with services seven times a day. From Békéscsaba, it's faster to take an express train to Mezőtúr and change for Szarvas there.

GYULA
- *pop 35,800*
- *area code ☎ 66*

A town of spas with the last remaining medieval brick castle on the Great Plain, Gyula is a wonderful place to recharge your batteries before crossing the border into Romania just four km to the east. It has a large student population, and something always seems to be going on here.

A fortress was built at Gyula (the name comes from the title given to tribal military commanders among the ancient Magyars) in the 14th century, but it was seized by the Turks and held until 1695. Like Békéscsaba, Gyula came into the hands of the Harruckern family after the aborted Rákóczi independence war of 1703-11. They settled Germans and other groups in different sections of Gyula, and the names have been retained to this day: Big and Little Romanian Town (Nagy Románváros, Kis Románváros), German Town (Németváros) and Hungarian Town (Magyarváros).

Gyula refused to allow the Arad-bound railway to cross through the town in 1858 – a development welcomed by Békéscsaba, 20 km to the west. As a result, Gyula was stuck at the end of a spur and developed at a much slower pace; in 1950 the county seat was moved from here (after 500 years, Gyulans like to point out) to its sister city. Gyula is still seething and a strong rivalry persists between the two: from who should be allocated more county money to whose football team and sausage is better (for the latter, my vote goes to the leaner, spicier Gyulai).

But for better or worse, Gyula's spas, summer theatre in the castle and proximity to Romania attract far more visitors than Békéscsaba's scant offerings. And if we're counting local boys who made good, Gyula wins hands down. The composer Ferenc Erkel and the artists Mihály Munkácsy and György Kohán were all born here, and Gyula is the ancestral town of the 16th-century German painter Albrecht Dürer.

GREAT PLAIN

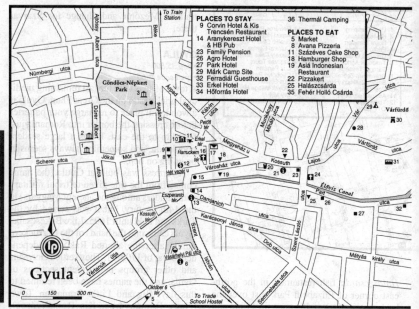

PLACES TO STAY
9 Corvin Hotel & Kis
   Trencsén Restaurant
14 Aranykereszt Hotel
   & HB Pub
23 Family Pension
26 Agro Hotel
27 Park Hotel
29 Márk Camp Site
32 Ferradiál Guesthouse
33 Erkel Hotel
34 Hőforrás Hotel

36 Thermál Camping

PLACES TO EAT
5 Market
8 Avana Pizzeria
11 Százéves Cake Shop
18 Hamburger Shop
19 Asiá Indonesian
   Restaurant
22 Pizzakert
25 Halászcsárda
35 Fehér Holló Csárda

Gyula

Orientation

Gyula is actually two towns: the commercial centre on Városház utca to the west and the Várfürdő (or 'Castle Bath') in a large park to the east. The areas are within easy walking distance of each other. The Élővíz Canal runs east-west through the centre of Gyula, from a branch of the Körös River to Békéscsaba and beyond.

Gyula's bus station is south of Eszperantó tér on Vásárhelyi Pál utca. Walk north through the park to the square and over the canal bridge to reach the town centre. The train station is at the northern end of Béke sugárút.

Information

Your best source of information is Tourinform (☎ 463 421) at Kossuth Lajos utca 7. It is open weekdays from 9 am to 5 pm (in summer to 7 pm as well as on Saturday to 1 pm). Gyulatourist (☎ 463 026), at Eszperantó tér 1, is open weekdays from 8 am to

4.30 pm. Ibusz (☎ 463 084), open from 9 am to 5 pm weekdays and on Saturday till noon, is upstairs at Vásárhelyi Pál utca 3/a next to the bus station.

There's an OTP bank branch at Hét vezér utca 2-6 west of Városház utca. The main post office is at Petőfi tér 1.

Things to See

Gothic **Gyula Castle**, overlooking a picturesque moat near the baths, was originally built in the mid-15th century but has been expanded and renovated many times over the centuries, most recently late in the 1950s. In the vaulted former chapel is a small **museum** tracing the history of the castle and city but it may still be 'resting'; be satisfied with a climb up the **Castle Tower** dating from the 16th century. The round squat **Rondella** next to the castle houses a café and wine bar.

The **György Kohán Museum**, in Göndöcs-Népkert park at Béke sugárút 35, is Gyula's

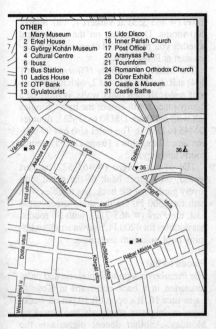

GREAT PLAIN

most important art museum with more than 3000 paintings and graphics bequeathed to the city by the artist upon his death in 1966. The large canvases of horses and women in dark blues and greens and the relentless summer sun of the Great Plain are quite striking and well worth a look.

The baroque **Inner Parish Church** (1777) on Harruckern tér has some interesting contemporary ceiling frescos highlighting events in Hungarian and world history – including an astronaut in space! The Zopf **Romanian Orthodox church** (1812) to the east in Gróza Park has a beautiful iconostasis (you can get the key from the house to the right of the church entrance), but for contemporary icons at their kitschy best, no place can compare with the **Mary Museum** at Apor tér 11, open daily except Monday from 9 am to noon and 1 to 4 pm from March to October and mornings only the rest of the year. Ask Tourinform about how to get the key. You've never seen the Virgin in so many guises.

On the same square at No 7 stands the **birthplace of Ferenc Erkel**, who composed operas and the music for the Hungarian national anthem. It's now a museum. The **Dürer Exhibit** at Kossuth Lajos utca 17 is devoted to the Ajtóssy family (whose name is derived from the Hungarian word for 'door'). They emigrated from Gyula to Germany in the 15th century and changed their name to Dürer (from the German word for 'door', *Tür*).

An interesting – and very unusual for Hungary – museum is **Ladics House** at Jókai Mór utca 4, the perfectly preserved and beautifully furnished mid-19th century residence of a prosperous bourgeois family. Guided tours (in Hungarian only) start every half-hour or so and offer an excellent look into what life was like in a Hungarian market town in those days.

Next door the **Százéves** cake shop and museum facing Erkel tér is both a visual and culinary delight. Established in about 1840 (no doubt Mrs Ladics bought her petits-fours here), the Regency-blue interior is filled with Biedermeier furniture and mirrors in gilt frames. It is one of the most beautiful cukrászdák in Hungary, and is open daily from 10 am to 8 pm.

Activities
The Castle Baths are in a 30-hectare park east of the city centre and count a total of 20 pools. The nine pools inside the spa are open all year from 8 am to 7 pm; the 11 outdoor ones can be used from May to September. There are rowing boats for hire on the castle moat in summer.

A company called Galopp (☎ 463 032) offers horse riding, lessons and coach tours out at the Farm Museum (Tanyamúzeum), Kétegyházi út, south-west of Gyula in Szentbenedek. It is open daily from April to October from 9 am to 5 pm.

Special Events
The biggest event of the year is the Gyula Theatre Festival, with performances in the castle courtyard starting in mid-June.

Places to Stay

Camping Of Gyula's two camp sites, *Márk* (☎ 463 380) at Vár utca 5 is the more central with great views of the castle, but it's tiny and only for caravans and tents; there are no bungalows. The charge is 1000 to 1500 Ft per site and it's open from mid-April to September. *Thermál Camping* (☎ 463 704) at Szélső utca 16 has a huge camping ground that is open year-round; sites cost 1675 Ft. The 20 four-bed rooms in the adjoining motel cost 3250 to 4900 Ft depending on the season.

Private Rooms & Hostels Gyulatourist can book you into a private room from 1200 Ft or an entire apartment with kitchen and living room from 2500 Ft. The *trade school* (☎ 463 822) south-east of the bus station at Szent István utca 38 has dormitory beds available for 650 Ft from mid-June to late August and at weekends year-round.

Pensions The central *Family* (☎ 463 725) is a small, seven-room pension at Kossuth Lajos utca 13 with doubles with shared shower for under 2000 Ft. Near the baths, the *Ferradiál* (☎ 463 146), a former trade union holiday house at Part utca 7/c, charges 930 Ft per person for one of its 60 bathless rooms.

Hotels The most charming hotel in Gyula is the *Aranykereszt* (☎ 463 194), alongside the canal at Eszperantó tér 2. Its 20 rooms all have telephones, TVs and minibars, and there's a popular restaurant and a bar with two tenpin bowling lanes. Singles/doubles are 3450/3900 Ft. More central (but less interesting) is the new 22-room *Corvin* hotel (☎ 362 044) at Jókai utca 9-11 with doubles from 2500 Ft.

There are plenty of hotels in or around the Várfürdő, all of them sprawling, modern affairs with the requisite outlets and satellite TVs. Room rates vary widely depending on the season, but generally the most expensive times are from June to September and over the Christmas and New Year holidays.

The closest hotel to the spa – in fact, it is connected by a corridor – is the sprawling *Erkel* (☎ 463 555) at Várkert 1, with almost 400 rooms. Depending on the season and whether you're in the old or new wing, doubles start at DM46.

The bizarre 178-room *Hőforrás* (☎ 361 544) at Rábai Miklós utca 2, with its rainbow roof and scalloped outer walls, is more of a family place south-east of the baths. Singles (all with bath) are DM30 to DM35, doubles DM45 to DM50. The hotel also has 96 self-contained bungalows (from DM55), tennis courts and a gym.

The 61-room *Agro* (☎ 463 522) at Part utca 5, on a quiet bank of the canal with lovely gardens at the back, has doubles with bath for 5500 Ft. On the same street to the east, the *Park* (☎ 463 711), with 56 rooms, has doubles for 4200 Ft, its own small swimming pool, solarium and sauna.

Places to Eat

The *Pizzakert* is a popular pizzeria and pasta restaurant in a back courtyard at Kossuth Lajos utca 16. It's open till 10 pm on weekdays, midnight at weekends and closes on Monday. Another decent pizzeria is the *Avana* at Corvin utca 21, open till 11 pm. The *Hamburger Shop*, a takeaway place with burgers and salads on Városház utca, is the closest Gyula gets to a McDonald's. It's open daily to 10 pm.

The *Kis Trencsén* is an intimate restaurant with good Hungarian dishes upstairs at Jókai utca 9. The restaurant at the *Aranykereszt* hotel can be recommended both for its food and excellent service.

If you're staying near the castle and baths, the *Fehér Holló* at Tiborc utca 49 is a good choice for csárda-style Hungarian meals. It is open daily till midnight. The *Halászcsárda* on the corner of Part utca and Szent László utca next to the Agro hotel offers the usual fishy dishes.

Gyula can boast a restaurant superlative: it has the only Indonesian eatery in all of Hungary (including Budapest). If you crave a fix of gado-gado, lumpia and satay, head straight for the *Asia* at Városház utca 15 – Asiaphiles will quickly recognise the Toraja-style 'fly-away' roof outside. The Asia has courtyard seating in summer and stays open till midnight. The Indonesian dishes are, well, as authentic as you could expect in south-east Hungary.

You can't miss the cakes and décor at the *Százéves Cukrászda* at Erkel tér 1. The Things to See section has more details.

Gyula's main *market* for fruit, vegetables and other produce is on Október 6 tér southwest of the bus station.

Entertainment

Staff at the *Ferenc Erkel Cultural Centre* (☎ 463 544) in Göndöcs-Népkert park at Béke sugárút 35 can tell you what cultural events are on offer in Gyula.

The *Lido* at Városház utca 1 is a popular night spot open till 2 am (4 am at weekends). Decent pubs include the *HB* in the courtyard of the Aranykereszt hotel and the *Aranysas* at Kossuth Lajos utca 3.

Organ concerts are sometimes held at the *Inner Parish Church*.

Things to Buy

The Herceg Workshop next to the Aranykereszt hotel at Eszperantó tér 1 has a huge selection of handmade scissors, shears and knives.

There aren't many of these kinds of workshops left in Hungary.

Getting There & Away

With Gyula lying on an unimportant rail spur, buses are the preferred mode of transport. There are dozens each day departing for Békéscsaba and at least half a dozen go to Debrecen. Other destinations include Budapest (one a day), Eger (one), Kecskemét (three), Miskolc (one), Szeged (five), Szeghalom via Vésztő (four) and Vésztő (six). A bus bound for Oradea leaves Gyula on Tuesday, Thursday and Saturday at 9.30 am.

Gyula's link to the Békéscsaba-Szolnok-Budapest rail line is line No 128; 15 trains a day follow it to Békéscsaba. Travelling north on this line will get you to Vésztő, Szeghalom and eventually to Püspökladány, where you can change trains for Debrecen. The only international train from Gyula leaves for the Romanian town of Salonta three times day.

Getting Around

Bus Nos 2, 3 and 4, infrequent as they are, run from the train station down Béke sugárút to Eszperantó tér. Nos 1 and 4 carry on to the bus station.

Northern Uplands

The Northern Uplands (Északi Felföld) make up Hungary's mountainous region – foothills of the mighty Carpathians rolling eastward from the Danube Bend almost as far as Ukraine, 300 km away. By anyone's standards, these 'mountains' don't amount to much: the highest peak – Kékes in the Mátra range – 'soars' to just over 1000m. But in a country as flat as Hungary, these hills are important for environmental and recreational reasons and, if nothing else, they relieve the monotony of the Great Plain.

The Northern Uplands include five or six ranges of hills, depending on how you count. From west to east they are: the Börzsöny, the home of Hungary's Slovak community and best reached from Vác (see the Danube Bend chapter); the Cserhát; the Mátra; the Bükk; the Aggtelek (an adjunct of the eastern Cserhát region); and the Zemplén.

Most of the features of hilly regions elsewhere in Europe apply to Hungary's Northern Uplands. Generally, they are forested, though a large part of the lower hills are under cultivation (mostly grapes). Castles and ruins abound, and the last vestiges of traditional folk life can be found here, especially among the Palóc people of the Cserhát Hills and the Mátyó of Mezőkövesd south of the Bükk. The ranges are peppered with resorts and camping grounds, and it is a region famed for its wine; two of Hungary's best known tipples – sweet Tokaj and ruby-red Bikavér (bull's blood) from Eger – are produced here.

But the Northern Uplands are not always so idyllic. Here too are industrial Miskolc, once a socialist 'iron city that works' and now a shadow of its former self; and the polluted Sajó Valley; and the depressed towns of Nógrád County.

It's difficult to put a tag on each of the ranges, but they do differ from each other in many ways. The Cserhát Hills region (best reached from Balassagyarmat) is little more than rolling countryside north-east of Buda-

HIGHLIGHTS

- the rich collection of folk art at the Palóc Museum in Balassagyarmat
- the unusual Buddhist stupa in Sándor Kőrösi Csoma Memorial Park at Tar
- just about everything in Eger: its castle, architecture, wine and the Senator House hotel
- Hollókő's restored castle and living folk traditions
- hiking in the Zemplén Hills near Boldogkőváralja
- riding the narrow-gauge railway from Miskolc through the Bükk Hills to Lillafüred
- caving in the Aggtelek karst region
- wine tasting in Tokaj
- the magnificent Lipizzaner horses of Szilvásvárad
- the trompe l'oeil ceiling of the Great Library in the Calvinist College in Sárospatak

pest, but its valleys harbour some of the most traditional communities extant in Hungary. The Mátra region is Budapest's mountainous retreat, with endless accommodation choices; it's easiest to enter here from Gyöngyös. The Bükk Hills are rich in wildlife (a large part forms one of Hungary's five national parks) and Eger or Miskolc are the jump-off points, depending on which side you approach the area. Aggtelek, site of another national park, is famous for its karst caves. The Zemplén Hills are the most remote; Boldogkőváralja

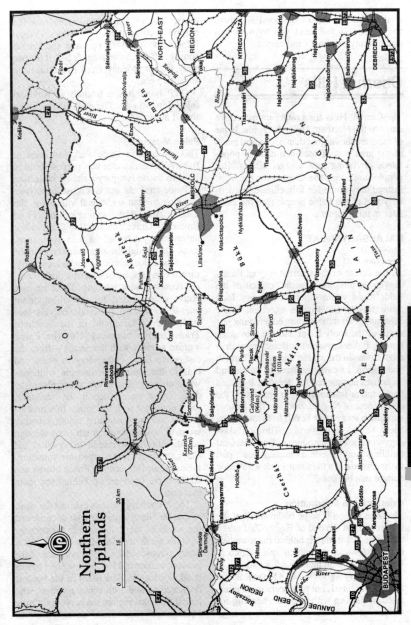

on the south-west side and Sátoraljaújhely to the north-east will lead you to mountain trails, sunny vineyards and castles.

Cserhát Hills

The Cserhát Hills are a rather unimpressive entry to the Northern Uplands region. None of them reaches higher than 650m, and much of the area is cultivated and densely populated, obviating any serious hiking. But people don't visit the Cserhát for the hills; instead they come for folk culture, particularly that of the Palóc people (see the aside later in this chapter).

BALASSAGYARMAT
• *pop 19,700*
• *area code* ☎ *35*

As the centre of the Cserhát region, Balassagyarmat bills itself as the 'capital of the Palóc', and while other places may look more folksy, the town's excellent Palóc Museum gives it the leading edge. Lying just south of the Ipoly River and the Slovakian border, Balassagyarmat suffered more than most towns in the region during the Turkish occupation, its castle reduced to rubble and its houses abandoned for decades. It gained back stature late in the 18th century as the county seat of Nógrád, but even that honour was taken away after WWII in favour of the 'new town' Salgótarján. Today Balassagyarmat's few baroque and neoclassical buildings and the odd monument don't pull in the crowds. It's the town's link with Palóc culture that beckons.

Orientation & Information
The train station is some 650m south of the town centre at the end of Bajcsy-Zsilinszky utca. The bus station is behind the town hall on Köztársaság tér, which splits Rákóczi fejedelem útja, the main drag, in two.

You can try Ibusz (☎ 312 415) at Rákóczi fejedelem útja 61, but they seem more interested in dealing with Magyars heading for Greece or the Canary Islands on package

tours. Instead, seek assistance from the helpful staff at the City Gallery (Városi Képtár) (☎ 300 186) opposite the former county hall at Köztársaság tér 5-7. It is open daily, except Monday, from 10 am till noon and 1 to 5 pm.

OTP bank has a branch at Rákóczi fejedelem útja 44. The post office can be found at No 24.

Palóc Museum
This museum in Palóc Park just west of Bajcsy-Zsilinszky utca was purpose-built in 1914 to house Hungary's richest collection of Palóc artefacts and is a must for anyone planning to visit traditional villages in the Cserhát Hills. The standing exhibit 'From Cradle to Grave' on the 1st floor, while unfortunately labelled only in Hungarian, takes you through the important stages in the life of the Palóc people and includes pottery, superb carvings, mock-ups of a birth scene, a classroom and a wedding. There are also votive objects used for the all-important *búcsúk*, or church patronal festivals (see aside under Máriagyűd in the Southern Transdanubia chapter). But the Palóc women's agility with the needle – from the distinctive floral embroidery in blues and reds to the almost microscopic white-on-white stitching – leaves everything else in the dust. Notice the cabinets in the 'wedding' room crammed with handmade folk masterpieces, and the graduating colour schemes worn by women from youth (red) through adulthood (blue) to middle (navy blue) and old age (black). An open-air museum, including an 18th-century **Palóc house** and stable, have been set up behind the main museum.

The **art gallery** upstairs exhibits the work of Oszkár Glatz, a painter who documented the world of the Palóc in oils for decades until his death in 1958. Much of his work is pretty syrupy, but the frightened face of the peasant woman in *The Chicken Thief* makes it all worthwhile. The room in the back is dedicated to two 19th-century writers who hailed from this region: the playwright Imre Madách and the satirical novelist Kálmán

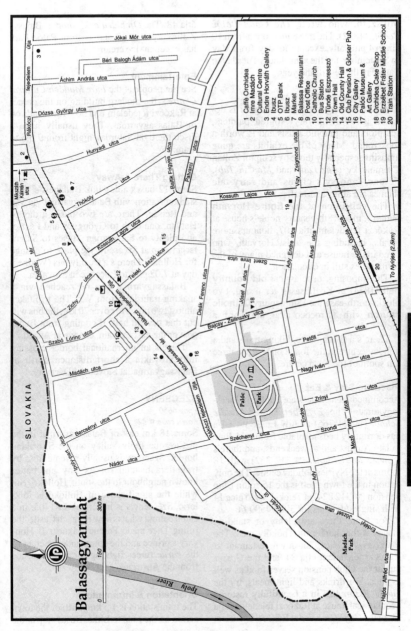

Balassagyarmat

SLOVAKIA

NORTHERN UPLANDS

Ipoly River

0   150   300 m

1 Caffé Orchidea
2 Imre Madách Cultural Centre
3 Endre Horváth Gallery
4 Ibusz
5 OTP Bank
6 Ibusz
7 Market
8 Balassa Restaurant
9 Post Office
10 Catholic Church
11 Bus Station
12 Tünde Eszpresszó
13 Town Hall
14 Old County Hall
15 Club Pension & Gösser Pub
16 City Gallery
17 Palóc Museum & Art Gallery
18 Orchidea Cake Shop
19 Erzsébet Fráter Middle School
20 Train Station

Jókai Mór utca
Béri Balogh Ádám utca
Áchim András utca
Rákóczi fejedelem útja
Dózsa György utca
Hunyadi utca
Baltik Frigyes utca
Pálvarci utca
Thököly
Miksztáth Kálmán utca
Kossuth Lajos utca
Kossuth Lajos utca
Vizy Zsigmond utca
Teleki László utca
Szent Imre utca
Ady Endre utca
Deák Ferenc utca
József A. utca
Bercsényi Gyula utca
Aradi utca
To Nyírjes (2.5km)
Zrínyi utca
Rákóczi fejedelem útja
Szabó Lőrinc utca
Madách utca
Köztársaság tér
Bajcsy - Zsilinszky utca
Petőfi
Nagy Iván
Zrínyi
Szondi
Palóc Park
Széchenyi utca
Endre utca
Mező Imre utca
Bercsényi utca
Nádor utca
Ipoly-part utca
Kóvári út
Madách Park
Hajós Alfréd utca
Erdélyi
József utca

Mikszáth, who wrote *The Good Palóc People* (1882). The museum is open from 10 am to 4 pm daily, except Monday, from May to September and the same hours Tuesday to Saturday the rest of the year.

Other Things to See
The **City Gallery** on Köztársaság tér is devoted to contemporary Nógrád painters, sculptors and graphic artists and is worth a look round. Many of the exhibits are quite amusing, especially those by sculptor Zoltán Csemniczky (*Bar Lady* and *Man in Tub*). Ferenc Jánossy's circus and fairy-tale themes are almost surreal.

The collection at the **Endre Horváth Gallery**, in an 18th-century noble's house at Rákóczi fejedelem útja 107, honours more locals, including the artist Horváth, who lived in the house and designed many of the forint notes still in circulation.

The imposing, neoclassical **old country hall** (1834) at Köztársaság tér 6 and, two blocks north-east, the 18th-century **Catholic church** with its rococo altar, are worth a look.

There's a fishing lake, hiking trails and a holiday centre in the forest of Nyírjes, three km south of the town centre.

Places to Stay & Eat
Accommodation choices are limited in Balassagyarmat. The *Erzsébet Fráter Middle School* (☎ 311 765) at Ady Endre utca 1/a has dormitory beds available from mid-June to late August and at weekends, and there's a cheap *tourist hotel* (☎ 312 352) with 18 rooms at the Nyírjes holiday centre. The only option in the town itself is the 15-room *Club* pension (☎ 312 824) at Teleki László utca 14 with singles/doubles for 3000/4500 Ft.

For food, there are plenty of stand-up places at the market on Thököly utca. The *Balassa* is a cheap sit-down restaurant at Rákóczi fejedelem útja 34, and the *Gösser* pub at the Club pension serves food as well as suds. For drinks and light meals, try the *Tünde Eszpresszó* in a beautifully restored neoclassical house at Rákóczi fejedelem útja 31, or the *Caffè Orchidea* at Rákóczi fejedelem

útja 48. The *Orchidea cake shop* at Bajcsy-Zsilinszky utca 12 across from Palóc Park has excellent ice cream.

Entertainment
See the people at the *Imre Madách Cultural Centre* – the modern building on the corner at Rákóczi fejedelem útja 50 – for what's on in Balassagyarmat. They usually have a disco there on Saturday night from 9 pm to 4 am.

Getting There & Away
Some 12 buses a day link Budapest's Népstadion station with Balassagyarmat via Vác and Rétság. There are two buses a day to Hatvan, one each to Gyöngyös and Pászto, and plenty to Salgótarján. Buses to Salgótarján stop at Szécsény, the place to change for Hollókő. There's a weekly bus (Wednesday at 7.02 pm) to Lučenec in Slovakia.

Balassagyarmat can be reached via a snaking train line from Vác. The trip takes almost two hours to cover 70 km; the bus will cut that time in half. If coming from Budapest or the east by train, change at Aszód.

There's an international border crossing into Slovakia a short distance north of Balassagyarmat at Slovenské Dármoty.

SZÉCSÉNY
• *pop 6850*
• *area code* ☎ *32*
Some 18 km east of Balassagyarmat in the picturesque Ipoly Valley on the Slovakian border, Szécsény is usually given a miss by travellers headed for its tiny but better known neighbour to the south, Hollókő. But while the significance of Hollókő is folkloric, Szécsény's is historical. In 1705, in a camp behind what is now Forgách Castle, the ruling Diet made Ferenc Rákóczi II Hungary's prince and the commander in chief of the *kuruc* forces fighting for independence from the Austrians.

Orientation & Information
The train station is 1.5 km north of the town centre on the road to Litke. Buses stop at the

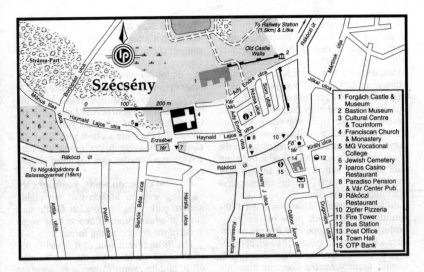

1 Forgách Castle & Museum
2 Bastion Museum
3 Cultural Centre & Tourinform
4 Franciscan Church & Monastery
5 MG Vocational College
6 Jewish Cemetery
7 Iparos Casino Restaurant
8 Paradiso Pension & Vár Center Pub
9 Rákóczi Restaurant
10 Zipfer Pizzeria
11 Fire Tower
12 Bus Station
13 Post Office
14 Town Hall
15 OTP Bank

station on Király utca east of the fire tower on Fő tér.

Tourinform (☎ 370 777) has an office in the Rákóczi Cultural Centre (☎ 370 860) on Ady Endre utca 12, which is open weekdays from 8 am to 4 pm. You'll find an OTP bank branch next to the town hall at Rákóczi út 86. The post office is at Dugonics utca 1, which leads south from Fő tér.

Forgách Castle

This imposing castle at the end of Ady Endre utca was built around 1760 from the remains of a medieval border fortress that had been blown to bits by vengeful Habsburg troops 50 years earlier. It passed into the hands of the aristocratic Forgách family in the mid-19th century. The Forgáchs made further additions, and today it houses an odd mixture of exhibits as the **Ferenc Kubinyi Museum**.

On the ground floor to the right of the entrance there's a small pharmaceutical exhibit as well as a few rooms done up much the way the Forgách family would have liked to see them decorated. Upstairs, beyond the Stone Age bones and chips, the reconstructed Neolithic house and the Bronze Age jewellery, is a ghastly hunting exhibit with any number of 'useful' items (napkin rings, cups, pistol butts, umbrella handles) carved and whittled from the carcasses of our furred and feathered friends. Guns figure prominently, of course.

Only a little less frightening is the **Bastion Museum** in the north-east tower, from where stretches of the original 16th-century castle wall can be seen to the west and south. Along with maps and displays on the original castle's historical role, the bastion contains an all-too-complete collection of torture implements: racks, yokes, stocks and a flogging bench.

Not just those of a nervous disposition will find refuge in the **Sándor Kőrösi Csoma Memorial House** near the main entrance. Kőrösi Csoma (1784-1842) was a Franciscan monk who travelled to Tibet and wrote the first Tibetan-English dictionary. The Dalai Lama paid homage to him by visiting Hungary on the 150th anniversary of his death and dedicating a Buddhist stupa and memorial park in his memory at Tar, south of Salgótarján (see that section).

Franciscan Church & Monastery

Parts of this Gothic Franciscan church at

NORTHERN UPLANDS

Haynald Lajos utca 7-9 date from the 14th century and the monastery has been returned to the church and restored to its former glory after years of neglect. In the sanctuary (the oldest section), your guide will point out (in Hungarian or German) 500-year-old carvings in the vaulted ceiling of saints, flowers and fruits (the carvings on the pillars were destroyed by the Turks when they occupied Szécsény in 1552) as well as where Muslims carved out a mihrab, or prayer niche, in the south wall. In the nave, the baroque main and side altars are actually wood, though they look like marble, and the richly carved pulpit is from the 18th century.

In the monastery (dating from the 17th-century, though with parts of the 14th-century church incorporated into it), you'll have a look at the monks' cells and, depending on what's open, the library, dining hall, Gothic oratory overlooking the church's interior, and/or the Rákóczi Room, where the newly appointed prince and military commander met with his war cabinet in 1705. The barely recognisable frescos are Gothic with some Turkish geometric designs added. The Franciscan church and monastery are open Tuesday to Saturday from 10.30 to 11.30 am and 1.30 to 4.30 pm; Sunday hours are 1 to 4.30 pm. Ring the bell to gain entry.

Other Things to See

You may think you're seeing things but, yes, the baroque **fire tower** (1700) dominating Fő tér is leaning – a result of shelling and bombing in 1944. The official estimate is 3°, but it looks a whole lot more than that to me.

A **monument to King Stephen** in Erzsébet tér near the Franciscan church bears a strange and plaintive inscription: 'Where are you King Stephen? The Hungarian people long for you.' Walk west from here along Haynald Lajos utca to see the sadly decrepit **Jewish cemetery** now being encroached upon by new housing.

The Palóc Riding School (☎ 370 350) at Nógrádgárdony south-west of Szécsény offers lessons and riding excursions.

Places to Stay & Eat

There's not a lot of choice in Szécsény. In summer and at weekends the *MG Vocational College* (☎ 370 573) at Haynald Lajos 9-11 has dormitory rooms available. The only other option in town is the *Paradiso* (☎ 370 427), a 17-room pension sitting atop the castle's cellar system at Ady Endre utca 14. Comfortable singles/doubles with bath are 2500/3800 Ft. There's a beer hall called *Vár Center* in the cellar below (notice the date 1648 carved on the arch overhead as you enter).

If worse comes to worst, you might try camping wild in Strázsa-part, an eight-hectare park west of Forgách Castle and close to where Ferenc Rákóczi took command of the anti-Habsburg forces.

The *Rákóczi* restaurant at Rákóczi út 95, south of the castle, serves the usual sludge till 10 pm; the *Iparos Casino* at Erzsébet tér 3 is a similar place with better (and cheaper) food. It closes at 9 pm. For something more upbeat, try the *Zipfer*, a decent pizzeria and cukrászda at Rákóczi út 85, or the restaurant at the *Paradiso* pension.

Getting There & Away

About 10 buses depart for Hollókő on weekdays and half a dozen at weekends. You shouldn't have to wait more than half an hour for buses to Balassagyarmat or Salgótarján (with a possible change for the latter at Litke). There are eight buses a day to Budapest and two or three to Pászto.

Szécsény is on a minor railway line linking it with Balassagyarmat and Aszód to the west and south-west and Lučenec in Slovakia to the north. To get to Vác from Szécsény by train, you must change at Balassagyarmat.

HOLLÓKŐ
• *pop 650*
• *area code* ☎ *32*

It may sound simplistic, but people either love Hollókő or hate it. To some, the two-street village nestling in a valley 17 km south-east of Szécsény is Hungary's most beautiful and deserves praise for holding on

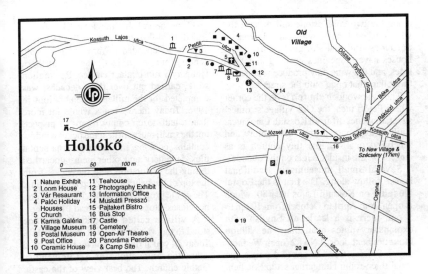

Hollókő

0   50   100 m

1 Nature Exhibit
2 Loom House
3 Vár Resaurant
4 Palóc Holiday
  Houses
5 Church
6 Kamra Galéria
7 Village Museum
8 Postal Museum
9 Post Office
10 Ceramic House
11 Teahouse
12 Photography Exhibit
13 Information Office
14 Muskátli Presszó
15 Pajtakert Bistro
16 Bus Stop
17 Castle
18 Cemetery
19 Open-Air Theatre
20 Panoráma Pension
   & Camp Site

to its traditional architecture and some old customs. Others see it as a staged tourist trap with paid 'performers' who make a mockery of Palóc culture. UNESCO agreed with the first view in 1987 when it put Hollókő on its World Cultural Heritage List – the first village in the world to receive such protection. What sets Hollókő (Raven Rock) apart is its restored 13th-century castle and the architecture of the so-called Old Village (Ófalu), where some 65 houses and outbuildings have been listed, declared historic monuments or deemed of 'village-scape' importance.

Most of what you see is, strictly speaking, not original. The village has burned to the ground many times since the 13th century (most recently in 1909), but the villagers have always rebuilt their houses exactly to plan with clay and wattle.

Despite what the tourist brochures (and some wishful guidebooks) tell you, women in traditional Palóc dress – red-and-blue embroidered skirts, ornate headpieces – are very thin on the ground these days; if you want to see people walking around in such finery, you'll have to travel a lot farther east to ethnic Hungarian towns such as Szék (Romanian: Sic) in Transylvania. Still, on Sunday mornings, important feast days like Easter, Easter Monday and 15 August, or during a wedding, you may get lucky and catch some traditional costumes.

Orientation & Information

Don't be disappointed as you ascend the hill into Hollókő: you're passing the Újfalu (New Village) on the right, scarcely 30 years old and of no particular interest. The bus stops on Dózsa György utca at the end of Kossuth Lajos utca; from there walk down the hill to the Old Village.

There's an information office (of sorts) called the Village Foundation (☎ 378 066) at Kossuth Lajos utca 68. If there's no one there, continue to the Kamra Galéria at Kossuth Lajos utca 86 for help. If something is 'on' in town – a wedding (rare) or a funeral (common in this ageing community) – everything will be shut for at least a few hours. You can change money at the post office at Kossuth Lajos utca 76.

Things to See

The village overall and its wonderful **folk architecture** are the main sights. Stroll

NORTHERN UPLANDS

along the two cobblestone streets, past the whitewashed houses with carved wooden porticoes and red-shingled roofs. Most houses have grapevines growing along the sides, and the wine they produce is stored in the cellars that open onto the streets.

The little wooden **church** is on the corner where Petőfi utca, the Old Village's 'other' street, branches off from Kossuth Lajos utca. Built as a granary in the 16th century and sanctified in 1889, the tiny church is as austere on the inside as it is on the outside.

Several small museums in traditional houses follow along. The first is the **Postal Museum** on Kossuth Lajos utca 80, which is open from April to October from 10 am to 5 pm; there is a leaflet in English with explanatory notes available. The **Village Museum** next door at No 82 (open Wednesday to Sunday from 10 am to 4 pm) is the usual three-room Hungarian setup (kitchen, fancy parlour, workroom) with folk pottery, painted furniture, embroidered pillows and an interestingly carved wine press dated 1872 in the back yard. But you could almost do better by peeking into the villagers' windows. A standing **nature exhibition** called 'The People and the Land' at Kossuth Lajos utca 99 (open from 9 am to 3 or 5 pm, closed Monday and Wednesday), deals with the flora, fauna and human inhabitants of the section of Bükk National Park surrounding the village.

Other Things to See

Hollókő Castle can be reached by following the trail up the hill across from the nature exhibit or from the bus stop by walking up to József Attila utca and picking up the marked west-bound trail from the car park. At 365m, the castle has a commanding view of the surrounding hills. To the south-east is Purga (575m), one of the highest 'peaks' in this part of the Cserhát, and to the north the Ipoly Valley. The hill to the east of the castle entrance is one of the best spots around for a picnic.

The castle was built at the end of the 13th century and strengthened 200 years later. It was taken by the Turks and not liberated until 1683 by the Polish King John III Sobieski (ruled 1674-96). It was partially destroyed after the Independence War early in the 18th century but is, in fact, one of northern Hungary's most intact castles. Restoration work, carried out over three decades, was completed for the millenary celebrations in 1996. Today there's not a whole lot more than a half-dozen empty rooms to inspect, but the small museum near the ticket window contains cooking implements, ornamental tiles, jewellery and other items unearthed during the restoration, and the views from the top of the pentagonal keep are stunning. The castle is open daily from 10 am to 6 pm, but closes altogether in the dead of winter.

A village called **Hollókőváralja** once stood to the west of the castle down the hill. Today all you'll find – if you look really hard – are the foundations of a 15th-century Gothic church. The best view of the castle looming over the town is from **Kerek Hill** (337m) north of the New Village.

There's a small but interesting **photography exhibit** documenting the village called 'From Easter to Christmas' on Kossuth Lajos utca opposite the information office. It's open from April to September.

Activities

The Village Foundation (see Orientation & Information) organises touristy folk-craft lessons, but if you'd like something a bit more authentic, see the dynamic manager of the Kamra Galéria (Studio Gallery) in the Udvarház at Kossuth Lajos utca 86. From pottery making and egg painting to gathering medicinal herbs and learning to thatch or ride a horse, she can organise it for you – or find someone who can.

There are some gentle walks into the hills and valleys to the west of the castle. *A Cserhát Turistatérképe*, the 1:60,000 Cserhát map (No 8) from Cartographia, will help you plan your route, but is not absolutely necessary.

Places to Stay

Private rooms are available at Kossuth Lajos utca 77 (1000 Ft for singles) and at the

Kamra Galéria (800 Ft per person for the upstairs apartment with a double room, kitchen and bathroom – as long as you help with the chores!). You can rent the entire farmhouse at Kossuth Lajos utca 98 from the owner, who lives at József Attila utca 2 near the bus stop.

The 10 *Palóc holiday houses* along Petőfi utca are the choice places to stay, but you should book well ahead in season through the Village Foundation office. Prices start at 1300/1500 Ft for a single/double room, and go as high as 5200 Ft for a traditional cottage for two people. House E at Petőfi utca 20, set back from the road in its own garden, is among the nicest. It costs 1950 Ft for two.

A rather obtrusive holiday complex called *Panoráma* (☎ 378 077) with a nine-room pension, five bungalows and a camping ground (May to August) is perched on the hill top off Sport utca south of the Old Village. Double rooms in the pension cost 2200 Ft, four-bed bungalows are 3000 Ft and camping costs 300/300/100 Ft per person/tent/car.

Places to Eat

There aren't many places to eat in Hollókő. The *Vár* at Kossuth Lajos utca 95 is a sit-down restaurant, but remember that this is still very much an early-to-bed, early-to-rise farming community: the Vár closes at 8 pm or so. Otherwise, try the restaurant at the *Panoráma* pension.

The *Muskátli*, a coffee shop that serves meals at Kossuth Lajos utca 61 is open Wednesday to Sunday to 6 or 7 pm. The little *teahouse* in the Múveszház beside the church at Petőfi utca 4 has a small *wine bar* in the cellar. The local hang-out for all ages is the *Pajtakert* (Barnyard), a little bistro at Kossuth Lajos utca 48 near the bus stop.

Entertainment

The *open-air theatre* on the hill south-east of the castle stages folk dance and music shows when the tour buses pull in. Check with the Village Foundation information office.

The Good Palóc People

The Palóc are a distinct Hungarian group living in the fertile hills and valleys of the Cserhát. Ethnologists are still debating whether they were a separate people who later mixed with the Magyars (their name means Cuman in several Slavic languages, suggesting they came from western Siberia) or just a Hungarian ethnic group which, through isolation and Slovakian influence, developed their own ways. What's certain is that the Palóc continue to speak a distinct dialect of Hungarian (unusual in a country where language differences are virtually nonexistent) and, until recently, were able to cling to their traditional folk dress, particularly in such towns as Buják, Hollókő, Rimóc and Őrhalom. Today they are considered the guardians of living folk traditions in Hungary. ■

Things to Buy

You might be put off by all the folk garbage being sold in some of the shops and by old women on the street, but the Loom House (Szövőház) at Kossuth Lajos utca 94 is a good place for finding hand-woven and embroidered goods; it's interesting to watch the women demonstrate how their enormous loom works. See if they have any of the old white-on-white embroidered tablecloths or napkins: the quality is light years from the new ones. The Kamra Galéria specialises in handicrafts and modern folk pieces of excellent quality.

You can buy decent handiwork from several individuals, including the women at Kossuth Lajos utca 51/b and the one at No 70 on the same street. The Ceramic House (Fazekasház) behind the teahouse on Petőfi utca has hand-thrown vases, jugs, candlesticks and decorative items. It is open from April to October.

Getting There & Away

Szécsény is the gateway to Hollókő, with some 10 buses a day heading there during the week and six at weekends. You can also catch one of about five buses a day to Salgótarján via Pászto.

NORTHERN UPLANDS

SALGÓTARJÁN
• *pop 49,300*
• *area code* ☎ *32*

After an idyllic day or two in Hollókő or any of the rural villages of the Cserhát, arriving in this modern city 25 km east of Szécsény is like stepping into a cold shower. Ravaged by fire in 1821 and by serious flooding 100 years ago, Salgótarján can boast almost no buildings that predate this century. And that's apparent as soon as you step off the train: row after row of concrete blocks and towers wall the city in from the picturesque Medves Hills.

Those hills have been exploited for their coal since the last century, and it is on this that Salgótarján's success is based. As in Miskolc, the Communists found the coal miners and steelworkers here sympathetic to their cause and were supported both during the Republic of Councils and after the war (though this did not stop the dreaded ÁVH secret police from shooting down over 100 people during the 1956 Uprising). For its support, Salgótarján was made the county seat in 1950 and rebuilt throughout the 1960s. Today the city faces high unemployment (the last mine closed in 1992), but it has nowhere near the depressed feel of other cities in the same position.

Except to see Salgó and Somoskő castles, and perhaps to hike in the Karancs Hills to the north-west (see the Around Salgótarján section), few travellers make their way to Salgótarján. Perhaps for that reason and the large, friendly student population – almost a dozen colleges and trade schools are located here – the city is worth a stopover.

Orientation & Information
Because it has virtually swallowed the town of Somoskőújfalu some 10 km to the north, Salgótarján feels like a large city. The train and bus stations are a short distance apart to the west of the city centre. The local bus station is on Bem utca.

All the big agencies have offices here. Nógrád Tourist (☎ 316 940), on the walkway above Erzsébet tér 5, can also help you with information about Hollókő and other towns in the county. It's open from 7.30 am to 5 pm on weekdays. Ibusz (☎ 314 831) keeps similar hours at Rákóczi út 10. Cooptourist (☎ 312 909), opposite at No 11 on the same street, is open weekdays from 9 am to 6 pm. Behind Cooptourist, at Mérleg utca 5, is Express (☎ 310 953), open 8.15 am to 4.30 pm on weekdays and 8.30 to 10.30 am on Saturday.

There's an OTP bank branch below Nógrád Tourist on Erzsébet tér and another at Rákóczi út 22. The main post office is on Klapka György utca 3.

Things to See
The **Mining Museum**, the city's only real sight, is on Zemlinszky Rezső utca 1, a short walk south-west of the bus station. Filled with geological maps and samples, old uniforms and a statue of St Barbara, the patron of miners, standing proudly next to old Communist banners calling for the nationalisation of the mines, the museum's style is somewhat outdated and it's not particularly interesting. But, across the street, an actual mine continues to be 'worked' by performers in unrealistically clean overalls, and you can wander through the pits, almost getting a feel for life below the surface as the signs wish you *Jó szerencsét!* ('Good luck!'), what miners here say to one another as they go to work. The museum is open from 9 am to 3 pm daily except Monday (10 am to 2 pm between October and March).

A set of steps west of the train station off Alkotmány út lead up to **Pipis Hill** (Pipishegy; 341m). Follow the stations of the Cross past the plinth of what was until not so long ago the Partisan Memorial Statue in Hungarian-Soviet Friendship Park for a great view of the city and surrounding hills. To the south-west at Kőváralja lies the rubble of **Baglyaskő Castle**, built on an extinct volcano in the early 14th century.

Places to Stay
Tóstrand Camping (☎ 311 168), about five km north-east of the centre of town just off the road to Somoskő, has two year-round motels with a total of 19 rooms priced from

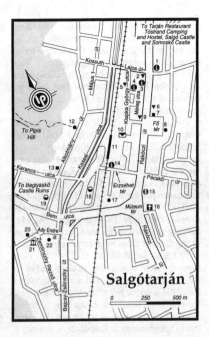

1700 to 2000 Ft for a double. A non-heated *motel* (1300 Ft) and a *hostel* affiliated with Hostelling International (650 Ft per person) are open from mid-April to mid-September. There's a boating lake, tennis courts and a pool nearby.

For *private rooms* in one of the city's many high-rises, ask Cooptourist; Nógrád Tourist deals with long-term accommodation only.

One of the better deals around is at the 24-room *Galcsik* pension (☎ 316 524), near the bus station at Alkotmány út 2. Singles/doubles with shower in this well maintained pension are 1980/2560 Ft.

The *Karancs* (☎ 410 088) at Fő tér 6, has 48 very ordinary rooms as well as a bar, restaurant and nightclub. Singles/doubles are DM58/68.

Places to Eat

The *Yellow* pizzeria next to Cooptourist on Rákóczi út and the *HB* pub behind on Klapka György utca are decent choices for cheap (if unexceptional) meals, as is the tiny *CZZ* restaurant opposite the Karancs hotel at Fő tér 1. For much better food, though, head for the restaurant at the *Galcsik* pension, which stays open nightly to 10.30 pm. The restaurant at the *Karancs* hotel has a Gypsy group playing big-band favourites at weekends.

The most popular cake shop in town is the *Godó* on Rákóczi út just north of the Karancs hotel.

Entertainment

The *Attila József Cultural Centre* (☎ 310 503) at Fő tér 5 is Salgótarján's highbrow cultural venue, but they'll be able to help you with information on more down-to-earth entertainment. (The statue of the doleful young man on the square outside the centre depicts the poet Miklós Radnóti, who was shot by his Nazi captors in 1944.)

Getting There & Away

Buses leave Salgótarján very frequently for Balassagyarmat and Szécsény. You can also get to Budapest (eight departures daily),

NORTHERN UPLANDS

Pászto and Eger (six each), Miskolc (two), Hatvan (three), Hollókő (five), Gyöngyös (five) and Parádfürdő (two) in the Mátra Hills.

A train line links Salgótarján with Hatvan and the main Budapest-Miskolc trunk to the south and, to the north, Somoskőújfalu and, in Slovakia, Lučenec.

AROUND SALGÓTARJÁN
Salgó & Somoskő Castles

There are some interesting walks in the area. **Salgó Castle**, eight km north-east of the city centre, was built atop a basalt cone some 625m up in the Medves Hills in the 13th century. After Buda Castle fell to the Turks in 1541, Salgó served as an important border fortress, but it too was taken 23 years later and fell into ruin after the Turks abandoned it late in the 16th century. The castle is remembered best for the visit made by Sándor Petőfi in 1845, which inspired him to write one of his best-loved poems, *Salgó*. Today you can just make out the inner courtyard, tower and bastion from the ruins, but views of Somoskő and Slovakia are excellent from this peaceful spot.

To visit the interior of **Somoskő Castle**, which is now in Slovakian territory, you must cross the border at Somoskőújfalu and follow a path east on foot to the castle. But most people will be content with what they can see from the Hungarian side. Whatever you do, don't follow my lead and slip under the broken fence for a 'do-it-yourself' tour: the Hungarian border guards were none too pleased when I re-emerged. Somoskő, built in the 14th century from basalt blocks, was able to hold off the Turkish onslaught longer than Salgó Castle, not falling until 1576. Ferenc Rákóczi used it during the independence war in 1706 and for that reason it was partially destroyed by the Austrians.

Somoskő Castle is much larger and more interesting than the Salgó one, and the Slovakians have restored much of it, with conical wooden roofs now topping two of the bastions. If you do get inside, you can walk around the inner castle, the remains of the palace and even into the casemates if the

entrance isn't blocked. Make sure you have a look at the basalt formations north-east of the castle; they are lava flows that have frozen into enormous 'organ pipes'. The only thing of importance on the Hungarian side is the **Petőfi Memorial Hut** built in honour of the poet's visit here in 1845 (no poem that time, though).

The adventurous with extra time might want to follow the marked trail from Somoskőújfalu along the Slovakian border for four km to 720m **Mt Karancs**; you can see the High Tatras from the lookout tower atop what is called the Palóc Olympus. Just make sure you have a copy of Cartographia's 1:60,000 *A Karancs, a Medves és a Heves-Borsodi-Dombság Turistatérképe* (No 11), the map that covers this area, a continuation of the Cserhát from Salgótarján east to Ózd.

To get to Salgó Castle, take bus No 11/b from the local bus station in Salgótarján to the Eresztvény recreational area. From here the castle is up the hill to the south-west, past the old Salgó hotel. An easier way to reach Salgó Castle, though, is to stay on the same bus to the terminus in Salgóbánya, the city's old mining district, and follow the path to the west. Still another route is to catch bus No 1 to Zagyvaróna. From the terminus there, go north along Örhegy utca and pick up the trail to the castle.

Bus No 11/a also goes to Eresztvény and then heads for Somoskő. You can catch bus No 11/a to Somoskő from the crossroads below the old Salgó hotel, but it's an easy walk between the two castles.

Buddhist Stupa

Travelling south some 22 km from Salgótarján on route No 21 toward Pászto, you may think you've driven through a black hole and arrived in South-East Asia. There, on a hillside to the east in the village of Tar, is a full-sized Buddhist stupa, its little chimes sounding and coloured pendants fluttering in the gentle breeze. It is part of **Sándor Kőrösi Csoma Memorial Park**, consecrated in 1992 by the Dalai Lama in memory of the early 19th-century Franciscan monk who became a Hungarian Bodhisattva (Buddhist

NORTHERN UPLANDS

saint). The stupa, with a revolving prayer wheel containing a tonne of sacred texts, has become something of a local tourist attraction. A Budapest-based Buddhist society (Karma Ratna Dargye Ling; ☎ 1-160 8847) runs a gift shop and snack bar (complete with non-vegetarian pizza) here and organises retreats and meditation courses. The train between Hatvan and Salgótarján stops in Tar.

Mátra Hills

The Mátra Hills, which boast Hungary's highest peaks (Kékes at 1014m and Galyatető at 964m), are the most developed and easily accessible of all the hills in the Northern Uplands. Indeed, at only 80 km from the capital, the region is very popular with Budapesters looking for fresh air. With all the accommodation and recreational options – from hiking and mushrooming in the autumn to hunting and skiing in winter – there's enough here to satisfy all tastes.

The Mátra Hills can be reached from other cities like Eger and Pászto, but Gyöngyös is its centre in every sense. It is also the capital of the Gyöngyös-Visonta wine-growing region, noted for its whites. While its rieslings, Leányka and sweet muscatel have all been praised, the Mátra's great contribution to the world of wine is Hárslevelű, a greenish-tinted white wine that is spicy and slightly sweet at the same time.

GYÖNGYÖS
• *pop 37,000*
• *area code* ☎ 37

A colourful small city at the base of the Mátra Hills, Gyöngyös (from the Hungarian word for 'pearl') has been an important trading centre since Turkish times and later became known for its textiles. Today, people come here to see the city's churches (the largest Gothic church in Hungary is here), visit its rich medieval library or to have a glass or two of wine and then head for the hills.

Orientation & Information
The bus station is on Koháry út, a 10-minute walk east of Fő tér, the main square. The main train station is on Vasút utca, near the southern end of Kossuth Lajos utca. Előre station, from where the narrow-gauge trains depart (see the Activities section), is at the start of Dobó István utca.

Egertourist (☎ 311 565) at Hanisz Imre tér 2 is open from 8.30 am to 5 pm on weekdays. Ibusz (☎ 311 861) at Kossuth Lajos utca 6 is open 8 am to at 4 pm. In summer Ibusz stays open to 6 pm on weekdays and to noon on Saturday.

You'll find a large OTP bank branch on Hanisz Imre tér near Egertourist; there's a Budapest bank at the southern end of Fő tér. The main post office is on the corner of Mátyás király utca and Páter Kis Szaléz utca north of the cultural centre.

Things to See
The **Mátra Museum** is housed in an old manor house in Orczy Garden that was once owned by a baron of that name. It's at Kossuth Lajos utca 40, east of Fő tér. The museum contains exhibits on the history of Gyöngyös, with much emphasis on Benevár, a 14th-century castle north-east of Mátrafüred and now in ruins, and the natural history of the Mátra region, including a gigantic reassembled mammoth. City lore has it that the wrought-iron railings enclosing the garden were made from gun barrels taken during the Napoleonic Wars.

St Bartholomew's Church is on the east side of Hanisz Imre tér, just a few blocks down Kossuth Lajos utca, a colourful street of pastel 19th-century houses. The church was built in the 14th century and is the largest Gothic one in Hungary. You'd hardly know it, though, with all the baroque work (including a curious upper-storey gallery inside) that was carried out 400 years later. The attractive little baroque building behind the church was once a **Jesuit school** (1752) and now serves as a music academy.

The **Franciscan church** on Barátok tere was built around the same time as St Bartholomew's, but it too has undergone

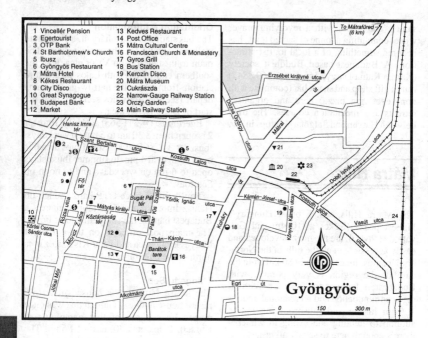

1	Vincellér Pension
2	Egertourist
3	OTP Bank
4	St Bartholomew's Church
5	Ibusz
6	Gyöngyös Restaurant
7	Mátra Hotel
8	Kékes Restaurant
9	City Disco
10	Great Synagogue
11	Budapest Bank
12	Market
13	Kedves Restaurant
14	Post Office
15	Mátra Cultural Centre
16	Franciscan Church & Monastery
17	Gyros Grill
18	Bus Station
19	Kerozin Disco
20	Mátra Museum
21	Cukrászda
22	Narrow-Gauge Railway Station
23	Orczy Garden
24	Main Railway Station

some major changes, with the frescoes and baroque tower added in the 18th century. The church's most celebrated occupant – well, second most to believers – is János 'the Blind' Bottyán, a heroic commander who served under Ferenc Rákóczi during the Independence War. The former monastery (1730), which is attached to the church, contains the **Széchenyi Memorial Library**, the only Hungarian historical collection to have weathered the Turkish occupation intact. Among its 16,000 volumes (you'll only get to see a handful of theological tomes) are 217 incunabula, some of the most valuable in the nation. The library is open from 9 am to 5 pm (closed Thursday and Sunday) and on Saturday till noon.

Gyöngyös was home to a relatively large Jewish community from the 15th century to WWII, and two splendid **synagogues** bear witness to that. The older of the two, a neo-classical monument built in 1816, is north of Vármegye tér. The renovated **Great Syn-agogue**, designed by Lipót Baumhorn in 1930, two decades after he completed his masterpiece in Szeged, is now a department store on the corner of Gárdonyi Géza utca and Kőrösi Csoma Sándor utca. There's a large **market** on Köztársaság tér south-west of Fő tér.

Activities

Two narrow-gauge trains depart from Előre station just beyond the Mátra Museum. One heads north-east for Mátrafüred, seven km away and the nicest way of entering the Mátra Hills. The other goes to Lajosháza, 11 km north of Gyöngyös. The latter offers no real destination, except a place to begin hiking – perhaps east along the Nagy Völgy (Big Valley) past a series of water catchments or north as far as Galyatető, Hungary's second-highest 'peak'.

The train schedules vary tremendously depending on the time of the year and day of the week and, though the timetables are

NORTHERN UPLANDS

prominently displayed, you can telephone for information on ☎ 312 453. Be advised that the Lajosháza train runs only on Saturday and holidays from May to September (maximum six trains a day) with extra ones on Wednesday and Friday from mid-June to August. Up to 10 trains daily make runs to Mátrafüred from April to October. During the rest of the year, count on about six trains on weekdays and up to nine on Saturday.

Places to Stay

The closest *camping ground* is at Sástó, three km north of Mátrafüred (see that section). In Gyöngyös, both Egertourist and Ibusz can book you a *private room* for about 800 Ft per person.

The 15-room *Vincellér* (☎ 311 691) at Erzsébet királyné út 22 is an attractive though rather expensive pension with singles/doubles for 3600/4600 Ft. The central *Mátra* (☎ 313 063), just off Fő tér at Mátyás király utca 2, is the city's only hotel and is at last getting a much needed face-lift. Its 40 rooms, all with shower or bath, cost 3000 to 4000 Ft for a single, or 4300 to 6000 Ft for a double, depending on the season.

Places to Eat

For a quick bite near the bus station, cross Koháry út to No 9 and the *Gyros Grill*. Another inexpensive place is the *Kedves* at Széchenyi utca 9 near the market.

The pub-restaurant at the *Mátra* hotel is one of the most popular places in town for lunch. Try one of the csülök dishes (trotters – and a lot better than they sound). Two other popular choices are the *Gyöngyös* restaurant at Bugát Pál tér 2 and the *Kékes* at Fő tér 7. The latter has a few vegetarian dishes.

The restaurant at the *Vincellér* pension remains very popular with locals. It's surprisingly inexpensive, and the service is friendly.

The *cukrászda* (cake shop) at the start of Mátrai út has excellent cakes and ice cream.

Entertainment

The *Mátra Cultural Centre* (☎ 312 282), a 'Finnish functionalist-style building', they say, with huge stained-glass windows at Barátok tere 3, is where Gyöngyös entertains itself. The big event is the Mátra Vintage Festival in late September.

There are several popular clubs within easy striking distance of the centre, including *Kerozin*, a 'techno-rave' venue at Kármán József utca 1, south of the Mátra Museum, and *City Disco* at Fő tér 9, popular at the weekend.

Getting There & Away

Bus Bus services are very good to/from Gyöngyös: you needn't wait for more than 20 minutes for buses to Budapest, Eger, Mátrafüred and Mátraháza. There are about a dozen buses a day to destinations farther into the Mátra like Parád and Parádfürdő, six buses to Recsk and about three to Sirok. You can also catch buses to Jászberény (12 daily), Hatvan (10), Szolnok (six), Salgótarján (five), Kecskemét (five), Miskolc (three) and Hajdúszoboszló and Tiszafüred (two each).

Train It's not so convenient to travel to/from Gyöngyös by train. The city is on a dead-end spur some 13 km from the main Budapest-Miskolc line (stop: Vámosgyörk). A dozen trains a day connect the city with Vámosgyörk.

GYÖNGYÖS TO EGER

Route No 24 wends its way through the Mátra Hills north of Gyöngyös and then cuts eastward; if you're under your own steam, it's a great way to get to Eger (60 km away) via some of the prettiest scenery in the Northern Uplands. Buses to Mátrafüred, Mátraháza, Parád and Parádfürdő are frequent (less so to Recsk and Sirok), but the best approach is by the narrow-gauge train that terminates in Mátrafüred.

Mátrafüred

• *area code* ☎ 37

Mátrafüred is a pleasant little resort at a height of 340m. Though there is a small **Palóc Collection** on exhibit near the centre at Hegyalja út 21, the main reason for coming is the many easy walks in the area.

Just arm yourself with a copy of Cartographia's 1:40,000 *A Mátra* map (No 14) before setting out.

From Mátrafüred, a trail leading northeast passes the ruins of **Benevár Castle** after half an hour or so and continues up to **Mt Kékes**, 12 km farther on. Another trail heading north-west hits the main road at Sástó, three km away, and then carries on up through the hills for another six km to Mátraháza.

Places to Stay & Eat The main accommodation in Mátrafüred is at the *Avar* (☎ 320 400), a 114-room monstrosity close to the narrow-gauge train station up sloping Parádi utca. It has a heated indoor swimming pool, sauna and a gym and rents bicycles. Singles are DM50 to DM65 and doubles DM60 to DM80, depending on the season and whether you're in a 'new' (renovated) or old room. At Béke utca 7, a former trade-union holiday complex of several buildings now called the *Hegyalja* hotel (☎ 320 027) has doubles with bath from 2270 to 3270 Ft, depending on the season and which building you're staying in. There are plenty of *food stalls* and the like opposite the train station; the *Benevár* next to the Avar hotel at Parádi utca 13 is an attractive csárda open till 11 pm.

Sástó
• *area code* ☎ 37

Sástó Camping (☎ 374 025) at Sástó is the highest camping ground in Hungary (520m) and certainly one of the most attractive. Centred around a small lake with rowing boats, fishing and a 54m-high lookout tower, the campsite complex (open from late April to mid-October) offers a wide range of accommodation – from 2nd-class bungalows for two/three people (1000/1500 Ft) and a double without bath in the 28-room motel (1500 Ft) to a cottage on the lake with bath, fridge and TV (3100 Ft). *Lángos stands* abound, and there is a *restaurant* and small *grocery shop*.

Mátraháza
• *area code* ☎ 37

Mátraháza, with 'Kékestető', the country's

centre for winter sport nearby, is built on a slight incline 715m above sea level and about five km from Sástó. This is an attractive spot to base yourself for short walks in the immediate area or more adventurous hiking farther afield.

Along the road to Mátraháza, you'll pass two big resort hotels originally built to attract foreigners. The 98-room *Bérc* hotel (☎ 374 102) has a large indoor swimming pool, health facilities, 10-pin bowling, tennis courts and bicycles for rent. Doubles with bath are 3100 to 3500 Ft. Make sure you get a 3rd-floor room with a balcony looking out onto the Kékes Hills. The more attractive *Ózon* (☎ 374 004), with 57 rooms (many with balconies) in a quiet park, is a relatively new place with all the mod cons. Singles are 3450 to 4100 Ft and doubles are 4900 to 5700 Ft.

In Mátraháza village, the old *Pagoda* (☎ 374 013) has dozens of differently styled rooms in four buildings spread out over a large garden. Prices vary, but expect to pay 2100/2900 Ft for singles/doubles with bath. Some 14 small rooms, with washbasin only, at the top of building B are 750 Ft per person. The *Sport* restaurant in building A is the town's restaurant.

Near the Pagoda, you'll see the end of a ski trail that runs down from Kékestető and Mt Kékes. In the absence of a lift, skiers wanting another go hop on the bus, which runs continuously up the mountain. The nine-storey **TV tower** is open to viewseekers; the old tower in front of it now houses the 18-room *Hegycsúcs* hotel (☎ 367 086) with singles/doubles for 1600/3200 Ft. You won't get any higher in Hungary than this. The 14-room *Édosz* inn (☎ 367 044) down the road toward Mátraháza has much more basic accommodation available at half the price.

Parádsasvár
• *area code* ☎ 36

The road divides about three km from Mátraháza, heading north-west to Mt Galyatető and north to Parádsasvár, where Hungary's most effective – and smelliest – *gyógyvíz* (medicinal water) is bottled. Stop for a glass if you can stand the stench of this sulfuric brew. The glass factory nearby produces high-quality Parád crystal; prices are slightly cheaper at the outlet here than in Budapest. There's a pension, called the *Vendégház 11/a* (☎ 364 148), up the hill from the factory at Kossuth Lajos utca 11/a with doubles from about 2500 Ft.

Parád & Parádfürdő

Parád and Parádfürdő run into each other and now almost make up one long town. You can't miss the **Coach Museum**, housed in the red marble Cifra stables of Count Károlyi at Kossuth Lajos utca 217 and one of the most interesting small museums in Hungary. (For the record, the word 'coach' comes from the name of the Western Transdanubian village of Kocs, where these lighter horse-drawn vehicles were first used in place of the more cumbersome wagons.) Inspect the interiors of the diplomatic and state coaches, which are richly decorated with silk brocade; the closed coach used by 19th-century philanderers on the go; and the bridles containing as much as five kg of silver. The museum is open 9 am to 5 pm between April and September and 10 am to 4 pm the rest of the year.

Palóc Days is a week-long folk and cultural festival held in Parád in early July.

Recsk & Sirok

The road continues on through Recsk, a place that lives on in infamy – like the prisons in Vác or on Fő utca in Budapest's District II – as the site of Hungary's most notorious forced-labour camp in the early days of Communism. Make a beeline for Sirok, effectively the last town in the Mátra Hills. The ruins of an early 14th-century castle perched on a mountain top provide superb views of the Mátra and Bükk hills and the mountains of Slovakia.

Bükk Hills

The Bükk (or 'beech', after the predominant tree species growing here) Hills are a green

lung buffering Eger and the industrial city of Miskolc. Although much of the area has been exploited for its ore for the ironworks of Miskolc and other towns of the scarred Sajó Valley to the east, a large tract – some 38,800 hectares – is now a national park. The Bükk teems with wildlife, and there are almost 500 caves in the mountains. The Bükk National Park Directorate (☎ 411 581) is in Eger at Sánc utca 6.

The Bükk Plateau, a limestone area rising to heights of between 800 and 900m, is particularly attractive. Following the winding road by car or bike (permission for this may be required, so ask at Tourinform or Egertourist in Eger) or a series of trails on foot from Szilvásvárad down to Lillafüred or Miskolc (springboards for the eastern Bükk) is an unforgettable experience. If you're lucky, you may come across a herd of the area's most celebrated inhabitants, the Lipizzaner horses.

EGER

- *pop 66,000*
- *area code ☎ 36*

Everyone loves Eger, and it's immediately apparent why: beautifully preserved baroque architecture gives the town a relaxed, almost Mediterranean feel; it is the home of the celebrated Egri Bikavér (Eger bull's blood) wine known the world over; and it is flanked by two of the Northern Uplands' most beautiful ranges of hills. Hungarians themselves visit Eger for those reasons and more, for it was here that their forebears fended off the Turks for the first time during the 170 years of occupation (aside).

The Turks came back to Eger in 1596 – more than four decades after their defeat – and this time succeeded in capturing the city, turning it into a provincial capital and erecting several mosques and other buildings until they were driven out at the end of the 17th century. All that remains of this architectural legacy – in fact, the Ottomans' northernmost in Europe – is a lonely little minaret, which still points its long, bony finger towards the heavens in indignation.

Eger played a central role in Ferenc

NORTHERN UPLANDS

The Siege of Eger

The story of the siege of Eger Castle is the stuff of legend. Under the command of István Dobó, 2000 Hungarian soldiers held out against more than 100,000 Turks for a month in 1552. As every Hungarian kid in short trousers can tell you, the women of Eger played a crucial role in the battle, pouring boiling oil and pitch on the invaders from the ramparts. Also significant was Eger wine, if we're to believe the tale. Dobó, it seems, sustained his soldiers with the vintage. When they fought on with increased vigour – and red-stained beards – rumours began to circulate among the Turks that the defenders were gaining strength by drinking the blood of bulls. Egri Bikavér was born.

Géza Gárdonyi's *Eclipse of the Crescent Moon* (1901), which describes the siege and is required reading in some schools, can be found in bookshops throughout Hungary. ∎

Rákóczi II's attempt to overthrow the Habsburgs early in the 18th century, and it was then that a large part of the castle was razed by the Austrians. Having enjoyed the status of an episcopal see since the time of King Stephen, Eger flourished in the 18th and 19th century, when the city acquired most of its wonderful baroque architecture.

Eger lies in the Eger Valley between the Bükk and Mátra hills. While it is not as convenient a springboard for either as Miskolc and Gyöngyös are, both ranges are accessible from here via Szilvásvárad – yet another reason for visiting this pretty, friendly area.

Eger (Erlau in German) is the perfect walking city: there's something interesting at every turn, and much of the city centre – with its 175 protected buildings and monuments – is closed to traffic.

Orientation

The centre of Eger and Széchenyi István utca, the main drag, are just a few minutes on foot to the east from the circular, 1960s-style bus station on Barkóczy utca. From the main train station on Vasút utca, walk north along Deák Ferenc utca. The Egervár train station, which serves Szilvásvárad and other points north, is a five-minute walk north of the castle.

Information

Tourinform (☎ 321 897), Dobó István tér 2, can supply all the brochures you care to carry and several of the staff speak fluent English. Tourinform is open weekdays from 9 am to 5 pm (6 pm in summer) and on Saturday to 2 pm. It can provide you with a pamphlet outlining bicycle tours in the Bükk National Park.

Egertourist (☎ 411 724) at Bajcsy-Zsilinszky utca 9 has accommodation information as does Cooptourist (☎ 311 998) at Dobó István tér 3. Express (☎ 427 865), good for hostel accommodation, is at Széchenyi utca 28. Most of these offices stay open till 4 or 5 pm on weekdays and keep Saturday hours till noon.

There's an OTP bank branch at Széchenyi utca 2, and the main post office is at No 22 of the same street. The bookshop at Széchenyi utca 12-14 has a decent selection of maps of the city and the Bükk and Mátra hills.

Eger Castle

The best overview of the city can be had by climbing up the cobblestone lane from Dózsa György tér to Eger Castle, erected in the 13th century after the Mongol invasion. It's open every day from 9 am to 5 pm except Monday, though you can visit the castle **casemates** seven days a week. Much of the castle is of modern construction, but you can still see the foundations of 12th-century **St John's Cathedral**, which was destroyed by the Turks.

The **István Dobó Museum** inside the 14th-century Bishop's Palace has models of how the cathedral looked in its prime, as well as furnishings like tapestries and porcelain. On the ground floor, a statue of Dobó takes pride of place in the **Heroes' Hall**. The 19th-century building on the north-west side of the courtyard houses an **Eger Art Gallery**, with portraits of leading contemporary Hungarians and several works by Mihály Munkácsy. Tours to the casemates (included

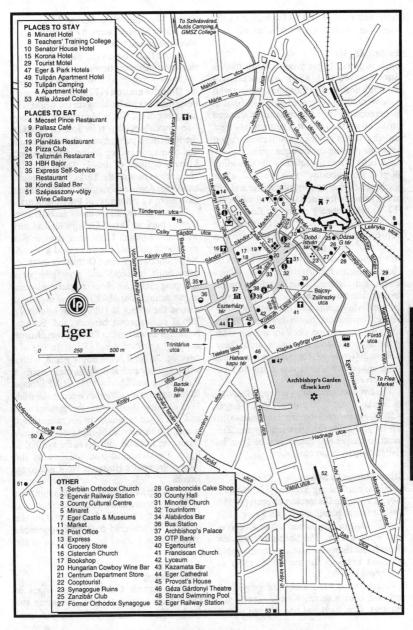

PLACES TO STAY
6 Minaret Hotel
8 Teachers' Training College
10 Senator House Hotel
15 Korona Hotel
29 Tourist Motel
47 Eger & Park Hotels
49 Tulipán Apartment Hotel
50 Tulipán Camping
   & Apartment Hotel
53 Attila József College

PLACES TO EAT
4 Mecset Pince Restaurant
9 Pallasz Café
18 Gyros
19 Planétás Restaurant
24 Pizza Club
26 Talizmán Restaurant
33 HBH Bajor
35 Express Self-Service
   Restaurant
38 Kondi Salad Bar
51 Szépasszony-völgy
   Wine Cellars

To Szilvásvárad,
Autós Camping &
GMSZ College

Malom utca

Mária utca

Jankovics Mihály utca

Bérc utca

Dárnay utca

Vitkovics Mihály utca

Kossuth Károly utca

Eger

Széchenyi István

Stream

Markhot F.

Dobó István utca

Leányka utca

Tünderpart utca

Csíky Sándor utca

Barkóczy

Sándor

Sándor

Mecset utca

Dobó
István tér

Dózsa
G tér

Almagyar utca

Magyar utca

Mercey István u.

Károly utca

Vörösmarty Mihály utca

Foglár

Érsek utca

Eszterházy
tér

Bajcsy-
Zsilinszky
utca

Kossuth Lajos utca

Fürdő
utca

Eger

0   250   500 m

Törvényház utca

Trinitárius
utca

Telekessy István

Klapka György utca

To Flea
Market

Hatvani
kapu tér

Hatvani

utca

Bartók
Béla
tér

**Archbishop's Garden
(Érsek kert)**

Sztoványi

Király

Kossuth István utca

Deák Ferenc utca

Eger Stream

Csatakály

Szépasszony-völgy

Hadnagy utca

Árpád

utca

Vasút utca

Ady Endre utca

Mocsáry Lajos utca

Mátyás király út

Sas utca

OTHER
1 Serbian Orthodox Church
2 Egervár Railway Station
3 County Cultural Centre
5 Minaret
7 Eger Castle & Museums
11 Market
12 Post Office
13 Express
14 Grocery Store
16 Cistercian Church
17 Bookshop
20 Hungarian Cowboy Wine Bar
21 Centrum Department Store
22 Cooptourist
23 Synagogue Ruins
25 Zanzibár Club
27 Former Orthodox Synagogue
28 Garabonciás Cake Shop
30 County Hall
31 Minorite Church
32 Tourinform
34 Alabárdos Bar
36 Bus Station
37 Archbishop's Palace
39 OTP Bank
40 Egertourist
41 Franciscan Church
42 Lyceum
43 Kazamata Bar
44 Eger Cathedral
45 Provost's House
46 Géza Gárdonyi Theatre
48 Strand Swimming Pool
52 Eger Railway Station

NORTHERN UPLANDS

in the entry fee of 160/80 Ft) built after the siege leave from outside the ticket office.

Eszterházy tér

Back in town, begin your walking tour at **Eger Cathedral** (1836), a neoclassical monolith designed by the same architect who later worked on the even larger cathedral at Esztergom. Despite the cathedral's size and ornate altars, the interior is surprisingly light and airy. If you're lucky, you'll chance upon someone playing the baroque organ.

Directly across the square is the sprawling Zopf-style **Lyceum**, now named after Károly Eszterházy (a bishop of Eger and one of the school's founders). The ceiling fresco (1778) in the **library** on the 1st floor of the south wing is a *trompe l'oeil* masterpiece depicting the Counter-Reformation's Council of Trent (1545-63) and a lightning bolt setting heretical writings ablaze. The library contains hundreds of priceless manuscripts and codices, some of which are on display. The **observatory** on the 6th floor of the east wing contains 18th-century astronomical equipment; climb three more floors up to the observation deck for a great view of the city and surrounding vineyards. There is also a 200-year-old camera obscura, a kind of periscope that allows you to spy on Eger unobserved.

The Lyceum's museums are open Tuesday to Sunday from 9.30 am to 1 pm. Tickets (150/50 Ft) are available from the desk to the left as you enter from Eszterházy tér. The frescoed chapel and ceremonial hall can be visited only by appointment.

Other Things to See

Continue north along Széchenyi István utca to No 15 and the **Cistercian church** (1743). The theatrical baroque altar sculpture of St Francis Borgia in gilt and white stucco is well worth a look. The **Serbian Orthodox church** and its enormous iconostasis of gold leaf and braid is farther north; enter at Széchenyi utca 59.

Retrace your steps along Széchenyi utca and east onto Knézich Károly utca to the **minaret**, 40m high and now topped with a cross. Non-claustrophobes will brave the 100 narrow spiral steps to reach the top. Mecset utca south-west of the minaret leads to central Dobó István tér, site of the town's market in medieval times.

On the southern side of the square stands the **Minorite church** (1773), one of the most beautiful baroque buildings in the world. The altarpiece of the Virgin Mary and St Anthony (the church's patron) is by Johann Kracker, the Bohemian painter who also did the fire-and-brimstone ceiling fresco in the Lyceum library. Statues of István Dobó and the Hungarians routing the Turks fill the square, and in the former monastery at Dobó István tér 6 there's a collection of **Palóc folk art**.

From Dobó István tér, cross the little Eger Stream back to Dózsa György tér and turn west onto Kossuth Lajos utca, another fine street with dozens of architectural gems. At No 17 stands the former **Orthodox synagogue**, built in 1893 and now part of a shopping mall. (An older neoclassical synagogue dating from 1845 and now in ruins is around the corner at Hibay Károly utca 7.) You'll pass several baroque and Eclectic buildings as well as the **Franciscan church** at No 14, completed in 1755 on the site of a mosque. At No 9 is the **county hall**, with a wrought-iron grid above the main door of Faith, Hope and Charity by Henrik Fazola, a Rhinelander who settled in Eger in the mid-18th century. Walk down the passageway, and you'll see two more of his magnificent works: baroque wrought-iron gates that have taken over from the minaret as the symbol of Eger. The wrought-iron balcony at the rococo **Provost's House** at No 4 is also by Fazola.

Eger's big **flea market** is to the south-east of the city centre at the end of Kertész utca. Just get off the bus (No 5) when you see the crowds. The covered **fruit and vegetable market** is on Katona István tér, east of the post office.

Wine Tasting

You can sample Eger's famous wines at many places around town, including the *Borkóstoló a Magyar Csikóshoz* – a local wine bar on Dobó István tér with a mouthful of a name that just means 'Wine Tasting at the Sign of the Hungarian Cowboy'. But why bother drinking here when you can do the same in the working cellars of the evocatively named **Valley of the Beautiful Women** (Szépasszony-völgy) so close by? The best time to visit the valley is the late afternoon on a warm day.

From behind the cathedral, walk south on Trinitárius utca to Bartók Béla tér and continue west along Király utca to Szépasszony-völgy utca. Veer to the left as you descend the hill past the camping ground and into the valley, and you'll see dozens of cellars – some with musicians, some with outside tables, others locked up tight as their owners party elsewhere. This is the place to sample the famous bull's blood (especially the GIA label) – the only red wine produced in Eger – or any of the whites: Leányka, Olaszrizling (particularly the Thummerer variety) and Tramini.

The choice of wine cellars can be a bit daunting, so take the following advice. If you want to meet South Africans, head for No 16. For schmalzy Gypsy music, No 38 is the one. But if you're interested in good wine, visit cellars 5, 13 and 23. Be careful though; those one-dl glasses (20 Ft) go down easily. If you need a taxi, the fare back to Dobó István tér will be about 300 Ft. Hours are erratic, but a few cellars are sure to be open till the early evening.

Other Activities

You can unwind in the Archbishop's Garden (Érsek kert), once the private reserve of papal princes. It has open-air and covered swimming pools (open from 8.30 am to 7 pm) as well as thermal baths dating from Turkish times. Enter from Fürdő utca off Petőfi tér, or from Hadnagy utca 3.

Farther afield, the artificial lake at Ostoros, about five km south-east of Eger, is a popular place to cool off on a hot summer's day. Frequent buses to Novaj will drop you off.

Bicycles can be rented from Mountain Bike Rentals (mobile ☎ 60-352 695) at Sólyom utca 28, or from Autós Camping (see Accommodation). Horse-riding enthusiasts should head for the Egedhegy Horse Farm (☎ 312 804) in Vécsey-völgy, north-east of the centre. The bus to Noszvaj (*not* Novaj) goes past the farm.

Organised Tours

Tours of Eger lasting about three hours leave from outside the Eger hotel, Szálloda utca 1-3, on Tuesday and Thursday at 10 am from early June to early October. The cost is 1100 Ft per person. For more information, ring ☎ 316 015 or contact Tourinform.

Special Events

Annual events include the Baroque Weeks in July, Eger Vintage Days in mid-September and the Lipizzaner Horse Festival held in both Eger and Szilvásvárad in early September.

Places to Stay

Camping *Tulipán Camping* (☎ 410 580), Szépasszony-völgy utca 7 (at the entrance to the Valley of the Beautiful Women), has two-bed caravans (DM20) and four-bed bungalows (DM30) with shared bath, as well as luxurious five-bed bungalows with private bath, kitchen and TV (DM60). Camping costs 800 Ft for two people. This site can get crowded, but it's an obvious first choice for those on foot as both the train station and the centre of town are less than a km away. (The little valley's wine cellars are within easy stumbling distance.) Campers can use the pool at the new Tulipán Apartment hotel (see Hotels) on the hill above the camping ground. The camping ground is open from April to September, and there's a snack bar on the premises.

Eger's other camping ground, *Autós Camping* (☎ 410 558) at Rákóczi út 79, four km north of Eger, is only of interest to people with cars. It also has a 40-room motel (DM19.50 per double) and 16 bungalows for DM20. Autós Camping is open from mid-April to mid-October.

Hostels In July and August, the *Gizella*

Berzeviczy Teachers' Training College (☎ 412 066) at Leányka utca 2 just above the castle has two and four-bed dormitory rooms with washbasins from 600 Ft per person and doubles with showers for 1800 Ft. Ask Express about other summer hostels including the *GMSZ College* (☎ 311 211) at Rákóczi út 2 and the *Attila József College* (☎ 310 259) at Mátyás király út 62.

Private Rooms Egertourist can organise private rooms for 1000 Ft per person or flats from 2000 Ft. Villa Tours (☎ 417 803) on Fellner utca near the Lyceum also has private rooms. If you arrive after the tourist offices are closed, try for a room at Almagyar utca 7 or No 8; along Mekcsey István utca south of the castle; or on Knézich Károly utca near the minaret.

Hotels The cheapest place in town is the rundown *Tourist* (☎ 429 014) at Mekcsey István utca 2, a county-run 'motel' with 48 rooms in three buildings (request a room in building C), which is about five minutes south of the castle. It has singles/doubles with shared bath for 1100/1700 Ft and doubles with private bath for 2800 Ft.

The *Korona* (☎ 313 670) with its entrance at Tündérpart utca 5, a quiet side street off Csíky Sándor utca, has 41 doubles from 3000 to 5000 Ft, depending on the season. It also has an excellent wine-cellar restaurant. The 38-room *Minaret* (☎ 410 020) at Knézich Károly utca 4 is a family-run hotel offering singles/doubles with shower for DM50/60.

The new *Tulipán Apartment* hotel (☎ 410 580) above the camping ground in Szépasszony-völgy has self-catering rooms for 3000 to 5000 Ft, depending on the size and the amenities.

If you want to splurge on accommodation in Hungary, save it for Eger and choose the *Senator House* (☎ 320 466), a delightful 18th-century inn with 11 rooms in the centre of Dobó István tér that many consider to be the best small hotel in provincial Hungary. Singles are DM40 to DM70 and doubles are DM60 to DM90, depending on the season.

The old-world *Park* (☎ 413 233) and its ugly modern sister next door, the *Eger* at Klapka György utca 3 (☎ same), have a total of 204 rooms, but make sure you get one of the Park's three dozen – preferably looking out on to the Archbishop's Garden. The hotels have all the facilities you'd expect at three-star prices: swimming pool, sauna, gym, bowling alley and three restaurants. At the Park, singles are DM61 to DM90 and doubles are DM79 to DM103. The Eger charges DM49 to DM72 for singles, DM63 to DM82 for doubles.

Places to Eat

Surprisingly, Eger is not overly endowed with restaurants, good or otherwise. The *Express*, at Pyrker tér 4 just north of the bus station, is a large self-service restaurant open till 8 pm. The *Planétás* at Zalár József utca 5-7 near Dobó István tér has good, reasonably priced food with lunches from only 200 Ft.

Two inexpensive places for a decent meal on Széchenyi utca are *Gyros* at No 10, with Greek salads and souvlakia, and the *Kondi* salad bar at No 2. The former is open late; the latter closes at 7 pm (4 pm on Saturday). For pizza, the *Pizza Club*, south of the castle at Fazolka Henrik utca 1, can be recommended.

The *HBH Bajor* at Bajcsy-Zsilinszky utca 19 serves reliable Hungarian-Germanic food in a bright and clean environment. The *Talizmán*, a wine-cellar restaurant at Kossuth Lajos utca 19, has become extremely touristy and is packed in summer with Germans and Austrians. Local people recommend the *Mecset Pince* near the Minaret hotel at Knézich Károly utca 8.

The *Fehérszarvas* beneath the Park hotel at Klapka György utca 3 is Eger's silver-service restaurant. But the Fehérszarvas (White Deer), with its game specialities and exposed kitchen, is really a place to enjoy in autumn and winter. In summer, dine at the open-air restaurant on the Park hotel's back terrace.

There are a couple of csárdas amidst the wine cellars (see Entertainment) in Szépasszony-völgy, including the vine-covered *Kulacs* and the more famous (and expensive) *Ködmön*.

For something sweet, try the *Garabonciás* cake shop across the street from the Talizmán restaurant at Kossuth Lajos utca 28. Another option is the *Pallasz* at Dobó István utca 20, a coffee shop in a small courtyard with a fountain.

There's a small *grocery store* at Széchenyi utca 38 open daily to 10 pm (to midnight on Friday and Saturday).

Entertainment
The *County Cultural Centre* on Knézich Károly utca across from the minaret, or the ticket office on Széchenyi utca 3, can tell you what concerts and plays are on in Eger. Venues are the *Géza Gárdonyi Theatre*, the *Lyceum*, and *Eger Cathedral*. From mid-May to mid-September there are organ concerts on Sunday at 12.45 pm in the cathedral.

Dobó István tér has wine bars and cafés with outside seating in summer, including the *Arany Oroszlán* at No 5 and the *Minorita* at No 7. *Alabárdos*, a pleasant bar at Érsek utca 7, stays open till midnight. Beneath the cathedral steps at Pyrker tér 3, a bizarre, cave-like place called the *Kazamata* offers pool, drinks and a disco till the small hours. Another popular place in town for a night out (presumably because it stays open till 4 am) is the *Pool* pub, quite a distance north of the city centre at Ráchegy utca 1-3. The *Zanzibár* on Dózsa György tér has go-go girls prancing around in G-strings.

Getting There & Away
Bus Bus services are good, with buses every 30 to 40 minutes to Felsőtárkány in the Bükk, Gyöngyös, Mezőkövesd, Noszvaj, Szilvásvárad and Bélapátfalva. Other destinations include: Békéscsaba (two buses daily), Budapest (12), Hatvan (eight), Kecskemét (three), Debrecen (three), Miskolc (10) and Szeged (two). Remember that the bus to Miskolc only goes through the Bükk via Felsőtárkány on Sunday at 7 am and 11.25

am. On other days it follows the boring E71 via Mezőkövesd.

Train Eger is on a minor railway linking Putnok and Füzesabony; you usually have to change at the latter for Budapest, Miskolc or Debrecen. There are up to five direct trains a day to and from Budapest-Keleti, though.

Getting Around
From the main train station, bus No 10, 11, 12 or 14 will drop you off at the bus station or town centre. For the flea market at the end of Kertész utca, take bus No 5.

You can order a taxi on ☎ 411 411 or ☎ 411 222.

AROUND EGER
Mezőkövesd
• *pop 18,300*
• *area code* ☎ *49*

Those interested in Hungarian peasant life and its traditions should make the easy day trip to Mezőkövesd, about 18 km south-east of Eger. Mezőkövesd is the centre of the Mátyó, a Magyar people famous for their fine embroidery and other folk art.

From the bus station in Mezőkövesd on Rákóczi utca, walk east along Mátyás király utca – Borsod Tourist (☎ 412 614) is at No 153 – to the **Mátyó Museum** in the cultural centre at Szent László tér 20. The displays explain the regional differences and historical development of Mátyó needlework: from white-on-white and blue-and-red roses to the metallic fringe that was banned in the early 1920s because the high cost was ruining some families. The Mátyó were not wealthy people; because most of their land was occupied by great estates, large numbers were compelled to sign up as seasonal labourers in the 19th and early 20th centuries. Across Szent László tér is the **Catholic church** with an overwrought romantic fresco of a Mátyó wedding (1961).

From Hősök tere to the west, enter any of the small streets running southward to find a completely different world: thatched and whitewashed cottages with old women outside stitching the distinctive Mátyó rose patterns. Interesting lanes *(köz)* to stroll along are Patkó köz, Kökény köz and Mogyoró köz, but the centre of activity is really Kis Jankó Bori utca, named after Hungary's own 'Grandma Moses' who lived and stitched her famous '100 roses' patterns here for almost 80 years. Bori's 200-year-old three-room cottage at No 24 is now a museum filled with needlework and brightly painted furniture. Other houses on the street that you can visit and watch the women at work are Nos 1, 12, 19 (the folk-art cooperative) and 32 – though the numbering system is a bit jumbled. Most of the work is for sale directly from the embroiderers, or you can buy it at the folk-art shop on the south-west corner of Szent László tér (open weekdays from 8 am to 4 pm).

With Eger so close, there's no point in staying overnight in Mezőkövesd. But if you miss your bus (unlikely – there are dozens every day) or you want to catch an early-morning train to Miskolc, check out the 10-room *Fáradt Vándor* (Tired Wanderer) pension (☎ 311 405) south-west of the bus station at Széchenyi utca 12, which has doubles with shower for 2200 Ft, or the similarly priced *Ádám* pension (☎ 431 100), south-east of the station at Nyárfa utca 1, which has five rooms in a converted farmhouse. For something to eat, try the *Vigadó* restaurant at Mátyás király utca 173 or the *Pizzeria Nero* south of Hősök tere at Eötvös utca 9.

SZILVÁSVÁRAD
• *pop 1800*
• *area code* ☎ 36

The western Bükk is most easily approached from Szilvásvárad, some 27 km north of Eger. The private domain of the profascist Count Palavicini (he razed an entire village in south-east Hungary in the 1920s when his tenants were acting up) until after WWII, Szilvásvárad is an easy day trip from Eger. It has the attraction of being an ideal base for hiking into the Szalajka Valley and the centre of horse breeding in Hungary, with some 250 prize Lipizzaners in local stables (see aside).

It is also the place to ride on one of Hungary's most delightful narrow-gauge trains.

Orientation & Information
Get off the train at the first of Szilvásvárad's two stations, Szilvásvárad-Szalajkavölgy, and follow Egri út north-east for about 10 minutes to the centre of town. The town's main station is about two km to the north. The bus from Eger will drop you off in the centre of town.

There are no tourist offices in Szilvásvárad, but those in Eger can provide you with whatever information you need as well as sell you Cartographia's 1:40,000 maps of the Bükk region: the Bükk Plateau (No 33), the northern section of the hills (No 29) and the southern part (No 30).

An OTP bank branch can be found at Egri út 30/a. The post office is a bit farther north at No 12.

Things to See & Do
Some people come to Szilvásvárad just to ride the **narrow-gauge railway** into the Szalajka Valley. The open-air, three-car train leaves seven times a day from May to September (nine times a day on weekends), with three departures daily in April and October (four at the weekend). The station is south of the open racecourse.

The little train chugs along for about five km, passing well-stocked trout tanks, streams and bubbling little waterfalls before reaching the terminus at **Szalajka-Fátyolvízesés.** You can either stay on the train for the return trip or walk back to Szilvásvárad for 1½ hours along well-trodden, shady paths, taking in the sights along the way. The open-air **Forest Museum** has some interesting exhibits, including a 16th-century water-powered saw and bellows once used by charcoal burners. It is open from April to October.

From Szalajka-Fátyolvízesés, you can walk for 15 minutes to **Istállóskő Cave**, where Stone Age pottery shards were discovered in 1912, or climb 958m **Mt Istállóskő**, the highest peak in the Bükk.

In Szilvásvárad, both the covered and the

The Magnificent Lipizzaners

Lipizzaners, the celebrated white horses bred originally for the imperial Spanish Riding School in Vienna under Habsburg rule, are considered to be the finest riding horses in the world – the *haute école* of dressage horses. And with all the trouble that's put into producing them, it's not surprising. They are very intelligent, sociable animals, quite robust and graceful.

Lipizzaners are bred for riding and show at Lipica in Slovenia; at Piber, north-east of Graz in Austria, for the Spanish Riding School; and in the US state of Illinois. The Lipizzaners at Szilvásvárad, on the other hand, are also raised as carriage horses. As a result they are bigger and stronger.

Breeding, as they say, is paramount. Some six families with 16 ancestors (including Spanish, Arabian and Berber breeds) can be traced back to the early 18th century, and their pedigrees read like those of medieval royalty. When you walk around the stables at the stud farm you'll see charts on each horse's stall with complicated figures, dates and names like 'Maestoso', 'Neapolitano' and 'Pluto'. It's all to do with the horse's lineage.

A fully mature Lipizzaner measures about 15 hands (that's about 153 cm) and weighs between 500 and 600 kg. They have long backs, short, thick necks, silky manes and expressive eyes. They live for 25 to 30 years and are particularly resistant to disease. But, like most horses, they are somewhat short-sighted (near-sighted) and they will nuzzle you out of curiosity if you approach them while they graze.

Surprisingly, Lipizzaners are not born white but grey, bay or even chestnut. The celebrated 'imperial white' does not come about until they are between five to 10 years old, when their hair loses its pigment. Think of it as part of the old nag's ageing process. Their skin remains grey, however, so when they are ridden hard and sweat, they become mottled and aren't so attractive. ∎

open **racecourses** put on Lipizzaner parades and coach races at weekends throughout the summer, but times are not fixed. You may find someone at the ticket office, or check the notice boards between the two race-courses.

If you're interested in doing some horse riding (from 1500 Ft per hour) or coach driving yourself, head for the **Lipizzaner Stud Farm** at the top of Fenyves utca. You'll learn more about these intelligent horses, and just how the stud ended up here after starting out in Lipica (now Slovenia) in the 16th century, by visiting the **Lipizzaner Horse-Breeding Exhibit** in an 18th-century stable, which you enter at Park utca 8.

The Protestant **Round Church** (1841), with its Doric columns and dramatic dome,

looks to some like a provincial attempt to duplicate Eger Cathedral. It's off Aradi vértanúk útja across the stream from Miskolci út. At Miskolci út 58, displays in a 17th-century farmhouse called **Orbán House** are devoted to the flora, fauna and geology of the Bükk National Park.

You can rent mountain bikes at the entrance to the park at Szalajka-Fatelep, an easy walk from the centre of Szilvásvárad. The charge is 100/550 Ft per hour/day.

Places to Stay

Hegyi Camping (☎ 355 207) at Egri út 36/a, a stone's throw from the Szilvásvárad-Szalajkavölgy train station, has small holiday houses for two for 2400 Ft. Camping

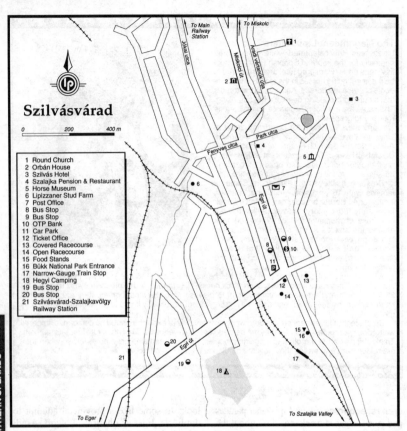

Szilvásvárad

0   200   400 m

1 Round Church
2 Orbán House
3 Szilvás Hotel
4 Szalajka Pension & Restaurant
5 Horse Museum
6 Lipizzaner Stud Farm
7 Post Office
8 Bus Stop
9 Bus Stop
10 OTP Bank
11 Car Park
12 Ticket Office
13 Covered Racecourse
14 Open Racecourse
15 Food Stands
16 Bükk National Park Entrance
17 Narrow-Gauge Train Stop
18 Hegyi Camping
19 Bus Stop
20 Bus Stop
21 Szilvásvárad-Szalajkavölgy
     Railway Station

costs 300 or 400 Ft per tent and 400 Ft per person.

The *Szalajka* (☎ 355 257), a 12-room pension at Egri út 2, charges 1500 to 1800 Ft for a double room with washbasin (showers in the hallway). The 46-room *Szilvás* hotel (☎ 355 211), the former Palavicini mansion at Park utca 6, is the most interesting place to stay in town. Prices vary wildly from season to season and whether or not your room has a bath, a shower and/or a WC, but expect to pay from 2200 to 3400 Ft for a double. The hotel also has motel-style

accommodation in bungalows in the back for 2200 Ft.

Places to Eat

In summer, *food stalls* line the entrance to the park at Szalajka-Fatelep and also at the car park to the north. The restaurant at the *Szalajka* pension is one of the few sit-down eateries in town; it specialises in trout from the Szalajka Valley.

Getting There & Away

Buses to/from Eger are very frequent and,

though they stop at Mónosbél and Béla-pátfalva, they're faster than the train. Buses also go to Ózd (eight a day), Miskolc (two), Gyöngyös (two) and Putnok (three).

Seven trains a day link Eger with Szilvásvárad. If heading for Szilvásvárad from the centre of Eger, board the train at the Egervár station, north of the castle on Gárdonyi Géza utca. Most of these trains carry on to Putnok, from where you can enter Slovakia (via Bánréve) or head south-east for Miskolc.

AROUND SZILVÁSVÁRAD
Bélapátfalva
• *pop 3400*

On the train or bus to or from Szilvásvárad, you'll pass through this town which seems to stand out for no other reason than its giant (and ancient) cement factory that covers everything in fine white dust.

However, one of Hungary's most perfectly preserved Romanesque monuments is just a few minutes away: the **Bélháromkút Abbey Church**. Built by French Cistercian monks in 1232, it can be reached by walking east from the village centre for 1.5 km (follow the 'Apátság Múzeum' signs). Along the way you'll see another sign giving the address for the church key (*templom kulcsa*), which is at Rozsa utca 42 and available daily between 10 am and 4 pm. The church, built in the shape of a cross, is set in a peaceful dell just below Mt Bélkő. Don't miss the 19th-century painted **Calvary scene** nearby.

MISKOLC
• *pop 212,000*
• *area code ☎ 46*

Hungary's third-largest city – but running neck-and-neck with Debrecen for position No 2 – and traditionally its most important industrial centre, Miskolc is a difficult child to love. It is a sprawling, polluted metropolis ringed by refineries, cement factories and cardboard-quality housing blocks. A relatively wealthy mining and steel-making town and very 'red' under the old regime, Miskolc is now something of a dinosaur with few sights or attractions of its own.

Cistercian Monastery at Bélapátfalva

So why come to Miskolc? For one thing, its location at the foot of the Bükk Hills makes it an ideal place to start a trek or walk in the national park. The thermal waters of nearby Miskolctapolca are among the most effective in Hungary, and the western suburb of Diósgyőr boasts a well-preserved castle. And Miskolc proper is improving, with central Széchenyi István út now completely pedestrian and many buildings along the way getting a face-lift or at least a fresh coat of paint.

Orientation

Miskolc is a long, narrow city stretching east to west from the despoiled Sajó Valley to the foothills of the Bükk. The main drag, Széchenyi István út, is lined with some interesting old buildings; those around the so-called Dark Gate (Sötétkapu), an 18th-century vaulted passageway, are especially colourful. Almost everything of interest in central Miskolc is near or on this street.

The main train station (Tiszai pályaudvar) lies to the south-east on Kandó Kálmán tér, a 15-minute tram ride from the city centre. The bus station is on Búza tér, a short distance north-east of Széchenyi István út.

NORTHERN UPLANDS

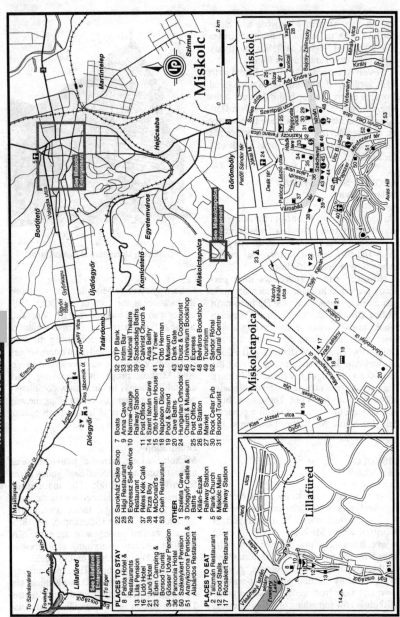

PLACES TO STAY
8 Palota Hotel &
   Restaurants
13 Lilla Pension
16 Lidó Hotel
21 Junó Hotel
23 Eden Camping &
   Borsod Tourist
34 Vasser Udvar Pension
36 Pannonia Hotel
50 Székelykert Pension
51 Aranykorona Pension &
   Alabárdos Restaurant

PLACES TO EAT
2 Tálizmán Restaurant
12 Food Stalls
17 Rózsakert Restaurant

22 Sárokház Cake Shop
28 Hági Restaurant
29 Expressz Self-Service
   Restaurant
37 Rétes Kék Café
38 Pizza Boy
44 McDonald's
53 Cseh Restaurant

OTHER
1 Szeleta Cave
3 Diósgyőr Castle &
   Baths
4 Killán-Észak
   Railway Station
5 Plank Church
6 Miskolc Main
   Railway Station

7 Boats
9 Anna Cave
10 Narrow-Gauge
   Railway Station
11 Post Office
14 Szent István Cave
15 Ottó Herman House
18 Napoclon Disco
19 Pool & Strand
20 Cave Baths
24 Hungarian Orthodox
   Church & Museum
25 Post Office
26 Bus Station
27 Market
30 Rock Cellar Pub
31 Borsod Tourist

32 OTP Bank
33 Intim Bar
35 National Theatre
39 Szabadság Baths
40 Calvinist Church &
   Aras Bélny
41 Ottó Power
42 Ottó Herman
   Museum
43 Dark Gate
45 Ibusz & Cooptourist
46 Universum Bookshop
47 Express
48 Belváros Bookshop
49 Tourinform
52 Sándor Rónai
   Cultural Centre

Information

Tourinform (☎ 348 921) has a hard-to-find office at Mindszent tér 1, but Borsod Tourist (☎ 350 666) at Széchenyi István út 35 is more central. Other agencies on Széchenyi István út include Cooptourist (☎ 328 812) at No 14; Ibusz (☎ 324 411) at No 18; and Express (☎ 349 400) at No 56. Most of the agencies are open from about 8 am to 4.30 pm on weekdays and to noon on Saturday.

OTP has a bank branch at Széchenyi István út 15. The main post office is on Hősök tere. The Belváros bookshop at Széchenyi István út 64 stocks some foreign-language publications and maps, including the Bükk and Zemplén maps from Cartographia. Universum at No 34 on the same street is another good bookshop.

Things to See

The Calvinist **Plank Church** (Deszka-templom), built in 1938, is a Transylvanian-style wooden church in the cemetery north of Petőfi tér; if you're not heading for North-East Hungary or into northern Romania, you should have a look at its interior. The key can be obtained from the parish office at Palóczy László utca 21.

The **Hungarian Orthodox church**, a splendid late-baroque structure at Deák tér 7, has an iconostasis 16m high with almost 100 icons. Make sure that the guide, who will escort you from the **Orthodox Museum** near the main gate, points out the Black Madonna of Kazan, presented to the church by Catherine the Great, and the jewel-encrusted Mt Athos Cross brought to Miskolc by Greek settlers late in the 18th century.

The **Ottó Herman Museum**, at Papszer 1 south of the centre, has one of Hungary's richest collections of Neolithic finds (many from the Bükk), a good ethnographical collection and a fine art exhibit. From here, take a stroll up leafy **Avas Hill**; the best approach is via Mélyvölgy utca, off Papszer, or Földes Ferenc utca, off Mindszent tér. Veer to the right along the narrow lane past some of the more than 800 wine cellars cut into the limestone. The **TV tower** at the top of the hill provides some superb views of the Bükk and,

on the rare clear day, even the Carpathians (if you can manage to overlook the ugly housing blocks and industrial wasteland to the west).

In a cemetery below the hill is the large Gothic **Avas Calvinist Church** (1410) with a painted wooden interior. The bell tower standing away from the church dates from the late 16th century. The key is in the parish office at Papszer 14.

A must-see is the four-towered **Diósgyőr Castle** in a suburb of that name west of the centre. Begun in the 13th century, the castle was heavily damaged early in the 18th century and was only restored – very badly in parts – in the 1950s.

There is a big **market** near Búza tér on Zsolcai kapu.

Activities

There's a horse-riding school at the Sárga Csikó hotel (☎ 368 471) in Görömböly, south of the city on route No 3 (Pesti út). Take bus No 4 from the bus station.

If you don't have time to visit Miskolctapolca's famous Cave Baths (see Around Miskolc), check out the turn-of-the-century Szabadság Baths and swimming pool at Erzsébet tér 4. It's open year-round till 6 or 8 pm every day except Monday, and till noon on Sunday. The Castle Baths on Vár utca in Diósgyőr are open till 6 pm in summer.

Special Events

An open-air theatre and music festival called Miskolc Summer is held in July and August at Diósgyőr Castle. The National Gypsy Gala takes place in June.

Places to Stay

In July and August, the *Bolyai College* (☎ 366 111) at the university in Egyetemváros has dormitory rooms available for 500 Ft. *Private rooms* for two or three people from Borsod Tourist or Ibusz cost 2400 Ft but will probably be in one of the housing projects ringing the city.

The *Gösser Udvar* pension (☎ 357 111), with seven rooms at Déryné utca 7, is not worth the 4000 Ft it charges for singles or doubles, but it's central and may be the only option in a town where accommodation is at a premium. Its restaurant and bar attract a young, noisy crowd.

The Gösser Udvar has a sister pension called the *Székelykert* (☎ 411 222) below Avas Hill at Földes Ferenc utca 4. The 10-room *Aranykorona* pension (☎ 358 400) nearby at Kis Avas Elsősor 19-20 is picturesquely situated among the Avas wine cellars, but it's a very dark walk home at night.

Miskolc's premier hotel is the *Pannonia* (☎ 329 811) at Kossuth Lajos utca 2. It has a restaurant, brasserie, the very popular Rori cake shop and 34 rooms, but is overpriced at 5300/9800 Ft for singles/doubles.

See Around Miskolc for accommodation options in the south-western suburb of Miskolctapolca.

Places to Eat

Among the cheapest places to eat at in Miskolc is the *Expressz* self-service restaurant at Széchenyi István út 107. There's a small pizzeria called *Pizza Boy* on Városház tér and a *McDonald's* can be found Széchenyi István út 10.

The terrace at the *Pannonia* hotel's pub-restaurant is a pleasant place for an evening meal in summer, but it can be pricey. A much cheaper place is the *Palotás* opposite at Kossuth Lajos utca 1, but it's gloomy and the attached wine bar attracts drunks. Near the bus station, the shocking-pink *Hági* restaurant at Zsolcai kapu 5 is an island in a sea of trashy pubs and pool halls. The *Cseh* restaurant in Science and Technology House on Corvin Ottó utca serves Czech and Slovakian dishes.

The *Alabárdos*, Kis Avas Elsősor 5, is supposed to be Miskolc's best restaurant, but it's really just a tarted-up Hungarian restaurant serving the same old things. Go instead to the restaurant at the *Székelykert* pension at Földes Ferenc utca 4, which has Transylvanian specialities, dishes rarely encountered at restaurants in Hungary.

In Diósgyőr, the *Talizmán* at Vár utca 14 can be recommended for its menu and pleas-

ant location on a chestnut-lined street just up from Diósgyőr Castle.

The *Rori* at the Pannonia hotel and the *Capri* at Széchenyi István út 16 are decent cake shops, but the best place for pastries in town is the *Rétes Kék* (Blue Strudel) café on Városház tér.

Entertainment

Theatre productions are staged at the *Sándor Rónai Cultural Centre* (☎ 342 485) at Mindszent tér 3. The *National Theatre* (1857), where the beloved 19th-century actress Róza Széppataki Déryné walked the floorboards, is at Déryné utca 1, while the Symphony Orchestra's *concert hall* is on Régiposta utca. Tickets for performances at both venues are available from the box office (☎ 329 600) at Kossuth Lajos utca 4. There are regular organ concerts at the baroque *Minorite church* (1734) on Hősök tere and at the *Avas Calvinist Church*.

The *Intim* at Déryné utca 4 is a popular bar among Miskolc students and a good place to meet people. The *Rock Cellar Pub* at Széchenyi utca 59 is another likely choice. There might be something going on at *Youth and Leisuretime House* (Ifjúsági és Szabadidő Ház) at Győrikapu 27.

Getting There & Away

Bus Some two dozen buses a day leave for Debrecen. If you're heading south, it is best to take the bus, though departures are infrequent: only one bus each day to Békéscsaba, Kecskemét and Gyula. There are about 10 buses a day to Eger, but if you're travelling on a Sunday, be sure to take the one at 6.25 am or 3.15 pm. These buses follow the scenic route through the Bükk Hills via Felsőtárkány, which is an excellent starting point for more mountain walks.

Train Miskolc is served by hourly trains from Budapest-Keleti, and some 15 depart for Nyíregyháza via Tokaj. Five of these trains carry on to Debrecen, but generally you'll have to change at Nyíregyháza. Eight trains leave Miskolc each day for Sárospatak and Sátoraljaújhely.

Daily international trains from Miskolc include those departing for Košice in Slovakia (six), Warsaw (one) and Kraków (two). There's one train daily to Romania (Oradea, Cluj-Napoca etc), but you'll have to change at Püspökladány. For Lvov, St Petersburg and Moscow, change at Nyíregyháza or Debrecen.

Getting Around
Tram Nos 1 and 2 begin at the train station and travel the length of the city, including along Széchenyi István út, before turning around in Diósgyőr. You can also reach Diósgyőr on the No 1 bus. To get to Miskolctapolca, board bus No 2 at Búza tér; bus Nos 12 and 22 are good for the university.

You can order a taxi by ringing ☎ 363 363 or ☎ 344 444.

AROUND MISKOLC
Miskolctapolca
• area code ☎ 46
The curative waters of the thermal spa in this south-western suburb, past the university about seven km from Miskolc's city centre, have been attracting bathers since the Middle Ages, though the gimmicky **Cave Baths**, with their 'mildly radioactive waters' and thrashing shower at the end, are relatively new arrivals (1959). The baths, at Pazár István sétány 1, are open every day from 9 am to 1 pm and 2 to 6 pm. The park strand in the centre of town has outside pools and a giant slide open in summer.

Miskolctapolca is Miskolc's recreational area (there are 20 tennis courts here), and there's a lot going on here in summer. Görömbölyi út, which flanks the strand, is lined with discos, pubs and small eateries (the *Napoleon* disco above the entrance to the strand on Aradi sétány is popular) that carry on till late, and there are more than a dozen hotels, pensions and tourist houses nearby. *Éden Camping* (☎ 368 917) at Károlyi Mihály utca 1 has bungalows accommodating four people for 4200 Ft. It's open from May to mid-October. Borsod Tourist (same ☎), which has an office at Éden Camping, can book you a *private*

room, though there are 'Zimmer frei' and 'szoba kiadó' signs everywhere here. The top hotel here is the rather pretentious 100-room *Junó* (☎ 364 133) at Csabai utca 2-4, a modern glass-and-concrete structure with tennis courts and a disco called the Bridge. Singles are DM61 to DM71 and doubles are DM68 to DM78, depending on the season.

The 54-room *Lidó* (☎ 369 800) at Kiss József utca 4 is bunker-like with doubles for half the price of the Juno. The *Rózsakert* restaurant on Aradi Sétáng is a decent place for a meal while the *Sarokház* at Thaly Kálmán utca 3 is good for cakes and ice cream.

Bus No 2 serves Miskolctapolca from Búza tér in Miskolc.

Lillafüred
• area code ☎ 46
Lillafüred, at 320m above sea level, lies at the junction of two valleys formed by the Garadna and Szinva streams 12 km west of Miskolc. Lillafüred has been a resort since the early part of this century and sights as such are few. But it is a pleasant break from Miskolc and the springboard for walks and hikes into the eastern Bükk Hills.

Some people travel to Lillafüred just to take the **narrow-gauge train** from Miskolc. It's one of the most enjoyable little train trips in Hungary and, as you loop through the forest, you can almost reach out and touch the beech and chestnut trees.

Caves There are three limestone caves in Lillafüred: **Anna Cave** near the Palota hotel; **Szent István Cave** about 500m up the mountain road leading to Eger; and **Szeleta Cave** above the village on the road to Miskolc. The first two can be visited with a guide from 9 am to 5 pm (closed Monday and open 9 am to 2 pm from mid-October to mid-April). Szent István, with its stalagmites, stalactites, sinkholes and large chambers, is the best. Just beyond the cave at Erzsébet sétány 33 lies the **Ottó Herman House**, where the noted archaeologist, ethnographer and naturalist (1835-1914) did his research.

Foundry Lake (Hámor-tó), named after the proto-blast furnace set up here by a German in the early 19th century to exploit the area's iron ore, offers fishing and boating (150 Ft per hour) on its jade-coloured water.

Hiking Trails for hiking into the Bükk Hills are well marked, but if you're planning anything more serious than an afternoon constitutional, be sure to have a copy of the northern Bükk map from Cartographia and carry extra water.

A number of beautiful walks can be undertaken from the terminuses of the two lines of the narrow-gauge train at **Garadna** and **Farkasgödör-Örvénykő**, but accommodation is sparse in these parts and hikers had better be prepared to camp rough if they miss the train. Keep an eye open for charcoal burners and, in autumn, wild mushrooms.

There are *holiday houses* in Szentlélek and Bánkút, west and south-west of Garadna, where you can spend the night before setting off for **Mt Bálvány** (956m). From the Bánkút there are a number of excellent walks south to **Nagy-mező** and east to **Nagy Csipkés** (869m).

Hollóstető, six km south of Lillafüred, is another good base for hikes and has a *camping ground* and the 10-room *Hollóstető* inn (☎ 390 163). About 45 minutes to the east is Bükkszentkereszt, another quiet resort with excellent walks and the 22-room *Bükk* inn (☎ 390 165). Bükkszentlászló is about 1½ hours to the north. From here you can catch a bus back to Miskolc.

Places to Stay & Eat Apart from the options mentioned in the Hiking section, there are a few possibilities in Lillafüred itself. The town is dominated by the *Palota* (☎ 331 411), an odd mock-Gothic structure that's now a hotel again after a 40-year stint as a trade-union holiday home. Like it or not, the Palota has been synonymous with the town since 1930 when the 'haves' of Hungarian society would descend upon it for a summer of wining, dining and dancing; you won't be able to stop thinking about that 1980 film *The Shining* with crazy Jack Nicholson

lurking around every corner. Rates vary according to the season and whether the room has a shower, bath or shower and WC, but doubles range from a low of DM50 to a high of DM102. The hotel has two well-appointed restaurants (stained-glass windows and enormous fireplace in the rather posh *Mátyás Terem*) and a lovely back garden with a terrace.

The *Lilla* pension (☎ 379 299), in a park behind the Palota at Erzsébet sétány 7, has four doubles without bath for 1600 Ft. The tidy little restaurant with pictures of the dishes on the walls is a nice change from the grandeur of the Palota, and the staff are friendly.

There are several *food stalls* serving lángos and sausage near the narrow-gauge train station. The *Falatozó* bistro serves cheap, decent meals under the trees.

Getting There & Away From Miskolc you have two options for reaching Lillafüred: the bus or the narrow-gauge train. If you are returning to Miskolc, the best way to go is to take the bus up and the train back. Bus Nos 1 and 101 (express) from Miskolc terminate at Majális Park. Transfer here to bus No 5 or 15, which depart every half-hour or so for Lillafüred. The No 15 continues on to Garadna, Ómassa, Szentlélek and Bánkút. Bus No 68 runs every half-hour between Újgyőri főtér on Andrássy utca west of Miskolc's centre and Bükkszentlászló.

Kilián-Észak train station, where the little narrow-gauge train from Miskolc terminates, is off Kiss tábornok út in western Miskolc, almost in Diósgyőr. There are only a couple of weekday departures between October and the middle of April (twice that number in summer) and between six and eight at the weekend, so check the schedules carefully or call ☎ 370 663 for information. From Lillafüred, the train carries on a further six km to Garadna.

Another line of the narrow gauge branches off at Papírgyár – the smelly paper factory that polluted the Szinva Stream – and covers the 23 km between Kilián-Észak station and

Farkasgödör-Örvénykő. It runs three times a day from May to September.

Aggtelek Karst Region

If you thought the caves at Lillafüred were kid's stuff, head 60 km north to the hilly karst region of Aggtelek National Park. The Baradla-Domica caves network is the largest stalactite system in Europe, with 25 km of passageways (seven km of them in Slovakia), and was declared a dual-nation UNESCO World Heritage Site in 1995. The array of red and black stalactite drip stones, stalagmite pyramids and enormous chambers is astonishing and a must-see.

In the summer, a tour of the caves usually includes a short organ recital in the Concert Chamber and, if the water is high enough, a boat ride on the 'River Styx'. The underground lighting is quite effective, and you won't have difficulty recognising the odd formations of dragons, tortoises, xylophones and the like, which your guide will point out.

AGGTELEK
• *pop 600*
• *area code* ☎ 48

There are three entrances to the Baradla Caves – at Aggtelek village; at Jósvafő, six km to the east; and at Vörös-tó, just before Jósvafő. The entrance to what are called Jaskyňa Domica (Domica Caves) in Slovak is across the border, a couple of km to the north-west in Slovakia. Guided tours of the Baradla system depart from these four points, but all the Hungarian tours can be joined at the Aggtelek entrance, where you should start. In any case, Aggtelek is the most accessible of the three Hungarian entrances; it also has the greatest choice of accommodation, and offers the most rewards on a short tour.

Orientation & Information
The staff at the caves' ticket office, the Naturinform office (☎ 343 073) at the small museum to the left or the people at the

Baradla tourist hostel nearby can supply you with information; they'll also sell you a copy of *Aggtelek, Jósvafő és környéke* (Aggtelek, Jósvafő and Environs; No 1), an excellent 1:40,000 hiking map from Cartographia. For more detailed information, contact the Aggtelek National Park Directorate (☎ 350 006) at Tengerszem oldal 1 in Jósvafő.

Caves
The caves are open all year – from 8 am to 5 pm from mid-March to September and to 3 pm the rest of the year. Tours lasting about one hour (one km; 270 Ft) start at the Aggtelek entrance at 10 am, 1 pm and 3 pm with an additional tour at 5 pm in summer. Two-hour tours (2.5 km; 320 Ft) start from the Vörös-tó entrance in Jósvafő at 8.40 am, 1.20 and 2.50 pm. One-hour tours (230 Ft) are also available from Jósvafő at 3 and 5 pm (summer only). A bus (six or seven a day) will take you from just outside the Cseppkő hotel in Aggtelek to the Vörös-tó/Jósvafő entrance. The temperature at this level is usually about 10°C with humidity over 95%, so be sure to bring a sweater along.

You can also visit the caves from Domica in Slovakia. Between four and six tours a day (except Monday) leave from 9 am to 4 pm. A short/long tour costs Sk50/90 plus Sk30 extra for an English-speaking guide.

Serious spelunkers will be tempted by the five-hour (1700 Ft) and seven-hour tours (2400 Ft), which cover between seven and nine km and must be booked in advance through the park directorate. Participants should wear boots and dress warmly; they will be issued lamps and helmets. You must seek special permission from the directorate to explore the Béke and Rákóczi caves to the south-east. The cost is 2400 Ft each.

A small **museum** near the Aggtelek entrance has exhibits dealing with the flora and fauna of the karst caves and surrounding countryside.

Hiking
You can join up with some excellent hiking trails above the museum, affording superb views of the rolling hills and valleys. A

relatively easy six-km hike will take you to Jósvafő.

Other Activities

The park directorate organises a number of programmes, including village tours on foot (230 Ft per person) or by horse-drawn carriage (900 ft); and traditional crafts tours (900 Ft), bird-watching, horse riding (720 Ft per hour) etc.

Places to Stay & Eat

Baradla Camping (☎ 343 073), where you can pitch a tent (250 Ft plus another 250 Ft per person) or rent a four-person bungalow for 1680 to 2800 Ft, is next to the Aggtelek cave entrance. Accommodation in the eight-bed dormitory rooms of the attached *Barlang* tourist hostel (same ☎) costs 450 to 520 Ft per person. Double rooms are 1500 Ft.

A very friendly alternative is the eight-room *Familiar* pension (☎ 343 043) at Ady Endre utca 24, a 15-minute walk from the cave entrance. Accommodation costs from 1500 to 2000 Ft per person, depending on the season (the Familiar is open from May to September), and there's a large restaurant with some vegetarian dishes available.

The 72-room *Cseppkő* (☎ 343 075), on a scenic hill above the entrance to the caves, is the only hotel in the area and has a restaurant, bar, terrace with splendid views, tennis court and sauna/solarium. Doubles are 4700 Ft.

If you intend to join cave tours at both the Aggtelek and Jósvafő entrances, you may consider staying at the 31-room *Tengerszem* hotel (☎ 350 006), Tengerszem oldal 2, in Jósvafő, which has singles/doubles with shower for 2100/2800 Ft. Book through Baradla Camping.

There are a number of *food stalls* in the car park near the Baradla Caves entrance.

Getting There & Away

Direct buses leave from Miskolc, Gyöngyös and Eger for Aggtelek. They return to Miskolc from the Cseppkő hotel car park at 3.58 and 5.30 pm, and to Gyöngyös and Eger at 3 pm. There's also a bus to Budapest at just after 3 pm.

Aggtelek can also be reached from Miskolc by train – you want the one heading for Tornanádaska. The Jósvafő-Aggtelek train station is some 10 km east of Jósvafő (and 16 km from Aggtelek village); a local bus meets each of the seven daily trains to take you to either town.

In a pinch (or a hurry) you could catch one of three buses a day from Aggtelek to Ózd, four to Putnok, or five to Kazinbarcika, and pick up one of up to a dozen daily trains to Miskolc.

Zemplén Hills

The area of the Zemplén is not uniform. On the southern and eastern slopes are the market towns and vineyards of the Tokaj-Hegyalja region. The wine trade attracted Greek, Serbian, Slovak, Polish, Russian and German merchants, and their influence can be felt in the area's architecture, culture and wine to this day. The northern Zemplén on the border with Slovakia is the nation's wildest region – if that's a word you can use to describe anything in Hungary other than someone who has pounded too much *pálinka* on a Saturday night – and is full of castle ruins and dusty one-horse towns.

BOLDOGKŐVÁRALJA
• *pop 1300*
• *area code ☎ 46*

The train linking Szerencs (on the main Budapest-Miskolc-Nyíregyháza trunk line) with Hidasnémeti, near the Slovakian border, stops at more than a dozen wine-producing towns as it wends its way some 50 km up the picturesque Hernád Valley. Some of the towns, such as Tállya and Gönc, are interesting in themselves, while others serve as starting points for forays into the southern Zemplén Hills. But not one combines the two so well as Boldogkőváralja, a charming village with an important castle.

Orientation

From Szerencs, make sure you sit on the

right-hand side of the train to see the dramatic castle as it comes into view. The train stops on the other side of the highway about two km from the castle. You can follow the surfaced road to the left or climb any of the steep trails up from the village to reach the main entrance.

Boldogkő Castle

The main site in the village is Boldogkő (Happy Rock) Castle, perched atop a mountain with a splendid 360° view of the southern Zemplén Hills, the Hernád Valley and nearby vineyards. Originally built in the 13th century, the castle was strengthened 200 years later but gradually fell into ruin after the *kuruc* revolt late in the 17th century.

There's a tiny **museum** here with dusty exhibits explaining who was who and what was what, but walking through the uneven courtyard up onto the ramparts and looking out over the surrounding countryside in the evening is much more satisfying. It's easy to see how the swashbuckling 16th-century poet Bálint Balassi came to love this place and produced some of his finest work here. The castle is open April to October from 8 am to 6 pm.

Other Things to See

The **Regional History Exhibit**, on Kossuth Lajos utca and open from 10 am to 2 pm on Friday, Saturday and Sunday from May to October, has some interesting exhibits devoted to Balassi and local sons and daughters who made it good overseas (one set up the first Hungarian-language newspaper in the USA), as well as a display of folk dress and a fully equipped smithy.

Hiking

Hikers can begin their rambles from the castle's northern side. Marked trails lead to **Regéc**, about 15 km to the north-east via Arka and Mogyoróska, skirting mountains and castle ruins along the way. From here you can either retrace your steps to Boldogkőváralja or follow the road westward to the Fony train stop (six trains a day in each direction) about 10 km away.

The hardy and/or prepared may want to carry on another eight km north to **Gönc**, a pretty town where the special barrels used to age Tokaj wine have been made for centuries. Gönc is on the main train line back to Szerencs. Depending on which way you're hiking, make sure you're armed with the north or south section (No 22 or 23) of the Zemplén 1:40,000 tourist map.

Places to Stay & Eat

Accommodation options in Boldogkőváralja are limited since the county government closed the hostel inside the castle in 1993. The *Tekerjes* inn (☎ 387 701) at Kossuth Lajos utca 41 has eight rooms, but is open from April to October only. If it's full (or closed), try the old *Peasant House* (Parasztház; ☎ 387 730), a traditional little farmhouse for rent near the regional history museum at Kossuth Lajos utca 75. The house at Major utca 4 nearby has *private rooms*.

Aside from the restaurant at the *Tekerjes*, the only other place for a sit-down meal is the *Bodókő* on Kossuth Lajos utca on the way to or from the train station. The no-name little *büfé* under the spreading chestnut trees in the village centre is OK for a snack or a drink. Ignore the cranky goose that may step in looking for a handout.

Getting There & Away

Boldogkőváralja is on the train line connecting Szerencs with Hidasnémeti, and seven trains per day in each direction stop at the town. Only two of these are direct; the rest require a change (no wait) at Abaújszántó.

TOKAJ

• *pop 5300*
• *area code* ☎ 47

The wines of Tokaj, a picturesque little town of vineyards and nesting storks in the south-east corner of the Zemplén Hills, have been celebrated for centuries. Tokaj is, in fact, just one of 28 towns and villages of the Tokaj-Hegyalja, a 5000-hectare vine-growing region that produces wine along the southern and eastern edges of the Zemplén Hills. But the name of the town has stuck and is now

NORTHERN UPLANDS

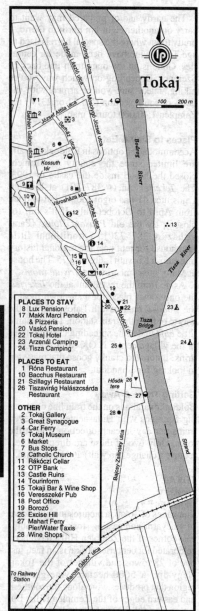

Tokaj

0   100   200 m

Bodrog River

Tisza River

Tisza Bridge

Hősök tere

Strand

PLACES TO STAY
8   Lux Pension
17 Makk Marci Pension
    & Pizzeria
20 Vaskó Pension
22 Tokaj Hotel
23 Arzenál Camping
24 Tisza Camping

PLACES TO EAT
1   Róna Restaurant
10 Bacchus Restaurant
21 Szillagyi Restaurant
26 Tiszavirág Halászcsárda
    Restaurant

OTHER
2   Tokaj Gallery
3   Great Synagogue
4   Car Ferry
5   Tokaj Museum
6   Market
7   Bus Stops
9   Catholic Church
11 Rákóczi Cellar
12 OTP Bank
13 Castle Ruins
14 Tourinform
15 Tokaj Bar & Wine Shop
16 Veresszekér Pub
18 Post Office
19 Borozó
25 Excise Hill
27 Mahart Ferry
    Pier/Water Taxis
28 Wine Shops

To Railway
Station

Baross Gábor utca

NORTHERN UPLANDS

synonymous with Hungary's most famous wine.

The area's volcanic soil, sunny climate and protective mountain shield are ideal for wine-making. Tokaj wines were exported to Poland and Russia in the Middle Ages and reached the peak of their popularity in Western Europe in the 17th and 18th centuries, gaining some pretty illustrious fans along the way. King Louis XIV called Tokaj 'the wine of kings and the king of wines', while Voltaire wrote that 'this wine could only be given by the boundlessly good God'.

In fact, to 20th-century Chardonnay drinkers, Tokaj may taste a bit old-fashioned and overly sweet, particularly the dessert wines, which are rated according to the number of *puttony* (butts, or baskets for picking the grapes) of sweet Aszú essence added to other base wines. But Tokaj also produces less-sweet wines: Szamorodni (not unlike dry sherry), Furmint and Hárslevelű, the driest of them all.

Orientation & Information

Tokaj's centre lies west of where the Bodrog and Tisza rivers meet. The train station is south of the town centre at the end of Baross Gábor utca; you can wait for a bus, but it's only a 15-minute walk north along Baross Gábor utca and Bajcsy-Zsilinszky utca to the main thoroughfare, Rákóczi út. Intercity buses arrive and depart from along Serház utca east of Kossuth tér. The main stop is in front of house No 30.

Tourinform (☎ 352 259) has an office at Serház utca 1. It is open weekdays from 9 am to 5 pm and on Saturday to 1 pm. OTP has a bank branch at Rákóczi út 35, and the main post office is at No 24 on the same street.

Things to See

The **Tokaj Museum** at Bethlen Gábor utca 7, open May to November from 9 am to 5 pm except Monday, leaves nothing unsaid about the history of Tokaj, the Tokaj-Hegyalja region and the production of its wines. Particularly interesting are the exhibits showing French, Italian, American and South African attempts to duplicate Tokaj wine; the Alsatian variety is said to be closest to the real thing. There's also a superb collection of liturgical art, including icons, medieval crucifixes and triptychs.

Just up the road, in an 18th-century Greek Orthodox church at No 15, the **Tokaj Gallery** exhibits works by local artists. It is open April to September from 10 am to 4 or 5 pm daily except Monday. Behind the gallery on Serház utca, the 100-year-old **Great Synagogue**, which was used as a German barracks during WWII, is once again falling into ruin after a partial renovation a mere five years ago.

Across the Bodrog River, what's left of 16th-century **Tokaj Castle**, which formed part of a defence triangle with the castles at Tállya and Szerencs until the Habsburgs levelled it, can be reached from the little car ferry on Bodrog-part.

The **market** is on Szépessi köz, east of the Tokaj Museum.

Wine Tasting

There are private cellars *(pincék)* offering wine tastings throughout town, including those at Rákóczi út 2, Óvári utca 36 and 40, and Bem József utca 2. Don't be intimidated if the cellars appear locked up tight; just ring the bell and someone will appear.

Start with 100-ml glasses; you may consume more than you think. If you're serious, the correct order of sampling Tokaj wines is: Furmint, dry Szamorodni, sweet Szamorodni and then the Aszú wines – from three to five or even the newfangled six-puttony variety.

The *Rákóczi Pince* at Kossuth tér 15 is a stand-up wine bar with all the Tokaj wines on offer, but for the ultimate in tasting locales, walk two doors down to the Pince's 600-year-old cellar at No 13, where bottles of wine mature in corridors several km long. Both places close at 6 pm. There's a very ordinary *borozó* at Rákóczi út 7.

You can see traditional *kádárok* (coopers) still at work at Rákóczi út 18 and 28 and at József Attila utca 12 near the Great Synagogue.

Other Activities

In summer, water tours of the Bodrog and Tisza rivers are available from the Mahart ferry pier at Hősök tere near the Tiszavirág Halászcsárda restaurant. Or you can just take a water taxi across to the grassy beach for a lazy afternoon of sunning and swimming in the Tisza River.

Kopasz-hegy (Bald Mountain) and its TV tower west of the town centre offer a stunning panorama of Tokaj and the surrounding vineyards, but the less ambitious will be content with the easy climb up Fináncdomb (Excise Hill) on Rákóczi út opposite Tisza Bridge.

Places to Stay

Tisza Camping (☎ 352 012), along the river just south of the bridge, has bungalows for about 2000 Ft (doubles). It also has its own restaurant, boat rentals and beach for swimming. *Arzenál* (☎ 352 640), on the opposite bank to the north, has bungalows and hostel accommodation. Both are open April to September, but be warned: they are plagued by mosquitoes.

Other accommodation choices are surprisingly limited in a town so well known abroad. *Private rooms* are available in various parts of town: just watch out for the signs along Óvári utca (Nos 6 and 38), Bem József utca and Bethlen Gábor utca. Rooms on offer along Hegyalja utca are convenient to the train station and are surrounded by vineyards.

The three-room *Vaskó* pension (☎ 352 107) at Rákóczi út 12 is as central as you can get. Singles/doubles are 2500 to 2700 Ft, depending on the season. The *Makk Marci* pension (☎ 352 336), just off Rákóczi út at Liget köz 1, has seven rooms, all with shower, for 2016 Ft (singles) and 3024 Ft (doubles). The *Lux* pension (☎ 352 145) to the north at Serház utca 14 is more expensive.

The only hotel in Tokaj is the garish 42-room *Tokaj* (☎ 352 344) at Rákóczi út 5, where the two rivers meet. Doubles with bath are 3600 Ft (avoid the noisy Rákóczi út side and choose a room on the river). A row of

NORTHERN UPLANDS

badly ventilated rooms with showers on the 4th floor cost 500 Ft less.

Places to Eat

Tiszavirág Halászcsárda at the start of Bajcsy-Zsilinszky utca serves decent fish soup and a lot of scaly things from the Tisza. The pizzeria at the *Makk Marci* is open till 10 pm and is a friendly place for a quick bite. For something more Hungarian try the *Bacchus* at Kossuth tér 17.

The *Szillagyi* at Rákóczi út 5 is actually the Tokaj hotel's restaurant. It's a pleasant enough place (if somewhat pricey); sit on the terrace along the Bodrog in summer, but be sure to bring plenty of insect repellent along. An up-market choice is the *Róna* at Bethlen Gábor utca 19 and it's open till midnight.

Should you get tired of all that wine, head for the *Veresszekér*, a congenial pub in a courtyard off Rákóczi út.

Things to Buy

Wine, wine and more wine – from a 10-litre plastic jug of new Furmint to a bottle of six-puttony Aszú – is available in shops and cellars throughout Tokaj, especially along Bajcsy-Zsilinszky utca and at the Tokaji Bar and Wine Shop at Rákóczi út 36. Just make sure it's corked tightly if pulled from a cellar cask.

Getting There & Away

Tokaj is not well served by buses. Seven a day go to Szerencs, the chocolate capital of Hungary, but it is just as easy to get there by train. Some 15 trains a day connect Tokaj with Miskolc and Nyíregyháza; change at the latter for Debrecen. To travel north to Sárospatak and Sátoraljaújhely, take the Miskolc-bound train (15 per day) and change at Mezőzombor.

In the summer, an alternative way to reach Sárospatak from Tokaj is on the Mahart ferry, departing from the pier at Hősök tere. Between April and November, boats usually sail on weekends at 7.30 am and 3.30 pm. The 36-km trip takes just under 2½ hours.

SÁROSPATAK

* pop 15,000
* area code ☎ 47

While not the gateway to the northern Zemplén that it may appear to be on the map (that distinction goes to Sátoraljaújhely 12 km to the north), the town of 'Muddy Stream' is renowned for its college and castle, the finest example of a Renaissance fort still standing in Hungary. Sárospatak is also a convenient stop en route to Slovakia.

Sárospatak has played a much greater role in Hungarian history than its diminutive size would suggest. A wealthy, wine-producing free royal town since the early 15th century, it soon became a centre of Calvinist power and scholarship and 200 years later the focal point for Hungarian resistance to the Habsburgs. The alumni of its Calvinist college, which helped earn Sárospatak the nickname the 'Athens of Hungary', read like a who's who of Hungarian literary and political history: the patriot Lajos Kossuth, the poet Mihály Csokonai Vitéz, the novelist Géza Gárdonyi.

Sárospatak is full of buildings designed by the 'organic' architect Imre Makovecz, including the cultural centre on Eötvös utca and the cathedral-like Árpád Vezér College on Arany János utca. Not all of them are appreciated by Sárospatakers.

Orientation & Information

Sárospatak is a compact city lying on the snaking Bodrog River and its attractive backwaters. The bus and train stations are cheek-by-jowl at the end of Táncsics Mihály utca, north-west of the city centre. Walk east through Iskola Park to join up with Rákóczi út, the main street.

Ibusz (☎ 311 244), at Rákóczi út 15, is the only travel agency in town. It is open weekdays from 8 am to 4 pm (6 pm in summer and on Saturday till noon). There's an OTP bank branch at Eötvös utca 3; the main post office is at Rákóczi út 45, near Béla király tér.

Rákóczi Castle

This castle should be the first port of call for any visitor to Sárospatak; enter the Várkert

(Castle Garden) by crossing over the dry moat at the southern end of Rákóczi út or from Szent Erzsébet utca. Although the oldest part of the castle, the renovated five-storey **Red Tower**, dates from the late 15th century, the Renaissance **palace** was built in the following century and later enlarged by its most famous owners, the Rákóczi family of Transylvania. They held it until 1711 when Ferenc Rákóczi's aborted independence war against the Habsburgs drove him into exile in Turkey and put the castle in the hands of Austrian aristocrats, including the Windisch-Grätz family.

Today the Renaissance wings of the palace and the 19th-century additions contain a **museum** devoted to the Rákóczi uprising and the castle's later occupants, with bedrooms and dining halls overflowing with period furniture, tapestries, porcelain and glass. Of special interest is the small, five-windowed bay room on the 1st floor near the Knights' Hall with its stucco rose in the middle of a vaulted ceiling. It was here that nobles put their names *sub rosa* (literally 'under the rose' in Latin) to the kuruc uprising against the Habsburg emperor in 1670. The expression, which means 'in secret', is thought to have originated here. You should also look out for the **Fireplace Hall** with its superb Renaissance hearth and, outside in the courtyard, the so-called **Lorántffy Gallery**, a 17th-century loggia linking the east palace wing with the Red Tower. It's straight out of *Romeo and Juliet*.

You can wander around the empty **casemates** of the castle on your own or visit the exhibit in the cellars of the east wing devoted to the history of wine and wine-making in the surrounding Tokaj-Hegyalja region. You can also now climb to the top of the Red Tower.

Other Things to See

Back along Szent Erzsébet utca, have a peek at the **Rákóczi Wine Cellar** built in 1684, but don't try to go in and have a glass unless you are in a group of at least five people and willing to pay 500 Ft each.

The **castle church** in Szent Erzsébet tér

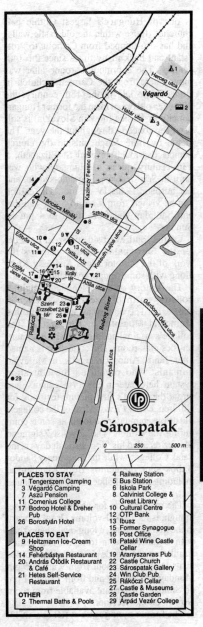

Sárospatak

PLACES TO STAY
1 Tengerszem Camping
3 Végardó Camping
7 Aszú Pension
11 Comenius College
17 Bodrog Hotel & Dreher Pub
26 Borostyán Hotel

PLACES TO EAT
9 Heitzmann Ice-Cream Shop
14 Fehérbástya Restaurant
20 András Ötödik Restaurant & Café
21 Hetes Self-Service Restaurant

OTHER
2 Thermal Baths & Pools
4 Railway Station
5 Bus Station
6 Iskola Park
8 Calvinist College & Great Library
10 Cultural Centre
12 OTP Bank
13 Ibusz
15 Former Synagogue
16 Post Office
18 Pataki Wine Castle Cellar
19 Aranyszarvas Pub
22 Castle Church
23 Sárospatak Gallery
24 Win Club Pub
25 Rákóczi Cellar
27 Castle & Museums
28 Castle Garden
29 Árpád Vezér College

is one of Hungary's largest Gothic hall churches (those within the old castle walls) and has flip-flopped from Catholic to Protestant and back many times since the 14th century. The enormous baroque altar was moved here from the Carmelite church in Buda Castle late in the 18th century; the 200-year-old organ from the former Hungarian city of Košice (now in Slovakia) is still used for concerts throughout the year. The statue by Imre Varga outside the church depicts the much revered St Elizabeth, a 13th-century queen of Hungary who was born in Sárospatak, riding side-saddle, and her husband Louis IV on foot. The church can be visited from 9 am to 5 pm Tuesday and Saturday and from noon to 4 pm on Sunday.

On the south-west side of Szent Erzsébet tér the **Sárospatak Gallery** displays the work of the sculptor János Andrássy Kurta along with some temporary exhibits.

The history of the celebrated **Calvinist college**, north of Szent Erzsébet tér at Rákóczi út 1, is on display at the **Comenius Memorial Museum** in the last of the college's original buildings, an 18th-century physics classroom. The collection is named after János Amos Comenius, a Moravian humanist who organised the education system here late in the 17th century and wrote the world's first picture textbook for children, *Orbis Pictus*. Most of the college's illustrious pupils are quoted at some point during the exhibit. The novelist Zsigmond Móricz recalled his 'dog-difficult days at the Patak College', while the missionary Sándor Babos sent mementos from Manchuria, including a pair of shoes for Chinese bound feet.

The main reason for visiting the college, though, is its 75,000-volume **Great Library** in the main building, a long oval-shaped hall with a gallery and a trompe l'oeil ceiling simulating the inside of a cupola. Guided visits leave on the hour from 9 am to 5 pm Monday to Saturday and from 9 am to 1 pm on Sunday. Tickets are available from room No 113 on the 1st floor.

The former **synagogue** at Rákóczi út 43, near the post office, is now a furniture store. Almost all of the 1200 Jews living in Sárospatak before the war died in Nazi concentration camps.

Special Events

Some events of the Zemplén Musical Days festival in late August take place in Sárospatak. The Bodrog Folk Dance Festival is held in July.

Places to Stay

Tengerszem Camping (☎ 312 744), across from the complex of thermal baths and pools called Végardó, also has 10 bungalows available from April to mid-October. Tengerszem is at Herceg utca 2, about two km from the stations, and can be reached by infrequent city bus from there or from the Bodrog shopping centre on Rákóczi út. *Végardó Camping* (☎ 311 639) in the same complex also has bungalows.

In summer, you might get a *dormitory room* at one of the teachers' colleges, preferably the lovely Art Nouveau *Comenius College* (☎ 312 211) at Eötvös utca 5-7, for about 500 Ft per person. Ibusz has *private rooms* and apartments available for between 1500 and 2000 Ft for two people.

The eight-room *Borostyán* hotel (☎ 312 611), in a restored 17th-century monastery within the castle walls at Szent Erzsébet utca 28, is a shadow of the marvellous place it once was and is now quite dumpy. Still, the prices are right: singles and doubles with bath are 2000 Ft, or 1500 Ft without. There are also dormitory rooms available in summer for about 800 Ft per person.

The *Bodrog* (☎ 311 744) at Rákóczi út 58 is a charmless, four-storey block with 50 rooms in the centre of town. It charges 4600 to 6350 Ft for a small single and 5600 to 7850 Ft for a double. All rooms have shower or bath, and there's a big restaurant and a beer bar. In a pinch, you might try the *Aszú* (☎ 312 657), a pension at Kazinczy Ferenc utca 27 with four doubles.

Places to Eat

The *Hetes* self-service restaurant at Kossuth

Lajos utca 57 is a cheap place for a meal, it's open 10 am to 3 pm on weekdays. The *Spaghetti Bar* in the cultural centre, popular with students, is open daily from 4.30 to 8.30 pm.

The *Fehérbástya* is an intimate little Hungarian restaurant at Rákóczi út 39, but an even better choice is the *András Ötödik* restaurant and café around the corner at Béla király tér 3.

The *Heitzmann* ice-cream shop at Rákóczi út 16/a has lickers lining up from dawn to dusk.

Entertainment

The staff at the anthropomorphic-looking *Sárospatak Cultural Centre* (☎ 311 811) at Eötvös utca 6, designed by Imre Makovecz in 1983, will fill you in on what's on in town. Be sure to ask about organ concerts at the castle church.

There's a disco at weekends in the cultural centre; the *Gomboshegyi Csárda* on route No 37 heading for Miskolc attracts an older crowd.

The *Aranyszarvas* at Béla király tér 2, which is something of a student hang-out and also called the Rock Gödör, stays open to 2 am. Other places popular with the young bloods of Sárospatak are the *Pataki Bor Vár* (the 'Patak Wine Castle' but really just a cellar) at the start of Szent Erzsébet utca, the *Win Club* at No 22 and the pub downstairs at the *Borostyán* hotel next door.

Getting There & Away

Bus Most of the southern Zemplén region is not easily accessible by bus from Sárospatak, though there is one bus a day to the pretty village of Erdőbénye, from where you can connect to Baskó and Boldogkőváralja. Other destinations include Budapest (one bus a day), Debrecen (two), Kisvárda (one), Miskolc (two), and Sátoraljaújhely (hourly).

Train To explore the southern Zemplén, you'd do better to take one of seven daily trains up the Hernád Valley from Szerencs and use one of the towns along that line such as Abaújkér, Boldogkőváralja or Korlát-Vizsoly as your base. For the northern Zemplén, take a train or bus (hourly) to Sátoraljaújhely.

Some nine trains daily connect Sárospatak and Sátoraljaújhely with Miskolc, and three or four of those continue on to Slovenské Nové Mesto in Slovakia, from where you can board a train to Košice. If you are coming from Debrecen, Nyíregyháza or Tokaj, change trains at Mezőzombor.

Boat In summer, the most pleasant way to get to Tokaj, 36 km to the south, is on the Mahart ferry. Between April and November, boats usually sail on weekends at 10.10 am and 6.10 pm. The trip takes about 2½ hours.

Getting Around

Hourly buses link the bus and train stations and the Bodrog shopping centre on Rákóczi út with the Végardó recreational centre to the north. You can order a taxi on ☎ 311 744.

SÁTORALJAÚJHELY

* pop 21,000
* *area code* ☎ 47

Sátoraljaújhely came into the possession of the Rákóczis in the 17th century (they lived on Kazinczy utca) and, like the family's base, Sárospatak, the city played an important role in the struggle for independence from Austria. It was not the last time the city would be a battleground. In 1919, fighting took place in the nearby hills and ravines between Communist partisans and Slovaks, and once again in the closing days of WWII.

Today Sátoraljaújhely (roughly translated as 'tent camp new place' and pronounced 'SHAH-toor-all-ya-ooey-hay') is a quiet frontier town surrounded by forests and vineyards and dominated by Magas-hegy, the 514m 'Tall Mountain.' Though definitely not worth a visit in itself, Sátoraljaújhely is a good base for trekking into the northern Zemplén hills and for crossing the border into Slovakia.

Orientation & Information

The bus and train stations sit side by side a km south of the city centre. From there, follow Fasor utca to Kossuth Lajos utca, past

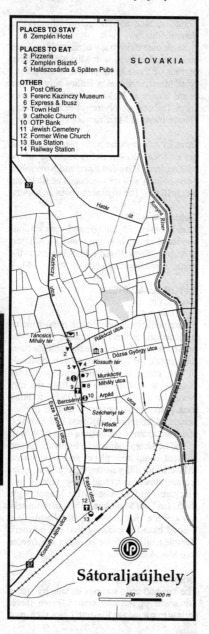

PLACES TO STAY
8 Zemplén Hotel

PLACES TO EAT
2 Pizzeria
4 Zemplén Bisztró
5 Halászcsárda & Späten Pubs

OTHER
1 Post Office
3 Ferenc Kazinczy Museum
6 Express & Ibusz
7 Town Hall
9 Catholic Church
10 OTP Bank
11 Jewish Cemetery
12 Former Wine Church
13 Bus Station
14 Railway Station

SLOVAKIA

Sátoraljaújhely

0   250   500 m

the old Jewish cemetery and Hősök tere, and continue until you reach Széchenyi tér. Two more squares follow – Kossuth tér and Táncsics Mihály tér – and then Kazinczy utca.

Express (☎ 322 563) and Ibusz (☎ 321 757) are a door apart at Kossuth tér 22 and 26. Both are open from 8 am to 4 pm on weekdays. There's an OTP bank branch at Széchenyi tér 13. For the post office, go to Kazinczy utca 10.

Things to See

The decrepit neo-Gothic former **Wine Church**, with seals of the Tokaj-Hegyalja towns in Zsolnay porcelain decorating its sides, greets you upon arrival at the bus or train station. Don't expect much from this Frankenstein's castle; its most recent incarnation was as a storehouse for discounted wine.

The baroque **Catholic church** (1792) on Széchenyi tér, with its stark interior, is not very interesting in itself, though it was here that the teachings of Martin Luther were first read aloud in public in Hungary. The same can be said for the **town hall** at Kossuth tér 5, but it too is remembered for a momentous event. In 1830, then-lawyer Lajos Kossuth gave his first public speech from the balcony looking down onto the square.

The **Ferenc Kazinczy Museum** at Dózsa György utca 11, named after the 19th-century language reformer and patriot who worked here, covers the history of the city, with emphasis on the Rákóczi family, as well as the natural history of the Zemplén region.

Places to Stay & Eat

Accommodation is very limited in Sátoraljaújhely. Try Ibusz for *private rooms* or Express for *dormitory accommodation* at the local college. There also may be a room available in the house at Dózsa György utca 17 or at Esze Tamás utca 20.

The 30-room *Zemplén* hotel (☎ 322 522), upstairs at Széchenyi tér 5-7, is an unattractive block sitting atop a supermarket, but as central as you'll find here. Doubles (no singles) with bath are 2500 Ft.

For something quick try the little *pizzeria* at Táncsics tér 3, open daily till 9 pm. A far less salubrious place is the *Zemplén Bisztró* at Dózsa György utca 2.

The *Halászcsárda* and the *Späten* side by side at Kossuth tér 10 offer fish dishes and Hungarian pub grub – in that order. The restaurant at the *Zemplén* hotel stays open daily to 10 pm.

Getting There & Away

There are frequent buses into the towns and villages of the northern Zemplén Hills, including three a day to Füzér, five to Hollóháza via Füzér, two to Telkibánya and one to Hidasnémeti, from where you can pick up trains north to the Slovakian city of Košice (six daily), south to Miskolc (12 a day), or to Szerencs and the towns along the western edge of the Zemplén.

Some nine trains a day link Sátoraljaújhely with Sárospatak and Miskolc; three or four of them cross the border with Slovakia at Slovenské Nové Mesto, where you can catch a train to Košice. If you are approaching Sátoraljaújhely from the south or east (Debrecen, say, or Nyíregyháza or Tokaj), you must change at Mezőzombor.

AROUND SÁTORALJAÚJHELY
Füzér & Hollóháza
• *area code* ☎ 47

An easy and thoroughly satisfying excursion into the Zemplén Hills can be made to see **Füzér** (pop 600), an idyllic little village, and the remains of the dramatic hilltop **Füzér Castle**, which dates from the 13th century. It's about 25 km north-west of Sátoraljaújhely. The medieval **Calvinist church** has a 19th-century painted ceiling similar to those found in the Tiszahát and Erdőhát regions of the North-East region.

From the village bus stop, follow the steep, marked trail and you'll soon come to the castle sitting 370m up on a rocky crag. The castle's claim to fame is that it was chosen as a 'safe house' for the Hungarian coronation regalia from Visegrád for a year or so after the disastrous defeat at Mohács in 1526. Like most castles in the area, it was heavily damaged by the Austrians after the unsuccessful kuruc revolt in the late 17th century, but parts of the chapel, a tower and the outer walls remain.

The Calvinist church – not the baroque Catholic church with silly contemporary murals of doom and gloom – is in the village centre; seek the church key from the house at Szabadság utca 17. The 50 ceiling panels were decorated with geometric patterns and flowers by a local artist in 1832.

You won't find a bed or much to eat in Füzér, though there is a small *grocery store* and *café* behind the bus stop.

From here you can return to Sátoraljaújhely or catch one of several daily buses for the nine-km trip to **Hollóháza** (pop 1100), Hungary's northernmost town and in third place after Herend and Zsolnay for its porcelain. Accommodation is in the decrepit but cheap 20-room *Castle* hotel (☎ Hollóháza 8) at Lászlótanya or the three-room *Éva* pension (☎ 305 038) at Szent László utca 4.

Starting a hike into the Zemplén from Füzér and Hollóháza is a good idea; several well-marked trails begin here, including the one that runs from the Castle hotel north-east to **Nagy Milic**, an 895m hill on the Slovakian border. Just make sure you're armed with drinking water, a sleeping bag and *A Zempléni Hegység Turistatérképe – Északi Rész*, Cartographia's 1:40,000 map (No 22) of the northern section of the Zemplén.

See the Sátoraljaújhely Getting There & Away section for transport information.

North-East

On the map, Hungary's north-east corner may appear to be a continuation of the Northern Uplands or even the Great Plain. But it is so different physically, culturally and historically from both that it is considered a separate region. Essentially North-East Hungary encompasses just one county (Szabolcs-Szatmár-Bereg) and is bordered by Slovakia, Ukraine and Romania, three countries with which it is trying to forge stronger economic and cultural ties.

The North-East is neither mountainous nor flat but a region of ridges and gentle hills formed by sand blown up from the Tisza River basin. Apart from the industries based around the city of Nyíregyháza, the area is almost entirely given over to agriculture – apples are the most important crop – with occasional stands of silver poplars and birch trees.

Before the regulation of the Tisza River in the 19th century, large parts of the North-East were often flooded and isolated by swamps. This helped to protect the area from the devastation suffered elsewhere during the Turkish occupation; as a result, the North-East has always been more densely populated than the Great Plain. This isolation saved the region's distinctive wooden churches and other medieval structures from oblivion.

Before WWII, the North-East was home to most Hungarian Jews living outside Budapest, and their erstwhile presence can be seen everywhere in the region's dilapidated synagogues and untended cemeteries.

But isolation has worked against the North-East and hindered development. Szabolcs-Szatmár-Bereg remains one of Hungary's poorest counties, with an unemployment rate more than twice that of the national average. It is also home to a large percentage of the country's 250,000 Gypsies (see aside). As a result, some Magyars refer to it disparagingly as 'Asiatic Hungary' or the 'black county' and advise visitors not to travel to such a 'backward' area.

HIGHLIGHTS

- the Gothic Calvinist church and bell tower, and the carved wooden altars at the Minorite church in Nyírbátor
- the enormous iconostasis at the Greek Catholic church in Máriapócs
- Szatmárcseke's ancient cemetery with its intriguing boat-shaped grave markers
- the narrow-gauge train trip from Dombrád to Nyíregyháza
- the 'folk baroque' painted wooden ceiling at Tákos' Calvinist church

In fact, the North-East's remoteness and the diverse cultural mix make it an interesting area to visit. If you want to see real village life – replete with dirt roads, horse-drawn carts laden with hay, thatched roofs and ancient churches – this is the place. There's nothing twee or artificial about the North-East; this is how much of provincial Hungary looked until WWII.

Nyírség Region

Two rivers – the Szamos and the serpentine Tisza – carve the North-East up into several distinct areas. The largest of these is the Nyírség, the 'birch region' of grassy steppes and hills that lies between Nyíregyháza, the

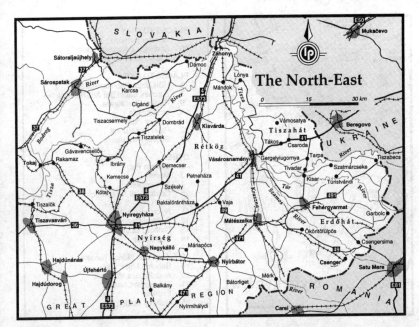

county seat, and the historical town of Nyírbátor. The life of the people was shaped by the Tisza floods and swamps that remained here all year long until just a century ago. But today the Nyírség is the most developed region of the North-East.

NYÍREGYHÁZA

- *pop 118,000*
- *area code* ☎ *42*

The capital of the Nyírség gets more than its share of bad press or worse: none at all. It's true that Nyíregyháza is the commercial and administrative centre of a poor area and misses out on a lot of the development and investment that goes to the cities of western Hungary. And it is not a particularly historical town; Nyíregyháza was the private domain for many centuries of the princes of Transylvania and was resettled by Slovaks in the late 17th century. But with its well tended squares and gardens and some interesting, newly renovated buildings, Nyíregyháza is

not a bad place to spend some time. It is also an excellent springboard for other Nyírség towns as well as northern Romania and Ukraine.

Orientation

Nyíregyháza's 'centre' is actually several interconnecting squares, including Kossuth Lajos tér, Hősök tere and Országzászló tér, surrounded by grey housing blocks and a ring road. Streets running north lead to Sóstógyógyfürdő, the city's sprawling recreational area of woods, parkland, the little Salt Lake (Sóstó) and a large spa complex.

The main train station is about two km south-west of the centre at the end of Arany János utca on Állomás tér. The bus station is just north of the train station on Petőfi tér.

Information

Tourinform (☎ 312 606) has an office here, but it is inconveniently located in the bowels of the county hall (building B) at Hősök tere

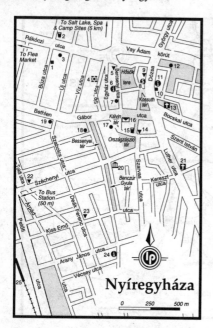

5 and hard to find. It is open weekdays from
8 am to 4 pm. Nyírtourist (☎ 409 344), at
Dózsa György utca 3 between the Szabolcs
and Korona hotels, is a more accessible
source of information and opens a half-hour
earlier on the same days. Express (☎ 311
650), at Arany János utca 2, seems more
interested in selling its outbound package
tours, but may help with basic information
and accommodation.

OTP bank has a branch at Dózsa György
utca 2 opposite Nyírtourist; the main post
office is at Bethlen Gábor utca 4 near the
town hall. You'll find a very good map shop
called Nyír-Karta at Kálvin tér 14.

Things to See

There are several churches in the inner city,
including the baroque **Evangelist church**
on Luther tér and, dominating Kossuth Lajos
tér, the neo-Romanesque **Catholic church**
(1904), with arabesque pastel-coloured tiles
inside.

A lot of the architecture in the centre is
worth more than a casual glance; visit the
Eclectic **county hall** (1892) with its splendid
Nagy Terem (Ceremonial Hall) on Hősök
tere, the blue and white Art Nouveau building housing a bank on Országzászló tér, or
the recently restored powder-blue **Korona
hotel** on Dózsa György utca. A must-see is the
bizarre **cultural centre** (1981) on Szabadság
tér, inspired by 'the principles of Japanese
metabolism', we're told. But it's not popular
in Nyíregyháza, and local people say they're
afraid to walk the corridors in the elevated
wings of this wobbly-looking, bridge-like
structure.

Real sights are limited in the centre. The
András Jósa Museum at Benczúr Gyula tér
2 has exhibits devoted to Nyíregyháza's
history since the Middle Ages. The **synagogue** at Mártírok tere 6, which still functions
as a house of worship, can be visited Monday
to Thursday from 8 am to 4 pm.

Nyíregyháza's most interesting sight is the

open-air **Museum Village** on Tölgyes utca in Sóstógyógyfürdő, open from 9.30 am to 4 pm (April to October) daily, except Monday. Though not as big as the skanzen at Szentendre, its reconstructed three-room cottages, school, draw wells and general store offer an easy introduction to the architecture and way of life in the various regions of Szabolcs-Szatmár-Bereg. All the nationalities that make up this ethnically diverse region are represented, including the Tirpák, a Slovak people who lived in isolated 'bush farms'. Some of these *bokor tanyák* are still being worked to the west of Nyíregyháza. The museum also has exhibits devoted to the Romantic, epic painter Gyula Benczúr and the novelist Gyula Krúdy, both sons of the city.

Far more interesting than the produce market on Búza tér, the **flea market** attracts Romanians, Poles, Gypsies and Ukrainians selling the usual diamonds-to-rust mixture of goods in a sea of sunflower-seed shells. A large selection of barnyard animals is available for those in the market. It is on Tokaji út, the north-west extension of Rákóczi út.

Activities
The park baths in Sóstógyógyfürdő, five km north of the city centre, is just the place to while away a hot summer's afternoon, with a half-dozen large pools of fresh and thermal-spring water, a sauna, solarium, and so on. It's open every day from 9 am to 7 pm.

The Sóstó Riding Club (☎ 479 704) at Tölgyes utca 1 in Sóstógyógyfürdő rents horses, and there are sightseeing flights available at the city's small airport (☎ 430 138), north-west of the centre just off Tokaji út.

Places to Stay
There are several camping grounds in Sóstógyógyfürdő, including *Fenyves* (☎ 402 036), which also has hostel accommodation for 600 Ft per person in four to six-bed cabins, and *Igrice* (☎ 479 705) at Blaha Lujza sétány. Its bungalows are about 2000 Ft and are available from May to September. Igrice is a short distance south-east of the former Krúdy hotel, a beat-up old pile on the lake

Sunflowers are common in the North-East

where political prisoners were held for a time under the Stalinists in the early 1950s. Have a look at the statue of the girl carrying a water jug in front and enjoy a local joke. If you walk to the left from behind the statue, you will see 'her' change to 'him'.

Nyírtourist and sometimes Express will arrange *dormitory rooms* at local colleges in summer from 600 Ft per person. If the agencies are closed, go directly to the *Teachers' Training College* (☎ 341 222) at Sóstói út 31/b or the *Sport College* (☎ 315 522) at No 24/a of the same street. The otherwise expensive *Paradise* hotel (☎ 402 011) at Sóstói út 76 is a member of Hostelling International and has dormitory accommodation from mid-April to mid-October.

Private rooms through Nyírtourist average 1200 Ft for a double.

The 15-room *Senátor* (☎ 311 796), near the produce market at Búza tér 11, has singles/doubles with bath for 2300/2800 Ft. Doubles without bath are 1600 Ft. The *Ózon* (☎ 402 012), a former Communist summer retreat near Sóstógyógyfürdő at Csaló köz 2, has 26 modern doubles from 3500 Ft.

The 62-room *Szabolcs* hotel (☎ 409 303) at Dózsa György utca 3 is a ghastly, gloomy place, but it's very central and the price is right: it costs 1000 Ft for singles with washbasin, 1100/1630 Ft for singles/doubles with shower and 2300 Ft for doubles with bath. For a splurge, head for the Szabolcs' former sister hotel, the lovingly restored *Korona* (☎ 409 300), next door at Dózsa György utca 1. It has 24 rooms scattered along seemingly endless corridors. Singles/doubles with all the mod cons are 5000/5800 Ft (plus 600 Ft if they make you take breakfast).

Places to Eat
The *City Grill* next to the post office at Bethlen Gábor utca 2 is fine for a cheap, fast meal, and there's a *McDonald's* at Zrínyi utca 4-6. Vegetarians should head for the *Zucchini Salad Bar* in the courtyard behind the OTP bank at Dózsa György utca 2.

For more comfortable surroundings, try the *HBH Bajor* pub-restaurant at No 6 of lovely Hősök tere, a decent choice for some well-prepared Hungarian dishes and a pint. The *Gösser*, a similar (but more cramped) place at Országzászló tér 7, has some Italian dishes, pizza and a salad bar. The *John Bull* pub-restaurant at the bottom of the Korona hotel is a little bit of ersatz England in far-flung north-eastern Hungary.

A good Hungarian-style restaurant is the cosy *Sasvár* at Kiss Ernő utca 25. The *Kispipa*, though a favourite among some locals, is dark and stale-smelling – did 1989 ever happen? It's at Dózsa György utca 6 next to the former Európa hotel, where Gypsy violinist Gyula Benczi played 'so warmly, so kindly, so melodiously' for half a century, according to the memorial plaque on the outside wall. The *Pater* at Széchenyi utca 37 serves meals with seating outside in the warmer months.

There's a 24-hour *grocery store* on Rákóczi út opposite the market.

Entertainment
Check with the staff at the lovely *Zsigmond Móricz Theatre* (☎ 310 810) at Bessenyei tér 13 or the *cultural centre* (☎ 411 822) at Szabadság tér 9 for current listings. And if there's a concert on at the *Èvangelist church*,

jump at the chance. The theatre ticket office (☎ 310 360) is at Országzászló tér 6.

The *John Bull* at the Korona hotel is a decent place for a pint, or try the more local *Unicum* opposite the market at Búza utca 2. For jazz, head for the *Fehér Narancs* (White Orange) at Pacsirta utca 20.

The most popular discos are the *Bahnhof Music Club* at Bethlen Gábor utca 24 and the *High Tech*, south-east of Kossuth Lajos tér at Szent István utca 7. There are club nights throughout the week at the cultural centre.

Getting There & Away
Generally, buses serve towns near Nyíregyháza or those not on a railway line – and there are very frequent departures to Nagykálló. Other destinations include Debrecen (three a day), Eger (one), Fehérgyarmat (four), Gyöngyös (one), Hajdúnánás (three), Kisvárda (four), Máriapócs (eight), Mátészalka (seven), Miskolc (two), Nyírbátor (seven) and Vásárosnamény (three). Towns in Ukraine served by bus are Beregovo (Tuesday, 11.45 am) and Užgorod (daily at 2.30 pm); buses also go to Baia Mare (Wednesday and Friday at 4 pm) and Satu Mare (daily at 1 pm) in Romania.

Five daily express trains link Nyíregyháza with Debrecen and Budapest-Nyugati, but you can count on at least one normal train an hour to Debrecen and about 10 to Miskolc. A total of seven trains depart Nyíregyháza each day for Vásárosnamény and six for Mátészalka, stopping at Nagykálló, Máriapócs and Nyírbátor en route. Two daily express trains (the Tisza and the Puskin) en route to Lvov, Kiev and Moscow also stop here.

Getting Around
Almost everything – with the exception of Sóstógyógyfürdő – can be easily reached on foot. Take bus No 7 or 8 from the train or bus stations to reach the centre of town; Nos 8 and 14 go to Sóstógyógyfürdő and pass the colleges on Sóstói út along the way. For the flea market, catch bus No 1 or 1/a; the former carries on to the airport.

You can order a taxi on ☎ 410 111.

AROUND NYÍREGYHÁZA
Nagykálló
• *pop 10,000*

This dusty (or muddy, depending on the season) town 14 km by train south-east of Nyíregyháza boasts some important listed buildings in its central square (Szabadság tér): a baroque **Calvinist church** with a separate Gothic bell tower originally built in the 15th century, and the splendid former **county hall** at No 13 done up in Zopf style and later turned into a notorious insane asylum. In October in alternating years, Nagykálló hosts the popular Two-Step Folk-Dance Festival.

But most visitors to Nagykálló are Jewish pilgrims who come to pay their respects at the **tomb of Isaac Taub Eizik** on the anniversary of his death (February or March, according to the Jewish calendar). Known as the 'Wonder Rabbi of Kálló', he was an 18th-century philosopher who advocated a more humanistic approach to prayer and study. His small tomb in the old Jewish cemetery on Nagybalkányi út can be visited, but you must seek the key from the house at Széchenyi utca 6 not far from the main square.

A bus meets each incoming train and goes as far as Szabadság tér. There's no accommodation in Nagykálló, but the *Belvárosi Eszpresszó* to the north of the square on Kossuth Lajos utca has sandwiches, the large *Kálló* restaurant is opposite the county hall and, on Szabadság tér itself, there's a small *bisztro* selling decent gyros and lángos. You can also reach Nagykálló by bus throughout the day from Nyíregyháza. At least two of these continue on to Máriapócs and Nyírbátor.

NYÍRBÁTOR
• *pop 14,000*
• *area code ☎ 42*

Nyírbátor, a town some 38 km south-east of Nyíregyháza in the centre of the lovely Nyírség region, is well worth seeing. It contains two Gothic churches built in the latter part of the 15th century by István Báthory,

the ruthless Transylvanian prince whose family is synonymous with the town. As the Báthory family's economic and political influence grew from the 15th to 17th century, so did Nyírbátor's. The town is also a music centre; the Nyírbátor Musical Days festival in July attracts visitors from all over Hungary.

Orientation & Information

Nyírbátor is compact, and everything of interest can be reached on foot. The train and bus stations are in the northern part of town on Ady Endre utca less than a km from the centre (Szabadság tér) via Kossuth Lajos utca.

The small Nyírtourist office (☎ 381 525) at Szabadság tér 14 is open weekdays from 8.30 am to 4 pm.

There's an OTP bank just across the road from the tourist office at the start of Zrínyi utca. The main post office is on the southwest side of Szabadság tér.

Things to See

The **Calvinist church**, on a small hill just off Báthory István utca, is one of the most beautiful Gothic churches in Hungary. The ribbed vault of the nave is a masterpiece, and the long lancet windows flood the stark white interior with light. The remains of István Báthory lie in a marble tomb at the back of the church; the family's coat of arms embellished with wyverns (mythical dragon-like creatures) is on top. The 17th-century wooden **bell tower**, standing apart from the church as was prescribed by Calvinism, has a Gothic roof with four little turrets. You can climb the 20m to the top 'at your own risk'. The pastor, who lives in the house just behind the church to the north, holds the massive medieval keys to the church and tower. Daily visiting hours are 8 am to noon and 2.30 to 4.30 pm (on Sunday from 10 am to noon and 3 to 4 pm).

The **Minorite church** on Károlyi Mihály utca is another Báthory contribution. Originally late Gothic, it was ravaged by the Turks in 1587 and rebuilt in baroque style 130

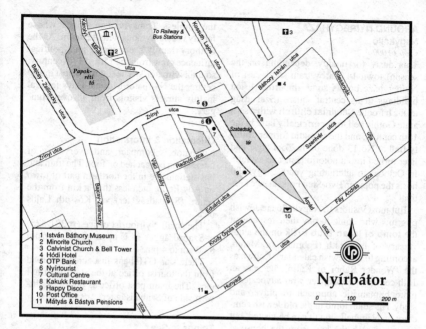

1 István Báthory Museum
2 Minorite Church
3 Calvinist Church & Bell Tower
4 Hódi Hotel
5 OTP Bank
6 Nyírtourist
7 Cultural Centre
8 Kakukk Restaurant
9 Happy Disco
10 Post Office
11 Mátyás & Bástya Pensions

Nyírbátor

0   100   200 m

years later. Five spectacular altars carved in Prešov (eastern Slovakia) in the mid-18th century fill the nave and chancel. The most interesting is the first on the left, the baroque **Krucsay Altar of the Passion** (1737), with its diverse portraits of fear, longing and devotion. To gain entry, ring the bell of the rectory door immediately left of the church entrance.

The **István Báthory Museum**, in the 18th-century monastery next to the church, has a very good ethnographic collection and some medieval pieces connected with the Báthory family and the churches they built. It's open daily except Monday from 9 am to 5 pm.

Places to Stay

Accommodation choices in Nyírbátor are limited; your best bet is to see Nyírtourist about arranging a *private room* (from 600 to 700 Ft per person).

The *Mátyás* pension (☎ 281 657) at Hunyadi

utca 8 has eight rooms but may now function just as a restaurant. Its flashy 15-room extension, the *Bástya* (same telephone number) next door, charges 3700/4400 Ft for singles/doubles. The only other place in Nyírbátor is the attractive *Hódi* hotel (☎ 281 012) in a small courtyard at Báthory István utca 12. Its 11 rooms have mini-bars, satellite TV and all the other features of a top-class place, and there's a small restaurant and bar. Singles/doubles are 4500/5000 Ft.

Places to Eat

The *Tinódi* restaurant across from the train station at Ady Endre utca 14 is open till 10 pm, and there's a small *büfé* around the corner at Martinovich utca 21.

The *Mátyás* pension has a restaurant called the *Troféa* serving fish and game dishes. *Kakukk* at Szabadság tér 24 is the only real restaurant in the centre. Its well prepared daily menu is very reasonable, but it closes at 9 pm.

NORTH-EAST

The Gypsies

The origins of the Gypsies (Hungarian: *cigány*), who call themselves Rom and speak Romany, a language closely related to several spoken today in northern India, remain a mystery. It is generally accepted, however, that they began migrating to Persia from India sometime in the 10th century and had reached the Balkans by the 14th century. They have been in Hungary for at least 500 years, and their numbers today are estimated at about 250,000.

Though traditionally a travelling people, in modern times Hungarian Gypsies have by and large settled down and worked as smiths and tinkers, livestock and horse traders and as musicians (see Music & Dance in the Facts about the Country chapter). As a group, however, they are chronically underemployed and have been the hardest hit by economic recession. Statistically, Gypsy families are twice the size of *gadje*, or 'non-Gypsy' ones.

Unsettled people have always been persecuted in one form or another by those who stay put and Hungarian Gypsies are no exception. They are widely hated and remain the scapegoats for everything that goes wrong in certain parts of the country, from the rise in petty theft and prostitution to the loss of jobs. Though their rights are inscribed in the 1989 constitution along with other ethnic minorities, their housing ranks among the worst in the nation, police are regularly accused of harassing them and, more than any other group, they fear the rightists' 'national revival'. You will probably be shocked at what even highly educated, cosmopolitan Hungarians say about Gypsies and their way of life. ∎

Entertainment

Concerts are held in the *Calvinist church* during the music festival in July, and organ recitals can be heard sporadically throughout the year. Nyírtourist or the people at the *cultural centre* (☎ 381 155) at Szabadság tér 7 should be able to help.

The *Happy* bar and disco, at the end of the big, sand-coloured town hall on Szabadság tér, is open till midnight on weekdays and at weekends till late.

Getting There & Away

There are very few long-distance buses trav-

elling to/from Nyírbátor; most just serve the small towns surrounding the city. These include Nagykálló (two), Nyíregyháza (three) and Máriapócs (six).

Six trains a day from Nyíregyháza call at Nyírbátor on their way to Mátészalka; 10 trains heading for Mátészalka from Debrecen also stop here. At Mátészalka, you can catch one of seven trains heading north for Záhony on the border with Ukraine, or three going south to Carei in Romania.

AROUND NYÍRBÁTOR

Máriapócs
• *pop 2000*

This town 12 km north-west of Nyírbátor contains a beautiful **Greek Catholic church**, with an unbelievably ornate gold iconostasis soaring some 15m up to the vaulted ceiling. Built in the middle of the 18th century, the church has been an important pilgrimage site almost from the start because of the **Weeping Black Madonna**, which now takes pride of place above the altar on the north side of the church.

Indeed, Pope John Paul II hurried here on his first visit to Hungary in August 1991 to pay homage to the miraculous icon. What he surely knew – but most others don't – is that this is not the original but a 19th-century copy. The real one is now in St Stephen's Cathedral in Vienna.

Buses from Nagykálló (two a day), Nyírbátor (five) and Nyíregyháza (two) will drop you off by the church. All the trains between Nyírbátor and Nyíregyháza stop at the Máriapócs train station, which is four km south of the town centre. Buses make the run between the centre and the station, but they are not very reliable.

Tiszahát & Erdőhát Regions

The most traditional parts of the county lie east and south of the Tisza River and are commonly referred to by their geographical locations: 'behind the Tisza' (Tiszahát) and 'behind the woods' (Erdőhát) of Transylvania. Because of their isolation, folk traditions have continued on here, especially in architecture. Some of the finest examples of Hungarian popular building and interior church painting can be found in this area – at least those that weren't moved to Szentendre's huge Open-Air Ethnographical Museum during the former regime. It is also the site of Hungary's most unusual cemetery.

With its rolling hills, ever-present Tisza and the soft silver-green of the poplar trees, this region is among the prettiest in Hungary. Unfortunately, it is also one of the most difficult to get around and, without your own transport, you should be prepared for long waits to connect between small towns. Distances are generally not great, though. For those of you not under your own steam, the best idea is to take the train or bus from Nyíregyháza or Nyírbátor to Vásárosnamény and use that as your starting point.

Information

Nyírtourist-Bereg Tourist (☎ 45-371 113) in Vásárosnamény is at Szabadság tér 9, some 1200m east of the train station. It generally handles the Tiszahát region east and north of the Tisza River. Nyírtourist (☎ 44-310 410) at Bajcsy-Zsilinszky utca 3 in Mátészalka is good for the Erdőhát.

Things to See & Do

Vásárosnamény This sleepy town of 9000 people, but it was once an important trading post on the lucrative Salt Road from the forests of Transylvania via the Tisza River and then across the Great Plain to Debrecen. Though it won't hold your interest for long, the **Bereg Museum** at Rákóczi utca 13 has a small, interesting collection of local embroidery, weaving and painted Easter eggs, a popular local art form. Keep an eye open for the famous Bereg cross-stitching, a blend of many different styles. The museum is open weekdays from 8.30 am to 4.30 or 5 pm and on Saturday and Sunday from 8 am to 4 pm.

Tákos The 18th-century wattle-and-daub **Calvinist church** in this village, eight km north-east of Vásárosnamény on route No 41, has a spectacularly painted coffered ceiling of blue and red flowers, a floor of beaten earth and an ornately carved 'folk baroque' pulpit sitting on a large millstone. Outside the church, which villagers call the 'barefoot Notre Dame of Hungary', stands a perfectly preserved **bell tower** (1767); it was almost carted off to Szentendre in the 1970s. The keeper of the keys lives in one of the houses just north of the church; if you're driving, sound the horn three times and she'll soon arrive at the church to let you in.

Csaroda A **Romanesque church** dating from the 13th century stands on Kossuth utca in Csaroda, some two km east of Tákos. The church is thought to have been founded by King Stephen, following his plan to have at least one church for every 10 villages in his domain. The church is a wonderful hybrid of a place with both Western and Eastern-style frescoes (some from the 14th century) as well as some fairly crude folk murals. On the short walk from the car park or bus stop, you'll pass two wooden **bell towers** of much more recent vintage. The key to the church is in the shop opposite the first tower.

Tarpa Six km farther east on route No 41 will take you to the turn-off for Fehérgyarmat. Another 10 km to the south is Tarpa, a town of 2500 people boasting one of Hungary's last examples of a horse-driven **dry mill**. The mill went through many incarnations – as a bar, a cinema and dance hall – before its renovation in the late 1970s. Still, it can't compare with the dry mill in Szarvas in south-east Hungary.

Szatmárcseke To get to this village, site of a cemetery with intriguing boat-shaped **grave markers**, travel another five km south to Tivadar and the Tisza River. After crossing the river, turn east and carry on another seven km north-east to Szatmárcseke. The carved *kopjafák* in the cemetery are unique in Hungary, and the notches and grooves cut into them represent a complicated language all of their own: it details marital status, social position, age etc. One of the few stone markers in the cemetery is that of Ferenc Kölcsey, who wrote the words to *Himnusz*, the Hungarian national anthem.

Túristvándi There is a wonderfully restored 18th-century **water mill** on a small tributary of the Tisza at Túristvándi, four km due south of Szatmárcseke. The surrounding forest park is the perfect place for a picnic.

Places to Stay

In Vásárosnamény, see Nyírtourist-Bereg Tourist for *private rooms* both in town and in other parts of the region from about 800 Ft. The *Tiszavirág* camp site (☎45-371 076) is across the river in Gergelyiugornya, and there's a new hotel in town called the *Marianna Center* (☎ 45-371 401), Szabadság tér 19, with doubles from 3000 Ft.

In Mátészalka, the *Szatmár* hotel (☎ 44-310 428) is at Hősök tere 8.

The *Kúria* (☎ 45-371 113), an old manor house now serving as an inn at József Attila utca 67 in Csaroda, has four three-bed rooms from 600 Ft per person. In Tarpa, the *Riviera* pension (☎ 42-343 028) is near the dry mill at Árpád utca 24.

In Tivadar, *Katica Camping* (☎ 44-363 859) at Petőfi utca 11 and *Diós Camping* (no ☎) on Tisza-part are both open from June to August.

In Szatmárcseke, the 13-room *Kölcsey* inn (☎ 60-355 233) at Honvéd utca 6 is a run-down old place on a quiet, leafy street. It's dirt cheap (doubles under 1000 Ft) but not a particularly pleasant place to stay, and it closes in winter. You'd do just as well by walking along the main street in the village and knocking at the door of any house with a *szoba kiadó* (or *Zimmer frei*) sign outside.

Getting There & Away

The ideal way to visit this part of Hungary is by car or bicycle (perhaps rented at one of the camping grounds in Nyíregyháza). If neither is an option, you can visit most of the places mentioned here by bus from

Vásárosnamény, Mátészalka or Fehérgyarmat. But departures are infrequent, averaging only two or three a day. Check return schedules from your destination carefully before setting out.

From Nyíregyháza, there are seven trains each day leaving for Vásárosnamény, and six for Mátészalka via Nagykálló and Nyírbátor. To reach Fehérgyarmat from Nyíregyháza by train, you'll have to change at Mátészalka (nine a day).

Rétköz Region

The Rétköz area north-east of Nyíregyháza lies somewhat lower than the rest of the North-East and was particularly prone to flooding. Agriculture was possible only on the larger of the islands in this mosquito-infested swampland, and the isolation spurred the development of strong clan ties and a wealth of folk tales and myths. That's all in the past now, and you won't see any more evidence of it than the once celebrated Rétköz homespun cloth. But you might get lucky...

KISVÁRDA
• *pop 19,000*
• *area code* ☎ 45

Kisvárda, 42 km north of Nyíregyháza and the centre of the Rétköz region, was an important stronghold during the Turkish invasions, and the remains of its fortress can still be seen. It's only 25 km from here to Ukraine and, if you're continuing onward, it's a much nicer place to stay the night than the border town of Záhony, where accommodation is virtually nonexistent.

Orientation & Information

Kisvárda's bus and train stations lie just over two km south-west of Flórián tér, the town centre. Local buses await arriving trains, but it's an easy, straightforward walk north along tree-lined Bocskai utca, Rákóczi utca and Szent László utca to town. The last stretch of Szent László utca is particularly colourful,

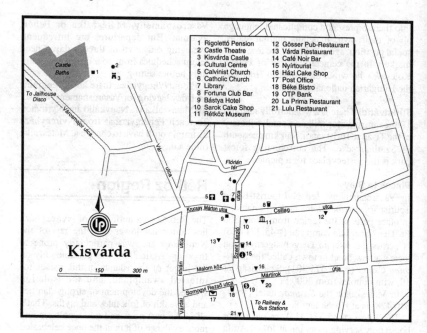

1 Rigolettó Pension	12 Gösser Pub-Restaurant
2 Castle Theatre	13 Várda Restaurant
3 Kisvárda Castle	14 Café Noir Bar
4 Cultural Centre	15 Nyírtourist
5 Calvinist Church	16 Házi Cake Shop
6 Catholic Church	17 Post Office
7 Library	18 Béke Bistro
8 Fortuna Club Bar	19 OTP Bank
9 Bástya Hotel	20 La Prima Restaurant
10 Sarok Cake Shop	21 Lulu Restaurant
11 Rétköz Museum	

Kisvárda

0   150   300 m

with virtually every building having had a face-lift or a fresh coat of bright paint applied in recent years. Some buses also drop passengers off at Flórián tér, and there's a schedule posted here.

Nyírtourist (☎ 405 241) is at Szent László utca 22. It's open from 8 am to 4 pm weekdays.

You'll find an OTP bank at the corner of Mártírok útja and Szent László utca. The main post office is at Somogyi Rezső utca 4.

Things to See & Do

Flórián tér offers the usual Gothic-cum-baroque **Catholic church** and a late 19th-century rosy-pink **Calvinist church** sitting uncomfortably close by. Far more interesting is the Zopf-style **town library** that is the pride of the square.

A short distance to the east of the square at Csillag utca 5 is the **Rétköz Museum**. Housed in a disused synagogue built at the turn of the century, the building itself is as interesting as the exhibits, with its geometric

ceiling patterns, blue and yellow stained glass and wrought-iron gates in the shape of menorahs. Lots of 'typical' Rétköz village rooms and workshops (a smithy, loom, etc) are set up on the ground floor of the museum, but the 1st floor has some interesting art, especially the paintings by Gyula Pál. Just inside the west entrance is a memorial tablet with over 1000 names of Jewish citizens of Kisvárda who died in Auschwitz. The museum is open daily except Monday from 9 am to noon and 1 to 4.30 or 5 pm.

The ruins of **Kisvárda Castle** are about 10 minutes by foot north-west of Flórián tér at the end of Vár utca. Though part of one wall dates from the 15th century, most of the castle has been heavily restored. A small exhibition room in a corner tower explains the history of the castle and the town. The courtyard is used as an open-air theatre in summer.

The **Várfürdő** beside the castle ruins on Városmajor utca is a small complex of fresh-

NORTH-EAST

water and thermal pools, with sauna and sunbathing areas. It's open May to September from 9 am to 7 pm.

Places to Stay

Nyírtourist can organise *private rooms* from 800 Ft, or you can stay at the *Rigolettó* pension (☎ 420 501), a rundown holiday house beside the castle ruins and baths at Városmajor utca 43. Rigolettó can accommodate about 60 people in multi-bed rooms in its main building, and there's a series of cramped cottages for about 1500 Ft (doubles).

A much better (and more central) choice would be the *Bástya* hotel (☎ 421 100) on the 2nd floor of the shopping arcade at Krucsay Márton utca 2. Its 18 double rooms cost 2000/2300 Ft without/with shower.

Places to Eat

The *Várda* restaurant, behind the hideous modern town hall at Szent László utca 15, is a dreary place to have a meal, but it's central and inexpensive. A better choice would be *La Prima*, with better-than-average Hungarian meals at Mártírok útja 3 and it's open daily till midnight. *Lulu* is a rather expensive Chinese restaurant at Szent László utca 47. The new kid in town is the *Gösser* pub-restaurant at the eastern end of Csillag utca just before the roundabout.

The coffee shop with the best cakes and ice cream in town is the *Házi* at Mártírok útja 2. *Sarok*, at Szent László utca 2, is a bit more central.

Entertainment

Plays are sometimes staged at the *Castle Theatre* in summer; check with Nyírtourist or the staff at the modern *cultural centre* on the northern side of Flórián tér. The cultural centre also has a small theatre.

The *Béke* is a seedy but friendly little bistro at Szent László utca 33 – just the place to stumble into in the early evening. A more up-market place is *Café Noir*, a bit farther north on Szent László utca. The video games and pool tables on the 1st floor of the *Fortuna Club* bar on Csillag utca (opposite

the Rétköz Museum) are the main draws for Kisvárda's young bloods.

The top dancing venue in town is the *Jailhouse Disco*, about 1.5 km north-west of the centre on Városmajor utca. It rages most nights from 9 pm to 3 am.

Getting There & Away

Kisvárda is not well served by buses with only a few destinations accessible including Dombrád (two a day), Sárospatak (one), Nyíregyháza (three) and Vásárosnamény (five).

The town is on the railway line connecting Nyíregyháza with Záhony, and you have a choice of 14 trains a day, some of which originate in Budapest. The two daily express trains headed for Ukraine and Russia also stop in Kisvárda before crossing the border at Záhony.

DOMBRÁD
• *pop 4700*

Rail buffs should consider the **narrow-gauge train** trip from this town on the Tisza River back to Nyíregyháza, some 50 km to the south-east. Buses connect Kisvárda with Dombrád, which is 14 km to the west.

There's not a whole lot to see or do when you get to Dombrád – an 18th-century church, a pontoon bridge across the river, a camping ground with the small *Dombrád* motel (☎ Dombrád 87), and a restaurant – but the 2½-hour ride will have train enthusiasts in ecstasy.

There are five trains a day running from Dombrád to Herminatanya, 28 km to the south-west, where you change trains for the final leg to Nyíregyháza. You'll only wait about 10 minutes for the connection, and the last train leaves Dombrád at 4.58 pm. All the trains call at the Sóstógyógyfürdő station and the one near the flea market (Vásártér) in Nyíregyháza before terminating at Nyíregyháza külső (abbreviated NyK on the timetable), the city's 'outer' train station on Kállói utca. The No 2 bus will take you to the centre of Nyíregyháza. The trains do *not* stop at the main station.

Glossary

If you can't find the word you're looking for here, try the Language section in the Facts about the Country chapter, or the Food and Drinks sections in the Facts for the Visitor chapter.

ÁEV – United Forest Railways
ÁFA – value-added tax (VAT)
Alföld – see *Nagyalföld*
autóbusz – bus
Ausgleich – German for 'reconciliation'; the Compromise of 1867
áutóbuszállomás – bus station
Avars – a people of the Caucasus who invaded Europe in the 6th century
ÁVO – Rákosi's hated secret police; later renamed ÁVH

bal – left
bejárat – entrance
borozó – wine bar
BKV – Budapest's city transport company
Bp – abbreviation for Budapest
búcsú – farewell; also, a church patronal festival
büfé – snack bar

centrum – town or city centre
Compromise of 1867 – agreement creating the dual monarchy of Austria-Hungary
Copf – a transitional architectural style between late baroque and neoclassicism (see *Zopf*)
csárda – a Hungarian-style inn/restaurant
csatorna – canal
csikós – cowboy from the *puszta*
csomagmegőrző – left-luggage office
cukrászda – cake shop or café

D – abbreviation for *dél* (south)
Dacia – Roman name for Romania and lands east of the Tisza River
db or **drb** – piece (used in shopping)
de – am (in the morning)

du – pm (in the afternoon)

É – abbreviation for *észak* (north)
Eclectic – an art style popular in Hungary in the Romantic period, drawing from varied sources
élelmiszer – grocery shop, provisions
előszoba – vestibule or anteroom; one of three rooms in a traditional Hungarian cottage
em – abbreviation for *emelet* (floor or storey)
erdő – forest
érkezés – arrivals
eszpresszó or **presszó** – coffee shop, often also selling alcoholic drinks and snacks; strong, black coffee
étterem – restaurant

falu – village
fasor – boulevard, avenue
felvilágosítás – information
fogas – pikeperch of Lake Balaton
folyó – river
fsz – ground floor
Ft – forint (see also *HUF*)

gyula – chief military commander of the early Magyar

hajdúk – Hungarian for *Heyducks*
hajó – boat
hajó llomás – ferry pier or landing
hegy – hill, mountain
HÉV – suburban commuter train in Budapest
Heyducks – drovers and outlaws from the *puszta* who fought as mercenaries/partisans against the Habsburgs
helyi autóbusz pályaudvar – local bus station
híd – bridge
honfoglalás – conquest of the Carpathian Basin by the early Magyars in the late ninth century

HTB – Hungarian Tourist Board (OIH in Hungarian)
HUF – forint (international currency code)
Huns – a Mongol tribe that swept across Europe, notably under Attila, in the 5th century AD

Ibusz – Hungarian national network of travel agencies
ifjúsági szálló – youth hostel
indulás – departures

jobb – right

K – abbreviation for *kelet* (east)
kamra – workshop or shed; one of three rooms in a traditional Hungarian cottage
kb – approximately
kékfestő – cotton fabric dyed a rich indigo blue
kemping – camping ground
Keokh – foreigners' registration office
kerület – district
khas – towns of the Ottoman period under direct rule of the sultan
kijárat – exit
kincstár – treasury
Kiskörút – the 'little ring road' in Budapest
kocsma – pub or saloon
komp – ferry
körút – ring road
köz – alley, mews
központ – town or city centre
krt – see *körút*
kúria – mansions or country house
kuruc – Hungarian mercenaries/partisans who resisted the expansion of Habsburg rule in Hungary after the withdrawal of the Turks (late 17th/early 18th centuries)

lángos – deep-fried dough with toppings
lépcső – stairs, steps
liget – park

Mahart – Hungarian passenger ferry company
Malév – Hungary's national airline
MÁV – Hungarian State Railways
megye – county
menetrend – timetable

mihrab – Mecca-oriented prayer niche
MNB – National Bank of Hungary
Moorish Romantic – an art style popular in the decoration of 19th-century synagogues

Nagykörút – the 'big ring road' in Budapest
Nagyalföld – the Great Plain (also called the *Alföld* or *puszta*)
Nonius – Hungarian horse breed
nosztalgiavonat – MÁV vintage steam train
Ny – abbreviation for *nyugat* (west)
nyitva – open

ó – see *óra*
OIH – Hungarian Tourist Board (OIH in Hungarian)
óra, abbreviated **ó** – hour, o'clock
oszt – abbreviation for *osztály* (department)
OTP – National Savings Bank
Ottoman Empire – the Turkish empire that took over from the Byzantine Empire when it captured Constantinople (Istanbul) in 1453, and expanded into southeastern Europe right up to the gates of Vienna

pálinka – Hungarian fruit brandy
pályaudvar – train station
Pannonia – Roman name for the lands south and west of the Danube River
panzió – pension, guesthouse
part – embankment
patika – pharmacy
pénztár – cashier
pénzváltó – exchange office
pince – wine cellar
porta – type of farmhouse in Transdanubia
presszó – see *eszpresszó*
pu – see *pályaudvar*
puli – Hungarian breed of sheepdog with shaggy coat
puszta – common geographical term for wilderness plains, see *Nagyalföld*
puttony – the number of 'butts' of sweet *aszú* essence added to other base wines in making Tokaj wine

racka – *puszta* sheep with distinctive corkscrew horns

rakpart – quay, embankment
repülőtér – airport
Romany – the language and culture of Gypsies

Secessionism – art and architectural style similar to Art Nouveau
sedile, sedilia – medieval stone niches with seats
sétány – walkway, promenade
skanzen – open-air museum displaying village architecture
söröző – beer bar or pub
stb – abbreviation equivalent to English 'etc'
strand – grassy 'beach' near a river or lake
sug rút – avenue
szálló, szálloda – hotel
sziget – island
szoba kiadó – room for rent
szűr – long embroidered felt cloak or cape worn by traditional Hungarian shepherds

Tanácsköztá rsaság – the 1919 Communist Republic of Councils under Béla Kun
táncház – an evening of folk music and dance
tanya – homestead or ranch
távolsági autóbusz pályaudvar – long-distance bus station
tér – town or market square
tere – genitive form of *tér* as in *Hősök tere* ('Square of the Heroes')
tilos – prohibited
tista szoba – parlour; one of three rooms in a traditional Hungarian cottage
tó – lake
toalett – toilet
Trianon Treaty – 1920 treaty imposed on Hungary by the victorious Allies, which reduced the country to one-third of its former size, allowing for the creation of new countries like Yugoslavia and Czechoslovakia

Triple Alliance – 1882-1914 alliance between Germany, Austria-Hungary and Italy – not to be confused with the WWI Allies (members of the *Triple Entente* and their supporters)
Triple Entente – agreement between Britain, France and Russia, intended as a counter-balance to the *Triple Alliance*, lasting until the Russian Revolution of 1917
turul – eagle-like totem of the ancient Magyars and now a national symbol

u – see *utca*
udvar – court
úszoda – swimming pool
út – road
utca – street
utcája – genitive form of *utca* as in *Ferencesek utcája* ('Street of the Franciscans')
útja – genitive form of *út* as in *Mártírok útja* ('Street of the Martyrs')

va, vm – abbreviations for *vasútállomás*
vágány – platform
vár – castle
város – city
vasútállomás – train station
vendéglő – a type of restaurant
vm – see *va*
Volán – Hungarian bus company
vonat – train

WC – toilet (see also *toalett*)

zárva – closed
Zimmer frei – German for 'room for rent'
Zopf – German and more commonly used word for *Copf*

Alternative Place Names

The following abbreviations are used:
(C) Croatian
(E) English
(G) German
(H) Hungarian
(R) Romanian
(S) Serbian
(Slk) Slovak
(Slo) Slovene
(U) Ukrainian

Alba Iulia (R) – Gyula Fehérvár (H), Karls-
    burg/Weissenburg (G)

Baia Mare (R) – Nagybánya (H)
Balaton (H) – Plattensee (G)
Belgrade (E) – Beograd (S),
    Nándorfehérvár (H)
Beregovo (U) – Beregszász (H)
Braşov (R) – Brassó (H), Kronstadt (G)
Bratislava (Slk) – Pozsony (H), Pressburg (G)

Carei (R) – Magykároly (H)
Cluj-Napoca (R) – Kolozsvár (H), Klausen-
    burg (G)

Danube (E) – Duna (H), Donau (G)
Danube Bend (E) – Dunakanyar (H),
    Donauknie (G)
Debrecen (H) – Debrezin (G)

Eger (H) – Erlau (G)
Eisenstadt (G) – Kismarton (H)
Esztergom (H) – Gran (G)

Great Plain (E) – Nagyalföld, Alföld or
    Puszta (H)
Győr (H) – Raab (G)

Hungary (E) – Magyarország (H), Ungarn (G)

Kisalföld (H) – Little Plain (E)
Komárom (H) – Komárno (Slk)
Košice (Slk) – Kassa (H), Kaschau (G)
Kőszeg (H) – Güns (G)

Lendava (Slo) – Lendva (H)

Lučenec (Slk) – Losonc (H)

Mukačevo (U) – Munkács (H)
Murska Sobota (Slo) – Muraszombat (H)

Northern Uplands (E) – Északi Felföld (H)

Oradea (R) – Nagyvárad (H),
    Grosswardein (G)
Osijek (C) – Eszék (H)

Pécs (H) – Fünfkirchen (G)

Rožnava (Slk) – Rozsnyó (H)

Satu Mare (R) – Szatmárnémeti (H)
Senta (S) – Zenta (H)
Sibiu (R) – Nagyszében (H),
    Hermannstadt (G)
Sic (R) – Szék (H)
Sighişoara (R) – Szegesvár (H),
    Schässburg (G)
Sopron (H) – Ödenburg (G)
Štúrovo (Slk) – Párkány (H)
Subotica (S) – Szabadka (H)
Szeged (H) – Segedin (G)
Székesfehérvár (H) – Stuhlweissenburg (G)
Szombathely (H) – Steinamanger (G)

Tata (H) – Totis (G)
Timişoara (R) – Temesvár (H)
Tirgu Mureş (R) – Marosvásárhely (H)
Transdanubia (E) – Dunántúl (H)
Transylvania (R) – Erdély (H),
    Siebenbürgen (G)
Trnava (Slk) – Nagyszombat (H)

Užgorod (U) – Ungvár (H)

Vác (H) – Wartzen (G)
Vienna (E) – Wien (G), Bécs (H)
Villány (H) – Wieland (G)
Villánykövesd (H) – Growisch (G)

Wiener Neustadt (G) – Bécsújhely (H)

Boxed Asides

Index

TEXT

LONELY PLANET PHRASEBOOKS

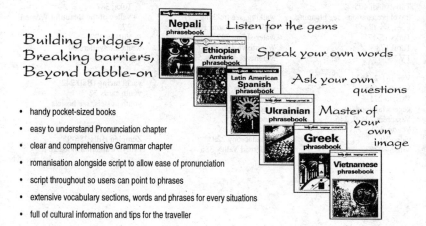

Building bridges,
Breaking barriers,
Beyond babble-on

Listen for the gems

Speak your own words

Ask your own
questions

Master of
your
own
image

- handy pocket-sized books
- easy to understand Pronunciation chapter
- clear and comprehensive Grammar chapter
- romanisation alongside script to allow ease of pronunciation
- script throughout so users can point to phrases
- extensive vocabulary sections, words and phrases for every situations
- full of cultural information and tips for the traveller

'...vital for a real DIY spirit and attitude in language learning' – Backpacker

'the phrasebooks have good cultural backgrounders and offer solid advice for challenging situations in remote locations' – San Francisco Examiner

'...they are unbeatable for their coverage of the world's more obscure languages' – The Geographical Magazine

---

Arabic (Egyptian)
Arabic (Moroccan)
Australia
  Australian English, Aboriginal and Torres Strait languages
Baltic States
  Estonian, Latvian, Lithuanian
Bengali
Burmese
Brazilian
Cantonese
Central Europe
  Czech, French, German, Hungarian, Italian and Slovak
Eastern Europe
  Bulgarian, Czech, Hungarian, Polish, Romanian and Slovak
Egyptian Arabic
Ethiopian (Amharic)
Fijian
Greek
Hindi/Urdu

Indonesian
Japanese
Korean
Lao
Latin American Spanish
Malay
Mandarin
Mediterranean Europe
  Albanian, Croatian, Greek, Italian, Macedonian, Maltese, Serbian, Slovene
Mongolian
Moroccan Arabic
Nepali
Papua New Guinea
Pilipino (Tagalog)
Quechua
Russian
Scandinavian Europe
  Danish, Finnish, Icelandic, Norwegian and Swedish

South-East Asia
  Burmese, Indonesian, Khmer, Lao, Malay, Tagalog (Pilipino), Thai and Vietnamese
Sri Lanka
Swahili
Thai
Thai Hill Tribes
Tibetan
Turkish
Ukrainian
USA
  US English, Vernacular Talk, Native American languages and Hawaiian
Vietnamese
Western Europe
  Basque, Catalan, Dutch, French, German, Irish, Italian, Portuguese, Scottish Gaelic, Spanish (Castilian) and Welsh

LONELY PLANET JOURNEYS

JOURNEYS is a unique collection of travel writing – published by the company that understands travel better than anyone else. It is a series for anyone who has ever experienced – or dreamed of – the magical moment when they encountered a strange culture or saw a place for the first time. They are tales to read while you're planning a trip, while you're on the road or while you're in an armchair, in front of a fire.

JOURNEYS books catch the spirit of a place, illuminate a culture, recount a crazy adventure, or introduce a fascinating way of life. They always entertain, and always enrich the experience of travel.

THE GATES OF DAMASCUS
Lieve Joris
Translated by Sam Garrett

This best-selling book is a beautifully drawn portrait of day-to-day life in modern Syria. Through her intimate contact with local people, Lieve Joris draws us into the fascinating world that lies behind the gates of Damascus. Hala's husband is a political prisoner, jailed for his opposition to the Assad regime; through the author's friendship with Hala we see how Syrian politics impacts on the lives of ordinary people.

Lieve Joris, who was born in Belgium, is one of Europe's leading travel writers. In addition to an award-winning book on Hungary, she has published widely acclaimed accounts of her journeys to the Middle East and Africa. *The Gates of Damascus* is her fifth book.

'Expands the boundaries of travel writing' – Times Literary Supplement

---

KINGDOM OF THE FILM STARS
Journey into Jordan
Annie Caulfield

Kingdom of the Film Stars is a travel book and a love story. With honesty and humour, Annie Caulfield writes of travelling in Jordan and falling in love with a Bedouin. Her book offers fascinating insights into the country – from the traditional tent life of nomadic tribes to the first woman MP's battle with fundamentalist colleagues. *Kingdom of the Film Stars* unpicks some of the tight-woven Western myths about the Arab world, presenting cultural and political issues within the intimate framework of a compelling love story.

Annie Caulfield, who was born in Ireland and currently lives in London, is an award-winning playwright and journalist. She has travelled widely in the Middle East.

'Annie Caulfield is a remarkable traveller. Her story is fresh, courageous, moving, witty and sexy!' – Dawn French

LONELY PLANET TRAVEL ATLASES

Lonely Planet has long been famous for the number and quality of its guidebook maps. Now we've gone one step further and in conjunction with Steinhart Katzir Publishers produced a handy companion series: Lonely Planet travel atlases – maps of a country produced in book form.

Unlike other maps, which look good but lead travellers astray, our travel atlases have been researched on the road by Lonely Planet's experienced team of writers. All details are carefully checked to ensure the atlas corresponds with the equivalent Lonely Planet guidebook.

The handy atlas format means no holes, wrinkles, torn sections or constant folding and unfolding. These atlases can survive long periods on the road, unlike cumbersome fold-out maps. The comprehensive index ensures easy reference.

- full-colour throughout
- maps researched and checked by Lonely Planet authors
- place names correspond with Lonely Planet guidebooks
  – no confusing spelling differences
- legend and travelling information in English, French, German, Japanese and Spanish
- size: 230 x 160 mm

Available now:
Chile & Easter Island • Egypt • India & Bangladesh • Israel & the Palestinian Territories •Jordan, Syria & Lebanon • Kenya • Laos • Portugal • South Africa, Lesotho & Swaziland • Thailand • Vietnam • Zimbabwe, Botswana & Namibia

LONELY PLANET TV SERIES & VIDEOS

Lonely Planet travel guides have been brought to life on television screens around the world. Like our guides, the programmes are based on the joy of independent travel, and look honestly at some of the most exciting, picturesque and frustrating places in the world. Each show is presented by one of three travellers from Australia, England or the USA and combines an innovative mixture of video, Super-8 film, atmospheric soundscapes and original music.

Videos of each episode – containing additional footage not shown on television – are available from good book and video shops, but the availability of individual videos varies with regional screening schedules.

Video destinations include: Alaska • American Rockies • Australia – The South-East • Baja California & the Copper Canyon • Brazil • Central Asia • Chile & Easter Island • Corsica, Sicily & Sardinia – The Mediterranean Islands • East Africa (Tanzania & Zanzibar) • Ecuador & the Galapagos Islands • Greenland & Iceland • Indonesia • Israel & the Sinai Desert • Jamaica • Japan • La Ruta Maya • Morocco • New York • North India • Pacific Islands (Fiji, Solomon Islands & Vanuatu) • South India • South West China • Turkey • Vietnam • West Africa • Zimbabwe, Botswana & Namibia

The Lonely Planet TV series is produced by:
Pilot Productions
Duke of Sussex Studios
44 Uxbridge St
London W8 7TG UK

Lonely Planet videos are distributed by:
IVN Communications Inc
2246 Camino Ramon
California 94583, USA

107 Power Road, Chiswick
London W4 5PL UK

Music from the TV series is available on CD & cassette.
For video availability and ordering information contact your nearest Lonely Planet office.

PLANET TALK

Lonely Planet's FREE quarterly newsletter

We love hearing from you and think you'd like to hear from us.

*When...*is the right time to see reindeer in Finland?
*Where...*can you hear the best palm-wine music in Ghana?
*How...*do you get from Asunción to Areguá by steam train?
*What...*is the best way to see India?

For the answer to these and many other questions read PLANET TALK.

Every issue is packed with up-to-date travel news and advice including:

- a letter from Lonely Planet co-founders Tony and Maureen Wheeler
- go behind the scenes on the road with a Lonely Planet author
- feature article on an important and topical travel issue
- a selection of recent letters from travellers
- details on forthcoming Lonely Planet promotions
- complete list of Lonely Planet products

To join our mailing list contact any Lonely Planet office.

Also available: Lonely Planet T-shirts. 100% heavyweight cotton.

LONELY PLANET ONLINE

Get the latest travel information before you leave or while you're on the road

Whether you've just begun planning your next trip, or you're chasing down specific info on currency regulations or visa requirements, check out Lonely Planet Online for up-to-the-minute travel information.

As well as travel profiles of your favourite destinations (including maps and photos), you'll find current reports from our researchers and other travellers, updates on health and visas, travel advisories, and discussion of the ecological and political issues you need to be aware of as you travel.

There's also an online travellers' forum where you can share your experience of life on the road, meet travel companions and ask other travellers for their recommendations and advice. We also have plenty of links to other online sites useful to independent travellers.

And of course we have a complete and up-to-date list of all Lonely Planet travel products including guides, phrasebooks, atlases, Journeys and videos and a simple online ordering facility if you can't find the book you want elsewhere.

www.lonelyplanet.com
or
AOL keyword: lp

LONELY PLANET PRODUCTS

Lonely Planet is known worldwide for publishing practical, reliable and no-nonsense travel information in our guides and on our web site. The Lonely Planet list covers just about every accessible part of the world. Currently there are eight series: *travel guides, shoestring guides, walking guides, city guides, phrasebooks, audio packs, travel atlases* and *Journeys* – a unique collection of travel writing.

EUROPE

Austria • Baltic States & Kaliningrad • Baltic States phrasebook • Britain • Central Europe on a shoestring • Central Europe phrasebook • Czech & Slovak Republics • Denmark • Dublin city guide • Eastern Europe on a shoestring • Eastern Europe phrasebook • Finland • France • Greece • Greek phrasebook • Hungary • Iceland, Greenland & the Faroe Islands • Ireland • Italy • Mediterranean Europe on a shoestring • Mediterranean Europe phrasebook • Paris city guide • Poland • Portugal • Portugal travel atlas • Prague city guide • Russia, Ukraine & Belarus • Russian phrasebook • Scandinavian & Baltic Europe on a shoestring • Scandinavian Europe phrasebook • Slovenia • Spain • St Petersburg city guide • Switzerland • Trekking in Greece • Trekking in Spain • Ukrainian phrasebook • Vienna city guide • Walking in Britain • Walking in Switzerland • Western Europe on a shoestring • Western Europe phrasebook

NORTH AMERICA

Alaska • Backpacking in Alaska • Baja California• California & Nevada • Canada • Florida • Hawaii • Honolulu city guide • Los Angeles city guide • Mexico • Miami city guide • New England • New Orleans city guide • Pacific Northwest USA • Rocky Mountain States • San Francisco city guide • Southwest USA • USA phrasebook • Washington, DC & the Capital Region

CENTRAL AMERICA & THE CARIBBEAN

Bermuda • Central America on a shoestring • Costa Rica • Cuba • Eastern Caribbean • Guatemala, Belize & Yucatán: La Ruta Maya • Jamaica

SOUTH AMERICA

Argentina, Uruguay & Paraguay • Bolivia • Brazil • Brazilian phrasebook • Buenos Aires city guide • Chile & Easter Island • Chile & Easter Island travel atlas • Colombia • Ecuador & the Galápagos Islands • Latin American Spanish phrasebook • Peru • Quechua phrasebook • Rio de Janeiro city guide • South America on a shoestring • Trekking in the Patagonian Andes • Venezuela

Travel Literature: Full Circle: A South American Journey

ANTARCTICA

Antarctica

ISLANDS OF THE INDIAN OCEAN

Madagascar & Comoros • Maldives & Islands of the East Indian Ocean • Mauritius, Réunion & Seychelles

AFRICA

Arabic (Moroccan) phrasebook • Africa on a shoestring • Cape Town city guide • Central Africa • East Africa • Egypt • Egypt travel atlas• Ethiopian (Amharic) phrasebook • Kenya • Kenya travel atlas • Morocco • North Africa • South Africa, Lesotho & Swaziland • South Africa, Lesotho & Swaziland travel atlas • Swahili phrasebook • Trekking in East Africa • West Africa • Zimbabwe, Botswana & Namibia • Zimbabwe, Botswana & Namibia travel atlas

Travel Literature: The Rainbird: A Central African Journey • Songs to an African Sunset: A Zimbabwean Story

MAIL ORDER

Lonely Planet products are distributed worldwide.They are also available by mail order from Lonely Planet, so if you have difficulty finding a title please write to us. North American and South American residents should write to Embarcadero West, 155 Filbert St, Suite 251, Oakland CA 94607, USA; European and African residents should write to 10 Barley Mow Passage, Chiswick, London W4 4PH; and residents of other countries to PO Box 617, Hawthorn, Victoria 3122, Australia.

NORTH-EAST ASIA

Beijing city guide • Cantonese phrasebook • China • Hong Kong, Macau & Guangzhou• Hong Kong city guide • Japan • Japanese phrasebook • Japanese audio pack • Korea • Korean phrasebook • Mandarin phrasebook • Mongolia • Mongolian phrasebook • North-East Asia on a shoestring • Seoul city guide • Taiwan • Tibet • Tibet phrasebook • Tokyo city guide

Travel Literature: Lost Japan

MIDDLE EAST & CENTRAL ASIA

Arab Gulf States • Arabic (Egyptian) phrasebook • Central Asia • Iran • Israel & the Palestinian Territories • Israel & the Palestinian Territories travel atlas • Istanbul city guide • Jerusalem city guide • Jordan & Syria • Jordan, Syria & Lebanon travel atlas • Middle East • Turkey • Turkish phrasebook • Yemen

Travel Literature: The Gates of Damascus • Kingdom of the Film Stars: Journey into Jordan

ALSO AVAILABLE:

Travel with Children • Traveller's Tales

INDIAN SUBCONTINENT

Bangladesh • Bengali phrasebook • Delhi city guide • Hindi/Urdu phrasebook • India • India & Bangladesh travel atlas • Indian Himalaya • Karakoram Highway • Nepal • Nepali phrasebook • Pakistan • Rajasthan • Sri Lanka • Sri Lanka phrasebook • Trekking in the Indian Himalaya • Trekking in the Karakoram & Hindukush • Trekking in the Nepal Himalaya

Travel Literature: In Rajasthan • Shopping for Buddhas

SOUTH-EAST ASIA

Bali & Lombok • Bangkok city guide • Burmese phrasebook • Cambodia • Ho Chi Minh city guide • Indonesia • Indonesian phrasebook • Indonesian audio pack • Jakarta city guide • Java • Laos • Lao phrasebook • Laos travel atlas • Malay phrasebook • Malaysia, Singapore & Brunei • Myanmar (Burma) • Philippines • Pilipino phrasebook • Singapore city guide • South-East Asia on a shoestring •South-East Asia phrasebook • Thailand • Thailand travel atlas • Thai phrasebook • Thai audio pack • Thai Hill Tribes phrasebook • Vietnam • Vietnamese phrasebook • Vietnam travel atlas

AUSTRALIA & THE PACIFIC

Australia • Australian phrasebook • Bushwalking in Australia • Bushwalking in Papua New Guinea • Fiji • Fijian phrasebook • Islands of Australia's Great Barrier Reef • Melbourne city guide • Micronesia • New Caledonia • New South Wales & the ACT • New Zealand • Northern Territory•Outback Australia • Papua New Guinea • Papua New Guinea phrasebook • Queensland • Rarotonga & the Cook Islands • Samoa • Solomon Islands • South Australia • Sydney city guide • Tahiti & French Polynesia • Tasmania • Tonga • Tramping in New Zealand • Vanuatu • Victoria • Western Australia

Travel Literature: Islands in the Clouds • Sean & David's Long Drive

THE LONELY PLANET STORY

Lonely Planet published its first book in 1973 in response to the numerous 'How did you do it?' questions Maureen and Tony Wheeler were asked after driving, bussing, hitching, sailing and railing their way from England to Australia.

Written at a kitchen table and hand collated, trimmed and stapled, *Across Asia on the Cheap* became an instant local bestseller, inspiring thoughts of another book.

Eighteen months in South-East Asia resulted in their second guide, *South-East Asia on a shoestring*, which they put together in a backstreet Chinese hotel in Singapore in 1975. The 'yellow bible', as it quickly became known to backpackers around the world, soon became *the* guide to the region. It has sold well over half a million copies and is now in its 9th edition, still retaining its familiar yellow cover.

Today there are over 240 titles, including travel guides, walking guides, language kits & phrasebooks, travel atlases and travel literature. The company is the largest independent travel publisher in the world. Although Lonely Planet initially specialised in guides to Asia, today there are few corners of the globe that have not been covered.

The emphasis continues to be on travel for independent travellers. Tony and Maureen still travel for several months of each year and play an active part in the writing, updating and quality control of Lonely Planet's guides.

They have been joined by over 70 authors and 170 staff at our offices in Melbourne (Australia), Oakland (USA), London (UK) and Paris (France). Travellers themselves also make a valuable contribution to the guides through the feedback we receive in thousands of letters each year and on our web site.

The people at Lonely Planet strongly believe that travellers can make a positive contribution to the countries they visit, both through their appreciation of the countries' culture, wildlife and natural features, and through the money they spend. In addition, the company makes a direct contribution to the countries and regions it covers. Since 1986 a percentage of the income from each book has been donated to ventures such as famine relief in Africa; aid projects in India; agricultural projects in Central America; Greenpeace's efforts to halt French nuclear testing in the Pacific; and Amnesty International.

'I hope we send the people out with the right attitude about travel. You realise when you travel that there are so many different perspectives about the world, so we hope these books will make people more interested in what they see. These are guidebooks, but you can't really guide people. All you can do is point them in the right direction.'
— Tony Wheeler

LONELY PLANET PUBLICATIONS

Australia
PO Box 617, Hawthorn 3122, Victoria
tel: (03) 9819 1877 fax: (03) 9819 6459
e-mail: talk2us@lonelyplanet.com.au

USA
Embarcadero West, 155 Filbert St, Suite 251,
Oakland, CA 94607
tel: (510) 893 8555 TOLL FREE: 800 275-8555
fax: (510) 893 8563
e-mail: info@lonelyplanet.com

UK
10 Barley Mow Passage, Chiswick,
London W4 4PH
tel: (0181) 742 3161 fax: (0181) 742 2772
e-mail: 100413.3551@compuserve.com

France:
71 bis rue du Cardinal Lemoine, 75005 Paris
tel: 1 44 32 06 20 fax: 1 46 34 72 55
e-mail: 100560.415@compuserve.com

World Wide Web: http://www.lonelyplanet.com